OUTLAW PORSCHE

AND THE ART OF REBELLION

Thomas Cortesi – Michaël Levivier

WELBECK

EMBRACE THE DIFFERENCE!

Does choosing a different way to drive make you a rebel or a non-conformist? I spent nearly 30 years in California and I can confirm just how deeply automotive modification is entrenched in American culture.

After World War Two, California was full of mechanical-minded war veterans who felt the need to express themselves creatively, and they used their savings to do it. That's how hot rodding was born in the USA in the middle of the 1940s. When Robert E. Petersen and Wally Parks founded *HOT ROD* magazine in 1948, it was the first monthly dedicated to automotive modification and customizing. That movement was the start of an emerging lifestyle and subculture, of which motor sports, such as NASCAR, drag racing and land speed racing were a part.

Over the years, some passionate followers even took inspiration from motorsports to come up with new trends for road vehicles. A prime example was the supercharged Pro Street Muscle Cars that were "street legal" versions of Super Stock or Pro Stock – categories that were part of drag racing in the 1980s. A decade later, the Trans-Am Championship in turn inspired the Pro-Touring treatment of those very same Muscle Cars.

Modification is part of the history of the automobile, and the Porsche community is no exception, despite what some of the brand's purists may think. After all, wasn't the first Porsche – 356 – a modded Beetle?

Some Porsche-oriented hot rodders have had a strong influence in the evolution of this culture, each bringing their own philosophy and identity. Starting with the Emory family: grandfather Neil, erstwhile builder of *rods* and *kustoms*; Gary, his son, a constructor of first generation 356s and 911s – long before the term Outlaw was even uttered in his workshop, Parts Obsolete, in Costa Mesa; grandson Rod, who continues the adventure by making Outlaws in his Emory Motorsport garage, opened in 1996. Not to mention Crees Huergas and Freemen Thomas, founders of the famous R Gruppe, and Rolly Resos, another founding member of that club of out-of-the-ordinary Porsche owners. And also Magnus Walker, nicknamed the Urban Outlaw ... All of them thrive on pure performance, on old-fashioned engine tuning, on the smell of burnt rubber or petrol from a boneshaking engine that may not be perfect, but still pounds like a race car hitting 7,000 rpm on the track at Laguna Seca.

At Singer Vehicle Design, also in California, they lean heavily on "newstalgia", by mixing technological prowess with aesthetic and mechanical perfection. The atmosphere may not be the same, but what is certain is that everyone is looking – first and foremost – for the pleasure of driving these cars they have built in their own image.

So when the term Outlaw is used, it is not necessarily talking about the law, it's more to with a rebellion against the intransigent representatives of a community of collectors who have seemed at times, let's say, intolerant. To be non-conformist is simply to oppose established practices. It is to act with a type of freedom, a different way of doing and being – and different is good!

GERRY BLYENBERG
Automotive presenter

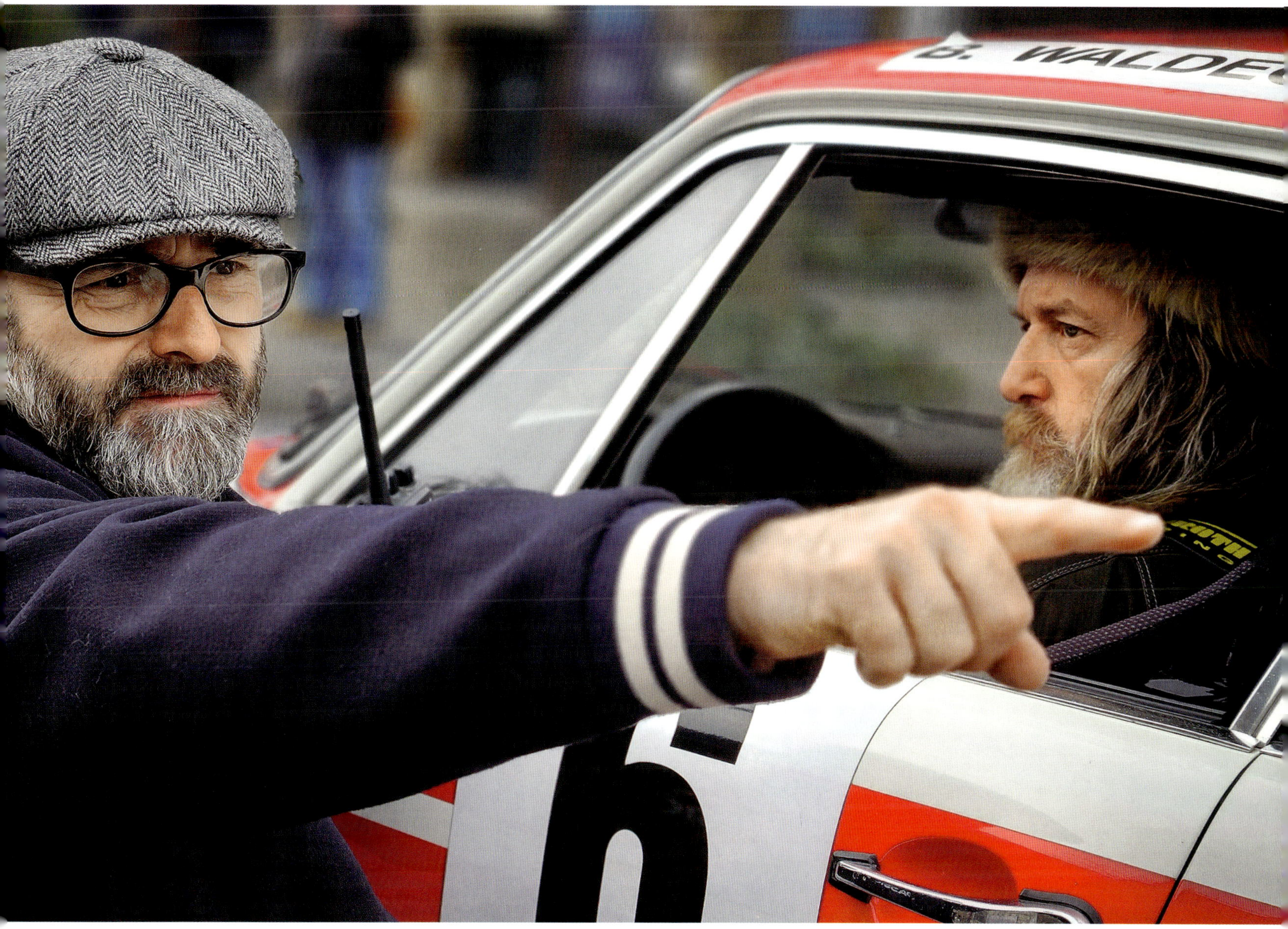

Gerry Blyenberg (left) with Magnus Walker – the Urban Outlaw – in- Paris.

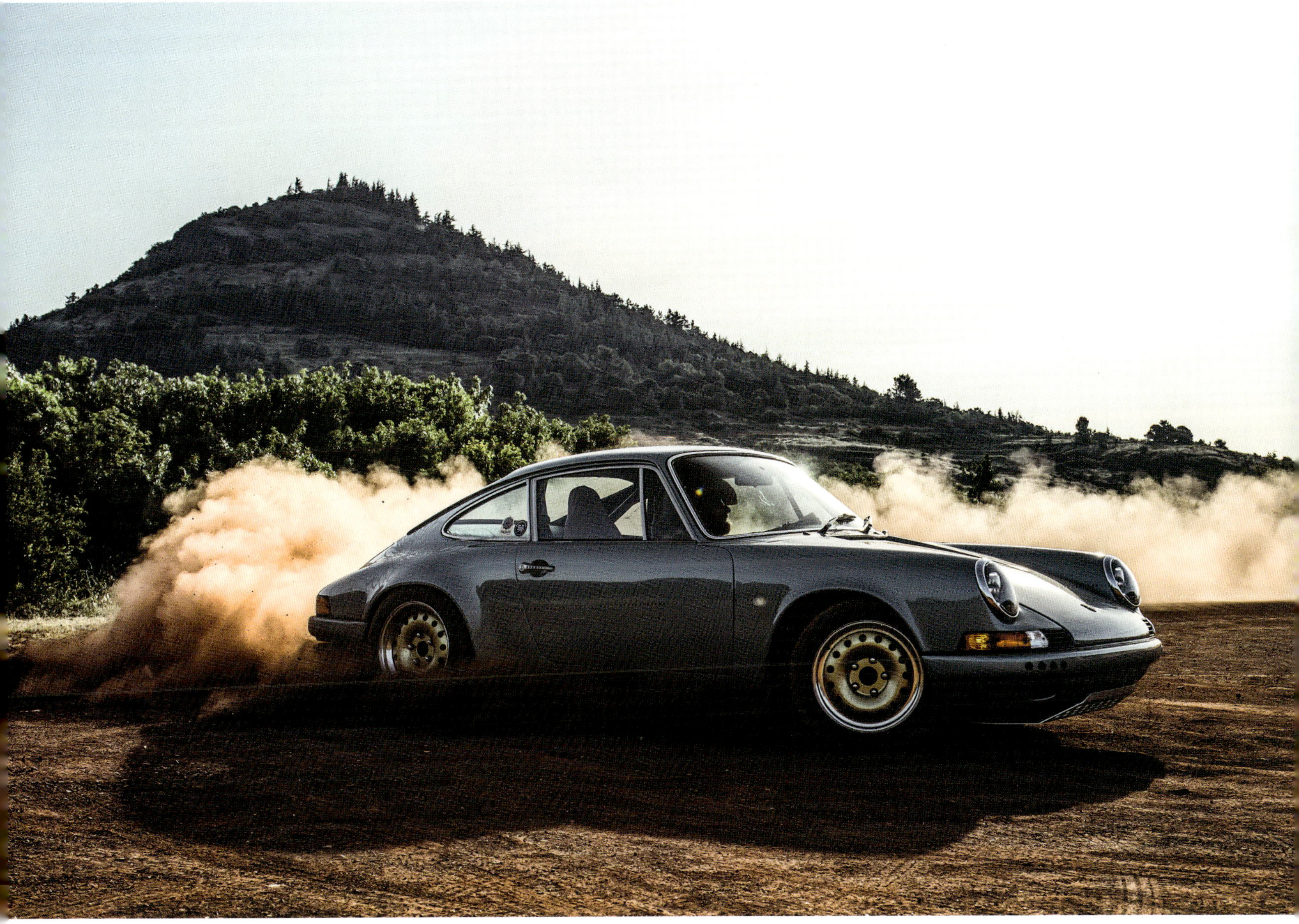

ORIGINS
BE OUTSIDE THE LAW

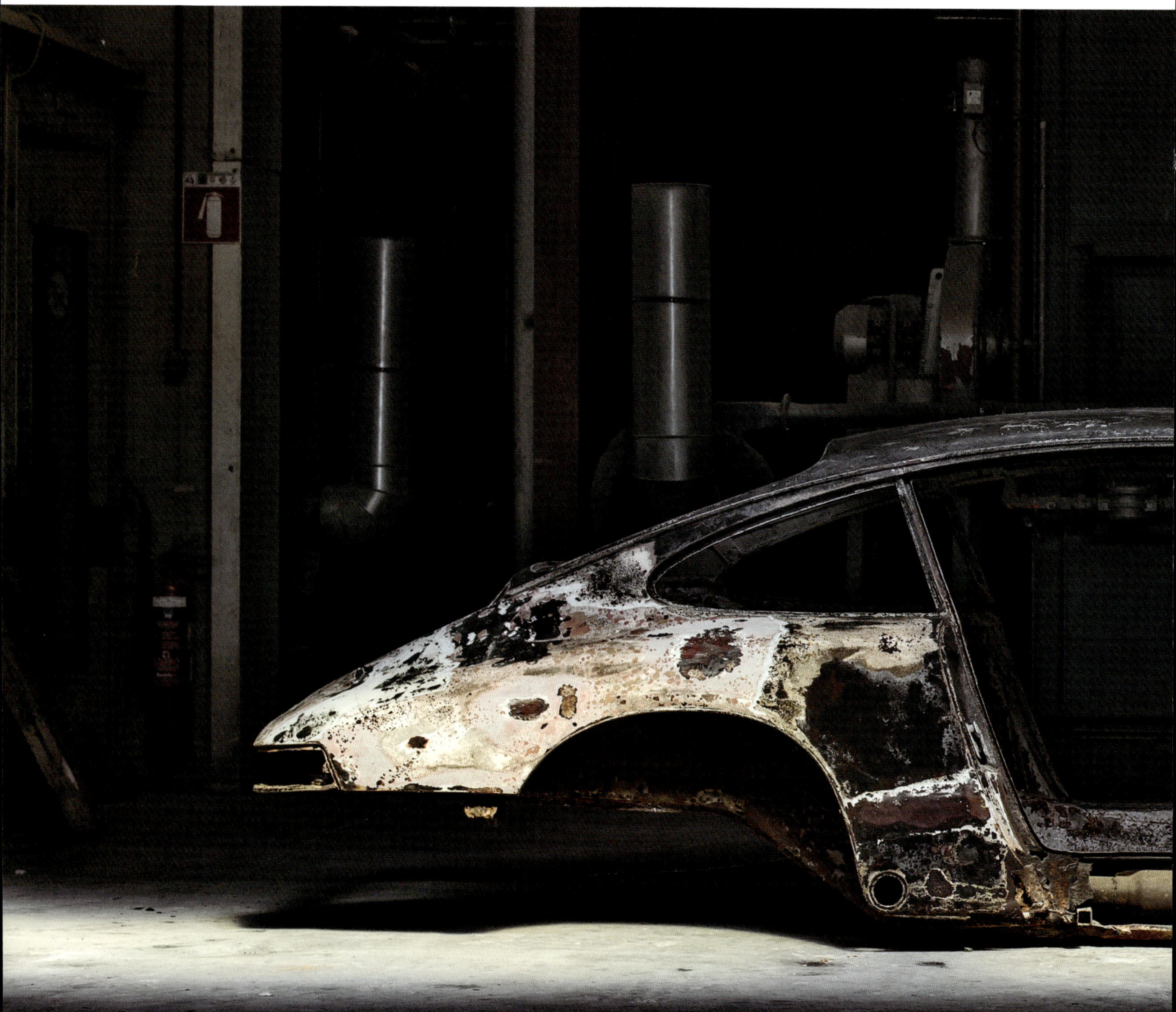

A Porsche that does not fit any category in the mind of the brand's purists – that's an Outlaw. Let's take a look at the genesis of the word that today means so much in terms of style and philosophy, and the customizing of these vehicles.

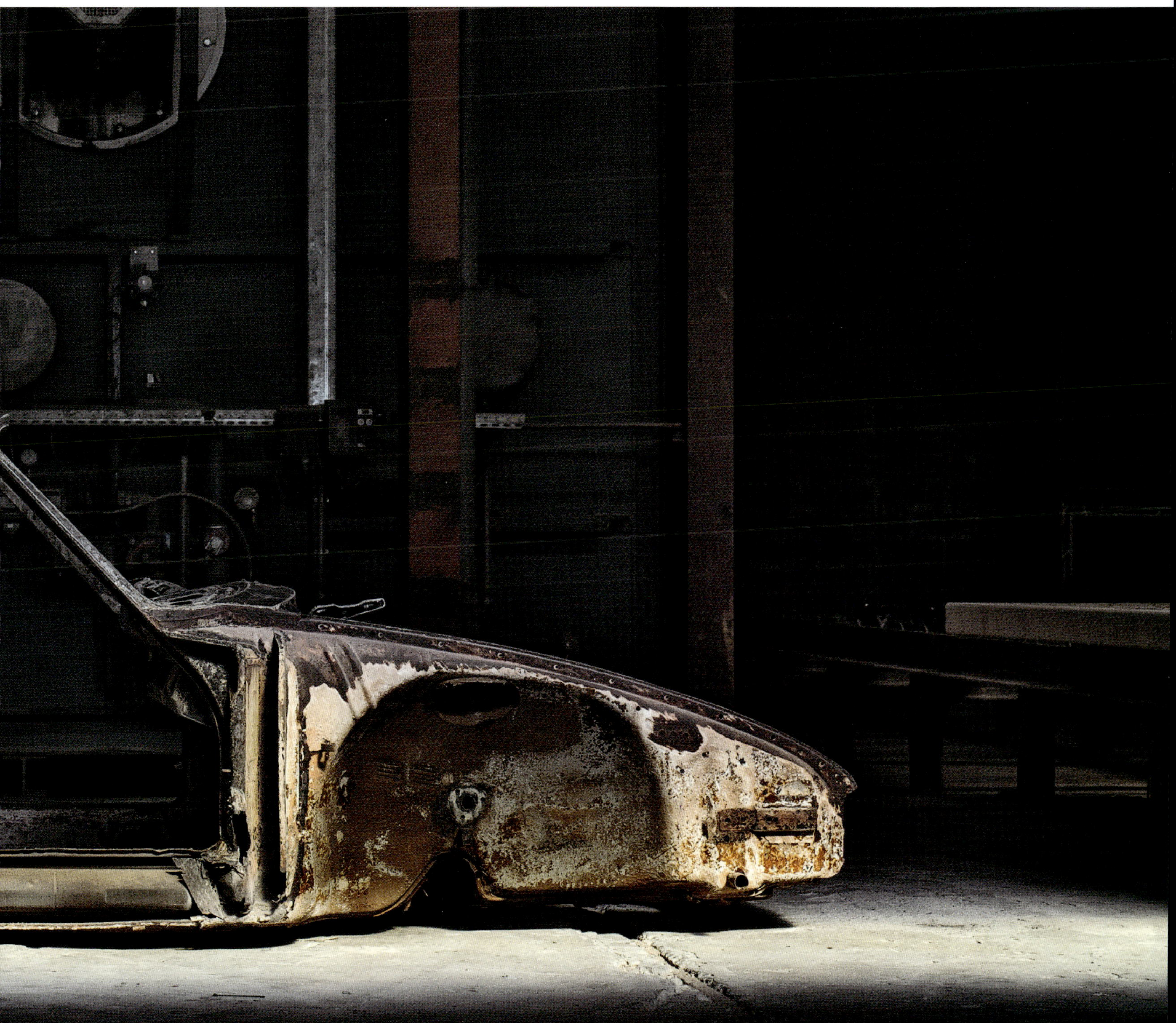

To own a Porsche Outlaw is literally to respect nothing. "Someone outside the established laws or rules" – the definition of the word is clear, it is all about not being constrained by the rules. For Porsche purists, for a very long time, no modification whatsoever was allowed. Hotted-up machines transgressed the rigid belief systems of such Porsche fundamentalists. No serious collectors would have been interested in cars like that. However, they were ideal for sports driving enthusiasts. And so, almost by chance – coming from California, a place long known for challenging established norms – the term emerged to describe Porsches that didn't really fit in with anything written in the rulebooks.

ORIGIN

The story begins in Burbank, Los Angeles County, California, with grandfather Neil Emory. He founded his automobile business in 1948. Very quickly the name became famous in hot rod culture through building high-performance cars, many of which are now collectors' items. His son Gary followed in his tyre tracks, and partnered with Porsche in 1960. It was a flourishing business and the names become inseparable. Gary Emory restores all sorts of Porsches, notably the iconic 356, which is a pretty old car these days. In 1996, grandson Rod Emory created Emory Motorsports in Oregon with his wife – all the while maintaining Emory Design in North Hollywood. The goal was

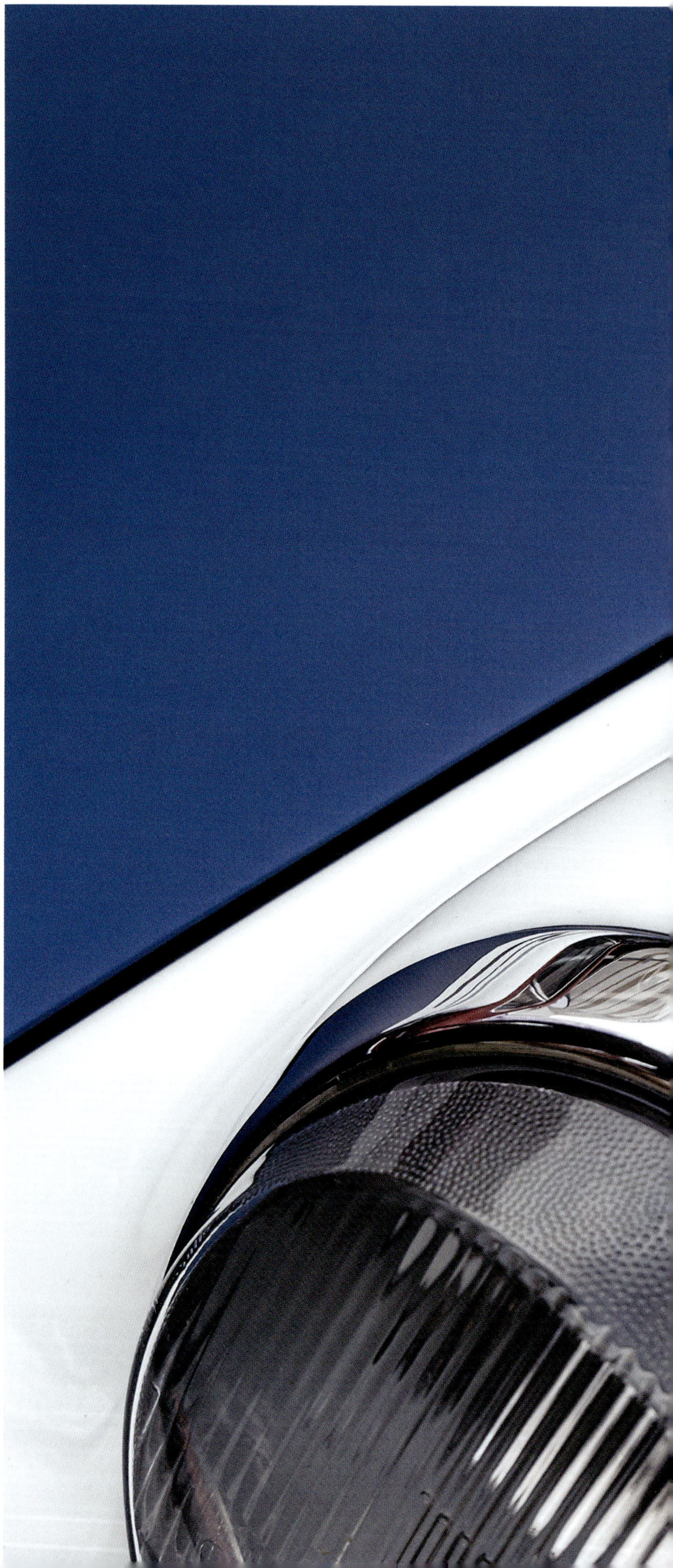

Opposite: Magnus Walker added a dedication to this beautiful Porsche Outlaw at the Rétromobile car show in Paris, in February 2024.

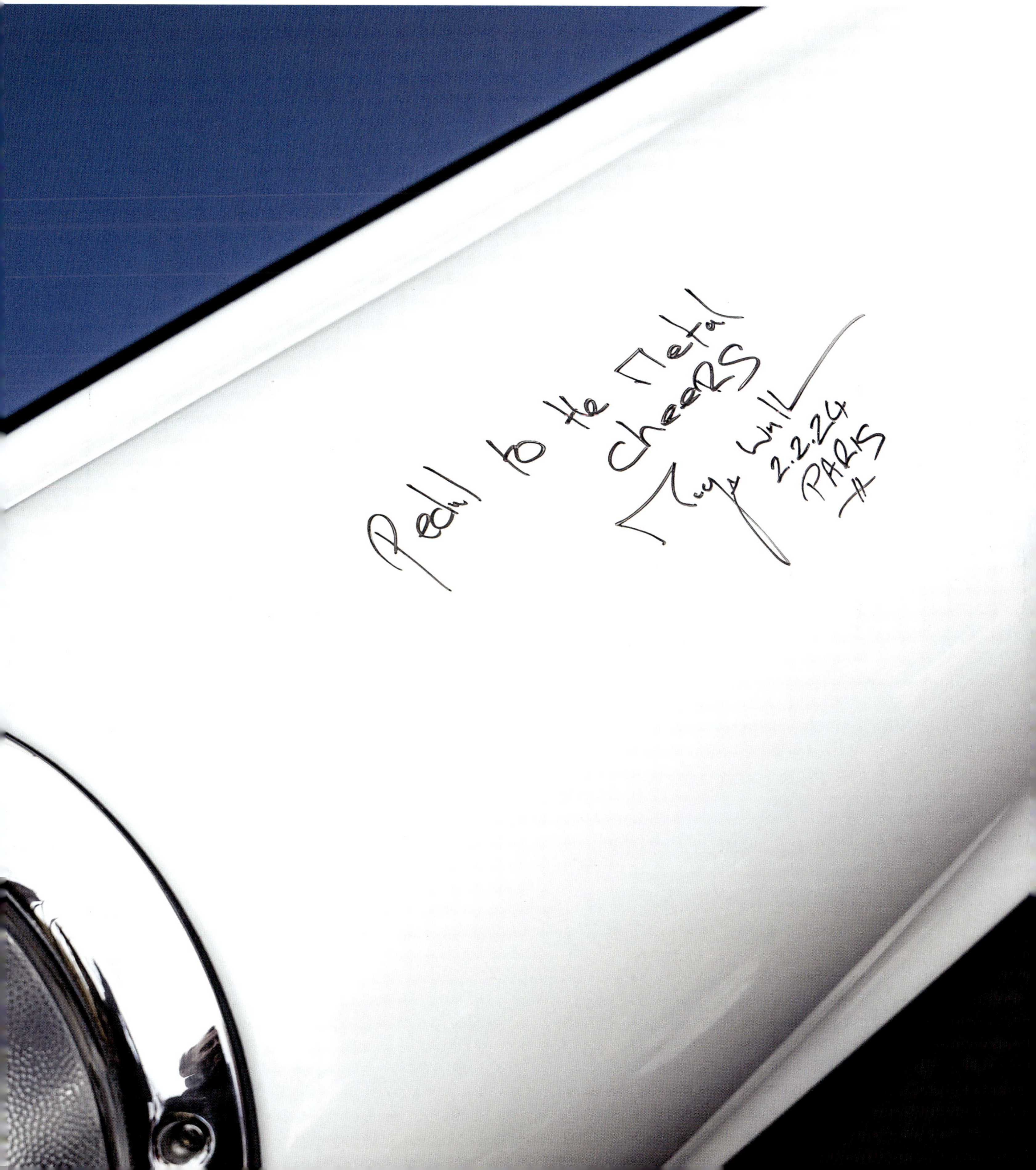

Pedal to the Metal
Cheers
2.2.24
PARIS

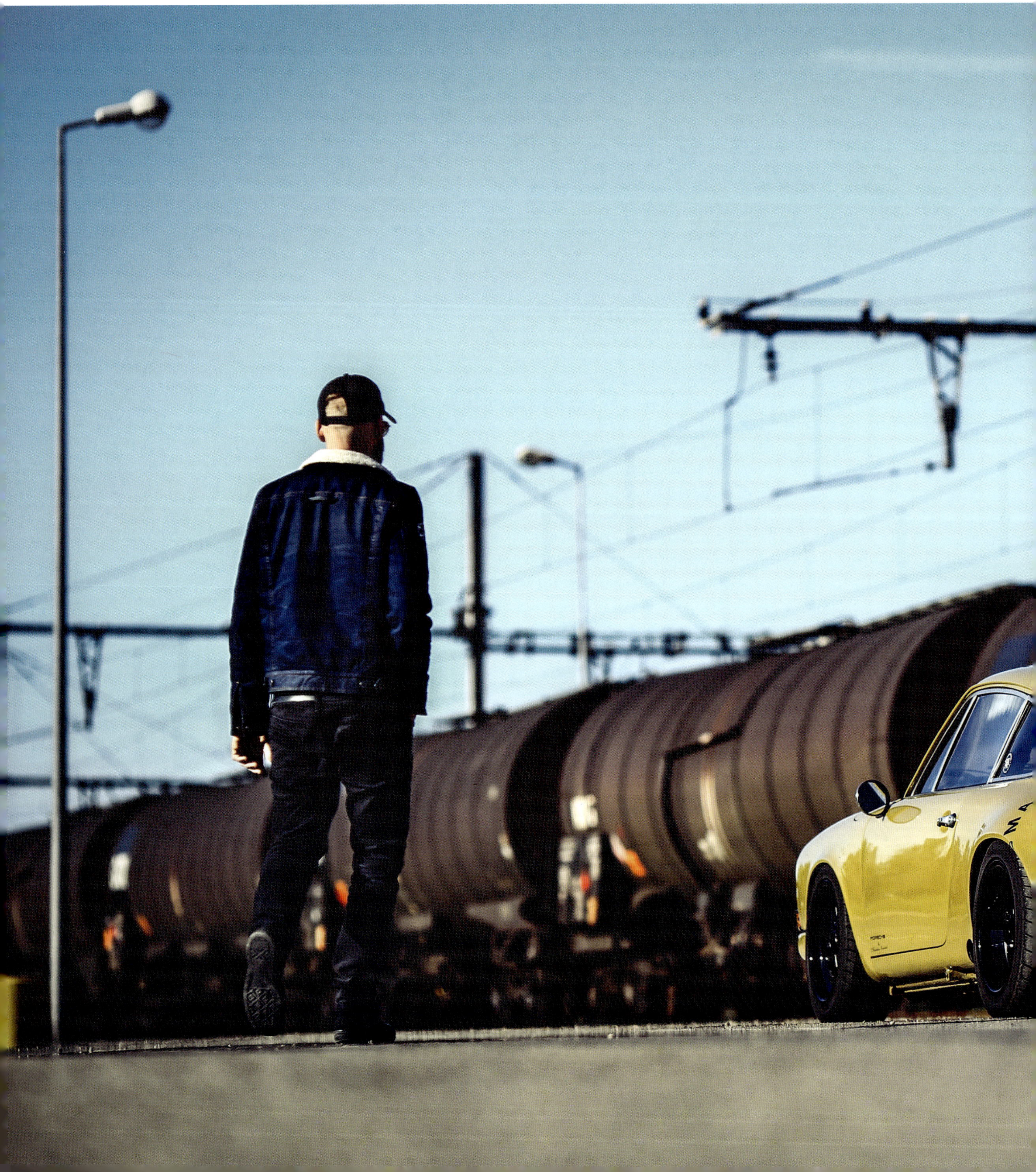

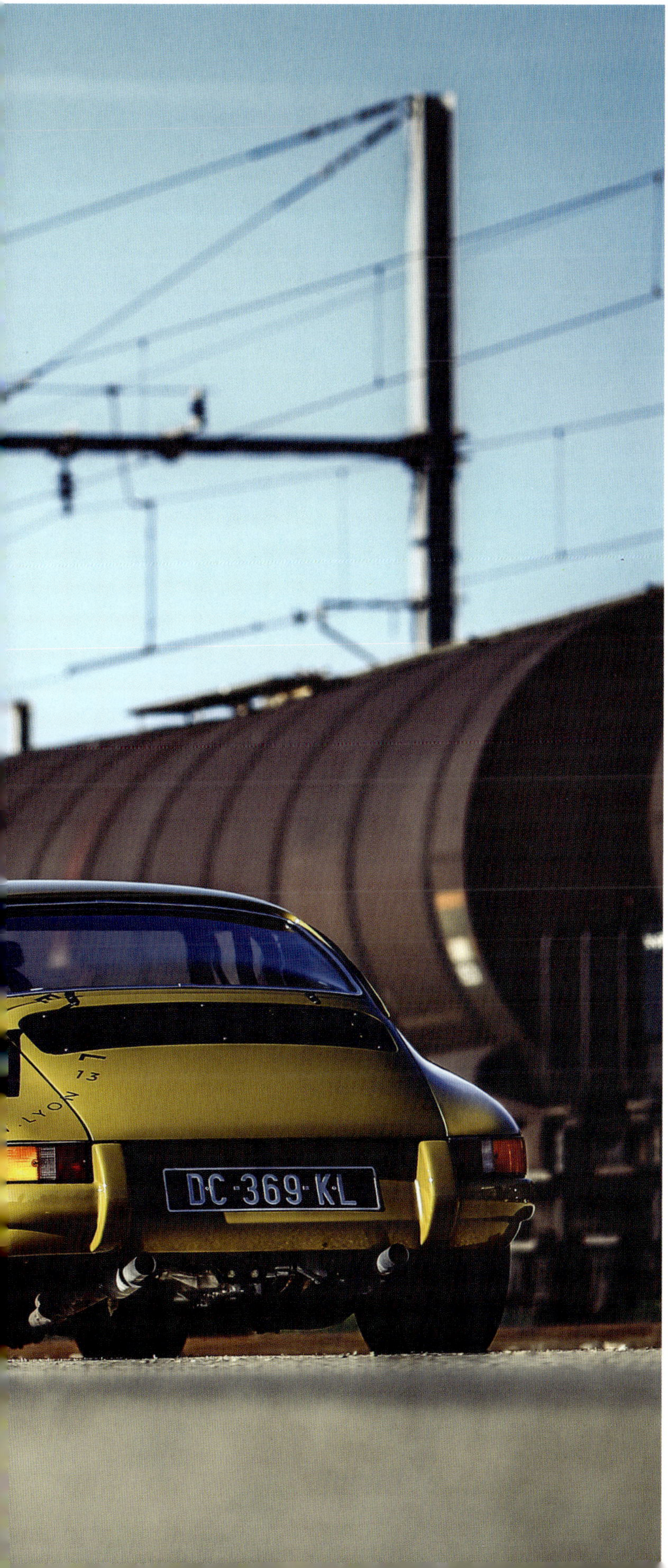

A PORSCHE OUTLAW BREAKS ALL THE RULES!

to continue his father's work by restoring Porsche 356s, but with a more personal touch, often inspired by racing. His first 356s were known as "Outlaws", because they shook up the established order of the automotive scene.

ANOTHER DIRECTION

So what precisely is a Porsche Outlaw? "I really have no idea," confesses Nicolas Quiles, founder of Machine Revival. "I don't really get what it means. An *Outlaw* is someone outside the law. So when you put yourself in that position, you don't go shouting it from the rooftops. Outlaw, when it comes to Porsches, is a term that was made up by bearded, tattooed guys who drive 911s ... And I completely fit that description," he says, laughing. "There are words that have appeared over time to describe things that were naturally occurring anyway, such as backdating, restomod or Outlaw." Backdating is when you give a car an older look. A restomod optimises the original configuration and makes it structurally more modern.

"I see it from the other direction," continues Nicolas. "When you start out on something new you don't immediately put a label on it and try to stick rigidly to it. An artist doesn't begin by saying to themselves: 'I'm going to make heavy metal orchestral music.' They make the music they want, and then other people come up with a name that describes what they perceive it to be. So, to start with, there is simply the desire to do something, without asking too many questions. I never started out with a goal of making Outlaw 911s. I just think about cars and I build them in the way I want to. Fifteen years ago, nobody had even heard the term Porsche Outlaw. I started out small, doing up all my own vehicles. I have always tried to personalize the things that belong to me. It comes from there, from my culture, from my influences. I've always loved rally cars. I was deeply affected by Group B cars (the most powerful rally category – created in 1982 and banned in 1986). I like motorbikes, Formula 1, cars in general and mechanics, even the more technical aspects of motoring. I like everything to do with racing: that is the biggest source of my inspiration. Over the years, I have been lucky enough to work on cars that are increasingly cool, classy and interesting, and on projects that keep getting better and better. Until I realized my dream: owning my own 911. And, like everything else, I modified it heavily."

INFLUENCES

Of all Nicolas' influences, one of them overtook the others and steered him in the direction he wanted to go: "Outlaw started out in California. Of course, there was Rod Emory to begin with,

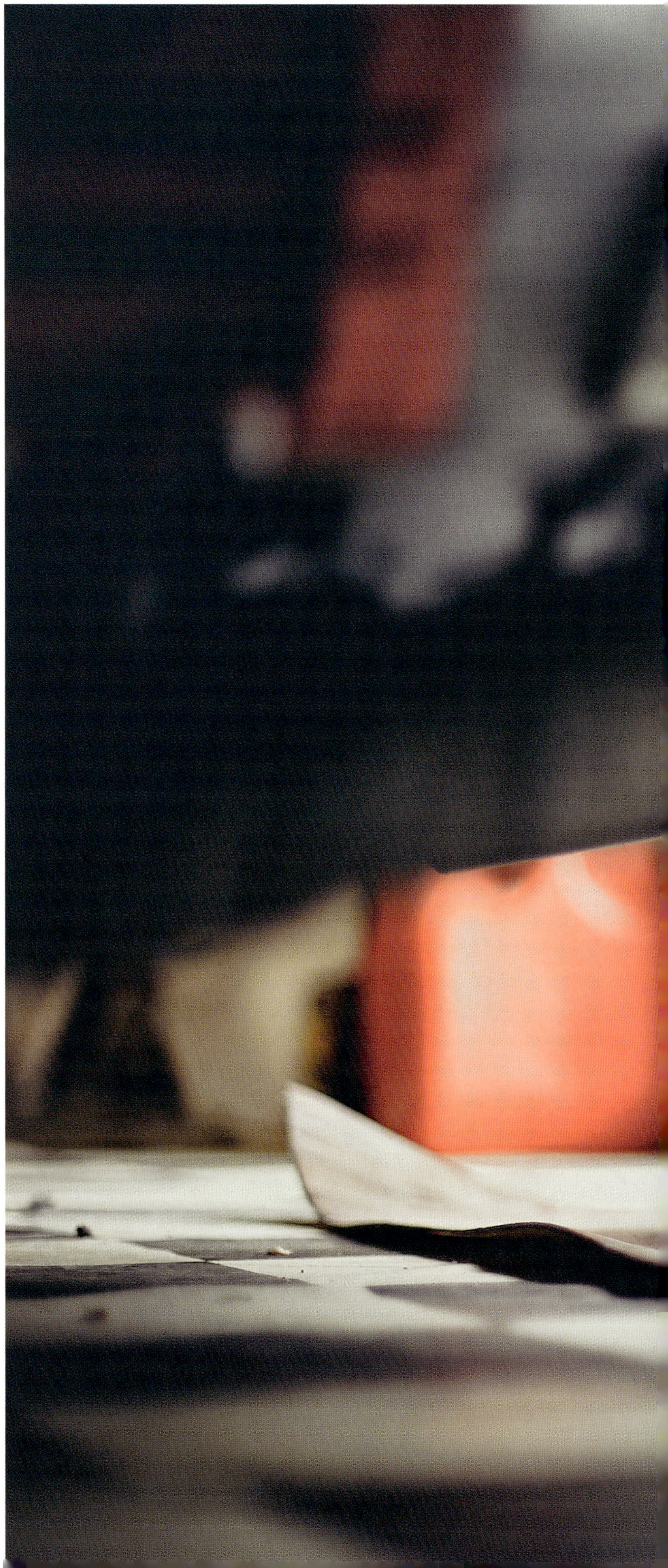

Opposite: Nicolas Quiles from Machine Revival, tool in hand!

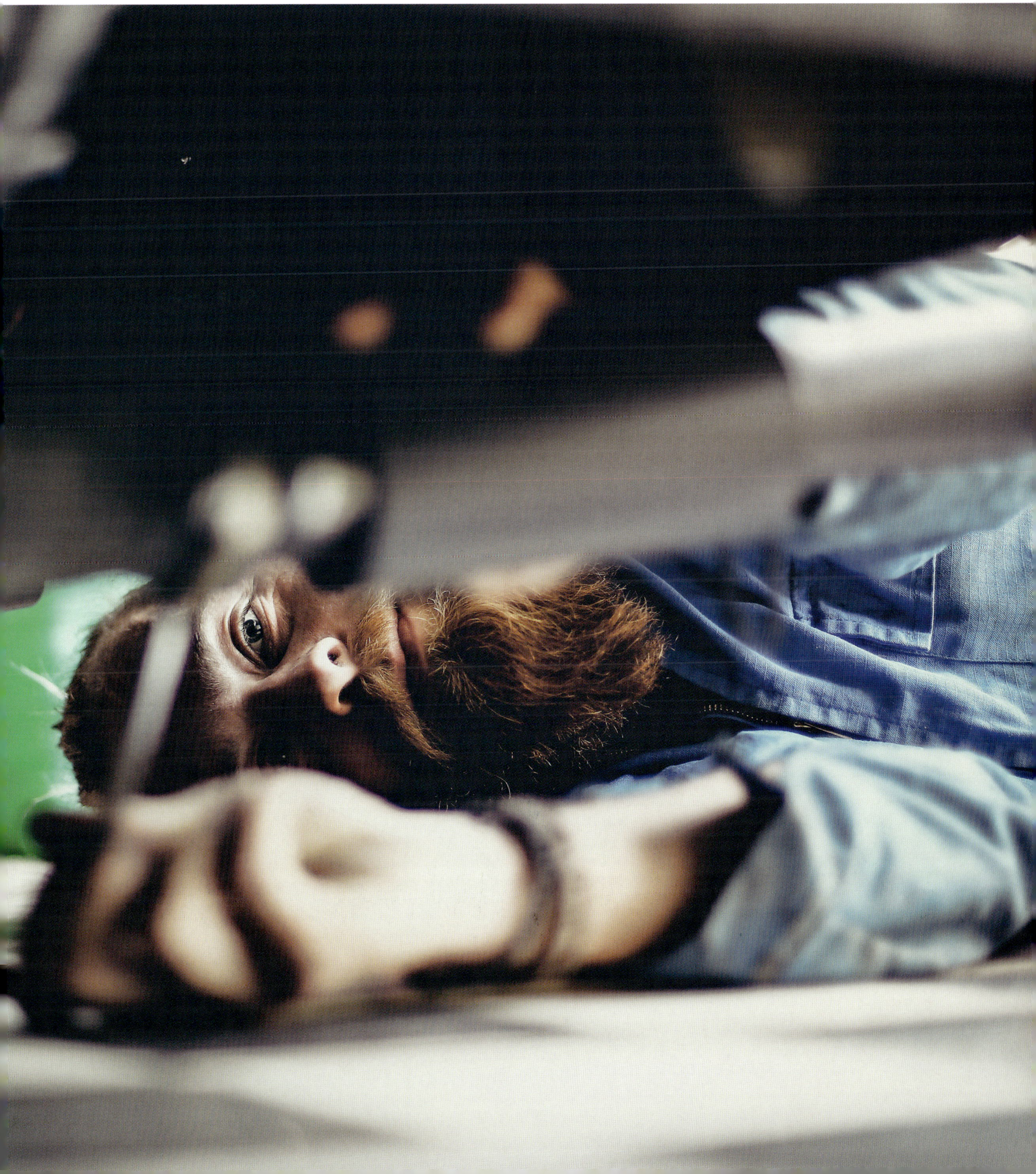

whose family legacy and Porsche 356 customizations played a key role in shaping the trend. But there was also – above all – the famous R Gruppe. That was a collective of Porsche owners who had classic models that they modified copiously. In an era that valued strictly stock Porsches, they took 1972 models and completely transformed them, making tuned-up cars with rally styling." R Gruppe was born in 1999 and became a highly influential club in the Porsche world. Each member – there by invitation only – devoted themselves to their own, highly personalized versions of old 911s. The goal was to push the technological boundaries of their cars. If you ask the members of R Gruppe how their cars came about, you will get a different answer from each one. But there will always be one thing in common: each 911 is a reflection of its owner. "I was looking for parts to get better performance out of my Porsches. Inevitably I ended up ordering from the United States. At that time, Rob Dickinson was modifying his own 911s – that was the start of Singer, now one of the most famous Porsche specialists." Its credo was to restore and reimagine 911s from 1989 to 1994

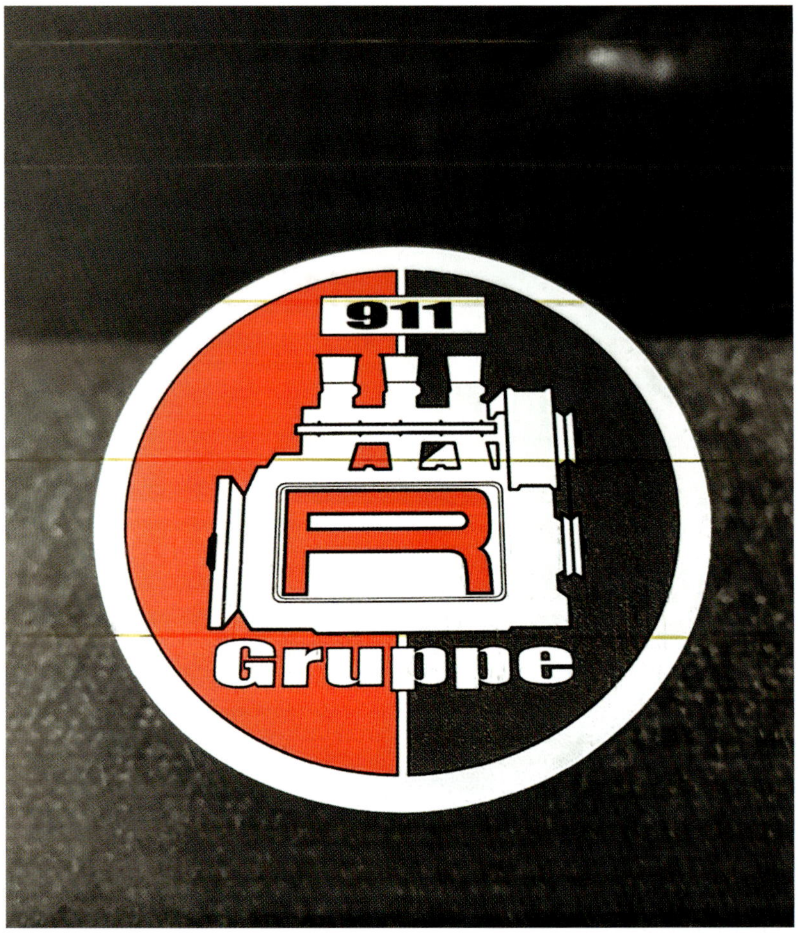

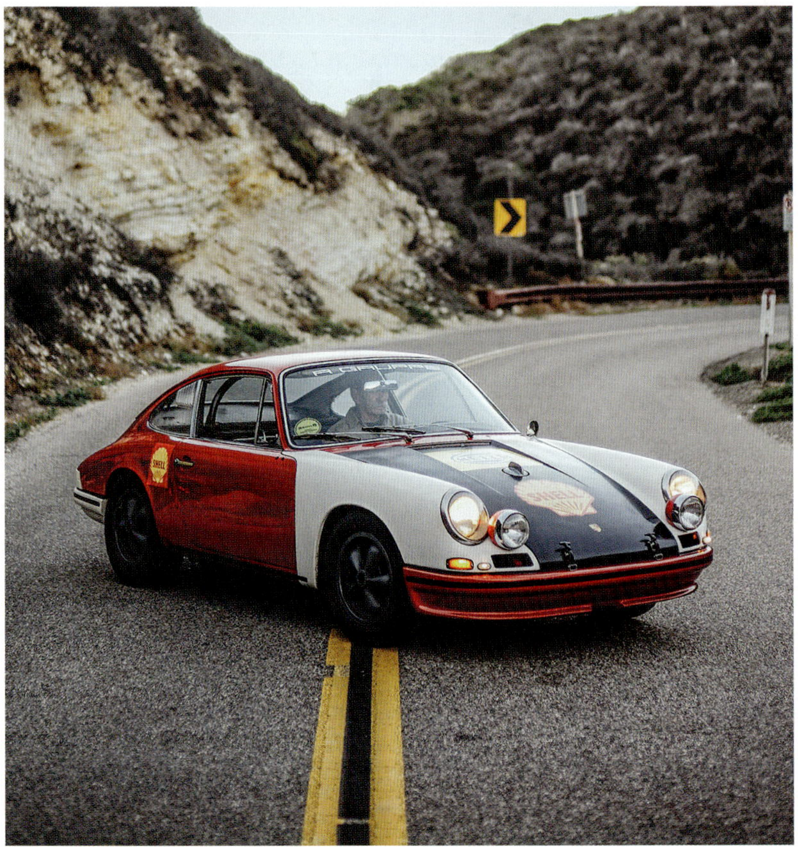

1. R Gruppe is a club of Porsche Outlaw enthusiasts based in California.

2. The 911 owned by Rolly Resos, one of the founding members of R Gruppe, alongside Cris Huergas and Freeman Thomas.

3. The famous MOMO steering wheel with Porsche logo – for a better ride!

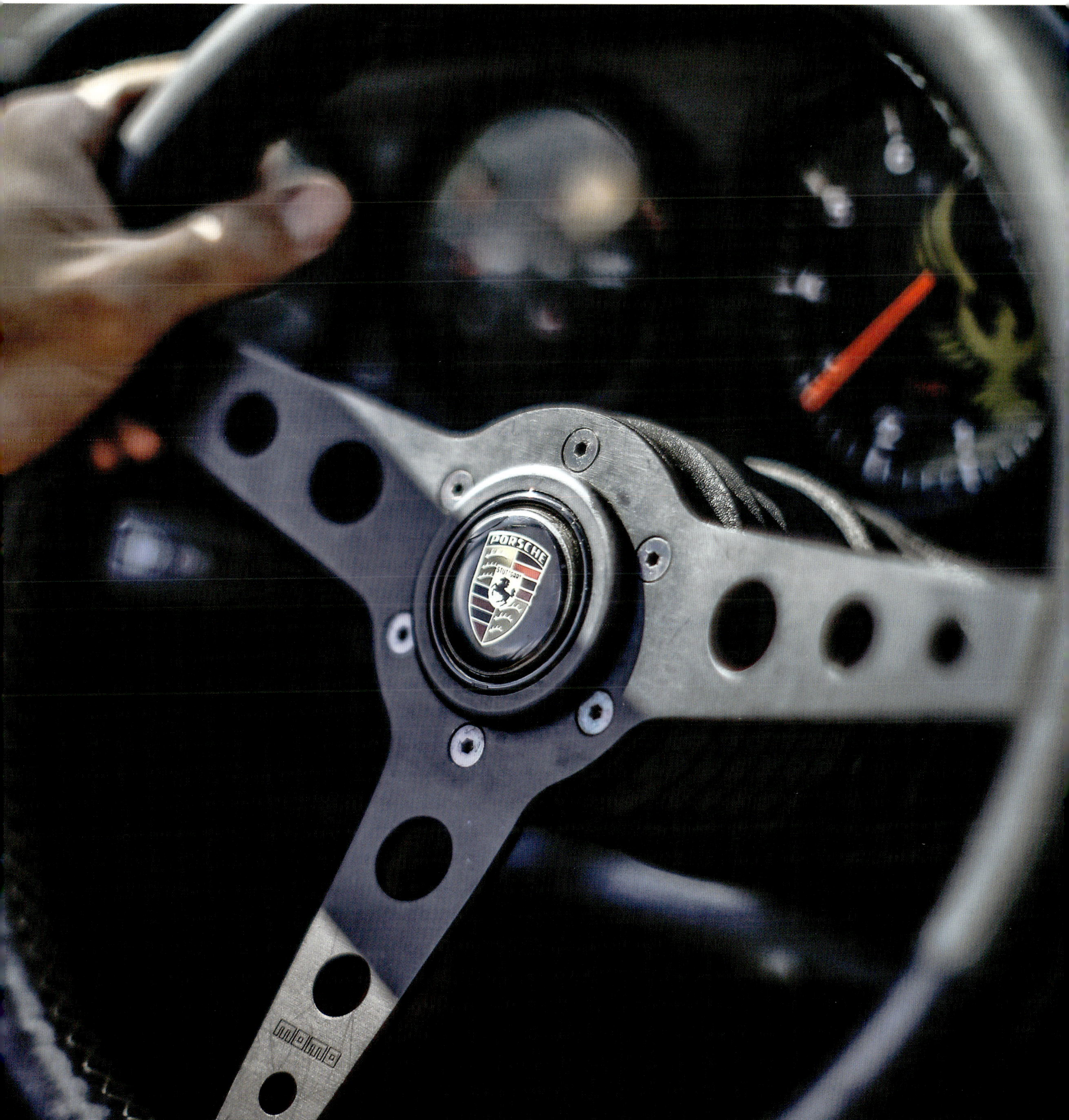
PORSCHE
momo

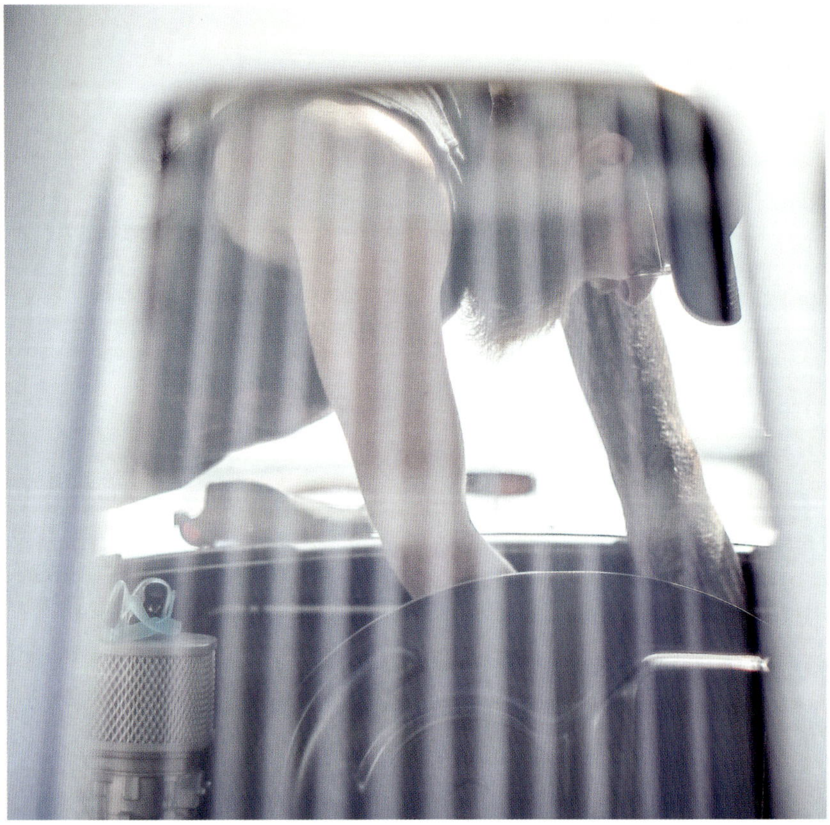

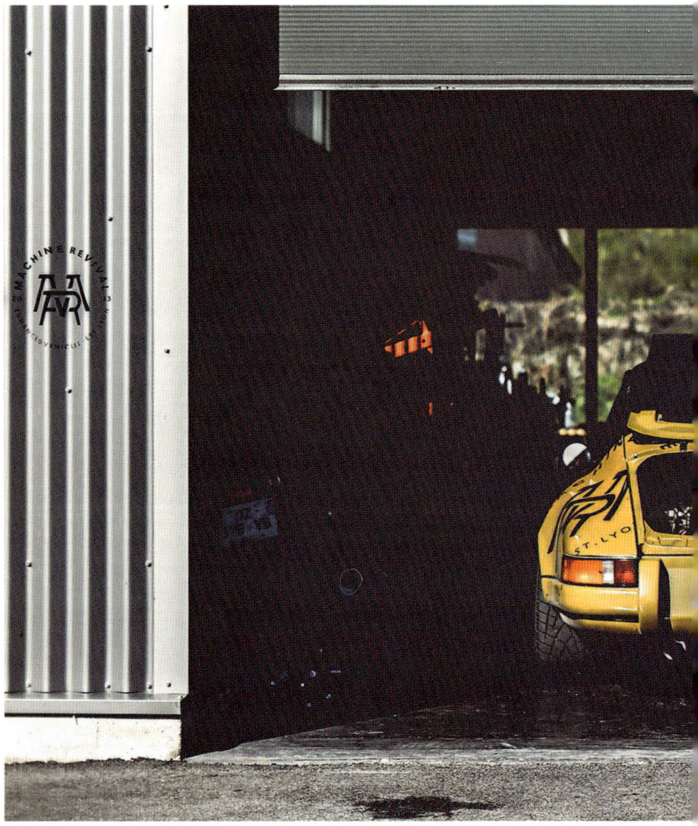

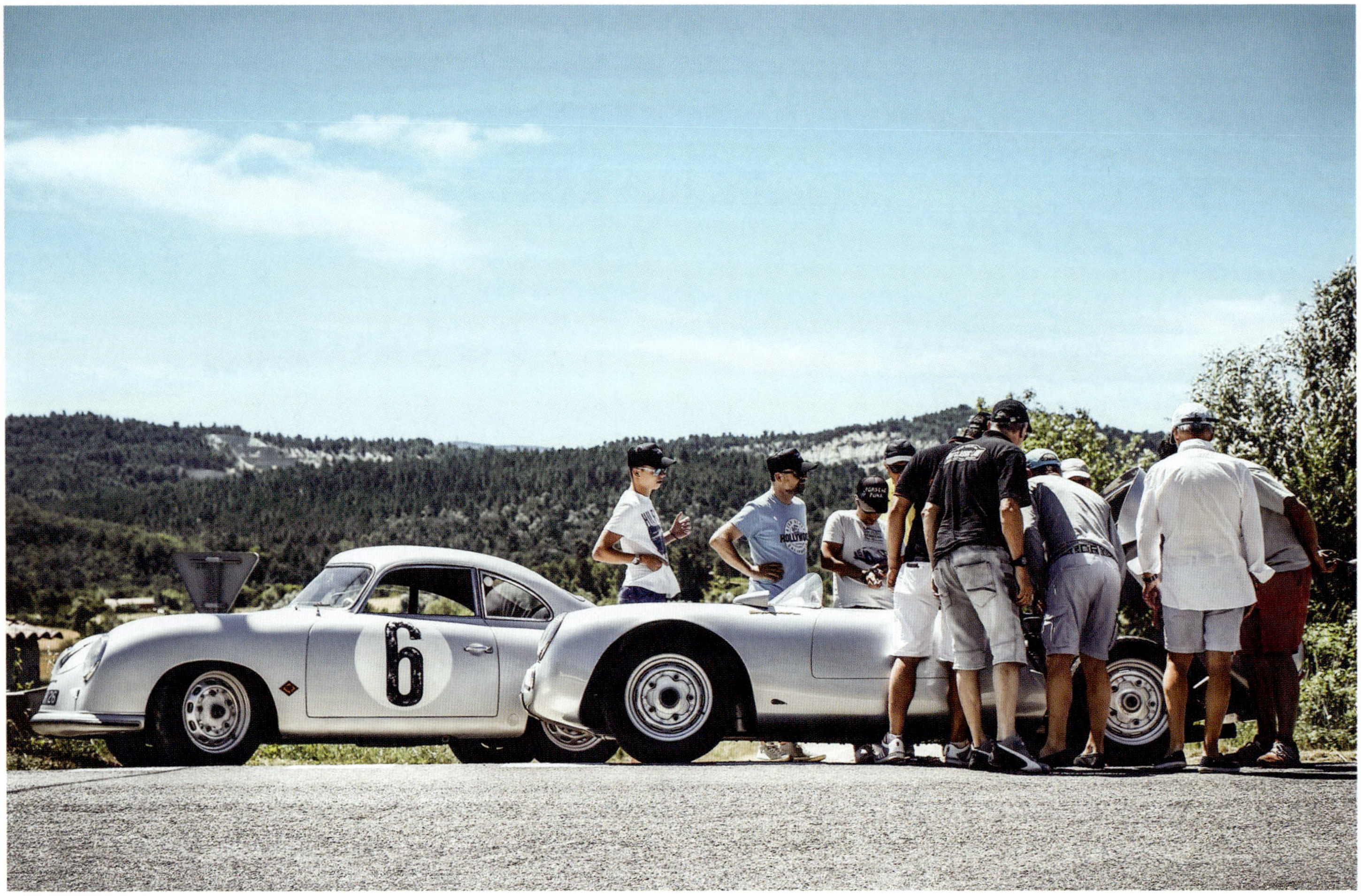

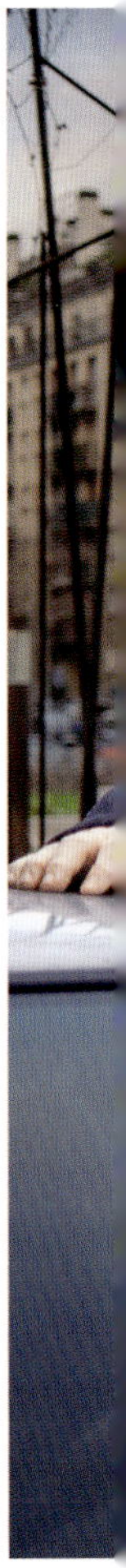

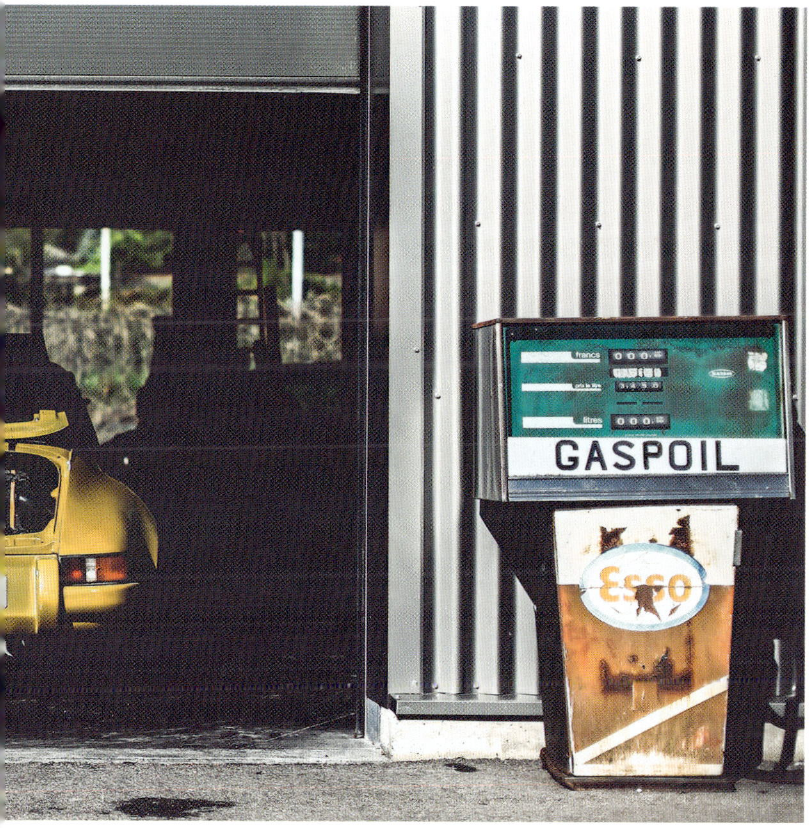

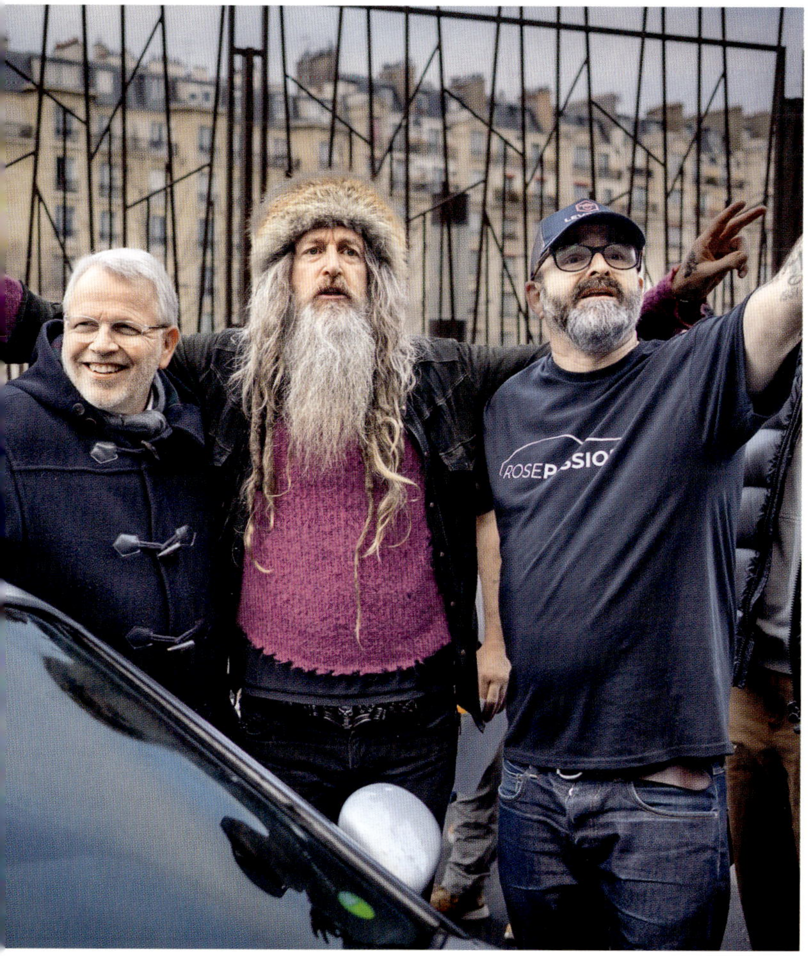

- based on the 964 chassis - and treat them with truly exceptional finishing. "Singer didn't even exist at that point, he was just having a bit of fun, before he became such a famous name in Porsche. There was also Magnus Walker, who was making 277, his Porsche 911, in Los Angeles. After he bought his complex in downtown LA, and after an incredible career in fashion (with Serious Clothing, which dressed Madonna, Alice Cooper, Bruce Willis, Jay-Z, Prince and many other stars) he made a name for himself with an extraordinary collection of Porsches. He did them up and talked about it on social media. It was the beginning of his explosion into the world of Porsche. All those people who had helped to create what we now call Porsche Outlaw without even knowing it - I came across them virtually at the beginning of their careers, when I started doing my own restoration work. That was before I even started Machine Revival."

1 2
3 4

1. The mechanics get to share their joy at plenty of meetings.

2. Driving a modified Porsche means keeping up with the regular maintenance of your ride.

3. From the 356 to the 550 Spyder: a single, shared passion.

4. Magnus Walker (centre) with Gerry Blyenberg and Philippe Delaporte, who drove around the world in a 928.

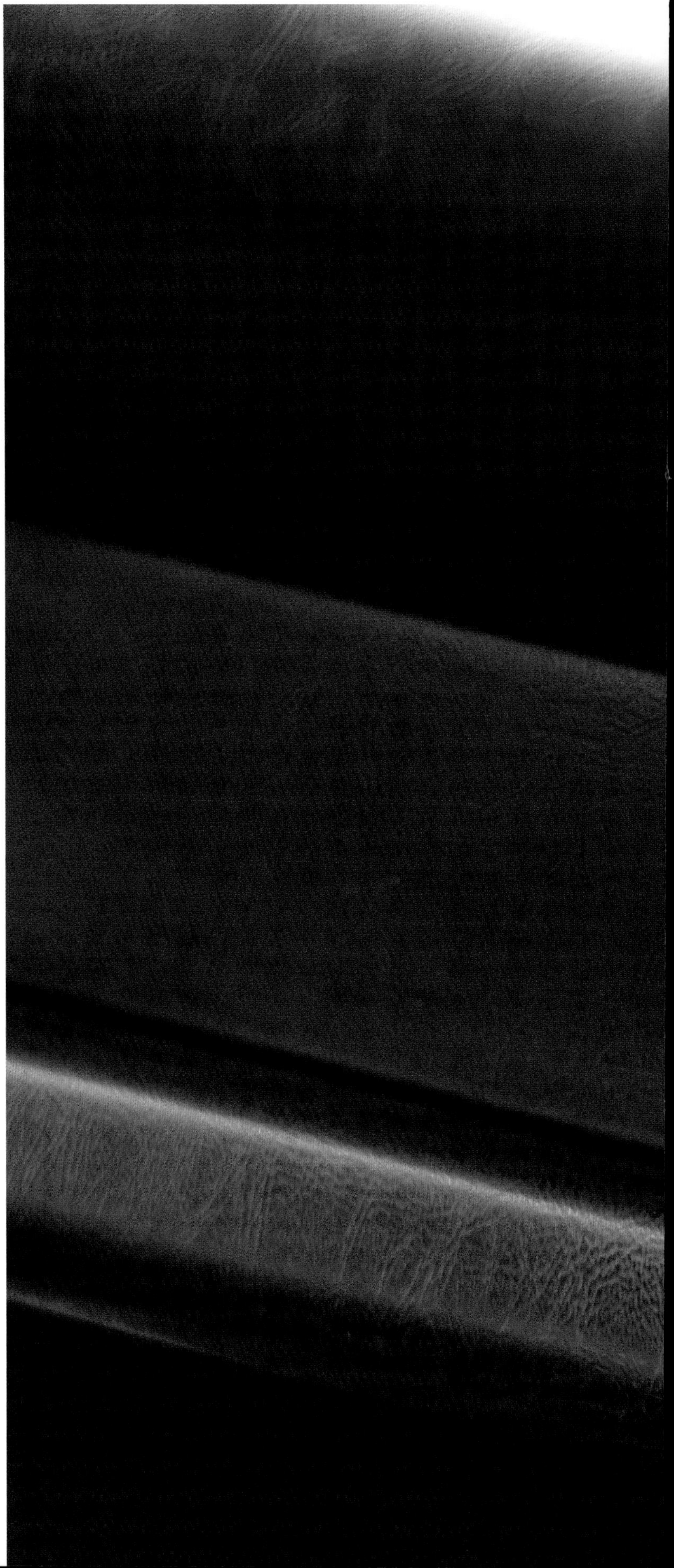

URBAN OUTLAW

The original idea behind an Outlaw wasn't some marketing ploy with a cool name to sound like bad boys, it was a genuine personal approach, as Magnus Walker explained in his book *Urban Outlaw*[1]: "Over time I gradually started to sell off anything that wasn't Porsche ... I'm just trying to explain how I came to own over 50 Porsches ... five grand here, six grand there, real inexpensive cars ... Early Porsches are fairly easy to modify and upgrade. Essentially, I am completely self-taught ... the quality of the cars I was working on continually improved. At that point, however, truth be told, my personality wasn't on the cars. Quite a few of these earlier cars are now cropping up for sale as 'an ex-Magnus Walker 911'.

"So, around 2010, I started a thread ... just a few words about my cars and Porsche stuff. I called it 'Porsche Collection – Out of Control Hobby' ... my posts seemed to tweak people's interest and began attracting quite a lot of attention and views ... The real turning point came when I started injecting a little more personality into

WORDS OF WISDOM FROM MAGNUS WALKER

1. *Magnus Walker, Urban Outlaw: Dirt Don't Slow You Down*, Bantam Press, 2017.

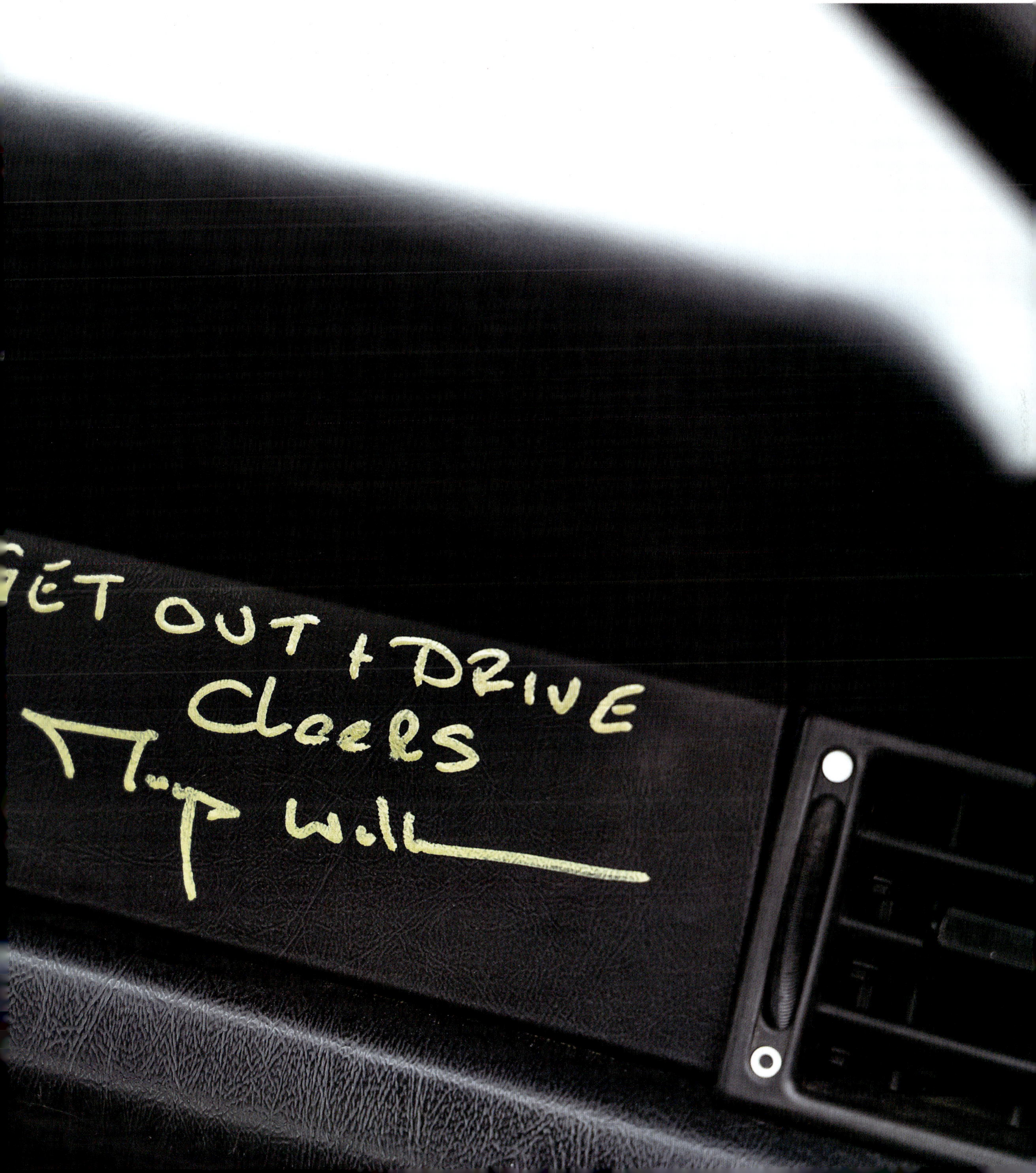
GET OUT + DRIVE
Cheers

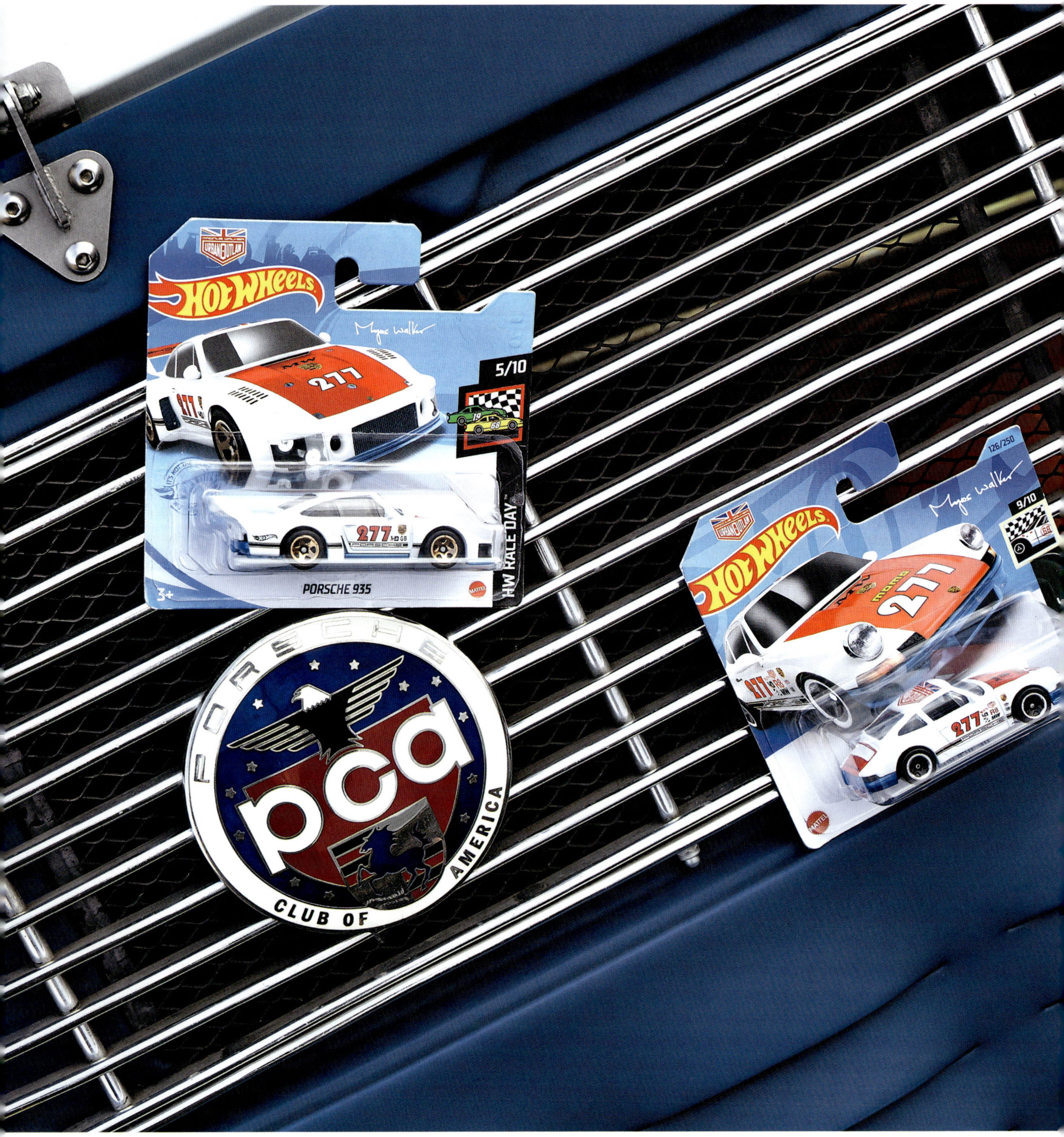
HOT WHEELS
URBANE OUTLAW
5/10
277
PORSCHE 935
HW RACE DAY
3+
MATTEL
PORSCHE
pca
CLUB OF AMERICA
126/250
9/10
MATTEL

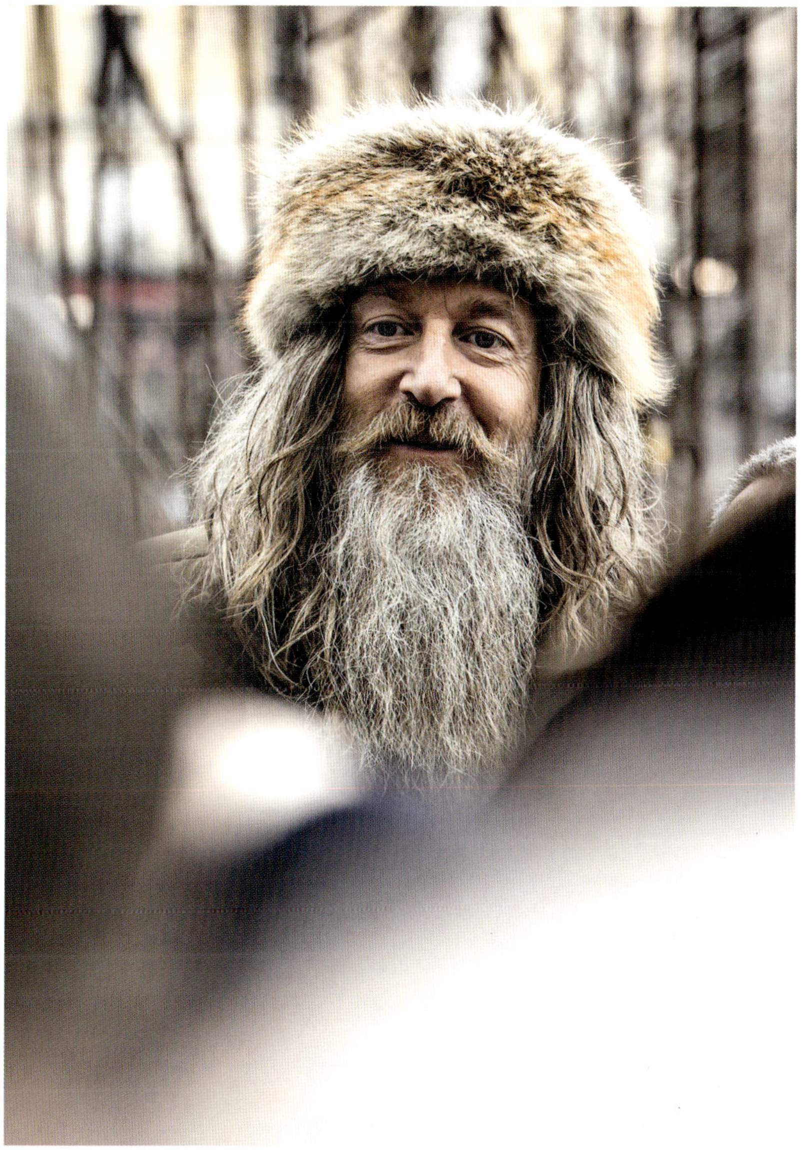

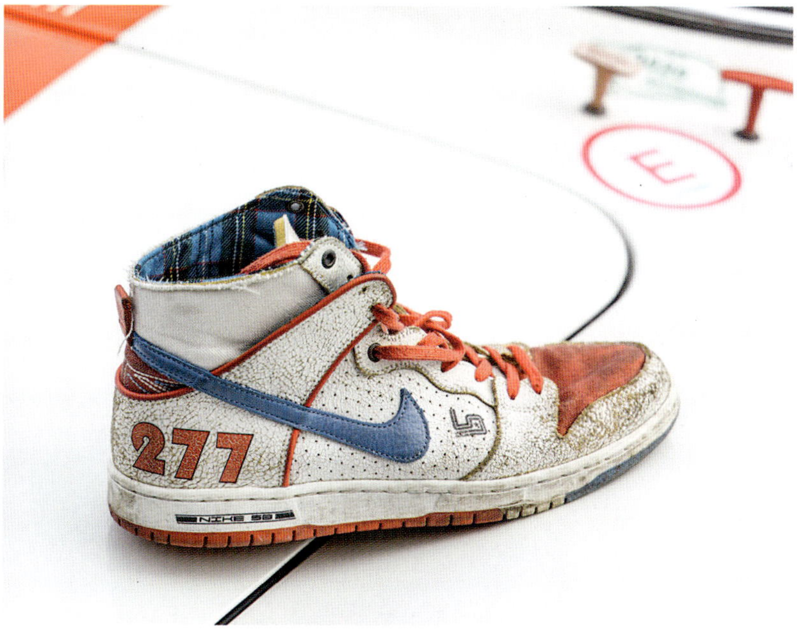

the cars." Until the day, when Maurice van den Tillard, the Dutch journalist who had a punk-rock culture similar to Walker's, started an article in *Total 911* magazine issue 83, with the words: "Meet Magnus Walker, the Urban Outlaw."

Walker continues, "I didn't come up with the term 'outlaw'. That had been around for a long time ... If you look up the definition of the word, it means someone who is beyond the normal confines of the law, 'a person who refuses to be governed by the established rules or practices of any group; a rebel, a non-conformist' ... That term has evolved beyond the history of renegades and criminals into more of a general description of an attitude and a lifestyle. With regards to cars, it was applied to people who were taking stock vehicles and working on them in a way that was outside of the norm, beyond the boundaries of standard factory specifications ... Rod Emory and his company, Emory Motorsports, are arguably the best-known proponents of that particular art. However, the outlaw instinct is the same regardless of what marques you are talking about – essentially what I'm doing with my Porsches is adding hot-rod touches and elements of customization that people have been doing for decades. That's the creative lineage that *Total 911* saw."

1	2
	3

1. Hot Wheels released their own version of the famous Porsche 277.

2. Magnus Walker, the undisputed star of the Porsche Outlaw vibe.

3. Even Nike chose to celebrate the famous 277– a Porsche 911 – with a pair of iconic sneakers.

USES

The most important thing in an Outlaw is the feeling you get from the car. "To start with I wasn't modifying my cars so they'd look cool," explains Walker. "[I was] always searching for better performance ... I would always drive the car to the track, thrash it around and then drive it back home ... for me that was just the natural thing to do ... [277] is a '71 911T ... I paid seventy-five hundred dollars for the car ... I very quickly made more and more modifications to the car ... I wanted to build my interpretation of a '73 RS replica ... I got the '73 RS Carrera fibreglass ducktail, repainted the car white and put black Fuchs on it ... These were not modifications for style or looks; I was doing all this so that I could continue to progress on the track ... I painted the Brumos stripes on the car. Brumos is my favourite race team and car dealership, one that has been in business for over 50 years. Their number-one driver, Hurley Heywood, won Daytona five times and Le Mans three times ... the red, white and blue Brumos livery also ties into my love of Americana, Evel Knievel ... I just wanted a low-digit number with sevens in it because I was born 7/7/67... I never wanted a big motor ... I can't physically keep my foot planted with 277's short-stroke, twin-plug 2-6 motor with about 230 horsepower, so why do I need 300 horsepower?

OUTLAW MEANS A REAL, SHARED DRIVING EXPERIENCE.

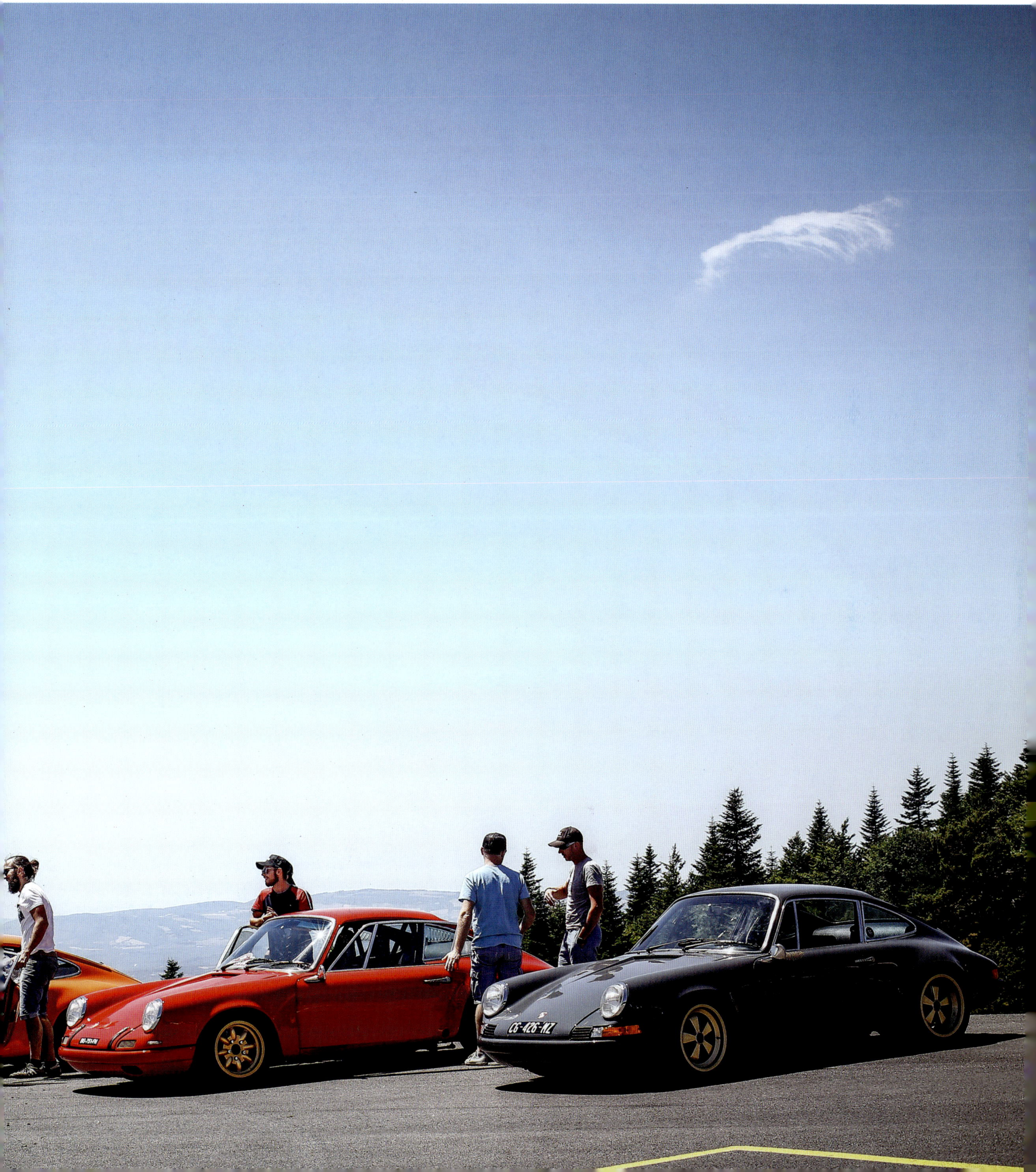

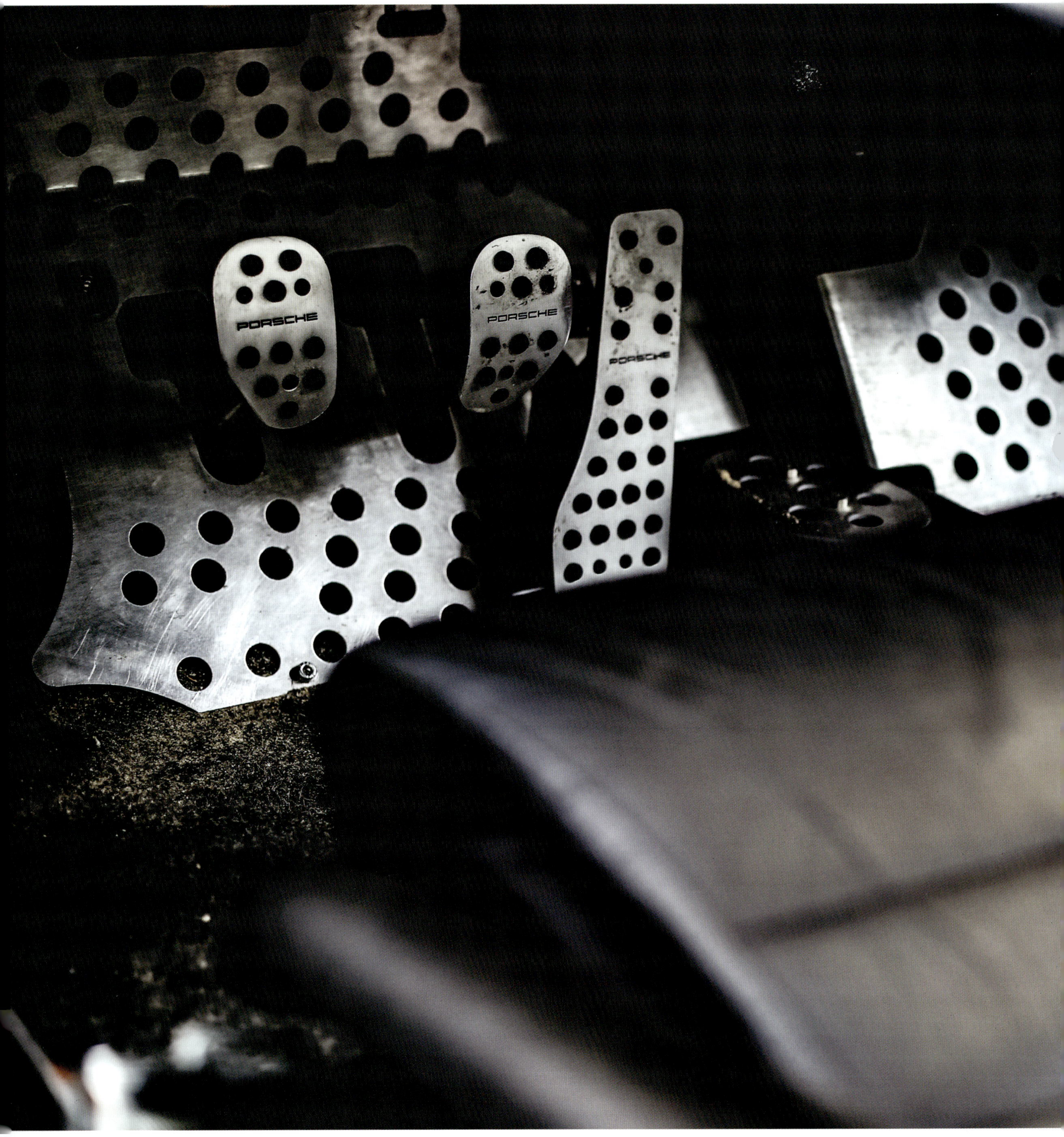
PORSCHE
PORSCHE
PORSCHE

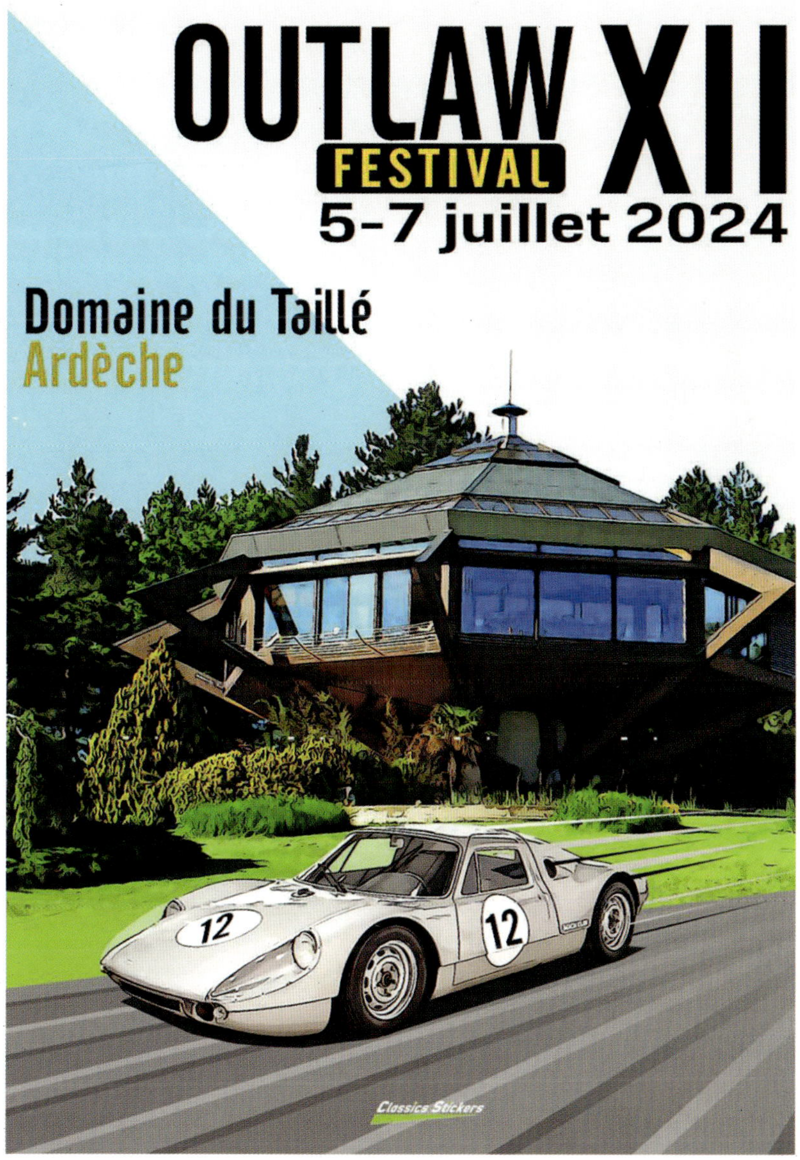

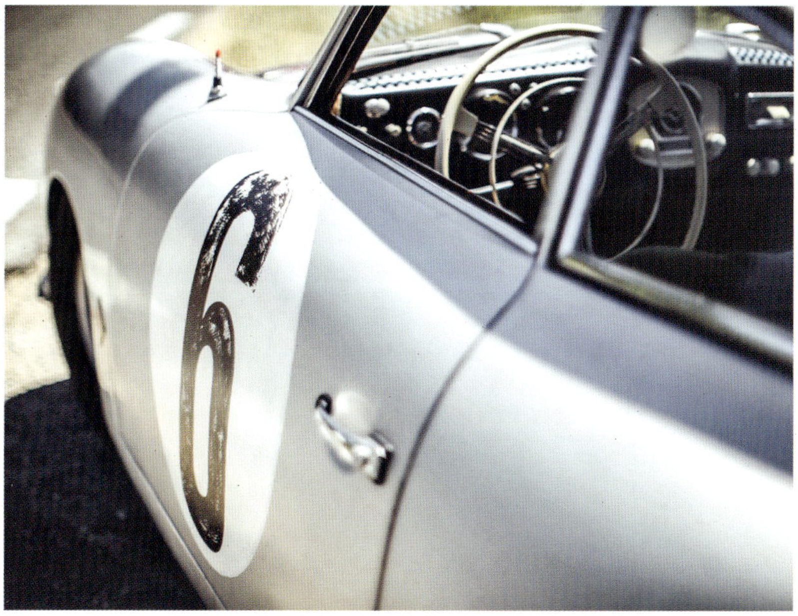

... In 277, you can keep your foot planted all the time, and I enjoy that ... There's nothing more intense than the feeling you get behind the wheel: with a car like 277 you smell the gas, you smell the oil, you just smell everything, you can almost taste the engine. You hear the wind, you know the seals don't work good, so it's ssssshhhhhh, there's all this road noise because there's not much insulation. It's the mechanical-ness, the creaky-ness, the throttle response, the squeaky brakes, the smell of the rubber, the oil, the smell of the brake pads when they get hot, it's all of that stuff ... to me it's an emotional high. Like I say, driving one of these machines uses all of your senses." And yet: "277 preceded all that; the car came before I was building outlaw Porsches."

GETTING POPULAR

It's an anthem to that raw, mechanical feeling and Nicolas agrees: "The advantage of starting out on your own is that you bring a completely personal approach. My goal was just to create cars and drive them! Hard driving in a 911 – with its rear-mounted flat-six – takes a lot of experience if you want to go fast. To show it true respect you have to push it to the limit. Your build should be a reflection of your culture. Mine is rock 'n' roll,

1 2 3

1. Aluminium Porsche-branded pedal set for that raw, metal-on-metal driving sensation.

2. Porsche Outlaw rallies are becoming ever more popular.

3. A 356 with race number on the door ... Which way to the starting grid?

and I also like things that are beautiful, handmade – quality craftsmanship. The cars are truly transformed; that is also why we call them Outlaws. They combine backdating for the vintage feel with restomod elements for performance, and it all comes together in an Outlaw – because the finishing touches are unique to each builder, each car, each owner. An Outlaw lives outside the rules, so you do what you want to do, and that's that. They are built to go from A to B, to go out and have a drink with your friends. It's just like café racer motorbikes. You do a lap and push yourself to the limit – that's the point! But there is a very strong community aspect to the movement. When I set up the company ten years ago, if you wanted to take a car to a Porsche rally to show what you were up to, they wouldn't even let you in. At the Porsche Paradise gatherings, even if you were registered in advance with a 3.2-litre 911, they'd make you park outside because your car was modified. It wasn't nice, truth be told. And that's how separate gatherings for modified

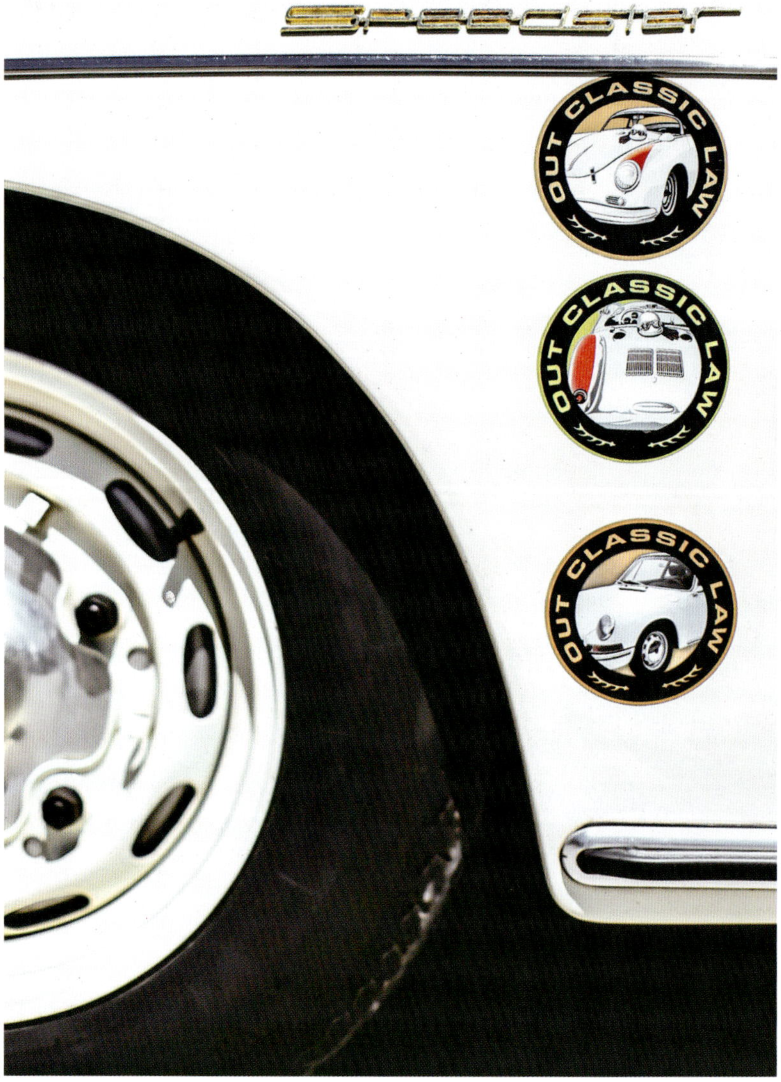

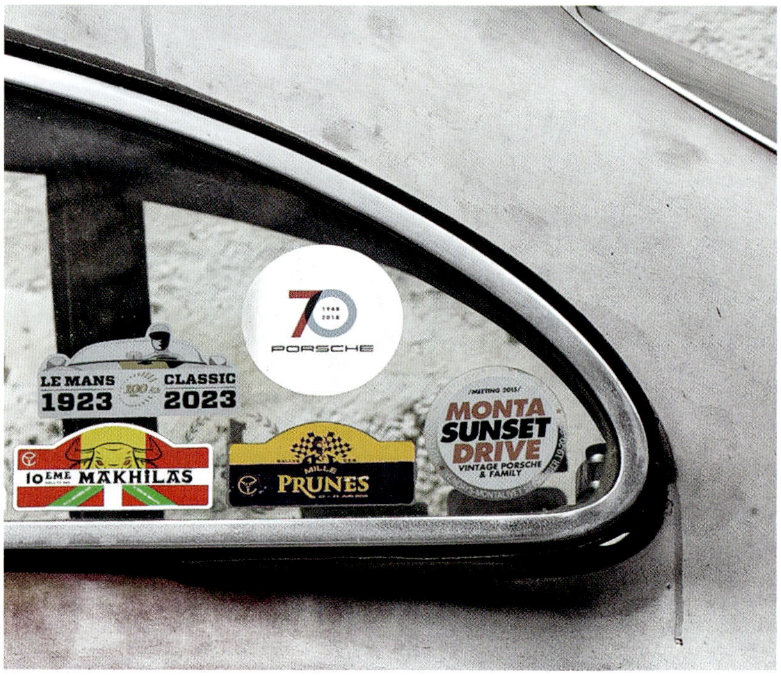

1. Stickers from the Out Classic Law adorn the left wing of this Speedster.

2. Meets are displayed on the rear quarter-light, including the Monta Sunset Drive.

3. Porsche Outlaws meet at the Monta Sunset Drive.

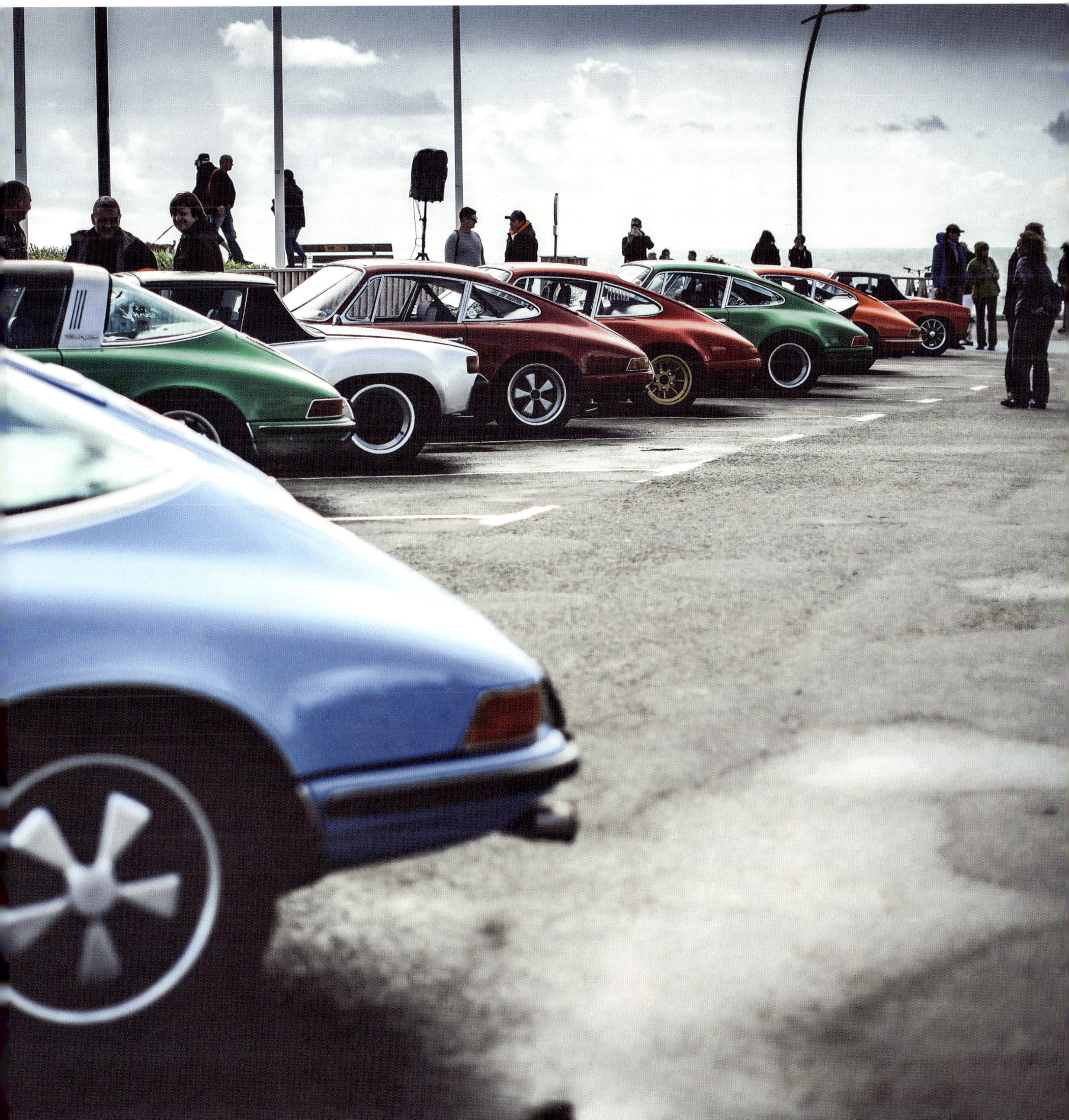

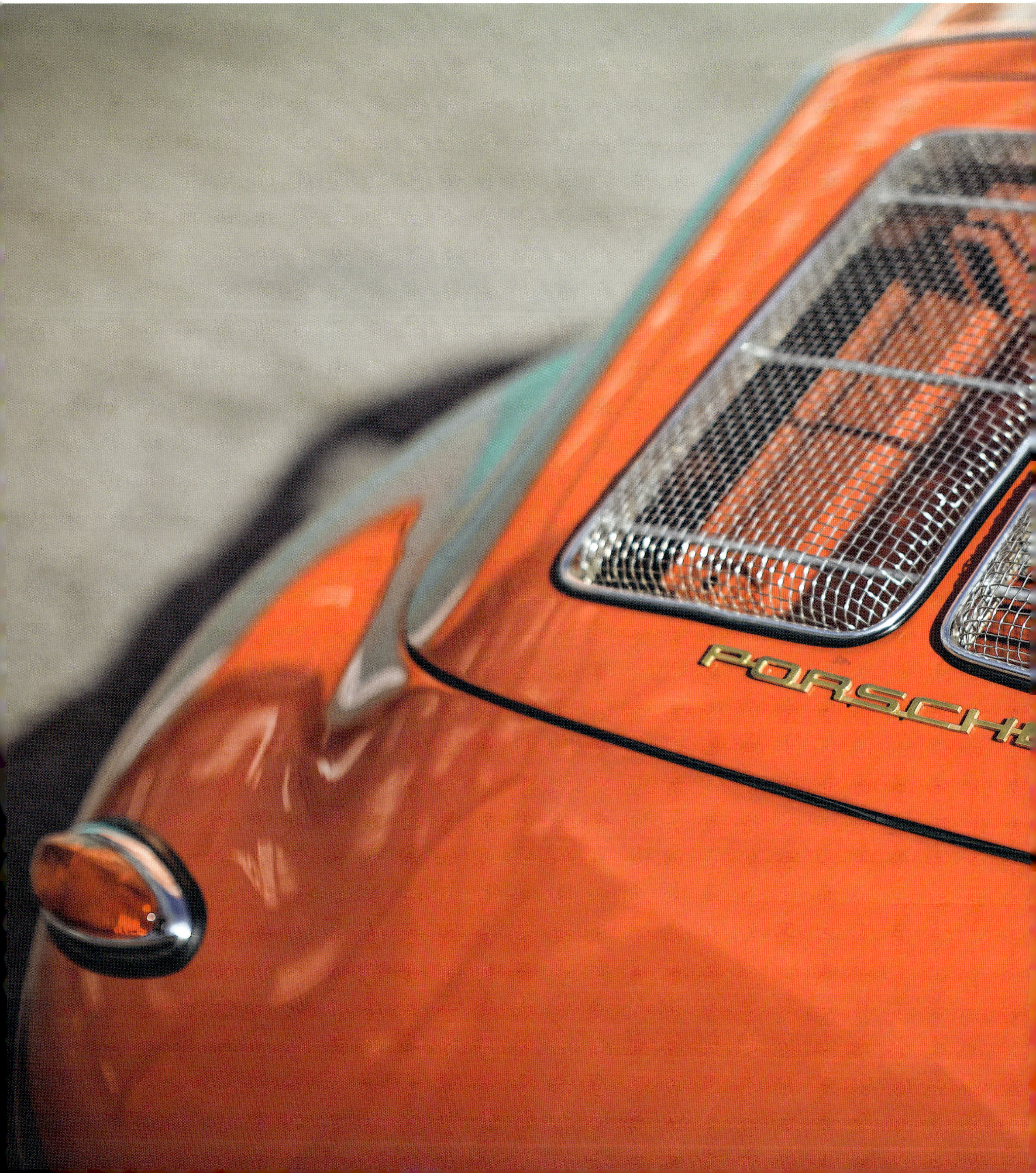
PORSCHE

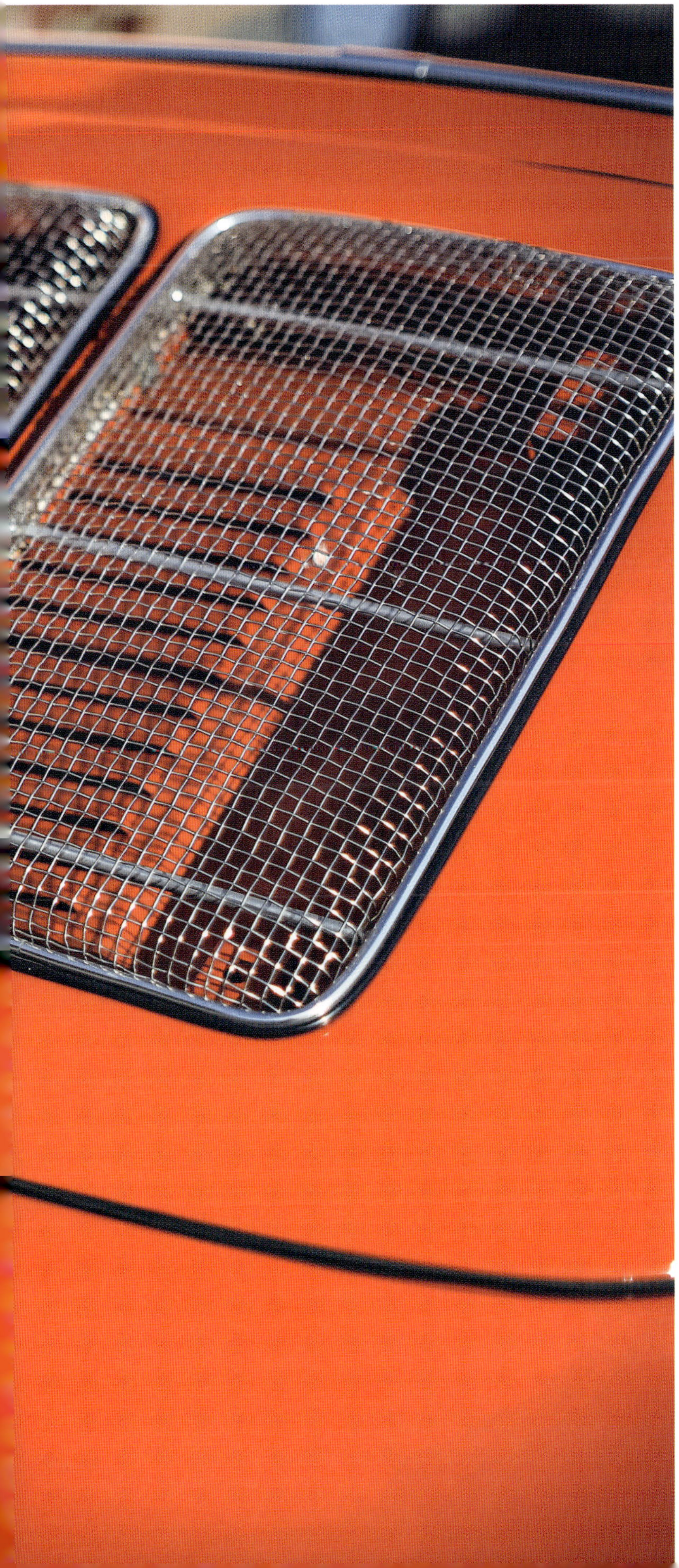

Porsches came about, a bit like speakeasies during the Prohibition era. Events such as the Monta Sunset Drive in Montalivet and the famous Out Classic Law, which first started in 2010, sprung up and have become more and more successful. The word Outlaw caught on and gained notoriety. The last Out Classic Law took place in early July 2024 in France.

And so, these customized Porsches – once rejected by the hardcore Porsche community – are now popular. These days, they even get invitations to official rallies. Porsche Paradise now showcases them, and a Porsche Outlaw parade takes place at Le Mans Classic. Everything has changed, and the term Outlaw has now become completely acceptable.

WHATEVER PORSCHE YOU HAVE, IT'S THE LOVE YOU HAVE FOR IT THAT MAKES IT WONDERFUL.

911

RED HOT

LEAP INTO THE PAST

This 911 looks like it could have come straight out of Magnus Walker's garage in LA. In fact it was built in Nantes, in France. The owner, Yvan, says every time he gets in it feels like stepping back in time, discovering distant, almost-forgotten emotions.

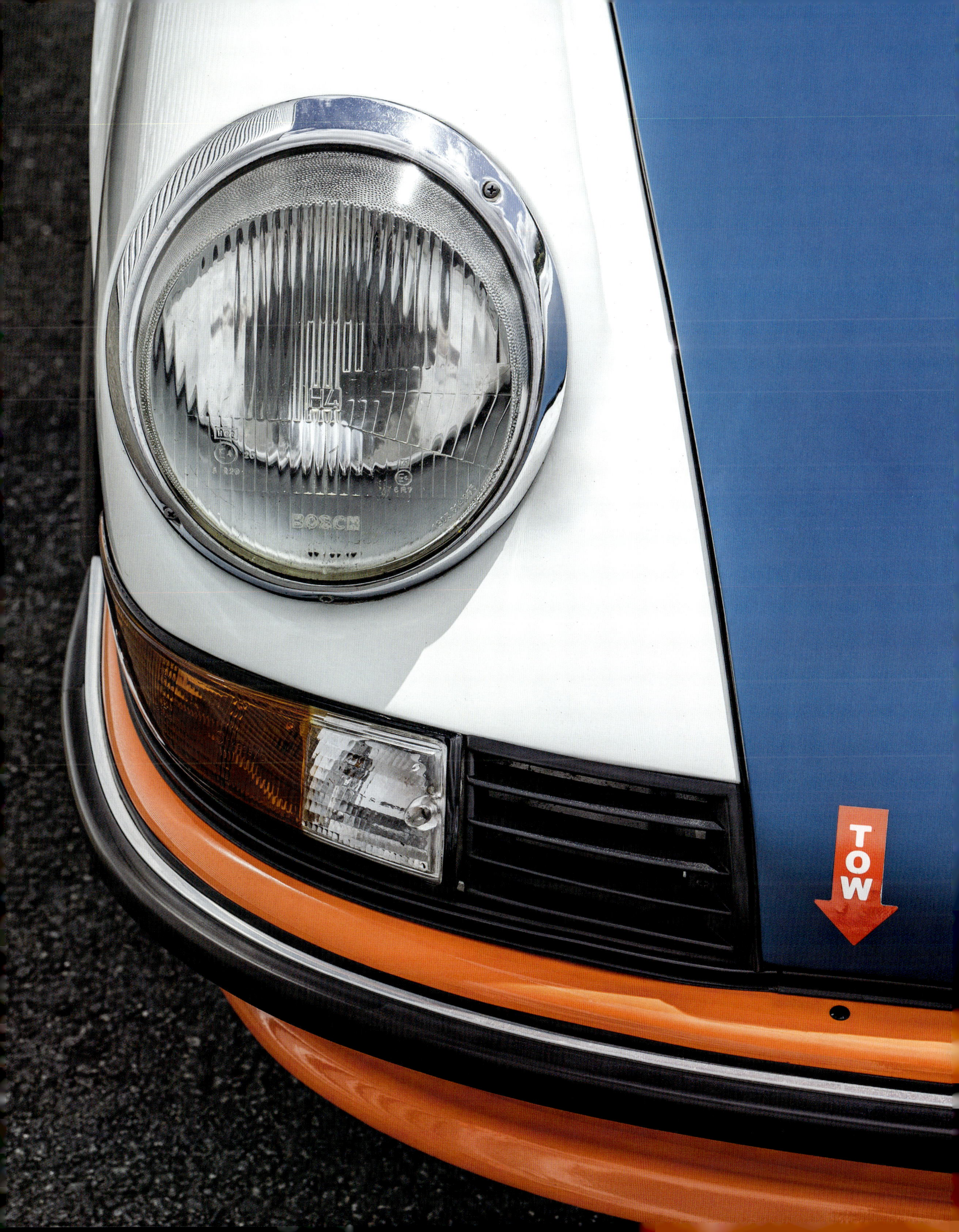
BOSCH
TOW

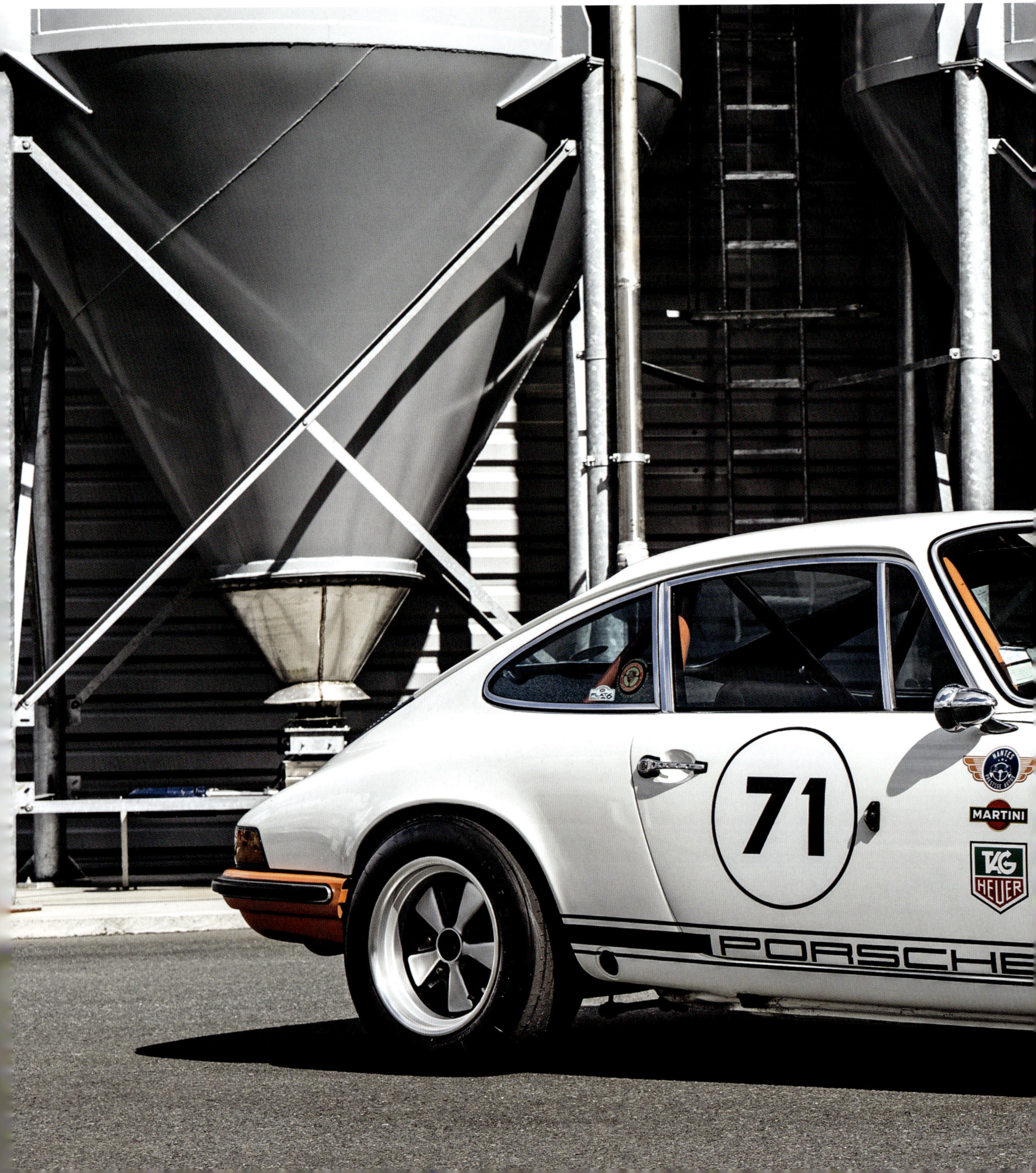
71
MARTINI
TAG
HEUER
PORSCHE

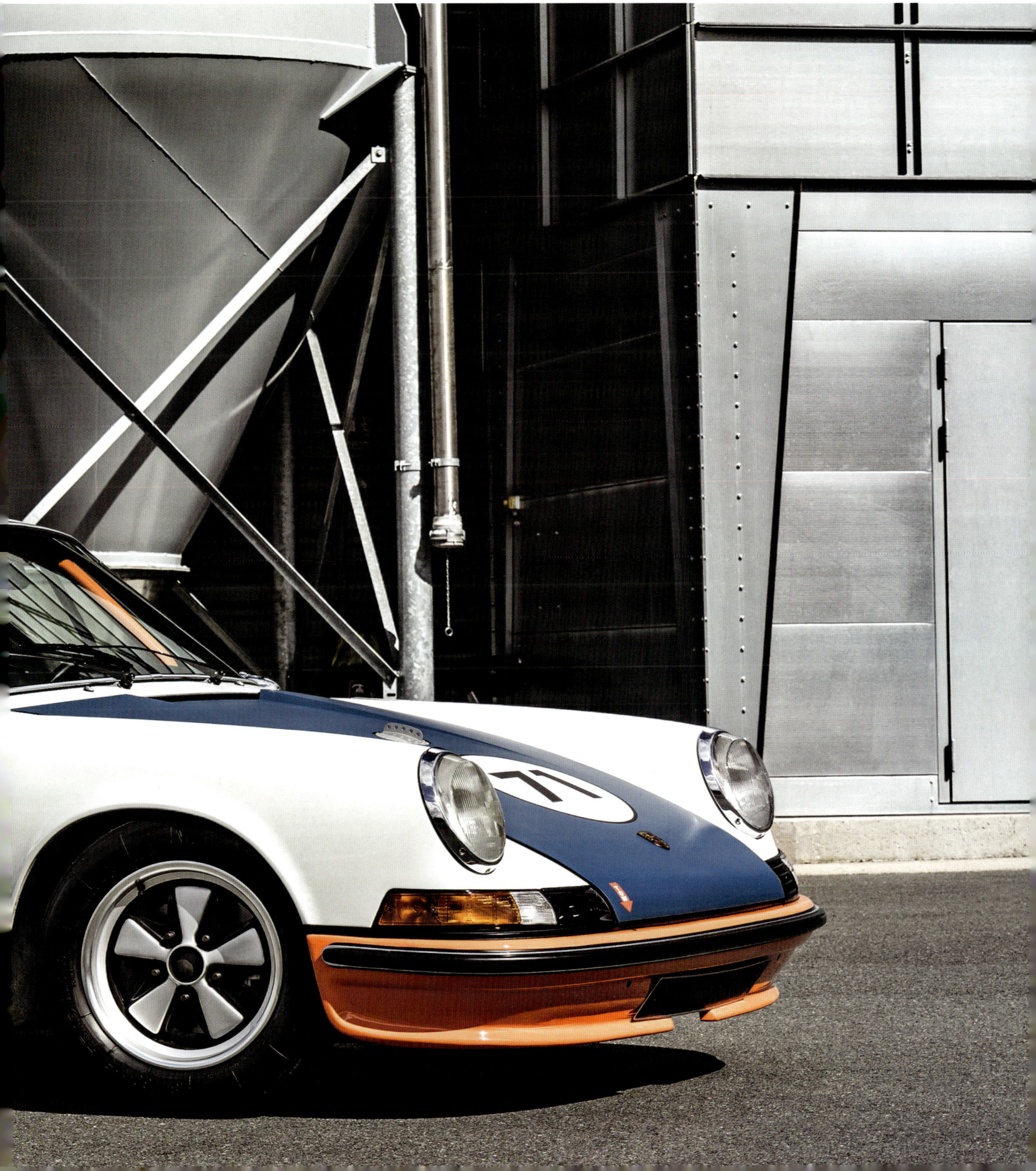

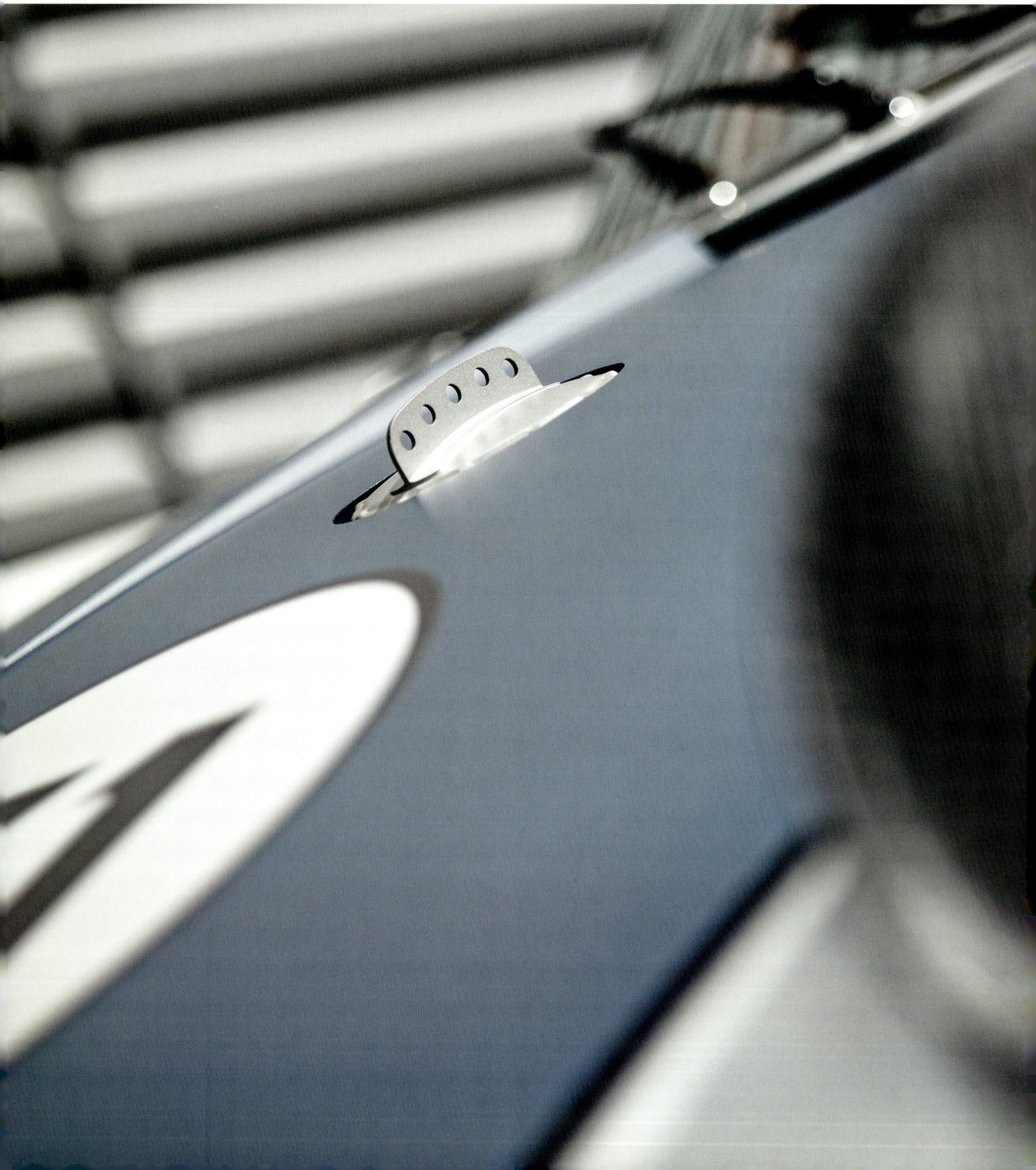

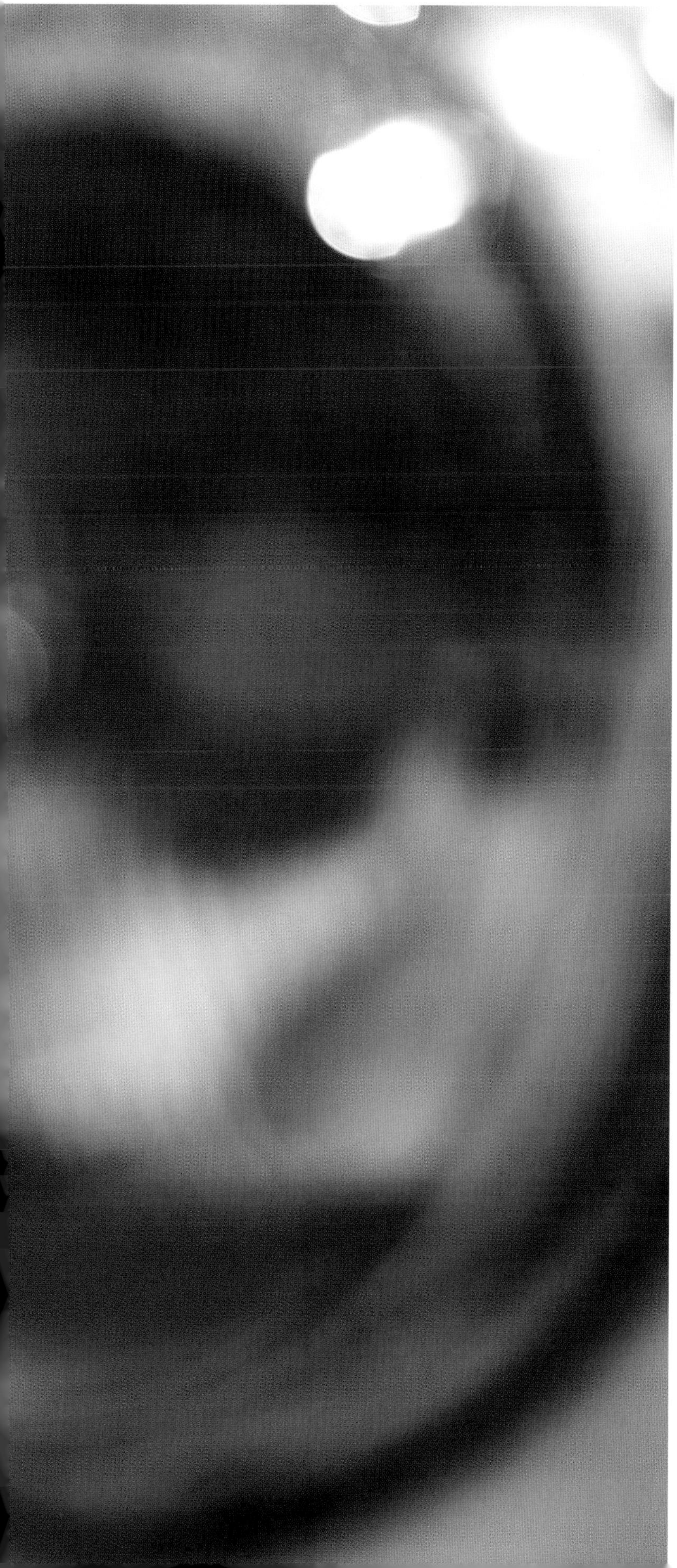

LARGE FUEL CAP IN THE MIDDLE OF THE HOOD – JUST LIKE A RACE CAR.

This Porsche Outlaw embodies the image that's most associated with this type of modified car. Possibly the best-known one is the 911 with 277 on it that was built by the famous, LA-based Magnus Walker and his Urban Outlaw Porsches. So at the beginning of February 2024, Yvan took his own pride and joy to the Rétromobile car show in Paris to meet the man who inspired his own outside-the-law Porsche. "It was a huge event," he said. "Magnus Walker is so popular it's unbelievable. He spent all day signing autographs, always with a smile and his pleasant human touch. I wasn't actually that much of a fan, because I'm more about the cars, but in spite of that shaggy look, he absolutely lives his passion for Porsches; it's what he cares about the most. I like that aspect of him, and he's a great character too." At one point, Walker approached Yvan's 911 and wrote a dedication on the left wing: "Pedal to the metal," he inscribed. "Unfortunately, the pen he used wasn't a permanent marker. So, in order not to lose the historic autograph, and using the skills I learned in my youth when restoring stained-glass windows in cathedrals, I set about recreating the signature identically on the roof above the driver's door. I added an Urban Outlaw sticker that I had picked up at the show." Yvan's Urban Outlaw was signed by the master!

Yvan bought the car in 2021. "I was looking for a Porsche and when the ad for this one came out, I jumped at the chance. It was there less than four days. It was love at first sight." It had been restored by the owner of the Nantes Prestige Autos garage, and it turned out to be a bit of a phoenix: "He found it in a field with a tree growing through the floor. He rebuilt it completely to give it this incredible Outlaw setup. It took more than four years to transform it into such a stylish machine. But then – for reasons of the heart – he sold it." It was originally a 1971 911 with a 2.2 T engine, hence the 71 on the doors and the bonnet: "I was born in 1972, so it's a little bit older than me." The Porsche was painstakingly put together and now has a 2.7-litre, flat-six engine, its power leaping from the original 125 hp to more than 250 hp!

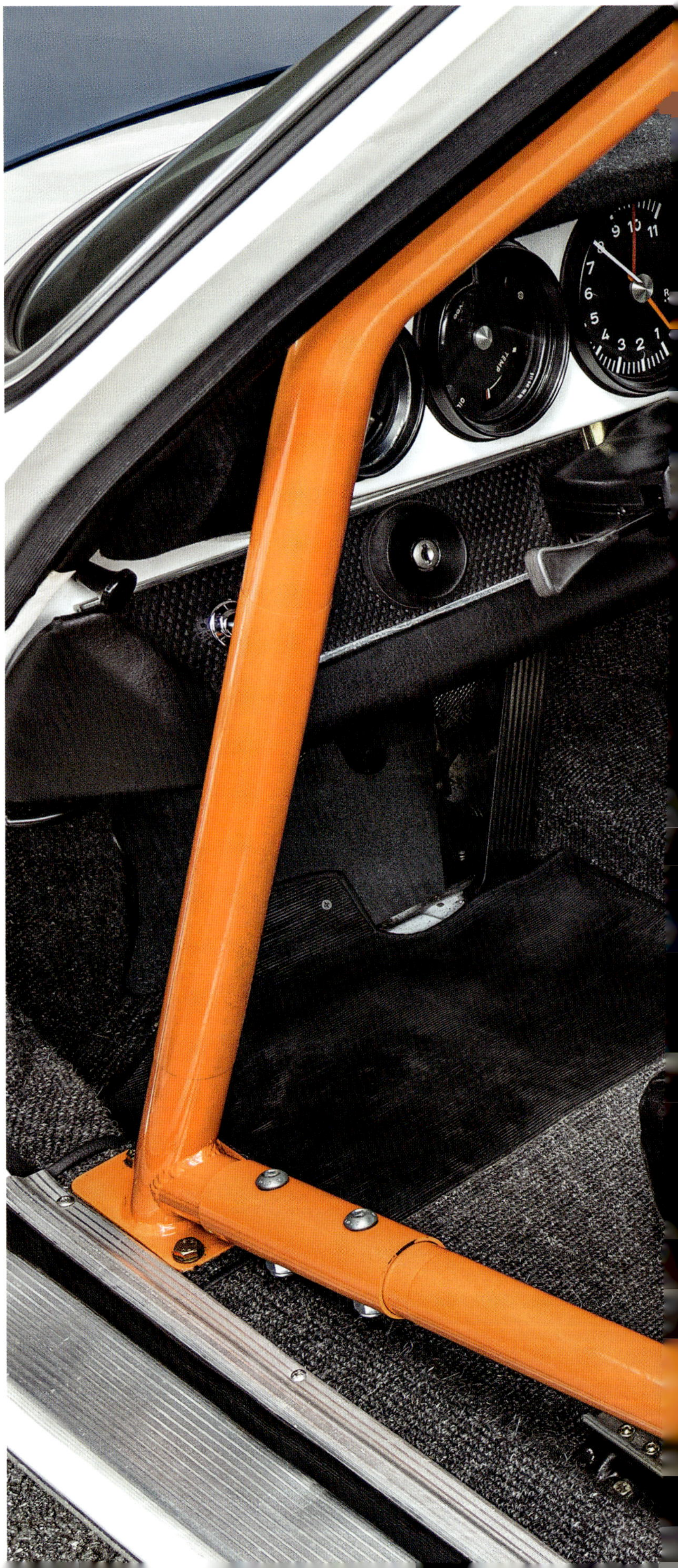

ORANGE ROLL BAR IN A METICULOUSLY MAINTAINED 911.

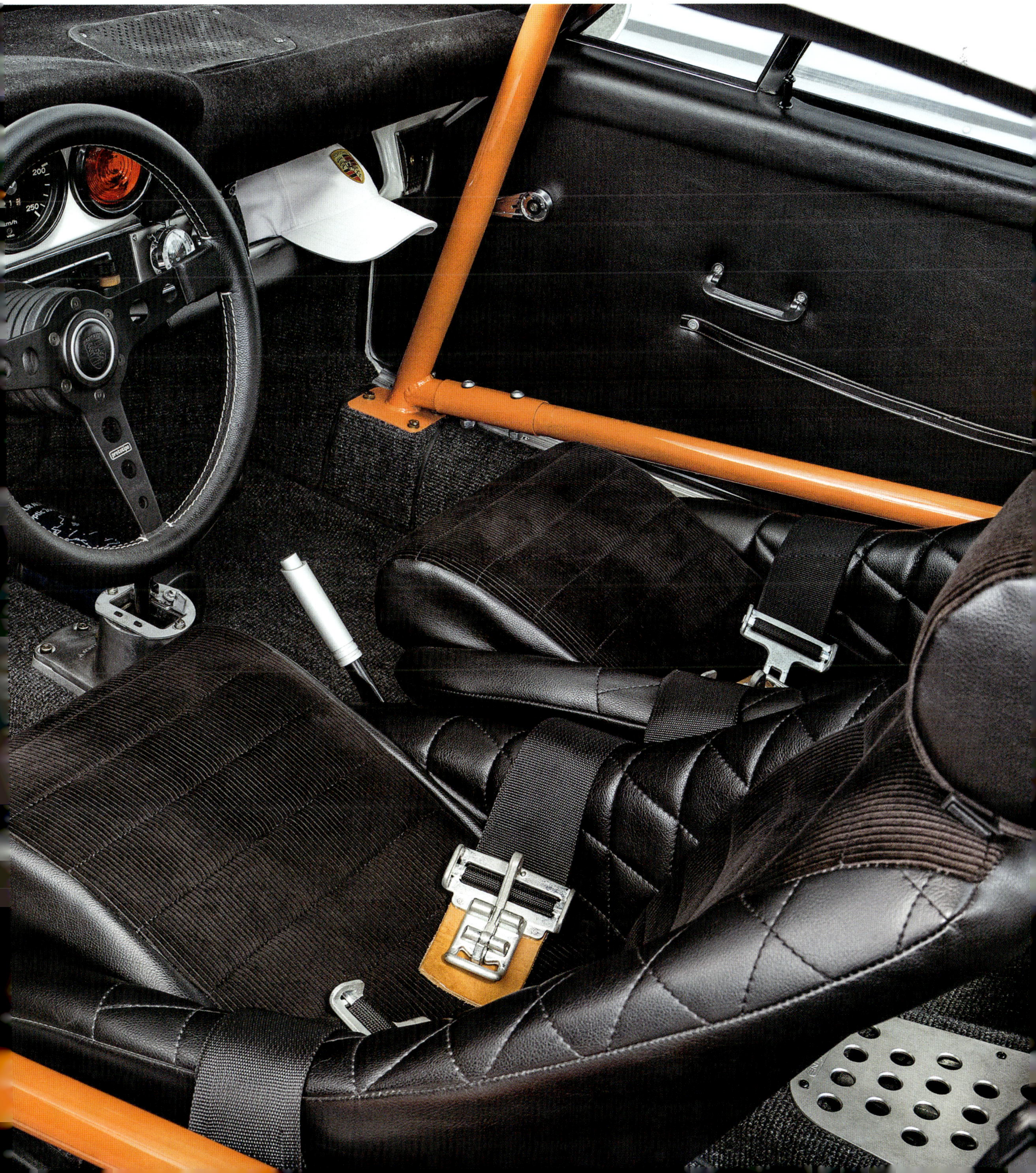

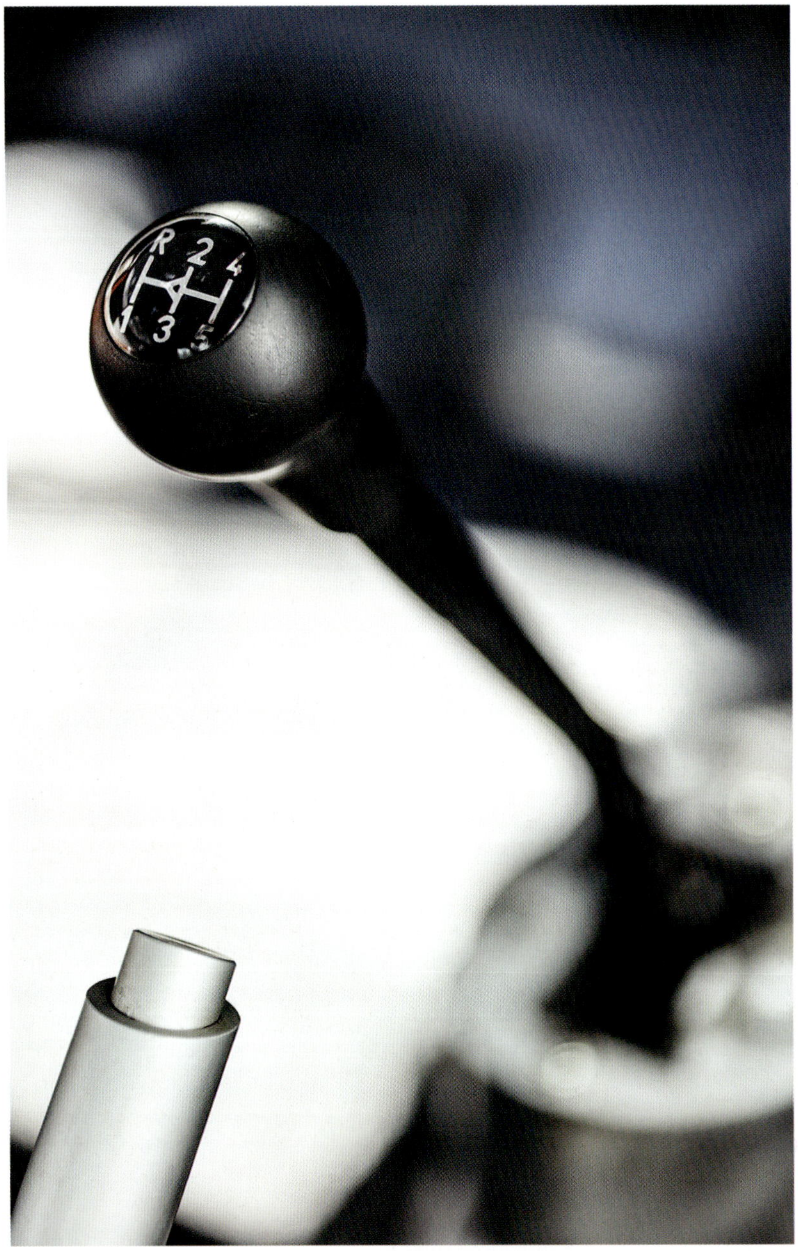

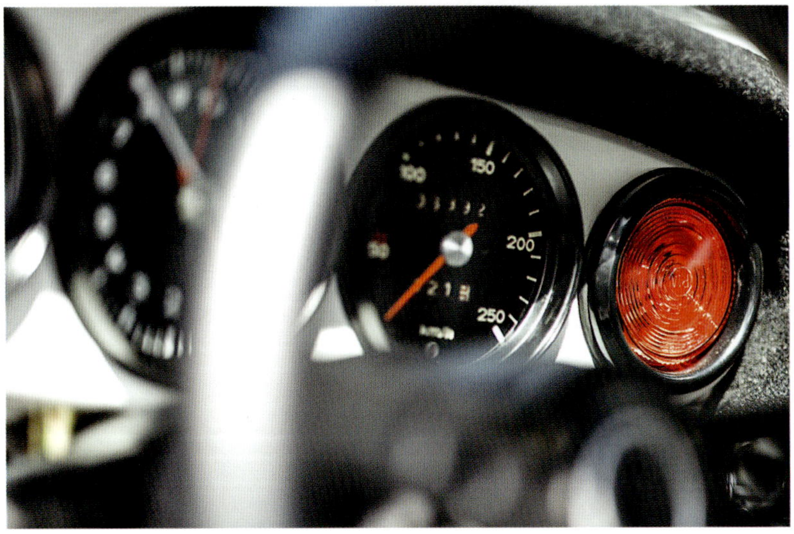

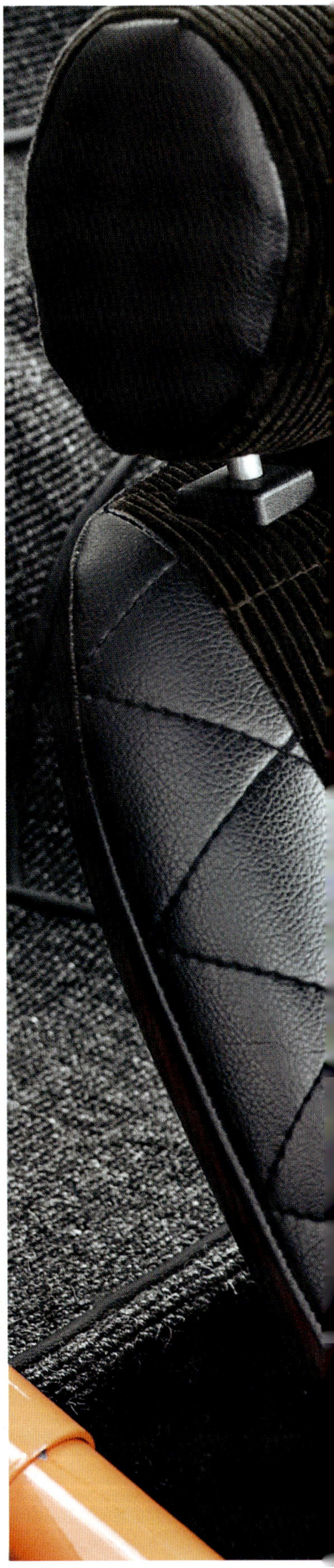

1 2 3

1. The original gear stick still controls the changes.

2. The clock was replaced with a red light to indicate low oil pressure.

3. Vintage seats welcome driver and passenger for a journey back in time.

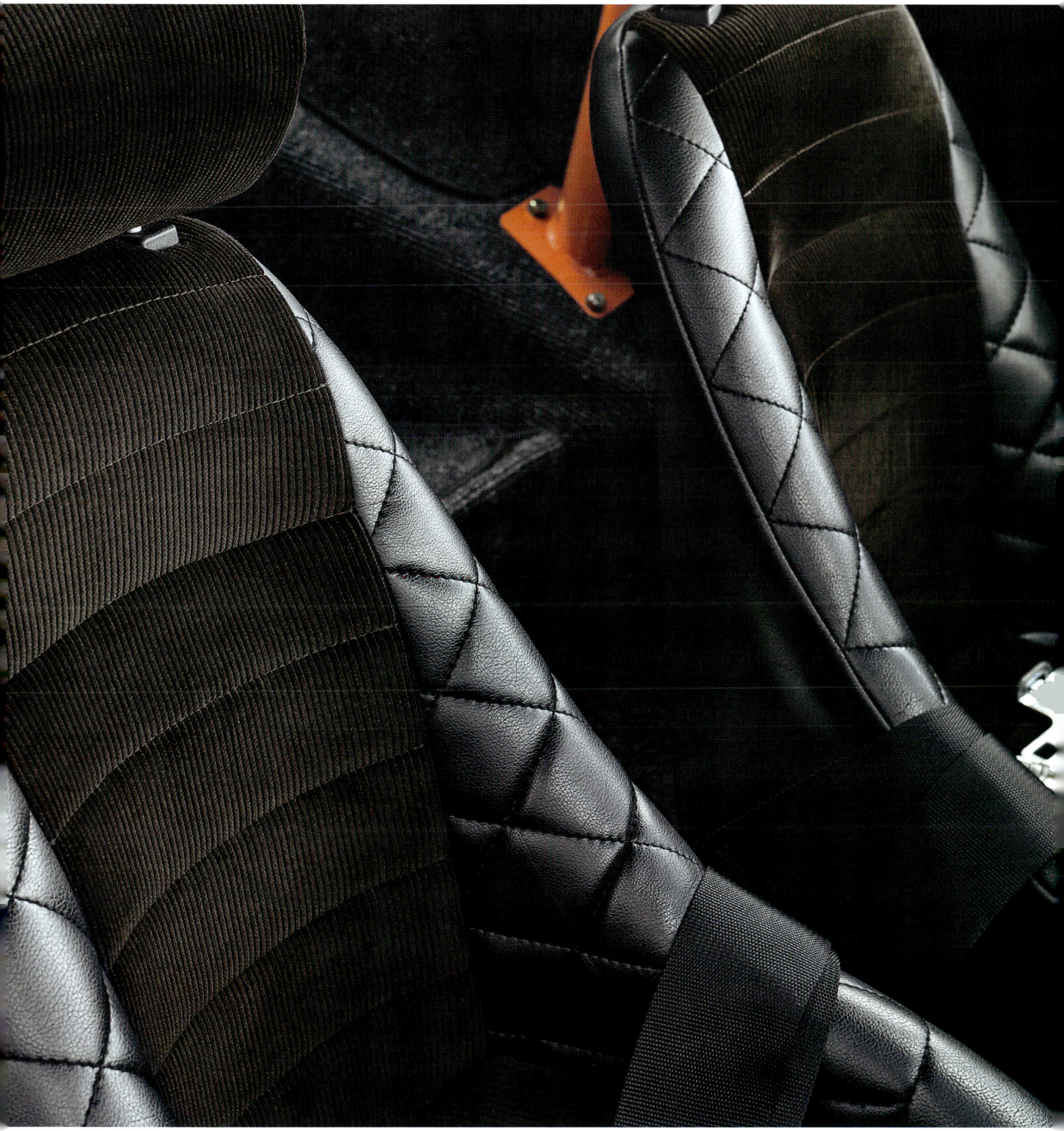

"It's a racing car with a roll cage, but I can use it on the road. The car's Outlaw side is very much present! Actually, it took me a long time to find an insurer who would provide cover. In the end I found two, including Aviva – now Abeille Assurance [Bee Insurance] – who specialize in non-original Beetles and VW Combis. The policy calls it a 'modified Porsche' and states that it doesn't have the original engine."

In addition to the high-power flat-six that's fed by two 40 mm Weber triple-choke carburettors, the entire running gear and suspension were taken from a 2.7 RS. "It is a narrow body, without any wing modification at all. The Fuchs rims are just a little wider, and in two shades of grey: slightly matt on the inside and glossy on the rim. The tyres are Michelin TB15s. They are road legal, but look like vintage racing tyres with matching tread patterns." Everything about this 911 evokes the spirit of Porsche without strictly adhering to the rules of a factory car. It's a beast from the track let loose on the road: "The colours are Porsche GP white and Gulf Orange – from the famous oil company – on the bumpers and the roll cage. To avoid copying Magnus Walker's car, which has a red hood and blue bumpers, the colours are reversed, with hood and trunk in a satin blue."

THE HUNT FOR LAP TIMES IS ON IN THIS 911, WHICH HAS THE SOUL OF A RACE CAR.

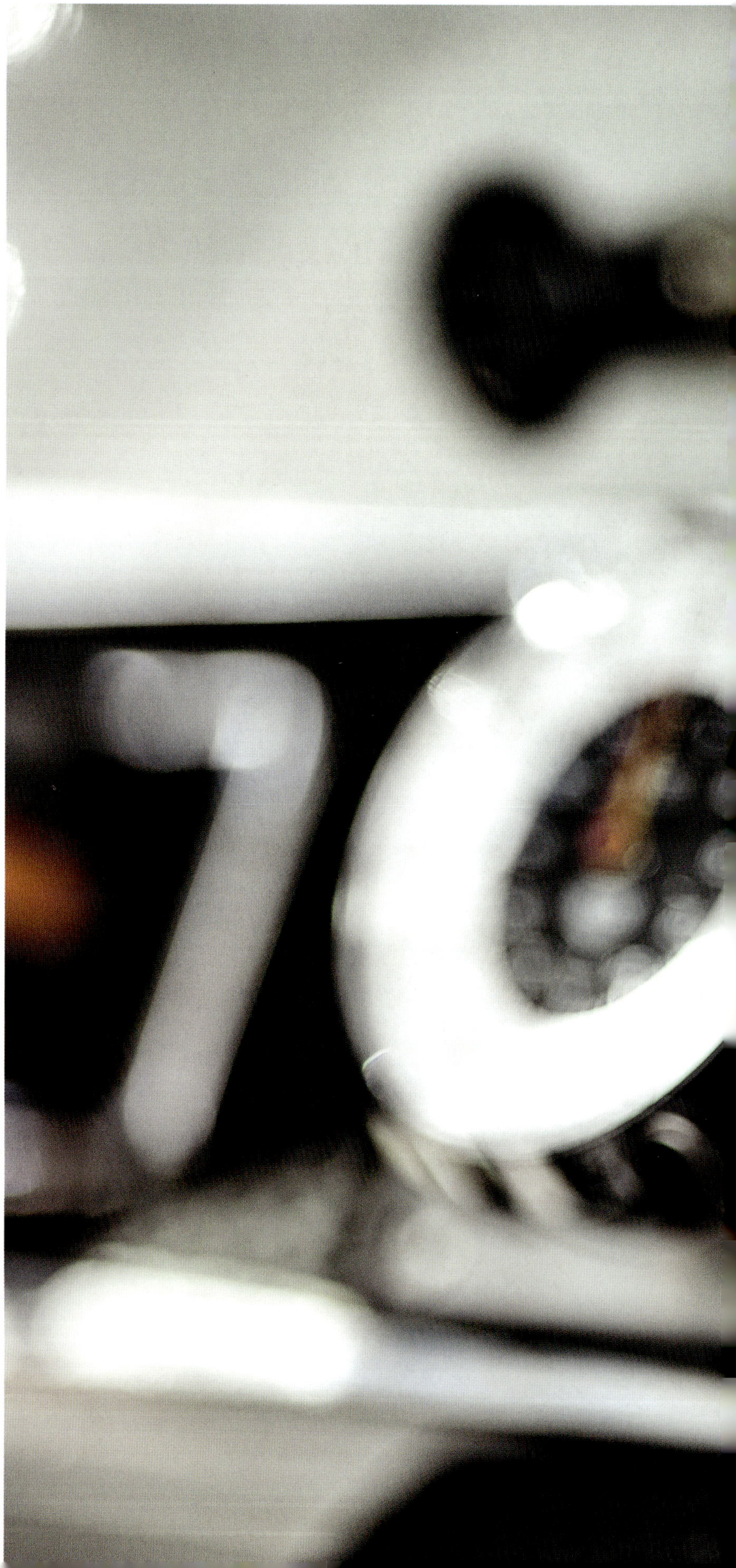

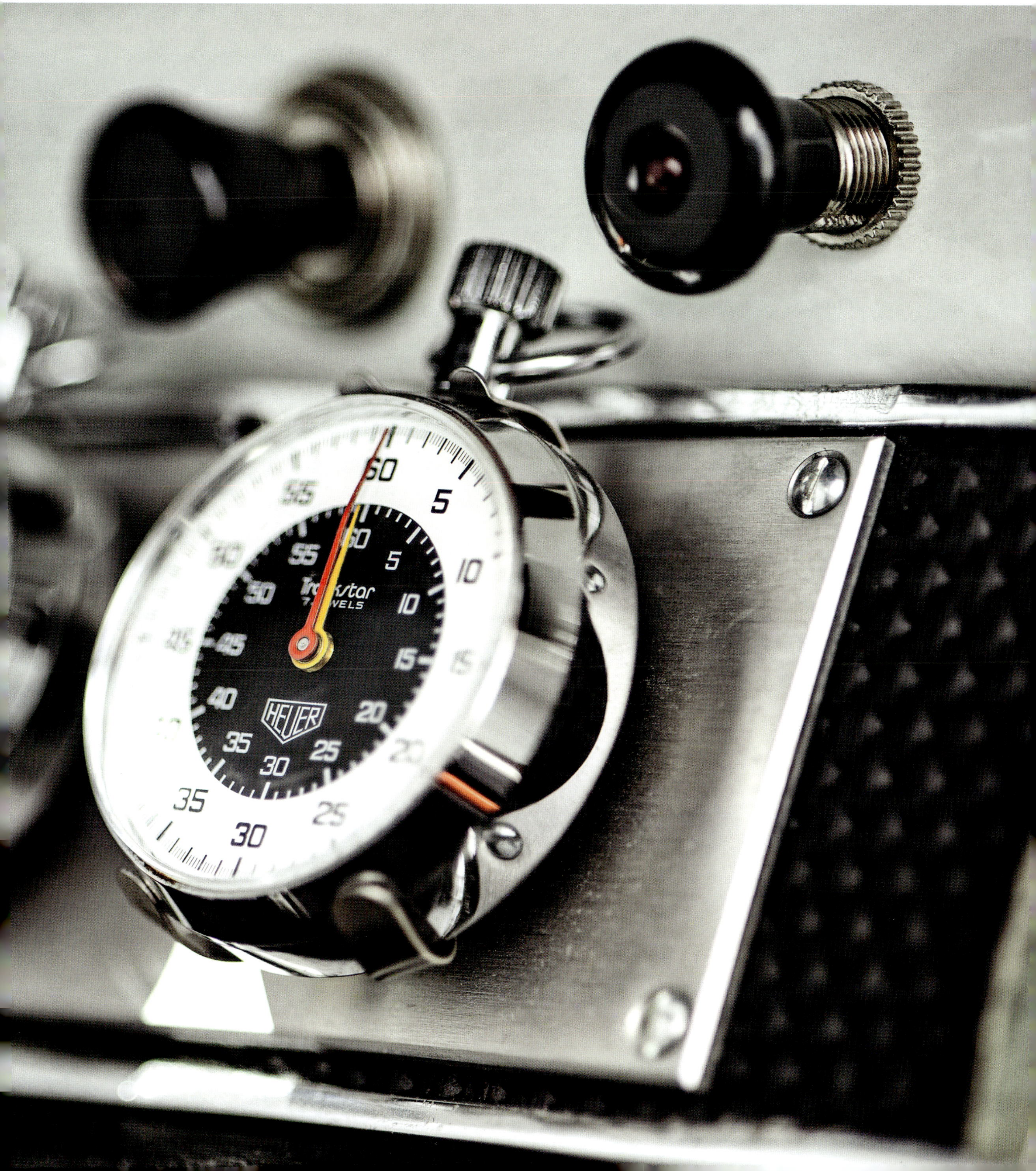
HEUER

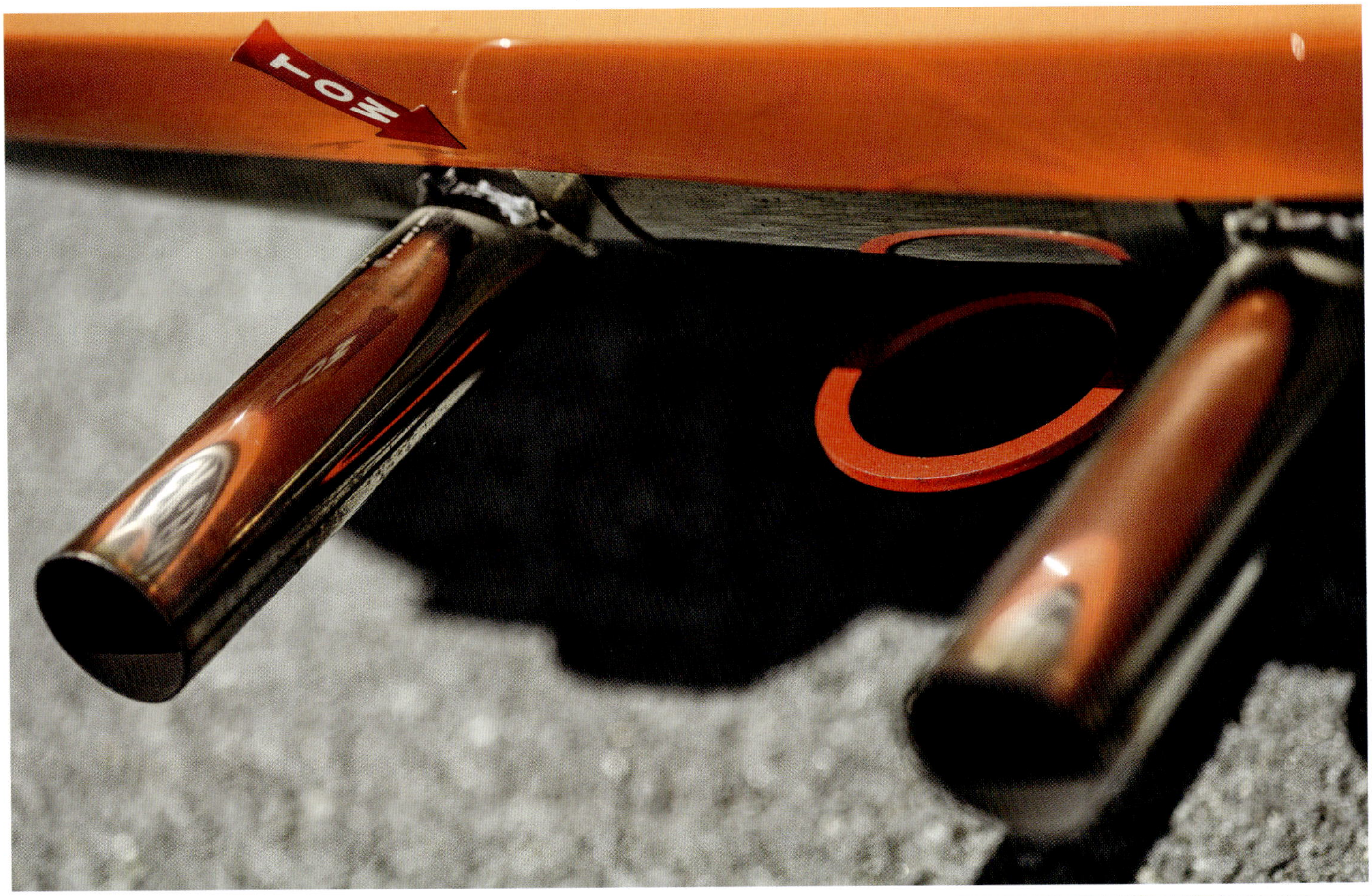

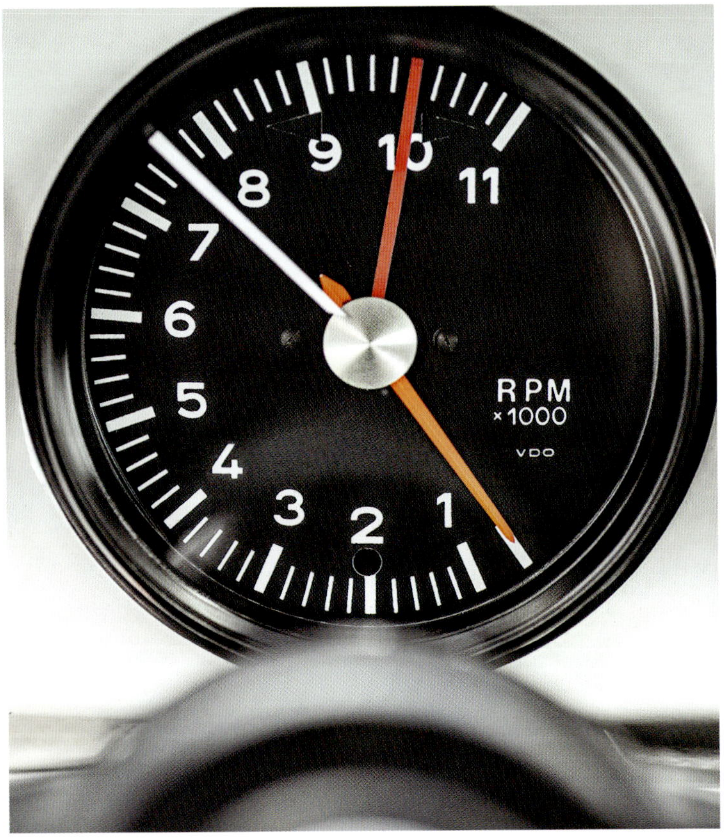
RPM
×1000
VDO

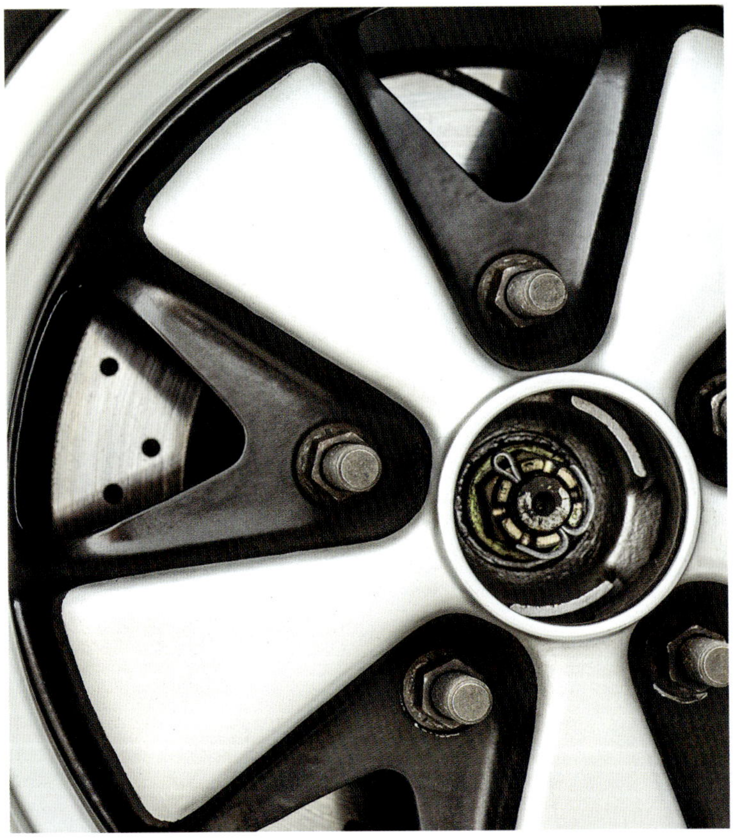

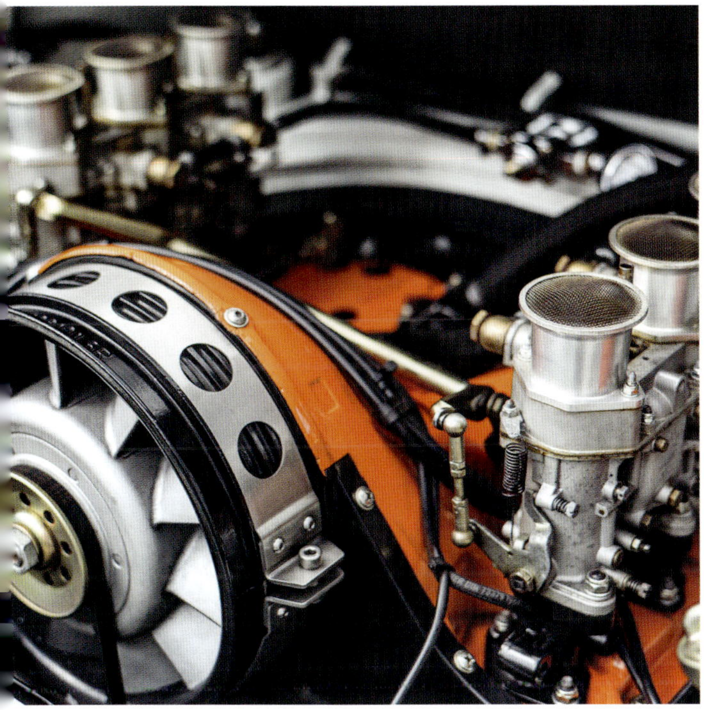

There are lots of little details that are reminiscent of the dreadlocked man from LA. "At the front is a large fuel cap right in the middle of the hood, just like on a race car. The door handles are perforated and there is a small light on each side to illuminate the number, just like in endurance racing. I added two more stylish bullet mirrors; the one on the right was missing completely. At the rear, on the metal engine hood, there are small vents to help the big flat-six breathe, just like Magnus has!"

Aesthetically, the collection of stickers and badges contributes to the car's spirit. The Porsche Club of America emblem sits proudly on the rear grille, just below the original, indispensable sticker of the famous R Gruppe, the American club that started Outlaw culture in California.

Inside, the attention to detail is just as lavish: attractive, vintage bucket seats in velvet and leather, with large seat-belt buckles for the driver and co-pilot – the only passengers allowed in the car. The steering wheel is a stunning MOMO Prototipo. It sits proudly in front of four of the five original dials – for racing, they took out the one on the right and replaced it with a big red warning light to show low oil pressure." Underneath, two analogue guages highlight the racing preparation detail which is found everywhere. "All the inside carpets are from a 2.7 RS," says Yvan. "Keeping with the racing spirit, you can see the gearbox linkage at the foot of the stick, and at the rear there is a latticed plate above the transmission – where the mechanical parts are visible – to allow heat to escape." Nothing is left to chance in this Outlaw, especially not Yvan's pleasure in driving it: "I go through an entire ritual. I take it out, prepare it, pamper it, warm it up gently. I listen to the engine idling with its magnificent sound, revving it a little. Then I take it for a drive, and it's like taking a journey back through time. They were so lucky to have cars like that in the 1970s. That's really what I enjoy most about this 911. Very few people have had the privilege of driving this Porsche, but I was determined to let Benjamin, my wife's son, do so. He died of cancer at the age of 23, two years ago. I wanted him to experience as many emotions as possible, so I let him take the wheel. He was a great kid and sharing that emotion with him was something really special."

911 RED HOT
BY THE NUMBERS

CREATION **1971**

FLAT CYLINDERS **6**

CC **2,700**

HP **250**

1. If you need to get it off the track, there's a red towing hook between the exhaust pipes of this 911.

2. The red zone is fixed at 10,000 rpm! Wanna give it a try?

3. The rims are genuine Fuchs, in two shades of grey.

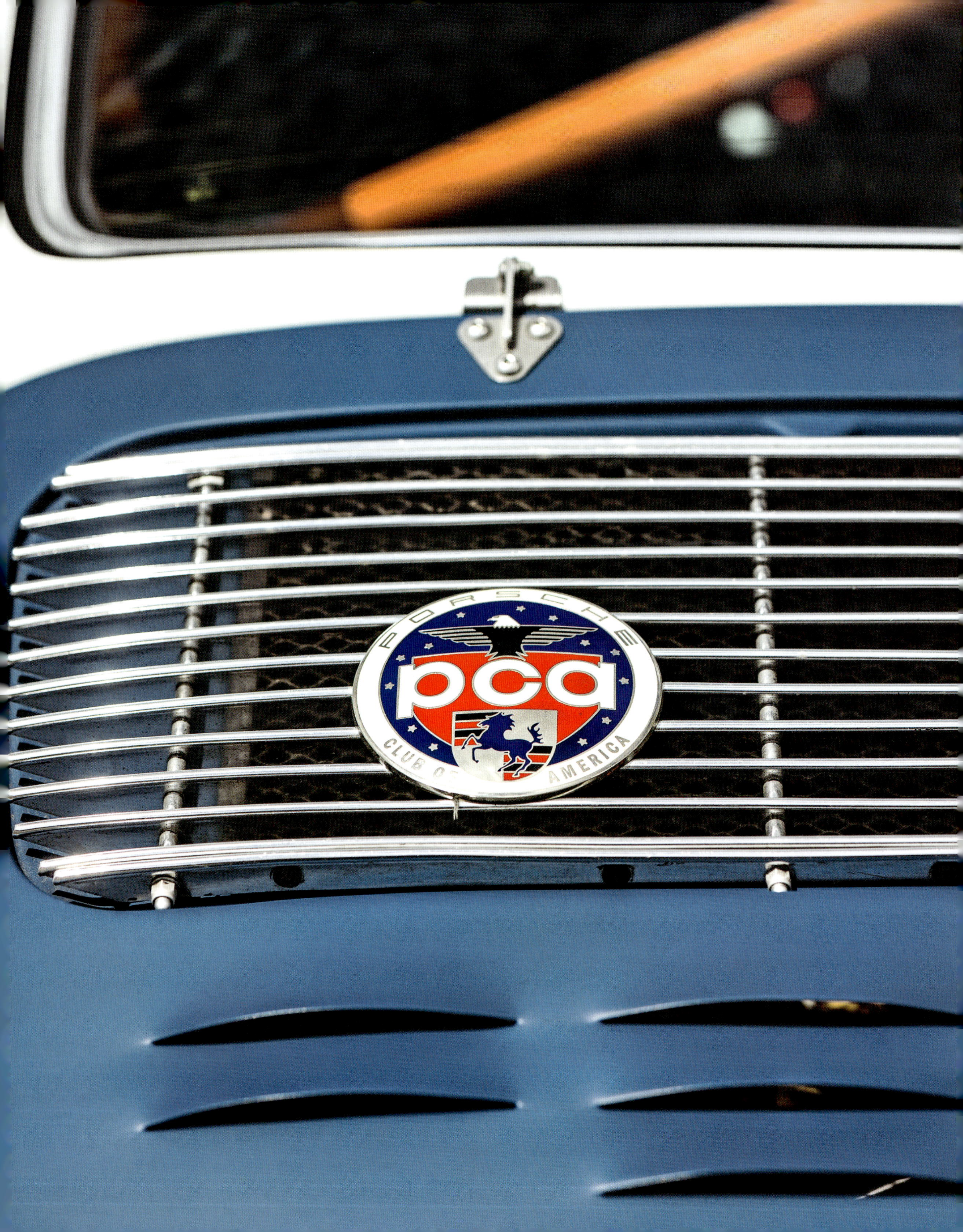
PORSCHE
pca
CLUB OF AMERICA

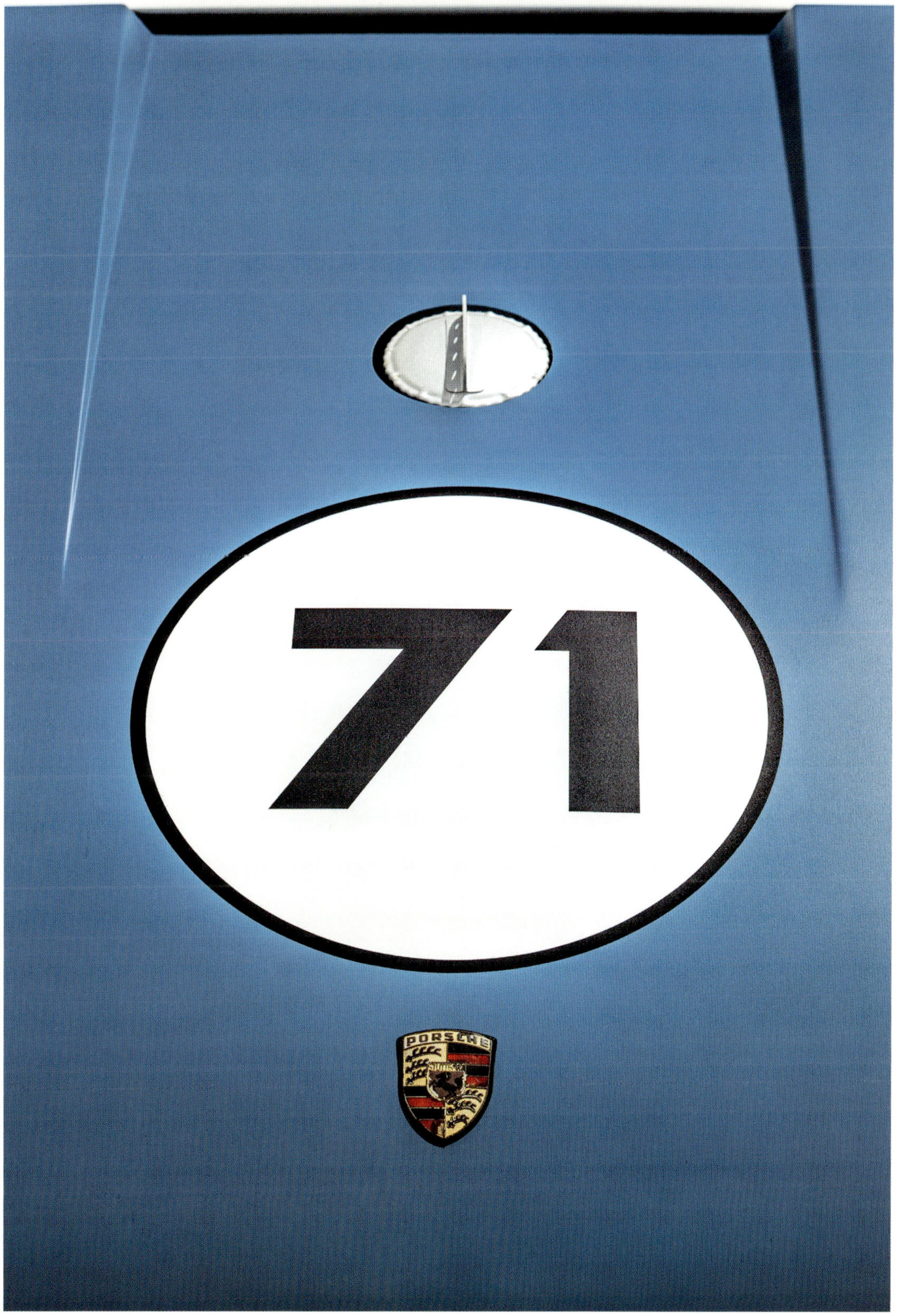

Above: 1971, the year this Porsche 911 was manufactured, starting life as a 2.2 T.

Opposite: The Porsche Club of America club emblem sits proudly on the engine grill above the small vents, Magnus Walker style.

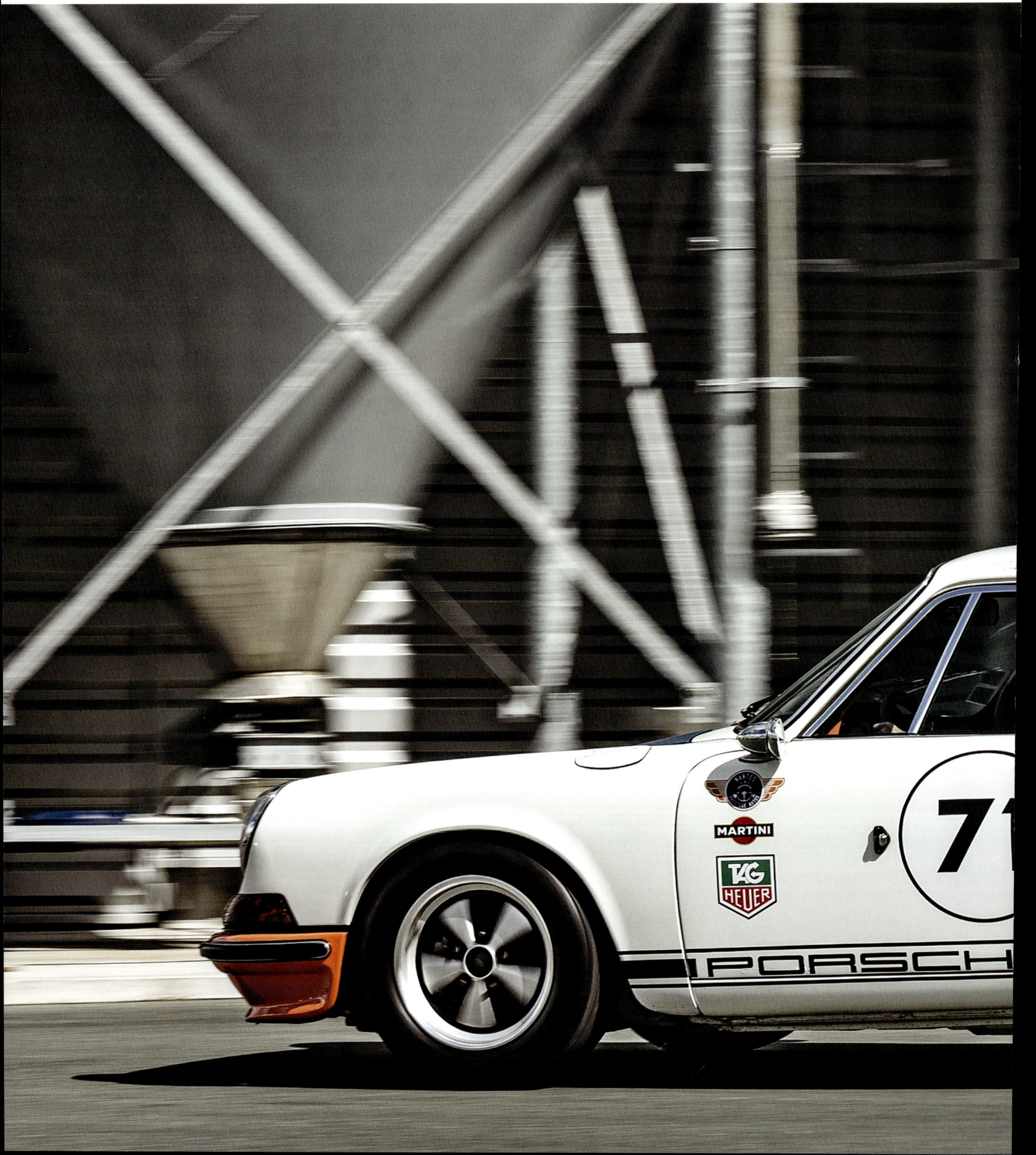
71
MARTINI
TAG
HEUER
PORSCH

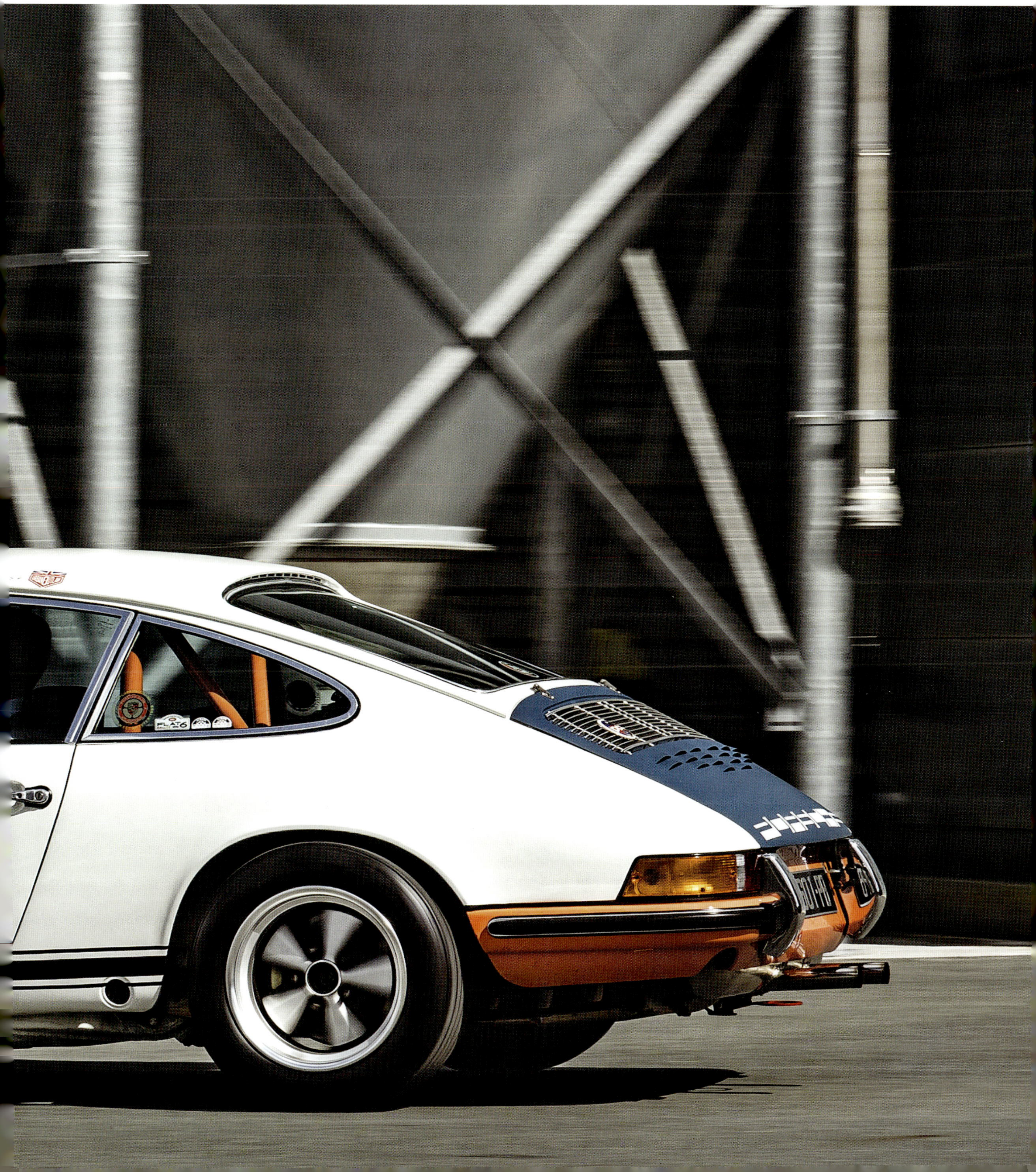

DESIGNER 924 CARRERA GT TURBO

INTERSCOPE

COMPLETELY DIFFERENT

Tanguy was 20 in 2020. His birthday present was a Porsche 924 Turbo in Carrera GT style, with a large helping of 935 Interscope! It was a car he had cherished since childhood. On the menu: roll bar, short box, 220 hp and a hydraulic handbrake ... All you need for a truly Outlaw driving experience.

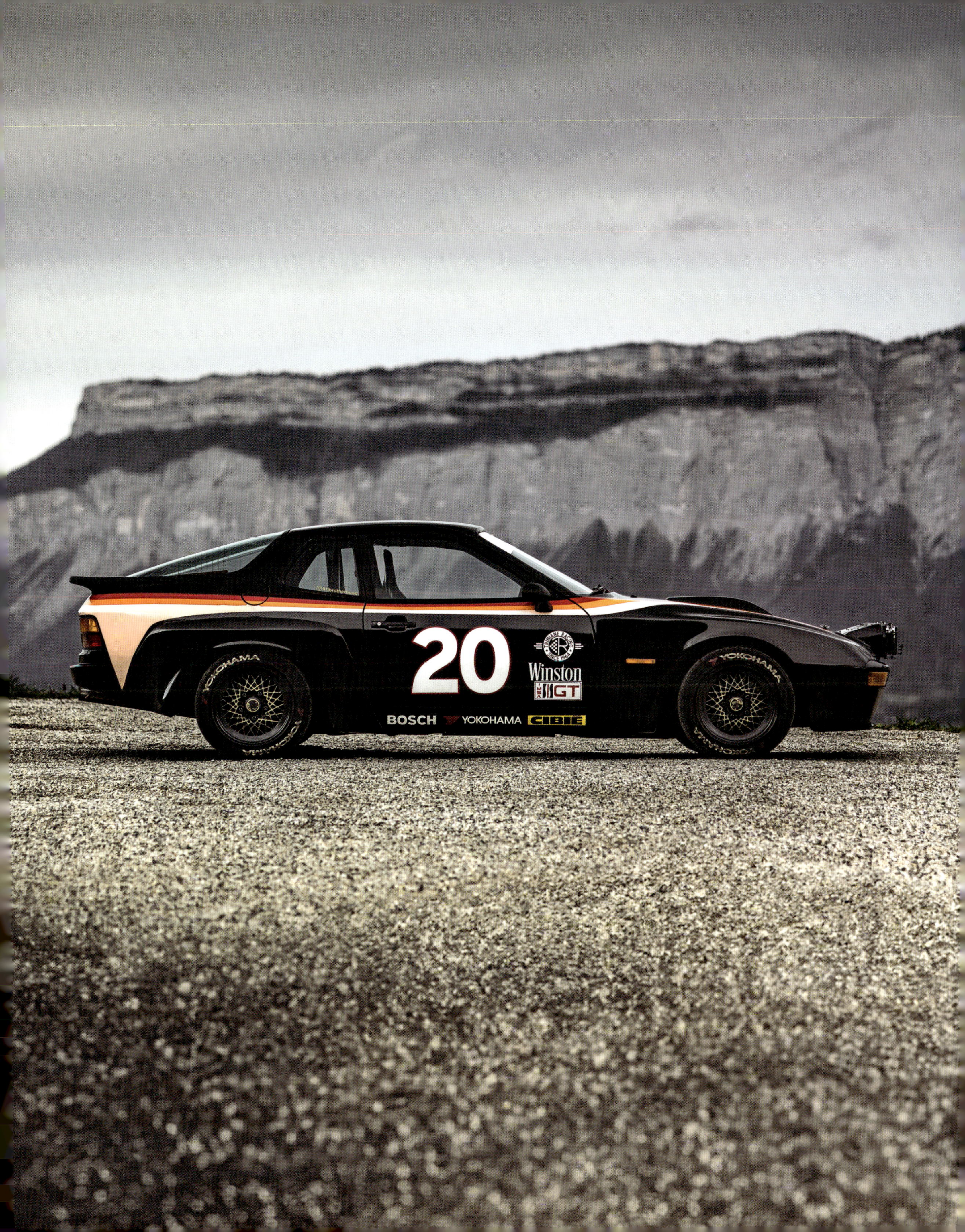
20
Winston
GT
BOSCH
YOKOHAMA
CIBIE

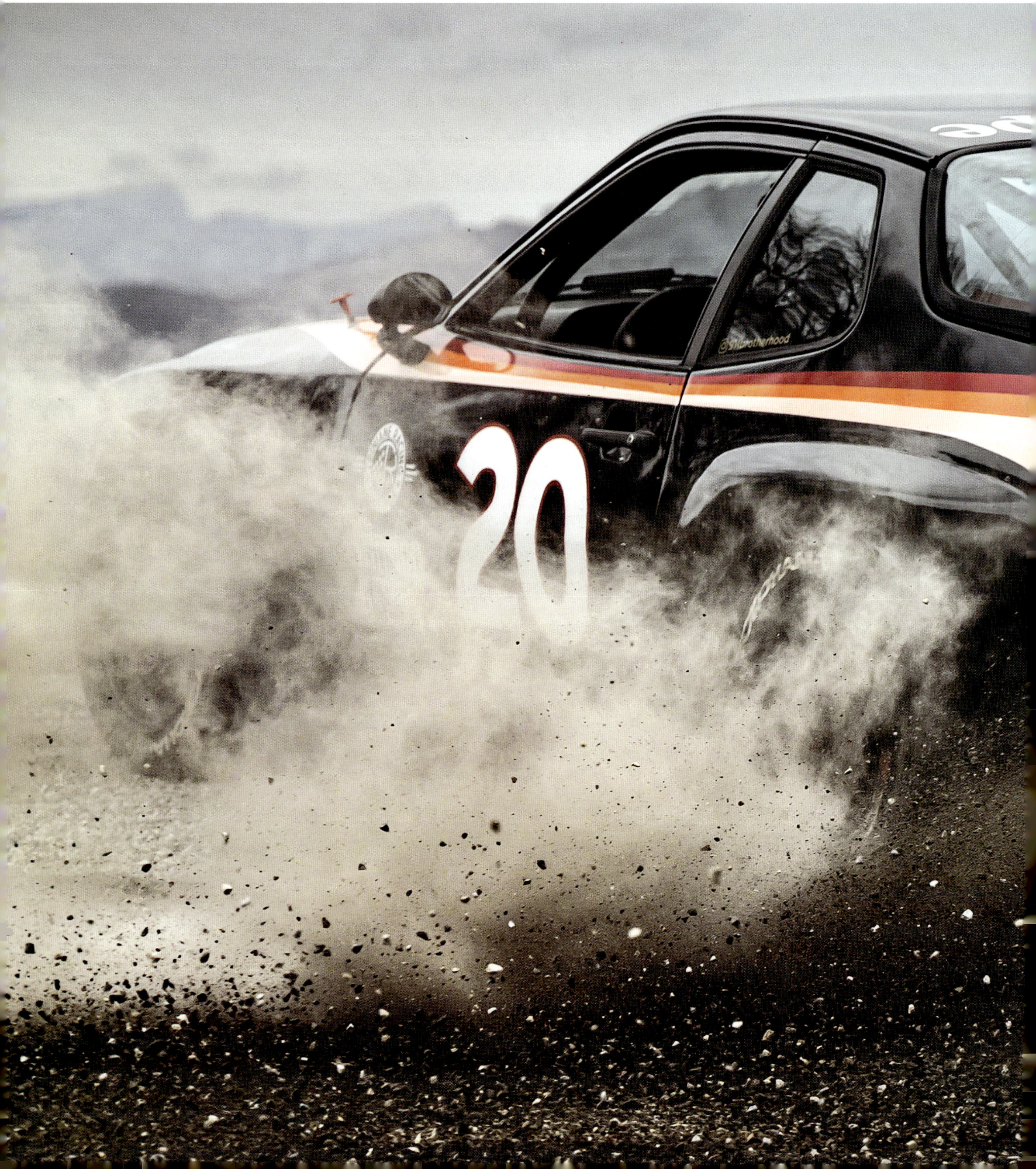
20
@911brotherhood

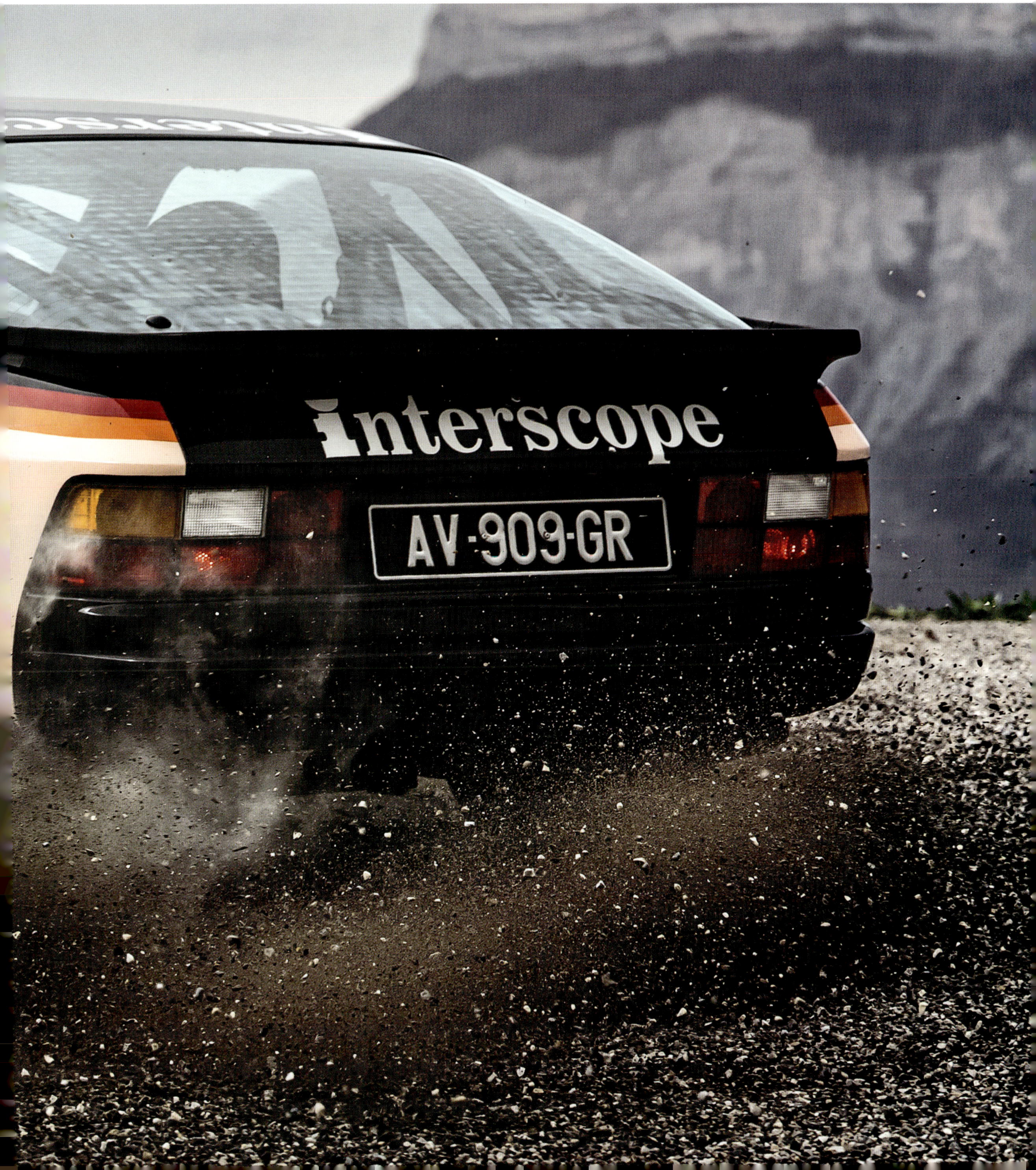
interscope
AV-909-GR

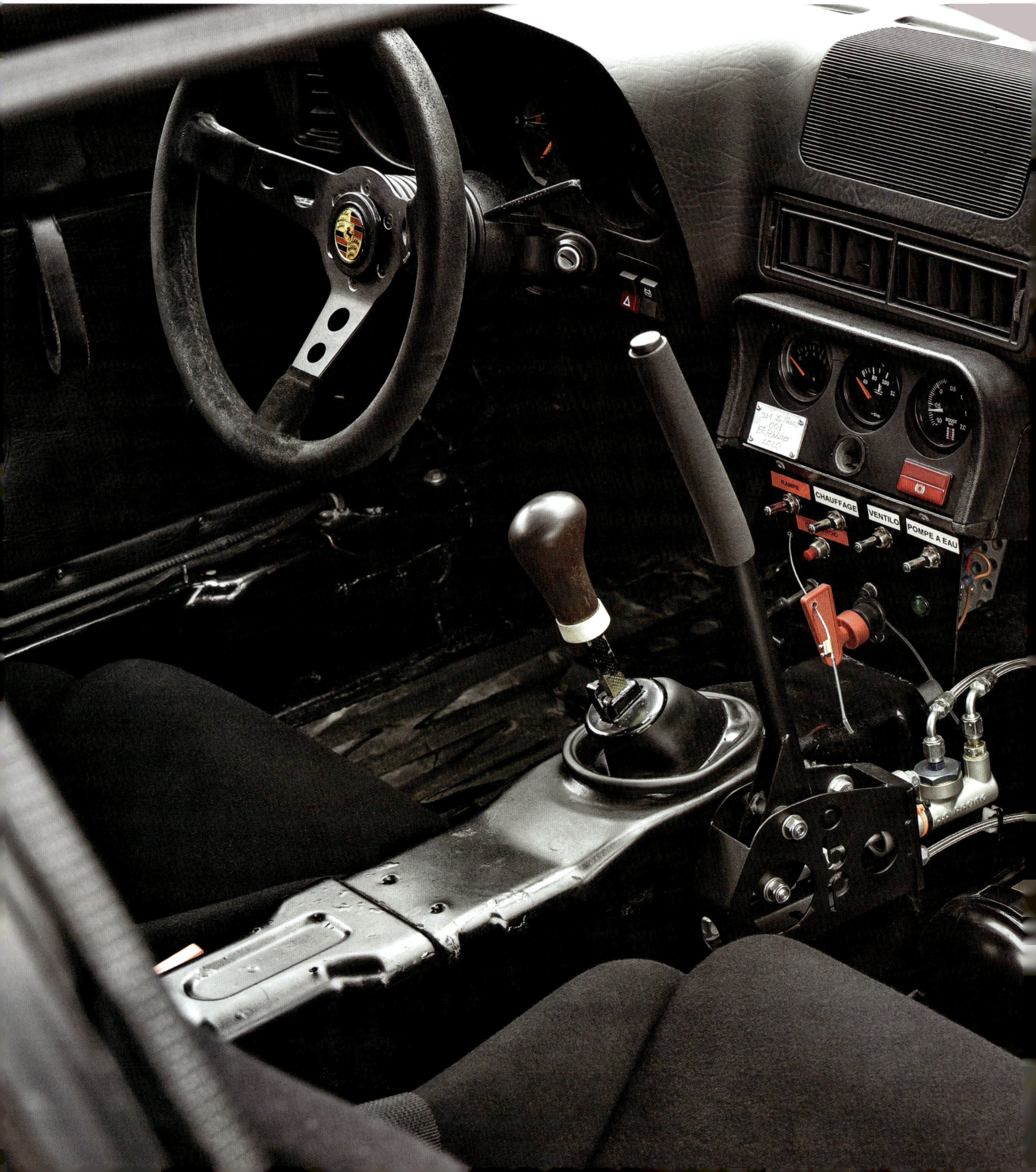
RAMPE
CHAUFFAGE
VENTILO
POMPE A EAU

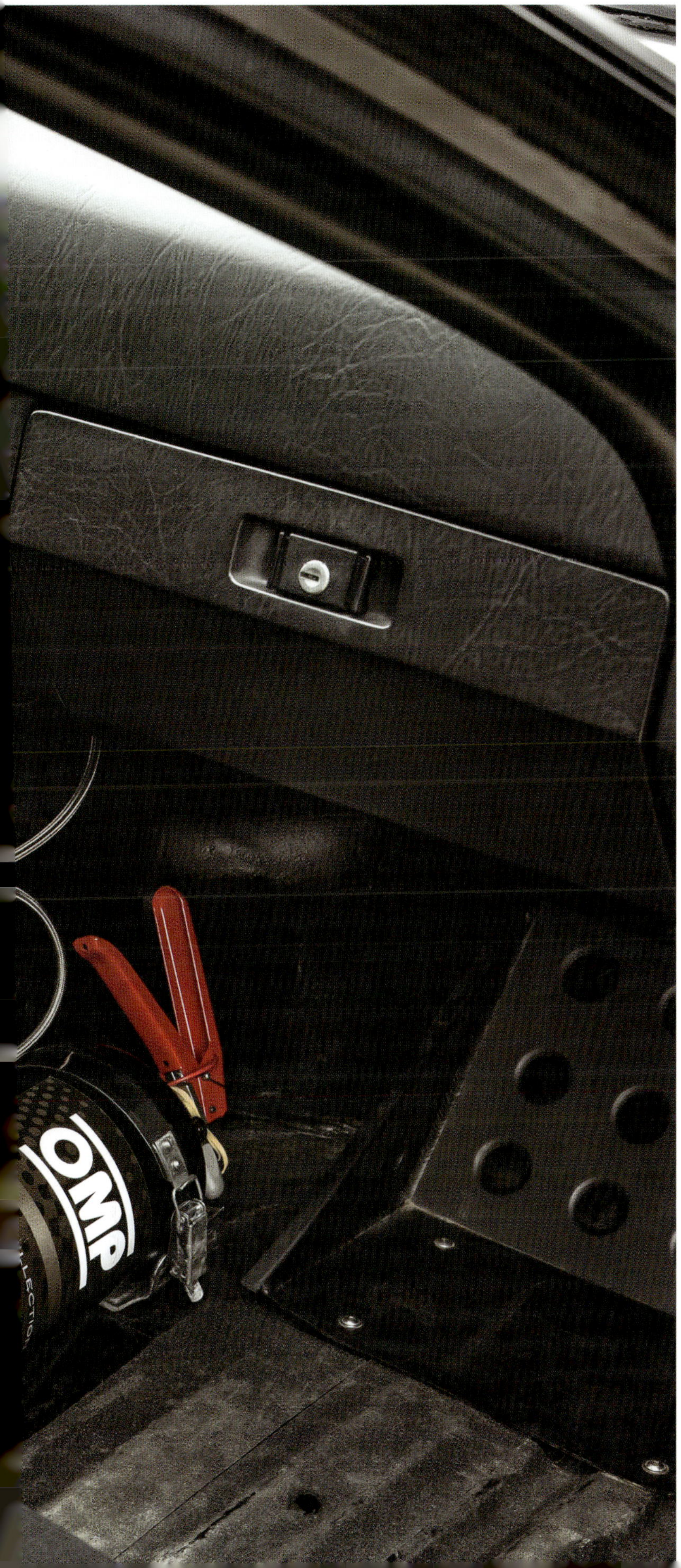

HYDRAULIC HANDBRAKE UP: THIS 924 DOESN'T MESS AROUND.

The 935 is a mythical beast, a Porsche like no other. With a flat bonnet that hid the 911's two signature headlights, bodywork with arches bulging like a bodybuilder and its hyper-impressive rear spoiler, the car excelled on every circuit in the world from 1976 until production ceased in 1981. Even then, its incredible longevity kept the wins going until 1984. In 1979, the Kremer Racing 935 won the prestigious 24 Hours of Le Mans. The first 935s were ultra-powerful, delivering a staggering 600 hp, then 780 hp, and finally reaching an astonishing 850 hp with the famous "Moby Dick" model. It was one of these cars – a 1978 935 driven by Ted Field, owner of the Interscope Racing team – that caused the young Tanguy to fall head over heels in love with motor racing. "My grandfather Alain was a fan of Porsche and car competitions," Tanguy reveals. "He drove a lot in rallies and had lots of racing cars in his garage. Notably, a

935 Interscope." The young Tanguy's sudden, overwhelming crush on that gargantuan-seeming car hit hard: "I was completely captivated, right from when I was little and I saw it driven into the garage with that enormous rear spoiler. It was a car that was so much wider than other 911s, with that amazing sound coming out of the rear-mounted, flat-six turbo. Ever since I was six years old, I've been drawing that car. It is completely different from anything else. It is so big, so beautiful. When you are small, it just screams power. It's almost unbelievable. Even today, I still get all emotional when I see it. It has always been my favourite Porsche."

For Tanguy's 20th birthday, his parents answered his prayers. "They gave me this Porsche 924 Turbo in Carrera GT style, in the colours of the 935 Interscope, for my birthday. Hence the 20, which is painted on the doors each side." It was an amazing gift – and plenty of people worked to make the project happen. "Whenever I drive this car, it always brings loads of emotions. My parents bought the car in May 2020, stripped it down completely and rebuilt the whole thing. They gave it to me the following 4 August. It was just crazy! Everyone worked on it: my mother, father, grandfather and even the mechanics from the family garage, Triniane Racing. It is a truly unique car." When it came to the build, Tanguy's parents didn't hold back, creating a car with a full interior roll cage – and a desire to do battle behind the wheel!

A 924 WITH A MEASURE OF INTERSCOPE – A TRIBUTE TO THE FABULOUS PORSCHE 935.

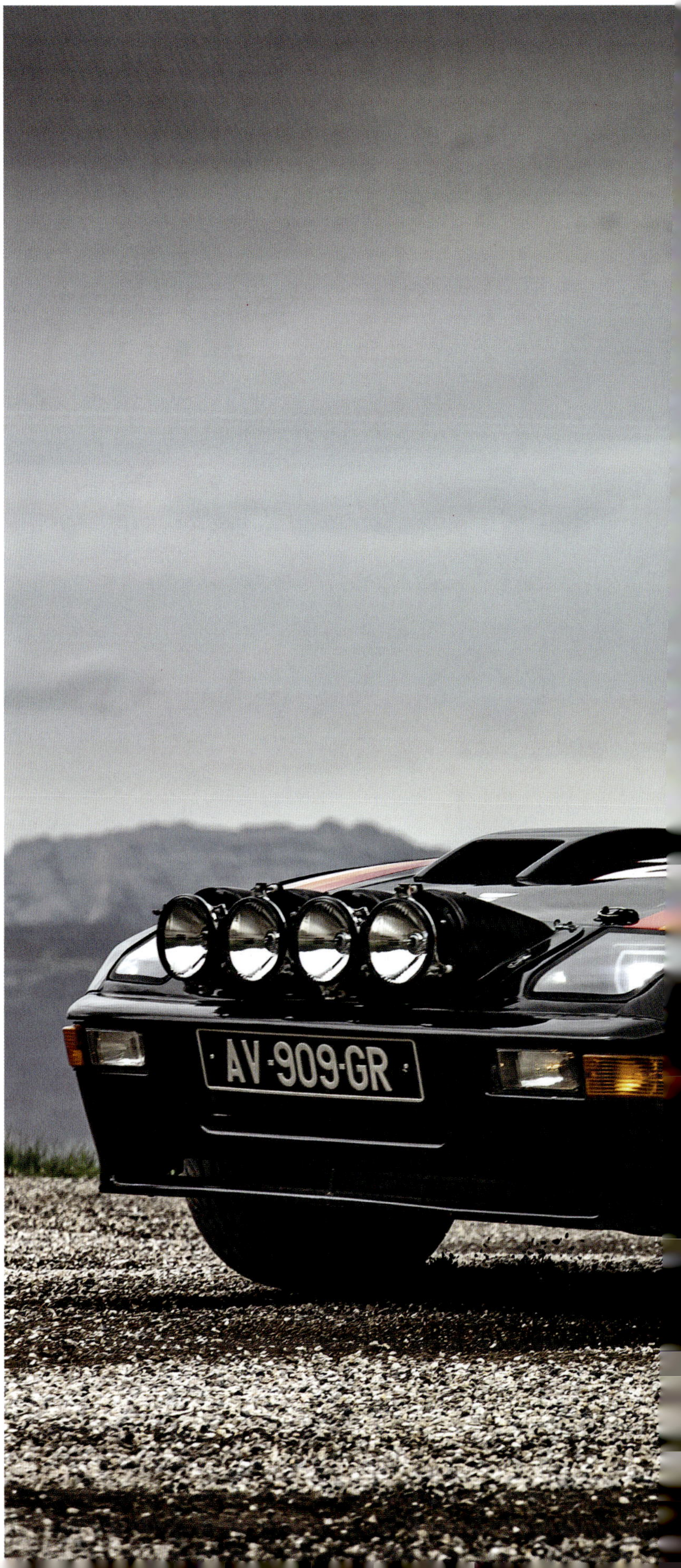

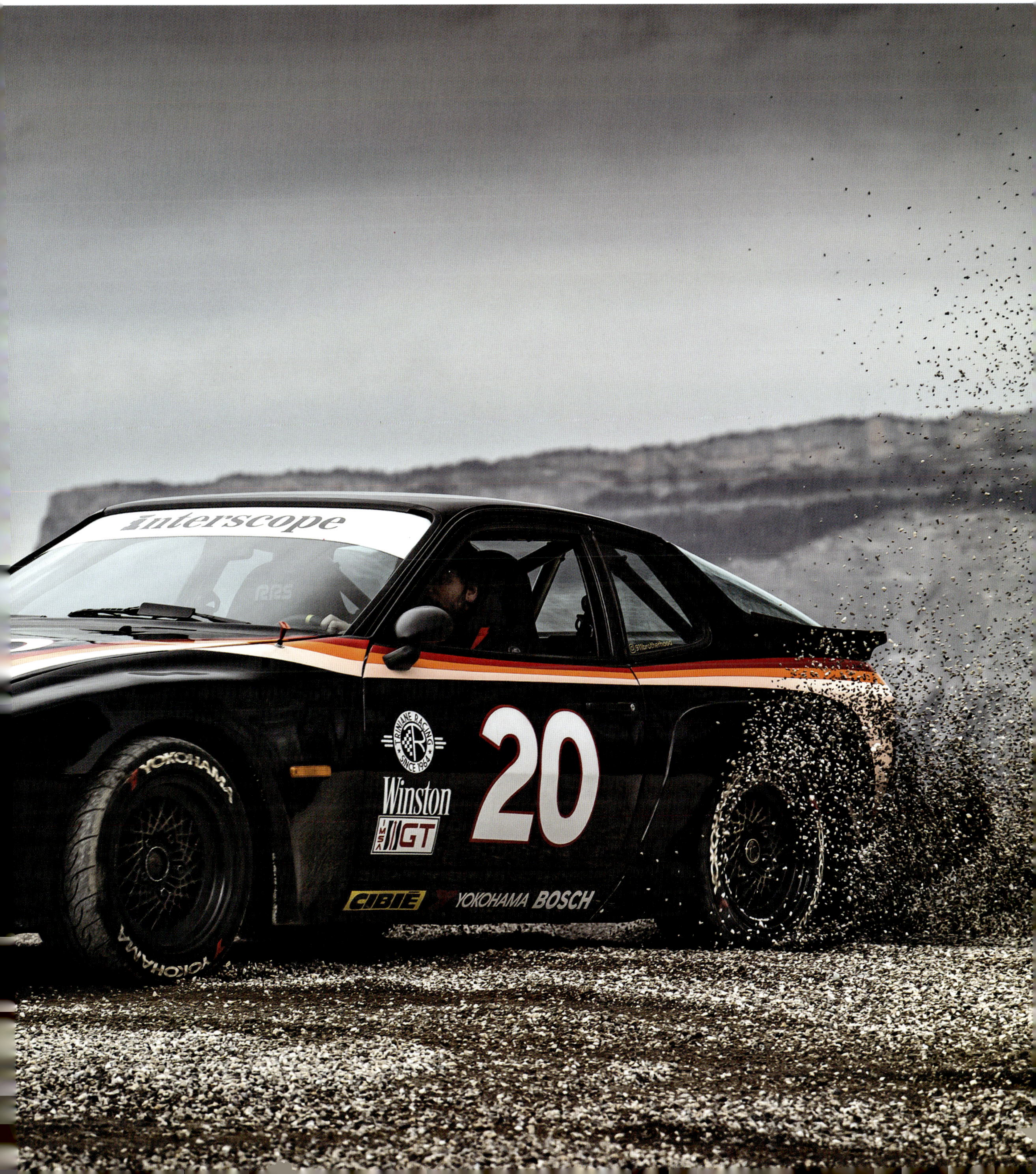
Interscope
20
Winston
IMSA GT
CIBIÉ
YOKOHAMA BOSCH
YOKOHAMA

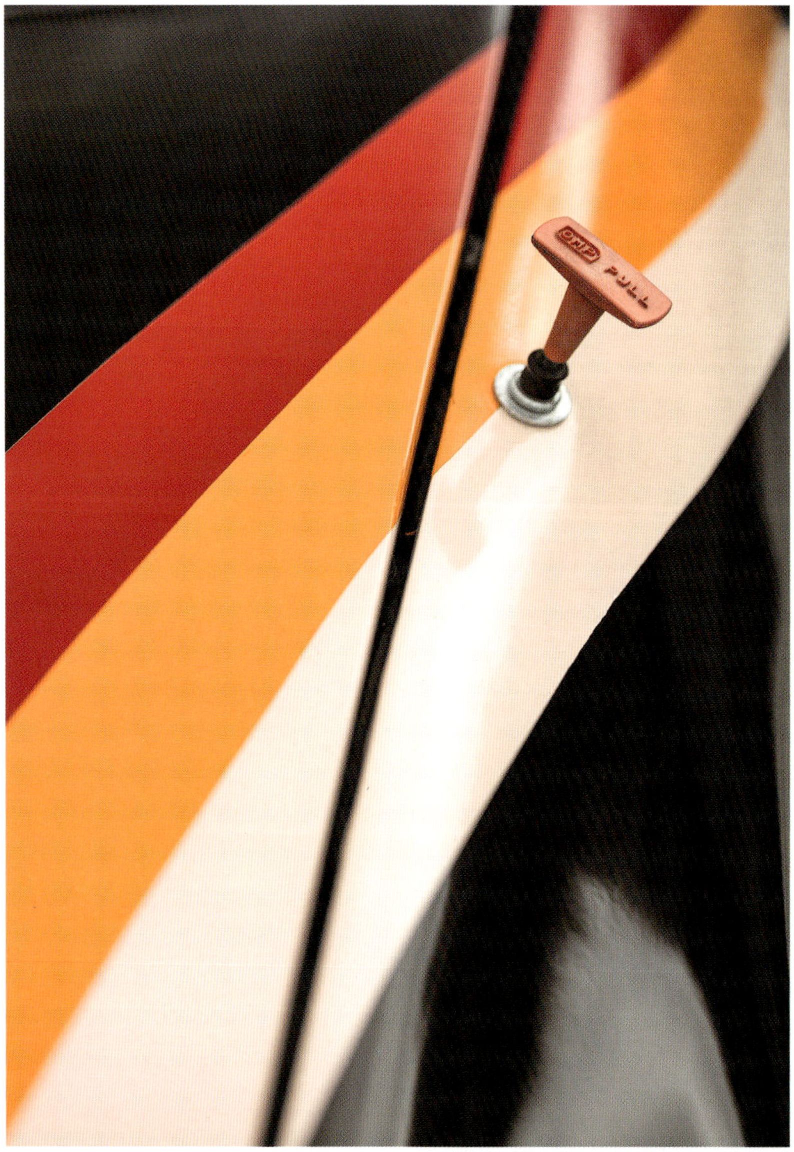

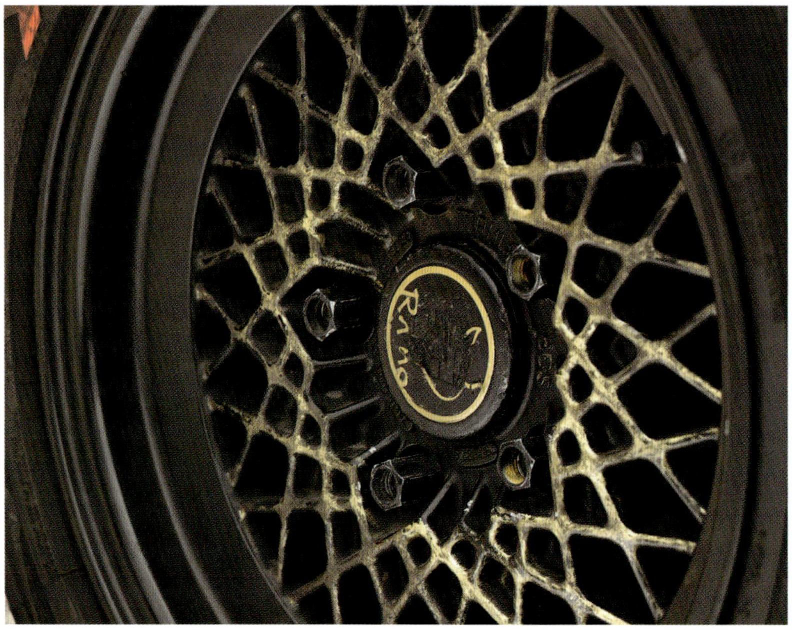

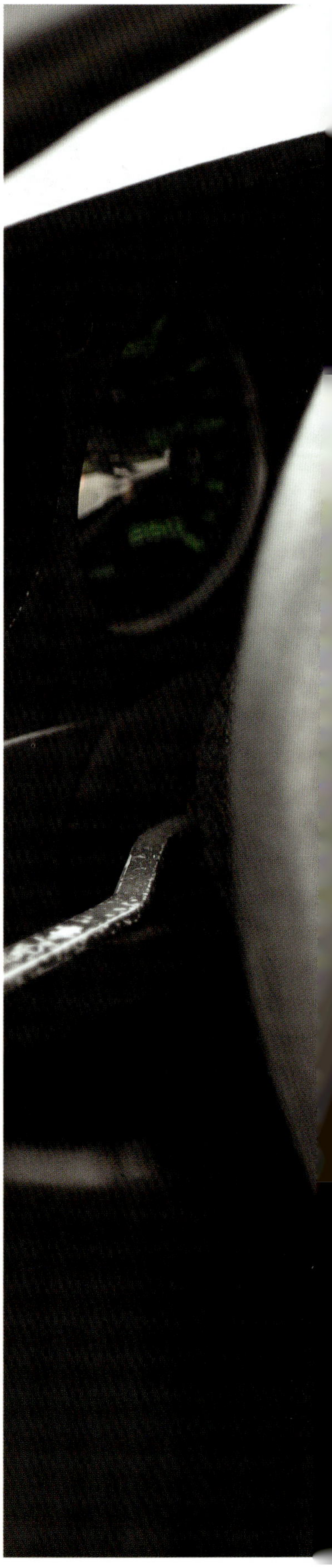

1. The pull-rod is used to operate the circuit breaker from outside ... just in case.

2. Four BBS wheels give this 924 the unmistakable look of a 935.

3. The steering wheel features a yellow marker at 12 o'clock, so you know where you are mid-drift.

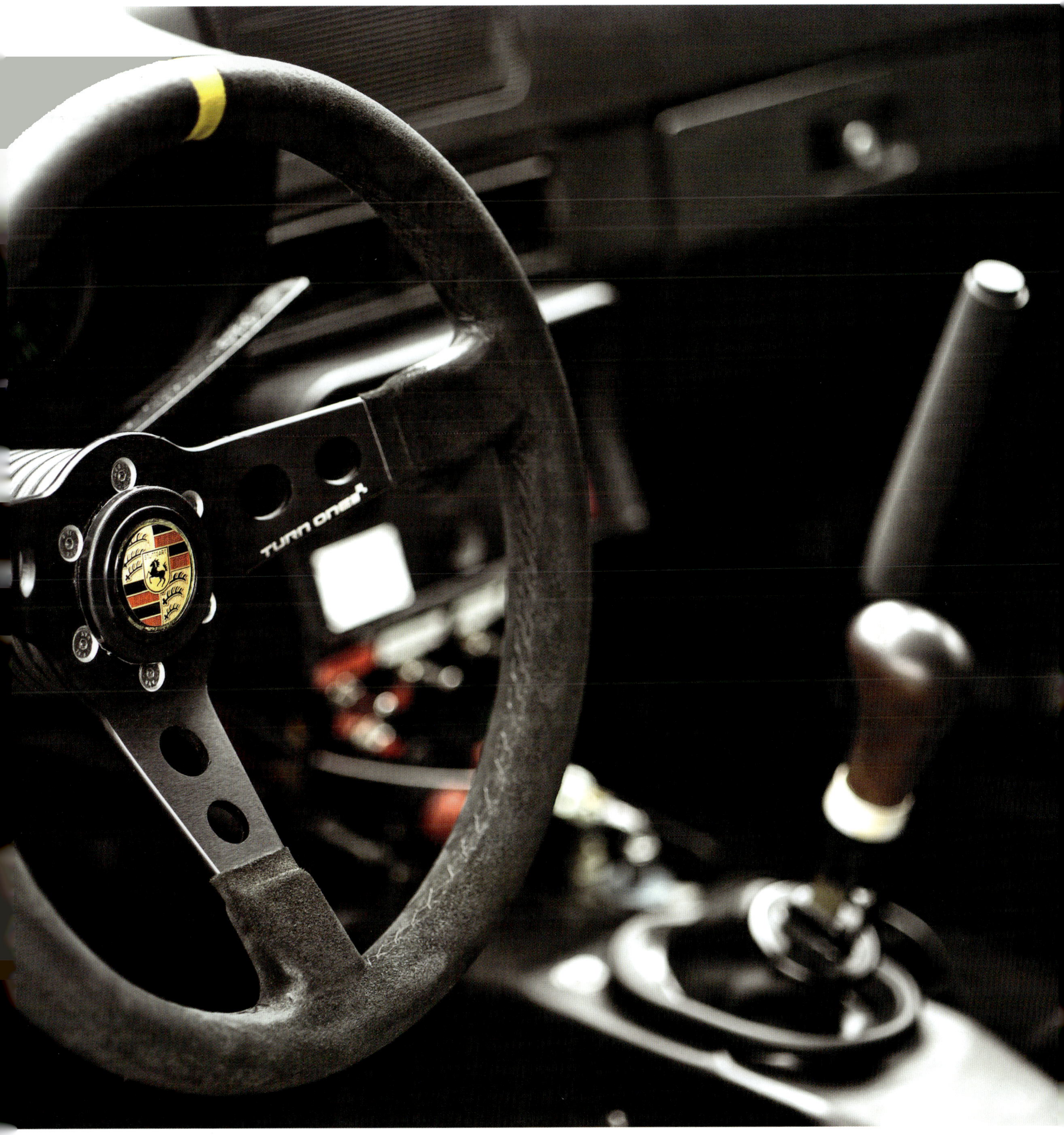
TURN ONE

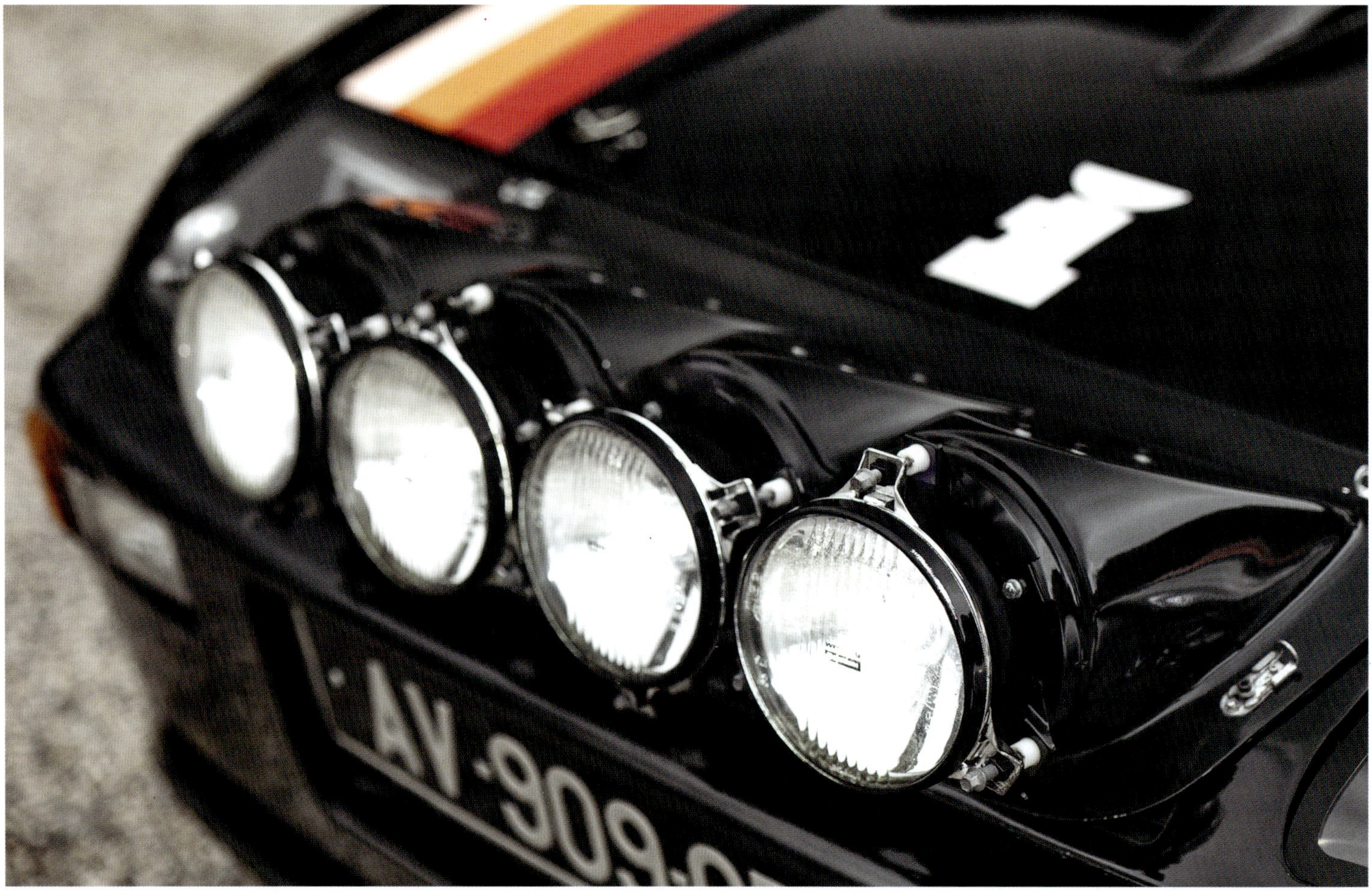
AV-909-0

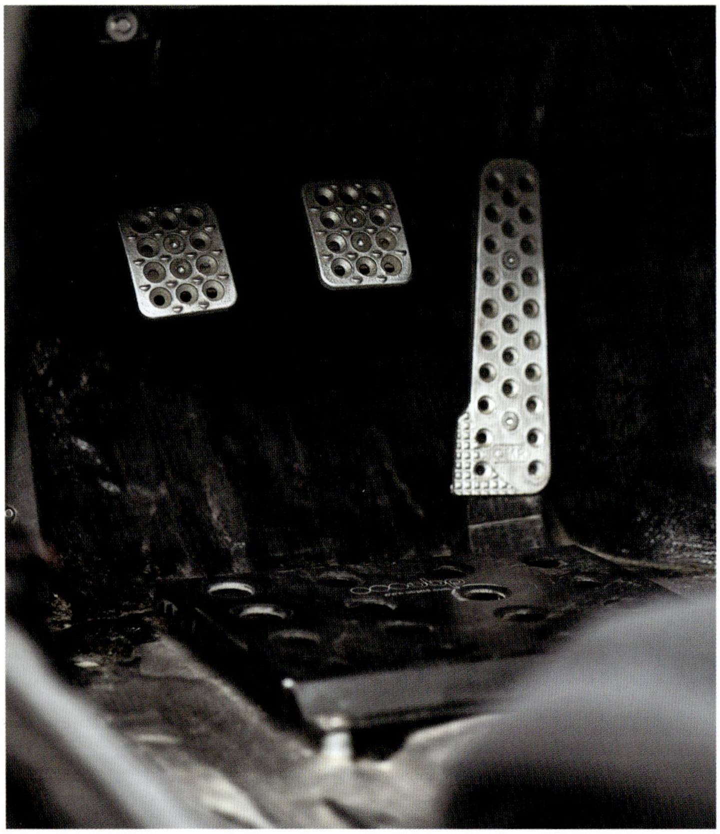

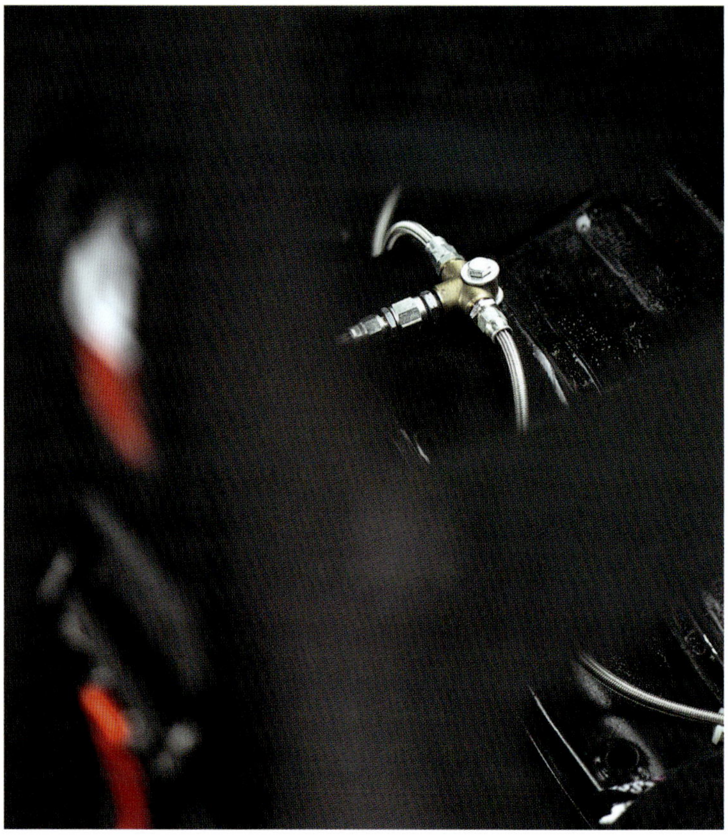

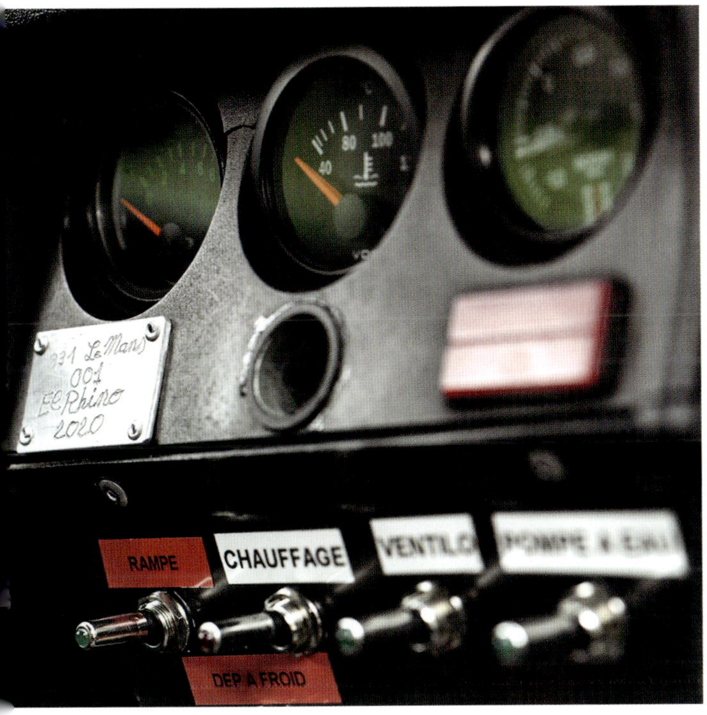

924 INTERSCOPE
BY THE NUMBERS

CREATION 1979

FLAT CYLINDERS 4

CC 2,000

HP 220

"The idea was to build a different kind of car – a bit of a mongrel in road-rally style – to mess around with near the house and to have fun pulling the handbrake! In winter I drive a lot on ice and snow." In short, it is a pure Outlaw, in use as well as design. "The 1979 924 was a Turbo model already. It had done a bit of rallying, hence the roll cage, but it had a white paint job. So they repainted it entirely in black and added a 1981 Carrera GT kit, giving it a more aggressive look – more reminiscent of the 935. They fitted the engine with a new turbo; it now pulls 220 hp." As for the interior, the concept was "racing", and nothing else. Everything is totally minimalist, with the soundproofing carpets removed: footrests, pedal kit, short-throw gearbox with specific limited-slip differential, custom gear knob, high-up hydraulic handbrake, water pump and auxiliary fan switches, circuit breaker, bucket seats, spare wheels, fire extinguishers ... Not a thing was left to chance. The side stripes on the body are the exact same colour scheme that gave the 935 its iconic, streamlined look. The headlights are no longer retractable, like on a standard 924, they are integrated into the grill as they were on the Carrera GT. Of course, being a 935, it's decked out with BBS wheels all round. "What I love about this car is that it's one of a kind. It is nothing like the other Porsches that I drive on the road or in rallies. It has an exceptional feeling when you are behind the wheel. To start with, it has incredible handling." On 924s, transmission is via the transaxle system: the gearbox and axle assembly is positioned at the rear axle, which, with the engine at the front, gives very favourable weight distribution. "The balance is much better than on a 911. It is slightly lowered and, above all, the front end is very responsive, with good camber. My parents are like magicians: they never fully reveal what they're working on with a car and they always keep their secrets. But this 924 Interscope they gave me is really a very different drive from any other car. And that's the way I like it!"

1. The row of long-range headlamps are for the rally spirit that runs through the entire Triniane family.

2. A pedal set that's hot as hell, with studs to keep your feet firmly fixed.

3. The car has been meticulously kitted out, just like a real race car.

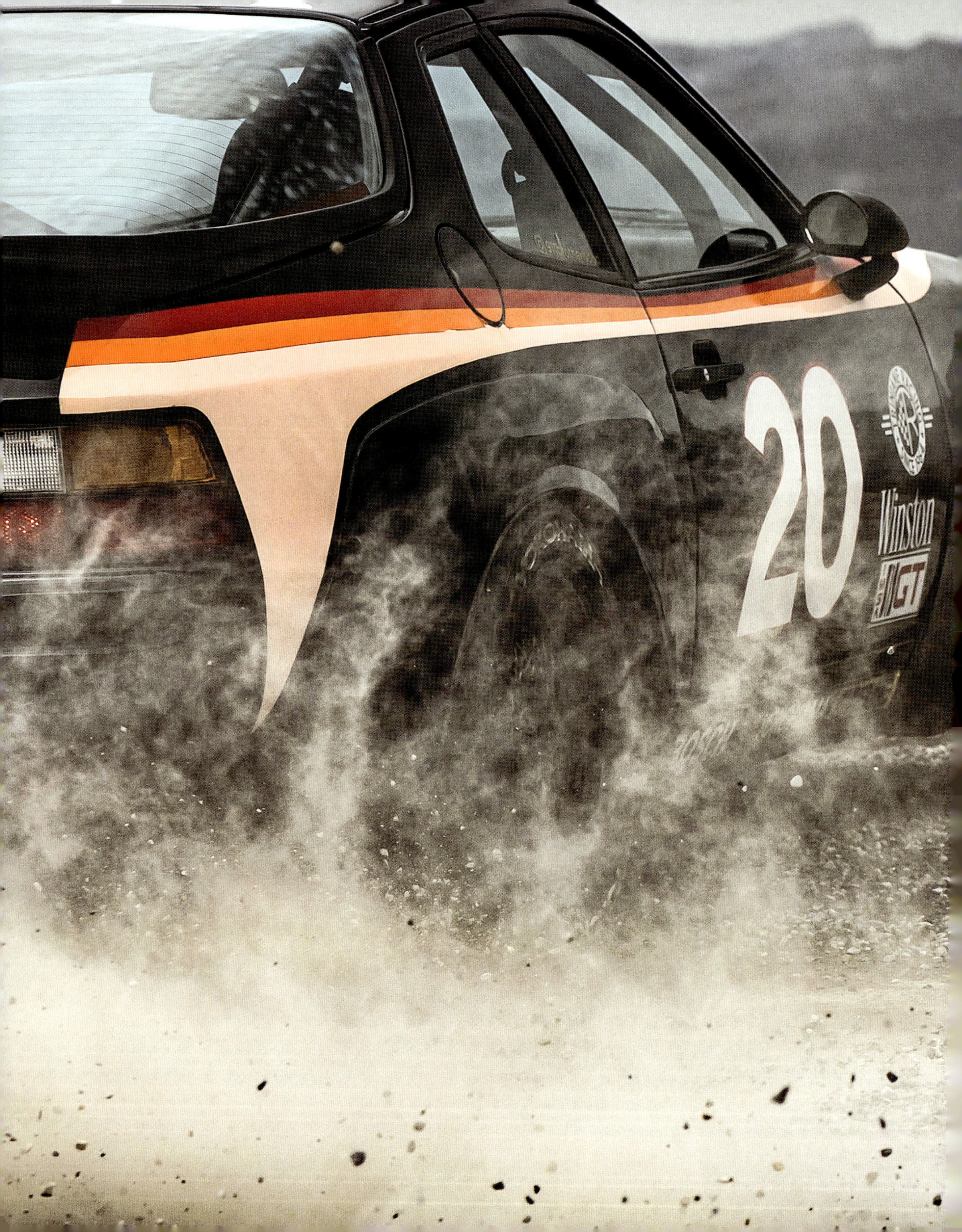
20
Winston
GT

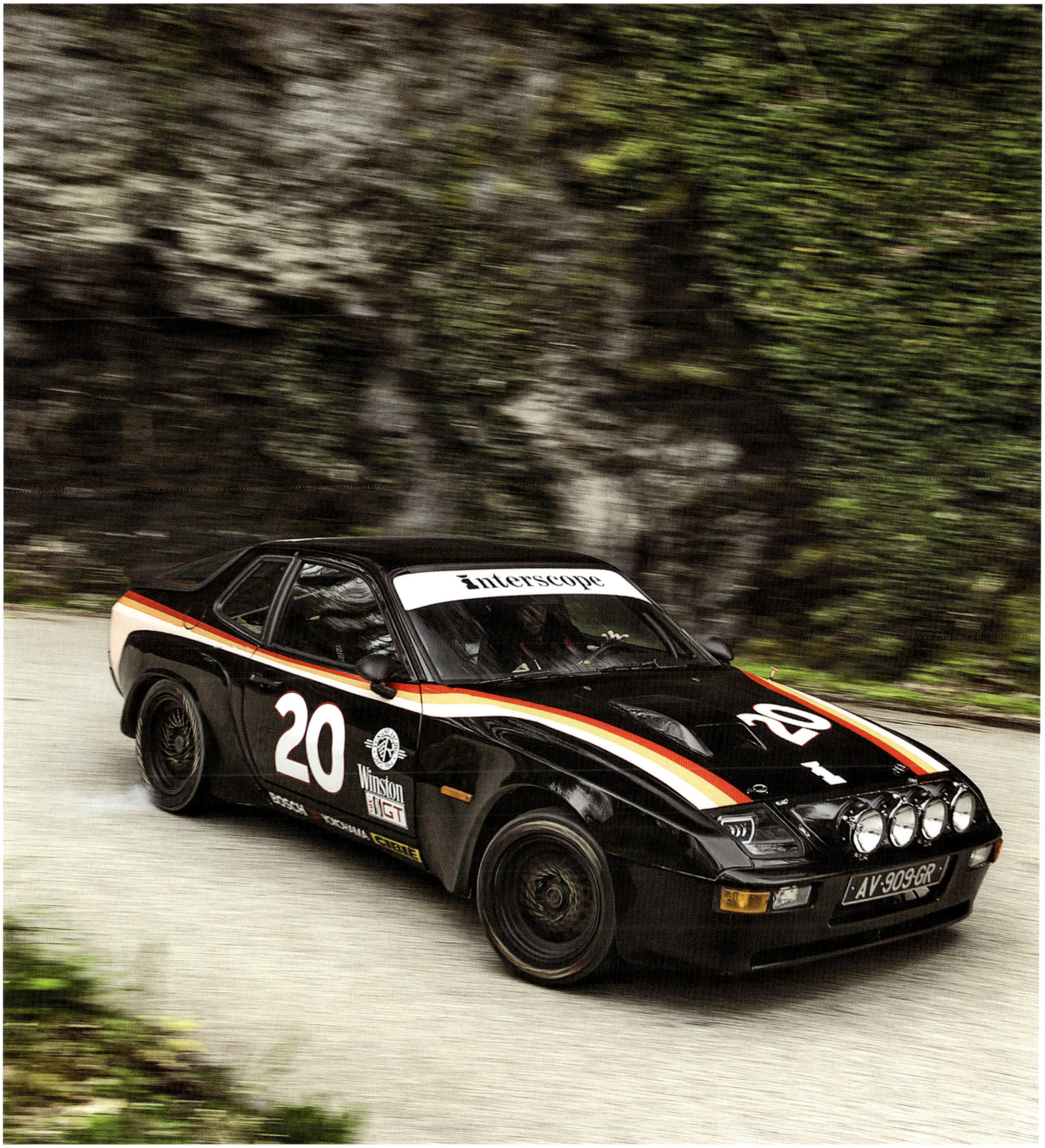

Above: This Porsche 924 sticks to the road – and loves a good sliding session on dry tarmac or gravel.

Opposite: The 924 Interscope is the ultimate car for learning to drive like a rally champ!

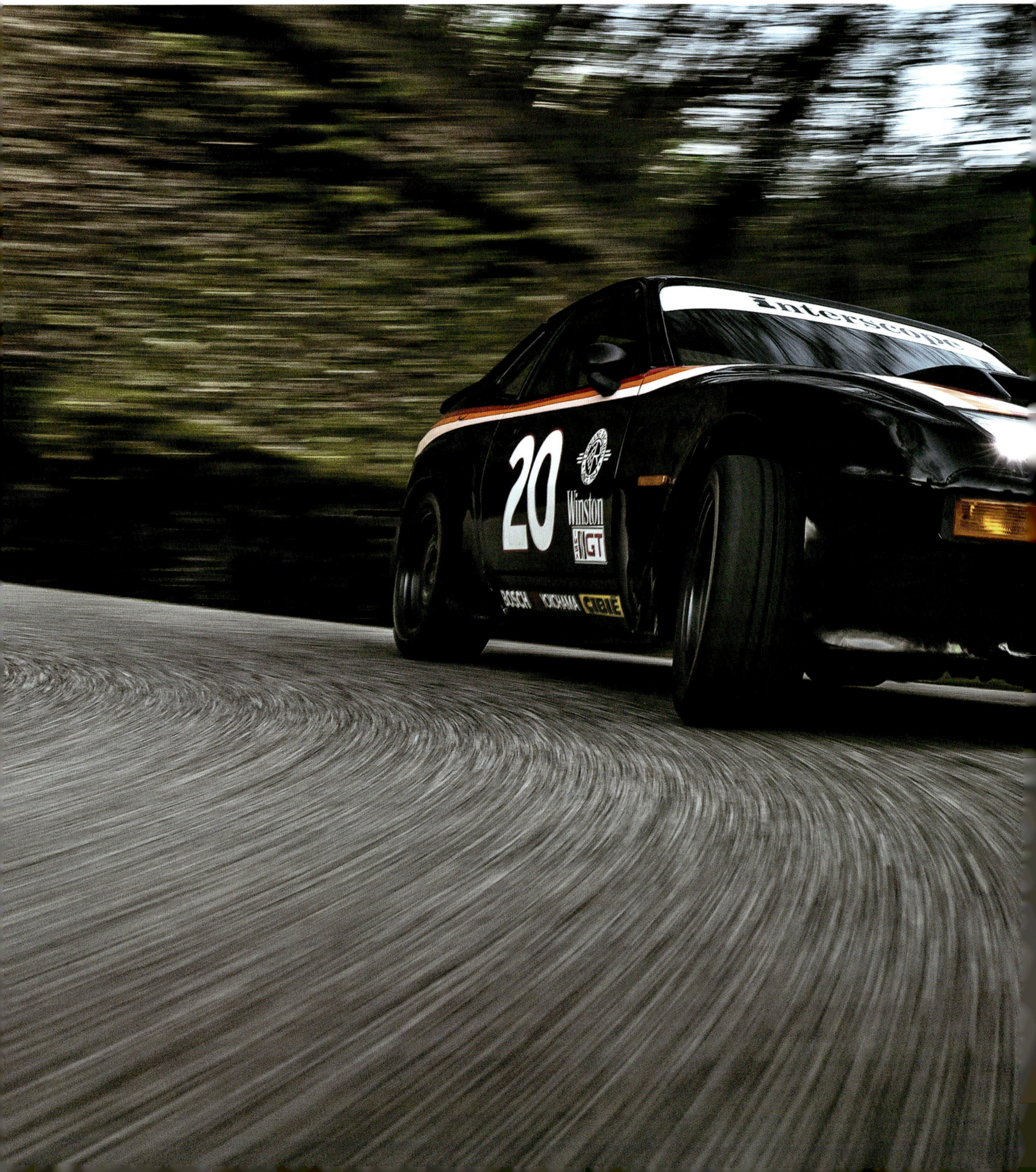
Interscope
20
Winston
GT
BOSCH
YOKOHAMA
CIBIE

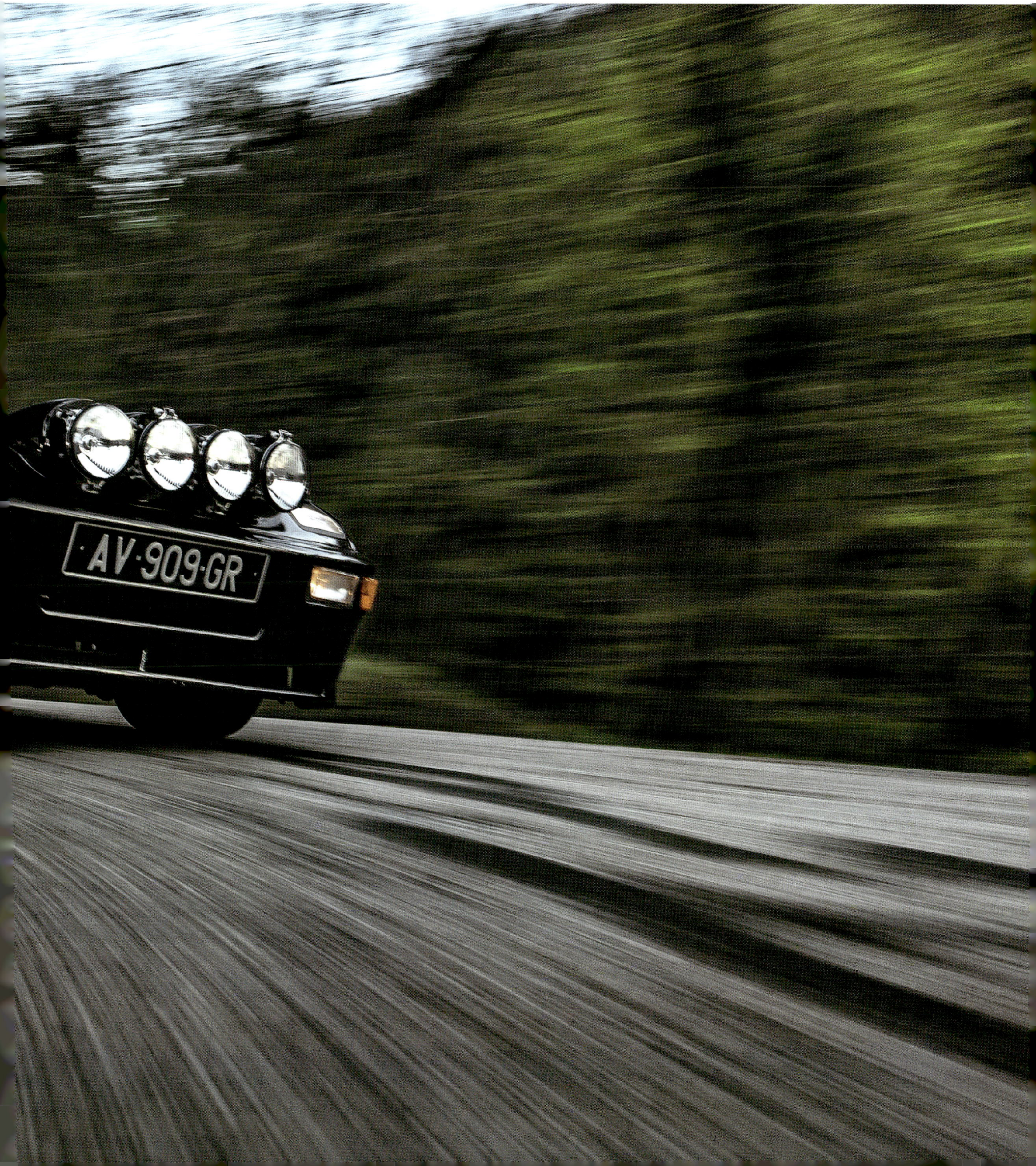
AV-909-GR

913 BLACK BIRD INNER GEEK

A tuned 1995 Porsche 993 engine in a 1967 912 body: the 913 Black Bird is a geek's dream, fuelled by Porsche fever and the "light is right" philosophy – an essential concept if you want to go as fast as possible.

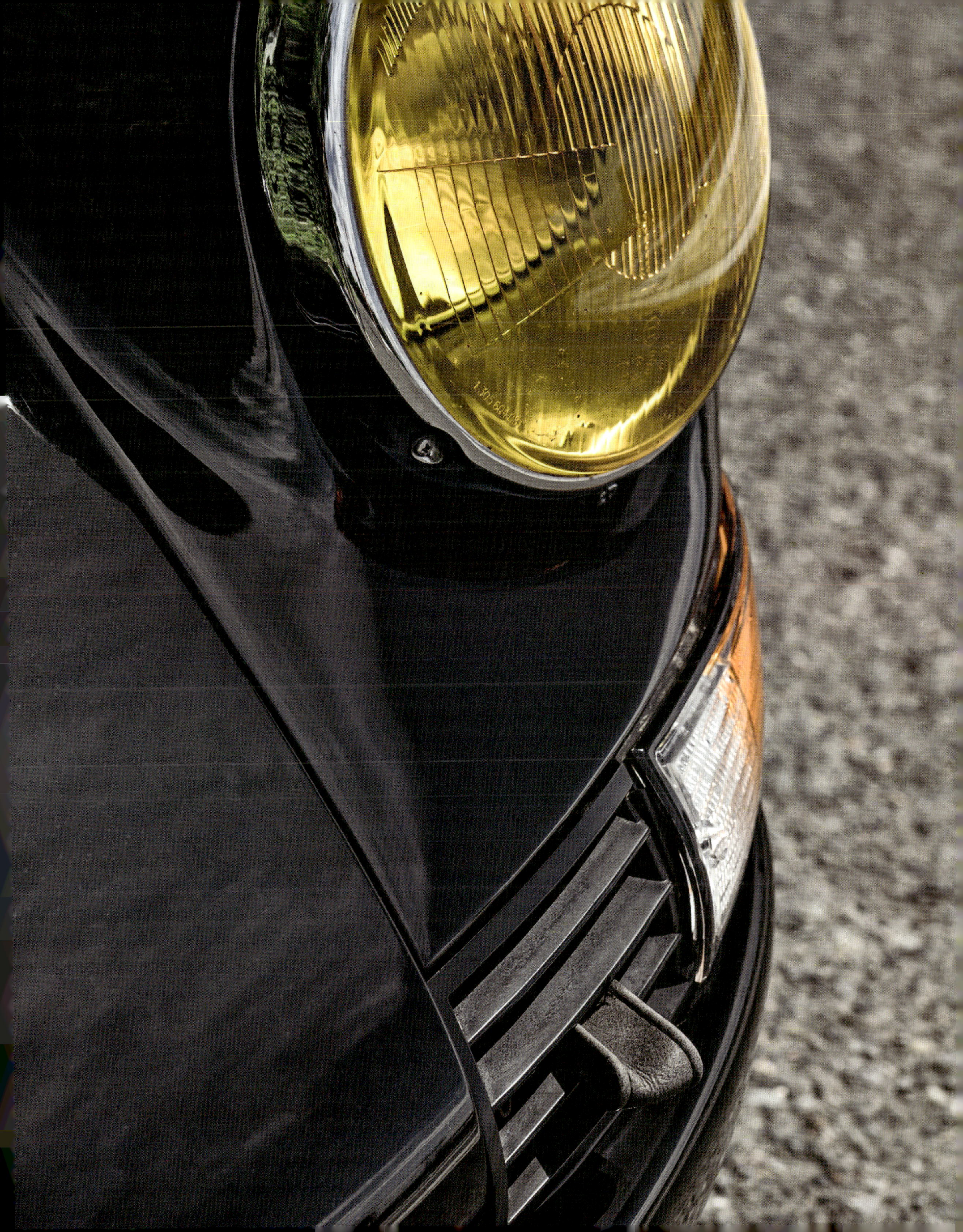

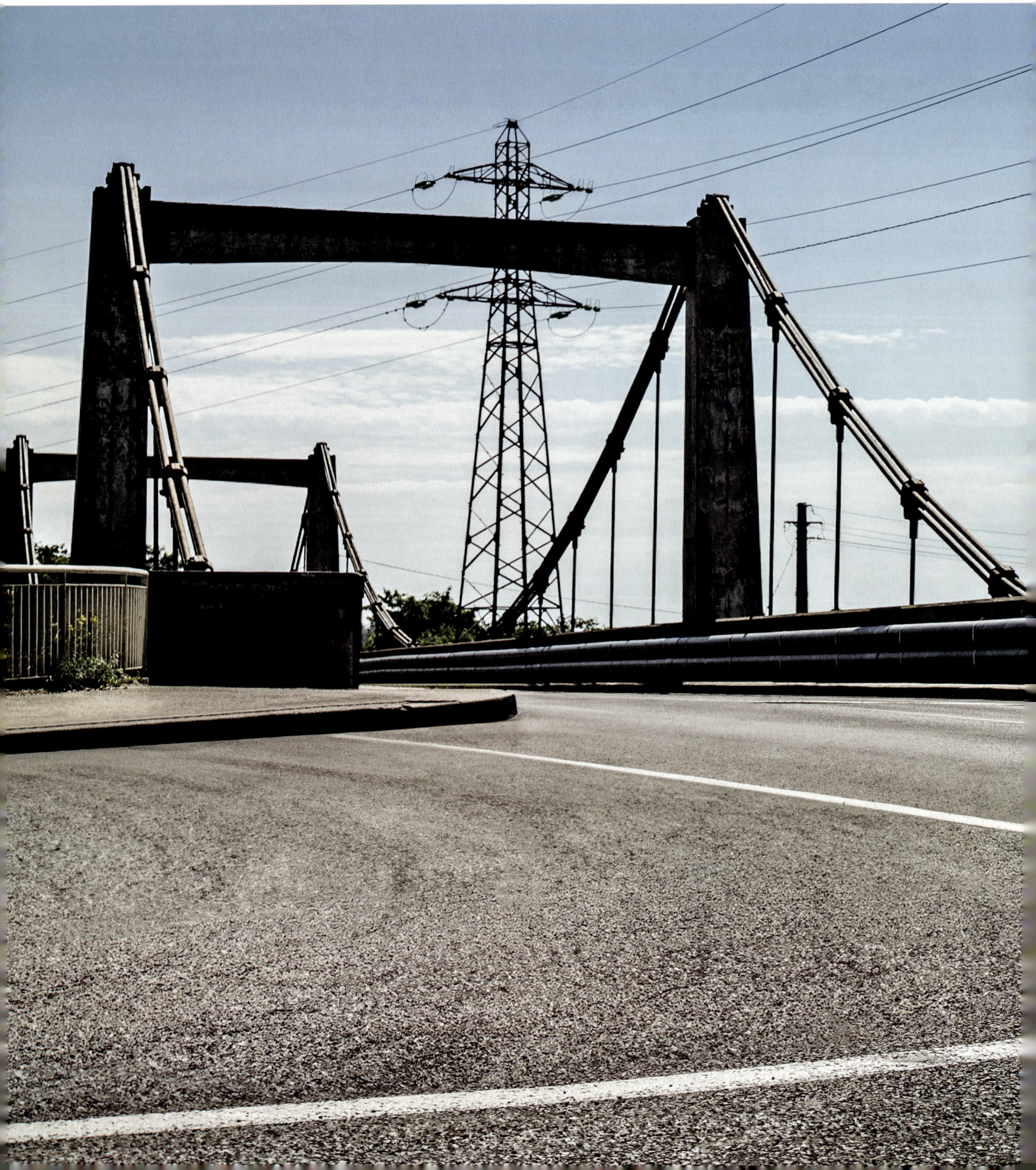

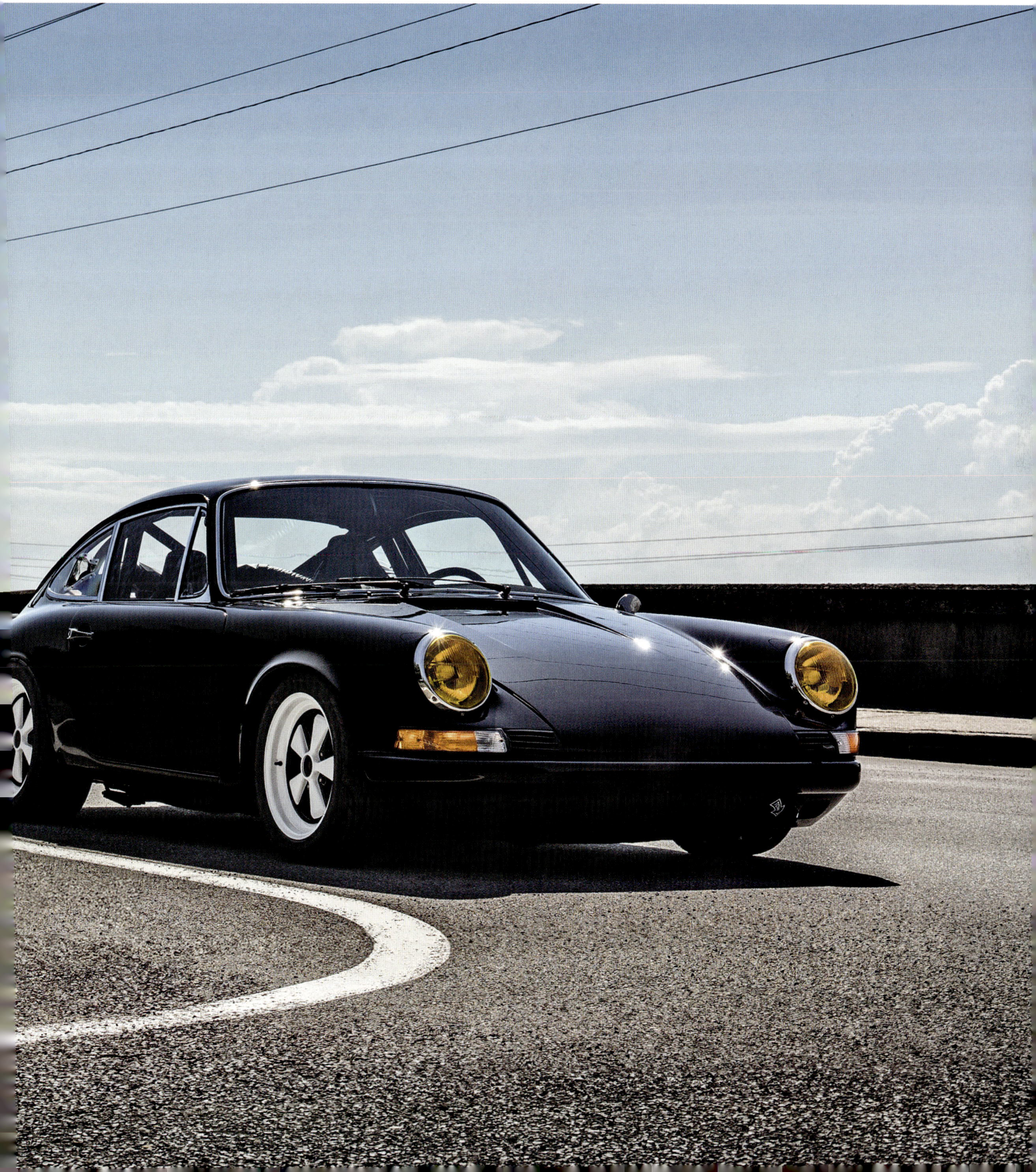

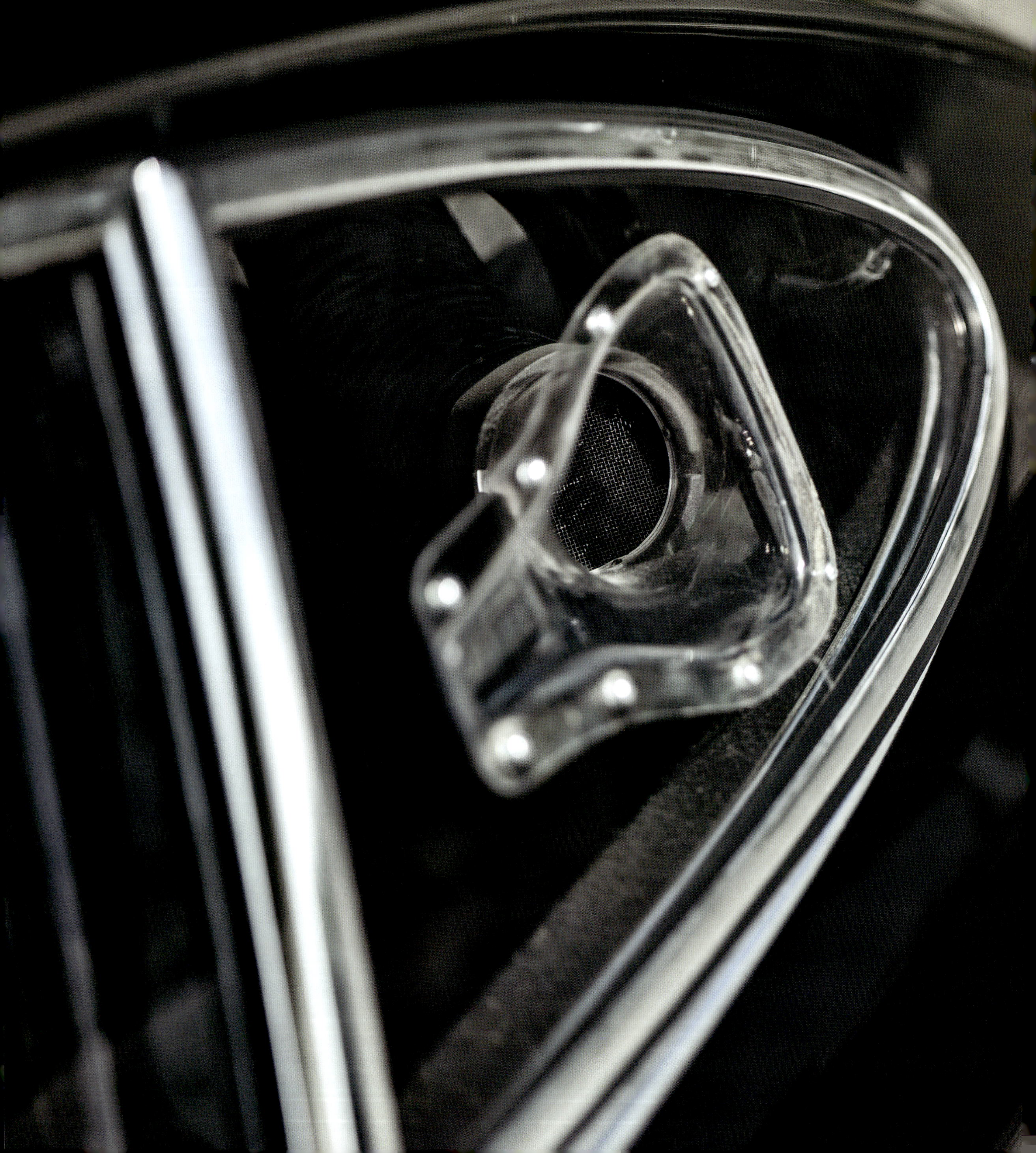

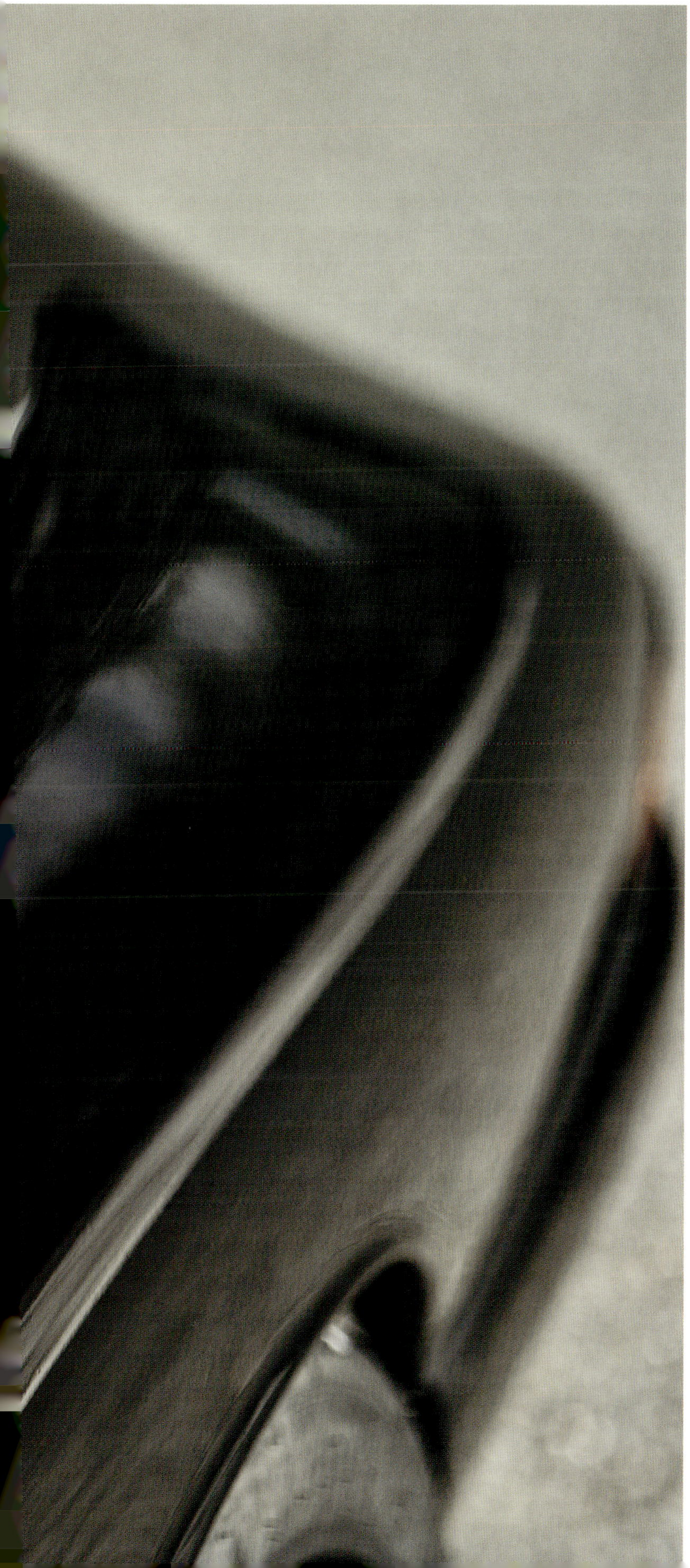

AIR FOR THE DYNAMIC INTAKE ENTERS THROUGH THE VENTS IN THE REAR QUARTER-LIGHTS.

The first Porsche truly designed for racing was the 911 R. It rolled out of the Stuttgart factory in 1967. Its power-to-weight ratio was unrivalled: weighing 230 kg (500 lbs) less than a 911 S, the car tipped the scales at 800 kg (1,764 lbs) and was powered by a 210 hp, flat-six engine borrowed from the 906. Only four prototypes and 19 production models were ever built. It's a very rare model that has become the stuff of legend. The project was spearheaded by Ferdinand Piëch, Ferdinand Porsche's grandson, who wanted the 911 to be as light as it possibly could be. The concept of "light is right" was also dear to Colin Chapman, the father of Lotus. And the owner of this car, Sylvain, made it his mantra, too. "I've always driven light cars: Ariel, Caterham, Lotus. But I'm also a big fan of Porsches," he says. "So I wanted to build myself a Porsche as close as I could get to a 911 R. I bought a bare 912 chassis, a 1968 model with no interior or engine. It was the famous short wheelbase version that disappeared the following year. I wanted to make it light and give it the biggest engine I could find. I ended up looking for a 3.6-litre flat-six from a 993. Not a 964 engine!" Produced between 1989 and 1994, the 964 gave way to the 993 that year, through to 1998. "The M64 engine from the 993 is different from the 964, despite the same reference number; it is much more responsive and has a higher rev count. I ended up finding one in Los Angeles, at LA Dismantler, which was a breaker's yard that only dealt in Porsches. I brought it back to France on a pallet, via Machine Revival, who completed the entire assembly. With the 912 shell and the engine from a 993, we called it a 913!" It was given the gentle name "Black Bird", not in reference to the military stealth aircraft – even though everything about it makes you think of that, with the intense black paintwork. It was actually a tribute to the "Yellow Bird" of Alois Ruf, the incredible German Porsche tuner who set a production car speed record in 1989, in front of a Porsche 959 and Ferrari F40.

Sylvain left nothing to chance in the pursuit of his dream: "We used a 3.2 SC gearbox because it has an external oil cooler. I wanted a 915 gearbox, that's what they're called, with a cable-operated clutch, because those boxes are lighter. Above all, the mechanical feel of the gear shift is very different from that of the G50 and G60 gearboxes that came afterwards: those 'boxes have hydraulic controls, which give a less springy gear change than the 915 and its shifter." Once the main components of the car had been assembled it was time to put them carefully

INSPIRED BY A 911 R, THIS SHORT WHEELBASE 913 BLACK BIRD IS GEARED FOR SPORT.

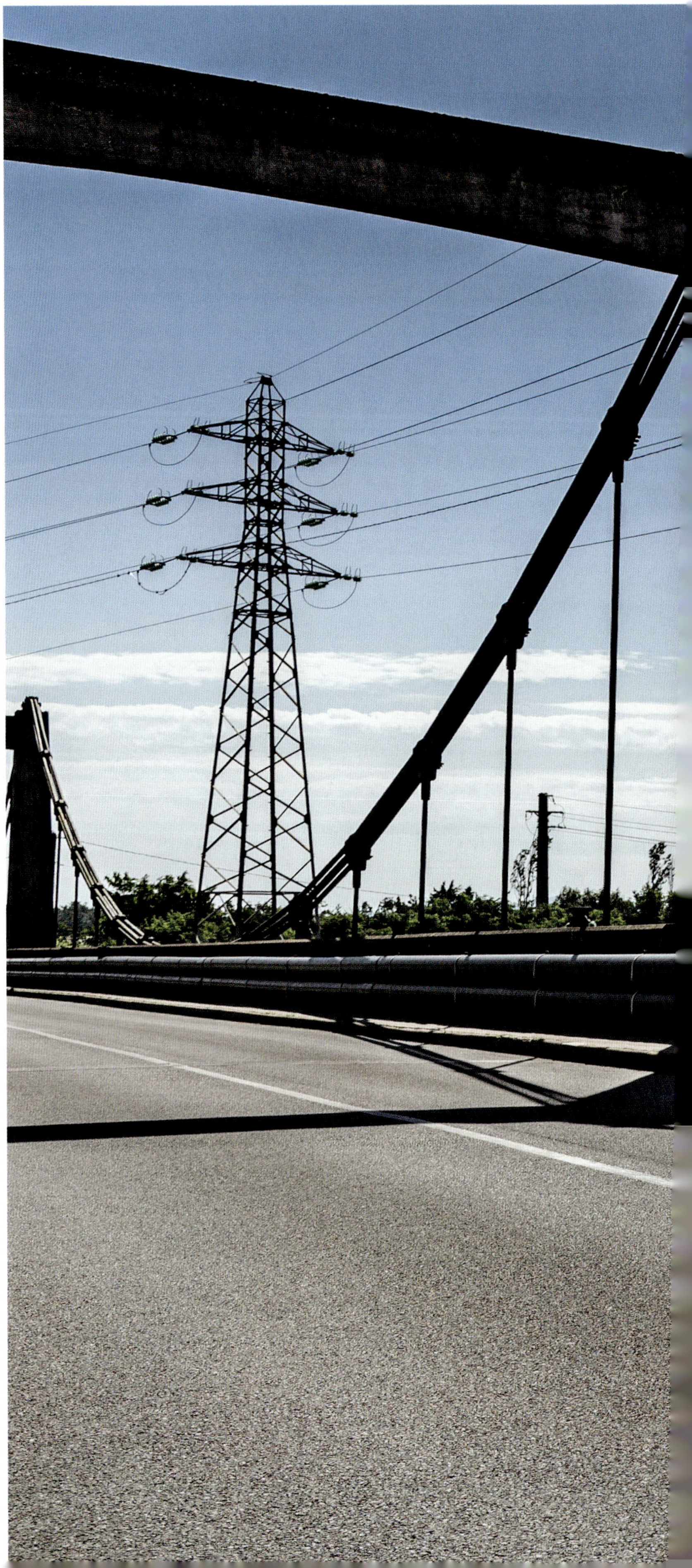

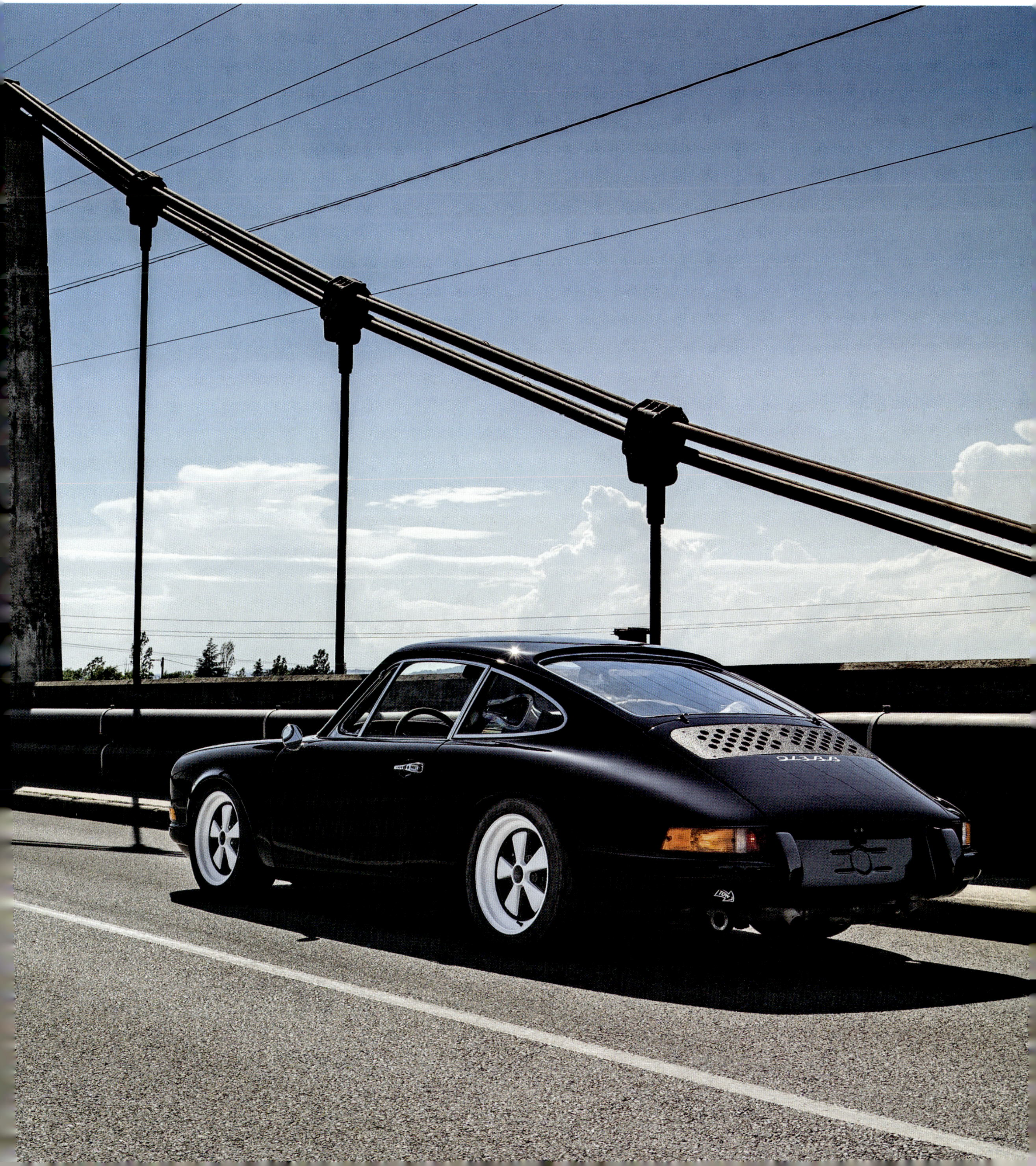

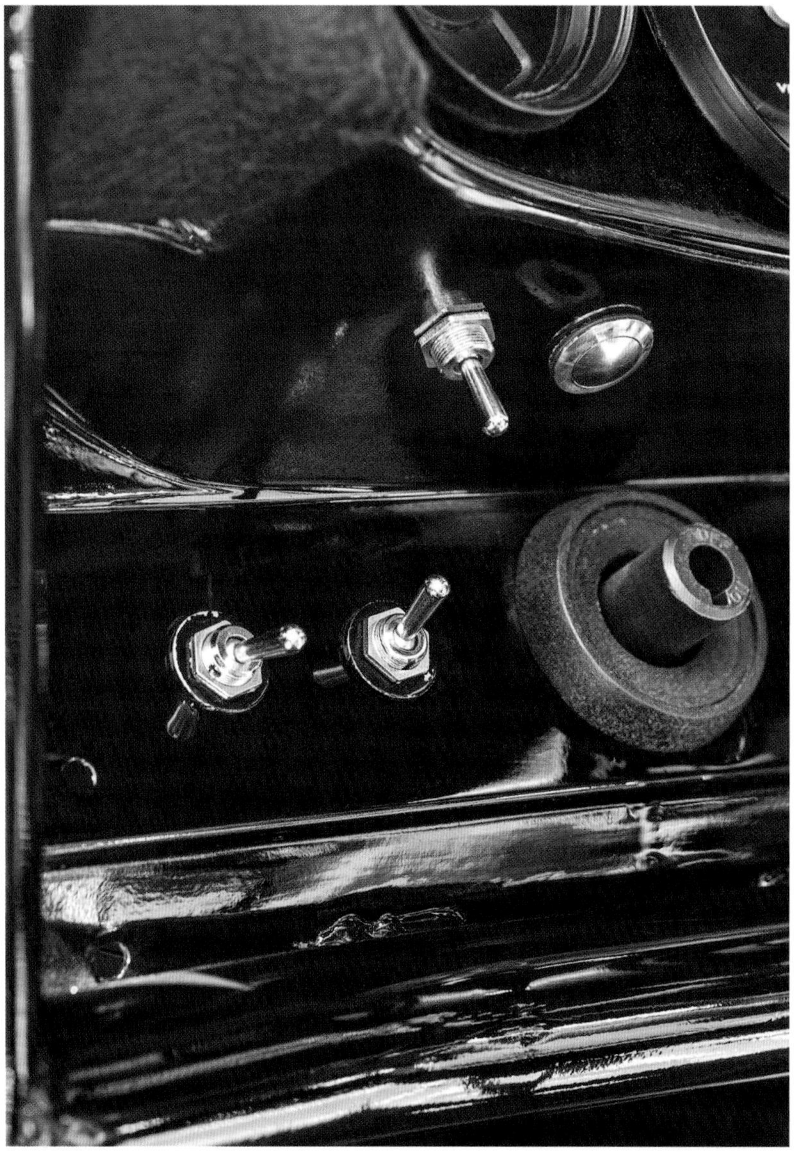

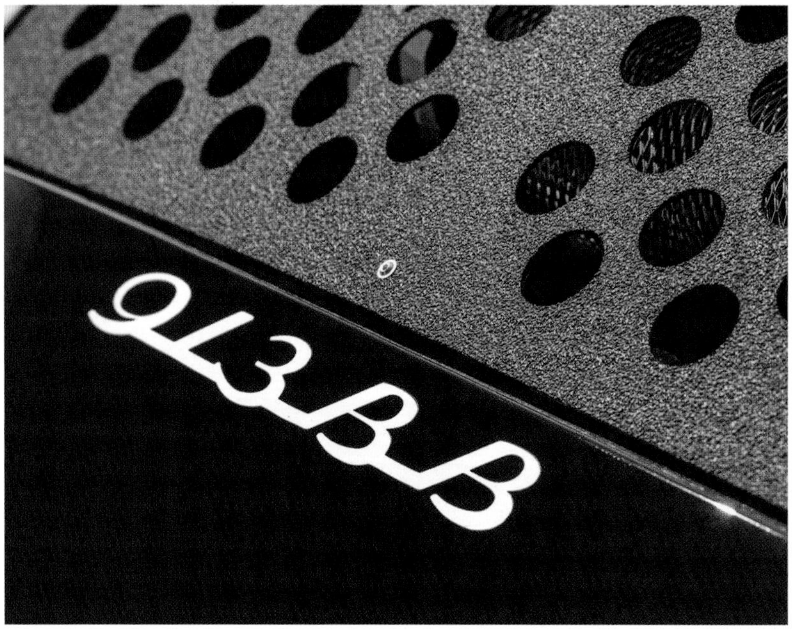

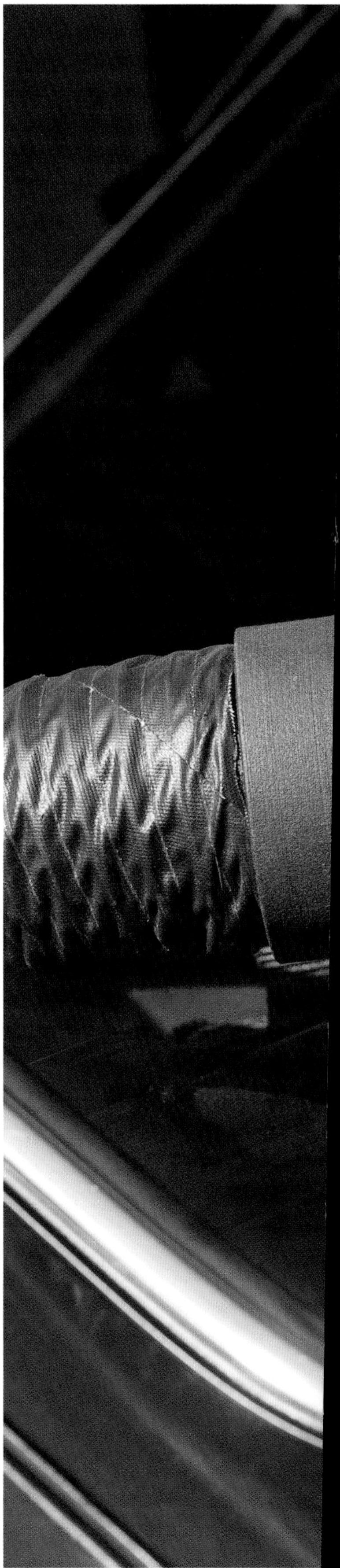

1. Back in Black, only the control levers bring colour to the cockpit.

2. 913 BB – it says so right there!

3. Two monstrous 3D-printed trumpets cover the performance plenum, which leads from the intake to suck air into the engine.

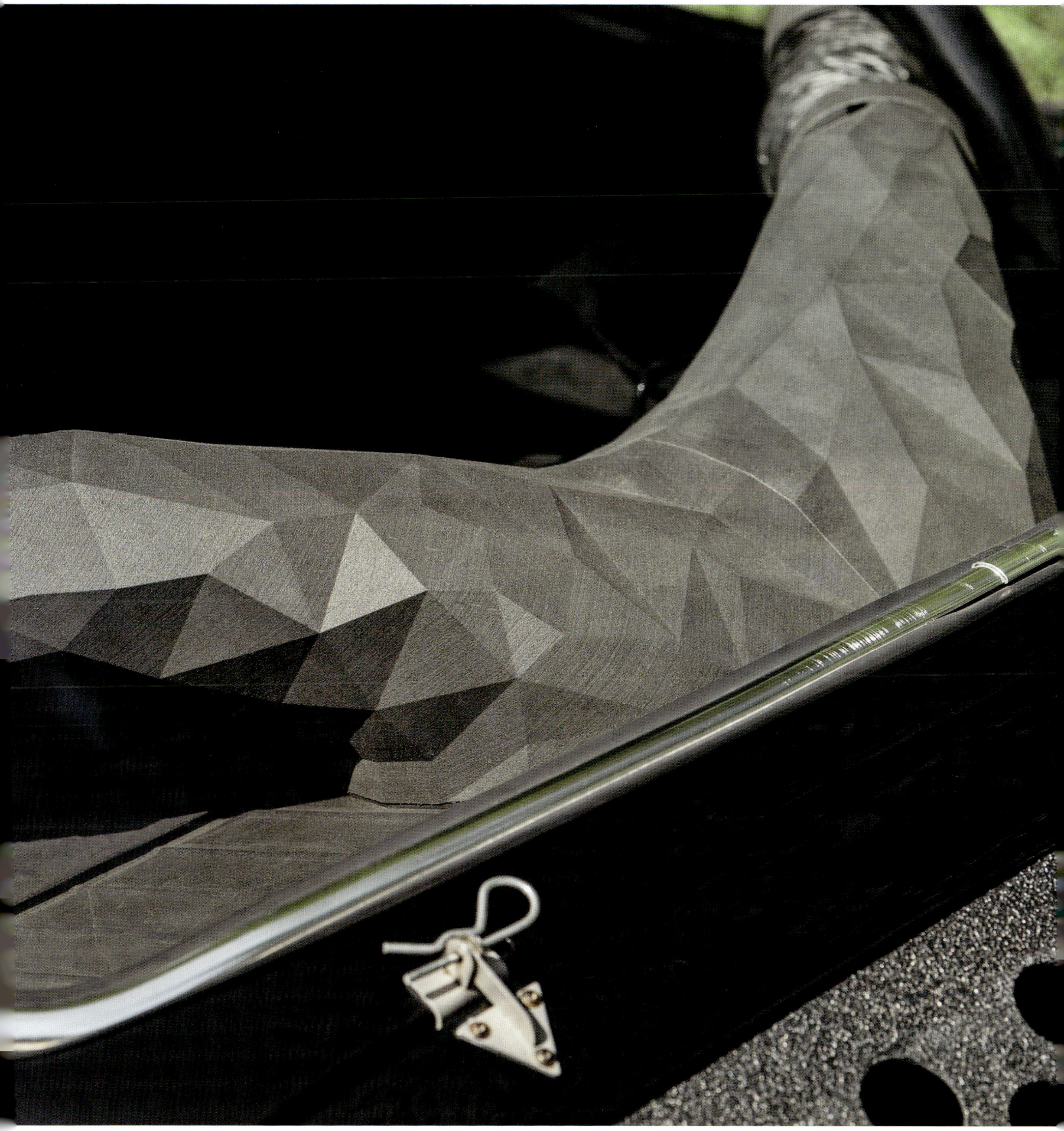

together without compromising the original concept: lightness. "The 912's body was completely rotten. It was rebuilt by replacing the steel with fibreglass parts, the front and rear hoods, bumpers, front wings and doors. Only the rear wings stayed in steel because you can't get those parts for short wheelbases. The roll cage was made by my friend at Bloodmotorsport, who is an expert. He has since moved to the US to make custom roll cages for drift cars. Today, the car weighs 890 kg (1,962 lbs) empty with a flat-six that pulls 317 hp!"

The engine has, of course, received the utmost care to bring it up to a very high-tech standard: "Originally, the engine produced 272 hp, but we added a dynamic intake, a programmable computer, electronic fuel injection and individual throttle bodies on each cylinder, which all helped to increase the power. We removed the distributor cap and replaced it with a twin electronic ignition system. For the dynamic intake, a performance plenum (like a large air chamber) was made to measure with 3D printing. Then two large intake trumpets were added on top, drawing air in through the side windows – they're clearly visible through the rear windows. They were 3D-printed using nylon-carbon powder sintering. That's a system that is stronger and thinner – but also more expensive – than printing filament, and it takes into account the aerodynamic flow inside the inlet."

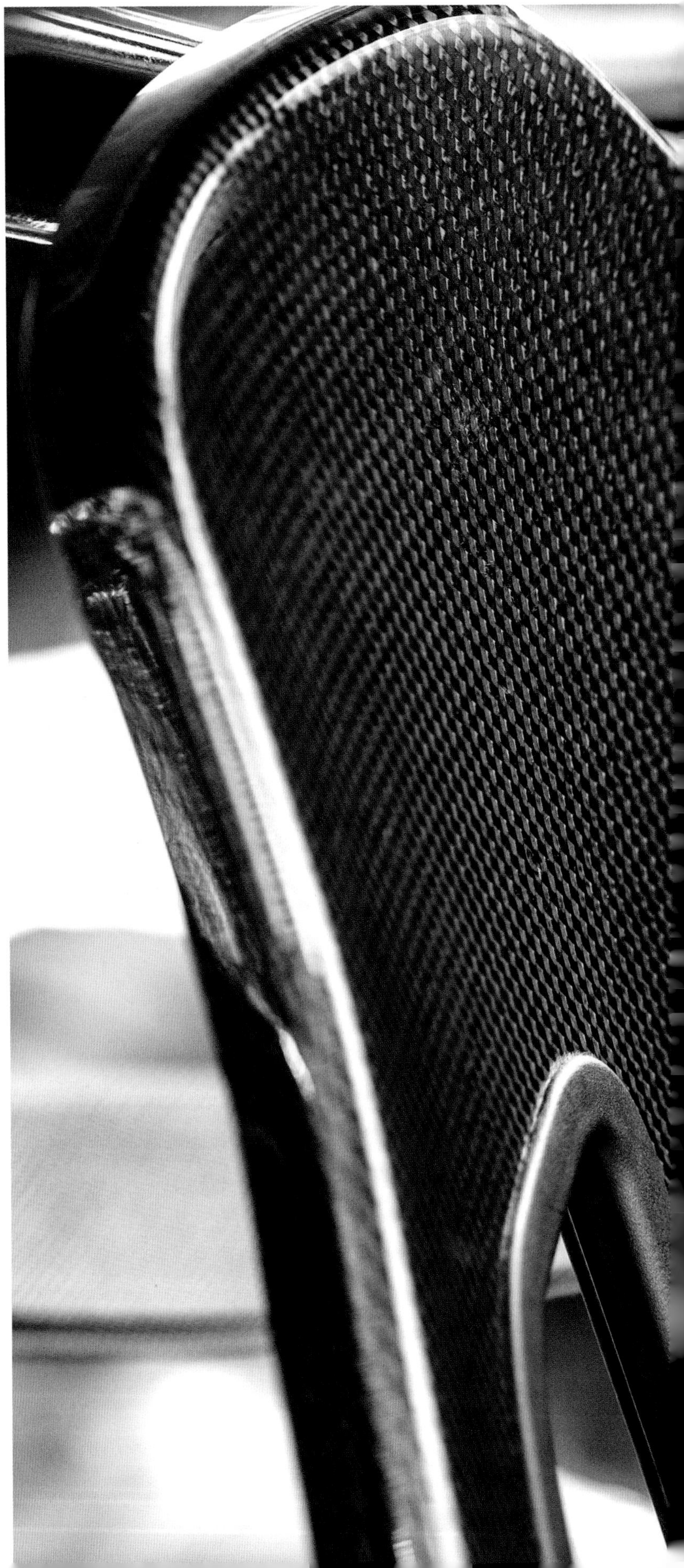

Opposite: The bucket seats are Tilletts, as seen notably in Caterhams. They are extremely light, at only 5kg (11 lbs) each.

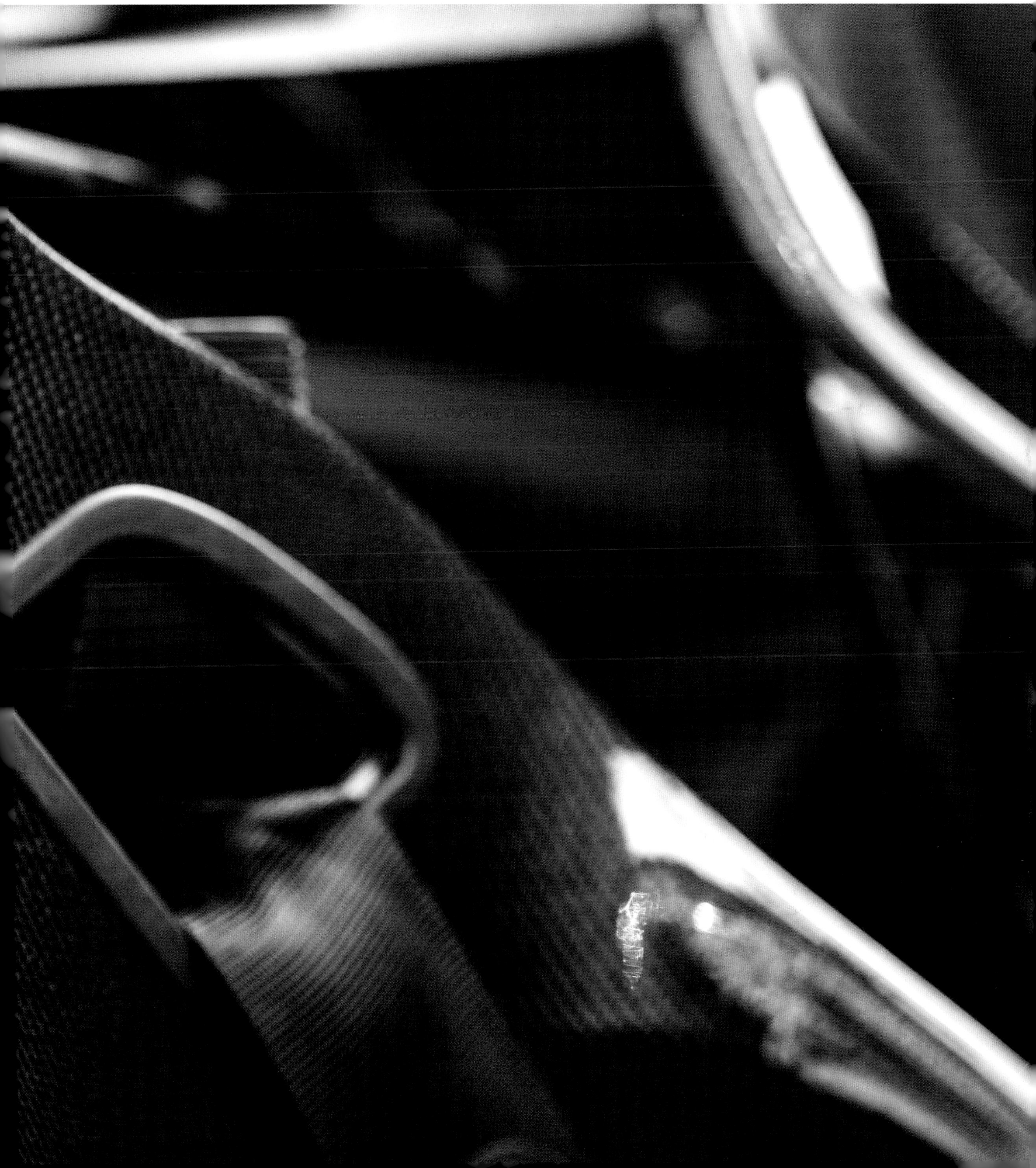

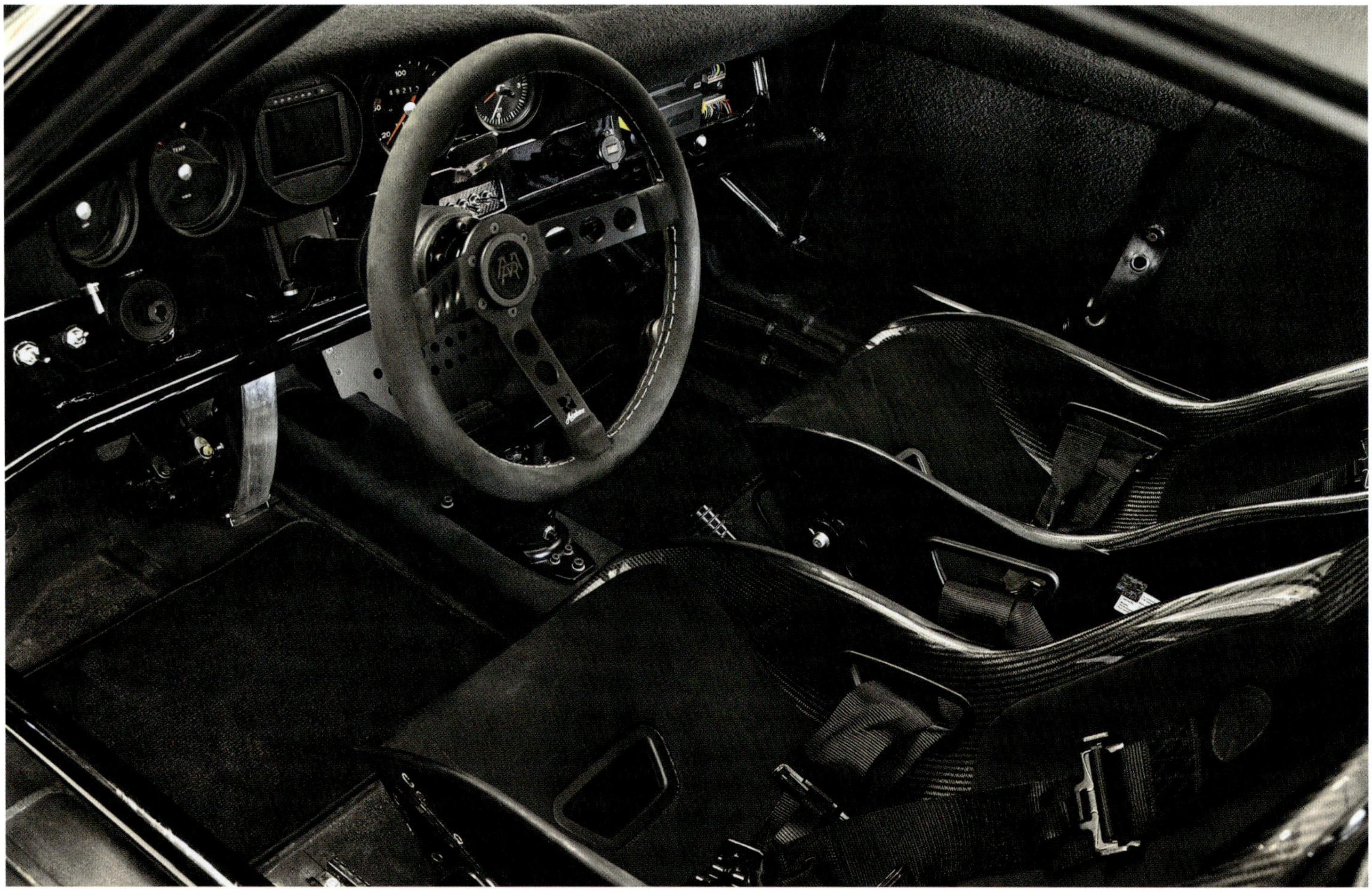

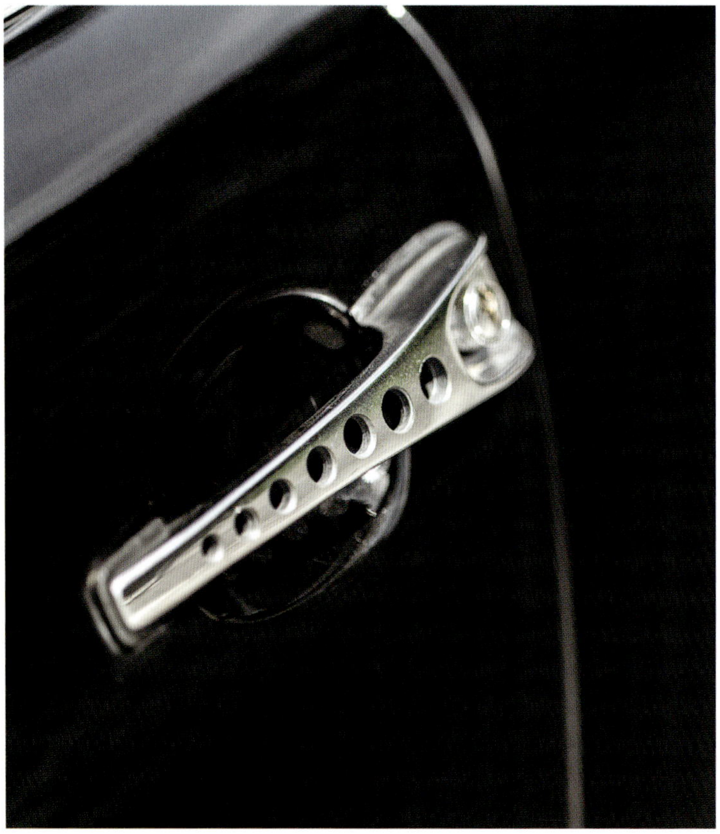

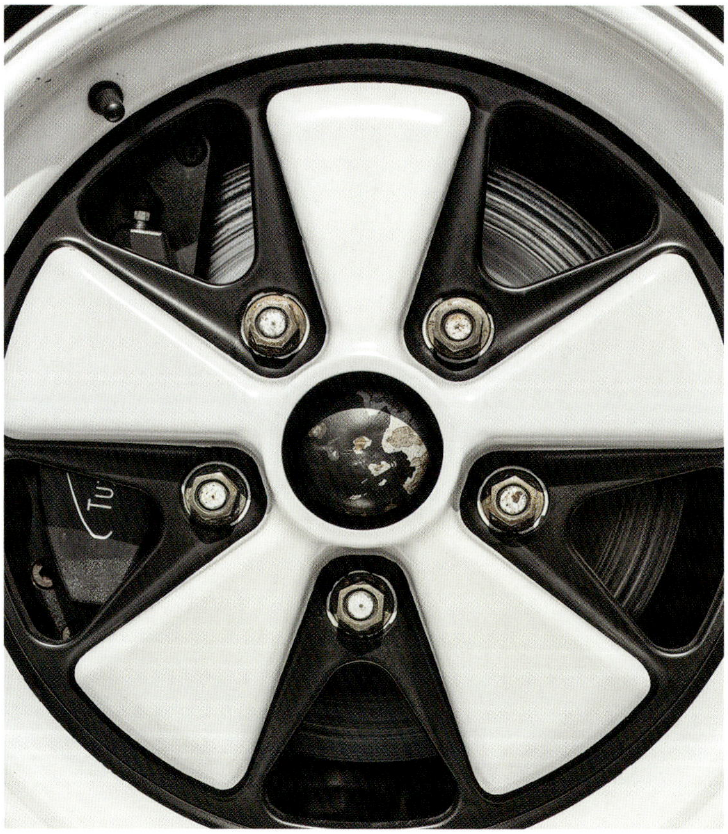

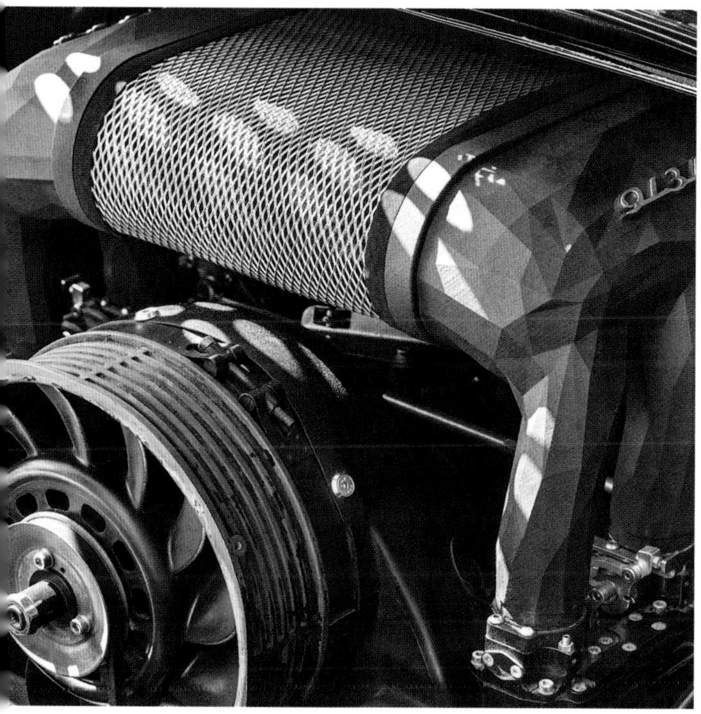

913 BLACK BIRD
BY THE NUMBERS

CREATION (EX-912) 1968

FLAT CYLINDERS 6

CC 3,600

HP 317

And the madness doesn't stop there: "The car is tuned for the track, with suspension and running gear from a 2.0-litre Cup model. Those are cars that race in the Peter Auto series." The category is for Porsche 911 2.0-litre short wheelbase cars that comply with pre-1966 FIA (Fédération Internationale de l'Automobile) regulations. "The braking system has been completely redesigned with rally car brakes: six pistons at the front and four at the back, connected by aviation hoses with a double adjustable lever on a racing pedal assembly." Even more, Sylvain's obsession reached the next level with the creation of completely unique rims: "It has 16-inch rims, which is a bit anachronistic, given that Porsches from that era were fitted with 14- or 15-inch rims. The four wheels were identical, as they had the same track width front and rear. The 911 R was fitted with 6-inch tyres at the front and 7-inch tyres at the rear, so it would have more grip on the drive wheels. To make sure you couldn't see that from the outside, Porsche designed the rear wheels with an inward offset. So they made a specific offset (ET, from the German *Einpress Tiefe*) on the Fuchs rims exclusively for this 911 R. They called it '7-inches deep'. I wanted to follow the same principle as Porsche back then, with 7-inches at the front and 8-inch at the rear. With an ET of 30, I was able to fit the 8-inch rims. But Porsche don't make them. So we asked Braid, the specialist manufacturer of light and strong forged competition wheels, to make some with those dimensions in a Fuchs-style design." The 913 Black Bird is a total geek machine! Meticulous, precise and knowing exactly what he wanted to do and where he wanted to go, this ambitious project took Yvan eight years to complete: "We started in 2015 and completed it in 2023. It wasn't exactly quick!"

The car has already clocked up more than 3,500 miles, including 2,500 on the track, as it is used for ride-alongs on circuits to promote *Vulcan* car magazine, where Sylvain is editor-in-chief: "The car is louder inside than out, which makes the enthusiasts I have on board absolutely delighted."

1. The Black Bird lives up to its name and the adage "light is right" is even demonstrated in the interior.

2. Door handles are perforated: the quest to save every ounce is evident throughout.

3. Made-to-measure wheels from the specialist Braid: 7 inch in front; 8 at the back.

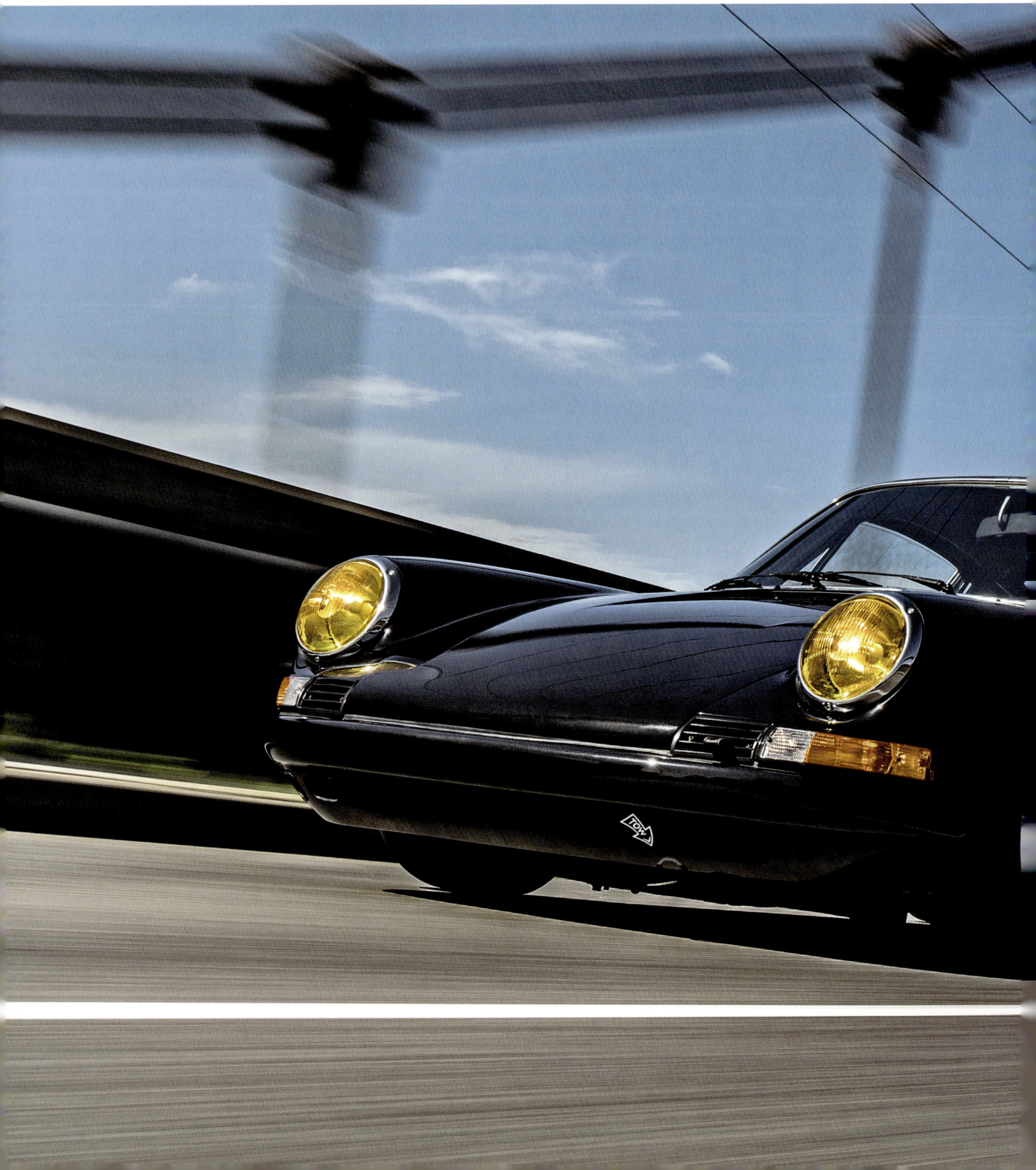
TOW

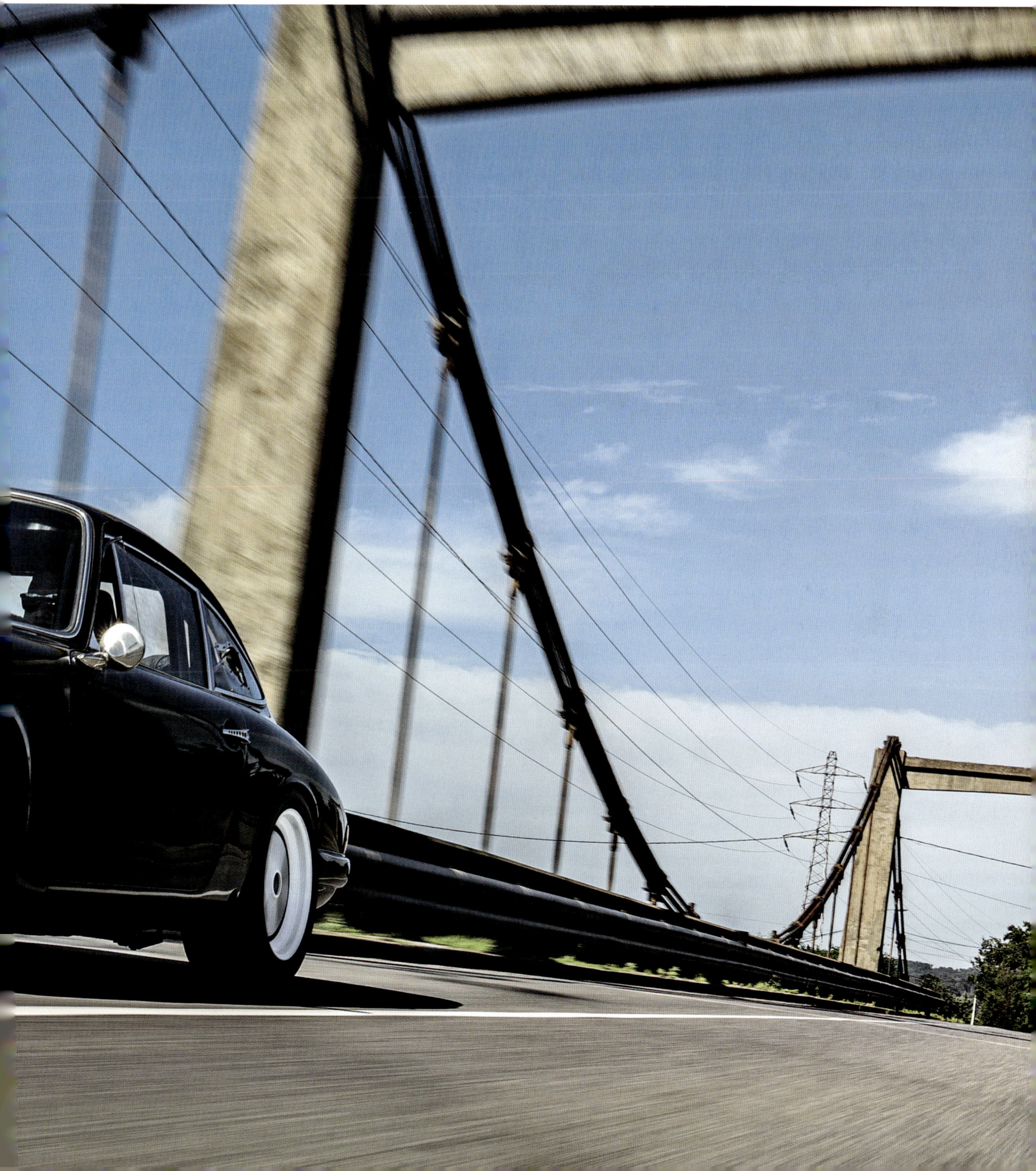

356 B-T5

RUSTY FLOWER

TIME CAPSULE

Some people may find it disrespectful that an old lady like this 356 has been left in such a state. But for owner Aymeric the opposite is true: he absolutely loves the patina, which, over the passage of time, makes for some old-fashioned, authentic charm.

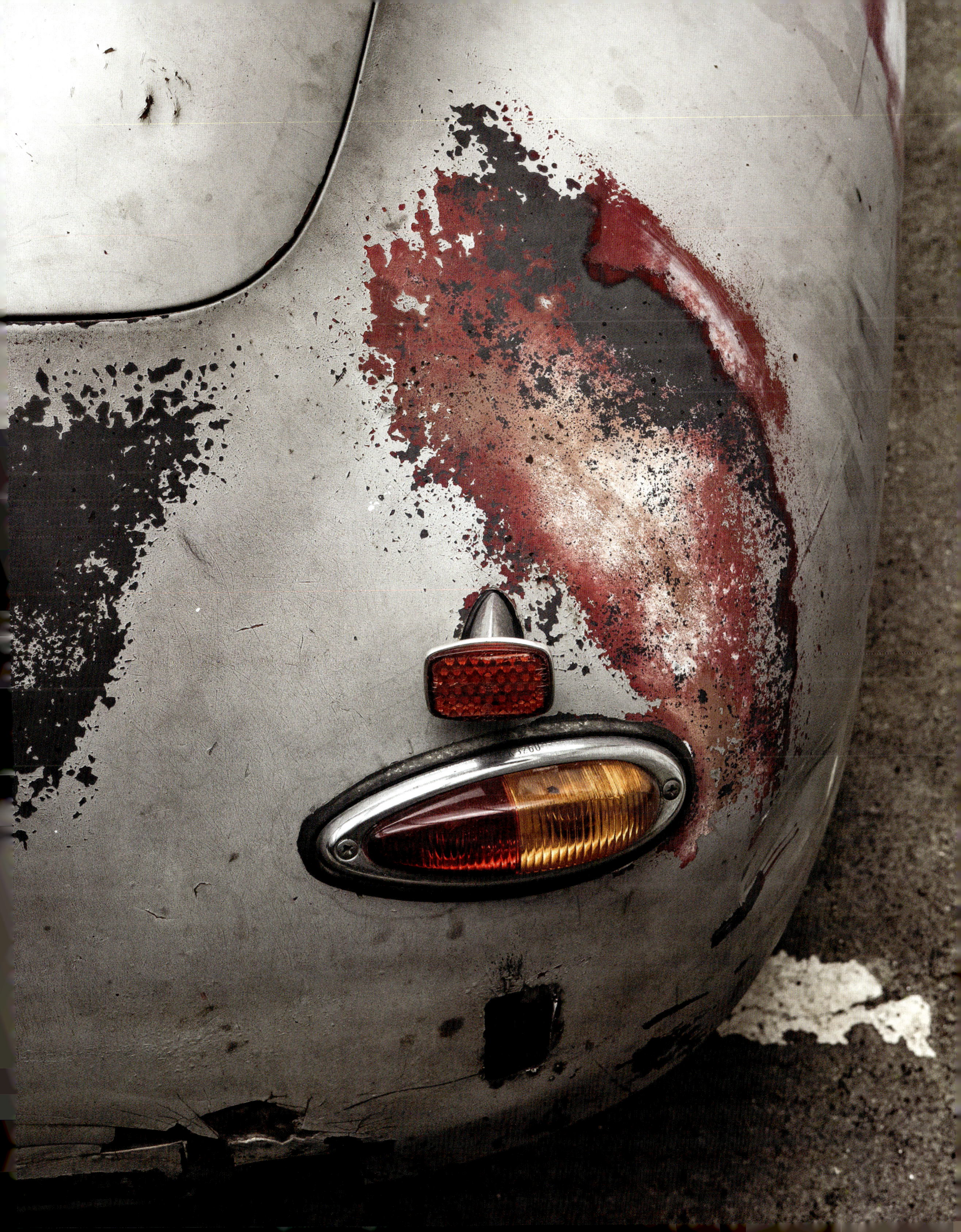

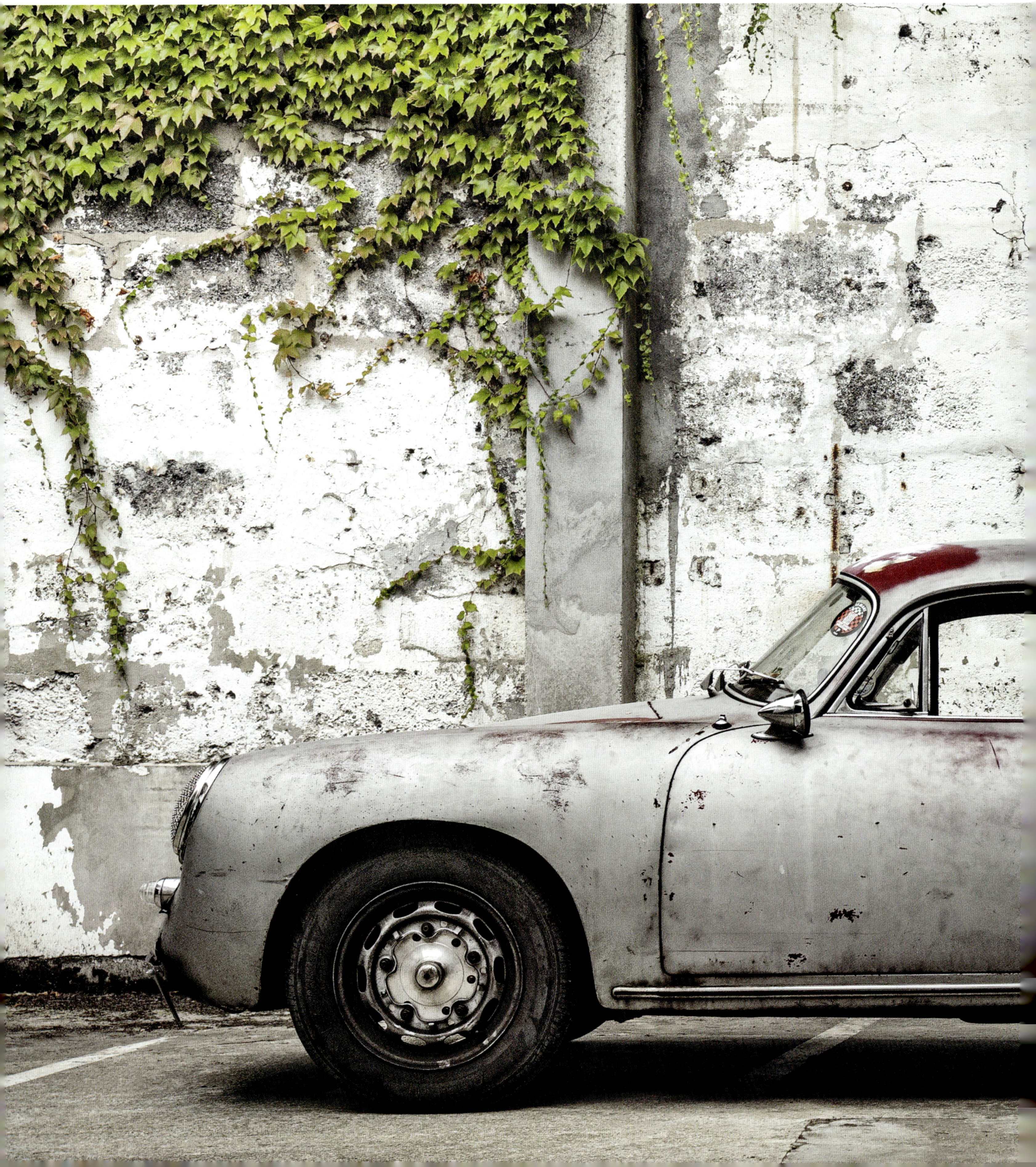

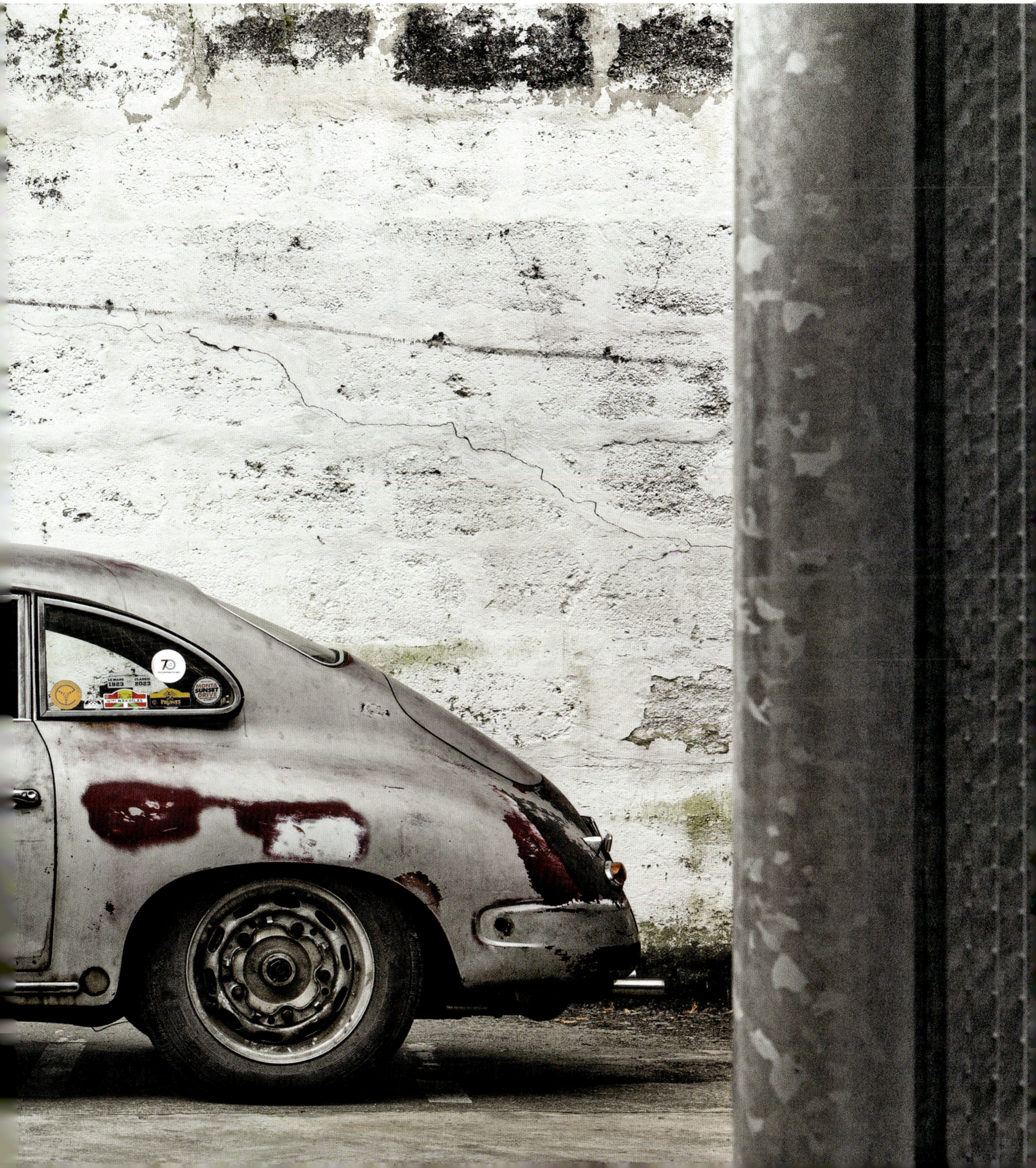
LE MANS 1923
CLASSIC 2023
MONTA SUNSET DRIVE
PRUNES

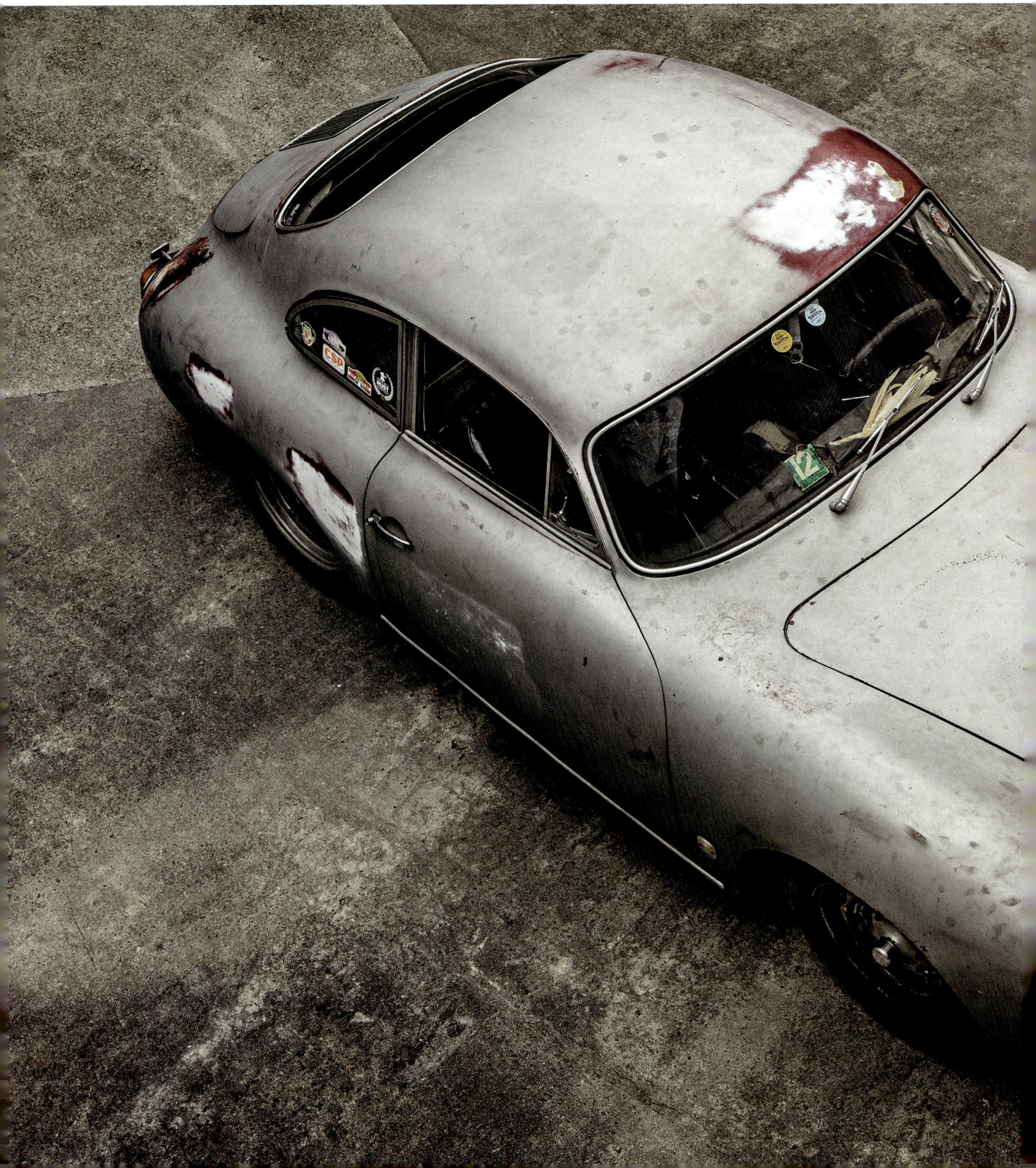
CSP
12

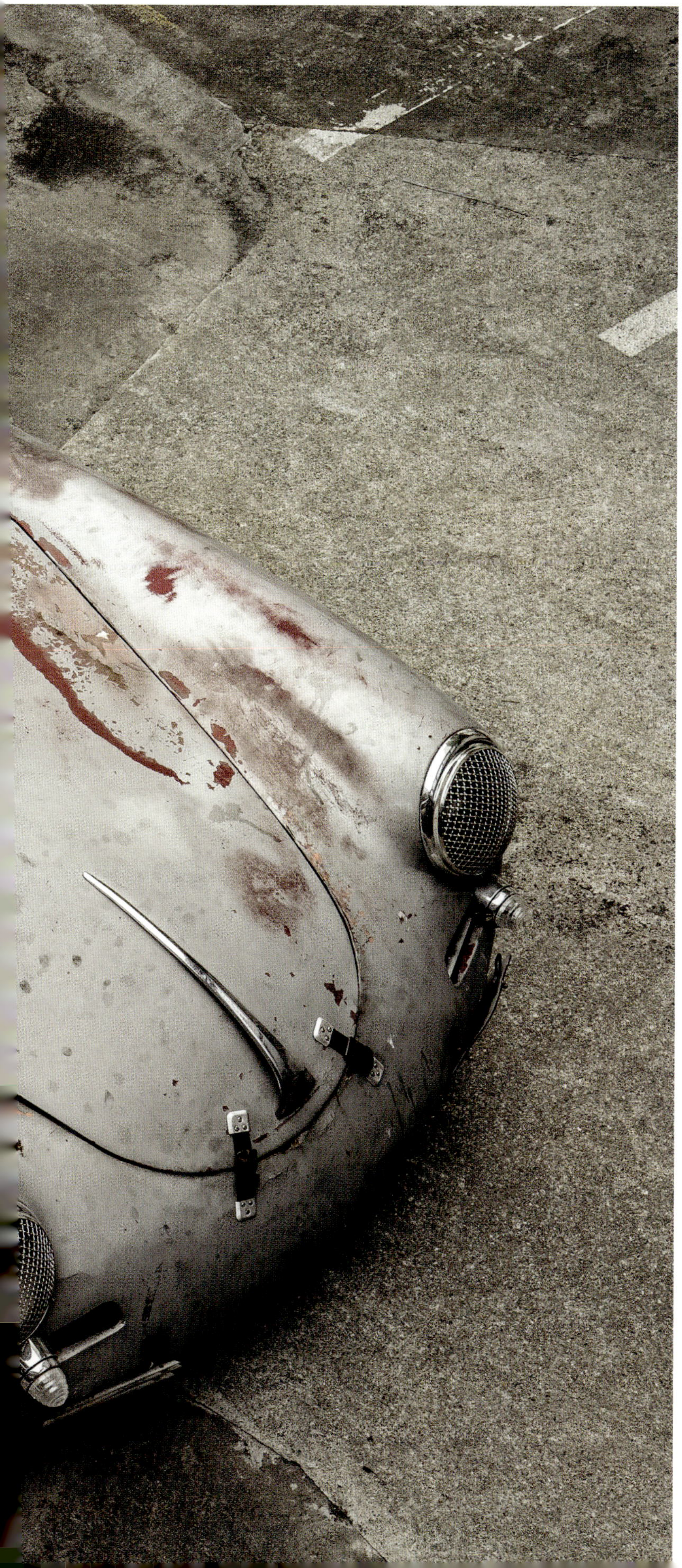

THIS "OLD LADY" IS OVER 64, AND REALLY LOOKS HER AGE.

"It is is a 1960 356 B-T5, with a flat-four, 1,600 cc engine – nickamed 'Dame' ('Lady') – that generates 60 hp!" Aymeric, the owner, is in love with the car, which has been kept in its original condition. The engine owes its name to its gentle character, compared to other, more powerful, engines. The story of this 356 is truly unusual, as it belonged to a descendant of a hugely famous, legendary figure from American history. "The first owner of the car in the US was Davy Crockett Junior, who was a relative of the trapper and politician from the early 19th century who became a popular American hero. I managed to keep hold of the original registration document. It was sold new in Florida, and then it went to Georgia, where it stayed, unused, from 1976. The 356 was imported into France in 2007 and someone bought it there, then I got hold of it in 2011. A few small jobs had been carried out, notably the rims had been sandblasted and epoxy had been painted, new tyres had been added, disc brakes at the front and an anti-rust treatment on the entire underside of the chassis. It had 35,000 miles on the clock.

But it could well have done 135,000 miles … I rebuilt the engine with Romain, a friend, who found it to be extremely clean on the inside."

Two small, weathered leather straps hold the trunk lid onto the front of the car. Pretty much all the paint has worn off. There are only a few spots here and there, a distant reminder of the scarlet coat the car once had. "Originally the car was coloured red before it had been painted grey in the 1970s. When I got it in 2011, the grey paint was starting to come off. In some areas that had been repaired you could see the sanded-down layers. But I never touched anything, I didn't even add a layer of varnish. I love it like this, and I want to keep it with this incredible patina intact for as long as I possibly can," says Aymeric, who is obviously totally passionate about this unique vehicle. "Not many cars are preserved like this, in such an original condition. Ever since I bought it, I haven't hoovered it once," he says, loud and proud. "I called it the 'Rusty Flower'. I do not know if that phrase exists or not, but I like the way the two words go together as they describe this 356 perfectly. It's almost like a time capsule that, over time, allowed the patina to develop and grow - particularly around the rear engine, which gets very hot."

But this 356 drives! Really well, in fact. "I use it regularly to go to gatherings such as the Grand Prix de Pau, the Circuit des Remparts d'Angoulême, the Monta Sunset Drive and the Le Mans Classic." It starts, drives and purrs perfectly.

FEW CARS ARE KEPT IN SUCH AN ORIGINAL CONDITION.

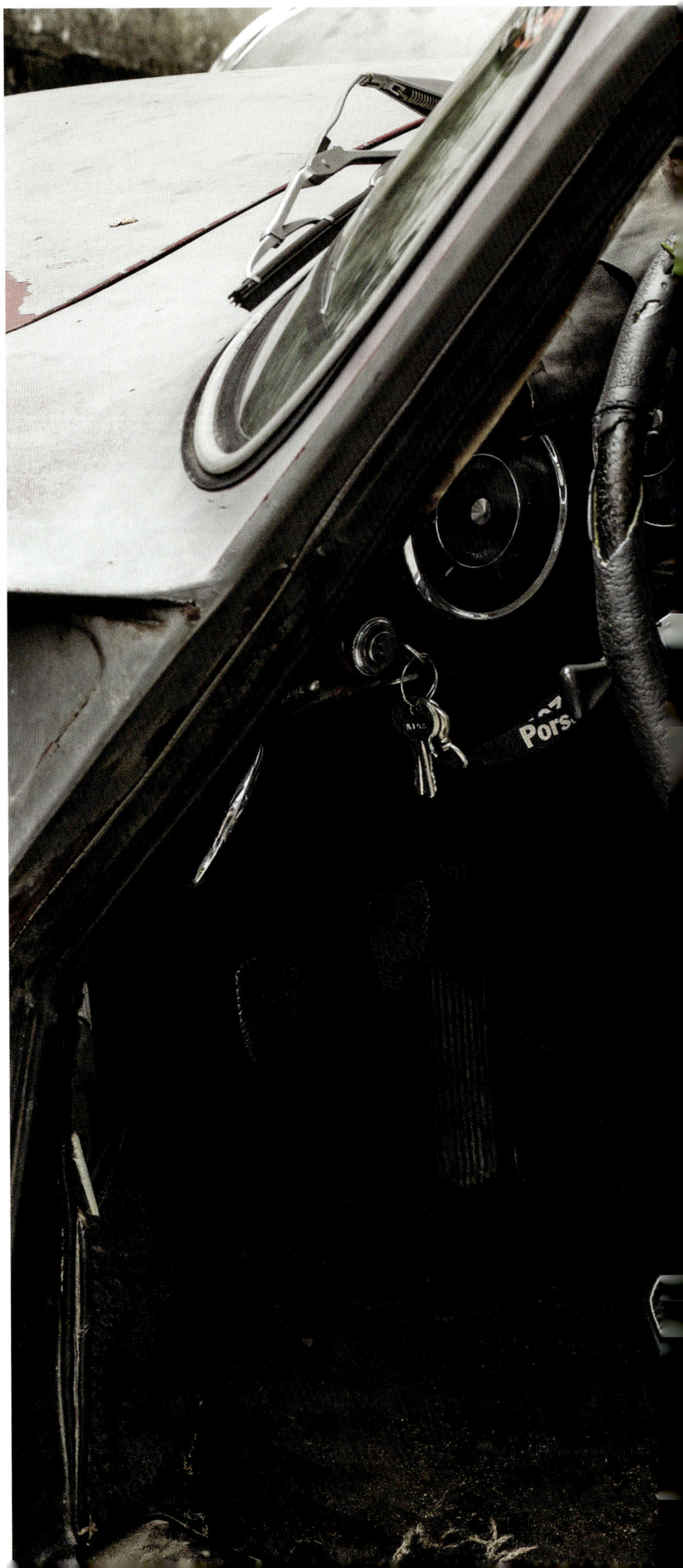

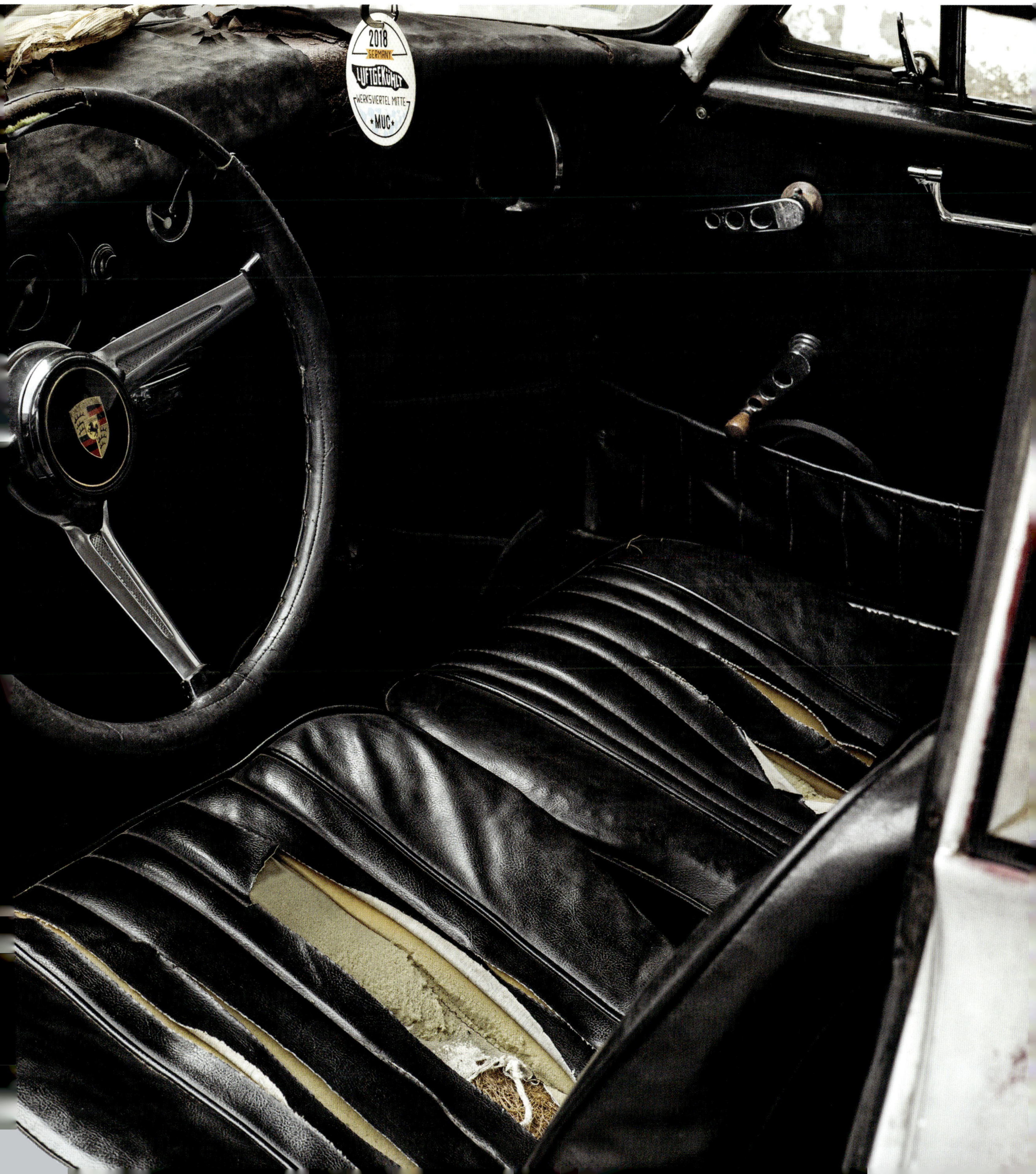
2018
GERMANY
LUFTGEKÜHLT
WERKSVIERTEL MITTE
MUC

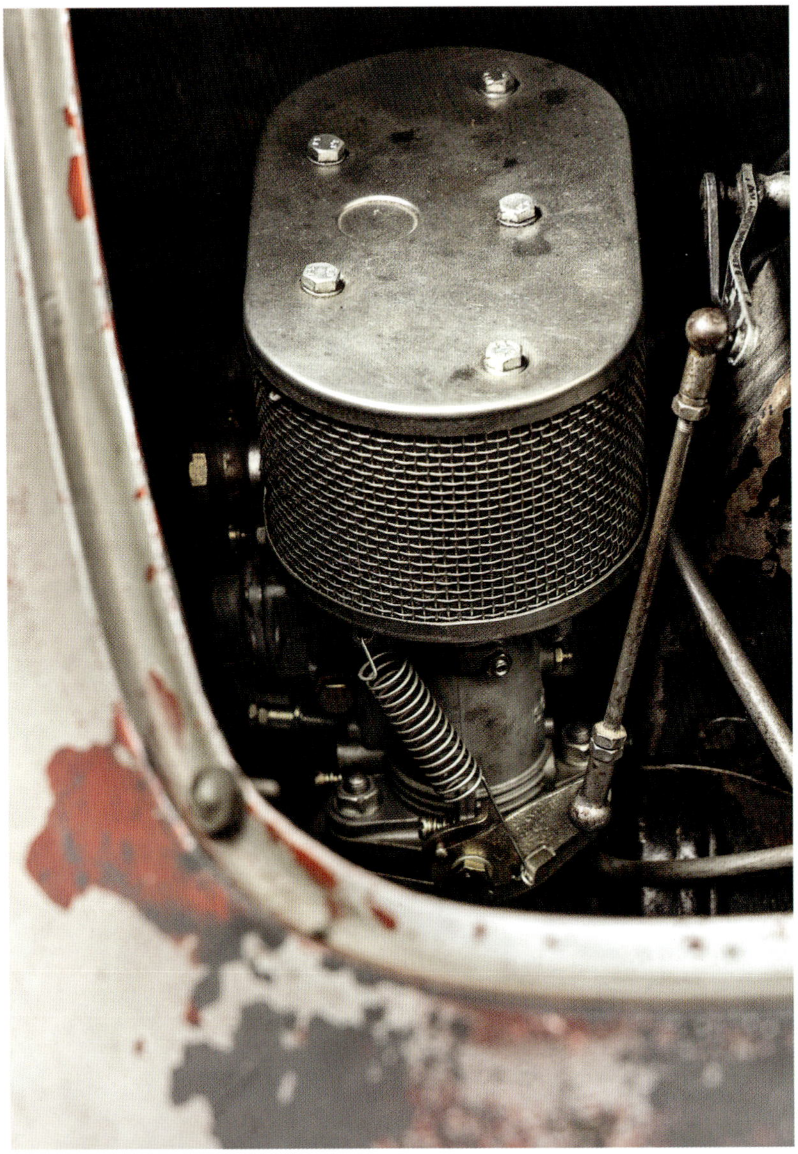

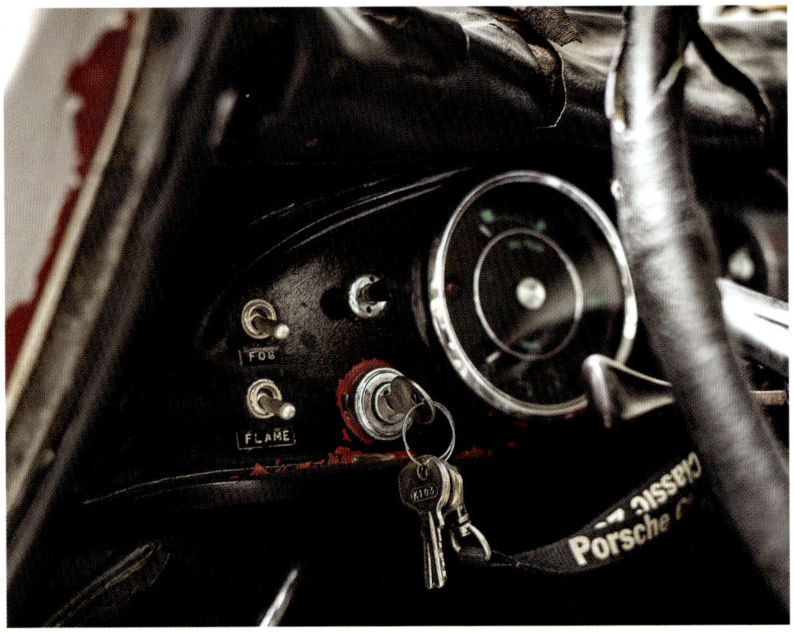

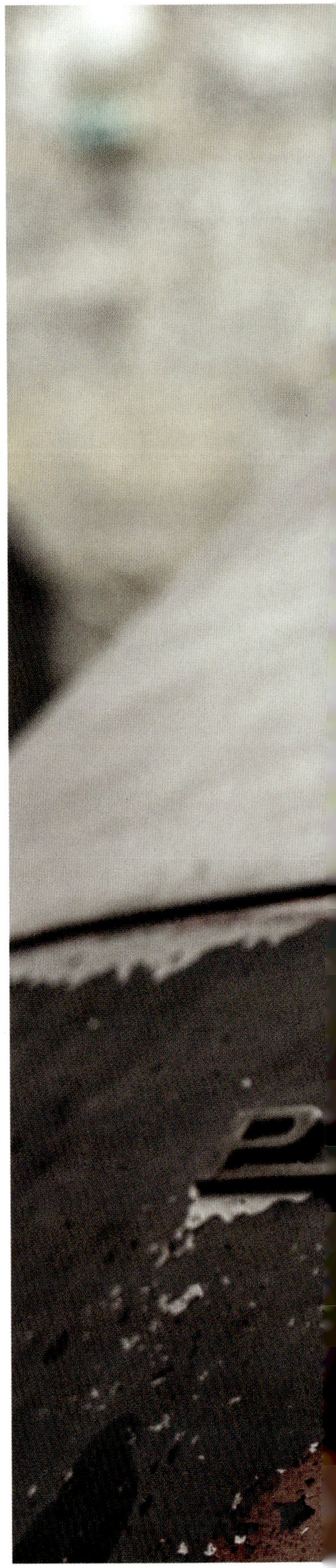

1. The original 60-hp engine has stood the test of time.

2. Ignition is on the left, as on any authentic Porsche.

3. The rear hood heats up considerably due to the engine, which allows the owner's much-loved patina to flourish.

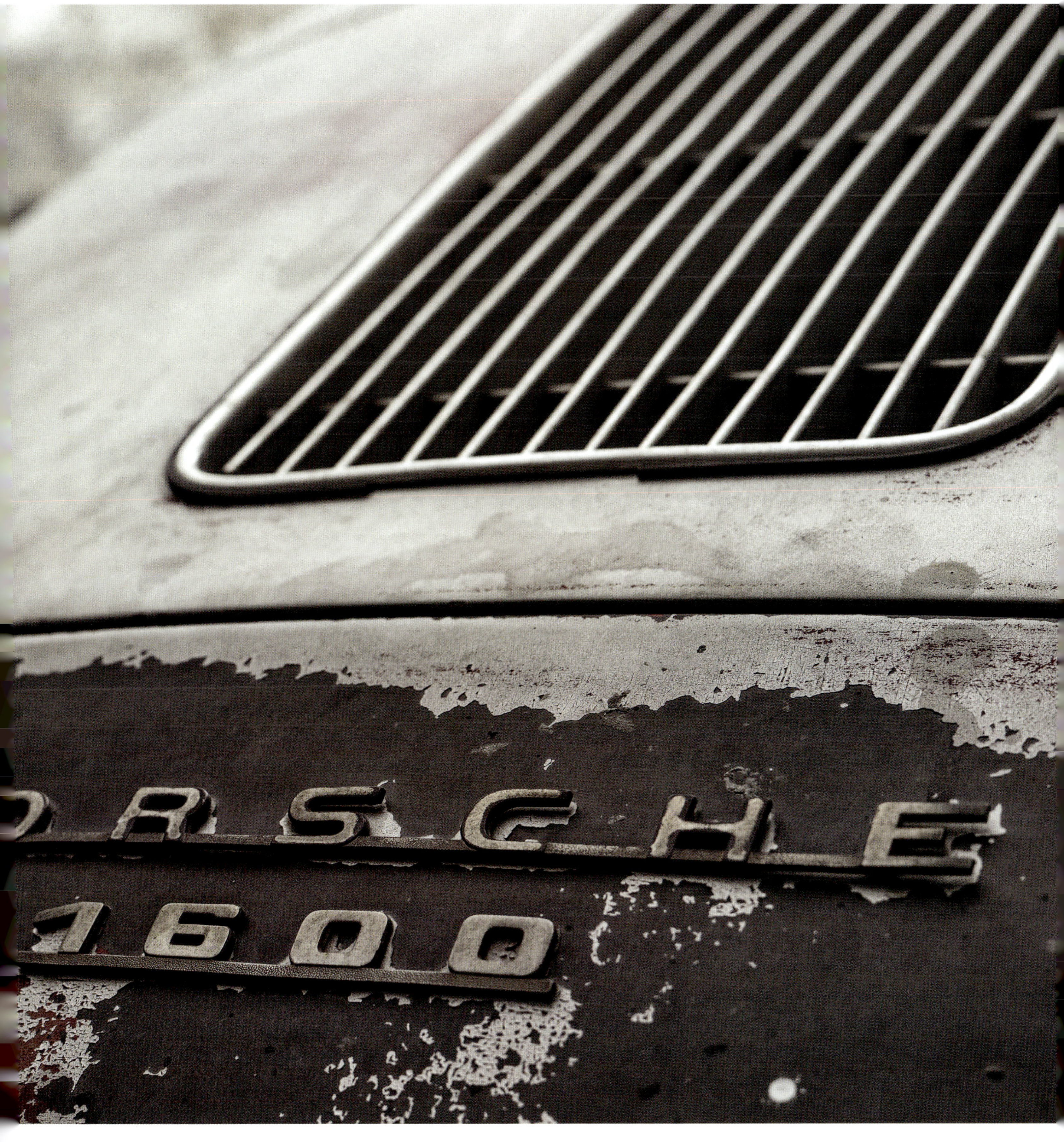
1600

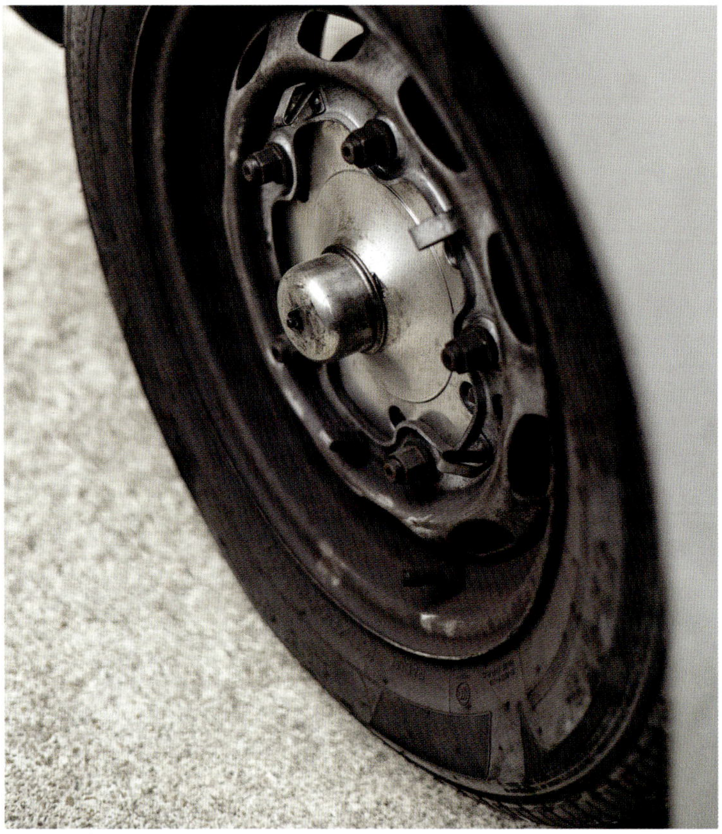

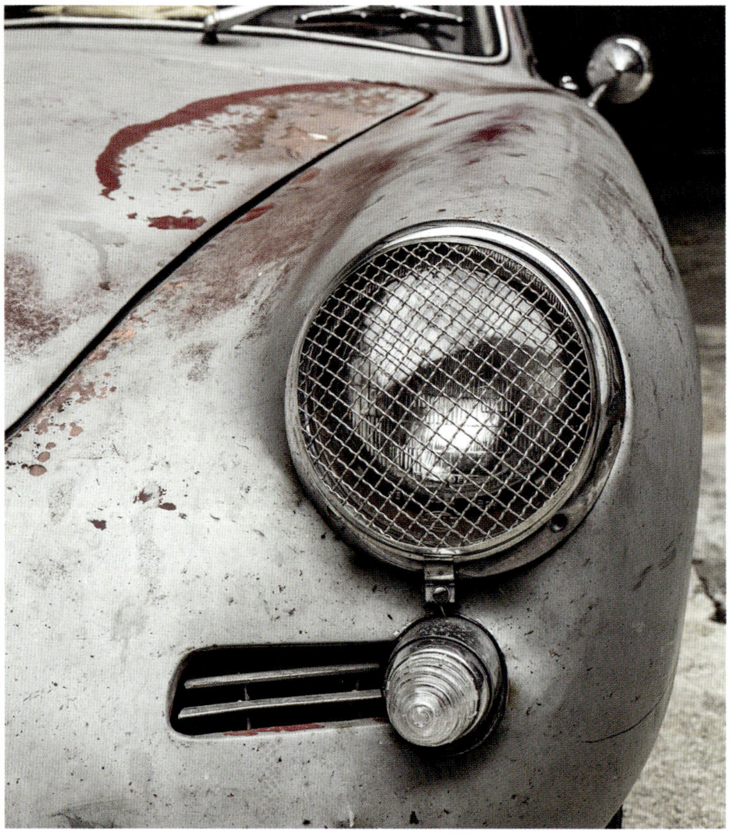

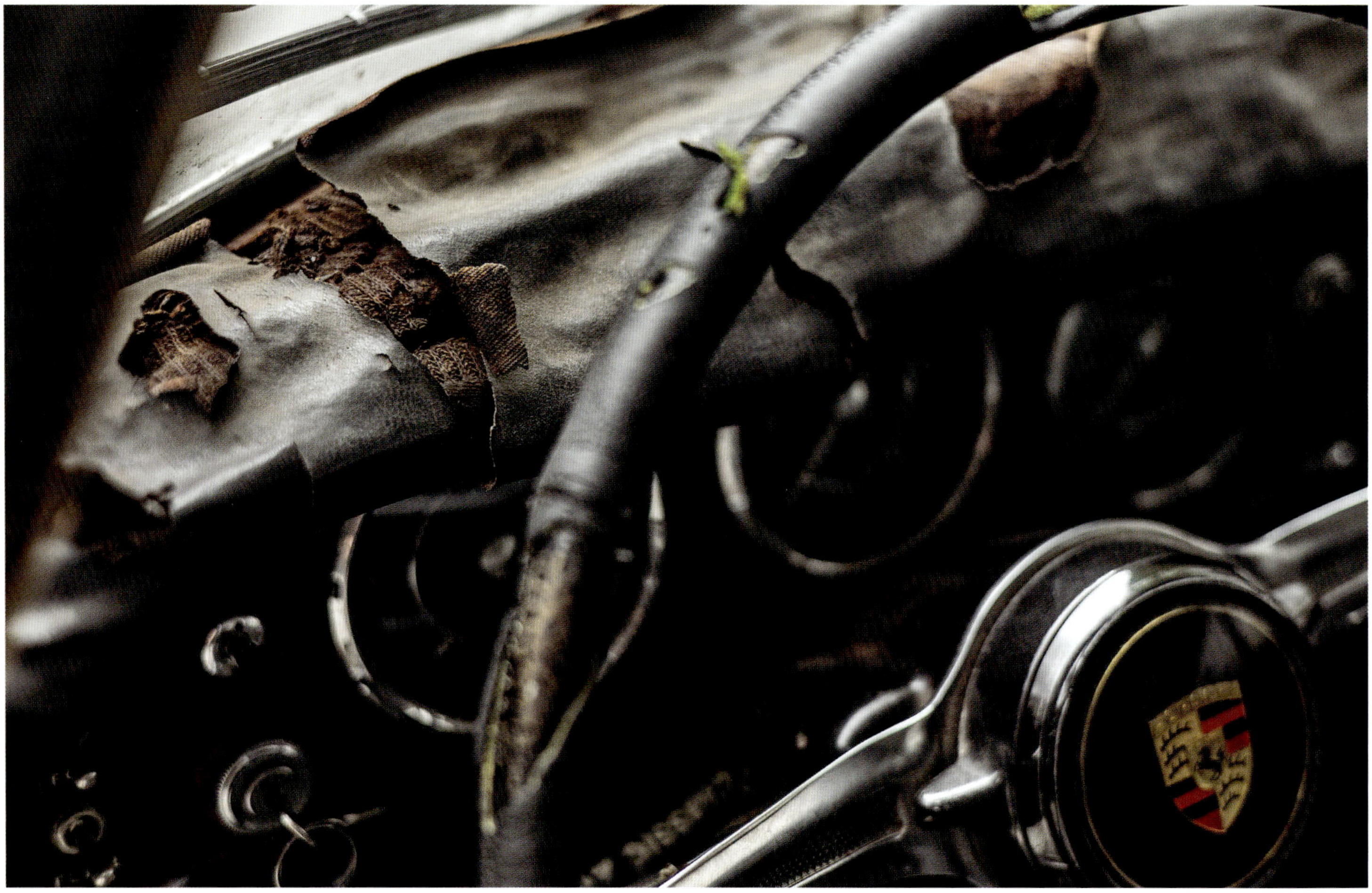

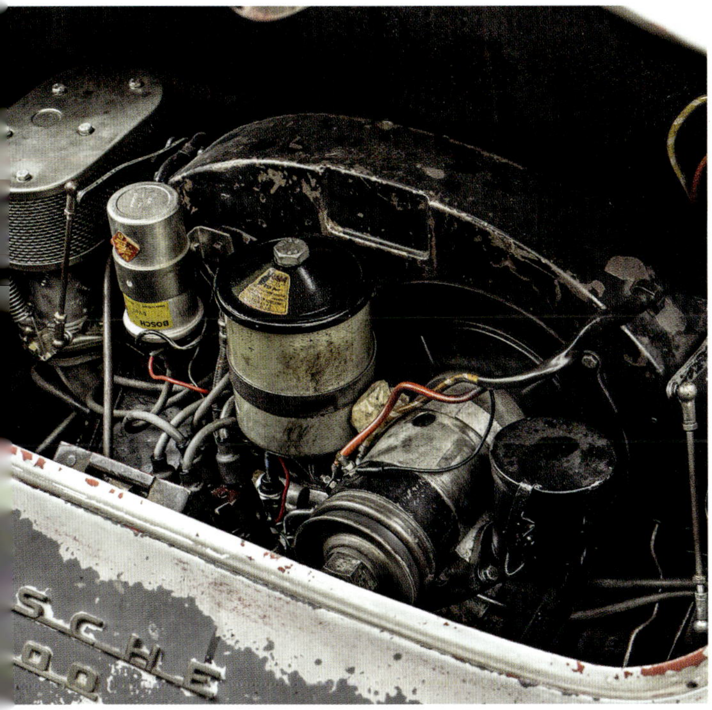

356 B-T5 – RUSTY FLOWER

BY THE NUMBERS

CREATION **1960**

FLAT CYLINDERS **4**

CC **1,600**

HP **60**

1 2 3

1. Bolted steel rims, *naturellement*!

2. The headlights are covered with mesh to protect them from gravel.

3. Bits of rusted wire wool fall on the driver's feet while at the wheel.

"Of course, there have been a few small accidents here and there. Little dings from low-speed manoeuvring or from when I renovated my house. Some floor varnish dripped down between the floorboards and onto the hood. I tried to rub it off but I couldn't get rid of it; I see it as part of its history, like a little scar, for example. She is like a grandmother, with beautiful wrinkles."

Aymeric also applied this philosophy to the interior of his car, which has very much retained the original styling. "Everything is functional; the chrome trim is in good condition. I left the odometer in miles, and the dashboard is thoroughly aged: the vinyl is ripped and flakes of rusted steel wool fall onto my shoes when I'm driving. The driver's seat has been broken, repaired and re-welded, and you can see foam padding coming out of the seat. But it's a conscious decision: I don't want a new seat that would clash with the rest of the car. I'll find another old seat some time. It's all part of the patina."

Better still, this 356, with its authentic wear and tear, has even completed a lap of the 24 Hours Le Mans circuit: "I had the opportunity to go round at the Le Mans Classic. There were about 60 Porsches on the starting grid. A whole load of supercharged GT3RSs with 400, 500, 600 horsepower. I got plenty of laughs in my old 60-hp car. I was left behind by the pack very quickly. Just me and another 356, a little older than mine. We were right at the back, by ourselves on that magical circuit. I pushed it to the limit, trying to catch up. Whenever I put the brakes on it veered from side to side. We realized afterwards that one of the wheels was loose and needed tightening. The chassis has a bit of play in it, so you have to drive it like you would ski: lean into the turns, but once you're steady, it's pure joy."

Aymeric has an even more Outlaw project planned for his 356: a high-performance engine! "I bought a Porsche engine that was mounted on an industrial machine. It's a flat-four and it was used on various things, including a combine harvester. It was sitting on a pallet in a garden. I had it done up and mounted it in my 356 between 2016 and 2020. Unfortunately, it started to seize as I was on my way to Angoulême. So I replaced it with the original engine, with a plan to rebuild that old industrial motor and beef it up a bit. I increased the displacement, rebuilt the camshafts and crankshaft, replaced the carburettors. The goal? Around 115 hp! Now I just need to put it back in ..."

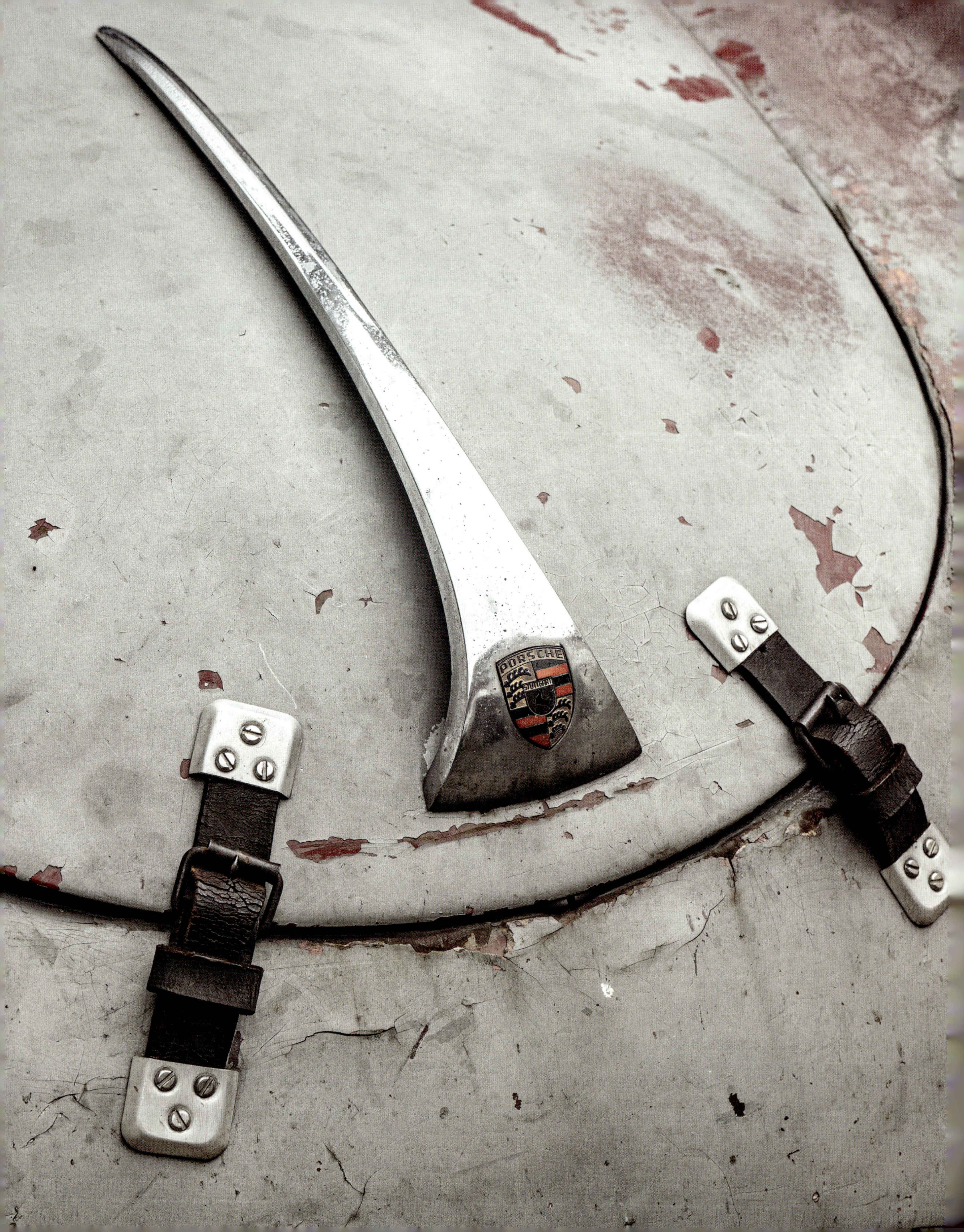
PORSCHE
STUTTGART

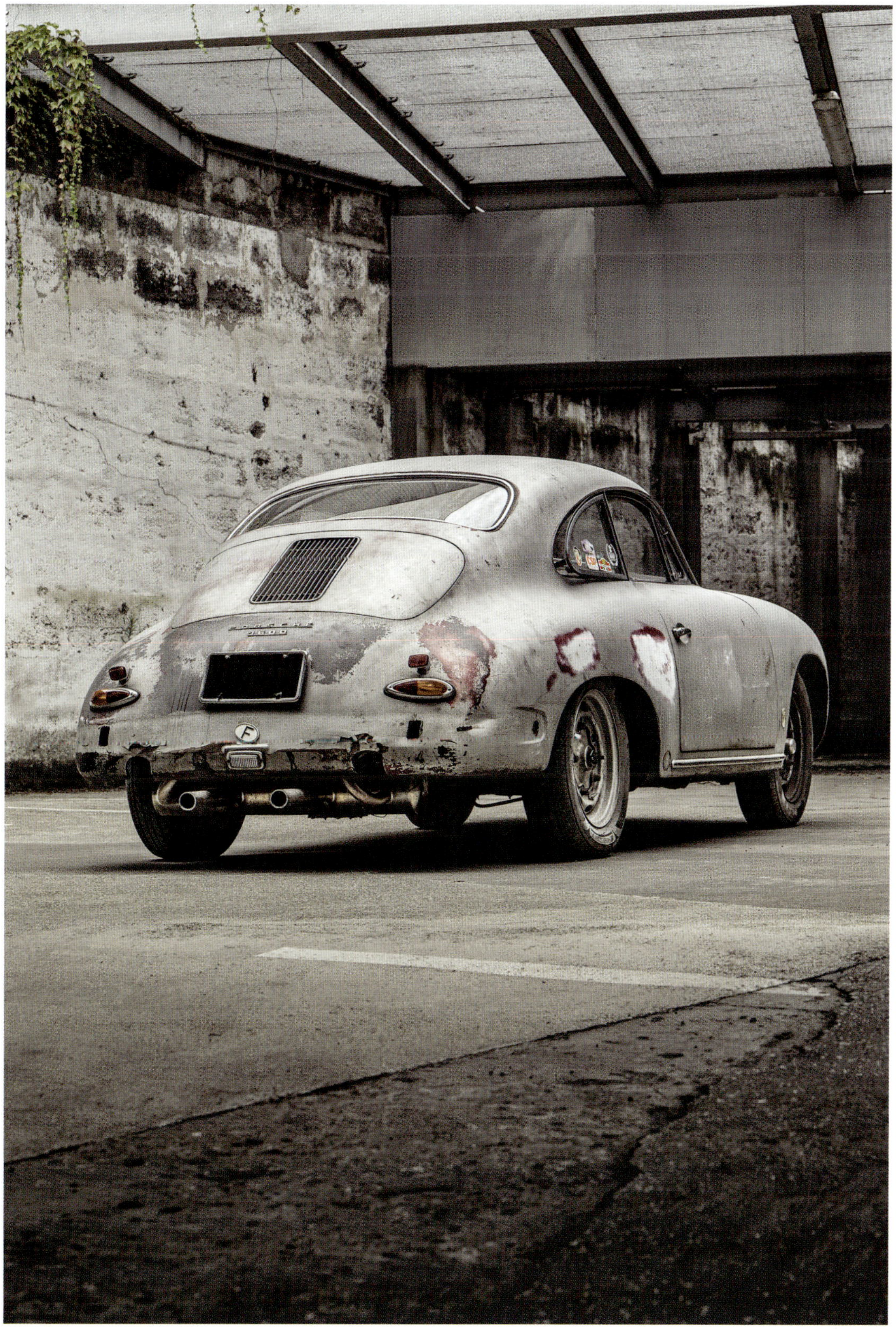

Above: No matter the condition of the "Rusty Flower", a 356 always has amazing style!

Opposite: Worn leather straps hold the front hood of this Porsche in place.
The logo has kept its original colours, albeit slightly faded.

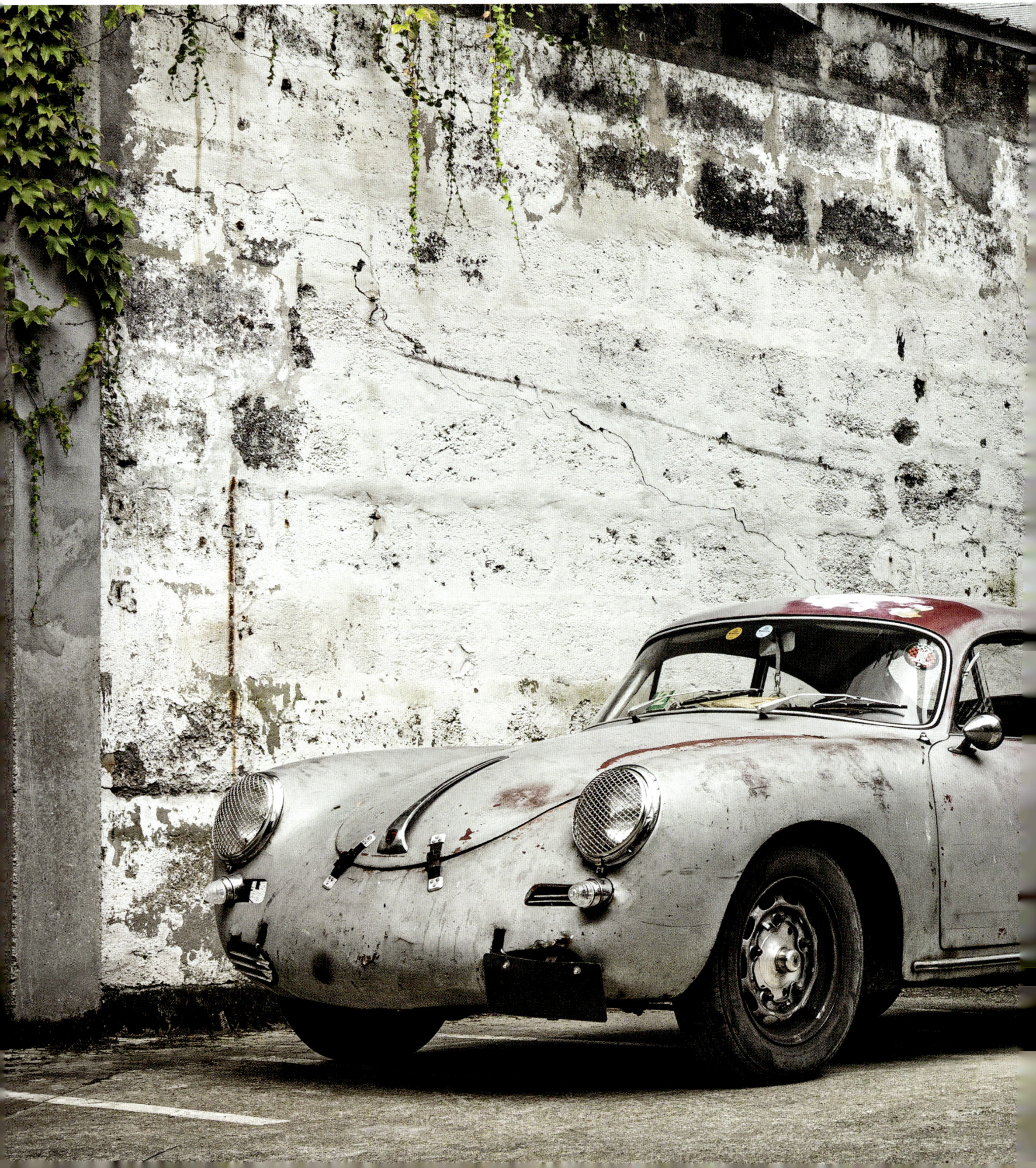

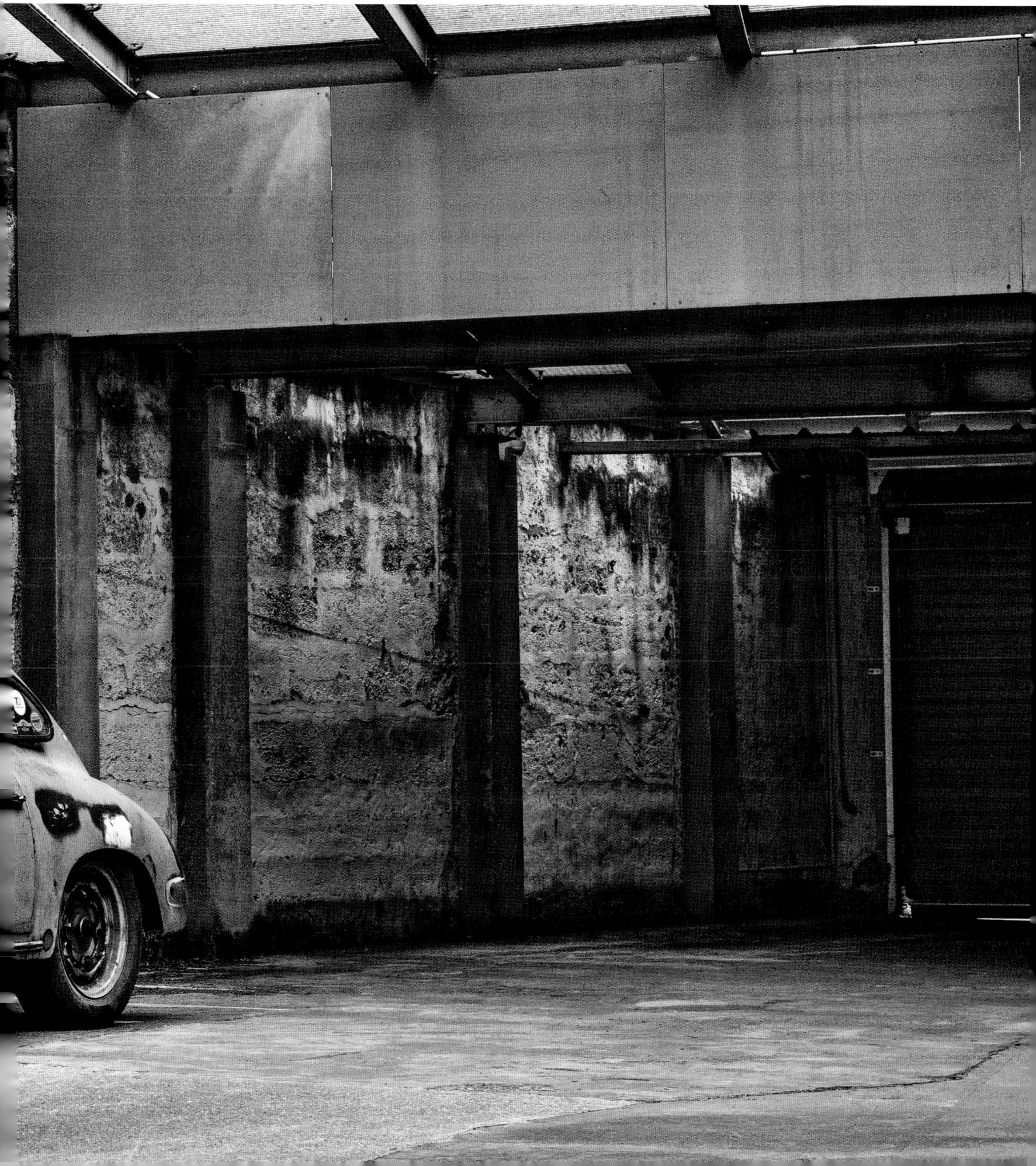

911 ART CAR TESTIMONY

Turning your Porsche 911 into a canvas for contemporary art is an idea that purists may find shocking. This totally outlaw, punk-style creation bears the signature of the graffiti artist Woo Ghost, based on an original idea by Aymeric.

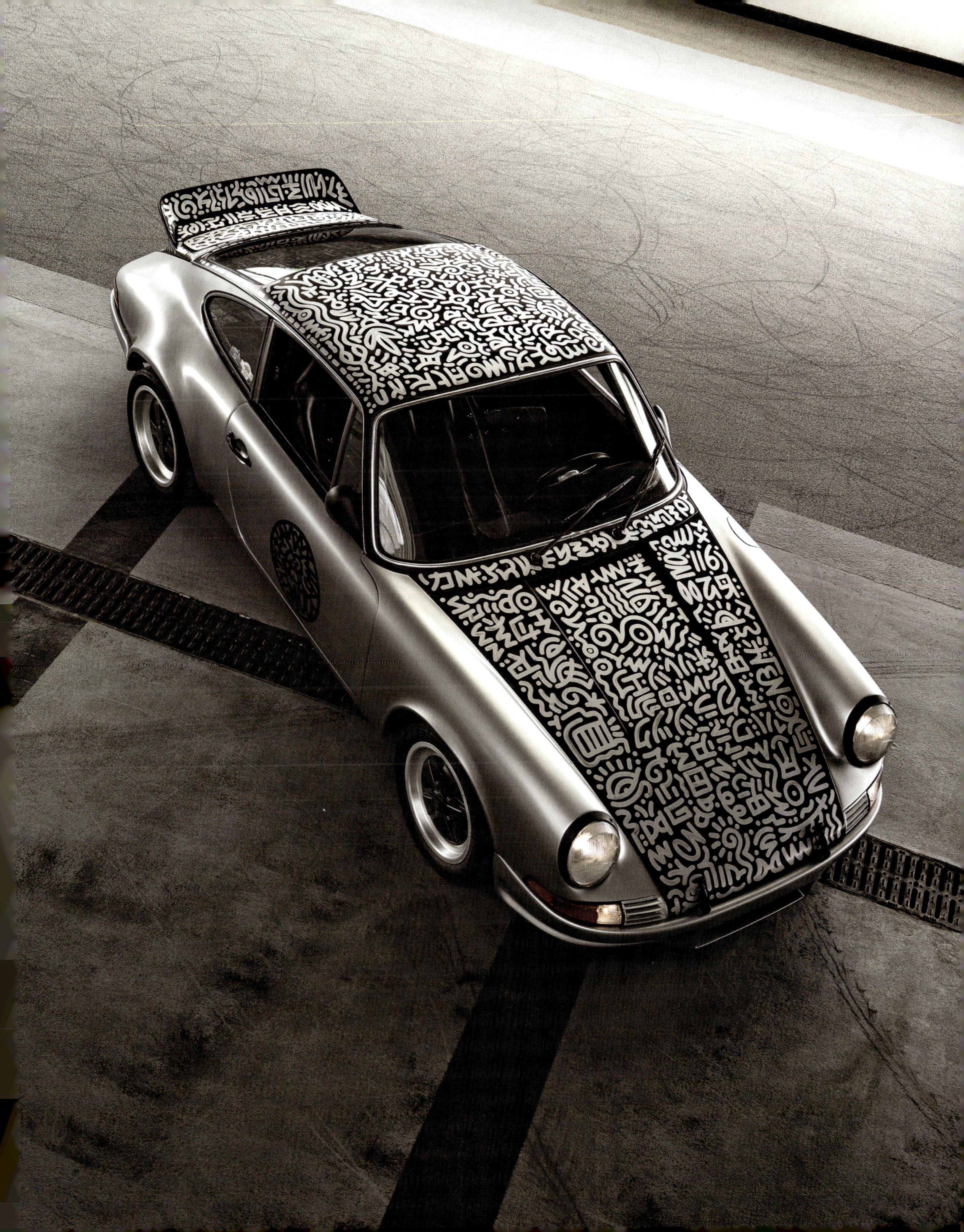

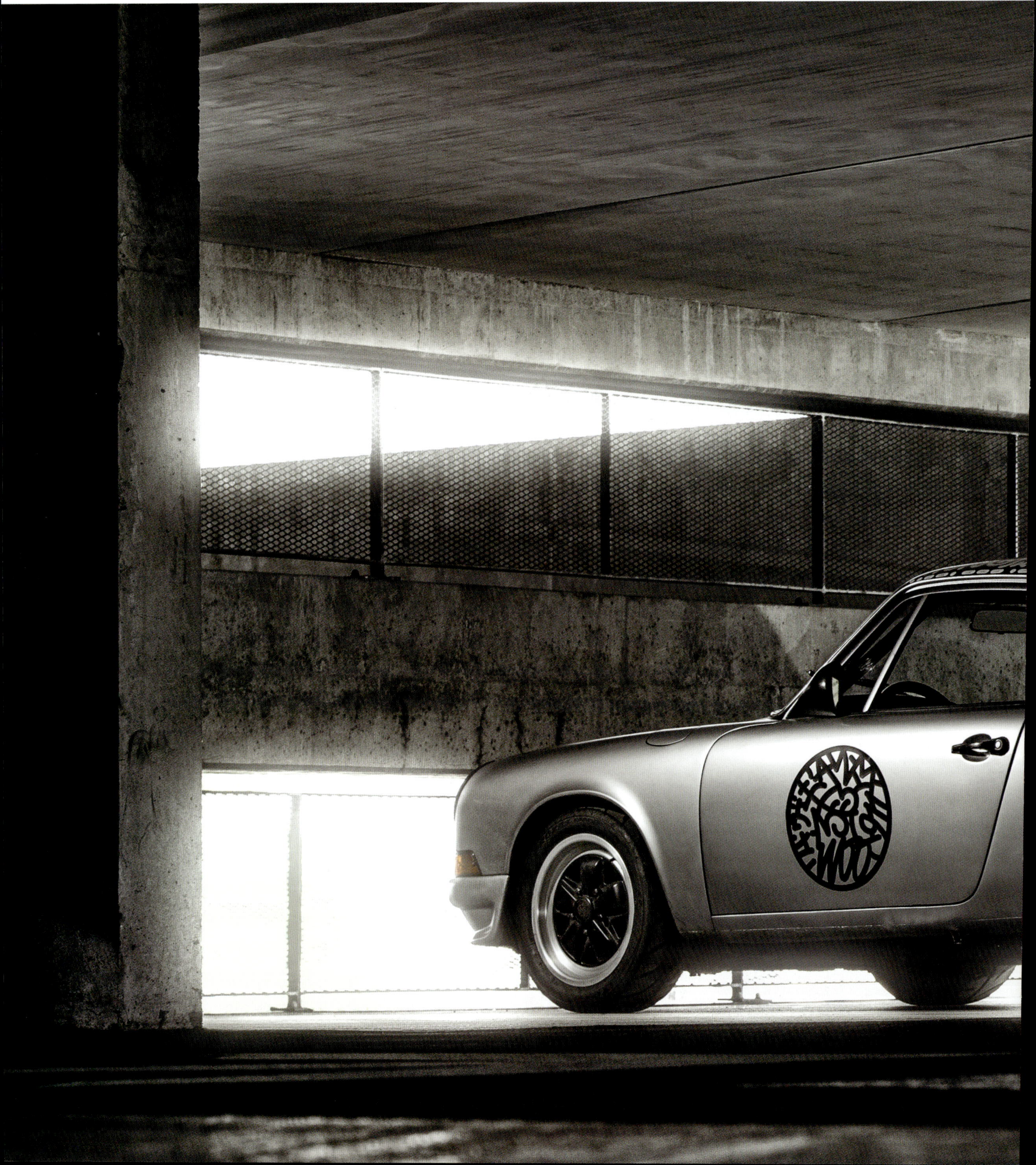

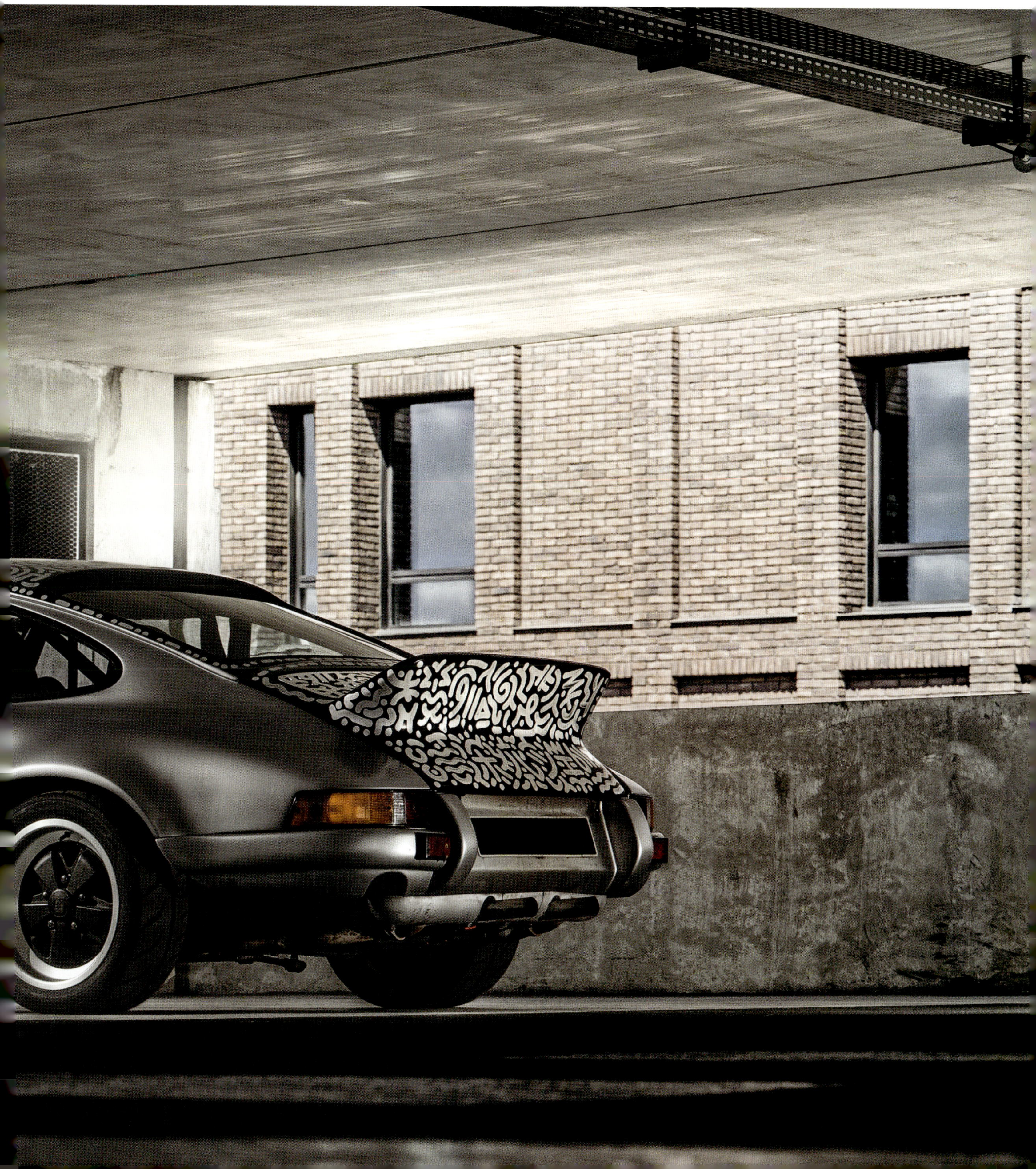

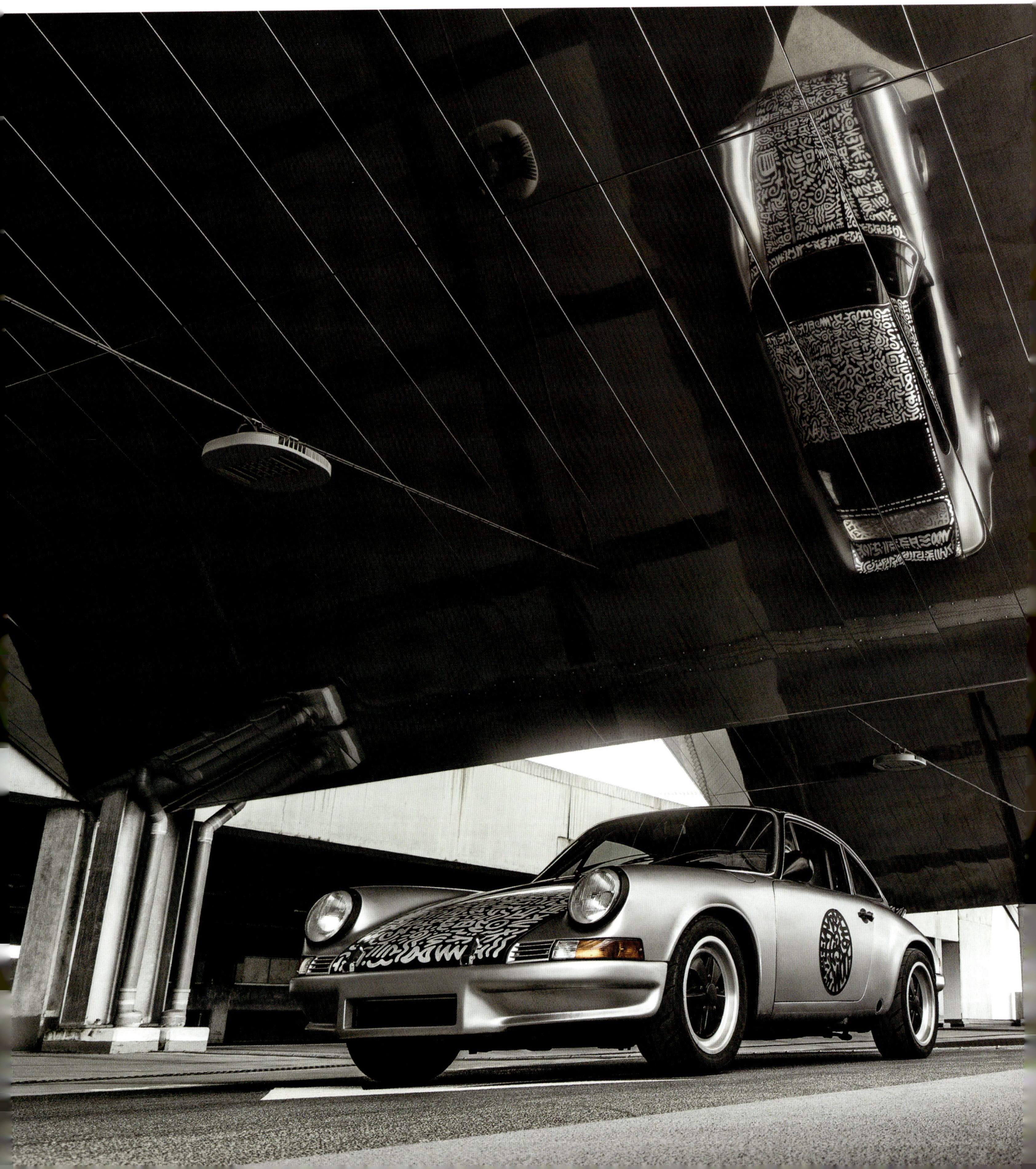

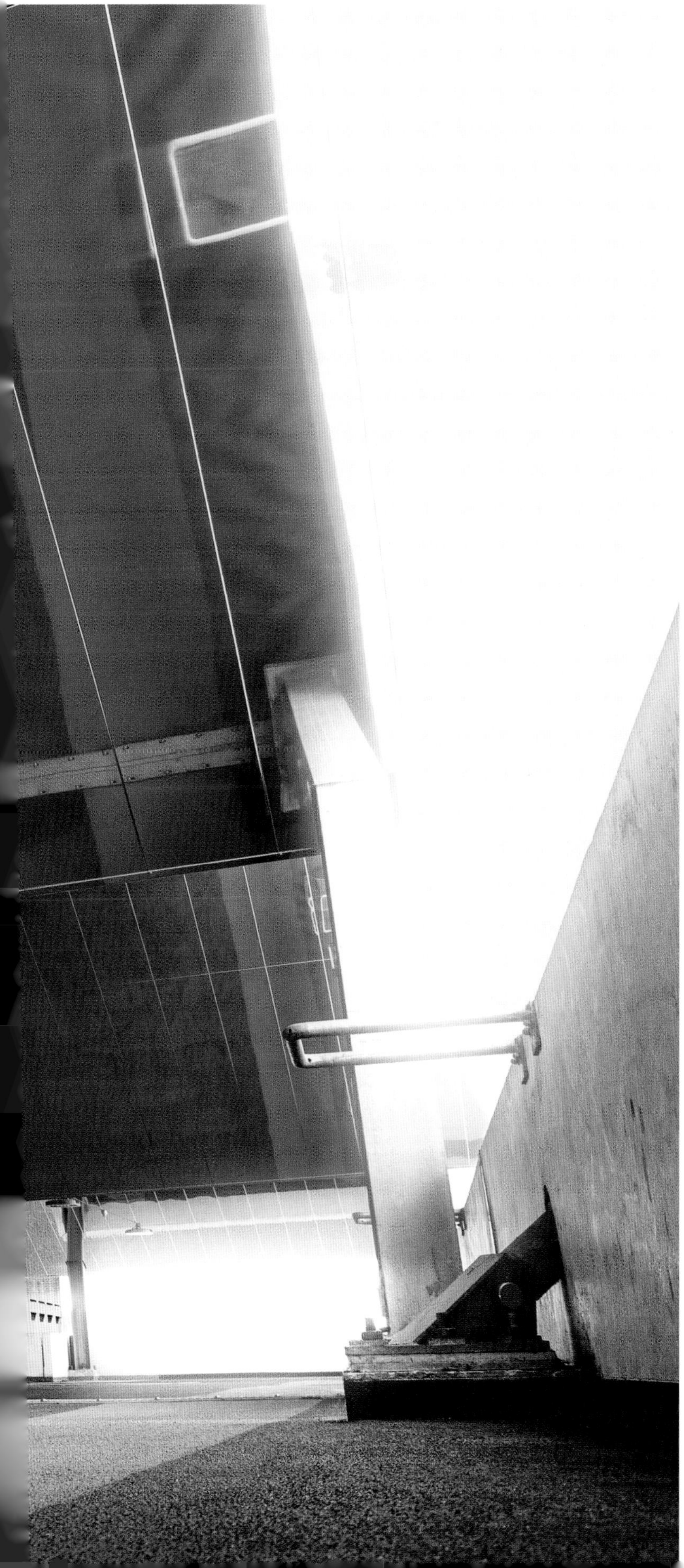

THE ARTISTIC ASPECT OF THIS PORSCHE 911 MEANS IT GETS ATTENTION WHEREVER IT GOES.

To start with, it wasn't a very desirable Porsche, or particularly good-looking. It was a 1971 911 2.2 E that put out 155 hp, but whose elegant silhouette had been altered by the ravages of time, making it an odd, rather unsightly machine. A 1973 2.4 S engine, with an output of around 190 hp, had replaced the original flat-six. The bodywork had been altered in the style of a 2.7 RS. "The rear sheet-metal wings had been widened," explains its owner, Aymeric – who also owns the 356 Rusty Flower. A ducktail spoiler had been added, as well as RS fibreglass bumpers and small tyres with somewhat unattractive ATS rims. The standard 911 yellow had been painted over in an ugly light blue-grey, seemingly applied with a roller. A roll bar replaced the rear seats, officially making it a two-seater, according to the registration document. All the inside carpet had been stripped out, leaving a very basic interior. "I bought this 911 in a job lot with a 912. I then sold the 912 to a friend so I could put this Porsche engine in a car for track racing without spending too much money. But it didn't work out very well: I had to rebuild the entire engine, then the fuel-injection pump ... I had so many problems with that car. I think I ended up overpaying for the 911, especially considering it was in 2016, when the second-hand market was on a high. All for a car that wasn't actually all that nice." However, Aymeric had an idea: to try his hand at driving on the track! "The car was built for action: that's the essence of the brand – the sporty side. The looks were not that important. But after going to a few events, it really began to get to me. So I thought about a cost-effective alternative to give it a new lease of life without getting a new, full paint job – that would have meant taking the whole thing to pieces." One thing led to another, and an exciting idea took shape: "To look for a graphic designer who could put their art on this 911. I needed to find someone, come up with a theme that I liked and that made sense in relation to the car, and make sure that the decoration was consistent with the lines of the 911 and its era. It wasn't easy, because in the world of graffiti, there's so much variety. I did a lot of research, but nothing really grabbed my attention." Then, one day, Aymeric bumped into an old friend who had worked in design and was now working in art. "His name was Sam, but his artist name was

THIS CAR IS MADE TO GO ALL OUT: IT IS THE VERY ESSENCE OF THE PORSCHE BRAND.

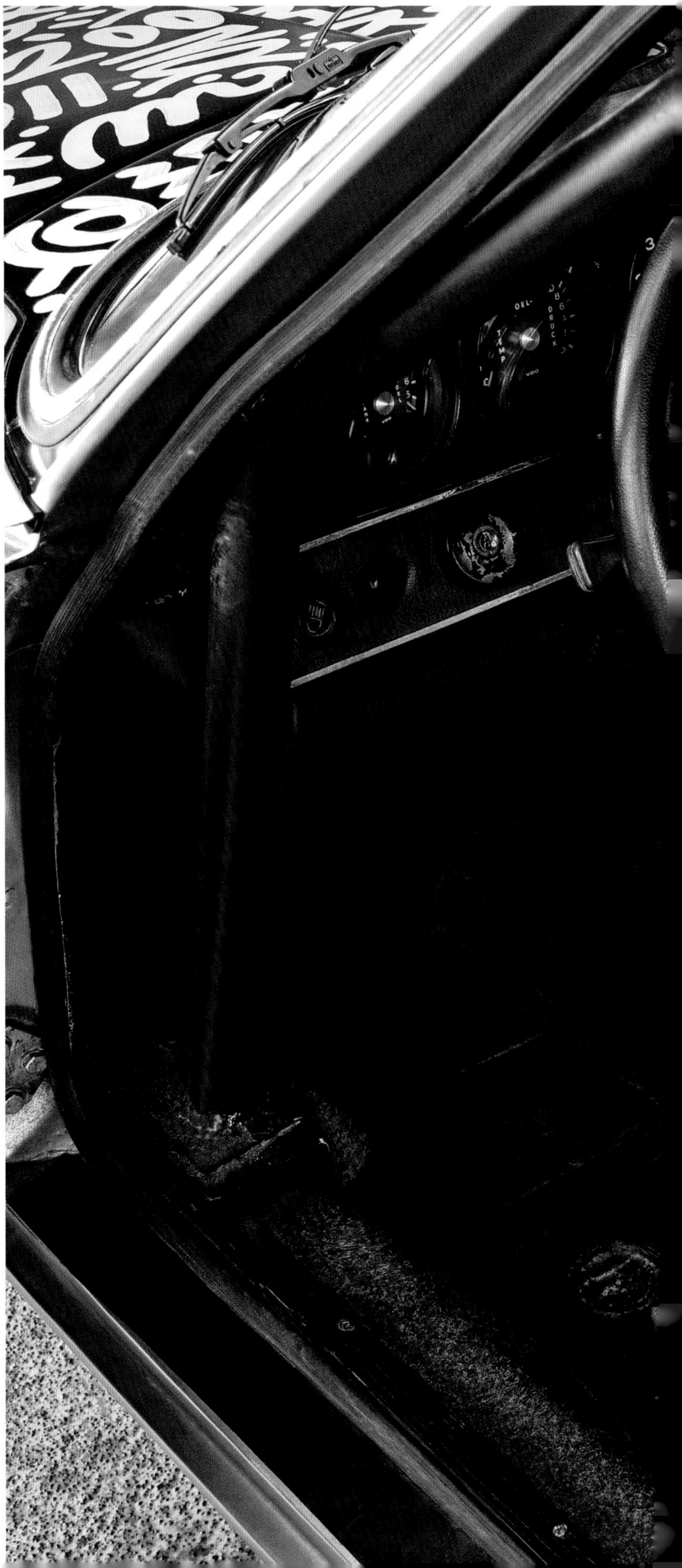

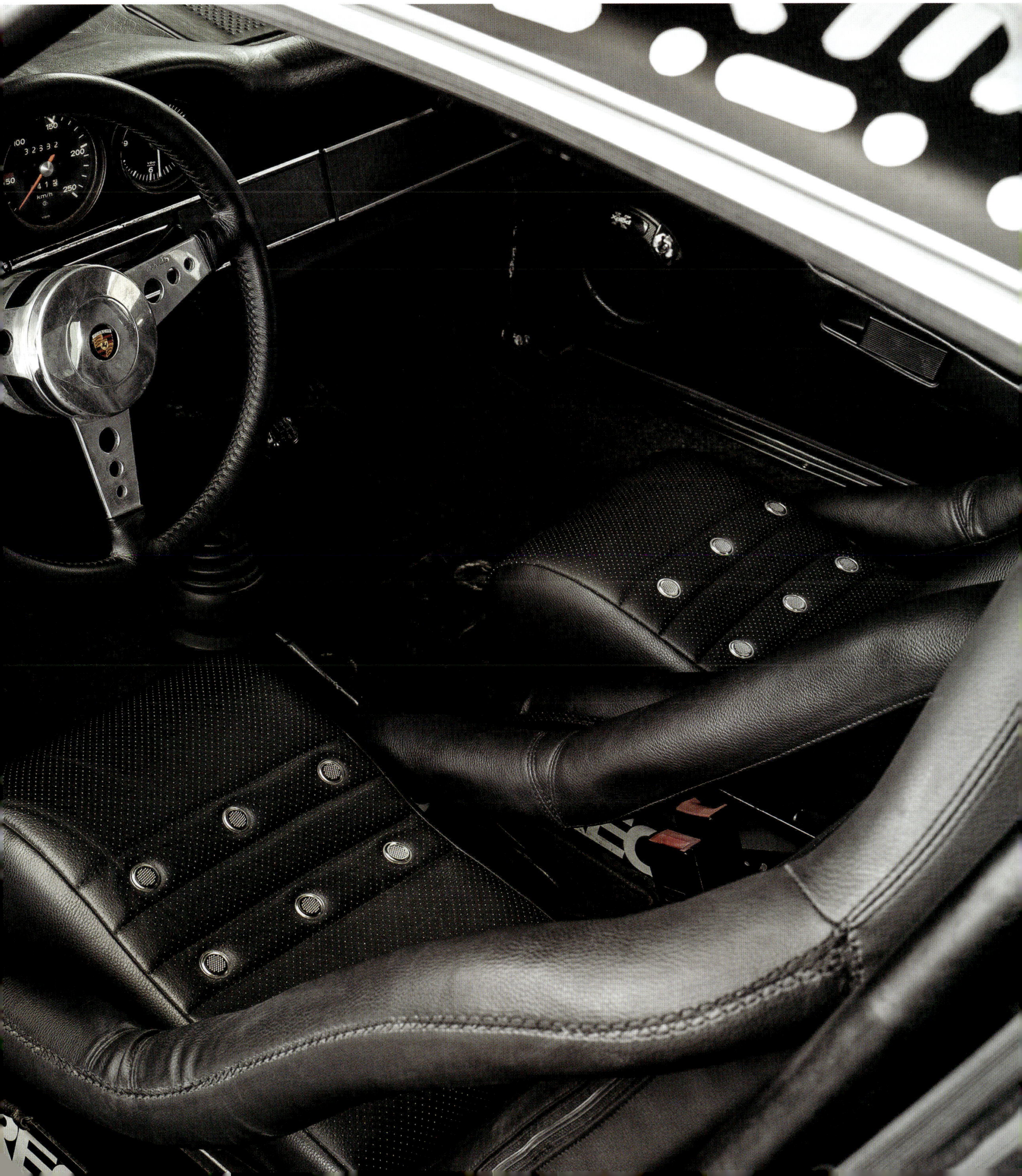

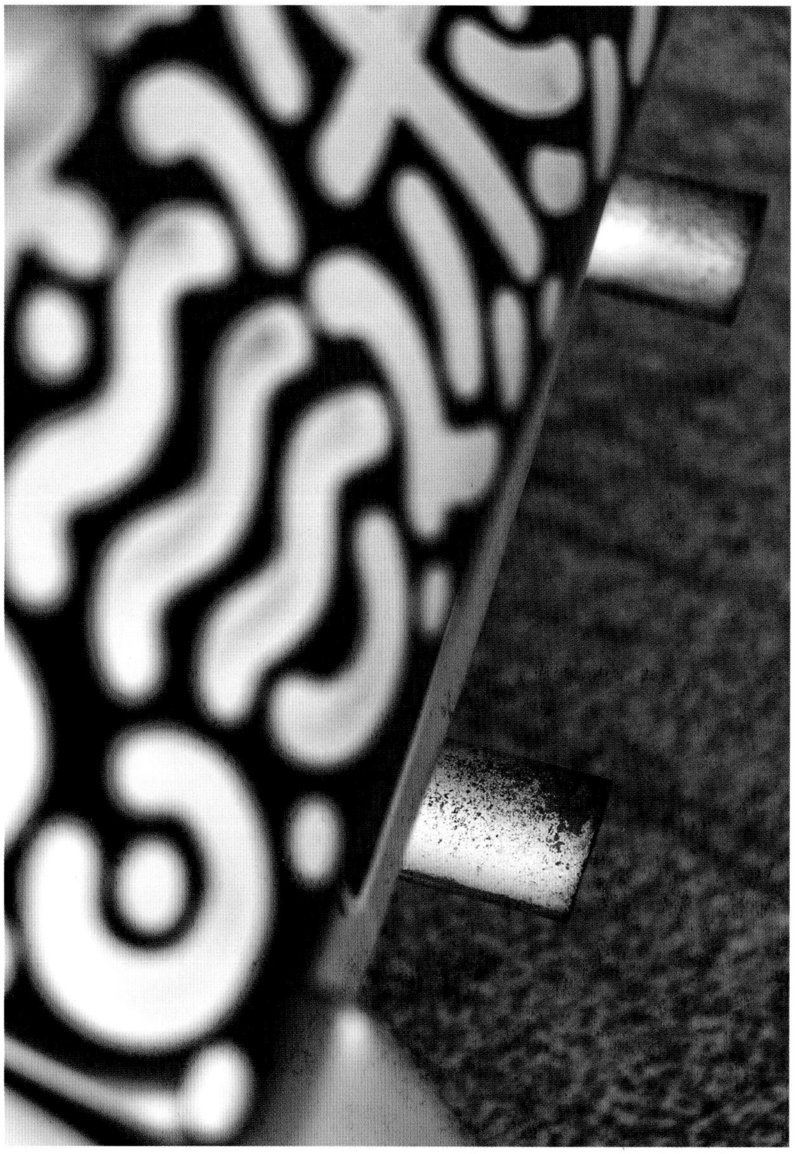

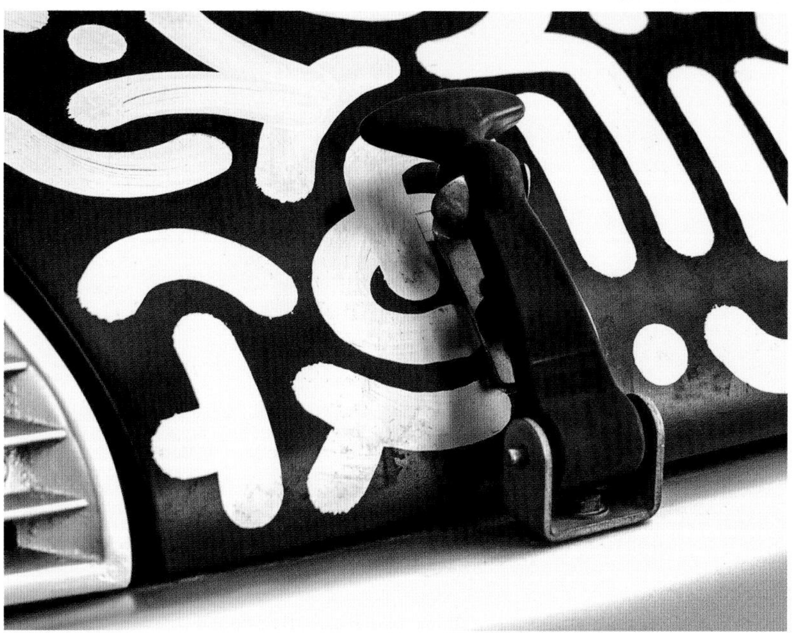

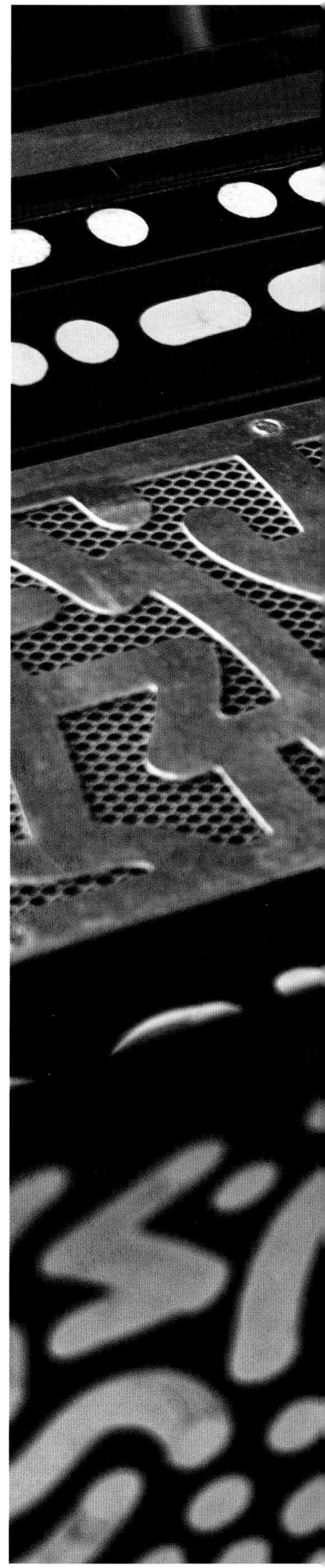

1. The exhaust pipes bear the marks of a life lived hard.

2. Ensuring the front hood doesn't budge is an important point.

3. The aluminium grill perfectly matches the overall styling of this 911.

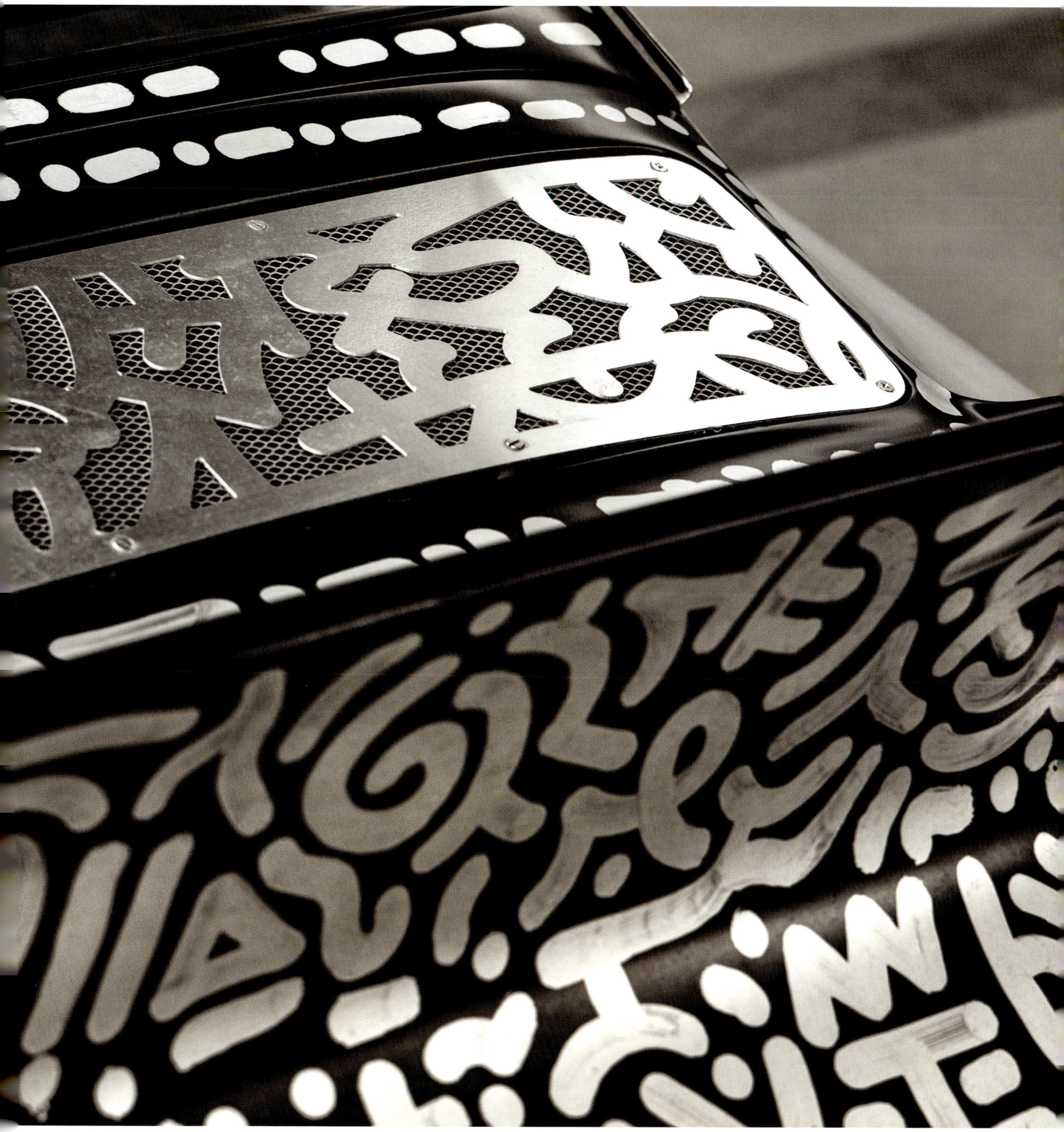

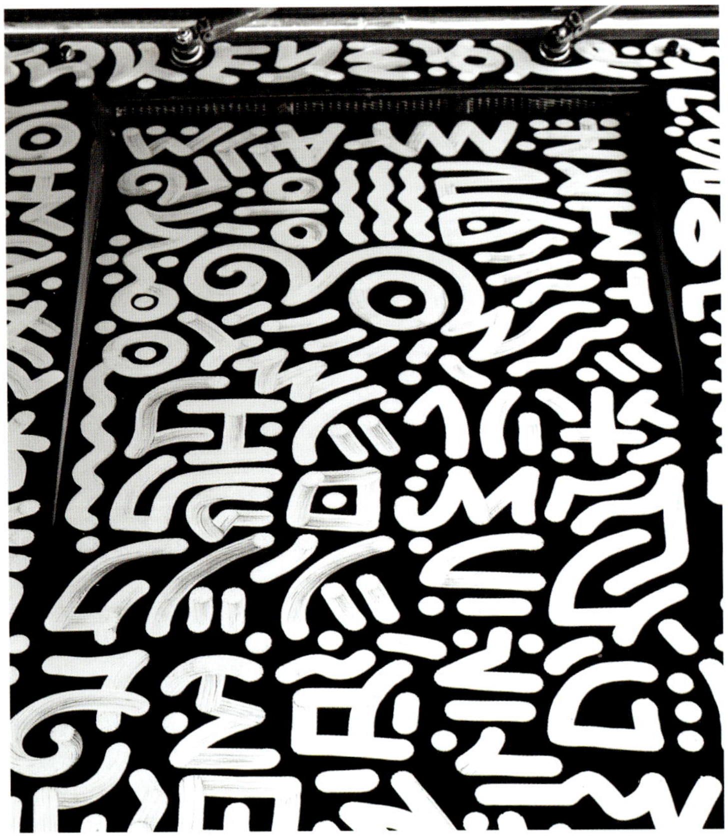

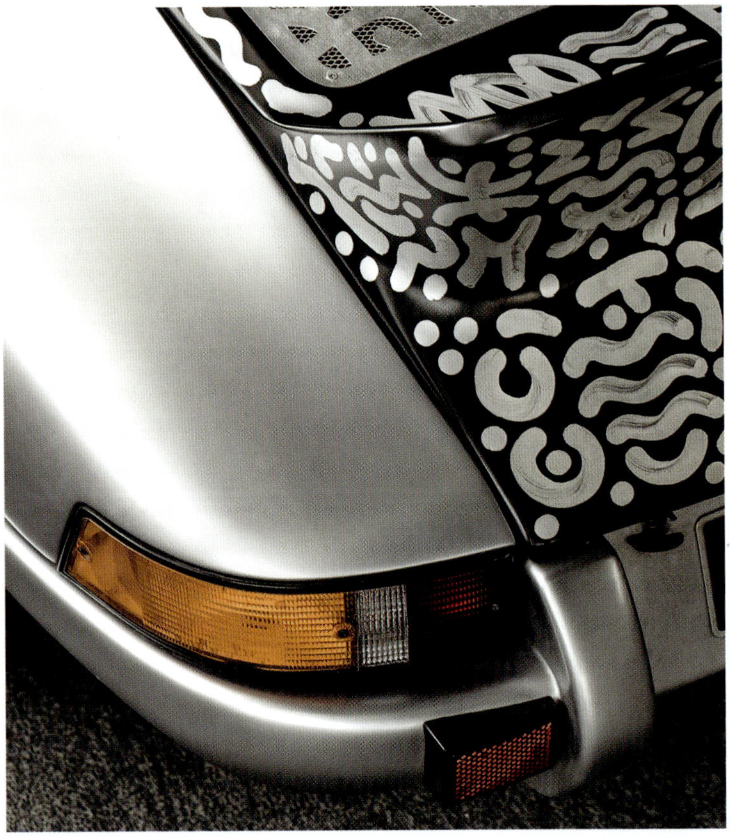

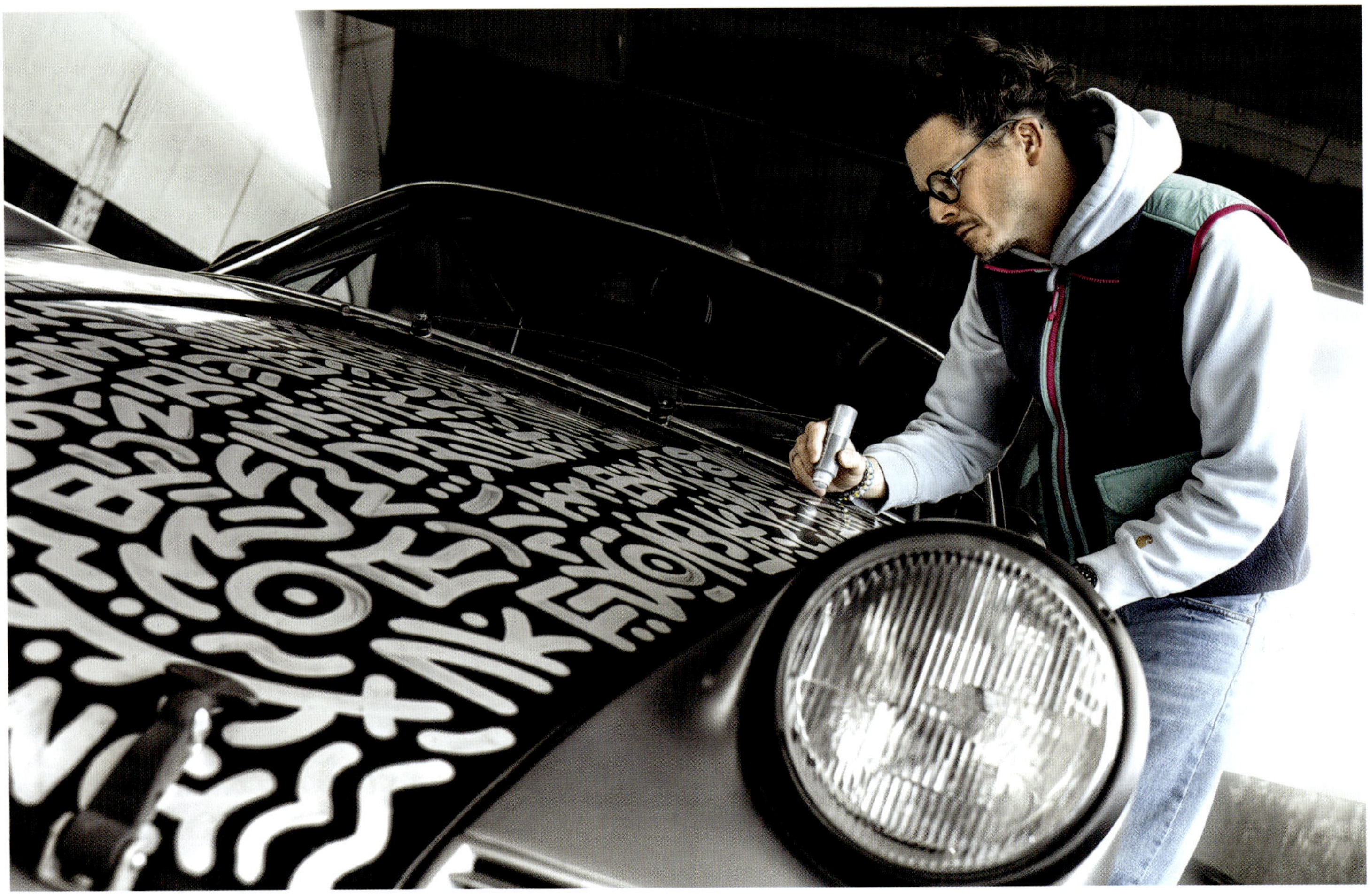

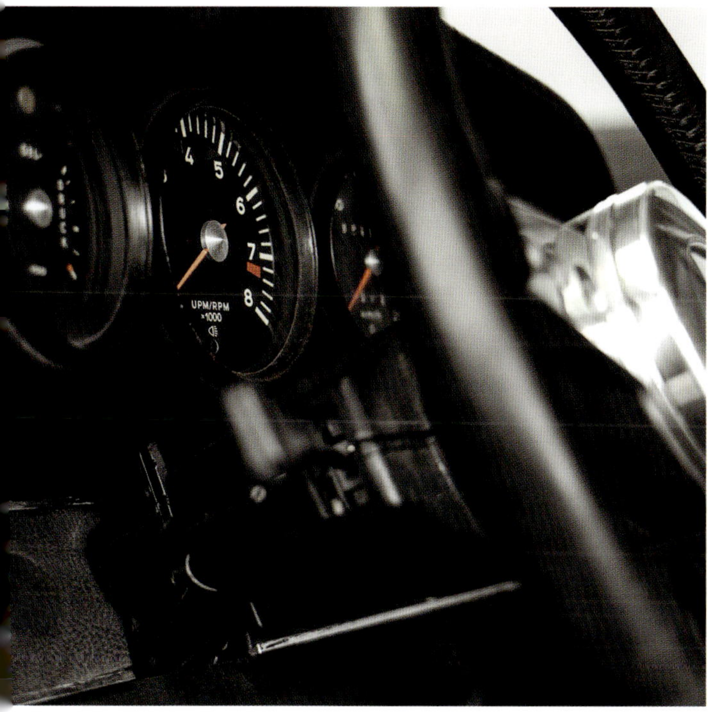

911 ART CAR
BY THE NUMBERS

CREATION 1971

FLAT CYLINDERS 6

CC 2,400

HP 190

Woo Ghost. He was enthusiastic about the idea, and we worked extensively together on the project. We got a body shop to repaint the sides of the car in a shade of grey and the front and rear hoods and roof in a shade of black which would highlight the artwork. However, when it comes to the artistic side, Sam is best placed to explain what he did." "I'm not really a petrol head," explains the artist, "but I have always liked the aesthetics of cars. I have a particular affinity for older things, vintage objects - stuff with the essence of the 1980s. On that, Porsche never changed. The lines always remained true to themselves. They kept their identity without ever straying. And the design is incredible: both feminine and masculine, it is a completely gender-free car, and exceptionally appealing. The curves in my drawings are similar. If you take a curve, it is feminine; an angle is very masculine. My work is inspired by Asian calligraphy - Chinese and Japanese - but it also includes hieroglyphs and pre-Columbian symbols. It is a mixture of drawing and writing, with mostly rounded shapes. There are some angular shapes, and it incorporates other codes, such as Morse; that's how I created the 911. When I started on the car, I had no plan in mind, I was working on instinct, but I knew that I wanted to have Morse code around the edges, to tell a story. So I wrote down a lot of automotive language: speed, elegance, the word Porsche. I like the idea that you don't get the meaning straight away, you have to take some time to think about it in order to understand it. Otherwise, you'd just take it all in at face value, like looking at a photograph." To write on his metallic, mechanical canvas, Sam used paint markers with broad, bold, thick lines: "I was inspired by Keith Haring, an artist I've felt a strong connection with since I was a kid," Sam continues. "We used silver ink to produce a two-tone car. The bodywork technician then varnished over the whole lot, to keep it intact and to make sure it would never be covered over. It is not just decoration, it is a work of contemporary art." It is an artistic statement of its time - and one that goes like hell!

1 2

3

1. Inspired by Keith Haring, the silver design is a perfect match for the 911.

2. Not just decoration,this is a work of contemporary art.

3. Sam, alias Woo Ghost, signed this mechanical canvas - an artistic statement for this automotive era.

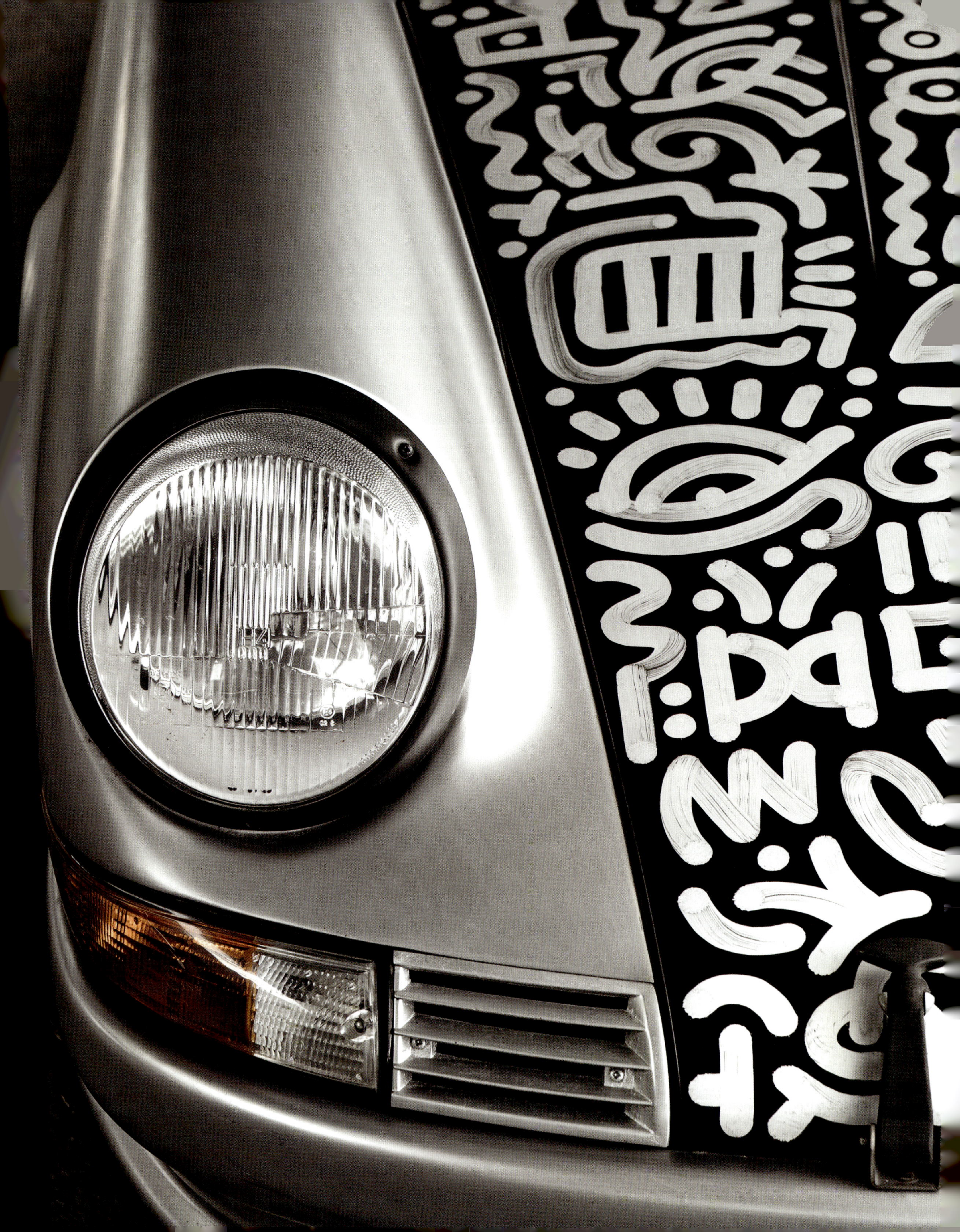

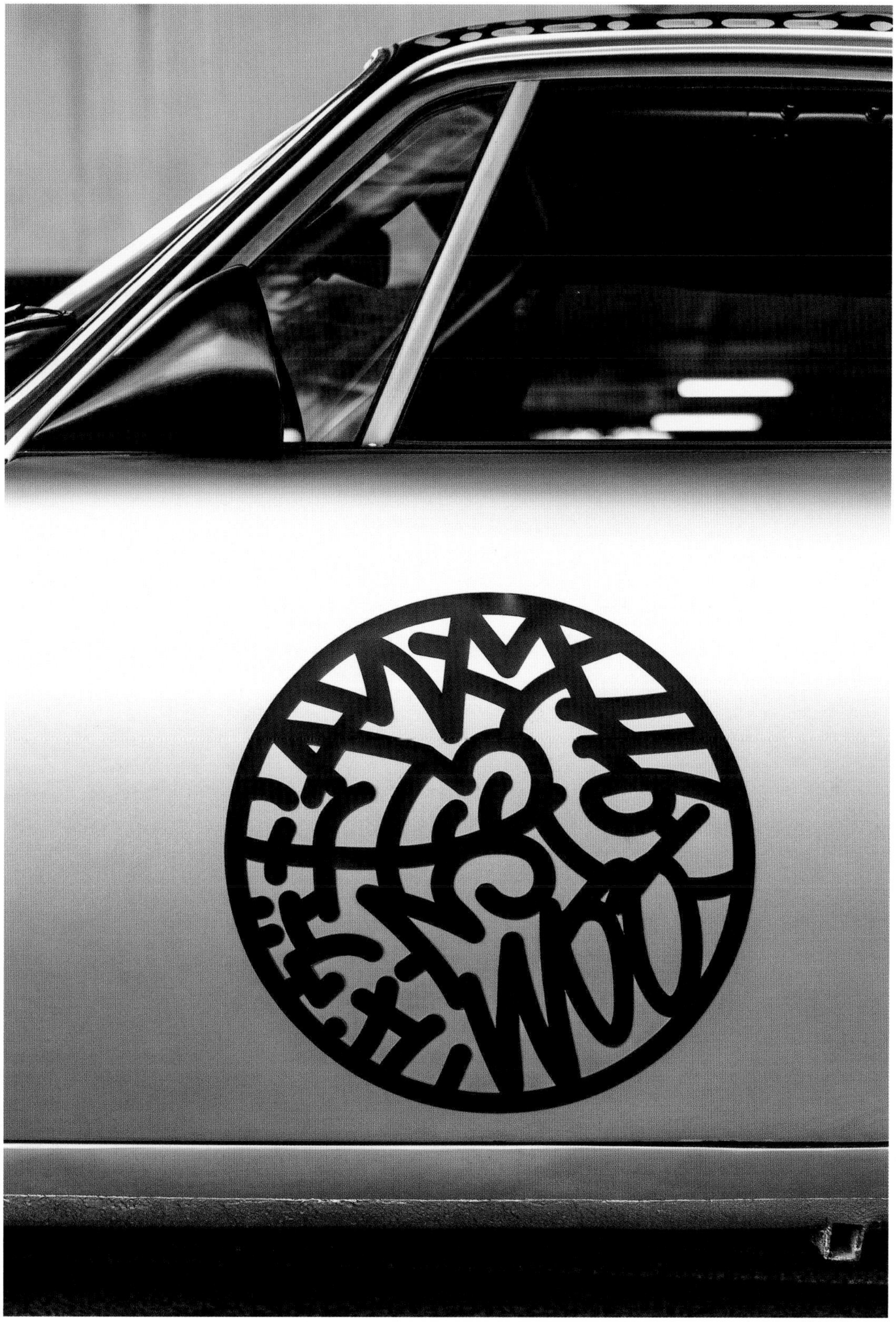

Above: To add a racing touch, the famous numbered circle on the doors has been replaced with one of Woo Ghost's graphic designs.

Opposite: Alongside the iconic headlight, Woo Ghost's graffiti brings a wholly unexpected dimension to a car with a legendary silhouette.

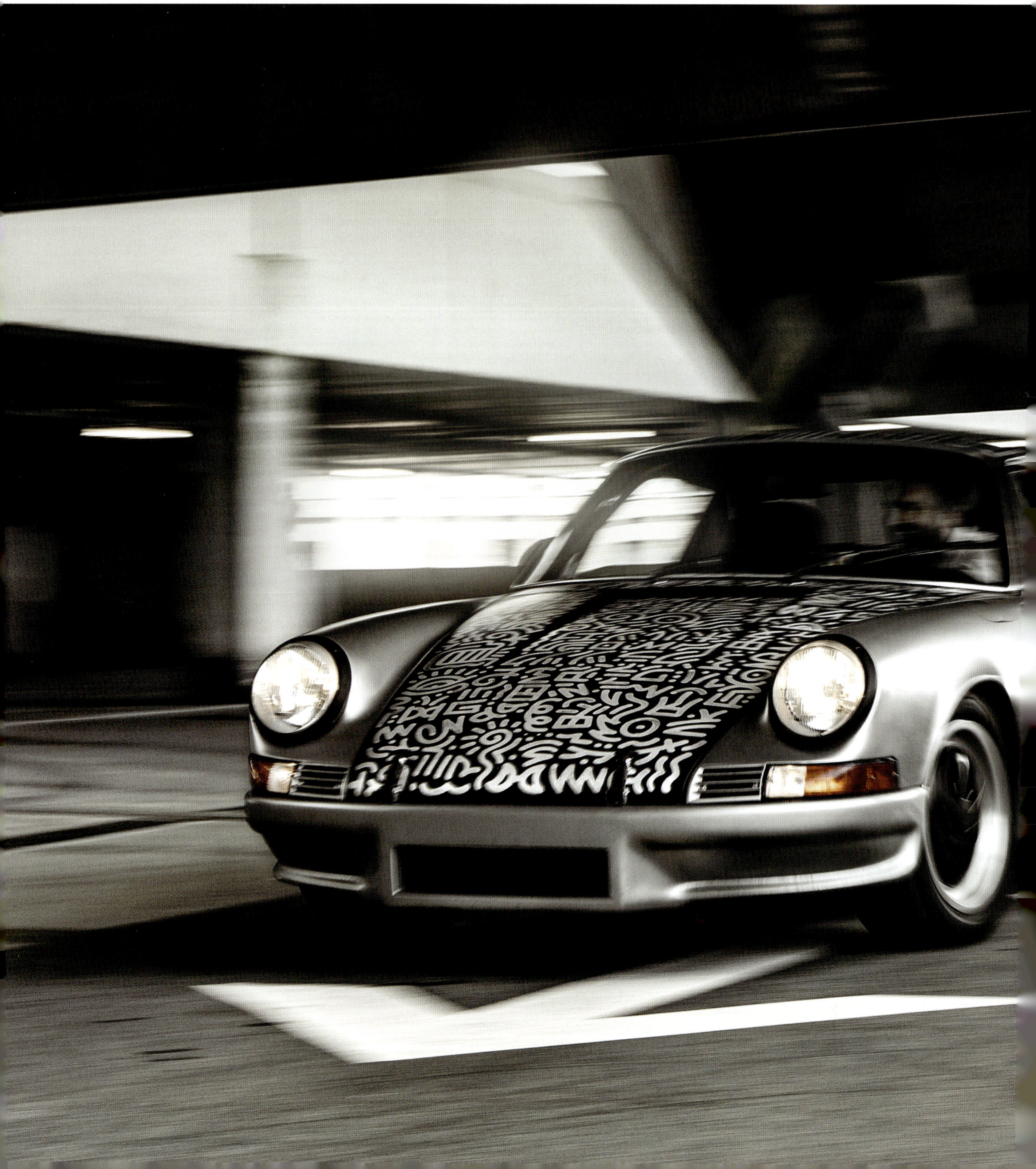

964 CARRERA 4 PEYOTE HALLUCINOGENIC

Peyote is a highly hallucinogenic Mexican cactus and it was the inspiration for the mad mutation of this 1989 Porsche 964 Carrera 4 into a rally car with a touch of Panamericana ... to drive to the beach in Greece!

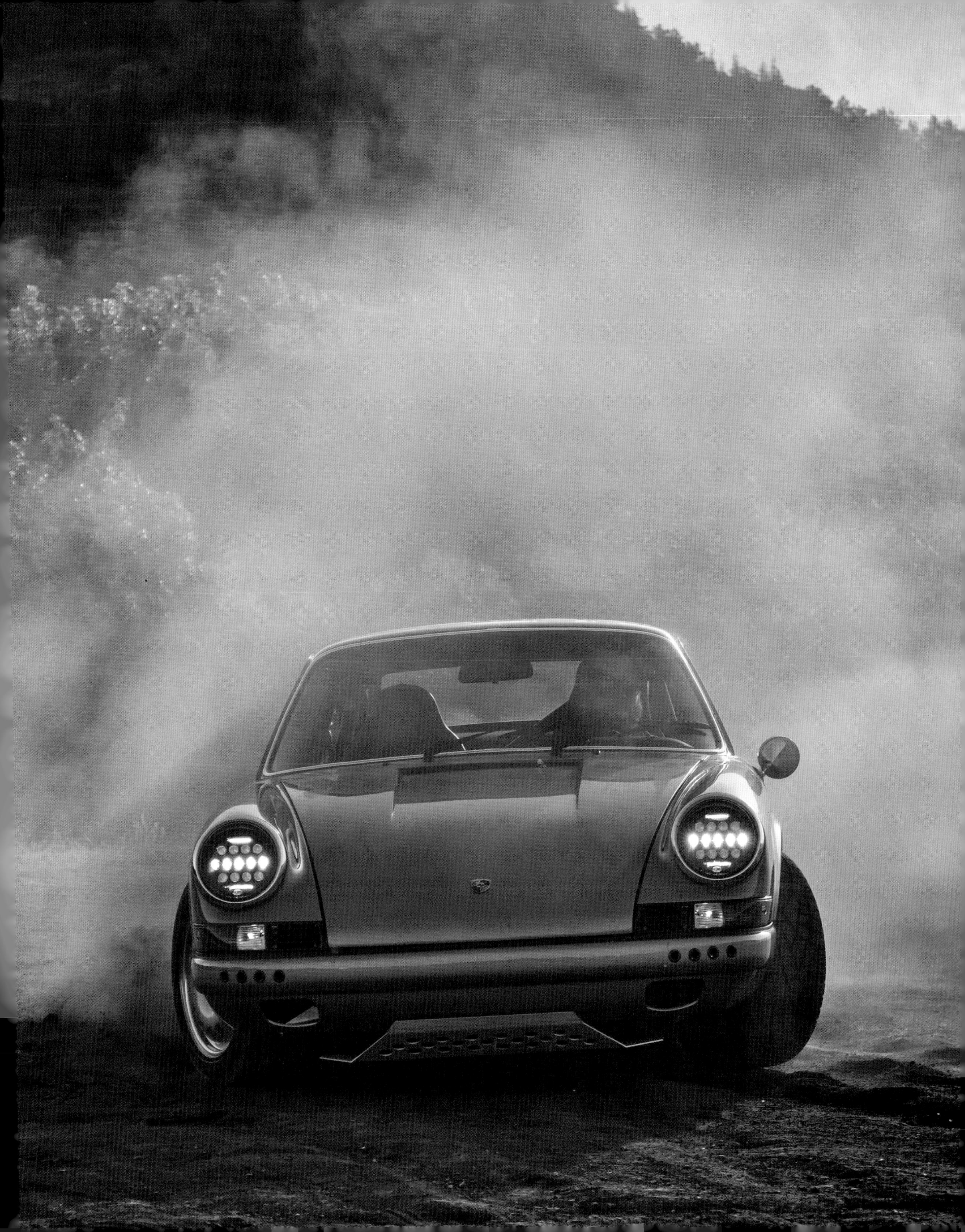

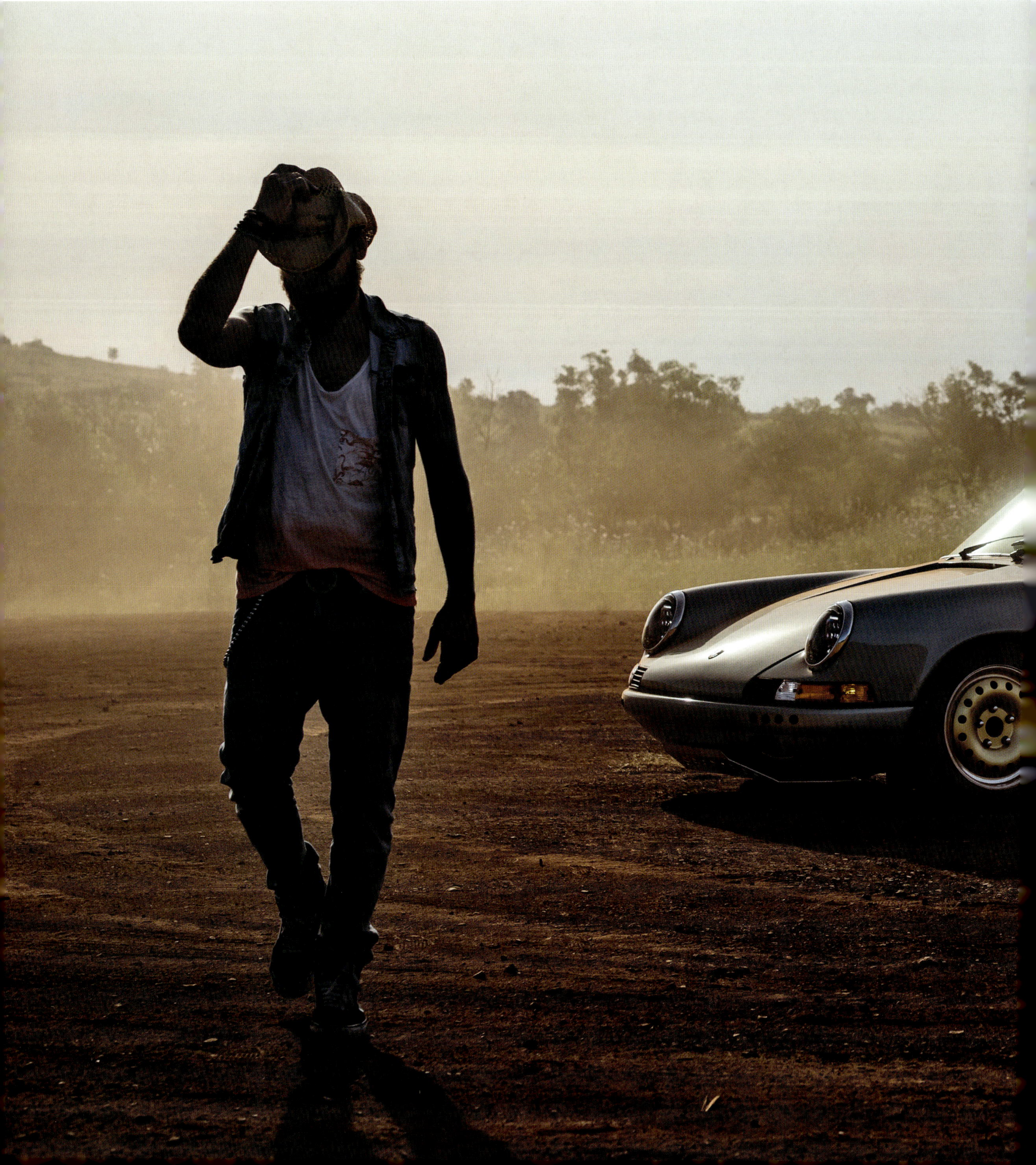

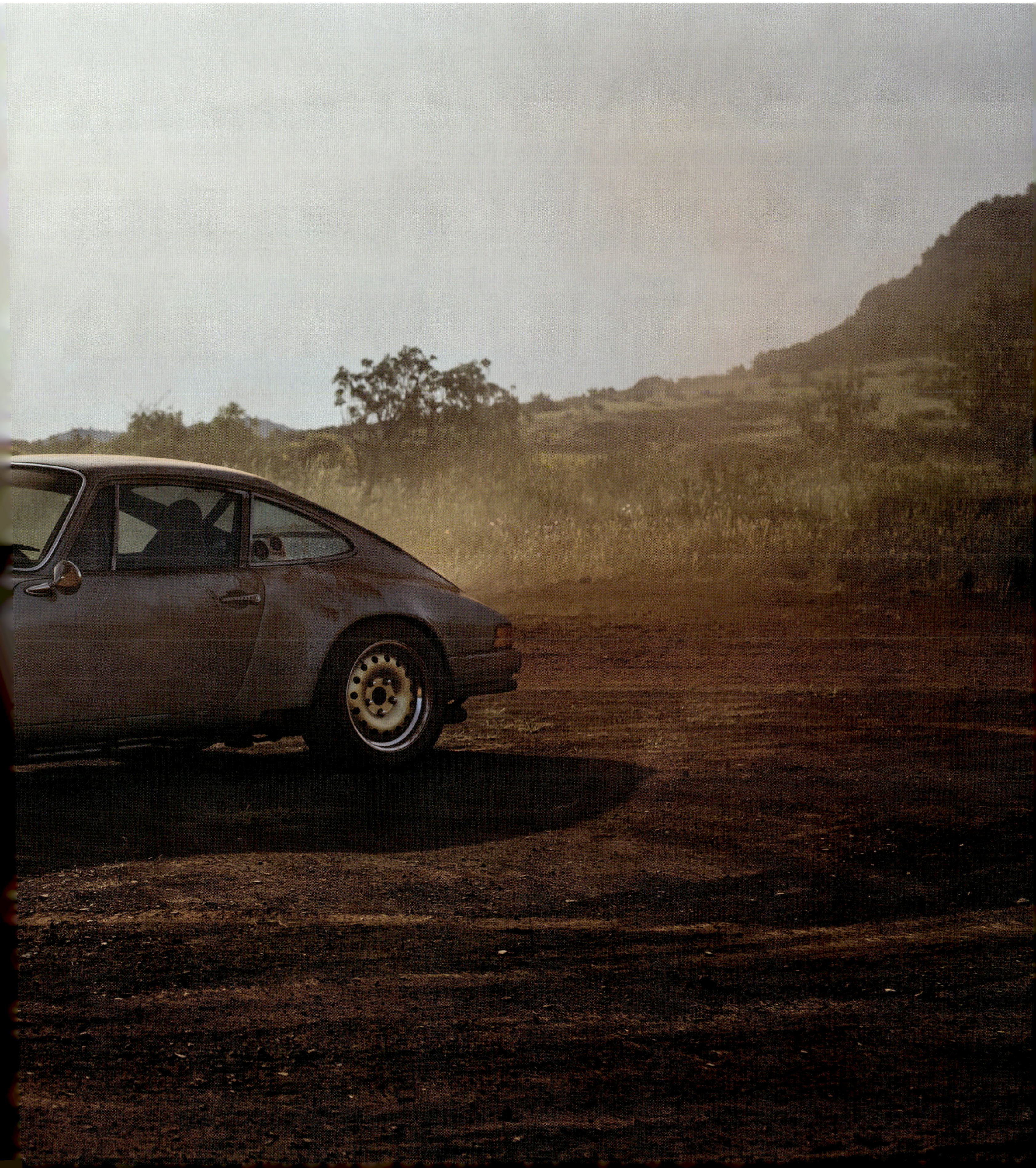

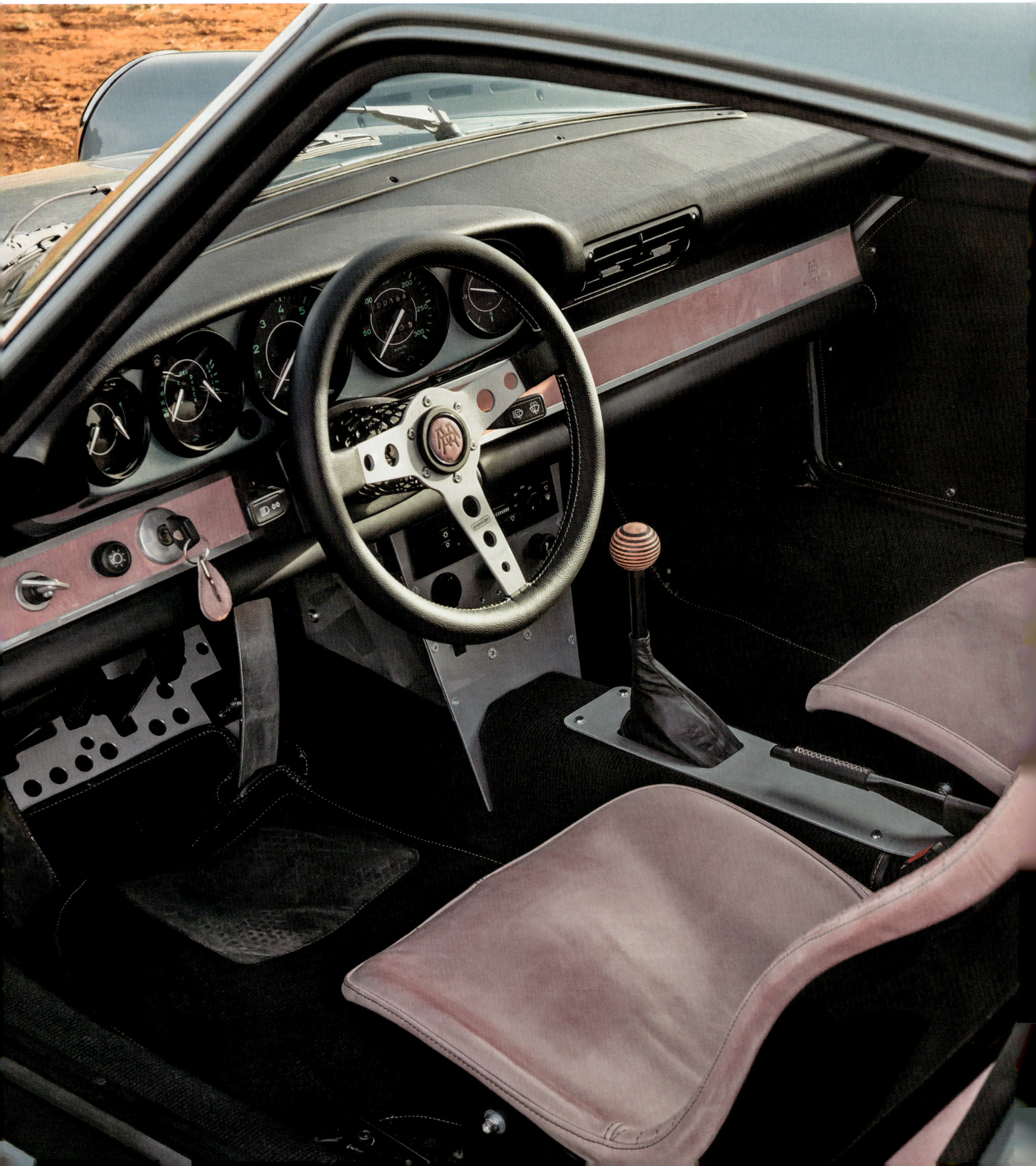

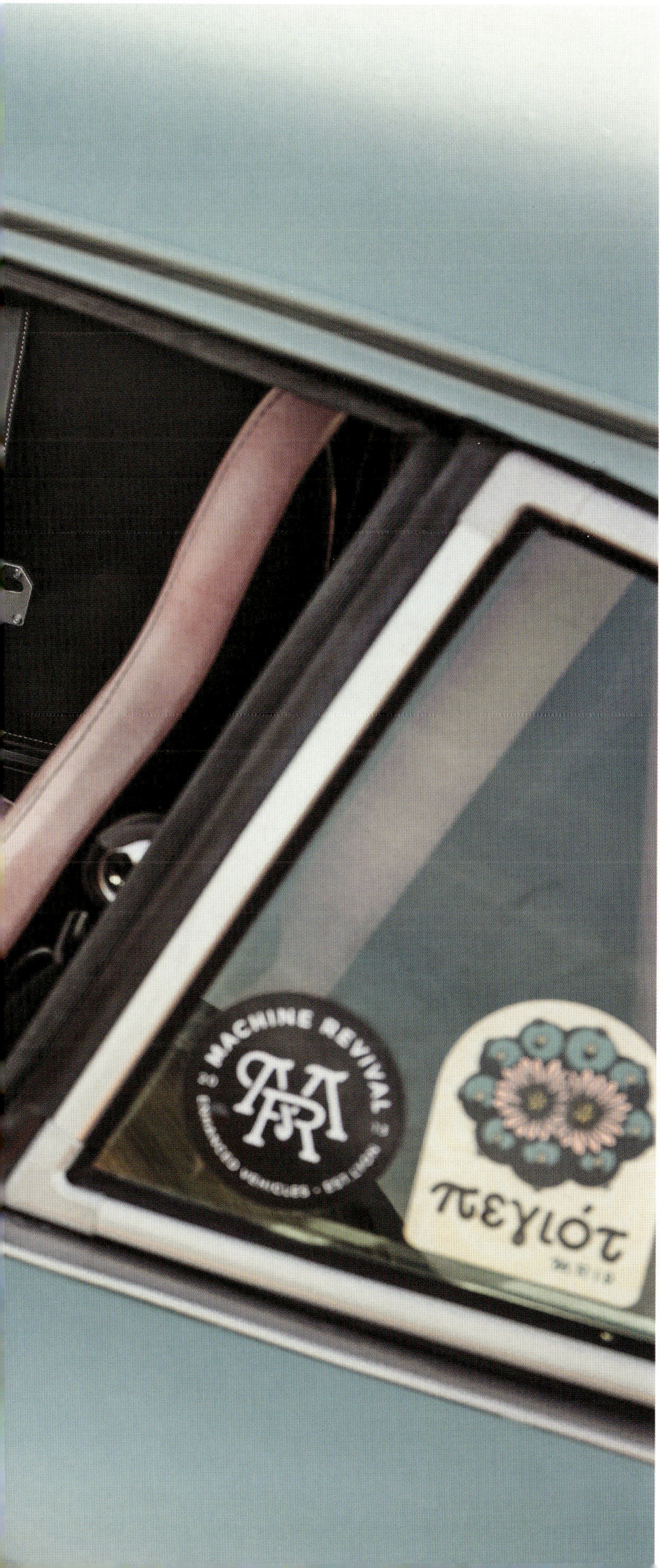

HALLUCINOGENIC: BETWEEN THE PINK INTERIOR AND THE BLUE-GREEN PAINTJOB, THIS CACTUS PACKS A PUNCH!

The *Lopophora williamsii* is a small, spineless cactus whose ceremonial use by Native Americans dates back more than 3,000 years, a ritual practice that still continues today among certain populations native to the semi-desert regions of southern Texas and Mexico. Also known as peyote, it grows along the coastal road of El Espinazo del Diablo – the Devil's Backbone. This small cactus, that rarely grows taller than five centimetres (2 inches) and looks a bit like a melon, is a powerful hallucinogen. And its distinctive feature is that it only flowers for three days, once every 30 years.

In 2019, when this 1989 Porsche 964 Carrera 4 began the transformation that would mark its 30th anniversary, the connection with peyote immediately became clear: a blossoming had begun and its flower was about to bloom. "The owner of this Porsche is Greek," says Nicolas Quiles, the main orchestrator of this highly non-conformist transformation. "We talked to him about what he wanted to do with the car, how he planned to drive it, in what conditions, in order to come up with very precise specifications. He wanted to drive it on the road but also to go to the beach in his usual manner, taking rough tracks over dirt, sand and stones. Hence a four-wheel-drive Porsche. We started working on a mood board to define the direction we were taking. Our idea was to build a car inspired by off-road rallies in Mexico, such as the Carrera Panamericana." This automobile race, also known as the Pan-am, launched in Mexico in 1950 and quickly became famous due to the involvement of all the major manufacturers of the time. It was cancelled in 1955, but reintroduced in 1988 in the shape of an automobile rally with classic cars. "We didn't want to come up with something for the Baja 1000, with huge headlights on the front. We wanted to keep it quite refined, but a car that could go anywhere. And while exploring the Mexican element, we eventually stumbled upon the incredible story of the peyote cactus. Artistic madness was unleashed! We talked to the client about it. He thought we were crazy, but since he liked our work, he gave it the green light anyway."

The car is finished in a shade of green with a hint of blue; actually quite close to the original

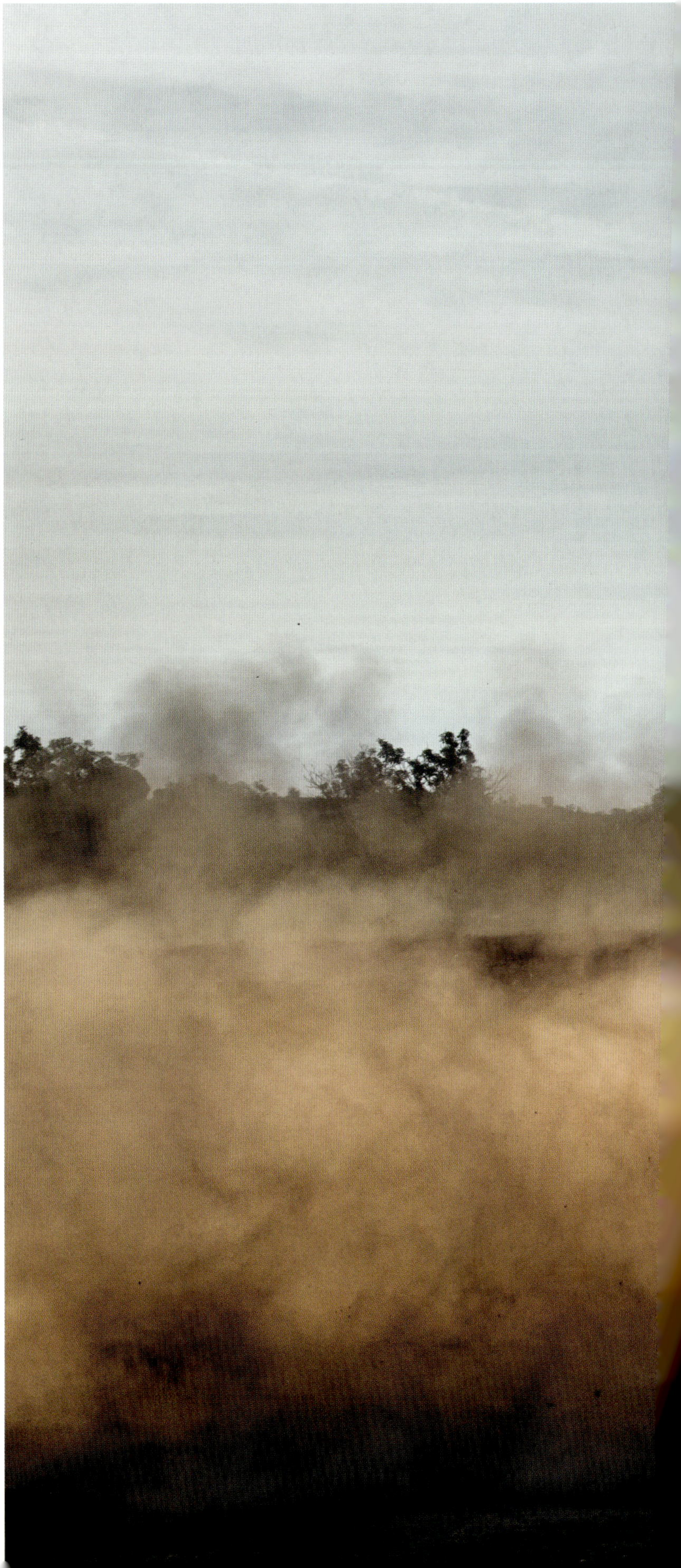

THIS RALLY-STYLED 964 CARRERA 4 LOVES A DUST CLOUD.

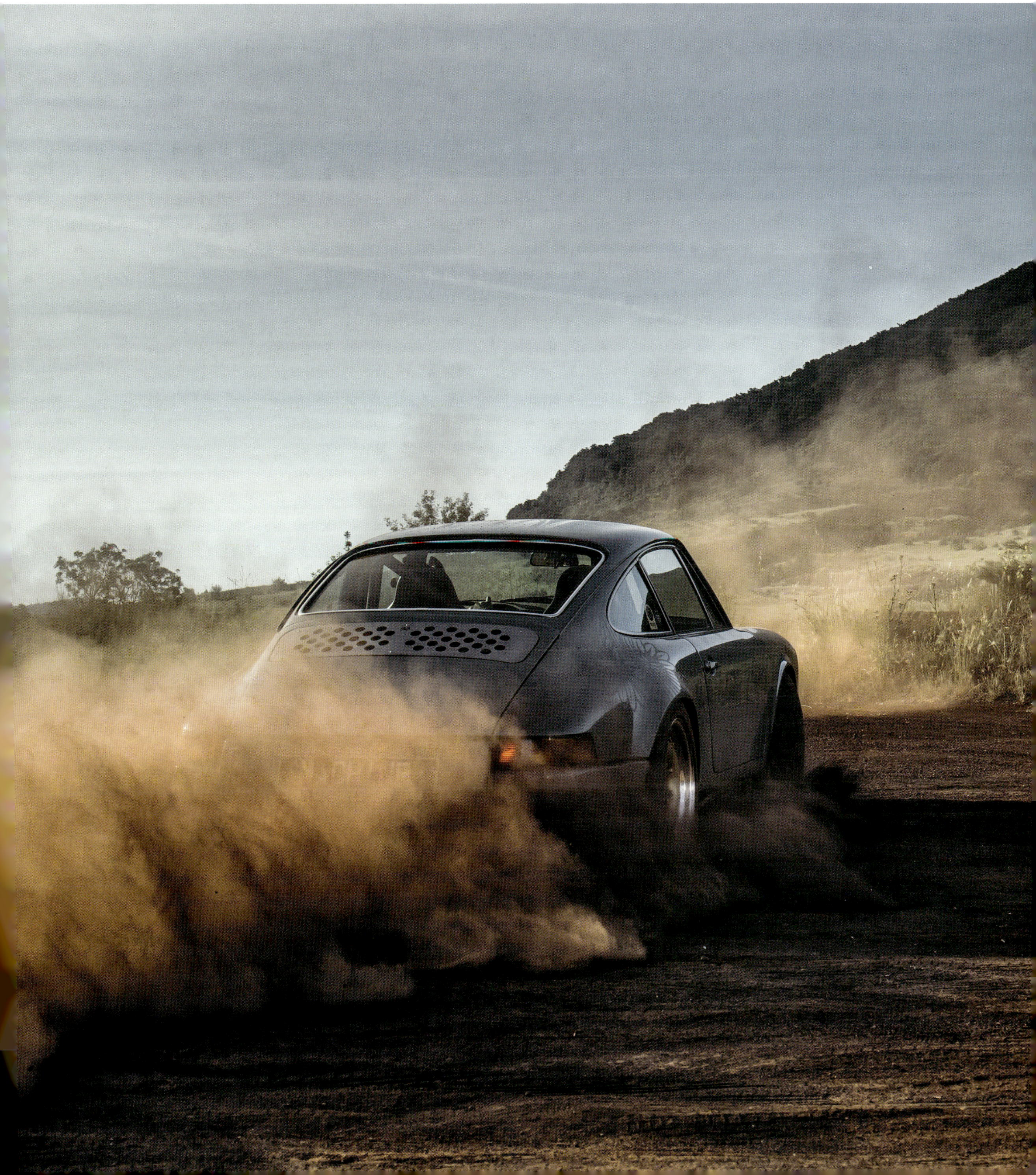

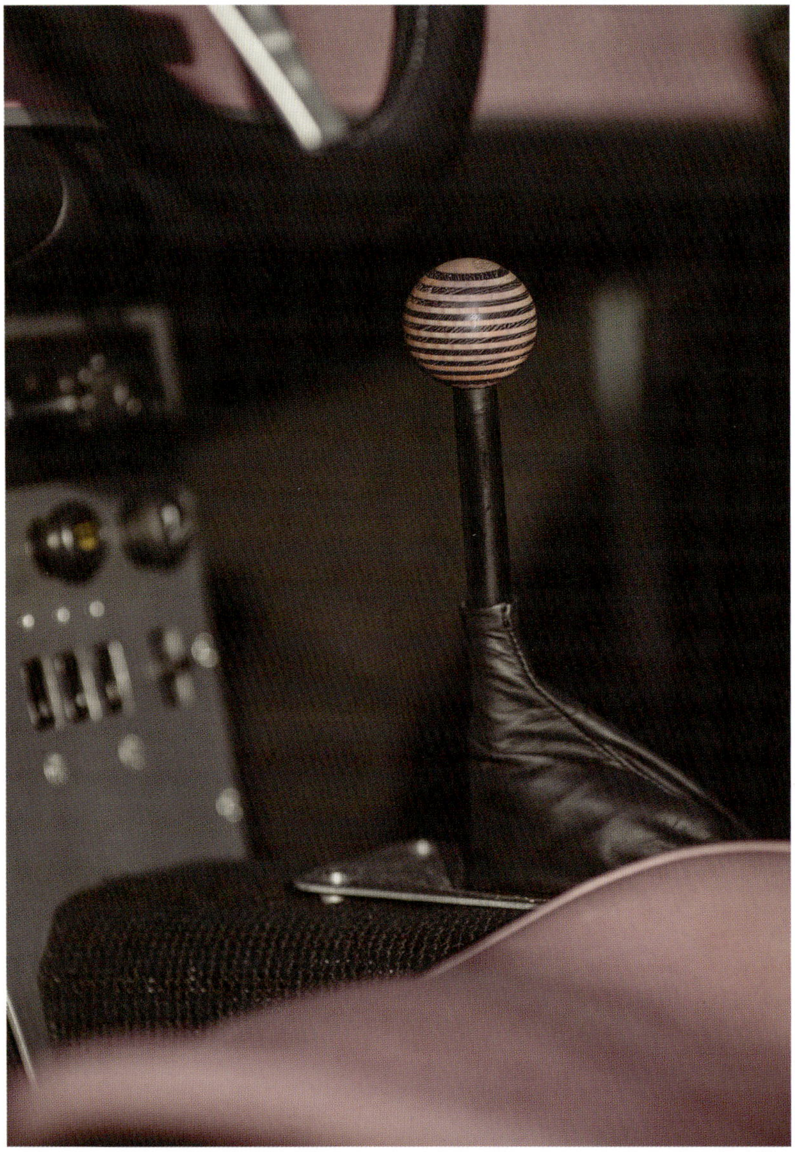

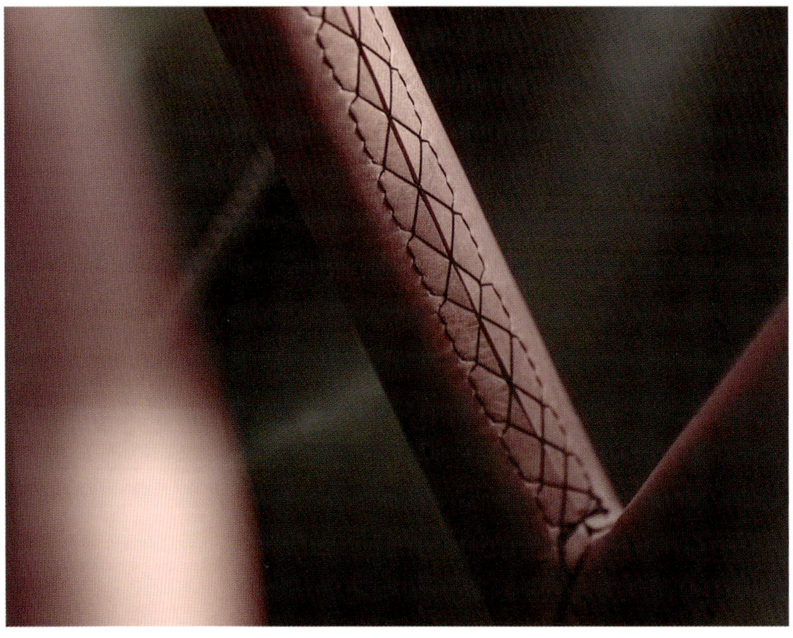

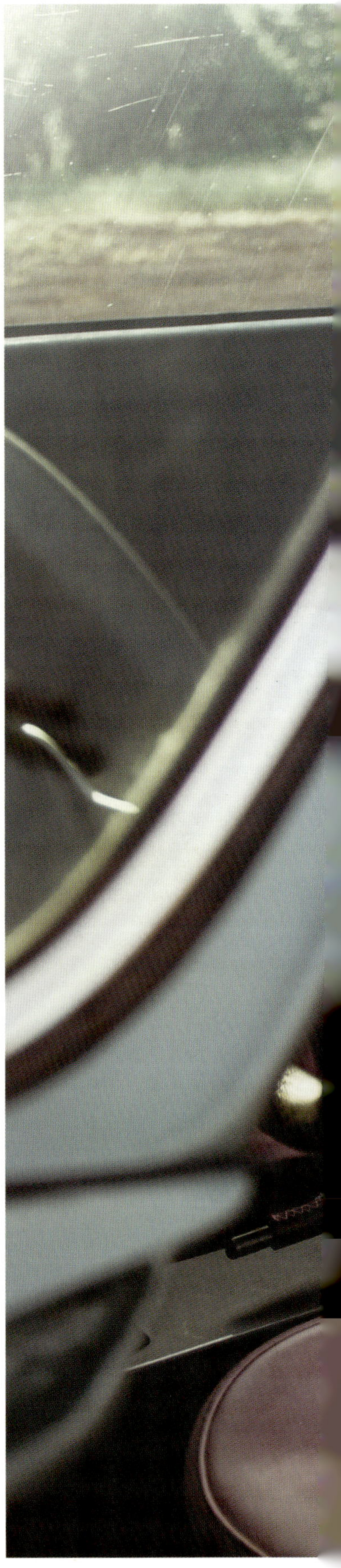

1. The gear shift knob is made of ... pink wood.

2. Completely upholstered in pink leather, the roll bar showcases some highly refined stitching.

3. The bucket seats have been reupholstered in the same beautiful fuchsia-pink leather.

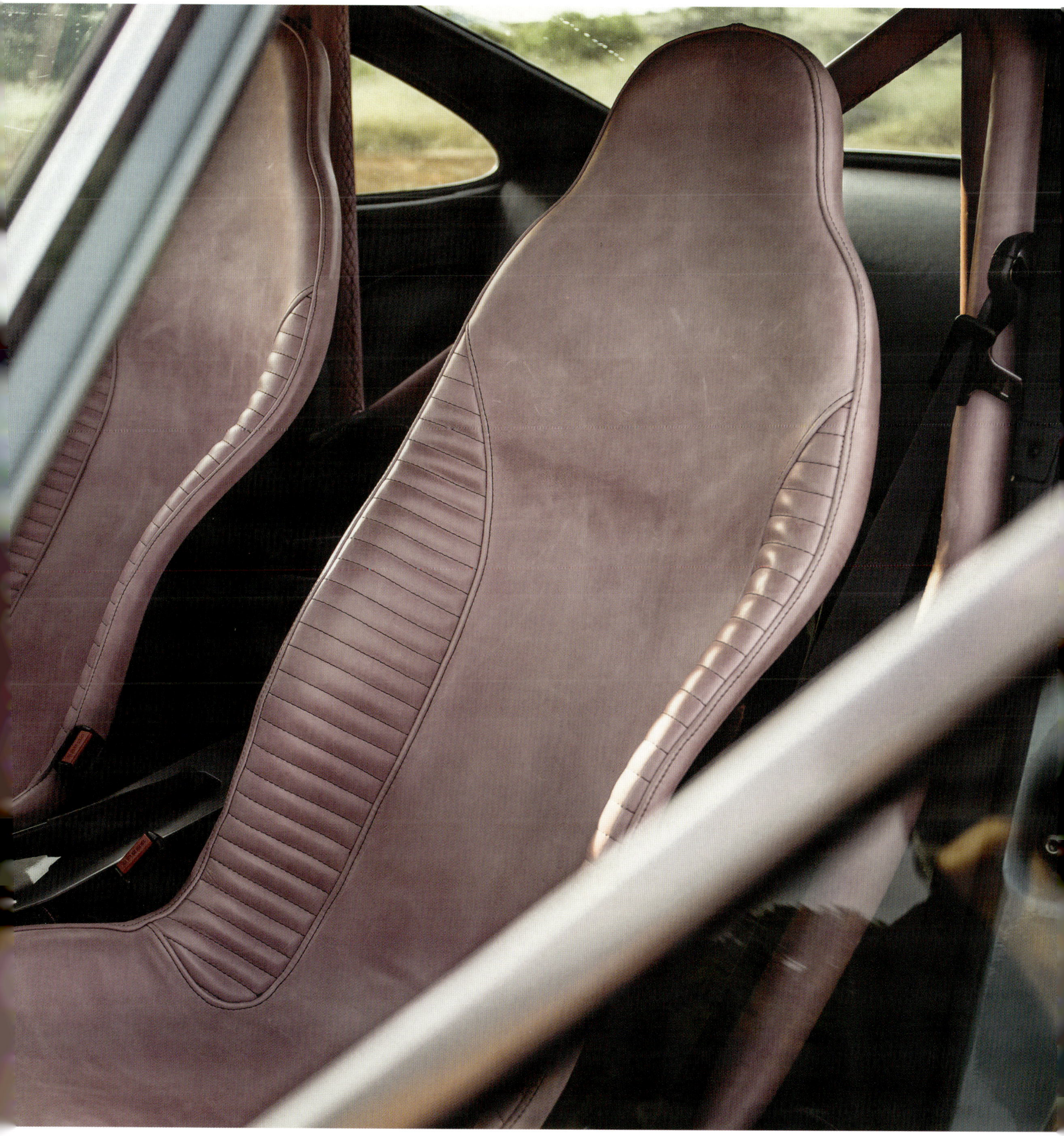

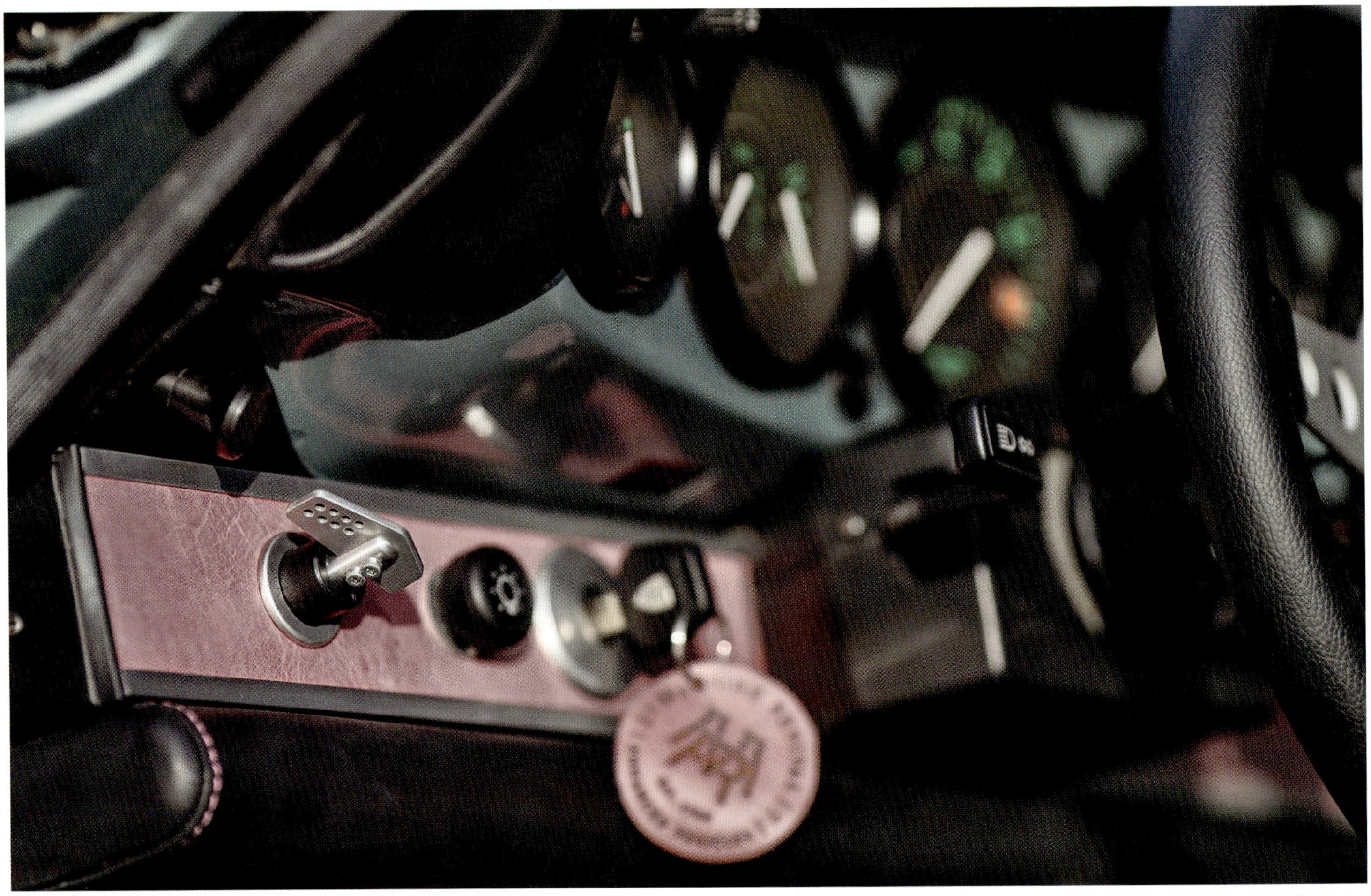

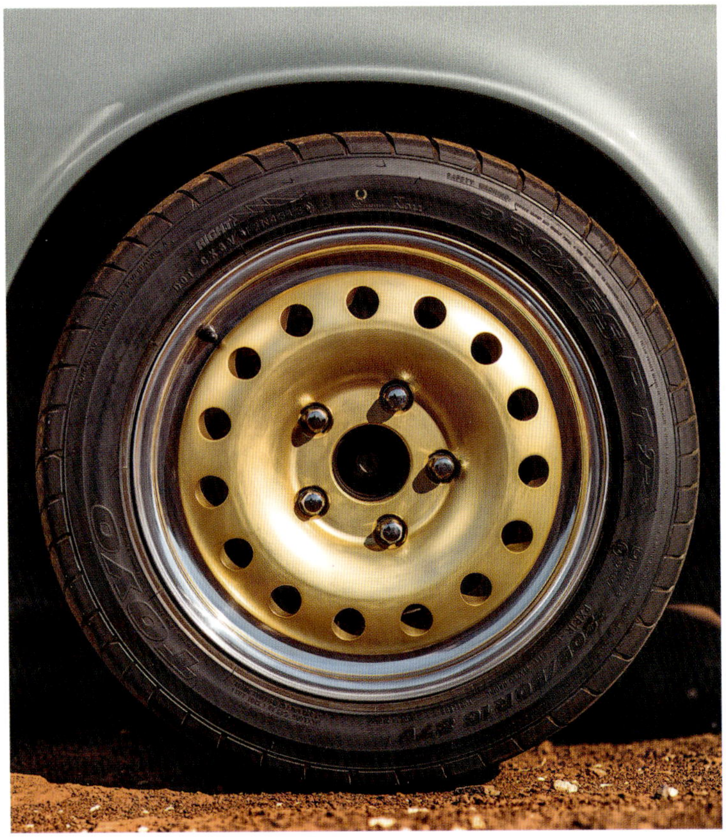

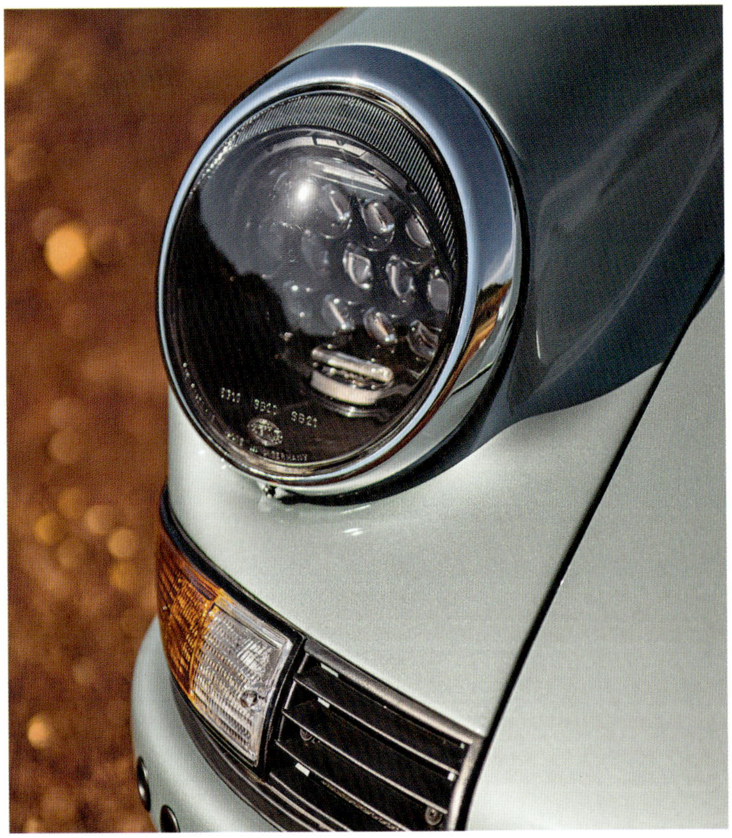

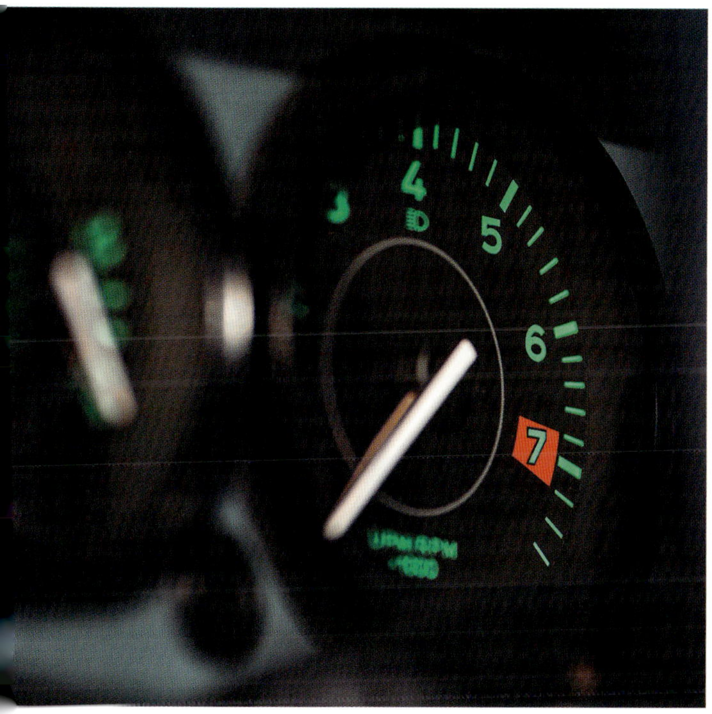

cactus. "The atmosphere and story surrounding the car – which came to us for a rebirth and blossoming after 30 years – are more important than the colour, which is simply a consequence of the project. The hallucinogenic nature of the cactus pushed our designers towards total extravagance; they wanted to have the interior lined entirely in pink, to resemble the peyote flower. The client gave the go-ahead for the fuchsia interior! But we didn't want to overdo it by having pink absolutely everywhere. With such a bold colour, the less you have the better it looks. And we chose black backgrounds to bring out the pink, using some absolutely stunning leather on the key components: the half roll bar, the seats, the strip under the dashboard, the gearstick, and some accent stitching throughout." On the outside, the 964 features a smooth, fluid design that lets it perform well on all types of surface. "We kept the original ride height, as Carrera 4s are already quite high. This effect is accentuated by the particularly minimalist treatment of the body line, making the profile look taller than a classic 964. We fitted perforated aluminium protective panels under the engine and the front hood, to safeguard the vulnerable parts of the car. The goal isn't to be able to drive over massive obstacles, but to cruise around without worrying too much about the surface you're on." To ensure excellent visibility, and keeping with the rally aesthetic, Nicolas fitted large LED headlamps into the housings, maintaining the car's elegance. As for the rims, he went with the classics he's so fond of: "They are three-piece aluminium wheels with custom offsets, designed to look like old, stamped-steel wheels. I enjoy that dual aesthetic – a wheel that has a simple enough look but that delivers serious performance."

911 PEYOTE
BY THE NUMBERS

CREATION 1989

FLAT CYLINDERS 6

CC 3,600

HP 290

1. Aluminium circuit breaker on pink leather, with matching stitching on the black leather beneath.

2. These aren't steel wheels; they're aluminium, for high performance.

3. Illumination comes from the very large LED lights fitted into the original housings.

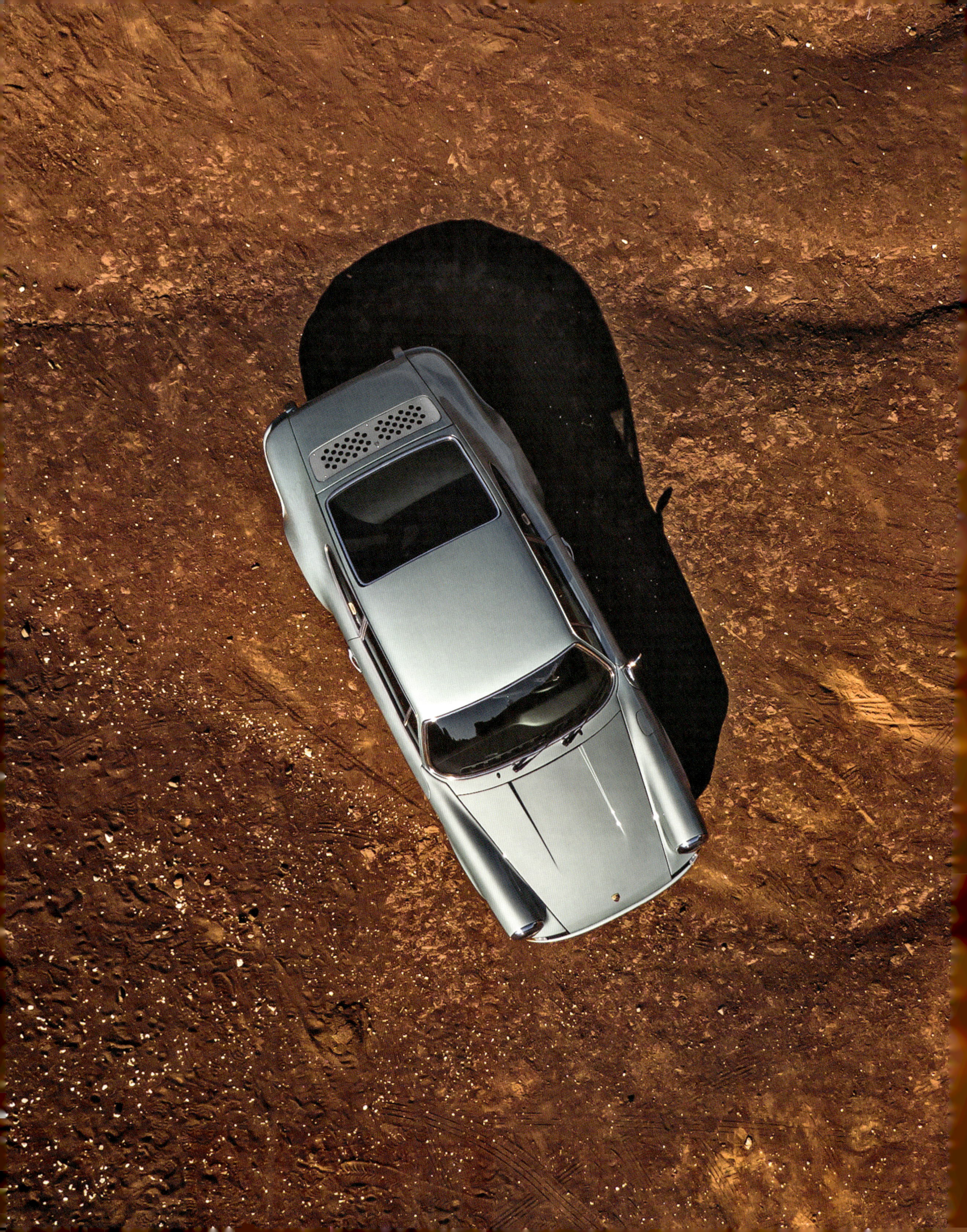

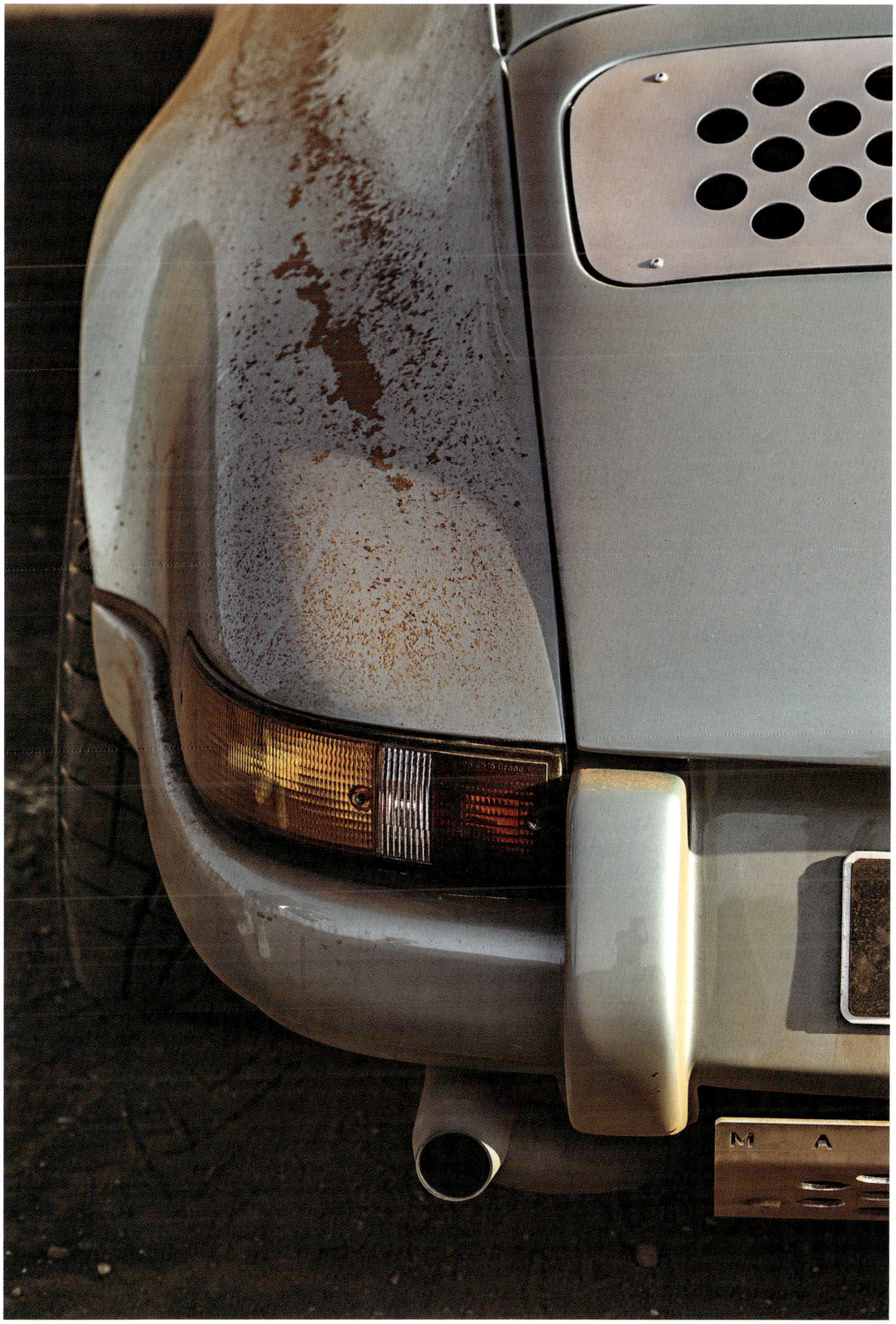

Above: On ochre-toned dirt, the peyote reconnects with a familiar element – and is soon covered in it.

Opposite: This drone shot offers a dreamlike view of the 911 that's inspired by a hallucinogenic Mexican cactus.

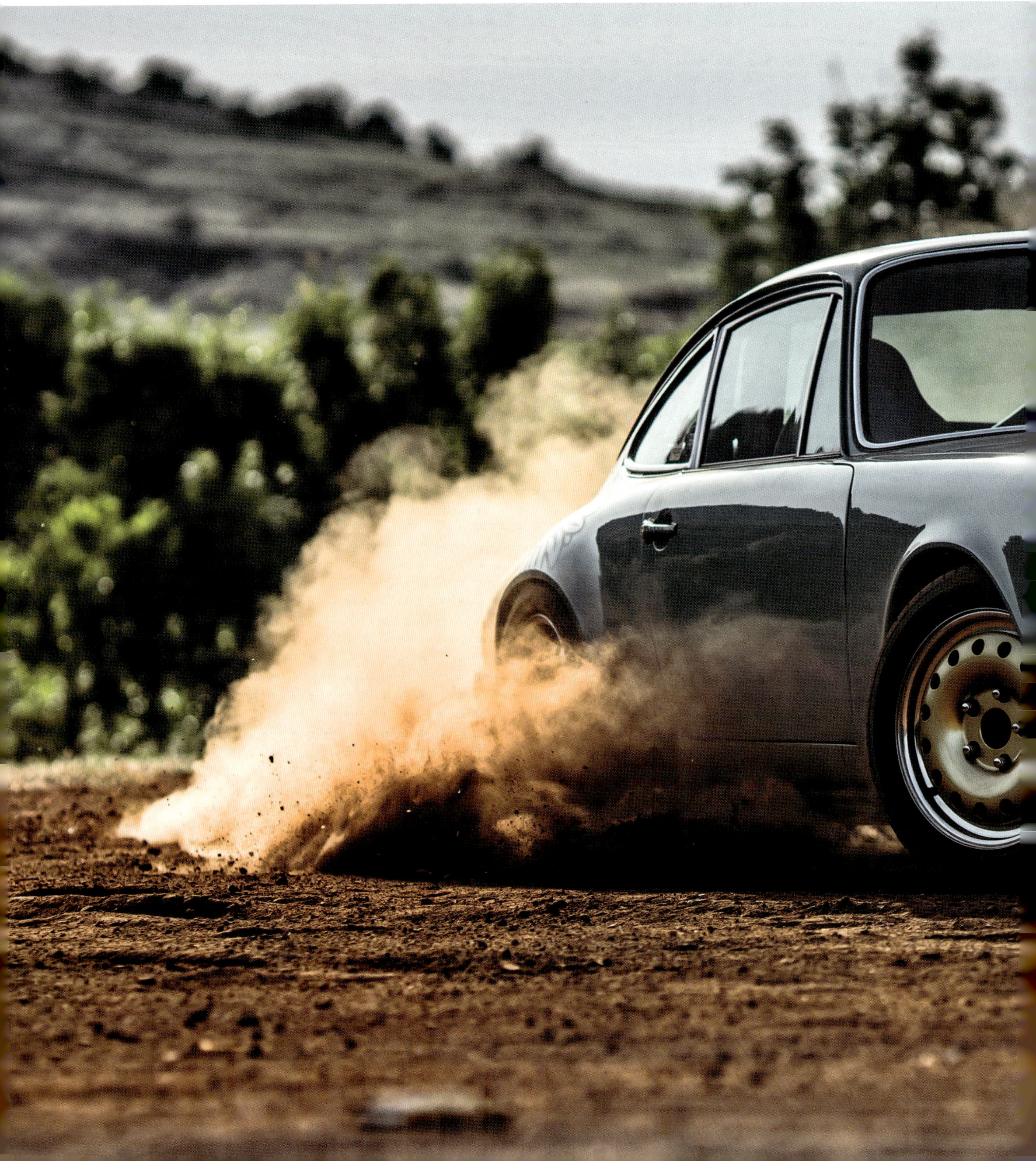

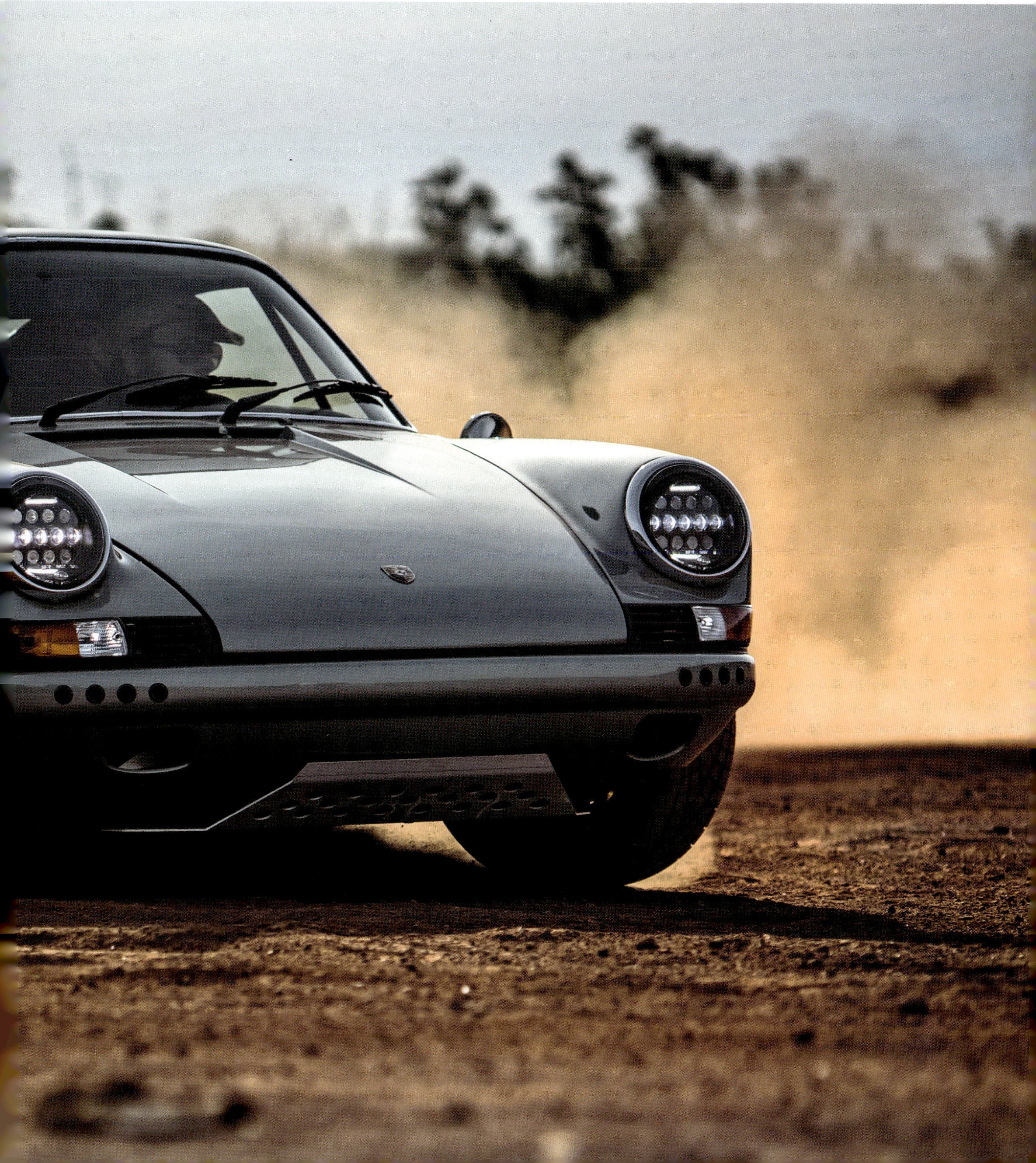

911 JAYA THE PEAK

It bears the name of one of the Seven Summits – the highest mountains on each of the seven continents. For a mountaineer, they represent the ultimate challenge. And with 2,000 hours of restoration behind it, the 911 Jaya was another: its 3.0-litre, flat-six engine gives 230 hp and the car weighs 948 kg (2,090 lbs). Get that harness on ...

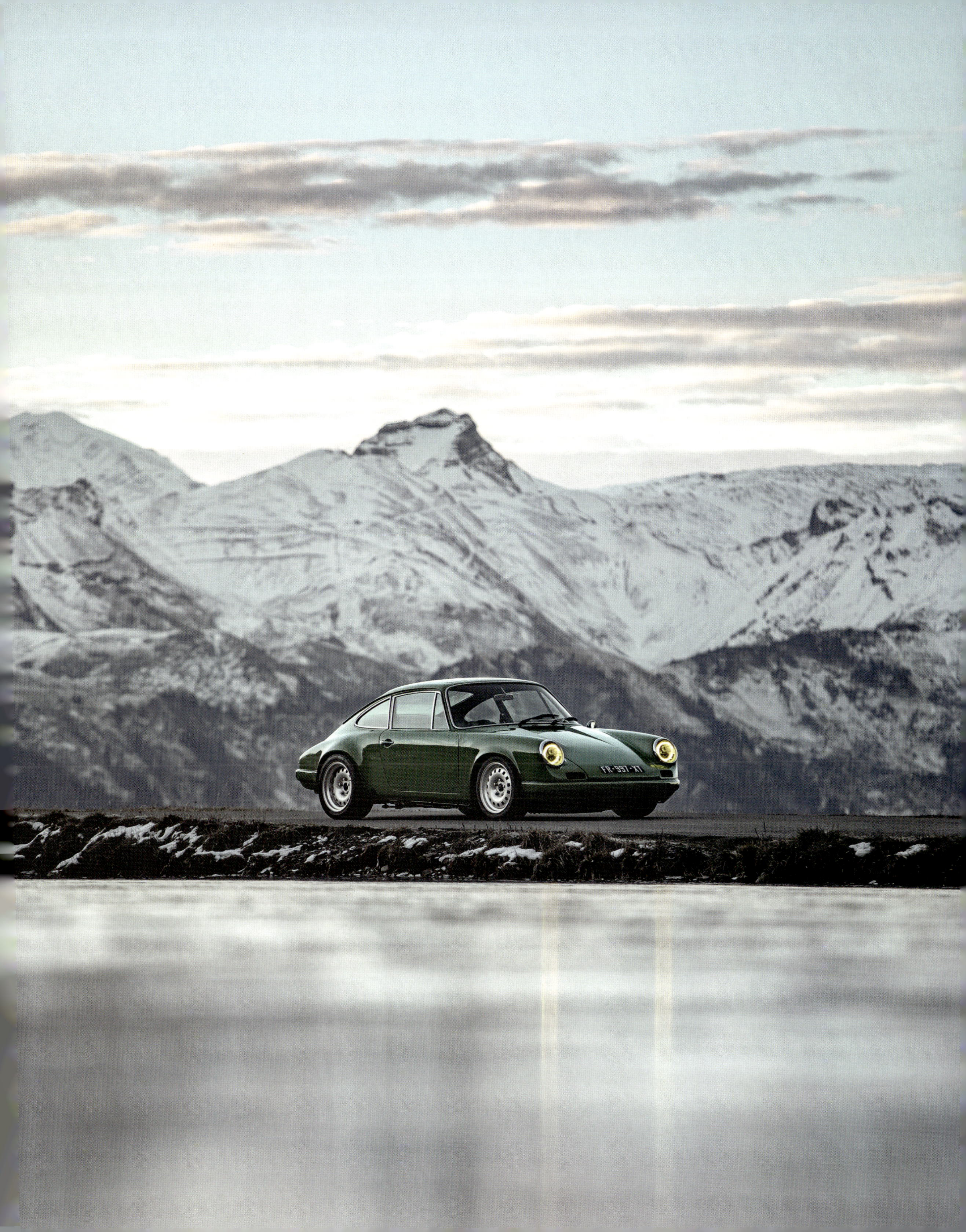
FR-997-XT

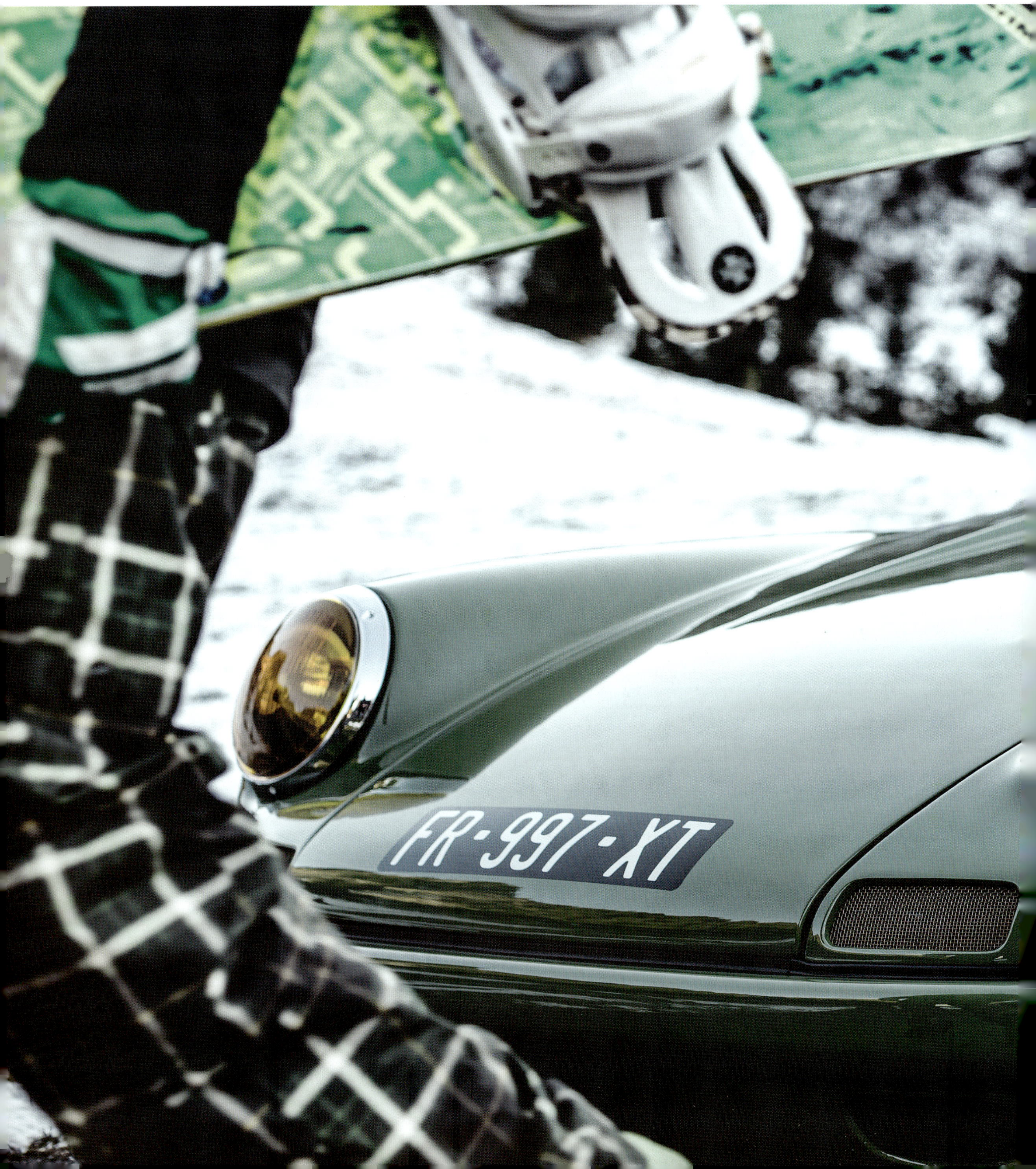
FR·997·XT

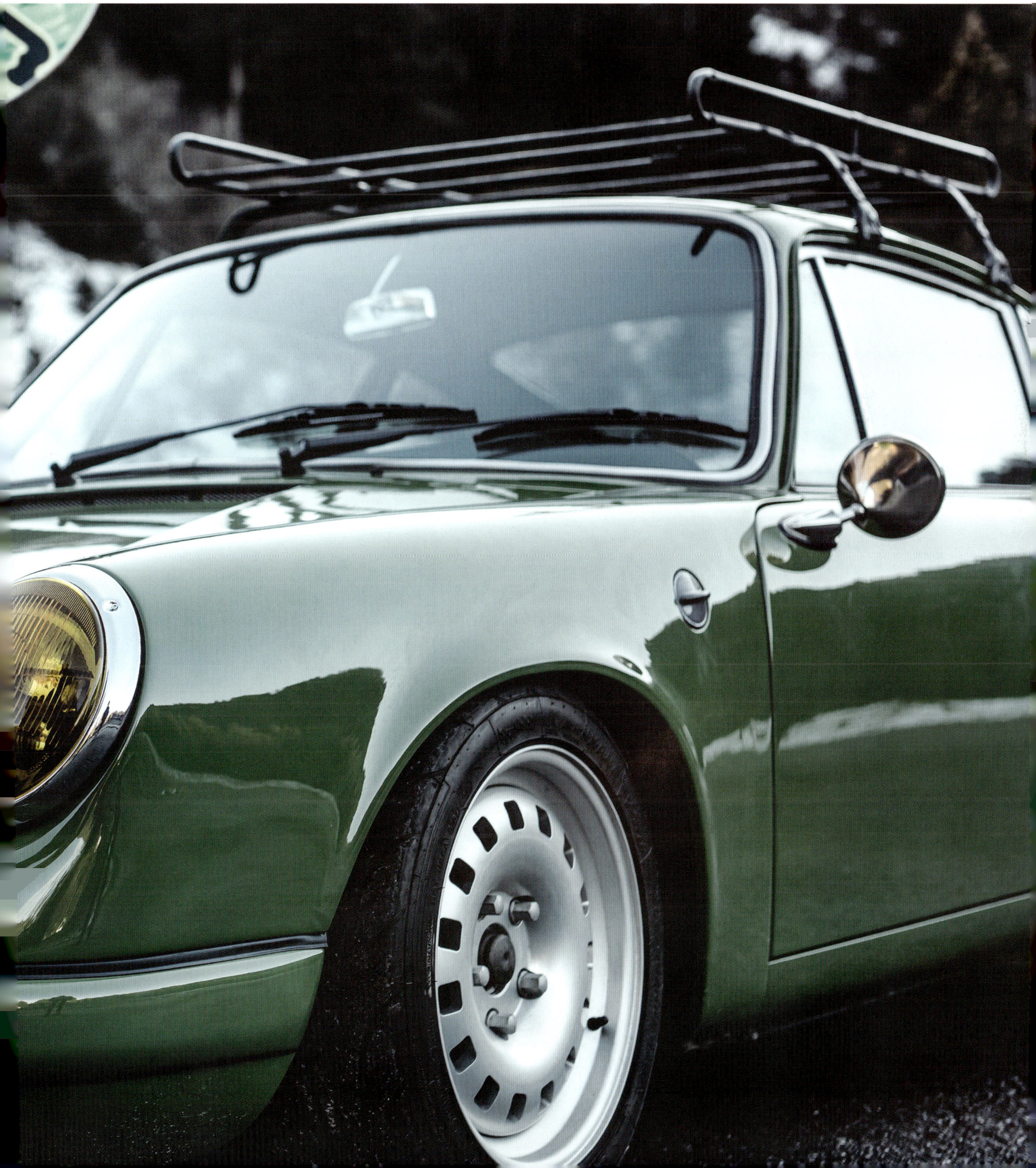

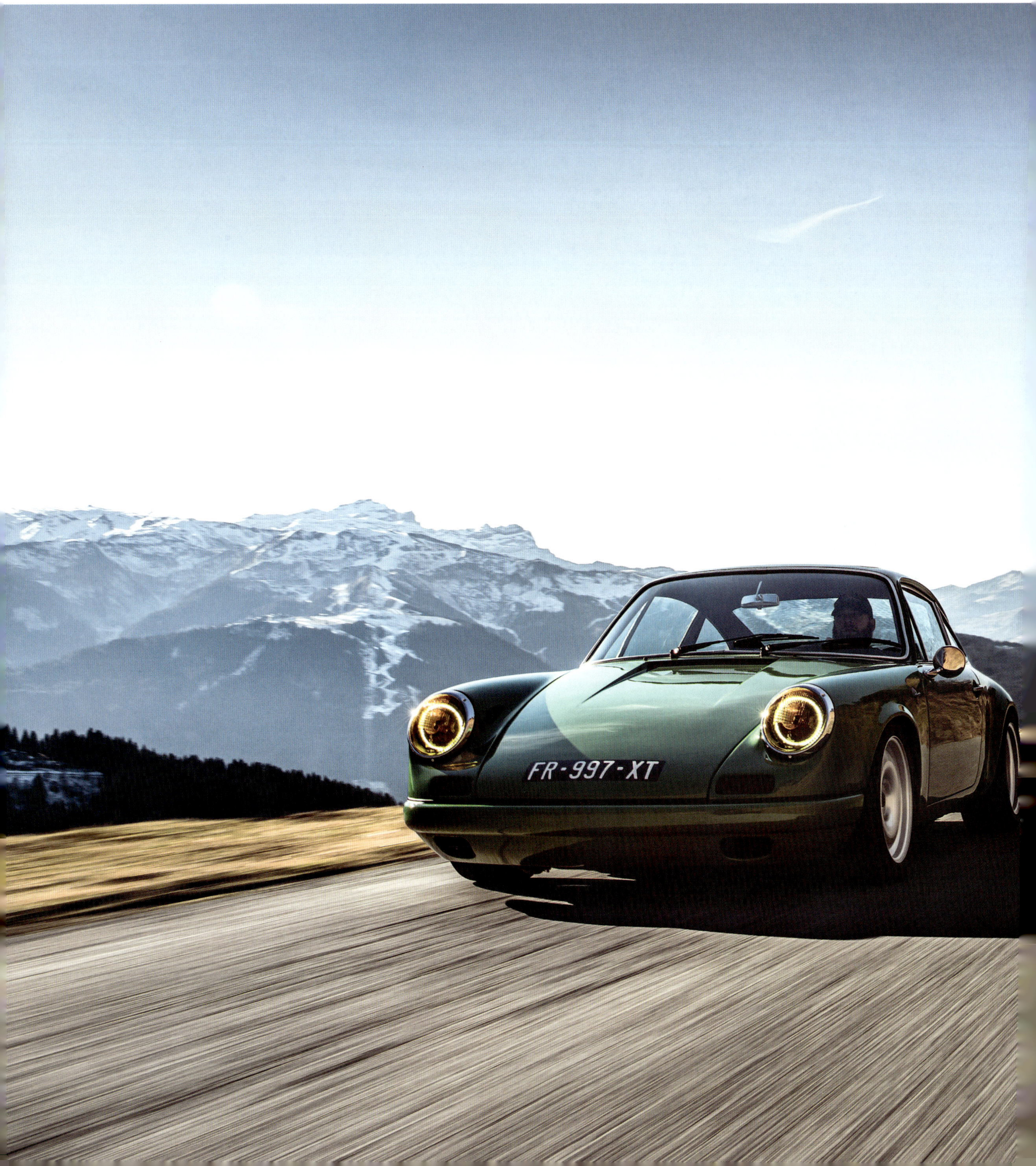
FR-997-XT

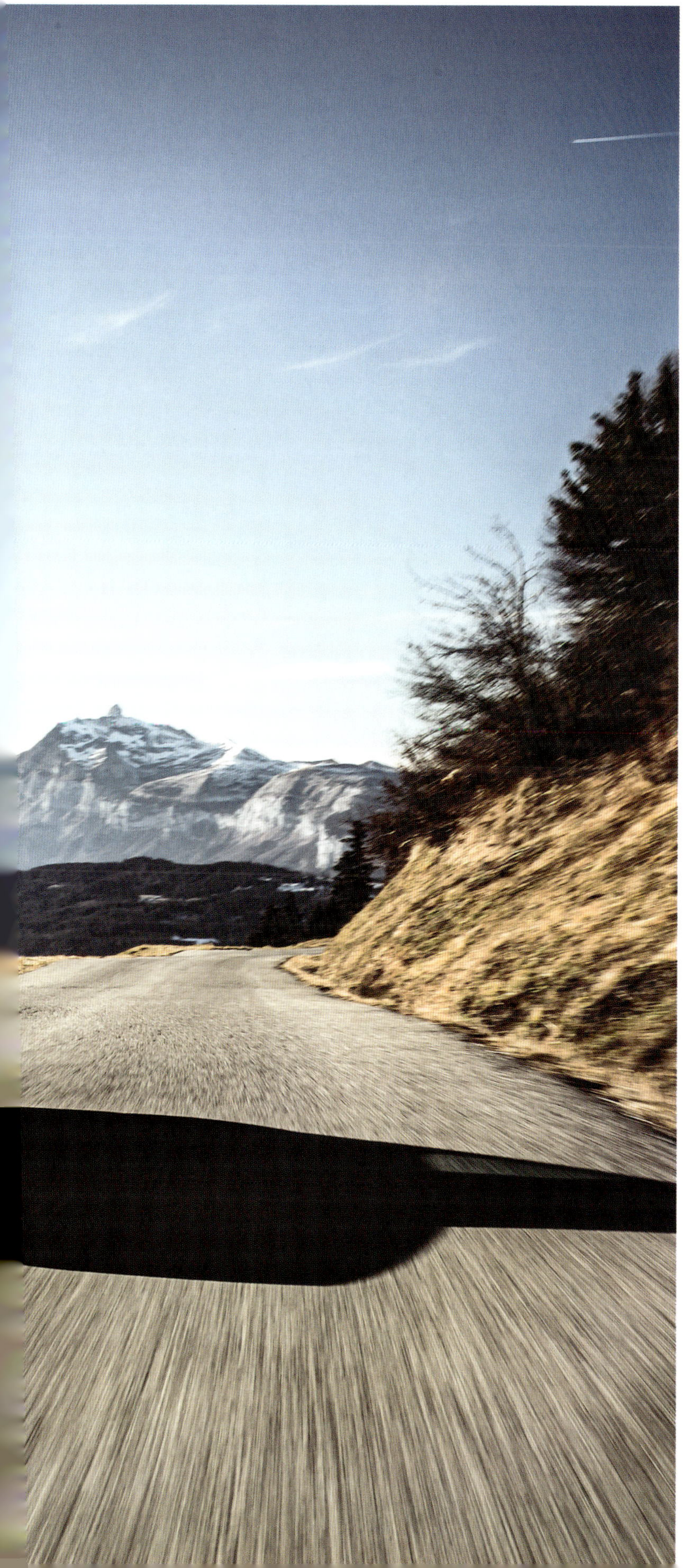

WITH AN EXTREMELY WELL REFINED SILHOUETTE, THE JAYA IS A RAW, WILD PEAK.

Dismantle, restore, improve, replace ... The level of challenge in breathing new life into this 1981 911 SC was akin to reaching the top of the peak it is named after: Jaya! The mountain Puncak Jaya, situated on the island of New Guinea, was discovered in 1623 but was believed to be insurmountable until 1962. With an altitude of 16,024 feet (4,884 m) Puncak Jaya is the highest point in Indonesia and the continent of Oceania. That is what makes it one of the Seven Summits – the ultimate goal for the best climbers in the world. Raw, wild and inspired by the great open spaces where nature draws its origins from the living earth, the Porsche 911 Jaya matches up perfectly with the spirit of the original mountain. And there's more than a touch of poetry and creation as a bonus. With nearly 2,000 hours of work put into its restoration, working on this 911 was akin to climbing a mountain, slowly but surely; but a goal worthy of the mammoth task.

Absolutely everything was redone. Starting with the shell, the rear wings were kept and fully restored, as were the doors. However, composite front and rear hoods and front bumpers were fitted in place of the originals. More than just the adaptation of a pre-1973 Porsche body kit, this restoration has taken refinement to the very top, even removing the front indicators, which were re-housed in the halogen headlight domes, which were powerful enough to dispense with additional optics. The silhouette is pared down to the extreme, and Jaya displays a unique style with its yellow headlights with a large luminous ring in the centre, further reinforcing the unmistakable sign of the 911. The lowered body, bumpers and entire bodywork are finished in a stunning, organic shade called Olive Green. The three-piece aluminium wheels reinterpret and build on the vintage look of the steel rims that were seen on early 911s. Behind these period, racing-style wheels, the chassis was optimized, new, firmer shock absorbers were installed and the braking system was replaced with modern components, featuring six-piston calipers at the front and four-piston calipers at the back, specially designed to fit inside the 16-inch wheels. The flat-six cylinder engine was totally refurbished, with a focus on reliability and engine refinement rather than astounding power output. New camshafts were fitted in the engine, along with a lightened flywheel to help it climb more quickly up the rev counter.

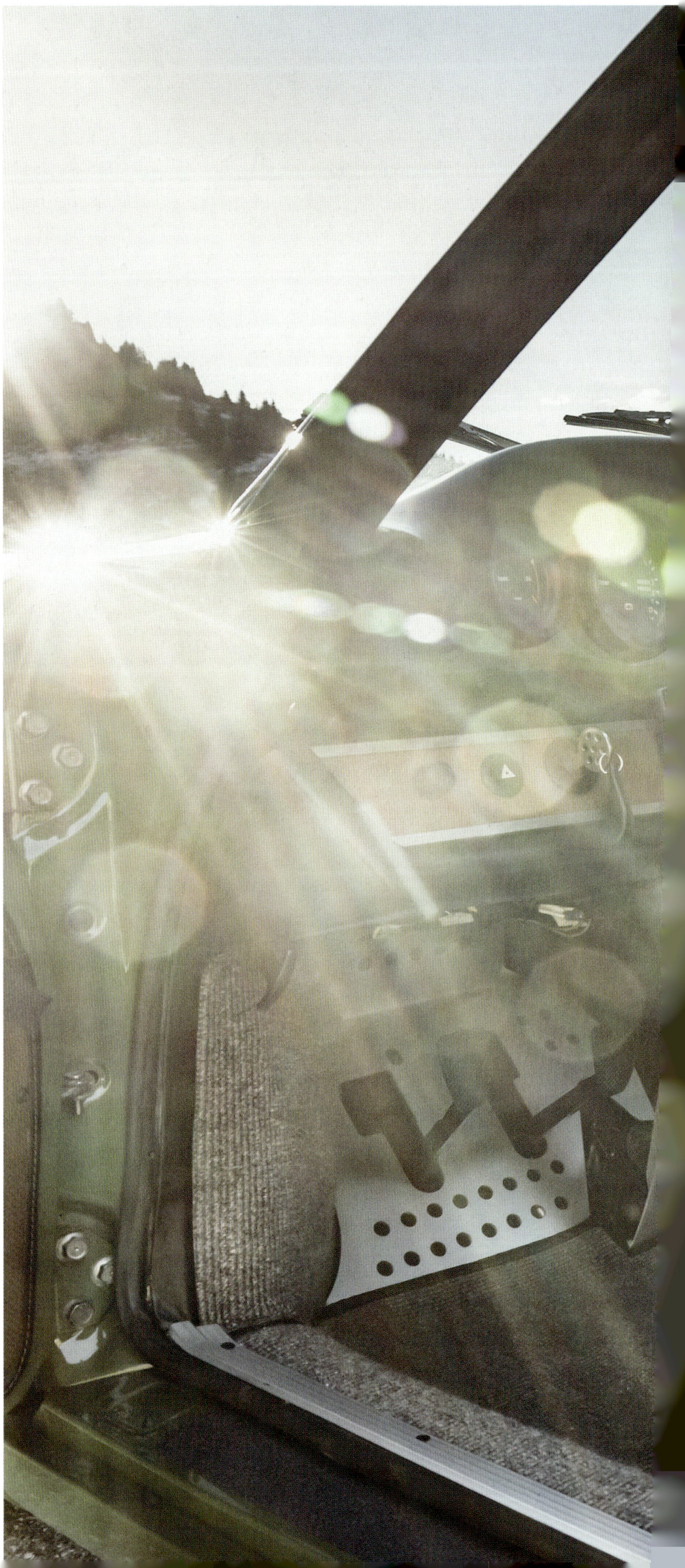

ORGANIC MATERIALS ARE PRESENT THROUGHOUT THE CABIN.

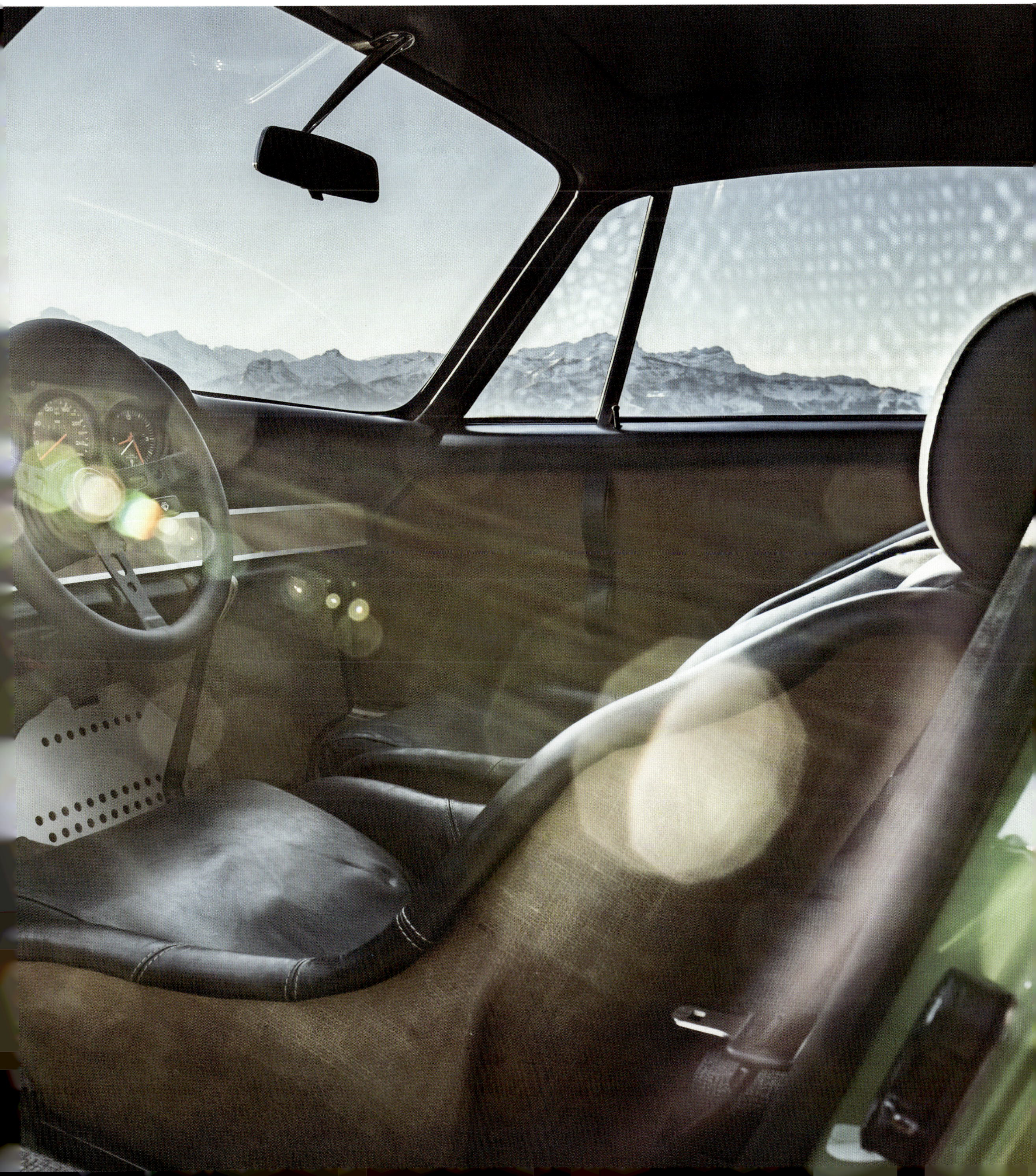

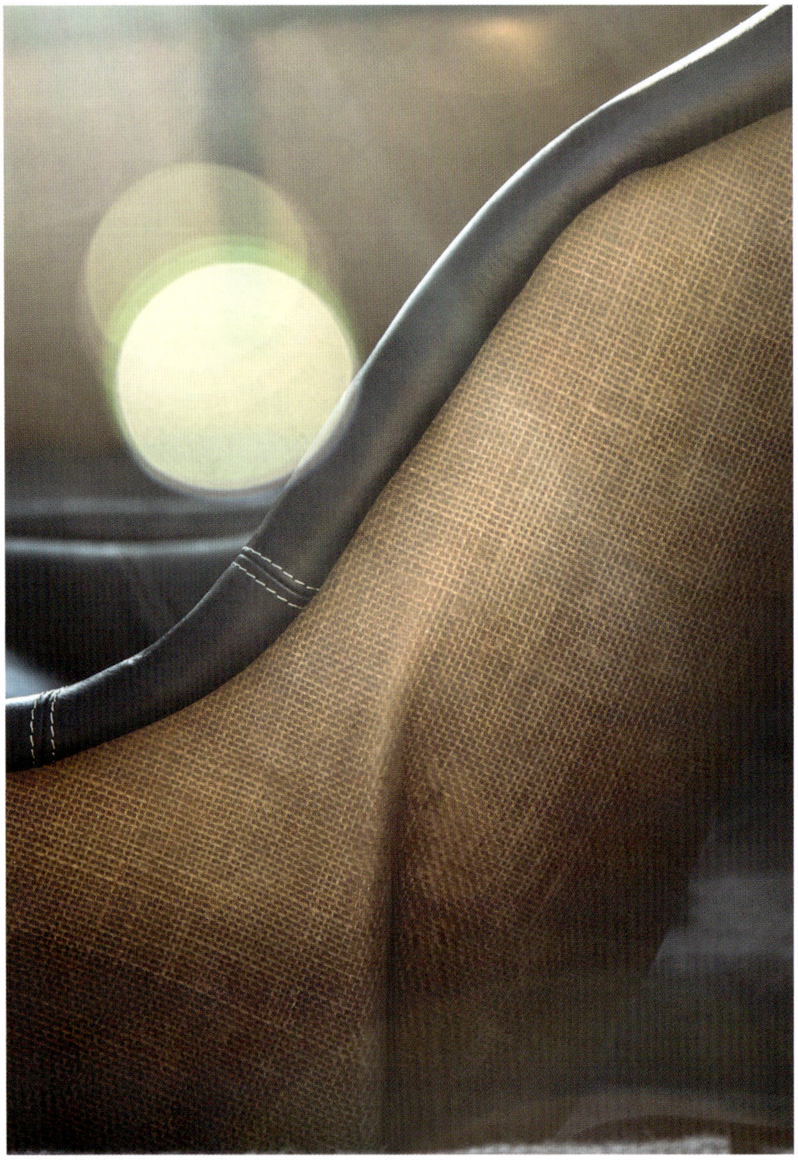

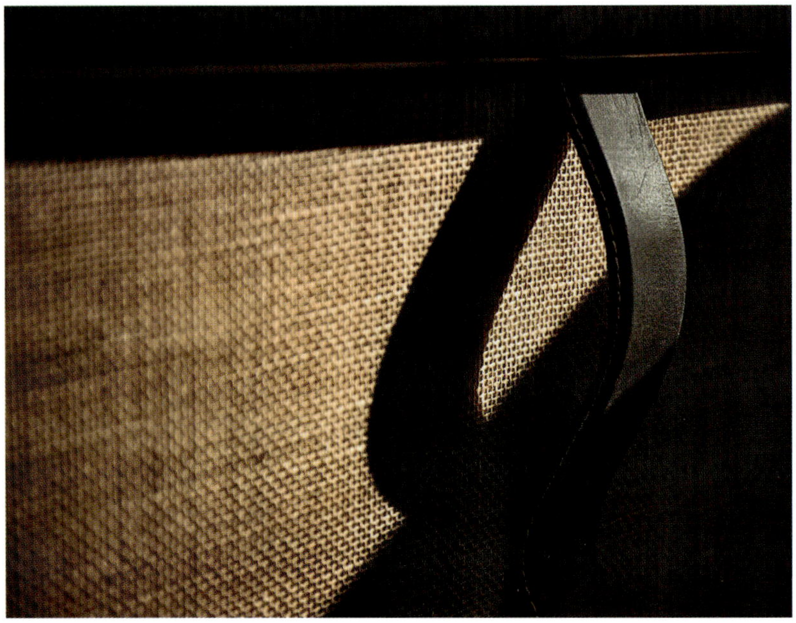

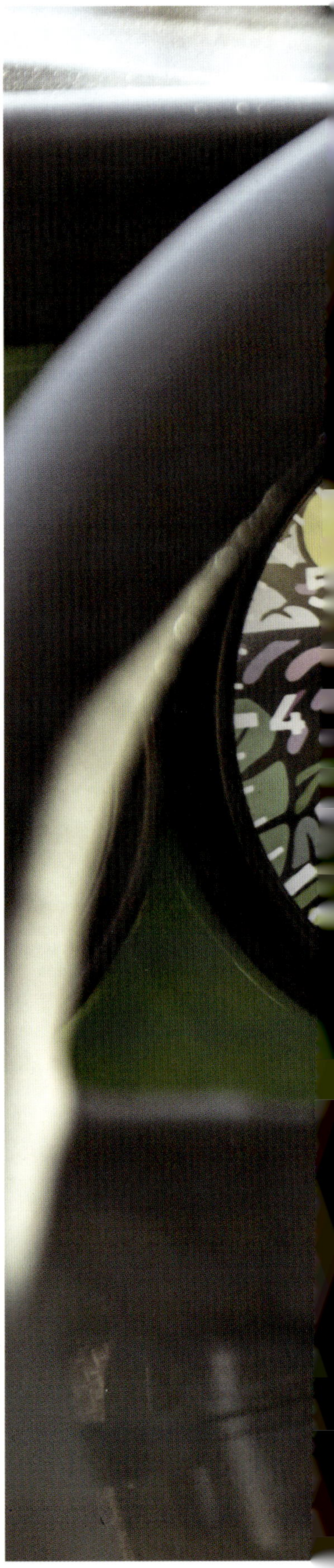

1. Linen fibres cover the backs of the bucket seats, with full-grain leather on the seats.

2. Organic fabric elegantly adorns the doors of this 911.

3. The soul of this Jaya is painted in the background of the tachometer.

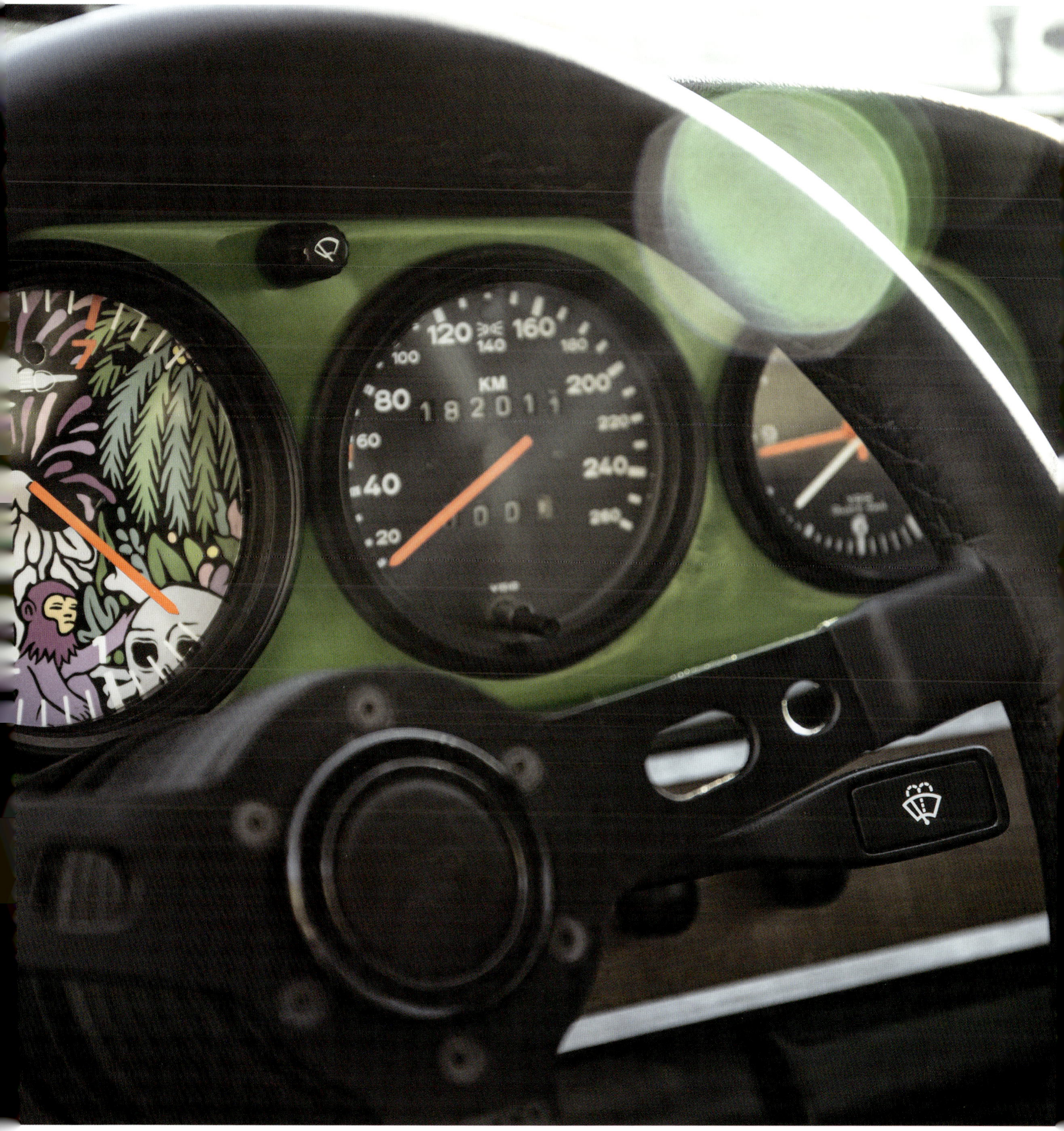

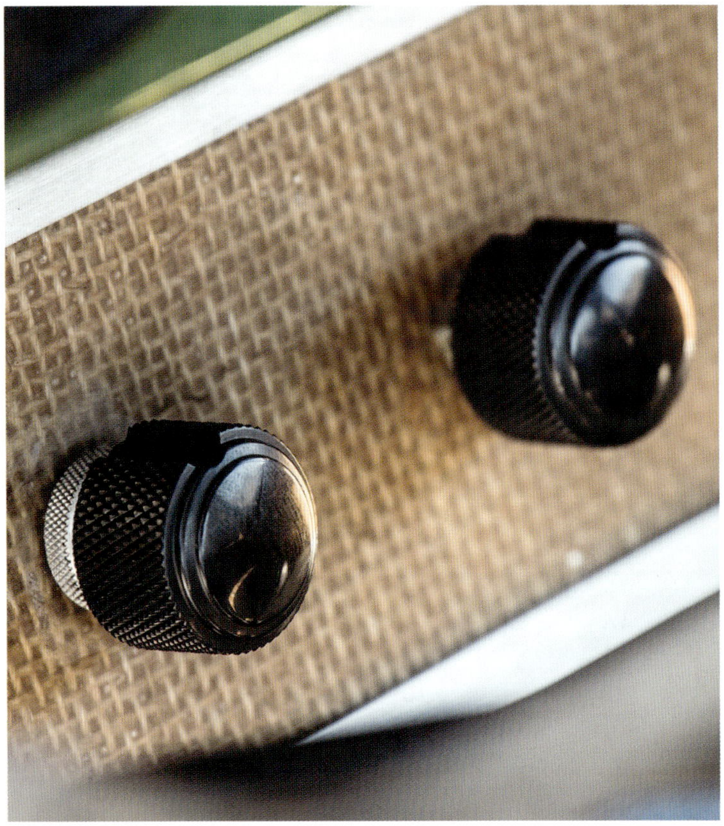

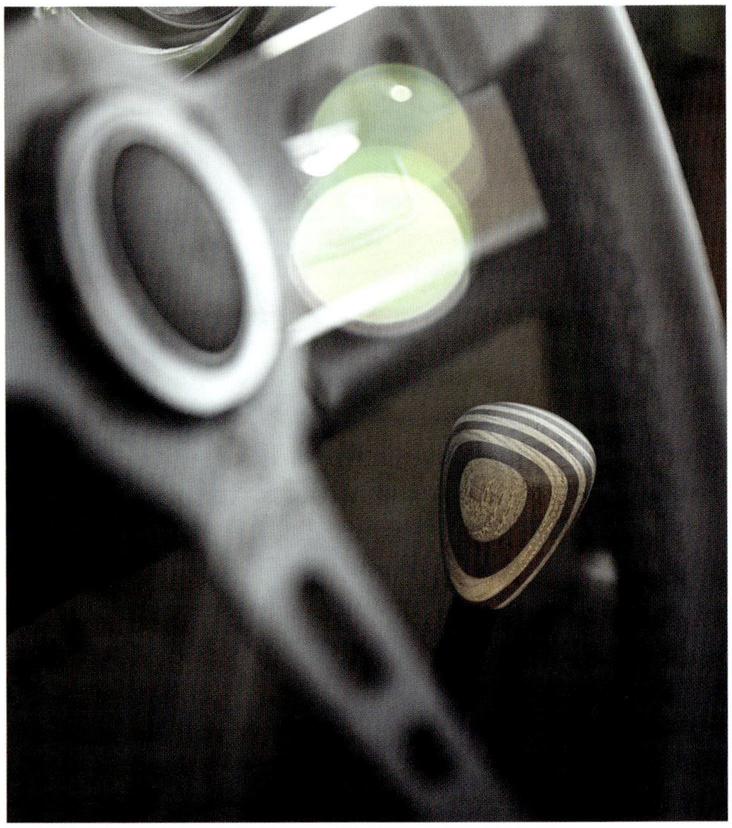

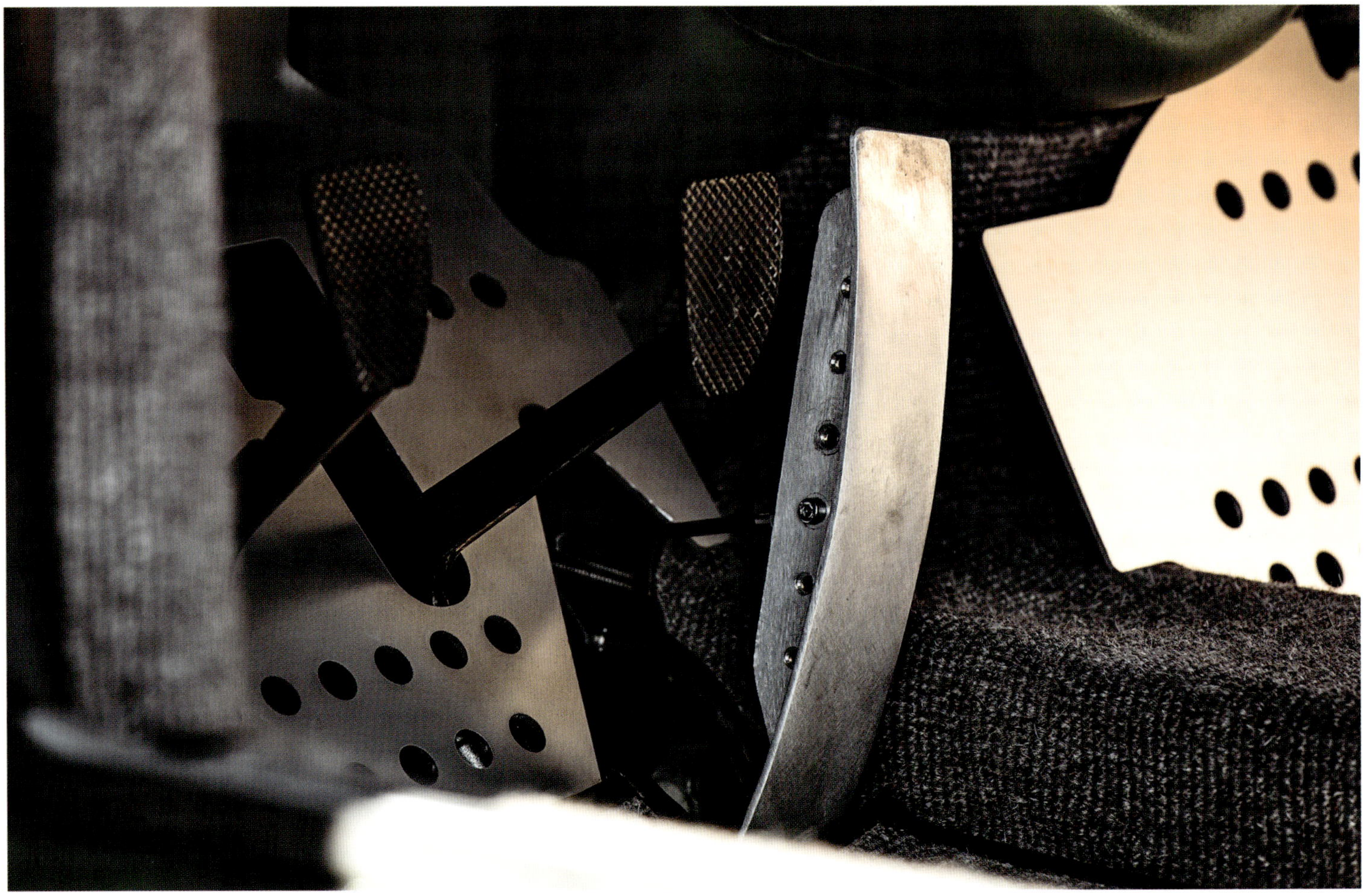

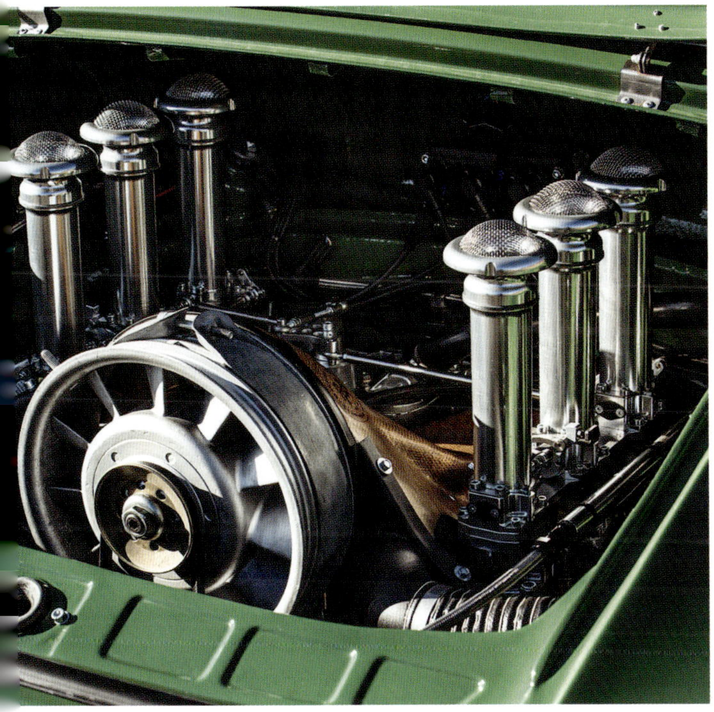

911 JAYA
BY THE NUMBERS

CREATION 1982

FLAT CYLINDERS 6

CC 3,000

HP 230

A modern injection system maintains high performance regardless of the level of the incline the car is faced with, and is topped by six intake trumpets that give this engine the appearance of the peaks to be scaled. Adapted for use with bioethanol, the injection system delivers a 15 per cent power increase compared to unleaded 98 (E5) petrol. With a custom-made exhaust, the 911 Jaya's original 3.0-litre engine gives 240 hp, ensuring that it is always reliable, however high the altitude you run at.

And inside, behind the ebony-coloured black-leather upholstery, the seats are covered in a linen fibre, for a fully organic look. This unique touch is also evident on the doors, which are entirely covered with the material, highly unusual for this type of interior. The dashboard strip also uses the fabric, as does the engine trim, which features a heat-resistant version made using resin fibres, but with the same appearance. Nothing was left to chance. Detail, synonymous with elegance, is present, even where it is not immediately visible. What does catch the eye when you are on board is the original VDO rev counter, which has been completely reconditioned: the background was hand-painted in a psychedelic theme depicting the flora and fauna of Puncak Jaya mountain. In hand, the gearknob is made from two coloured woods, Porsche 917 style. And down low, the aluminium accelerator pedal completes the racing spirit of this 911. And note, the 911 Jaya is not some gentle, exotic evocation of a distant peak – it's a speed demon that loves to be pushed to the limit! With a kerb weight of 948 kg (2,090 lbs) and the furious roar of the flat-six engine as it approaches 7,000 rpm, it stimulates all the senses and propels you on a unique driving adventure. The perfect combination of aesthetics, performance and usability, the 911 Jaya gives a truly sensory experience. Just like a mountaineer climbing a legendary mountain.

1 2 3

1. The switches are as minimalist as the rest of this Porsche.

2. The gearknob is machined in wood, Porsche 917 style.

3. The accelerator pedal is made entirely of aluminium, as is the guard plate.

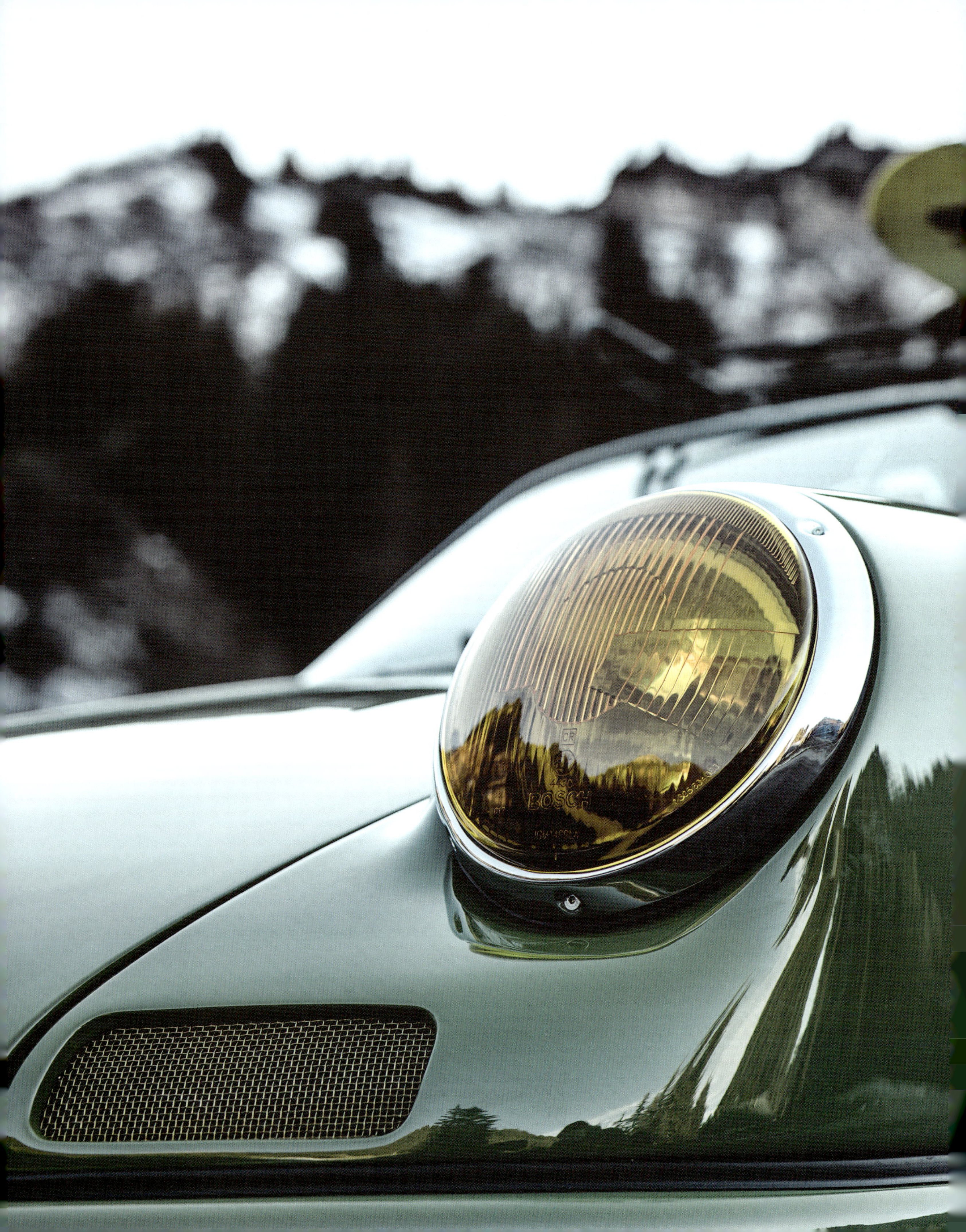
BOSCH

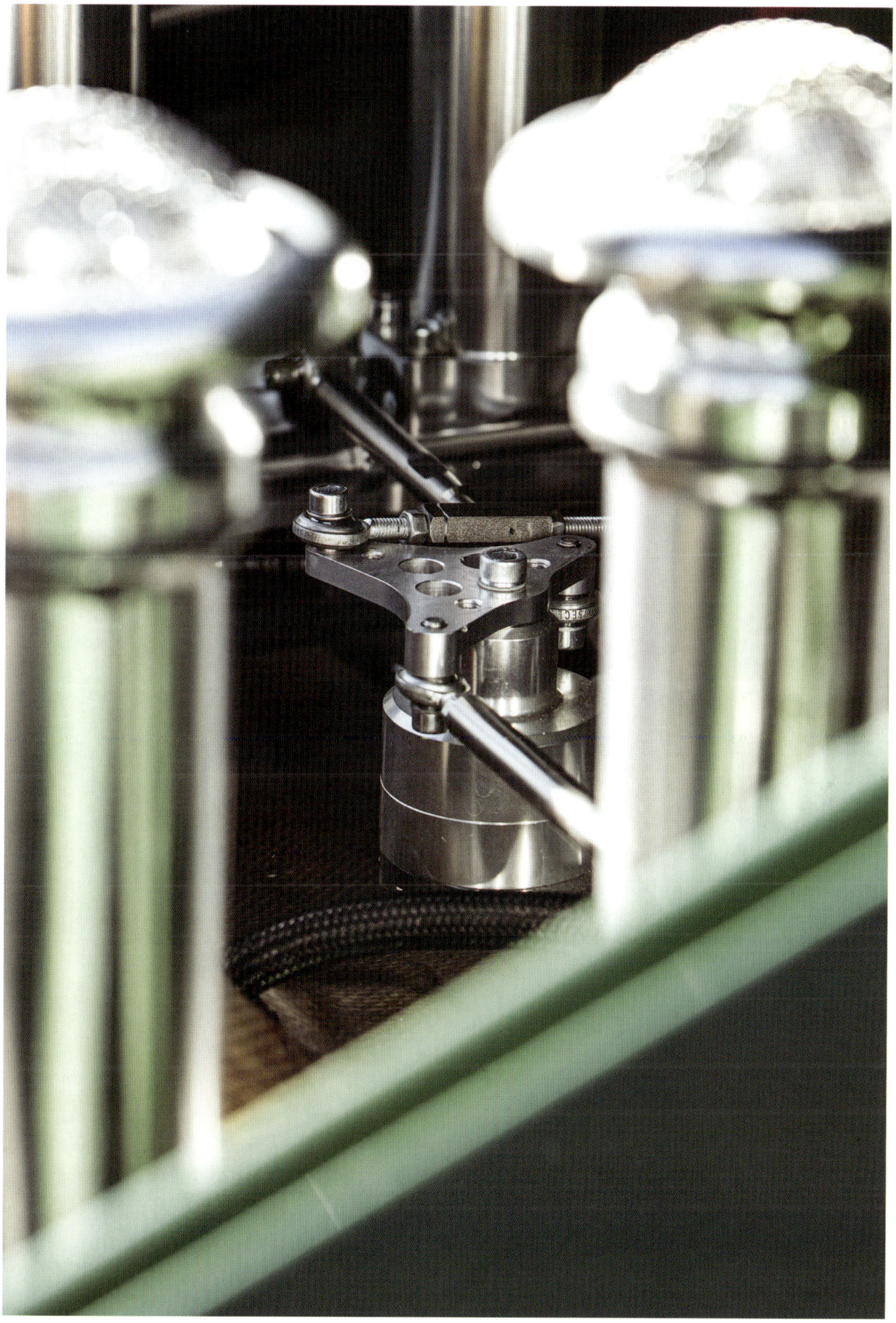

Above: In the middle of the six intake trumpets pointing to the sky, the mechanism for opening the intake valves is a work of art.

Opposite: The large yellow headlights give the Jaya a unique look – the indicators are integrated.

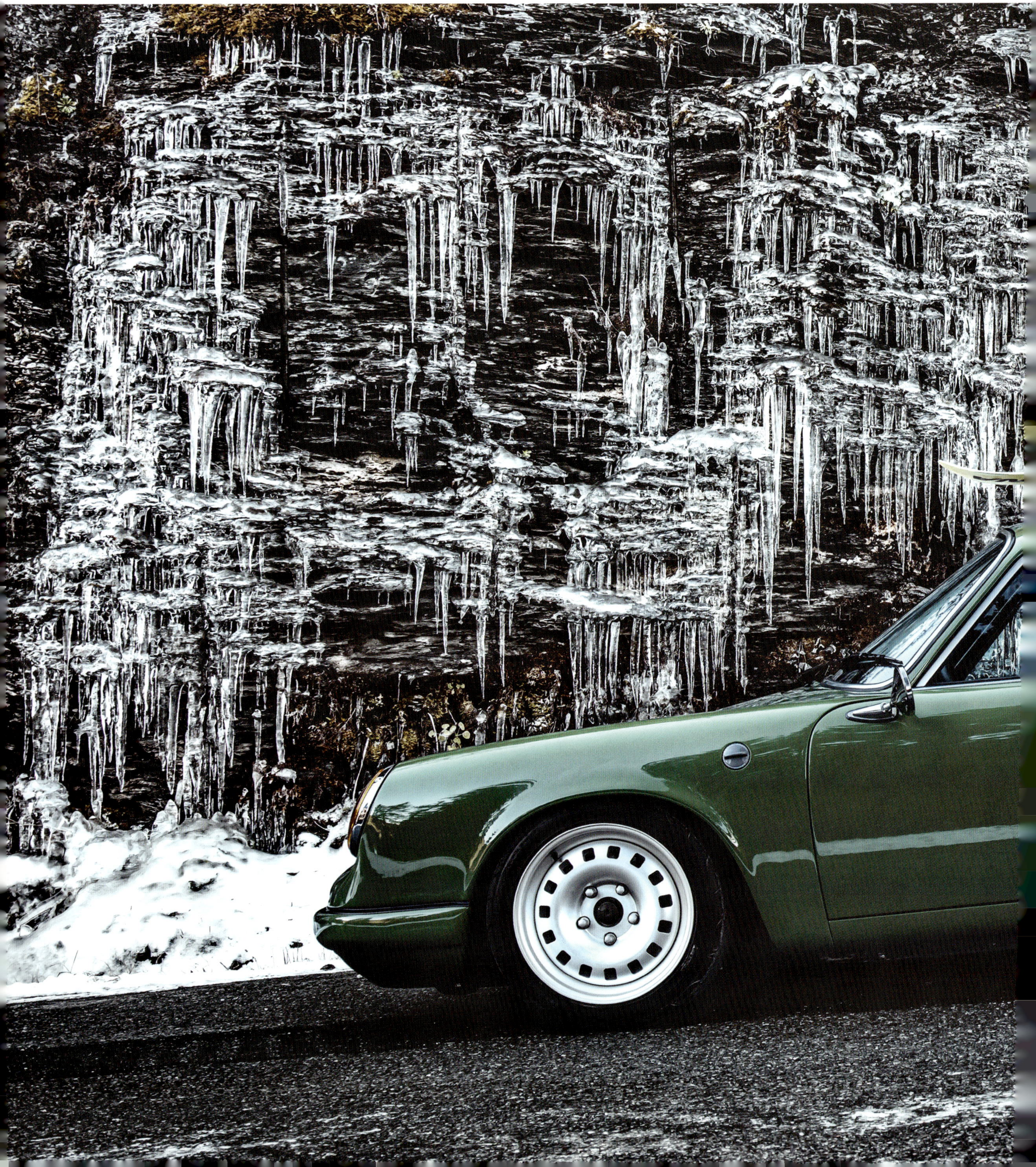

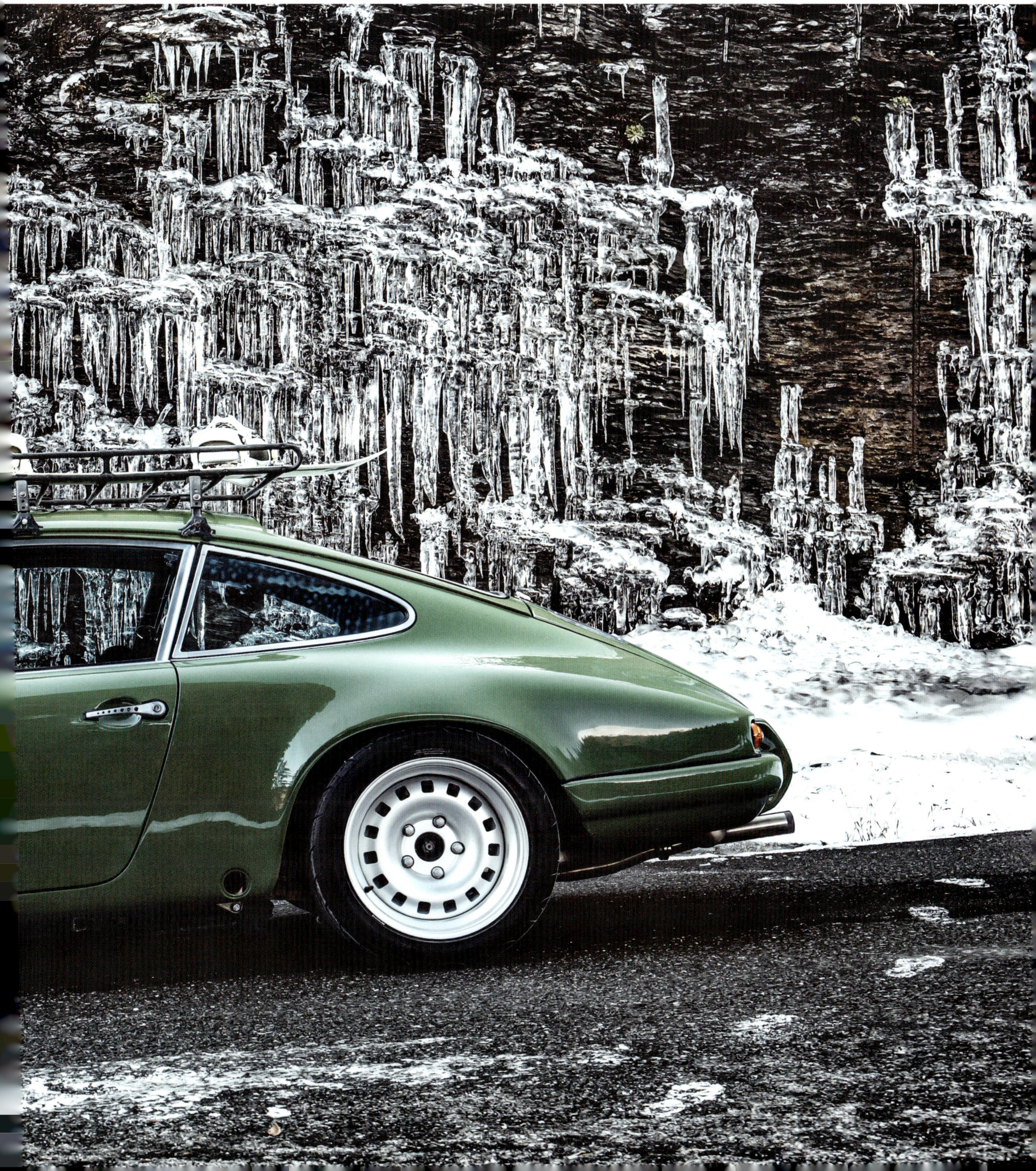

911 CARRERA
2.7 RST

A TASTE OF FREEDOM

Drive an old car, but with modern handling. Drive a sporty, chic, elegant car. Those were the goals set by Sylvie and Jean-Michel when they planned this sublime Porsche 911 2.7 RST. Mission accomplished!

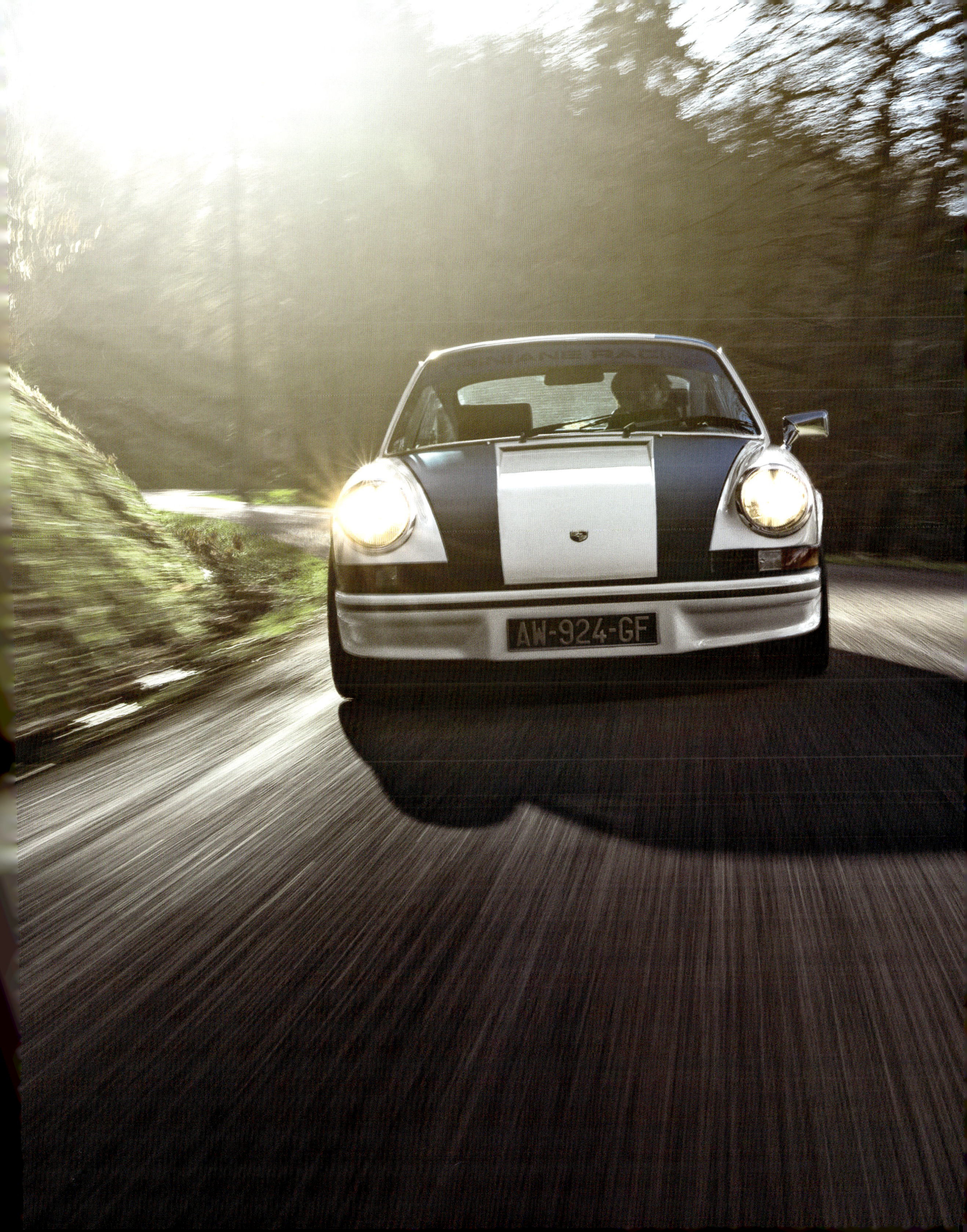
AW-924-GF

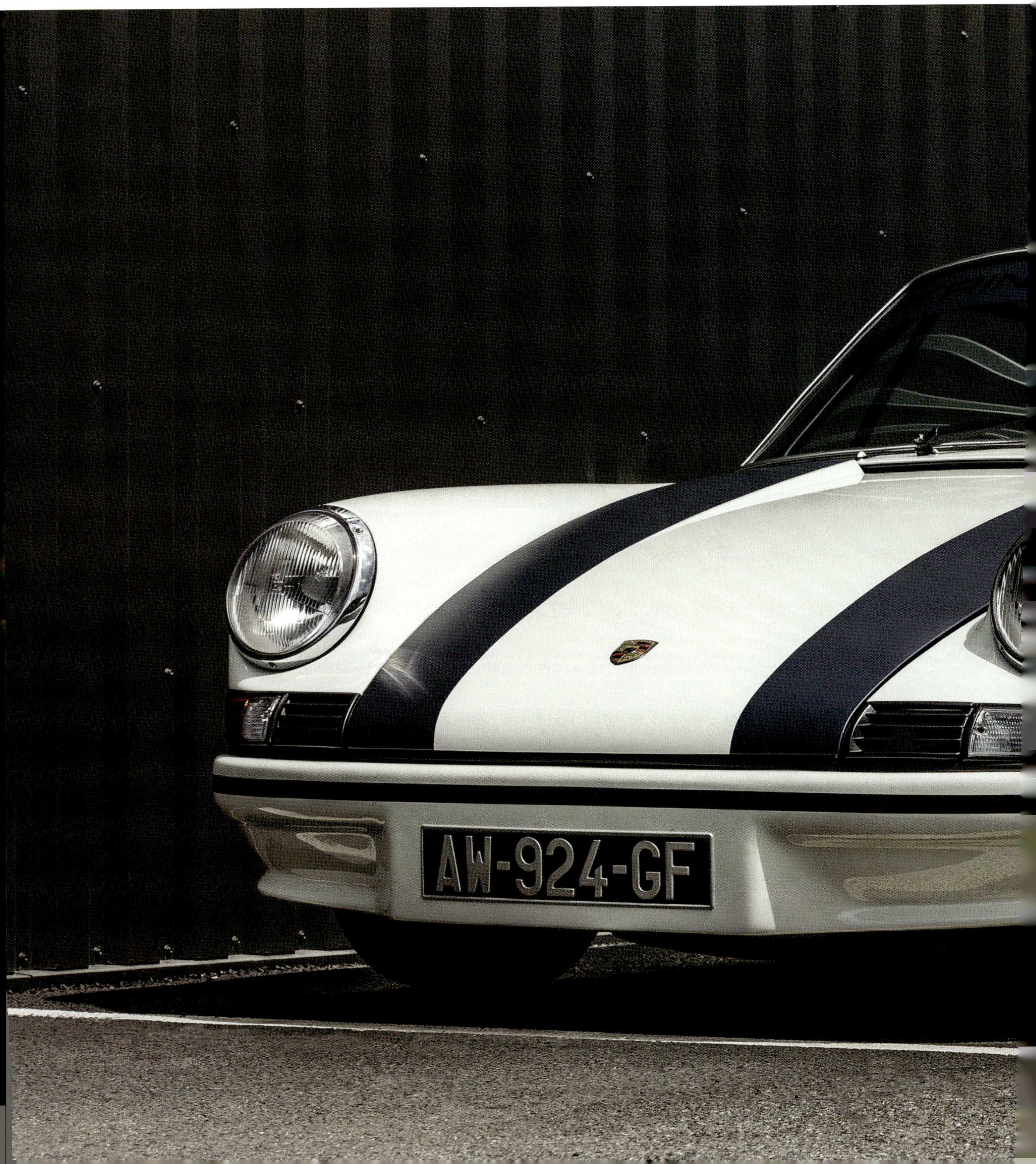
AW-924-GF

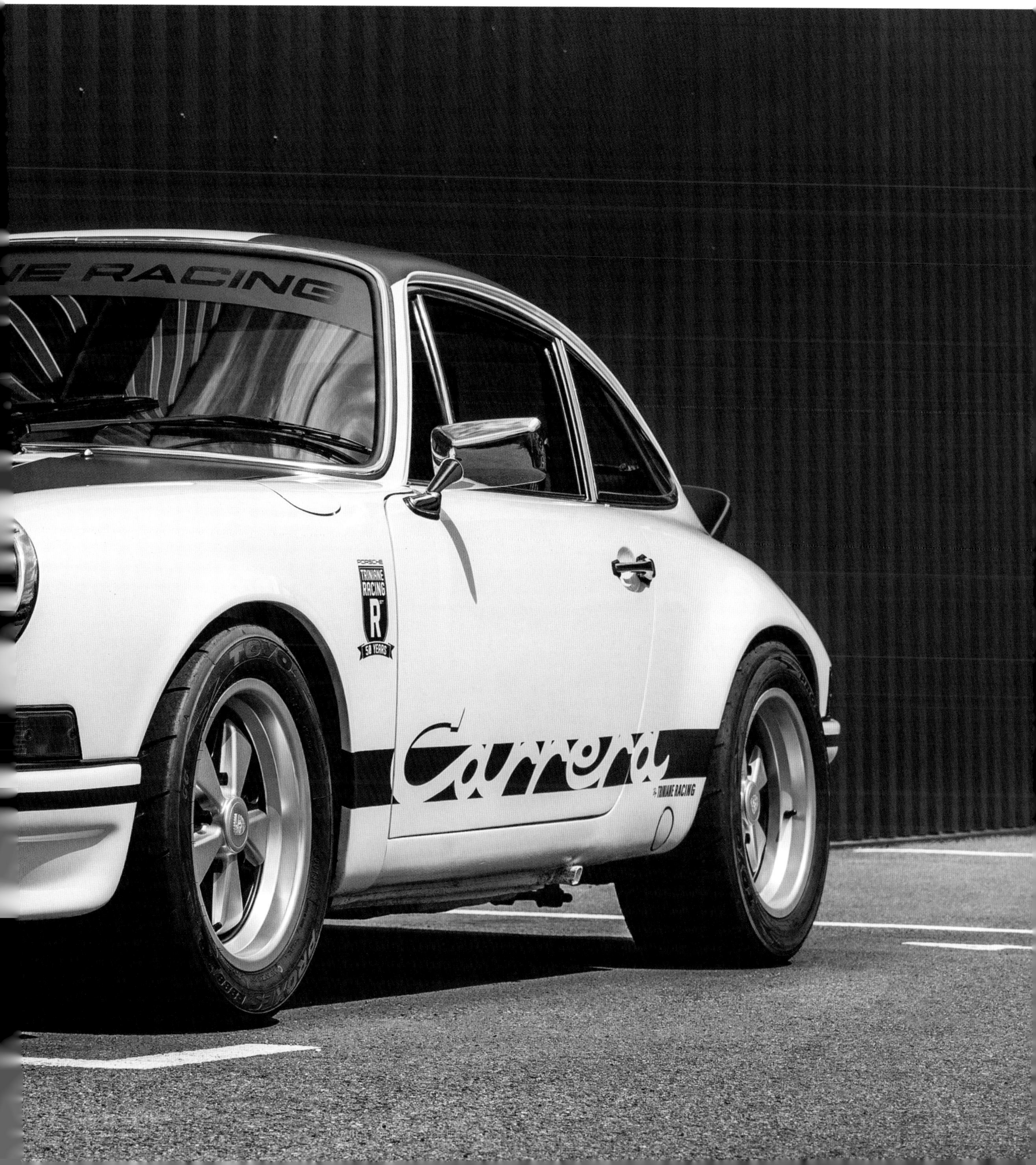

Carrera

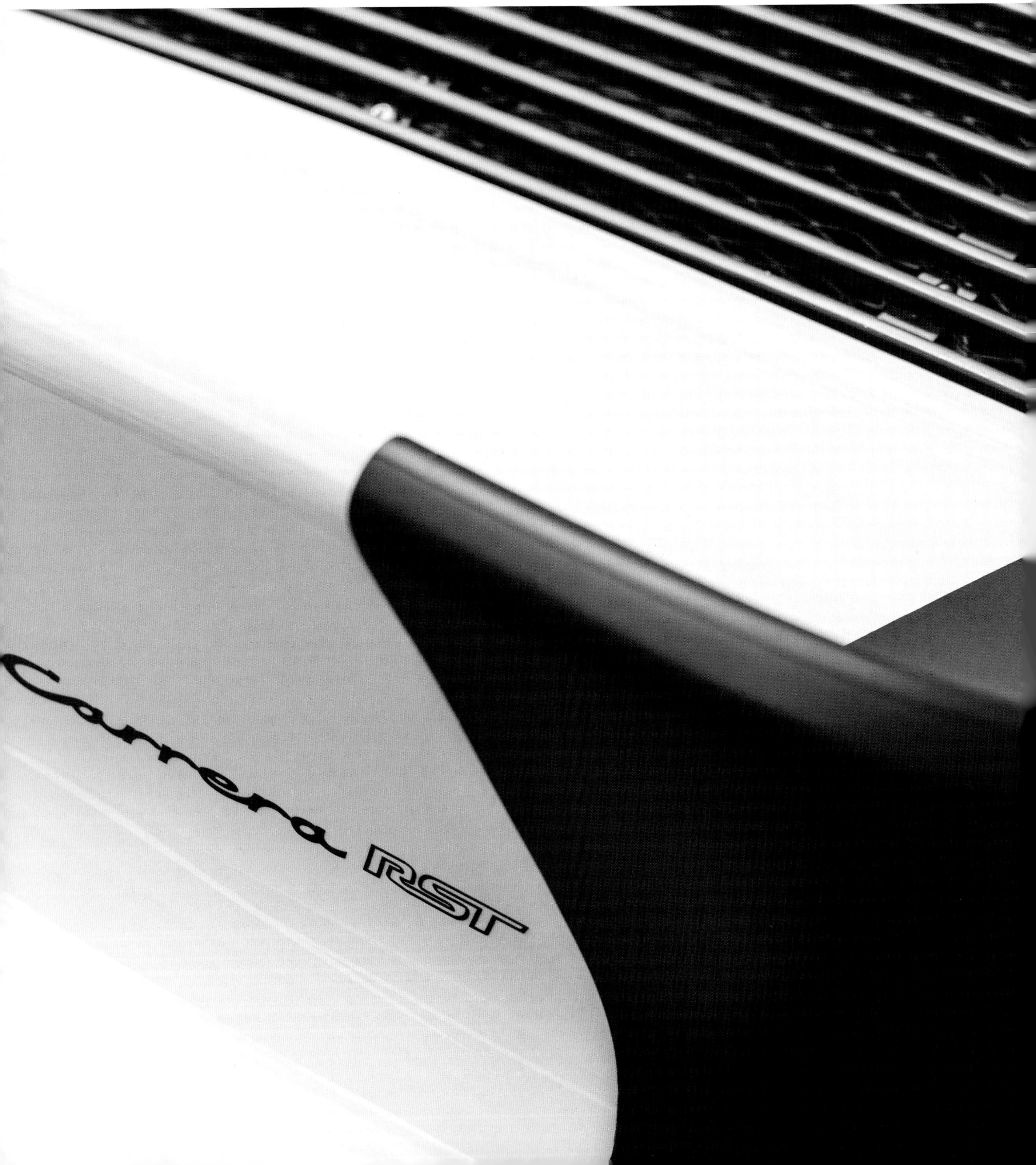
Carrera RST

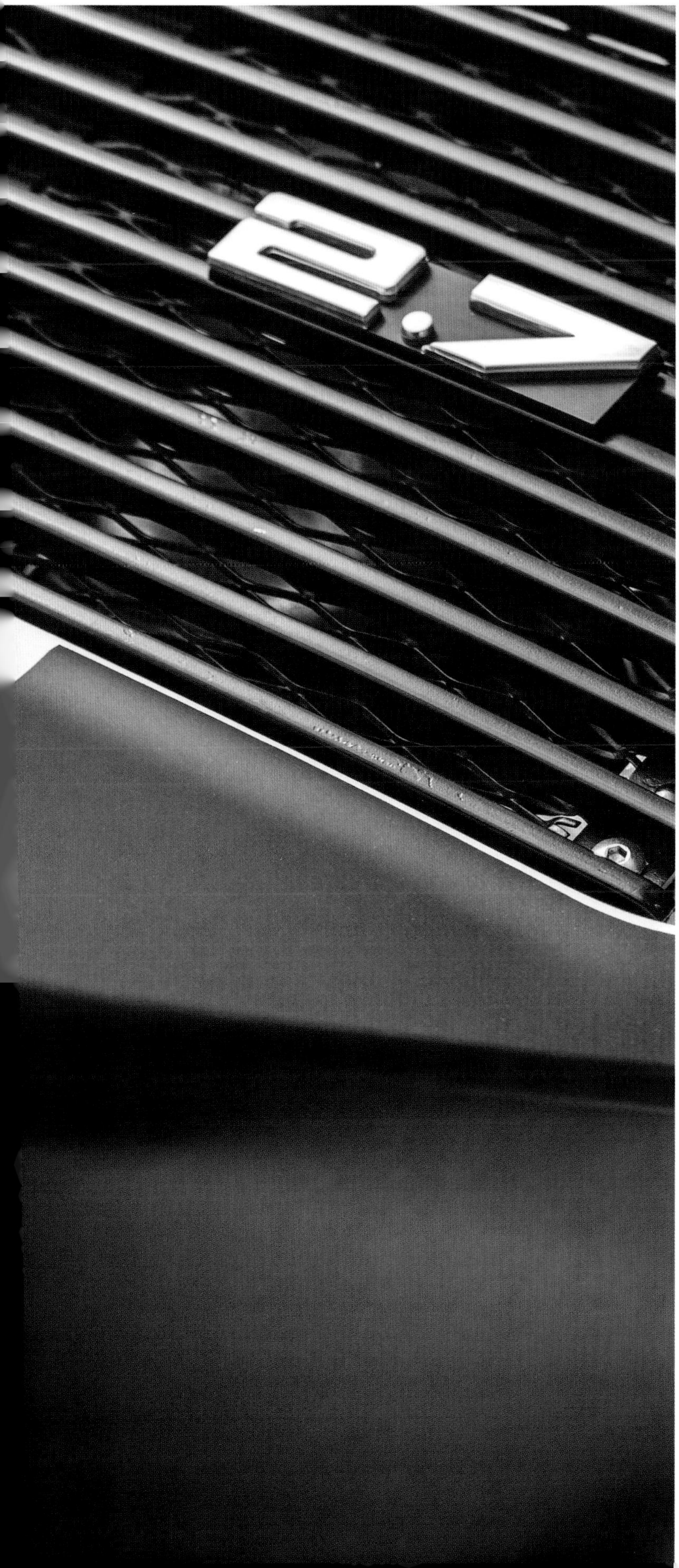

AN ODE TO THE 1973 PORSCHE 911 CARRERA RS 2.7, WITH A "T" FOR TRINIANE.

"The car was lifeless. And we decided to do something about it," explain Jean-Michel and Sylvie in unison. "We wanted to create the car we would hope to find, but that didn't exist," says the latter. "A chic, sporty, elegant Porsche 911, customized to take into account our 45 years of passion and expertise." It is worth noting that Sylvie was already in the game, since she comes from a long line of racing-car enthusiasts. Her grandfather, Raymond Triniane, took over the Moderne garage in Domène, in South-eastern France, in 1964, and handed down his passion for motor racing to his son Alain. After starting out in [Renault] R8 Gordini and other berlinettas in 1968, he began to get interested in Porsches, and in the 1980s he became a specialist in the marque. As for Sylvie, after more than two years spent travelling around the world, she began to support her father managing the company, and joined the garage in 1995. In 2016, Alain suffered a pulmonary embolism and his daughter took over the family business, which she – naturally – renamed Triniane Racing. From upkeep to restoration, she also focuses heavily on racing. Jean-Michel is an engineer at Schneider Electric and has been a massive fan of Porsche from a very young age. In December 2020, they came across just the right model for them to make into the car of their dreams: a 1974 Porsche 2.7 Carrera. It was burgundy in colour and had a roll bar inside, for taking part in historic rallies. The engine had been increased to 2.9, but there were a few parts missing. The owner wanted to get rid of it, so a deal was done. This Porsche was the first one of the G series, with the big bumpers, just after the beautiful F series. "That was my favourite," he says. It was an easy modification to the exterior styling. They then drew inspiration from the famous 1973 2.7 Carrera RS. With its rear spoiler, commonly referred to as the "ducktail", it was the fastest German production car of its time and without a doubt the most famous Porsche in the entire history of the brand. Only 1,590 units of this iconic car – the first to bear the Carrera name – were ever produced. Based on the 2.4 S, it was a playful, light and agile model, thanks to the increased engine capacity and the low weight of only 1,075 kg (2,370 lbs). It was reflection of its carefree, uninhibited era. One of freedom –

TAKE YOUR PLACE BEHIND THE WHEEL OF THIS STYLISH, SPORTY 911.

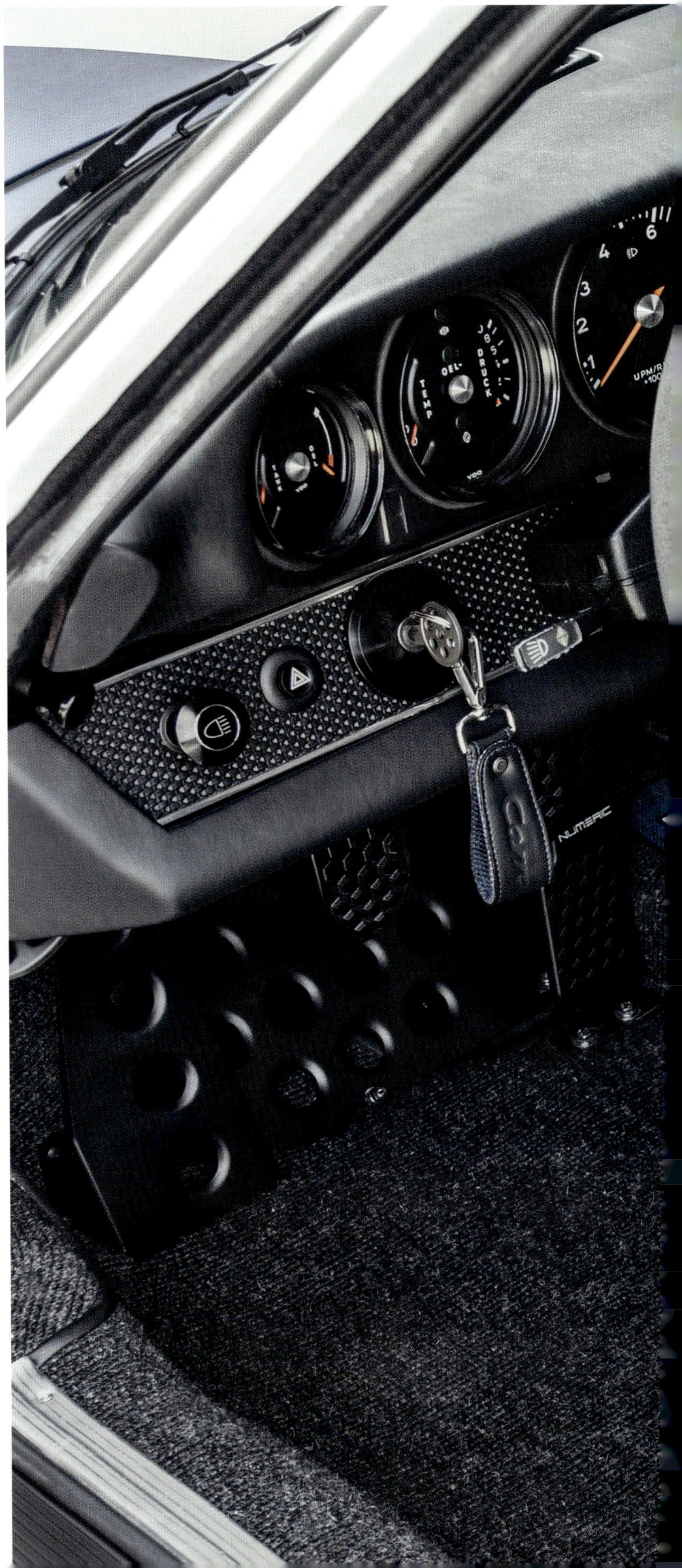

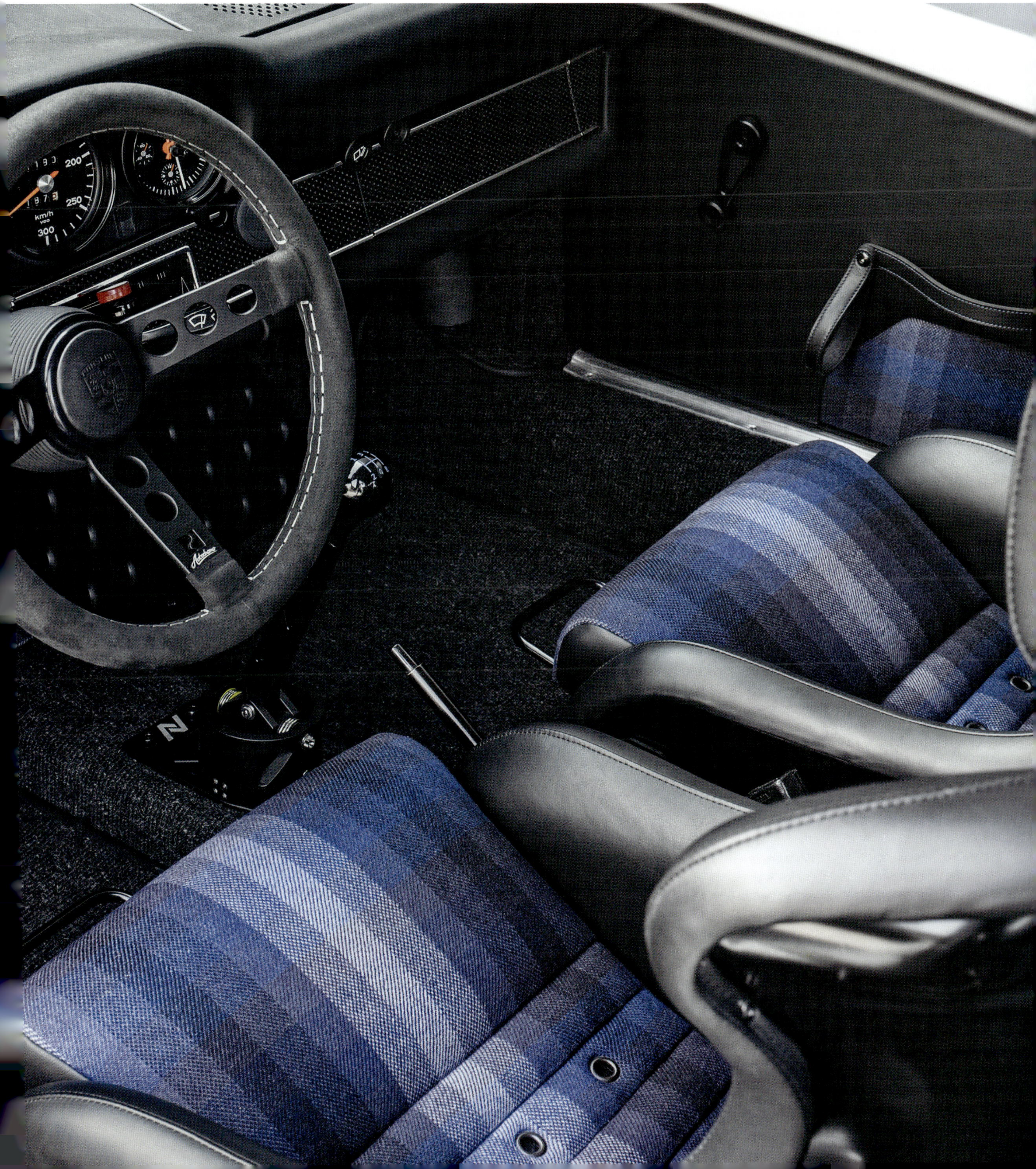
200
250
km/h
VDO
300

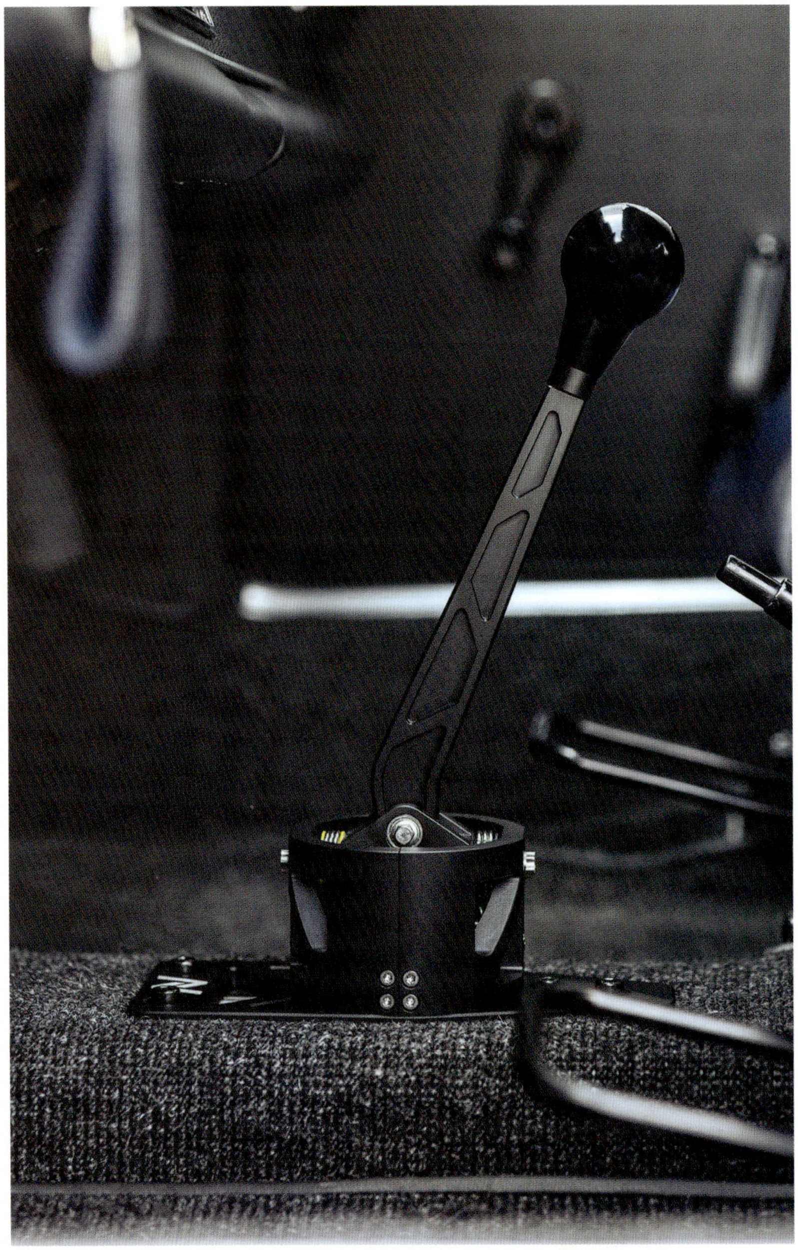

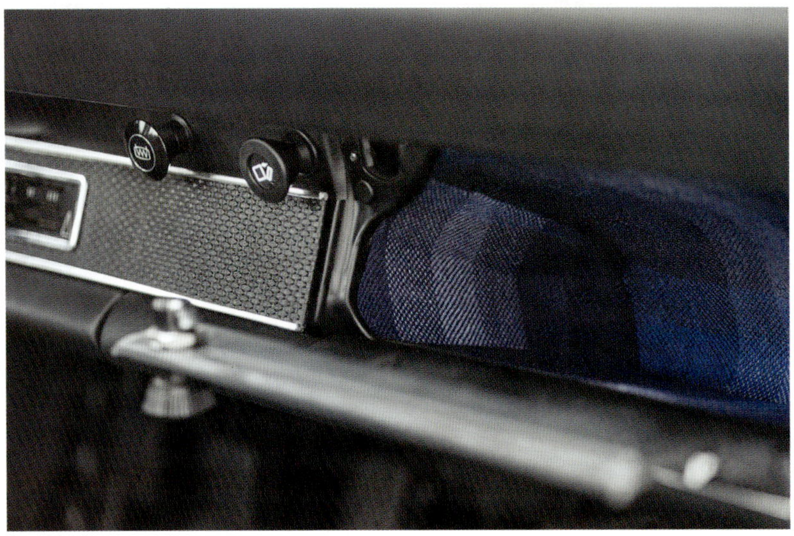

1. This Numeric short-throw shifter controls a type 915 gearbox.

2. The chic fabric in the glove box matches that used in the cabin.

3. The blue fabric is a type of Scottish tartan that was originally used on transaxle Porsches, such as the 944.

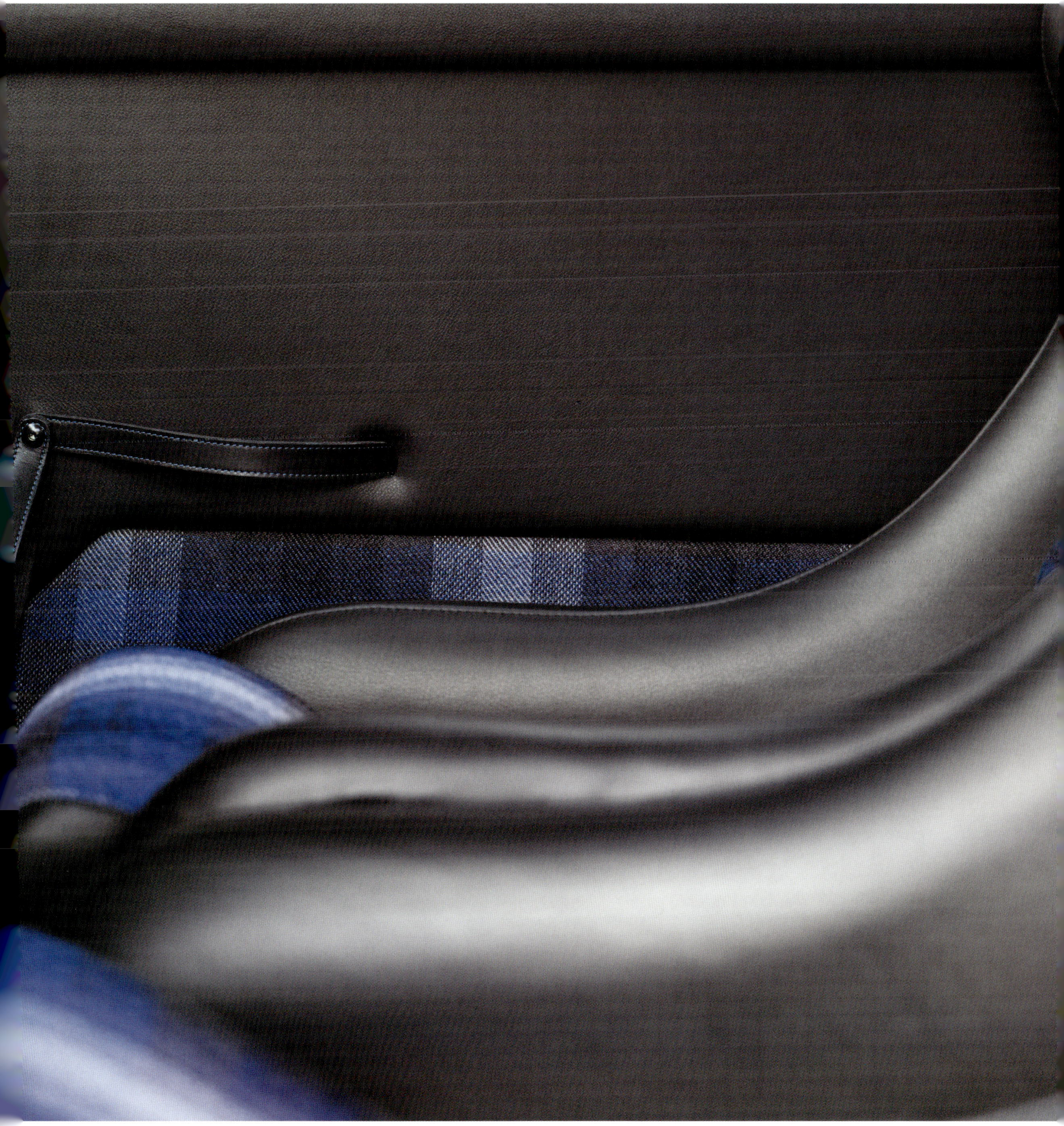

inevitably a word that resonates with Porsche enthusiasts. "To head out for a drive and enjoy the charm of a classic car, but benefiting from very dynamic handling" was the initial idea behind the project. The other was to "recreate the myth with a unique, and different, personalisation". Outlaw, here we come! But it couldn't be done just any old how …

Between June and October 2022, the project took shape, building up to its final phase. "The original paint was Porsche's 'Grand Prix White', and we restored it to its initial colour and added a 2.7 RS body kit. We kept the 2.9-litre engine, as it gives more torque and better roundness. But like the 2.7 RS, it has a smaller crankshaft, which makes for a more powerful engine compared to a 3.0-litre SC, for example." Forged Mahle pistons, 2.7 Carrera RS camshafts, Sachs Sport clutch, a sports exhaust system, 3.2-litre front radiator, high performance ignition coil … There is plenty to tuck into on the refurb menu! The same applies to the running gear, with new torsion bars and Bilstein "1000 Lakes" shock absorbers: "Same as rally Porsches were fitted at the time." The goal was to make a car that looked old but that had the handling of a modern motor. "It's like a skier on a slalom. We wanted our 911 to zip through the bends like they do through the gates – with precise, efficient handling. Our experience with racing cars, Porsche in particular, means we can tune motors to perfection, so they perform flawlessly."

THE ATTENTION TO DETAIL MATCHES THE CAR'S PERFORMANCE.

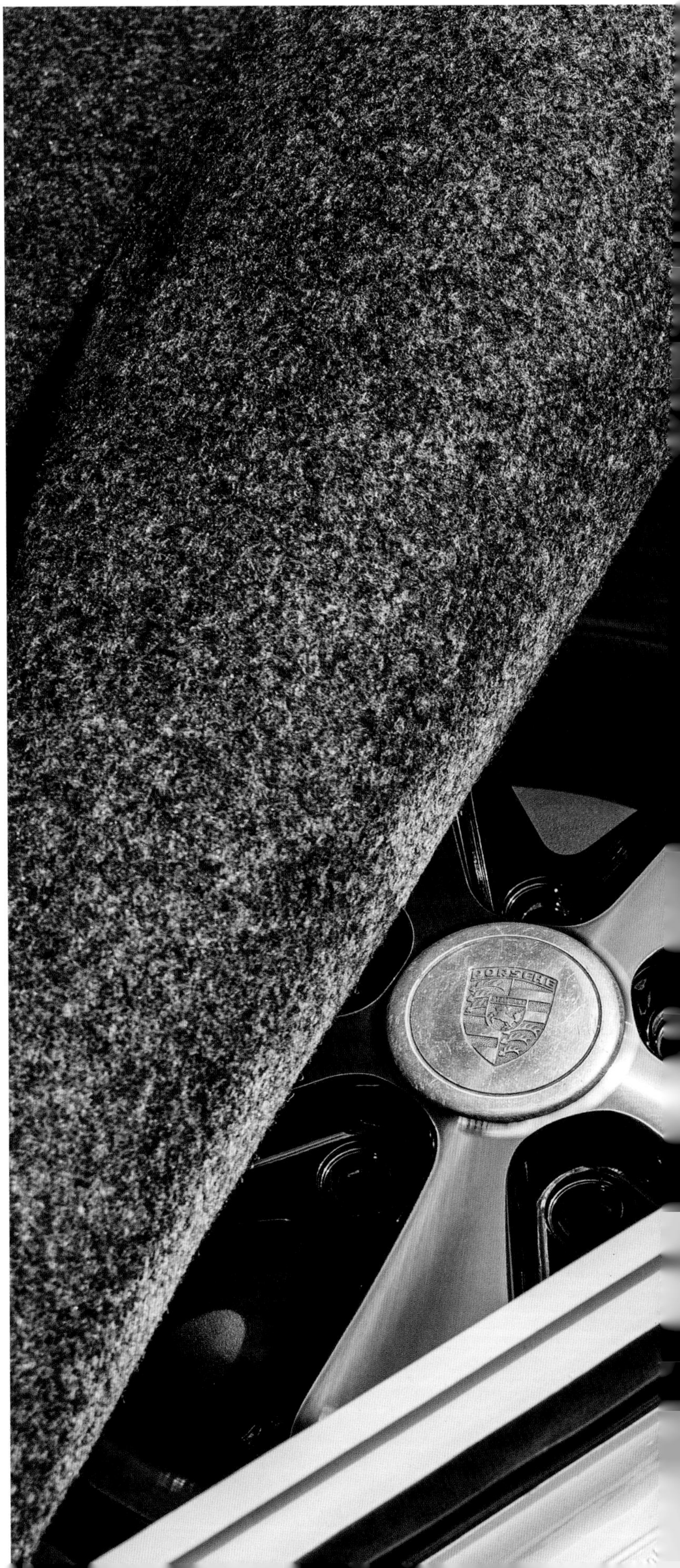

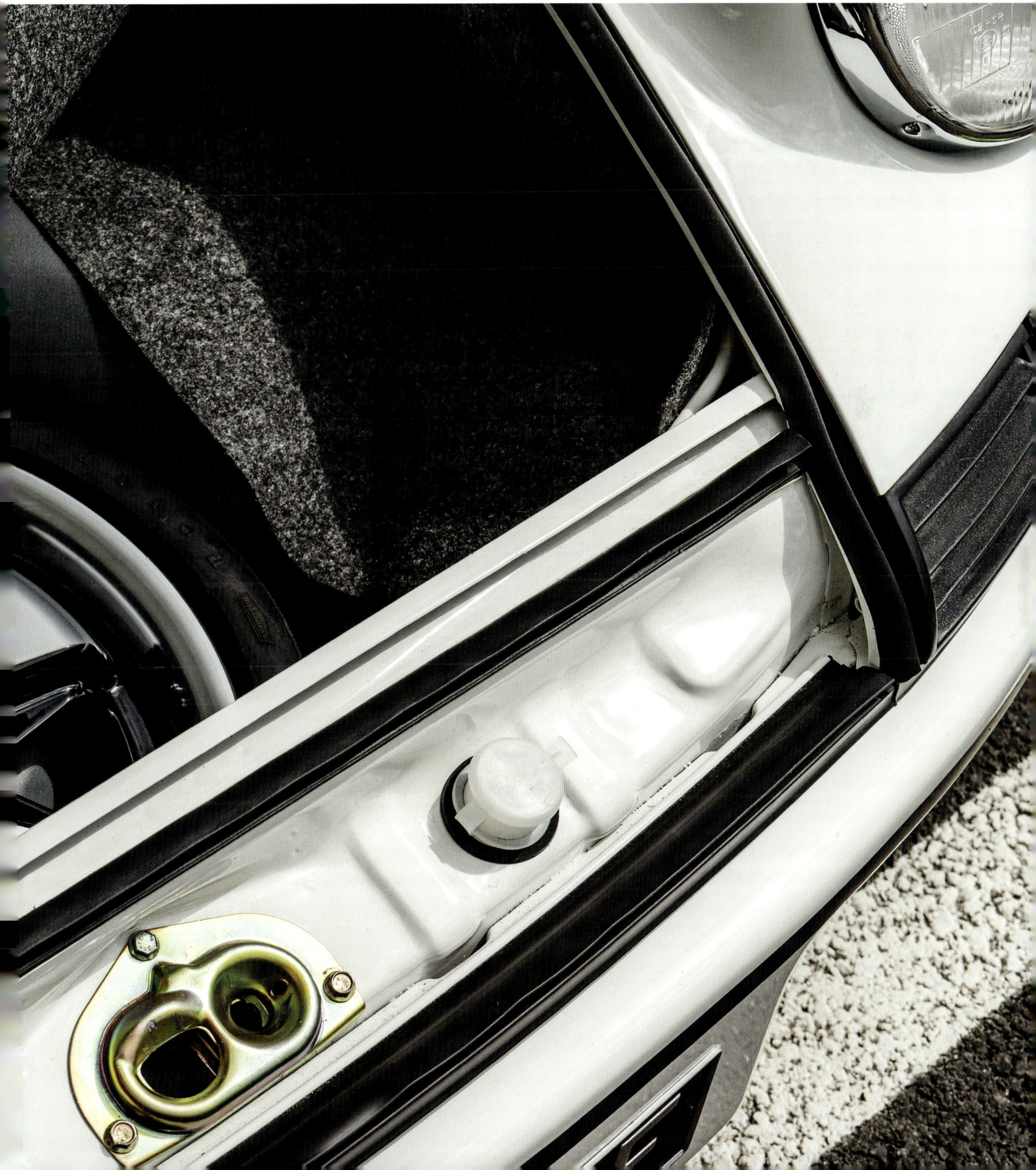

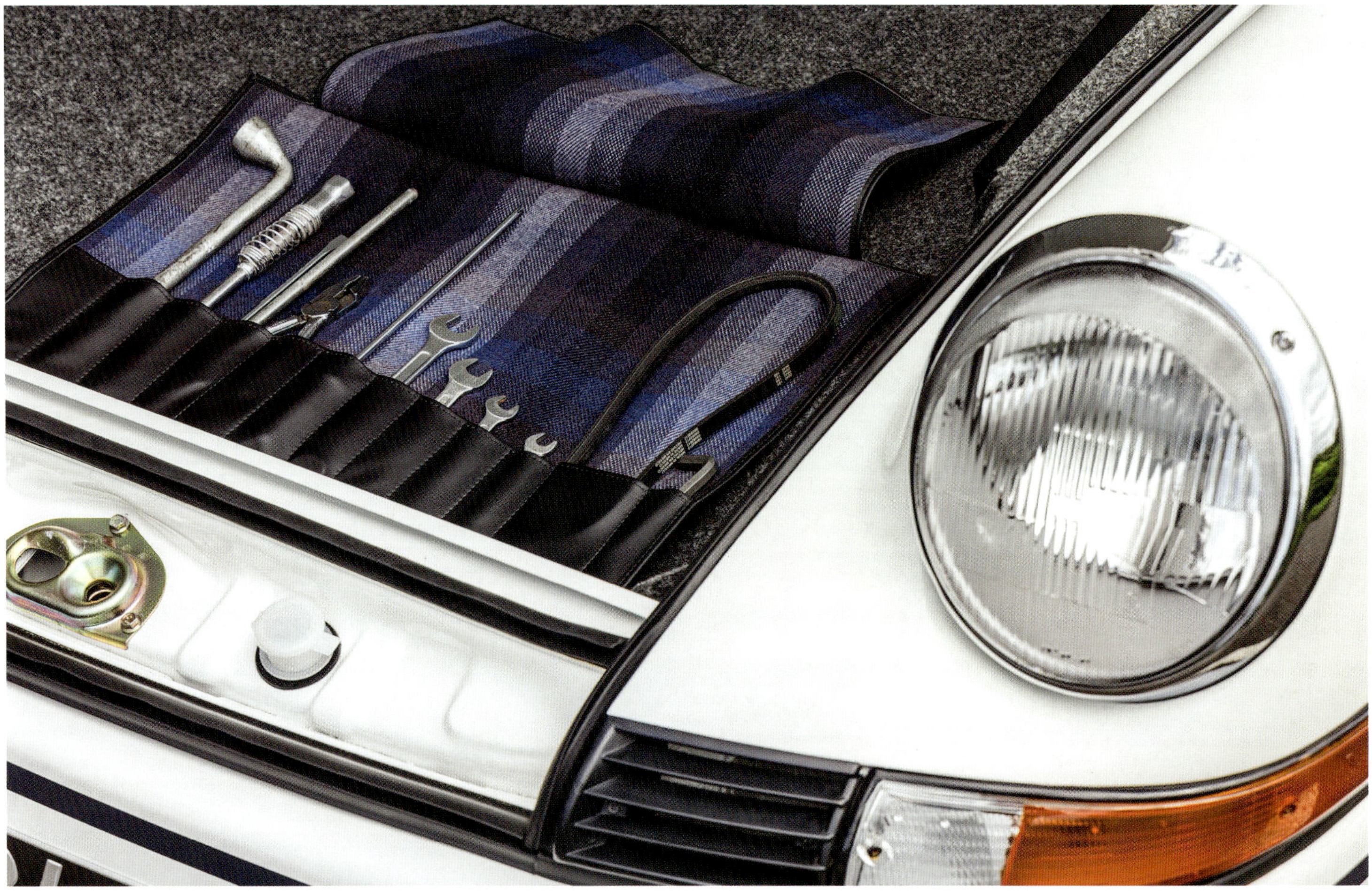

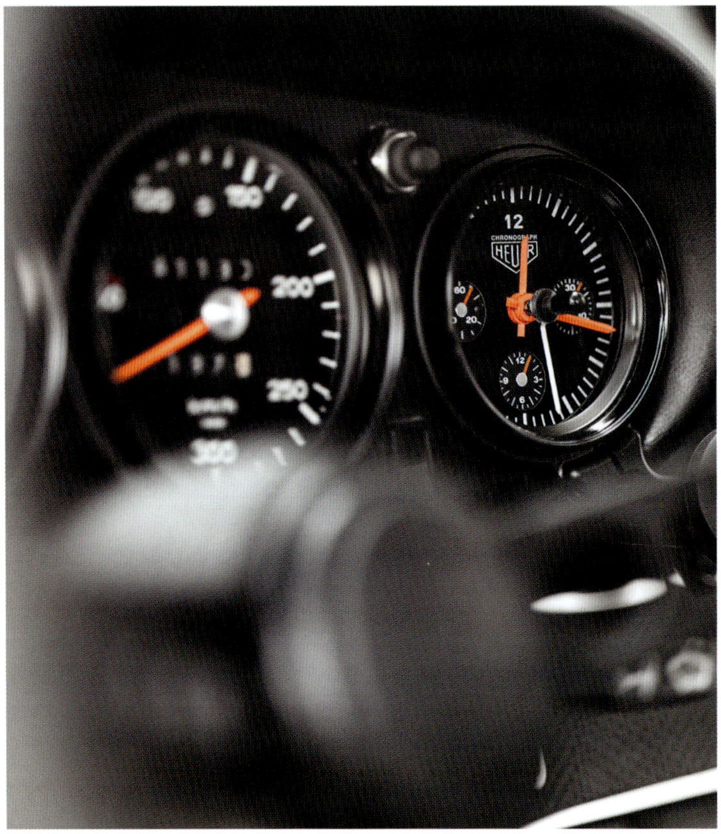
12
CHRONOGRAPH
HEUER

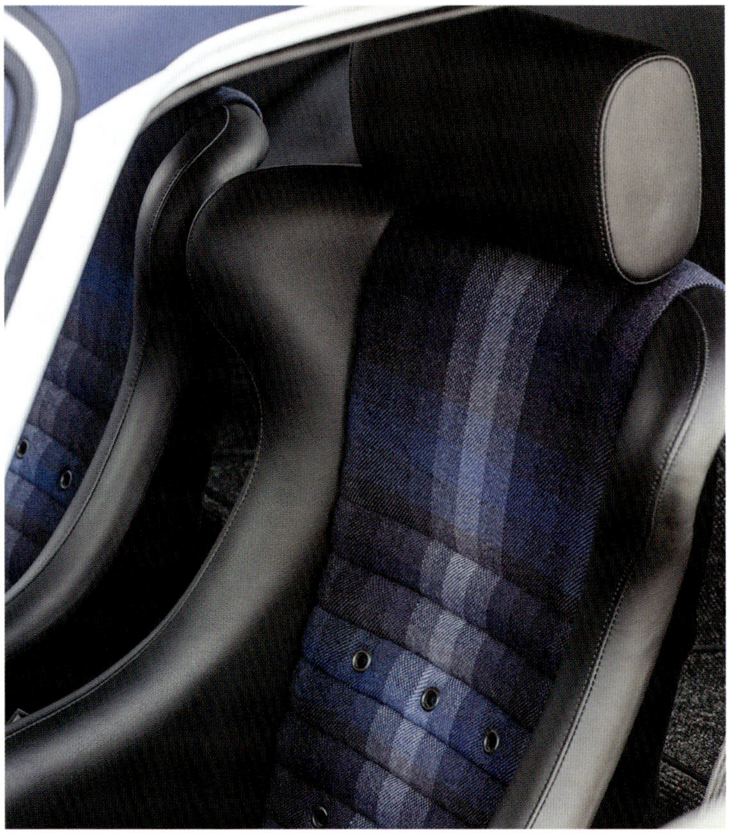

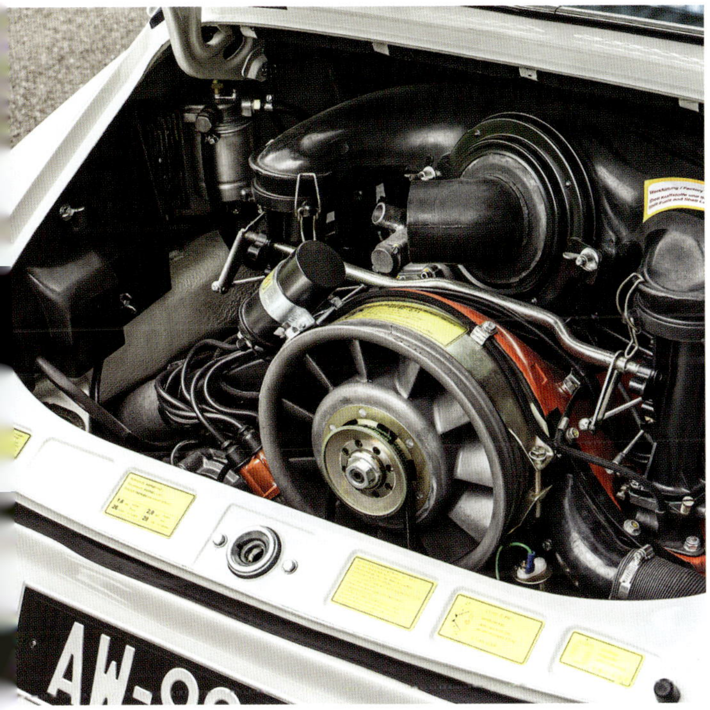

In terms of aesthetics, Sylvie and Jean-Michel opted for a design that set the car apart, while retaining the chic look of the bodywork: "It was Jean-Michel who had the idea for the two matte navy blue stripes painted on each side of the hood, running across the roof down to the spoiler. I gave it the green light!" The interior is minimalist, but stylish and comfortable. On the beautiful Singer-style bucket seats, a blue gradient fabric surrounds stainless steel circles. The soundproofing was retained, behind an elegant navy blue double carpet. Custom-made pedals and black anodised, perforated footrests for driver and passenger, adapted Autodromo steering wheel, custom-made dashboard with a 10,000 rpm rev counter and a speedo with 300 km/h (186 mph) at the end: the interior matches the car's sporty, tasteful exterior. The 911 RST is very much a joint achievement. It oozes character in every detail and weighs just 950 kg (2,094 lbs). It provides just the same driving pleasure that cars did back in the old days. And the bad-boy image is complemented by the performance of a well-tuned car that gives a precise, confident driving experience, all with the charm of a classic-era vehicle. Driving this 2.7 RST embodies a true spirit of freedom. And that, for us, makes it a real Outlaw!

911 2.7 RST BY THE NUMBERS

CREATION **1974**

FLAT CYLINDERS **6**

CC **2,900**

HP **240**

1. Everything has been designed so you can carry out repairs, with elegance and refinement.

2. This superb Tag Heuer chronograph is a fitting replacement for the original dial.

3. The beautiful bucket seats are inspired by American Singer models.

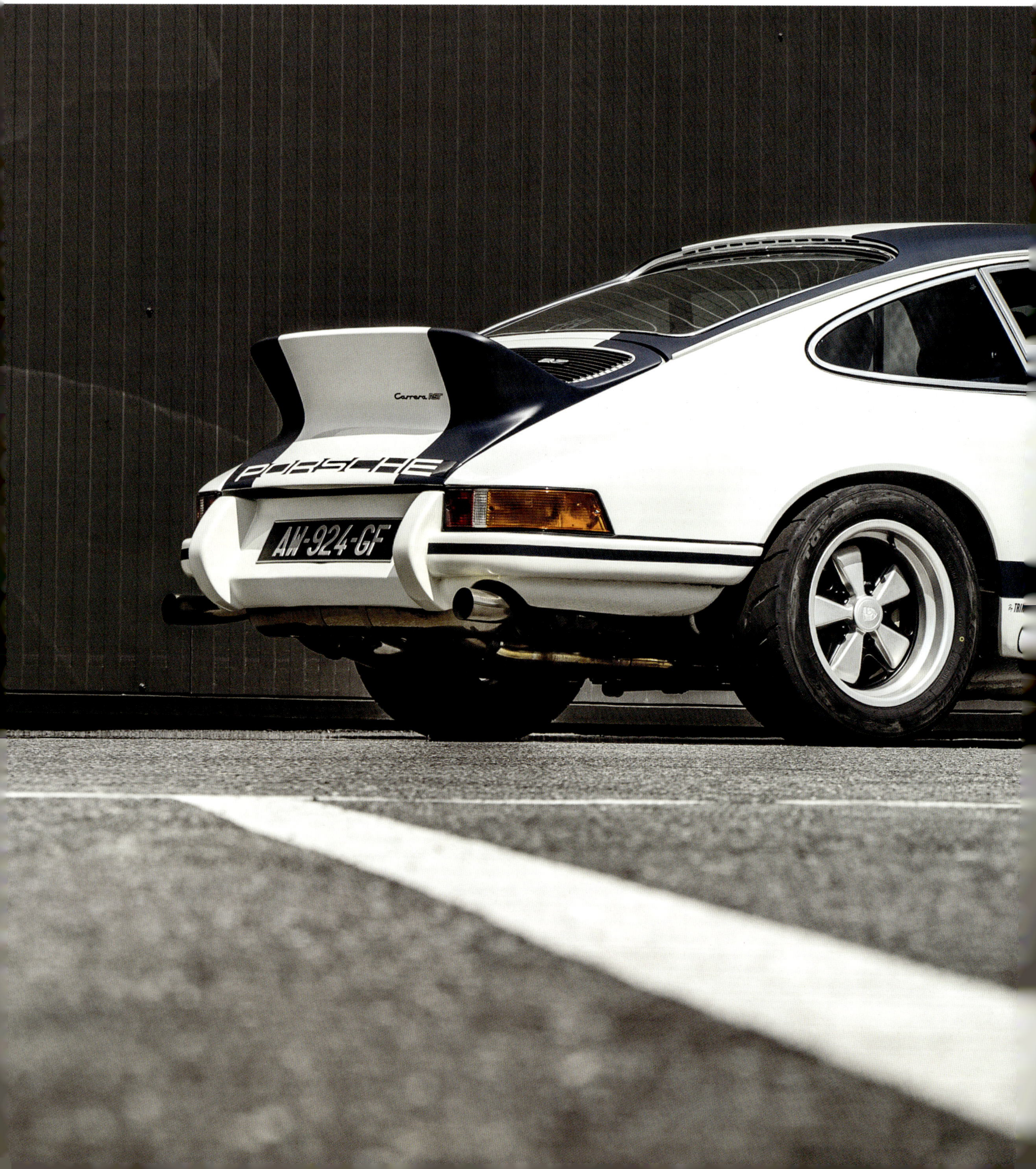
PORSCHE
AW-924-GF

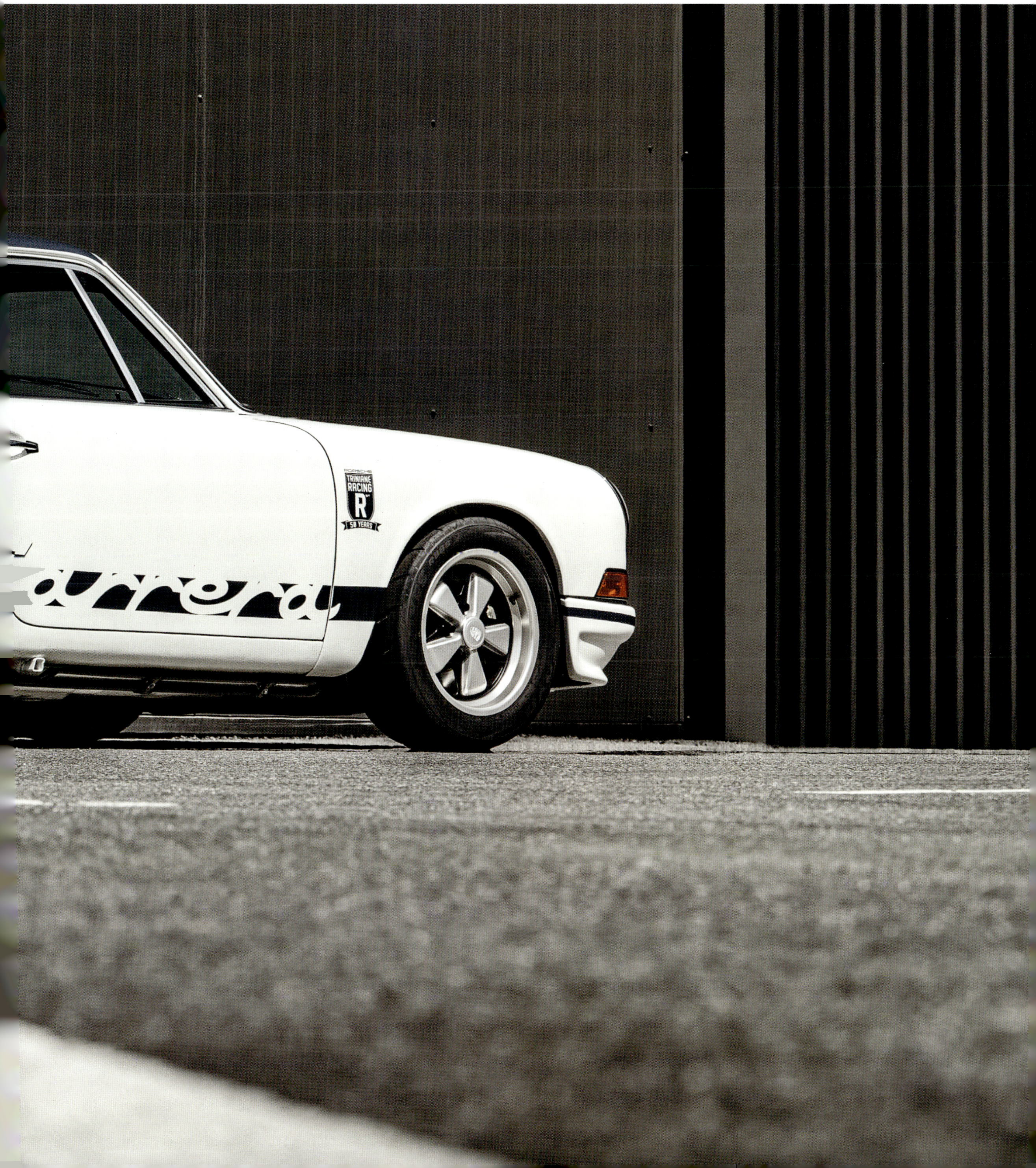

911 VOID BLACK GOLD

Interior frescoes evoke a black hole in which the driver is lost in the thrill of an extreme driving sensation. Enter the void!

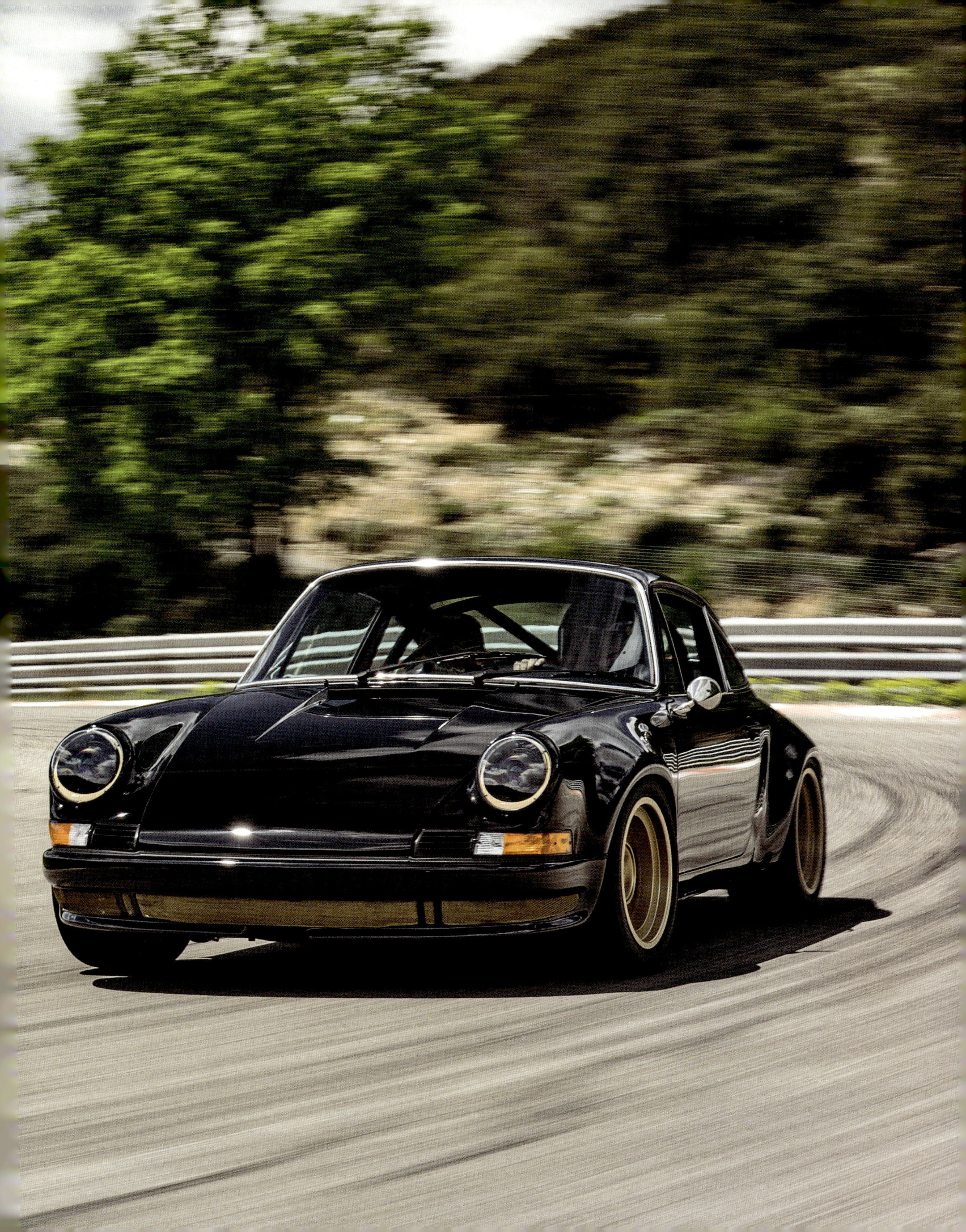

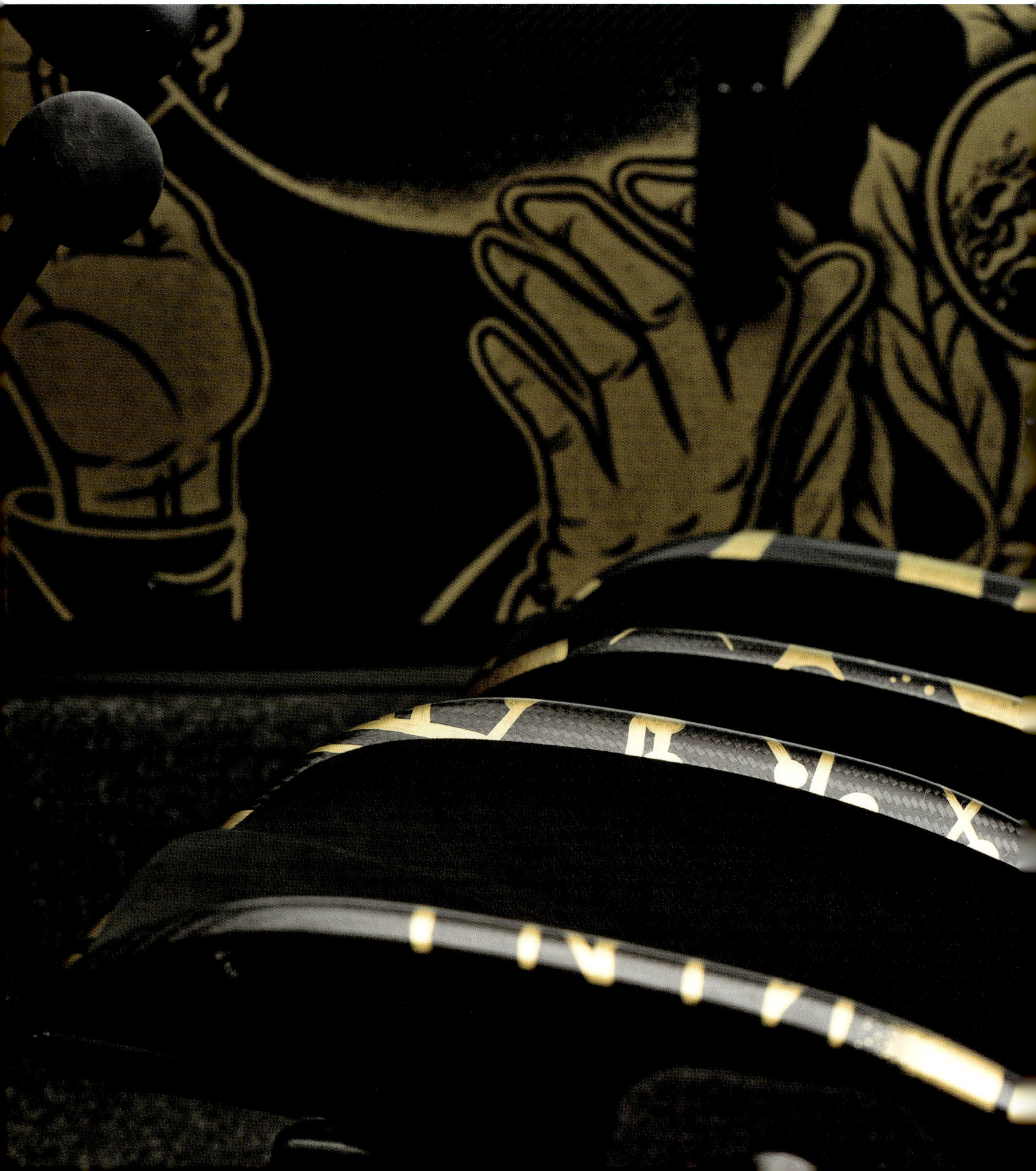

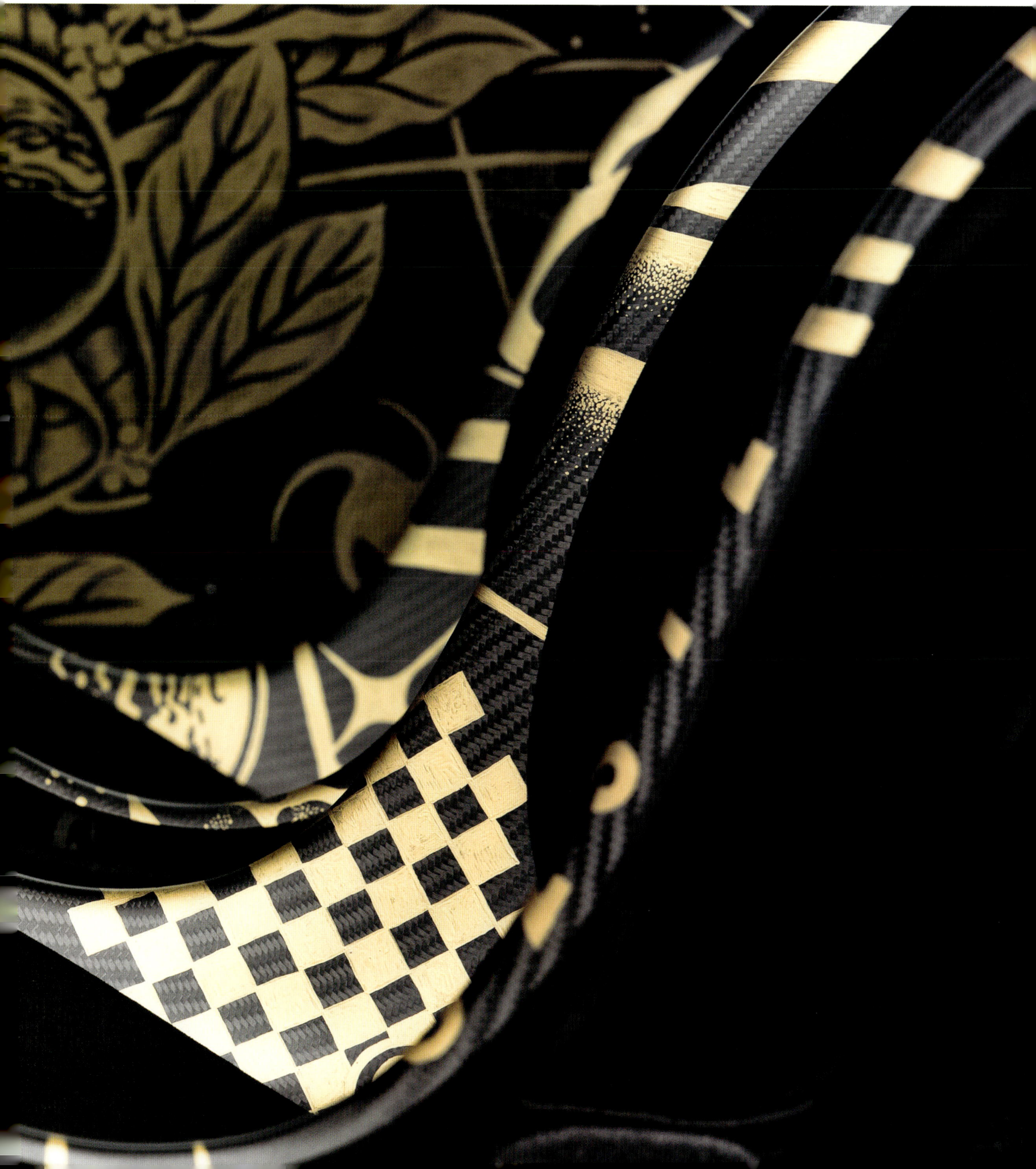

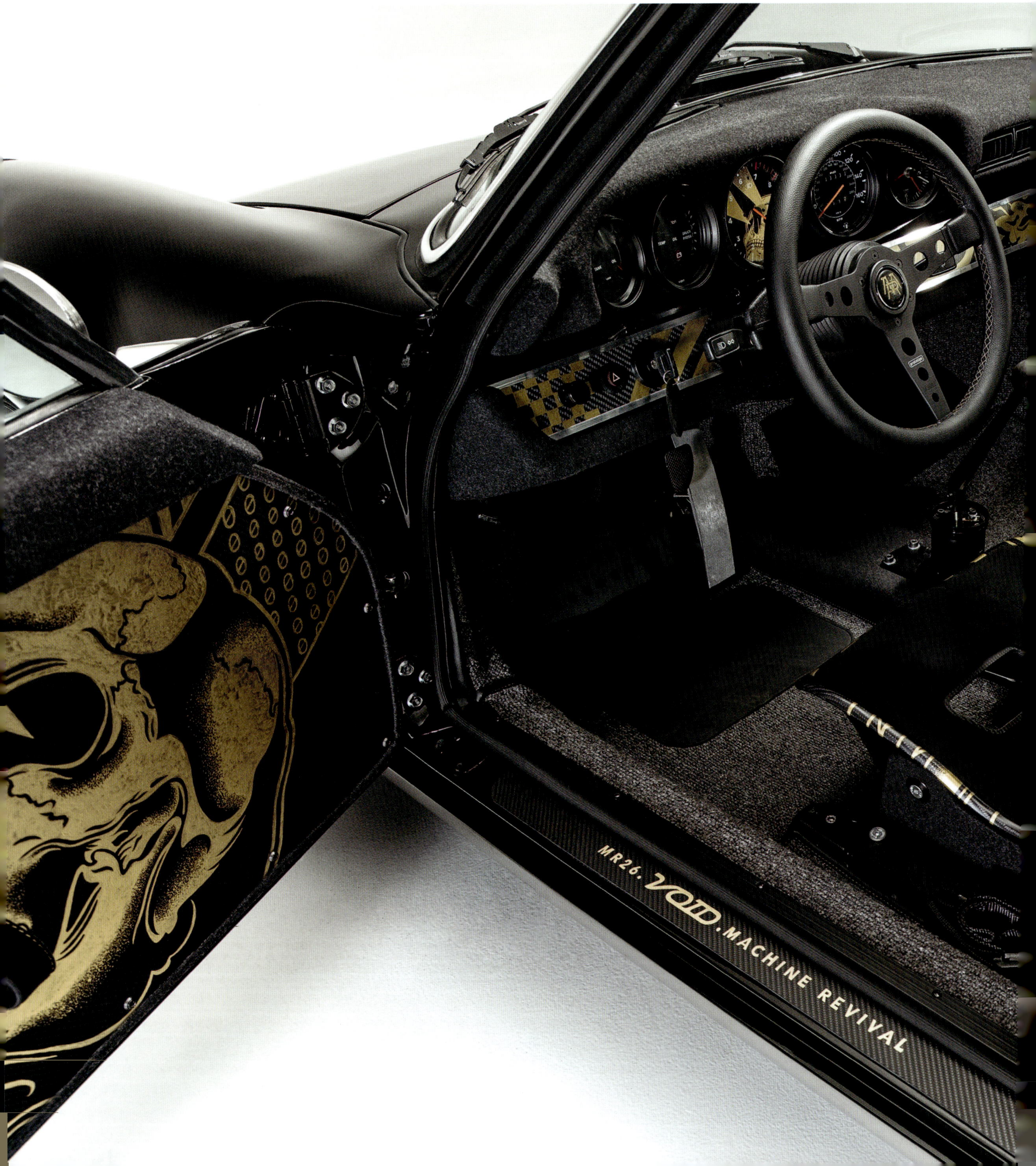
MR26. VOID. MACHINE REVIVAL

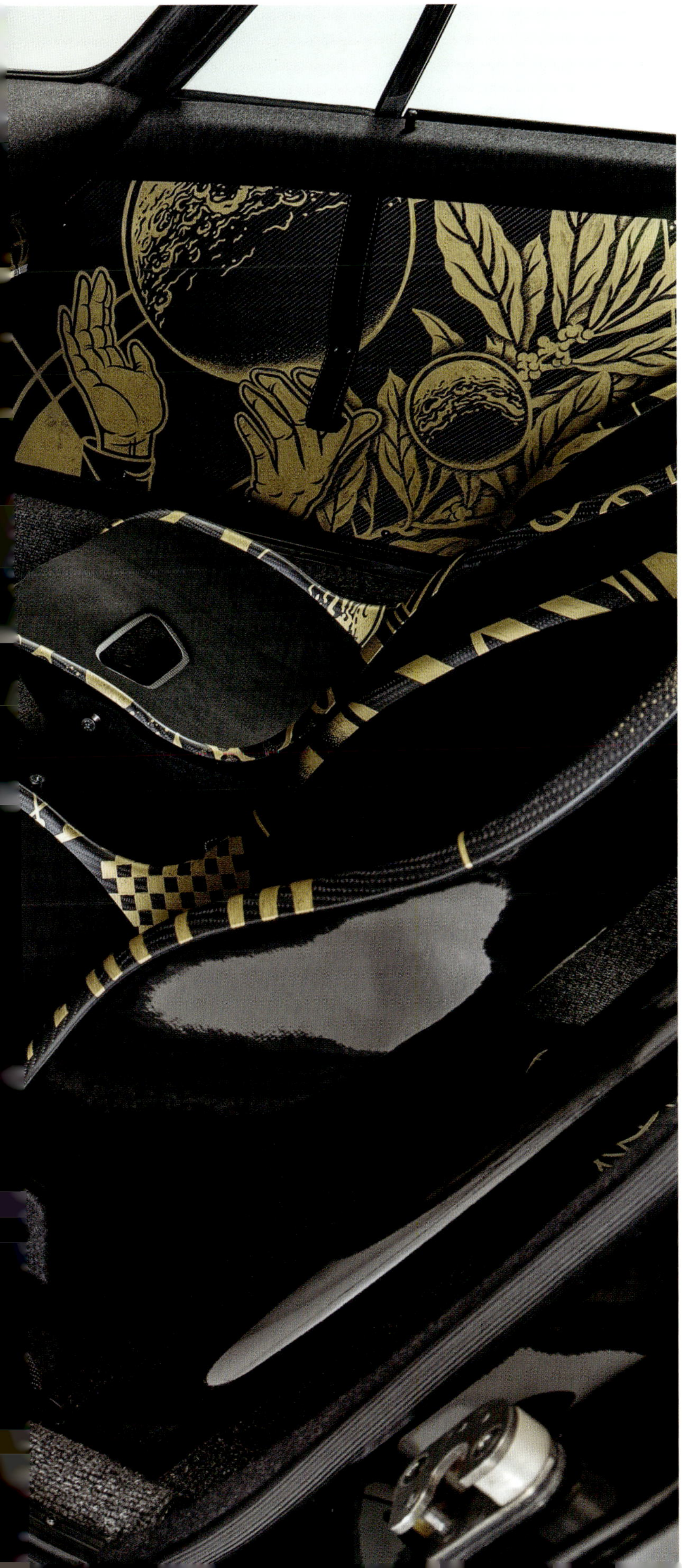

THE 911 VOID WAS BORN ON A PSYCHEDELIC MOOD BOARD.

The idea came from a theme. The vision was that of a black hole. No colour, no texture: everything blending into the universe and the deep darkness of space. "Void" means emptiness, nothingness. This Porsche could get lost in the dominant, dark environment and attain a sense of infinite purity. "That's where we were coming from in the creation of this 911. We came up with lots of ideas, pictures, materials, parts, and we put them all on a mood board," explains Nicolas Quiles, the boss of Machine Revival. "It was a kind of multi-faceted, varied board that combines all our inspiration behind the design of this creation. For us, this is an extremely important phase of intellectual stimulation." The design work is carried out in close collaboration with team members of various skill sets. "I work with Baptiste, our stylist, and Étienne, our designer. Strictly speaking he's not really a car lover, but he is passionate about what we create. His designs drew inspiration from distant worlds, which helped us to break away from the conventions of classic car design to create something truly different." For Void, the idea was to go for something really refined, very minimalist, based on black and gold. The visual theme of the interior is completely disconnected from the world of cars. "Étienne created a drawing board that showed the black hole sucking in elements, but in a totally psychedelic way. And that is what you see on the car's doors and seats. We drew on the visual language of the universe, the blend of absolute black and anthracite to evoke the mineral quality of planets, accented by touches of gold that illustrate the light of the stars in the galaxy." It is a way of conceiving automobile projects, together and without limits. "That is what I really like about this job," says Nicolas. "There is what we say about the car, but also our tortured-artist side that breathes life into projects such as this one."

But once the style has been defined, the idea must also work to make a car that is aesthetically consistent and balanced. "Once the theme was developed, we moved on to the car's set-up - to make sure it aligned with our universe. When a client comes to us with their own car, we first discuss the technical aspects before thinking about an aesthetic with its own specific rules, to come up with a coherent project. Void was an in-house project that allowed us to showcase our expertise. So we apply our creative process

IN THE PORSCHE GALAXY, THIS 911 REPRESENTS DARK MATTER.

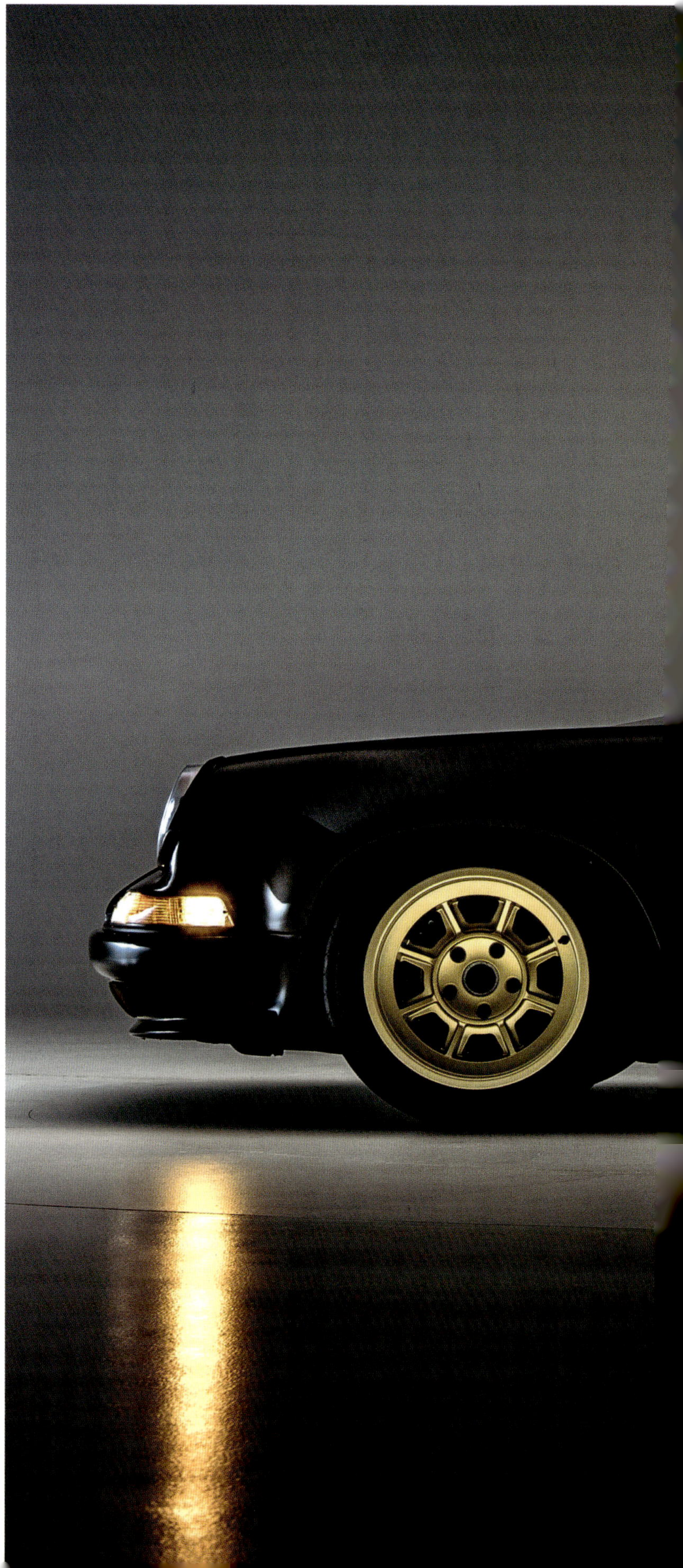

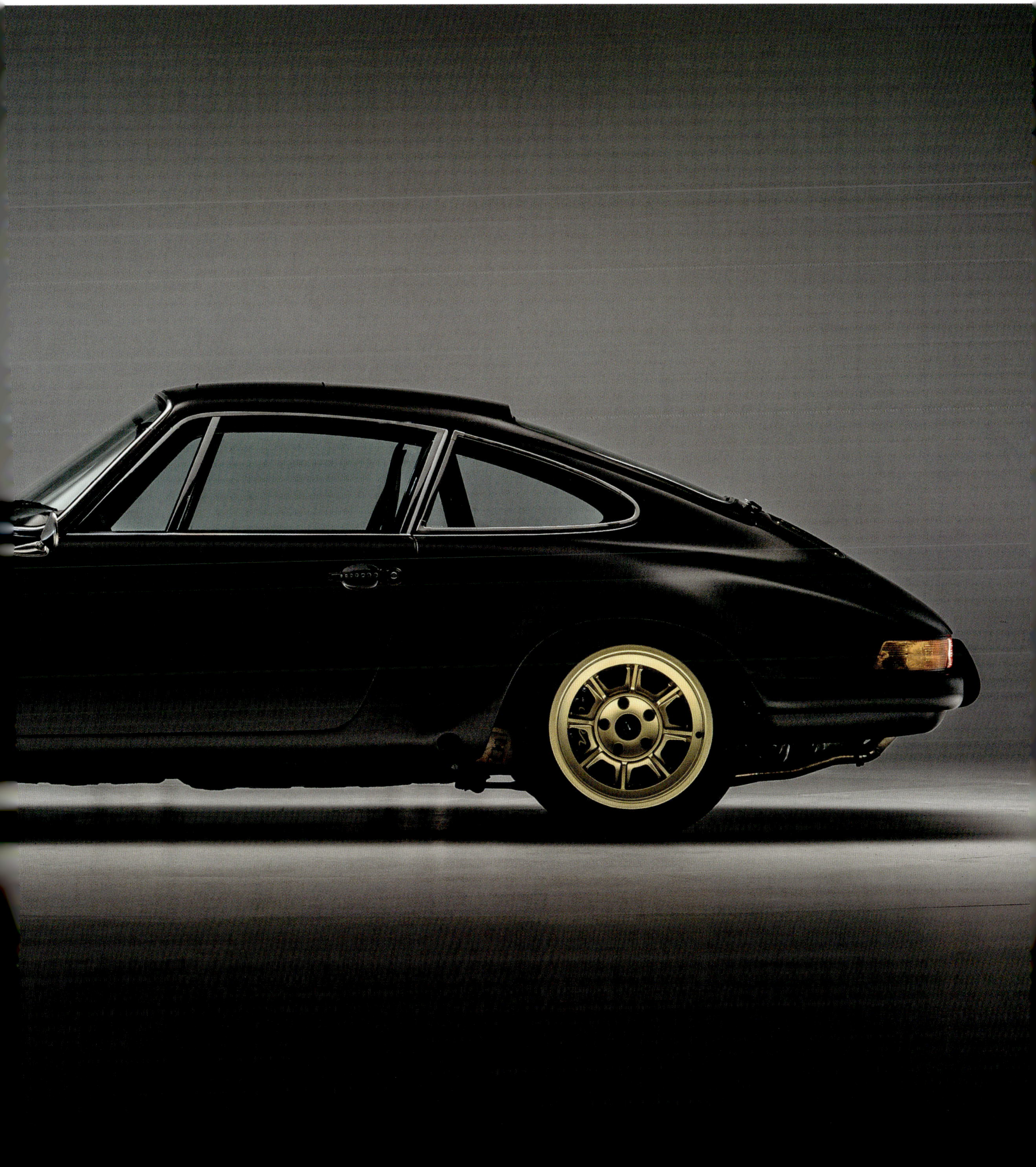

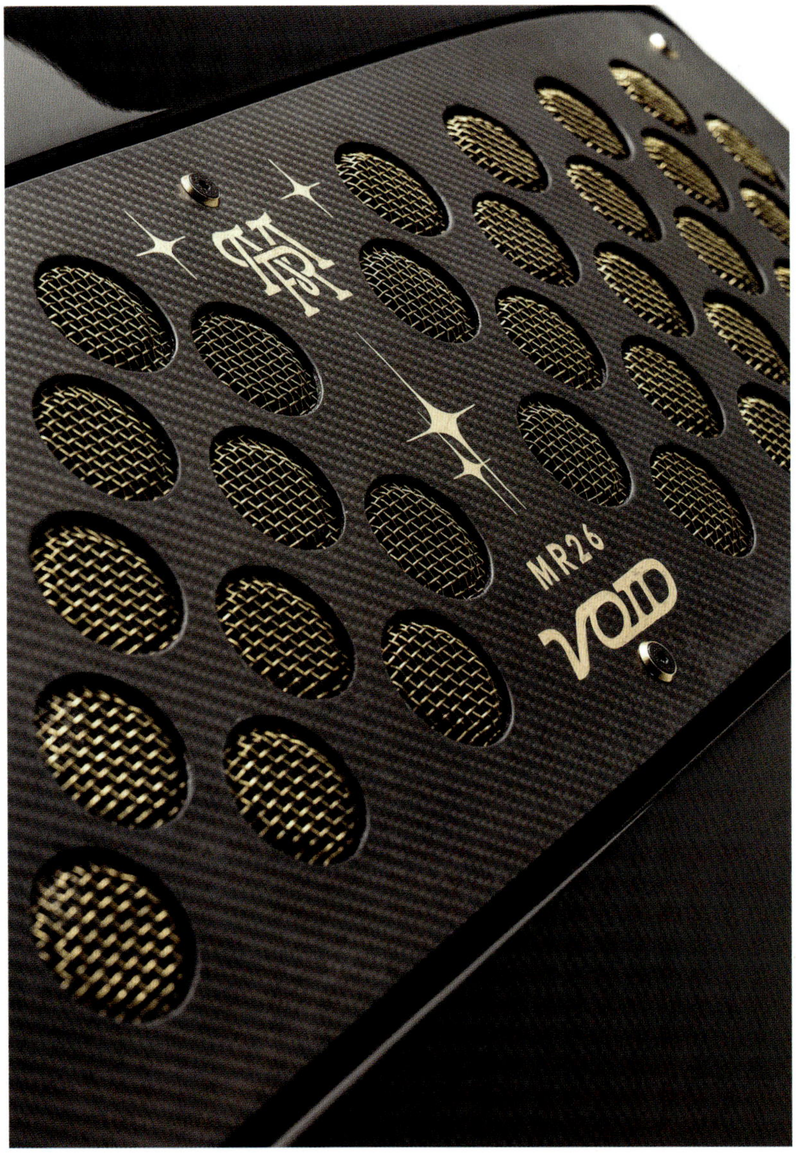

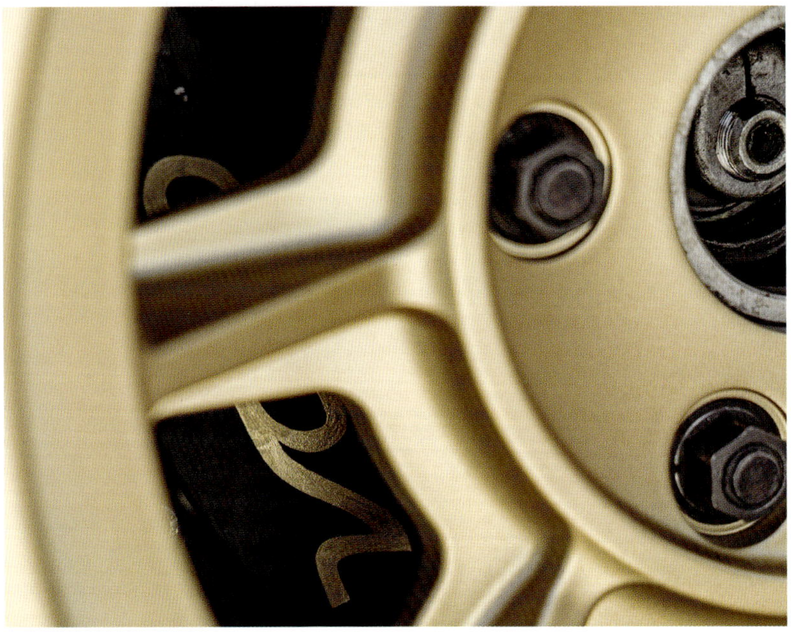

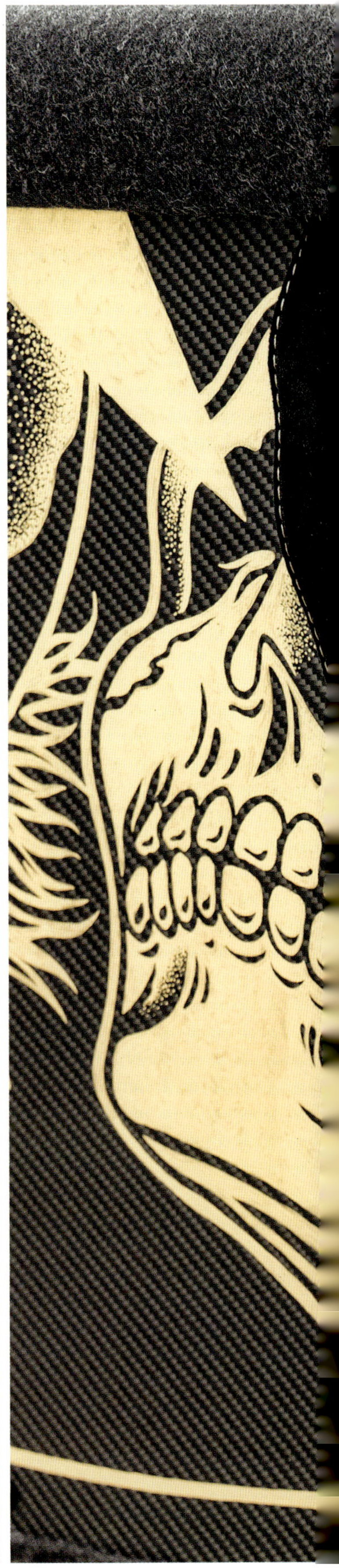

1. The perforated plate is like a kind of soundboard for the mechanics.

2. Campagnolo rims bring a raw edge to Void's design.

3. Inside the doors, infernal motifs complement the understated elegance.

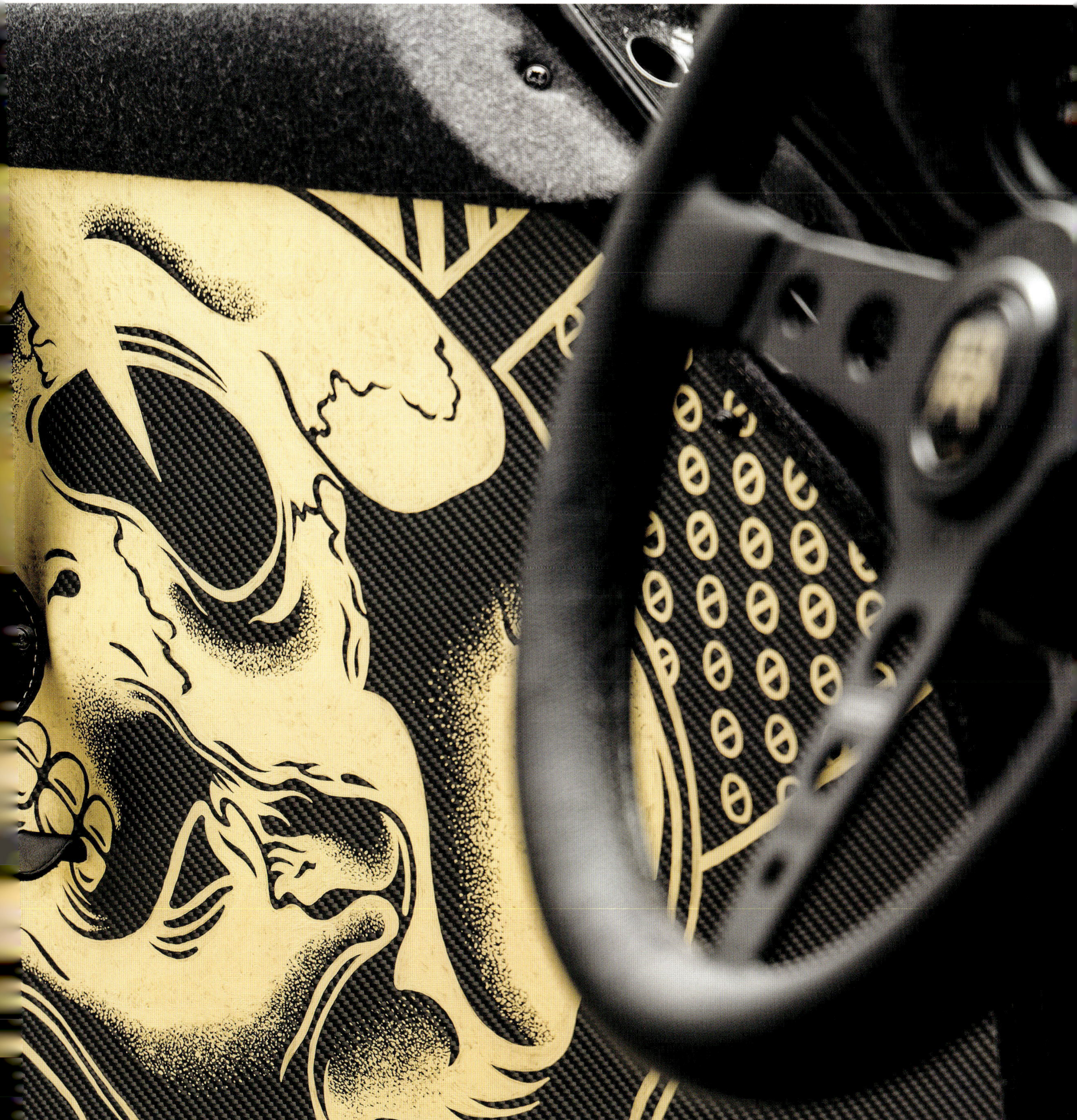

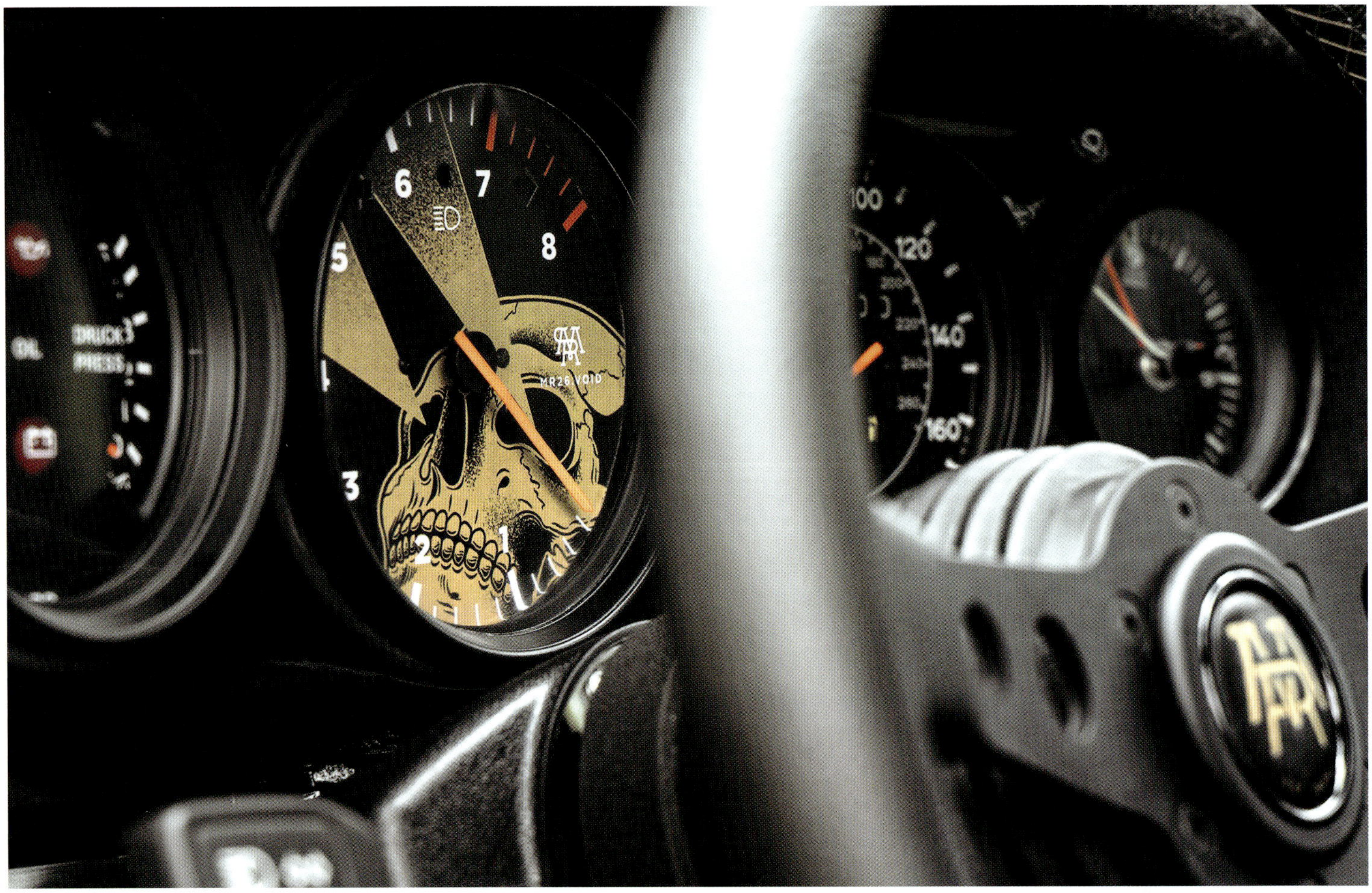
OIL
DRUCK
PRESS
MR26 VOID

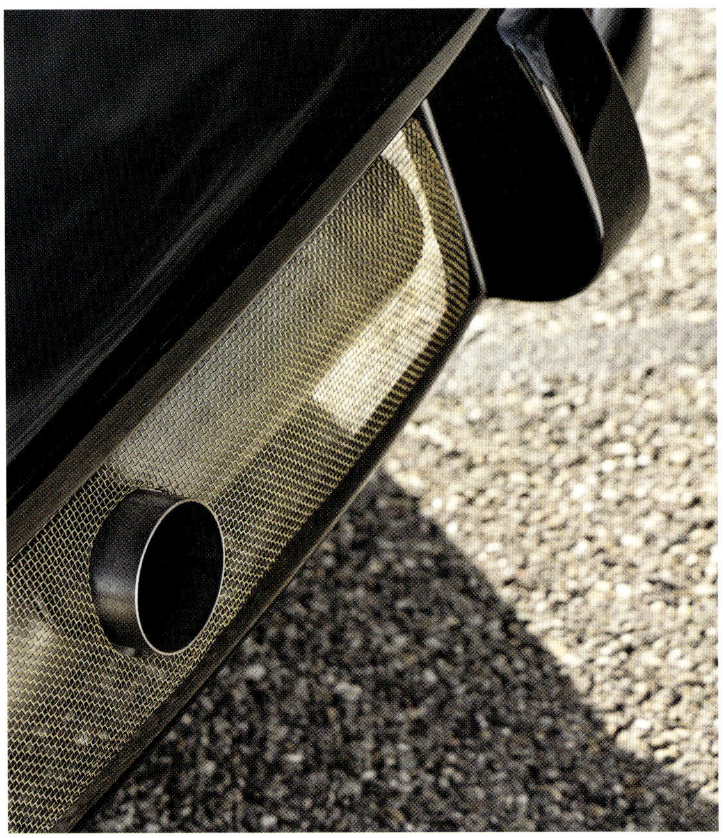

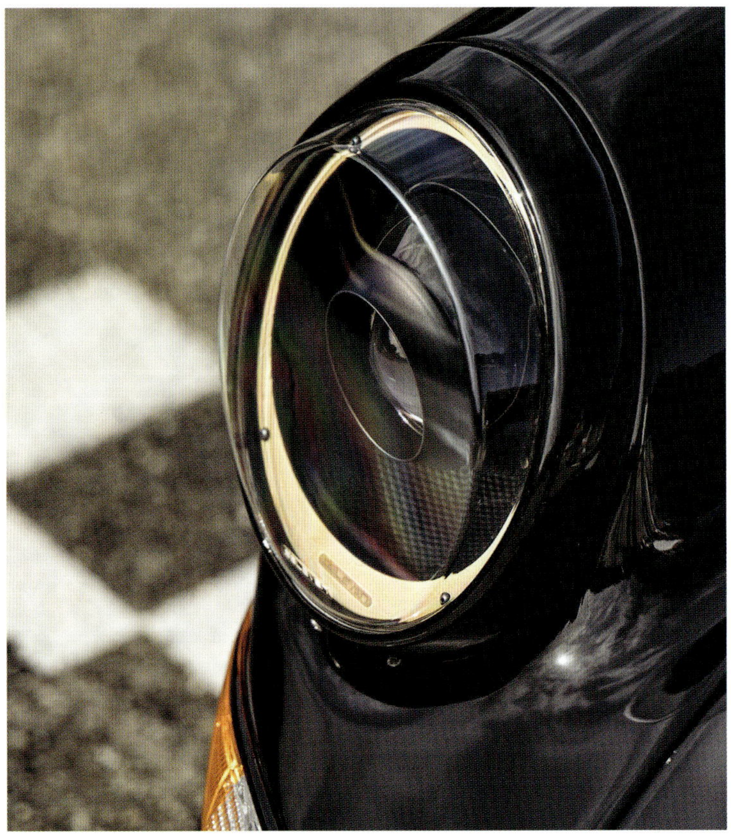

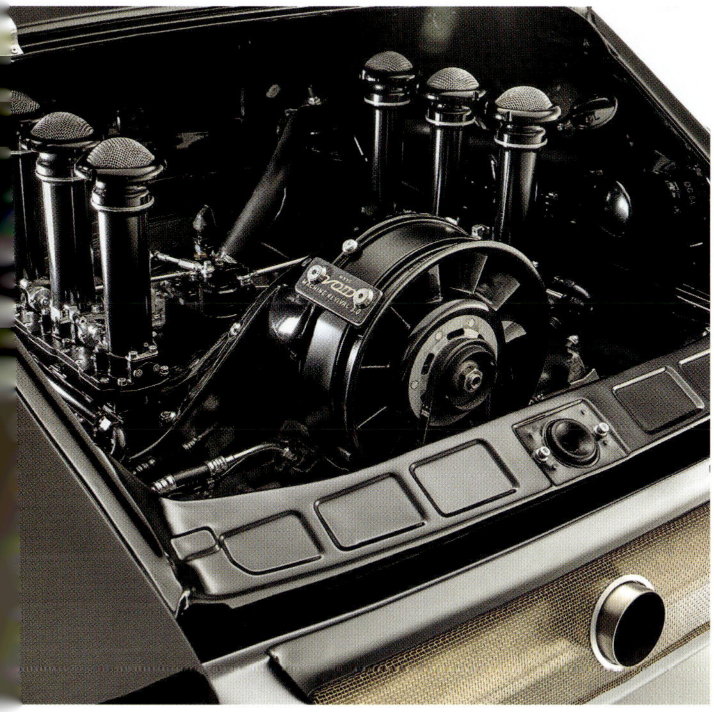

911 VOID
BY THE NUMBERS

CREATION 1982

FLAT CYLINDERS 6

CC 3,000

HP 297

in reverse. The end result is the same, but we don't really integrate all the elements at the same time. This flexibility gives us an even greater amount of artistic freedom on our projects." To match the initial concept of Void – a black hole – they had to figure out how technology could reflect the idea: "It had to be like a moment frozen in time behind the wheel of the car, when you are cut off from time, without any frame of reference – like being in space. We wanted it to be that when you get into the car time becomes irrelevant and you just concentrate on the sensation of driving." That first consideration focuses on the heart of this 911: the engine. "We didn't want a massive engine with staggering stats. Instead, we concentrated on the thing we felt was important: a sharp flat-six, where you can feel the raw mechanics. To get closer to the theme, we chose the engine that was the answer to all our dreams, from a 911 RSR. It is an engine with reasonable displacement but which revs very high, with plenty of mid-range torque and a sound that is utterly intoxicating. So we opted for a 3.0-litre engine that puts out nearly 300 hp in a car that comes in under a tonne, weighing 937 kg (2,066 lbs)." To achieve this power-to-weight ratio, all the 911's wings, bumpers and front and rear hoods are made of carbon Kevlar, but the initial shell remained unchanged. "We wanted a high-performance car that was capable of a fast time on the track, but that could also be used on the road, hence the half cage." Inside, the quest to shed every unnecessary pound continued the theme of absolute emptiness, but without compromising the extreme refinement of Machine Revival's hand-stitching. "We sought to optimize everything without falling into an obsessive pursuit of weight reduction. "The crucial element that we really focussed our efforts on was the seats: they each weigh 6 kg (13 lbs) instead of 25 kg (55 lbs). The goal was to make a car that is pleasant to drive, but still powerful and lightweight."

1 | 2 | 3

1. At the heart of the tachometer, psychedelic artwork registers the rising revs.

2. The exhaust is an aesthetic statement and emits a sound to shake the senses.

3. LED lighting brings the modernity needed for the contemporary use of this 911.

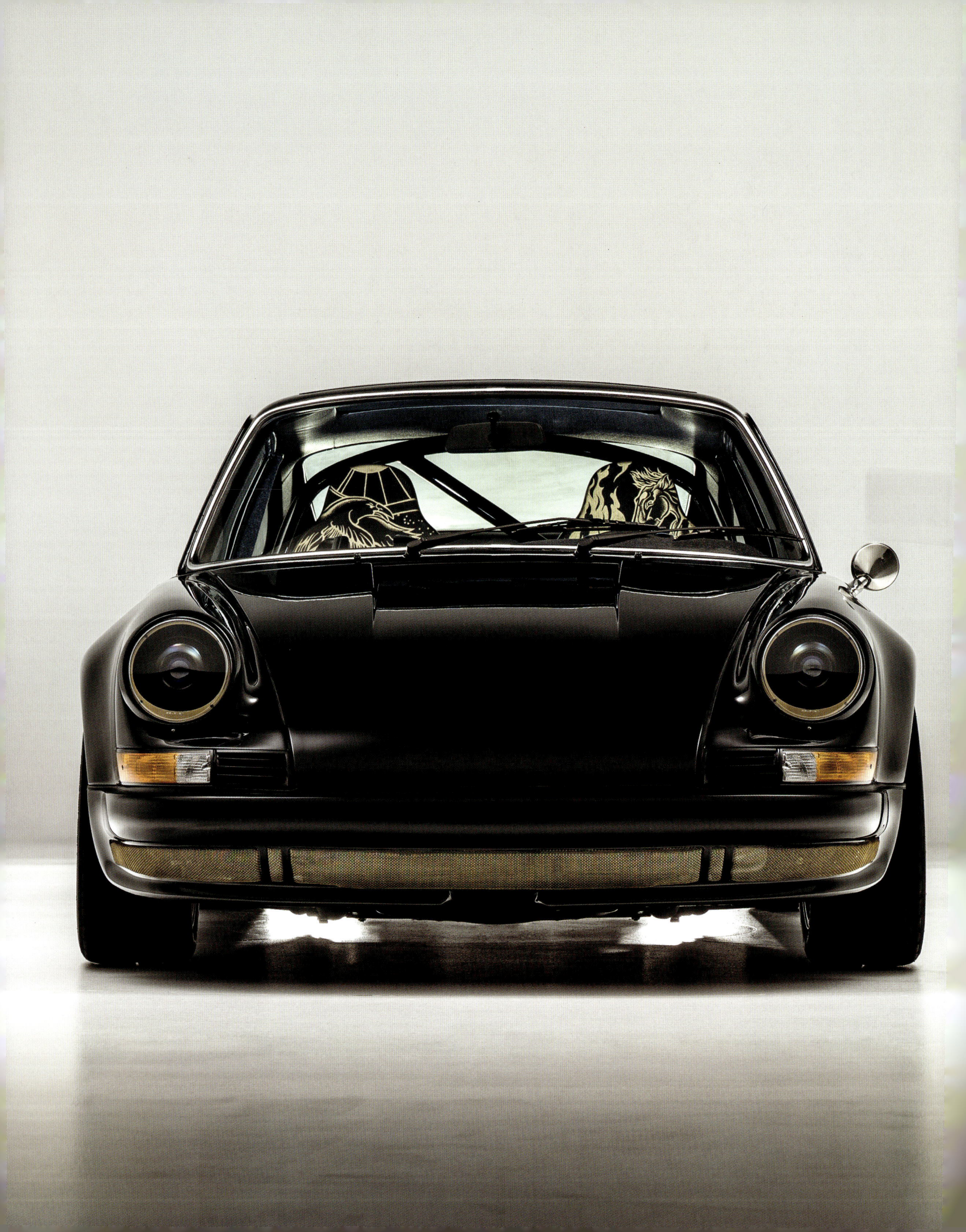

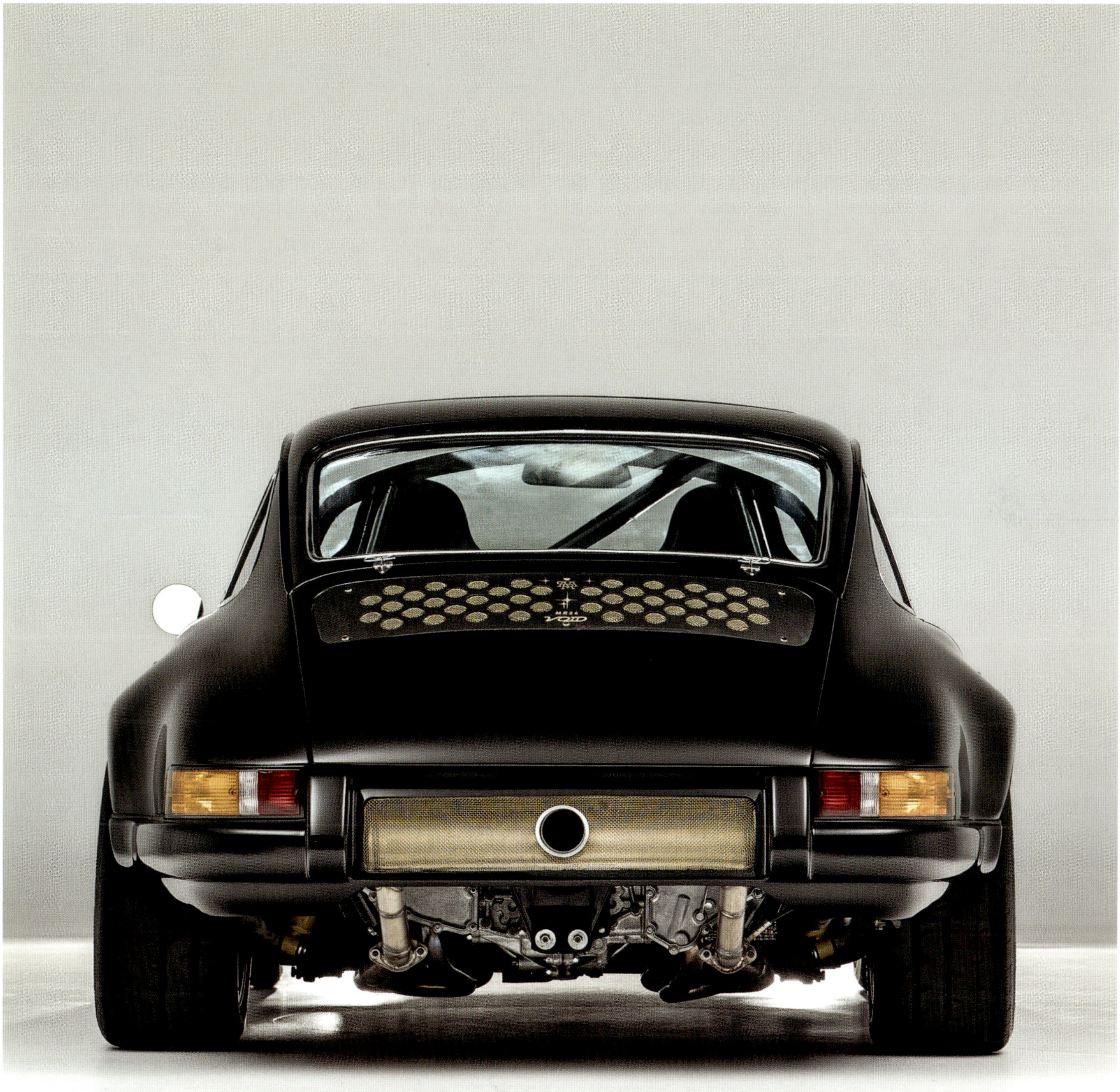

Above: With no driver assistance, this Porsche 911 awakens all five senses with a single turn of the key.

Opposite: In dominant black, lit up by a few touches of celestial light, the purity of this 911's lines make it glow.

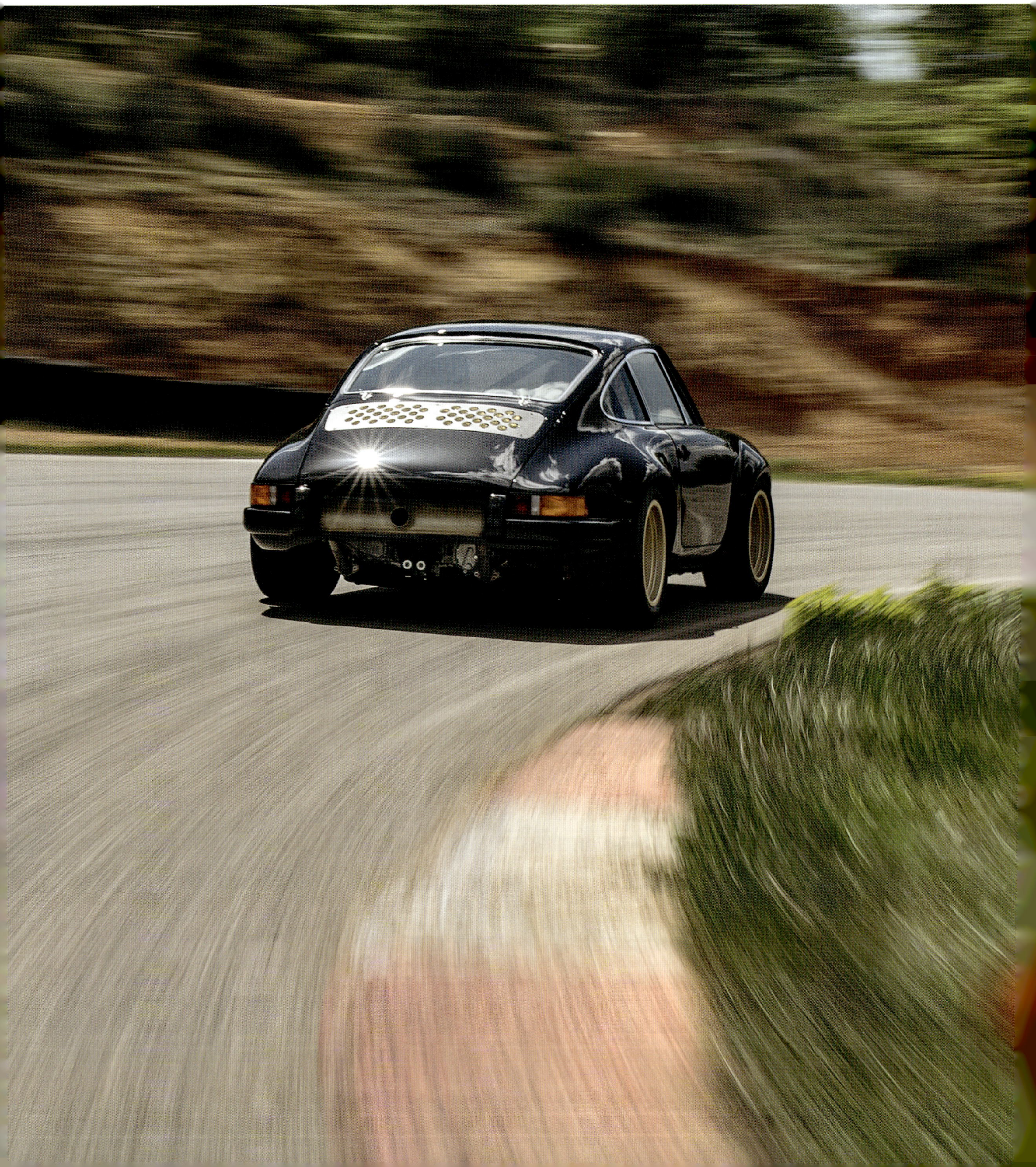

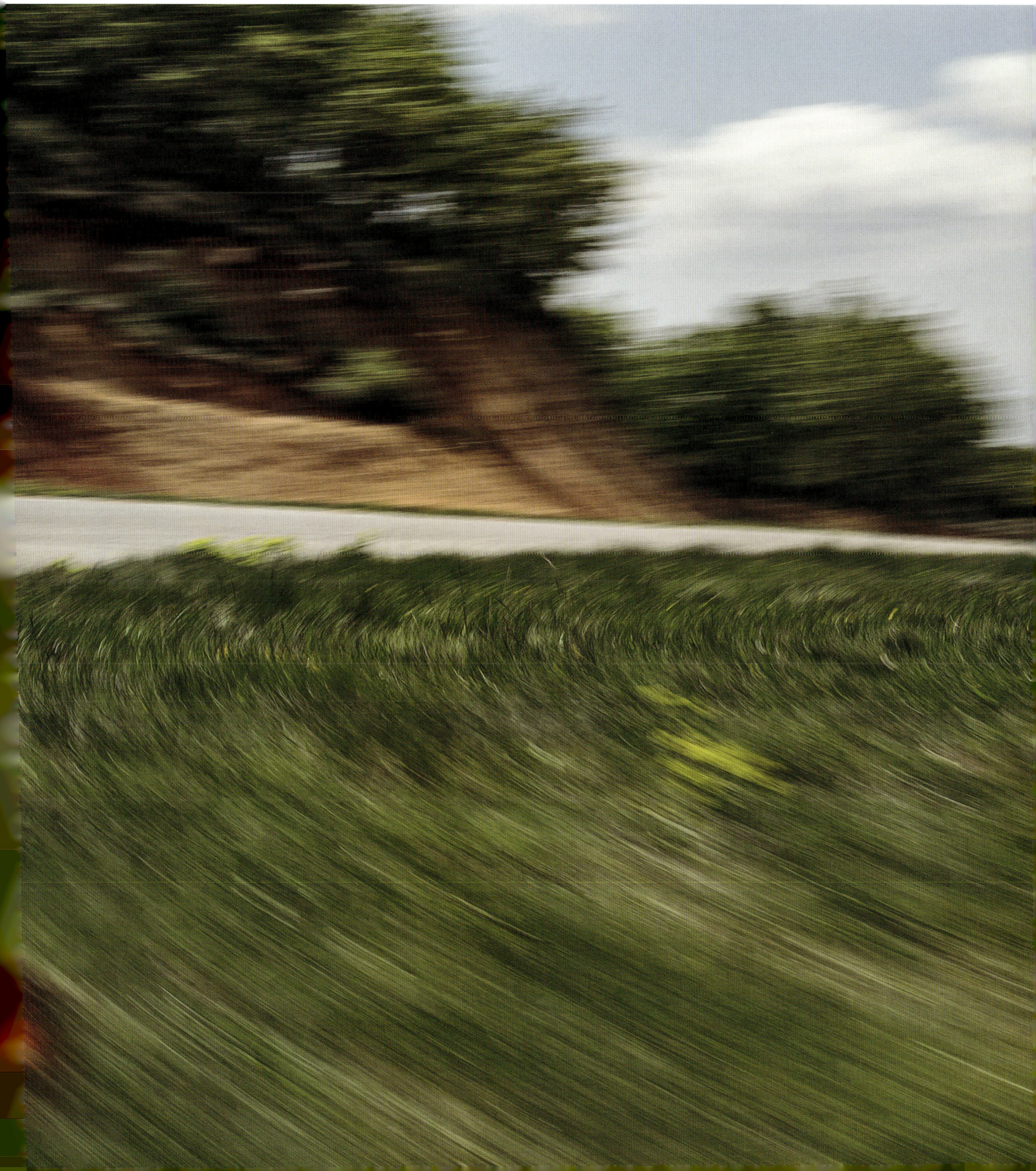

912 PATINA CARE-FREE

A 1965 912 with a sunroof is a very rare Porsche. This one's been around more than 60 years, and it still features its original Polo Red paint, with a pretty patina from which it takes its name.

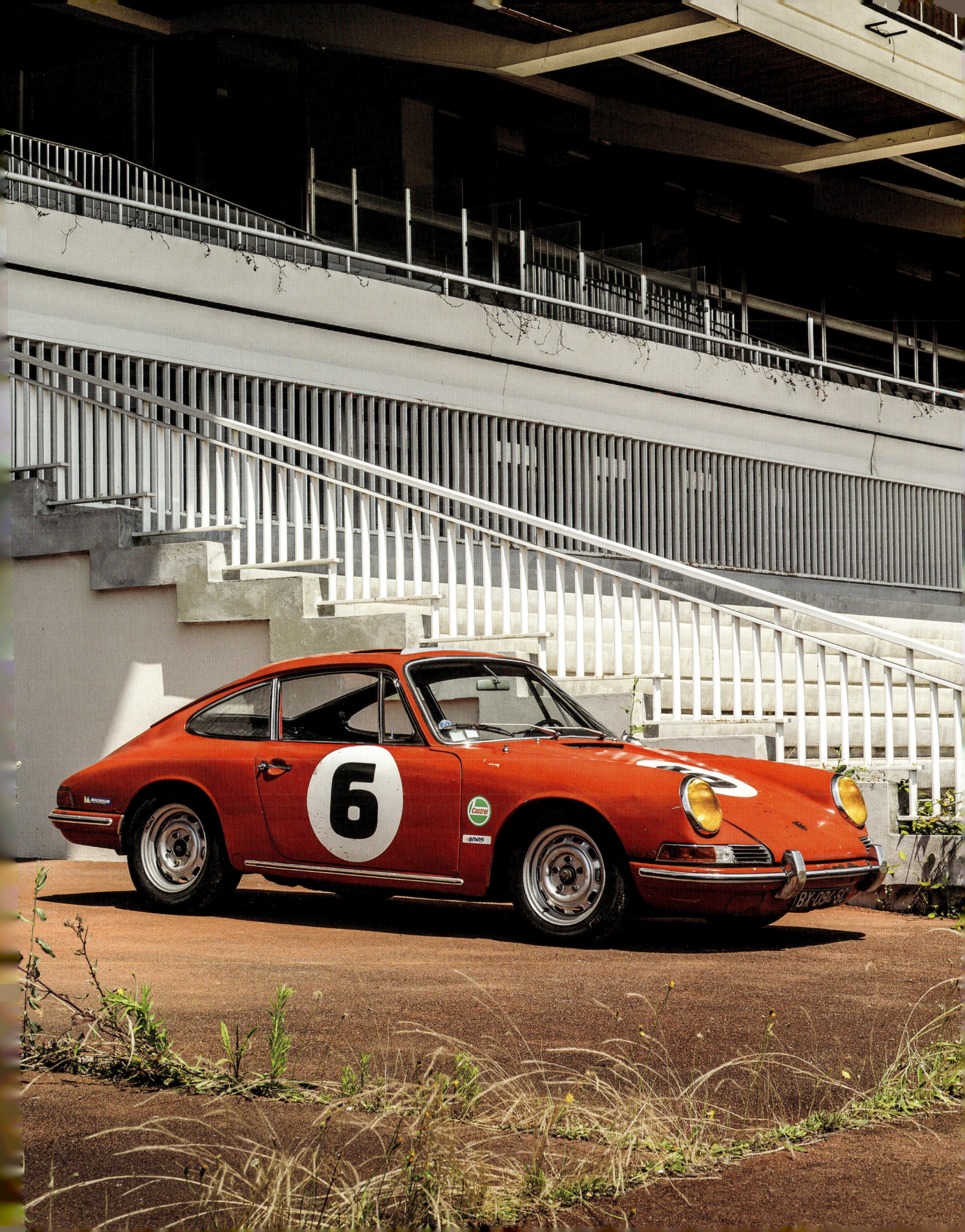
6
Castrol

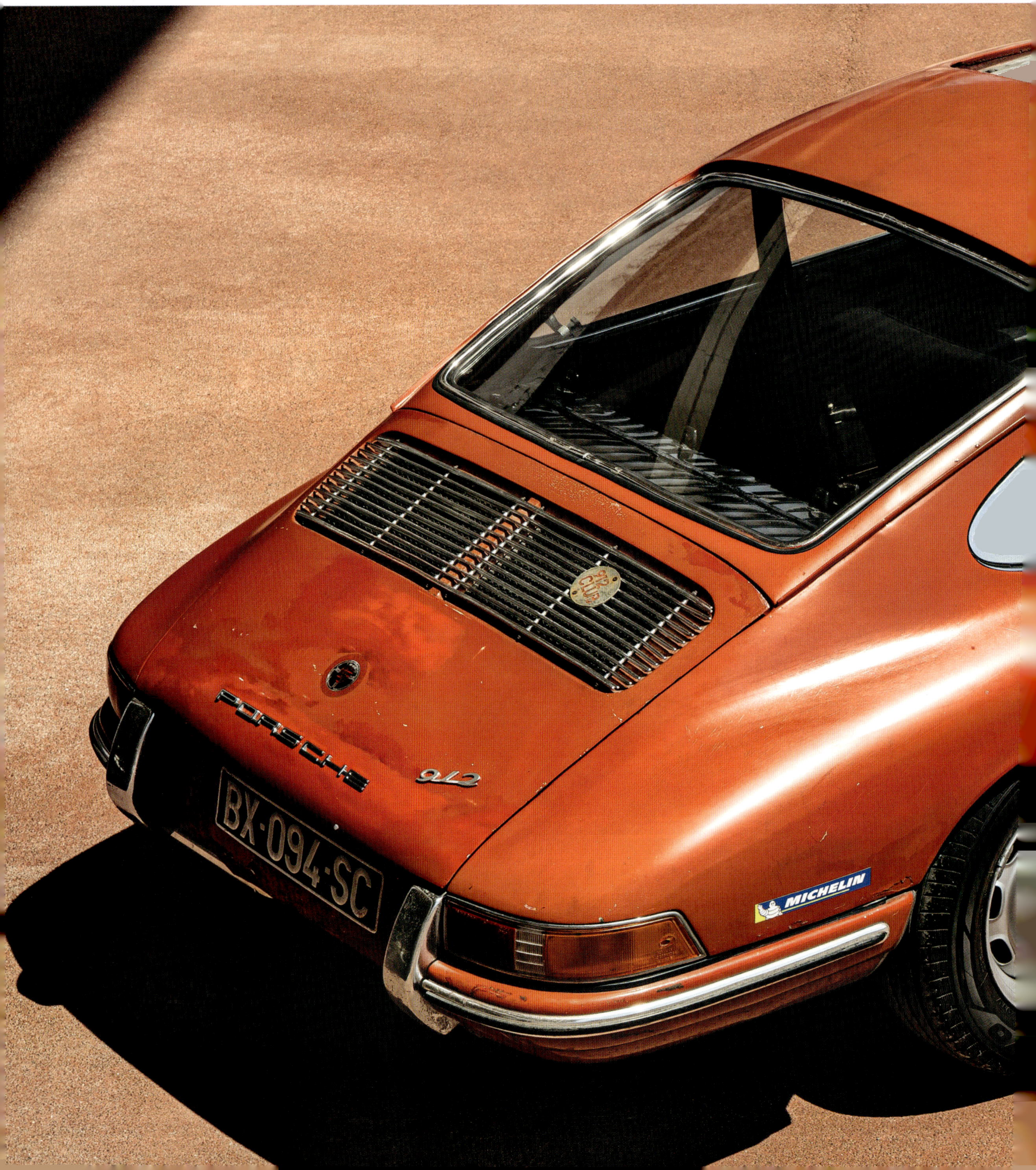
PORSCHE
912
BX-094-SC
MICHELIN

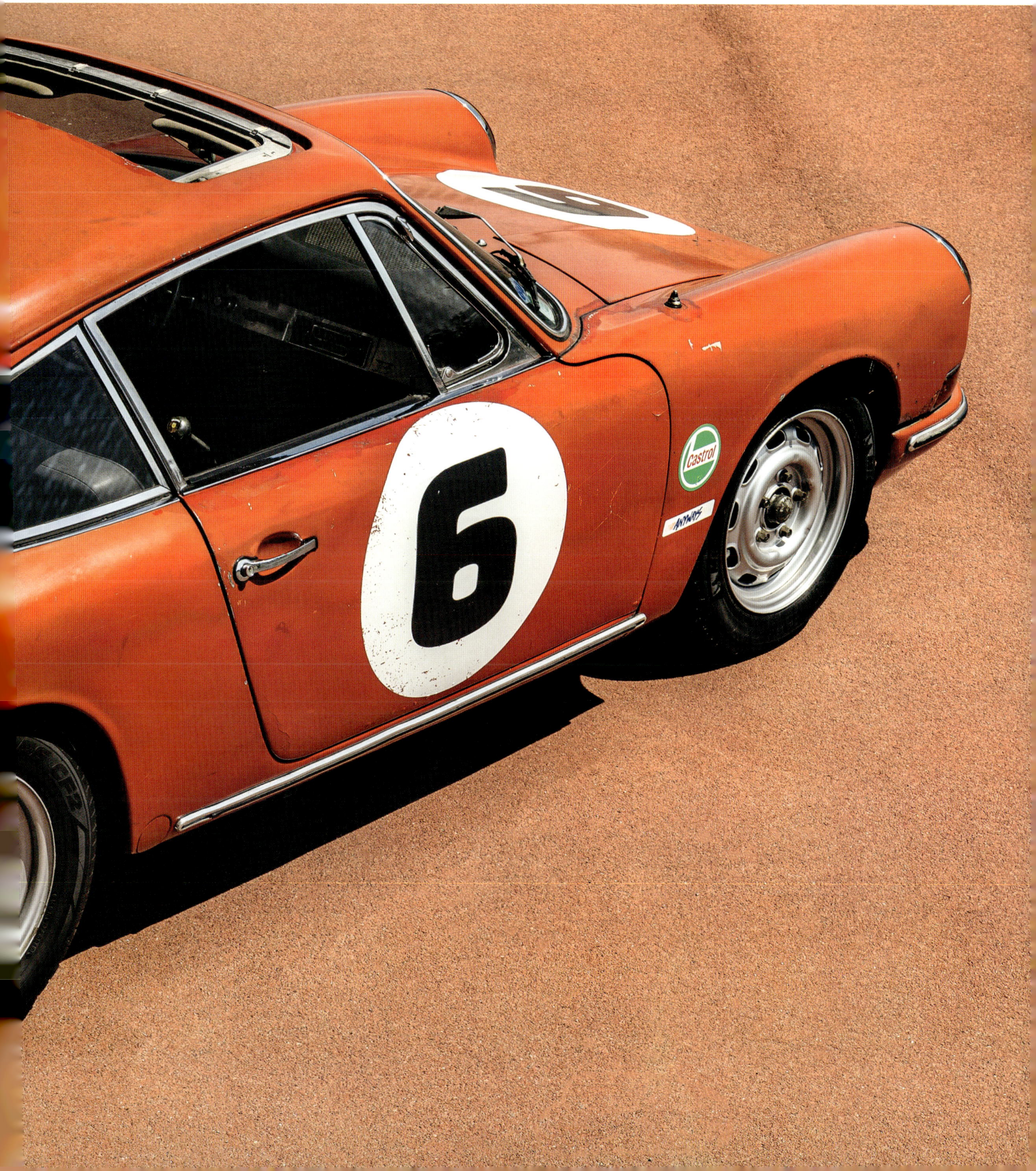
6
Castrol

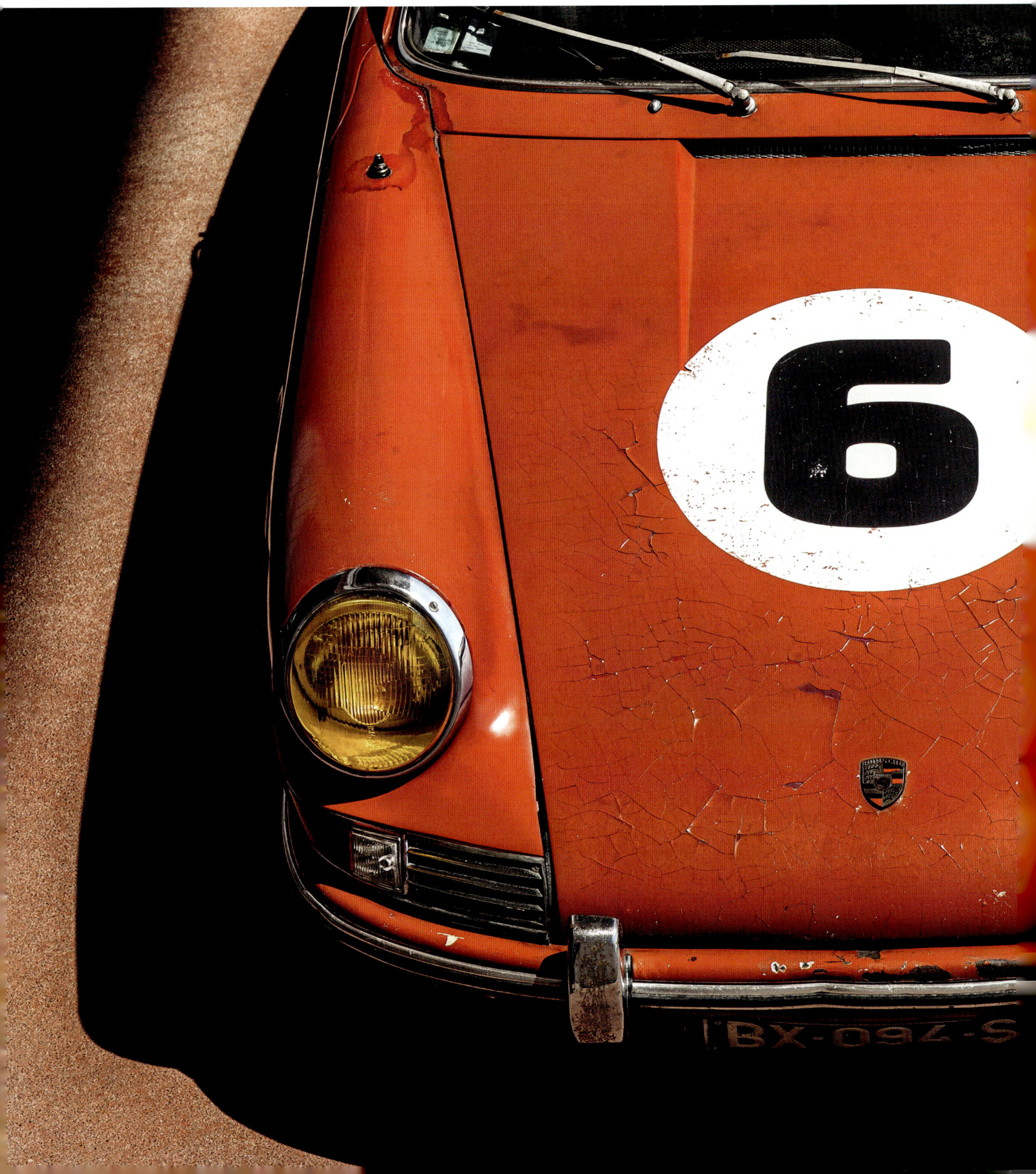
6
BX-094-S

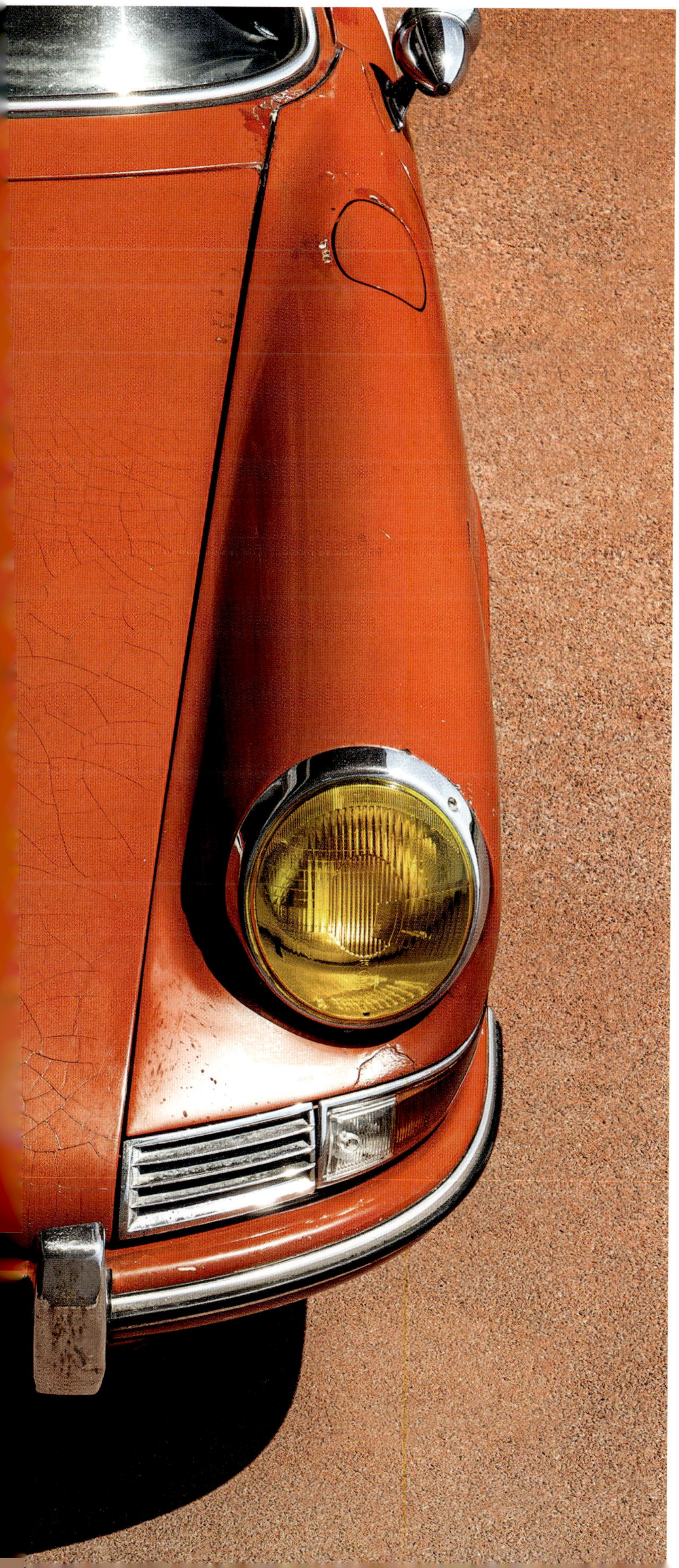

THE SHORT-WHEELBASE CHASSIS IS SYMBOLIC OF THE ESSENTIAL SPIRIT OF PORSCHE.

"It is a short wheelbase model," says Samuel, pointing at his Porsche. "It is one of the legendary aspects of the car: for me, that's what a real 911 is all about." However, this is a 912 from 1965, meaning that the famous - iconic - flat-six engine was replaced by the flat-four engine that featured in the first Porsche 356 models. "This car came under much criticism in France and Europe when it came out, whereas in the United States it was a bestseller. When the 911 came out in 1964 it didn't do well at all. As a result, the following year they released a 912 that had a smaller engine, which was less expensive, to try and gain acceptance for the new design, which broke with the style of the 356. The 1,600 cc, four-cylinder engine was detuned, its output dropping from 95 hp to 90 hp, because they realized that with the 356 SC engine, the 912 performed just as well - sometimes better – than a 2.0-litre 911 which had 130 hp." Samuel knows the history of the marque he idolizes by heart. As a child, he spent his time with Porsche specialists who rented a place from his father. And, inevitably, he comes back to the roots of his passion: "This short wheelbase is the very essence of Porsche! It was in construction until 1968 and gives an incredible sensation. It is really narrow and is amazingly pleasant to drive. That way of driving – you won't find it in any other car. And yes, I won the Ferdinand Cup in FC3, but this car has the true spirit of Porsche." Passionate about his 912, Samuel talks about just how much he enjoys driving it: "It is really light, weighing between 700 and 800 kg [1,543 and 1,764 lbs], and with the performance engine that was installed as soon as I got it in 2017, it has a displacement of 1,835 cc and 110 hp. I can keep up with plenty of 911s that have much higher horsepower."

In addition to the unrivalled driving pleasure of his 912, Samuel shares some of his car's finer points: "It has a sunroof, which is incredibly rare. The 912 was manufactured at the Karmann-Ghia coachbuilder's, apart from the models with a sunroof, which were made directly at Porsche.

AN ORIGINAL TREAT WITH A FEW EXTRA HORSEPOWER, FOR AN OUTLAW WHO'S NOT DONE YET.

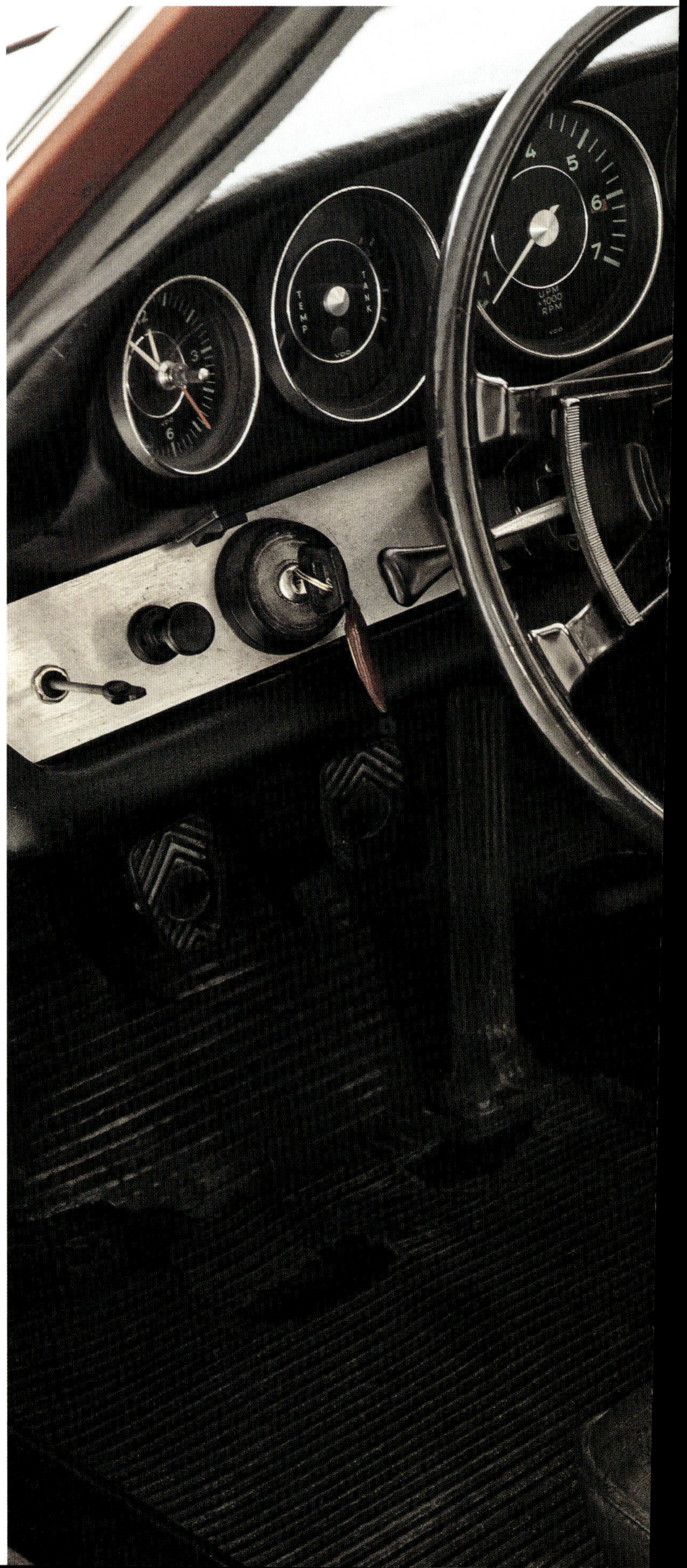

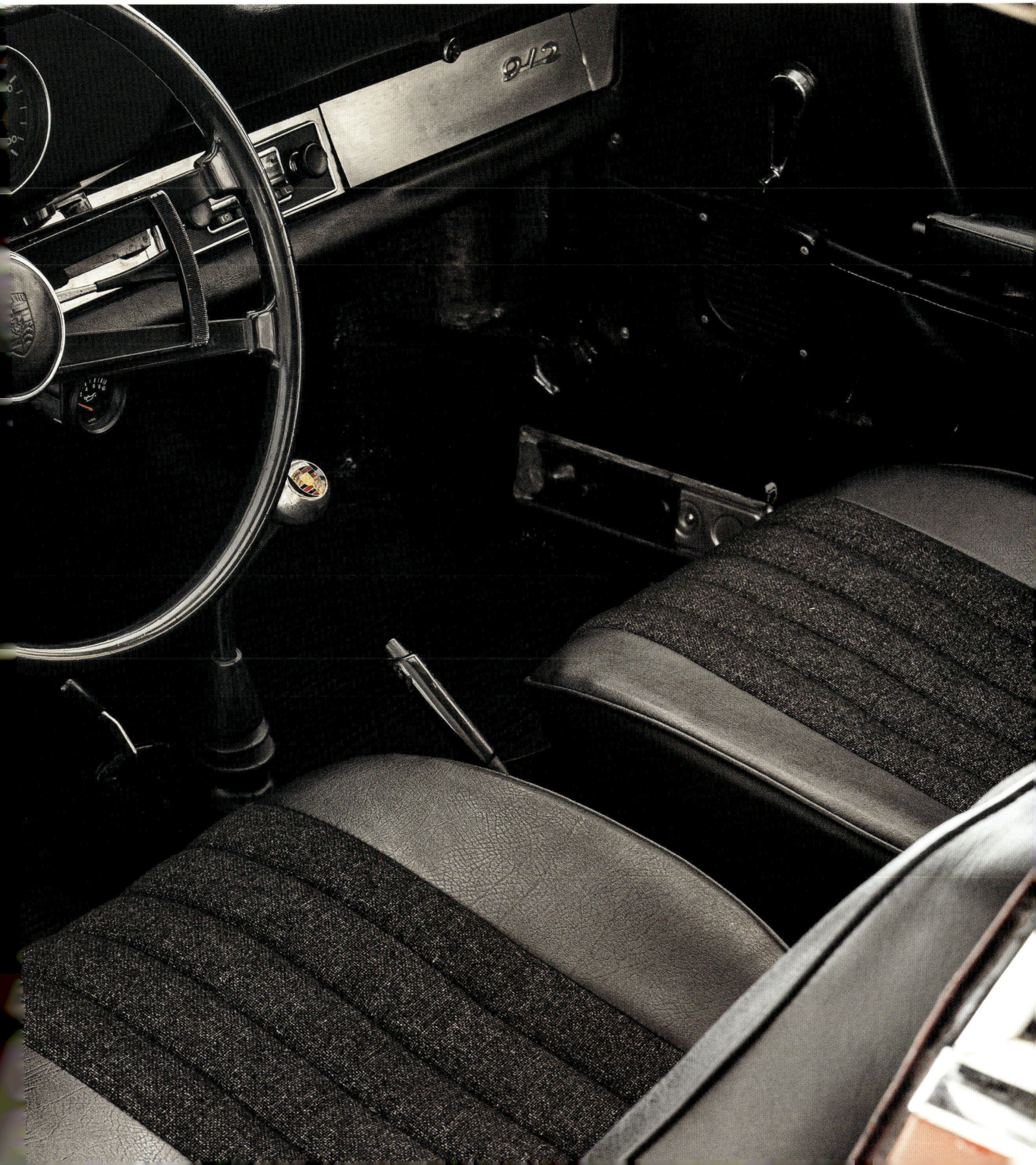

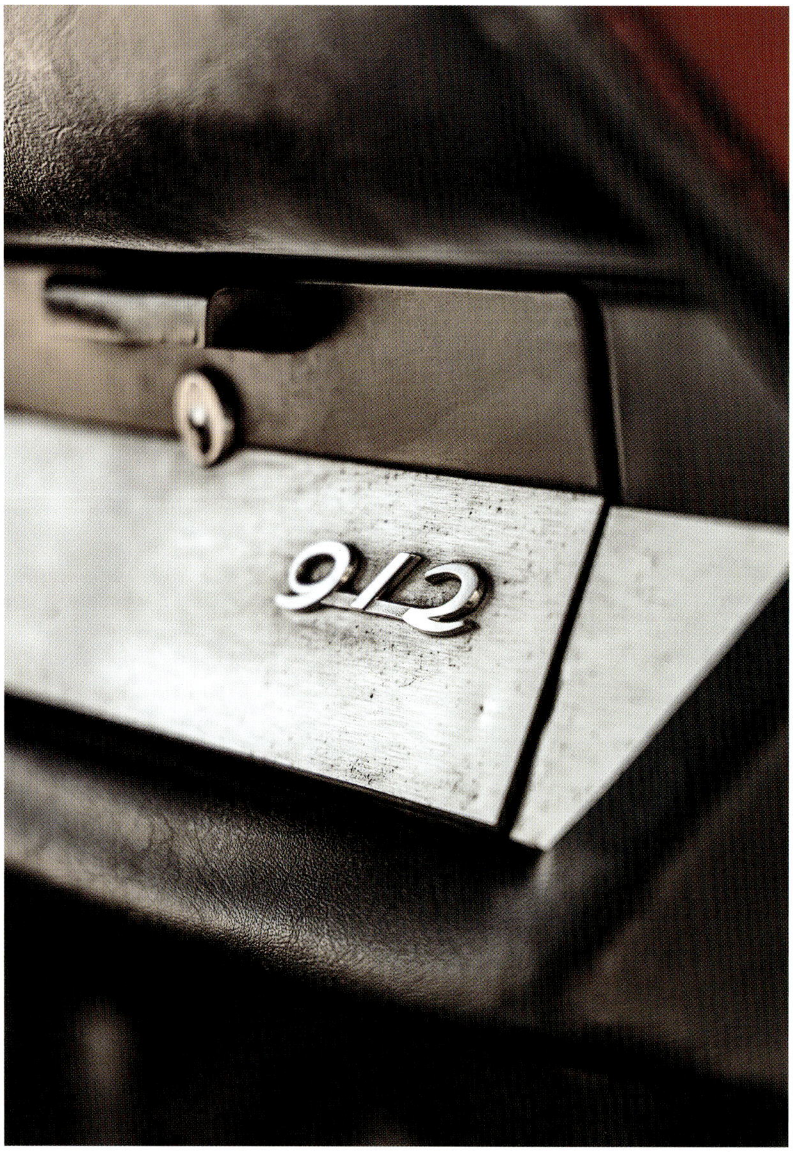

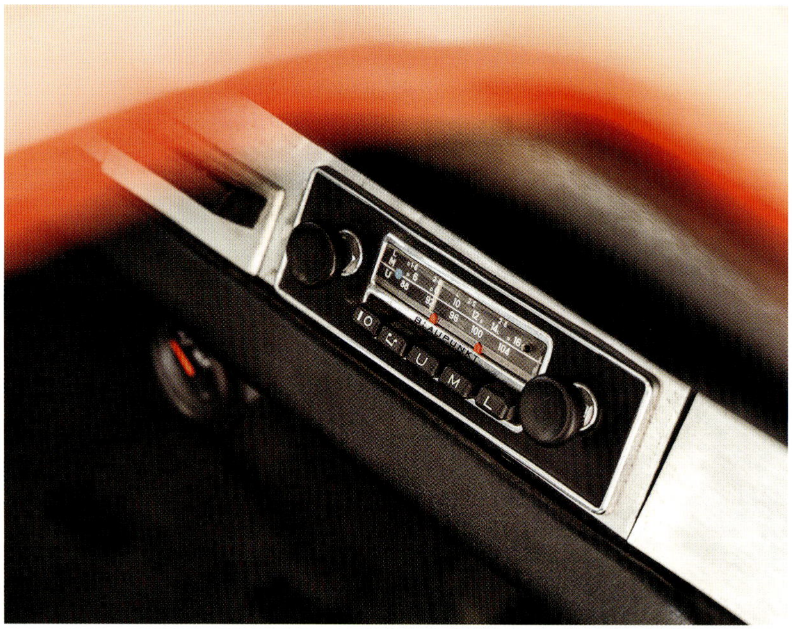

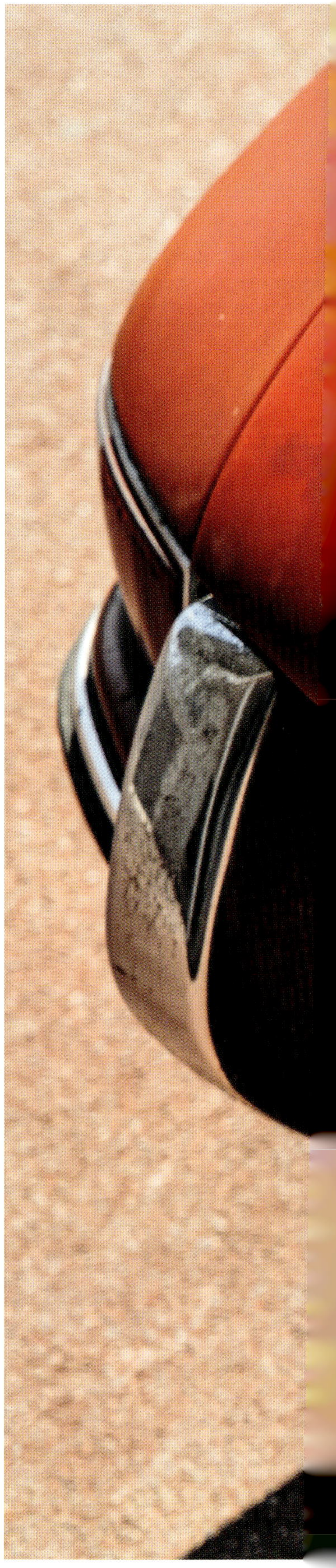

1. Not rated as highly as 911s, 912s are now much sought after.

2. The Blaupunkt radio can no longer tune into the short- and long-wave stations of the time.

3. The logo bears the name of Porsche dealer Jean Egreteaud, a former racing driver who died in 2023.

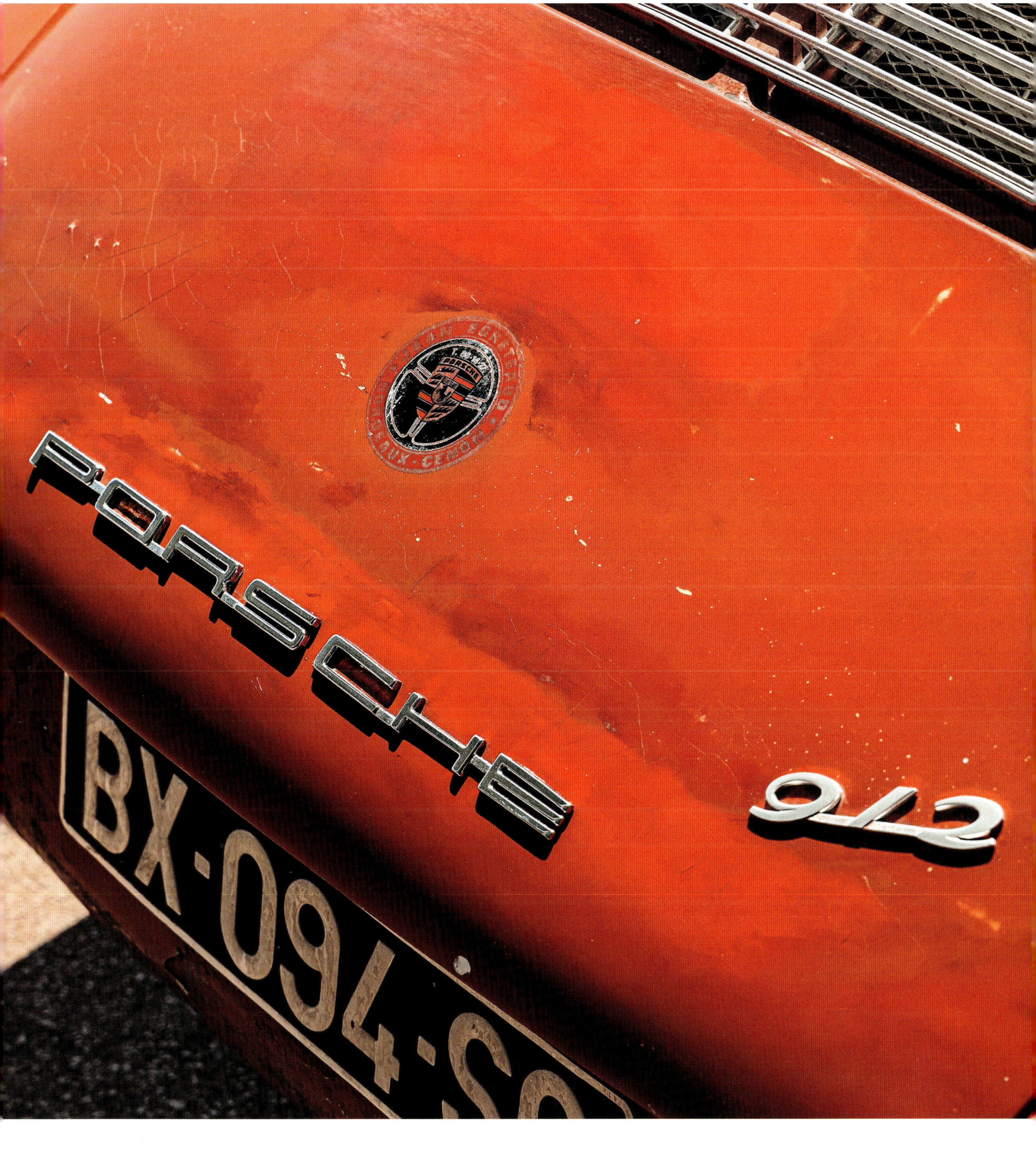
PORSCHE
912
BX-094-S

But because they preferred to sell 911s, they made the version with a sunroof really expensive, and it cost nearly as much as the six-cylinder-engine model. As a result, rather than offering a 912 with a sunroof, salesmen at the time directed customers towards the 911 without that option, giving the added bonus of a flat-six engine for the same price." After a photograph of a skateboarder jumping over his 912 at a Porsche gathering was published and shared, the former owners of this car called Samuel to tell him about its history. "The first owner was a doctor from Bordeaux, who frequently drove it up to Paris. He bought it brand new from the Porsche dealership in Bordeaux; I still have the original sticker with the old-style, six-digit telephone number on the rear cover. It really evokes the atmosphere of the time: a doctor in his car driving along with the sunroof open, the wind in his hair. One day, after many years of driving, the engine broke down. He entrusted it to one of his friends who had a garage in Paris, but the friend went bankrupt and the car ended up stored in a barn in Bordeaux, minus the flat-four engine. He took out the front seats, left the doors open and the 912 became a dog kennel!" It's unbelievable when you see the price of one of these cars today.

THE FISSURES ON THE HOOD OF THIS 912 LOOK LIKE SUN-BAKED, CRACKED EARTH.

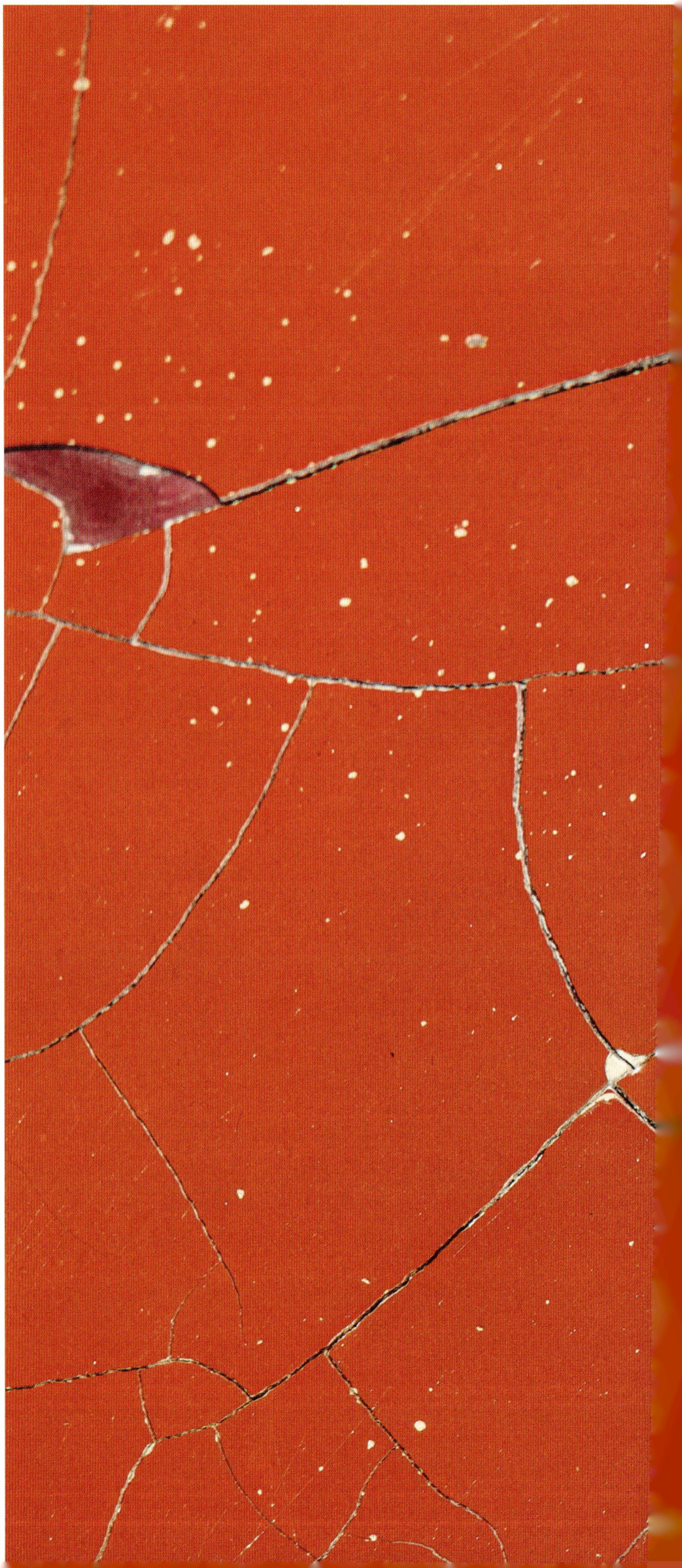

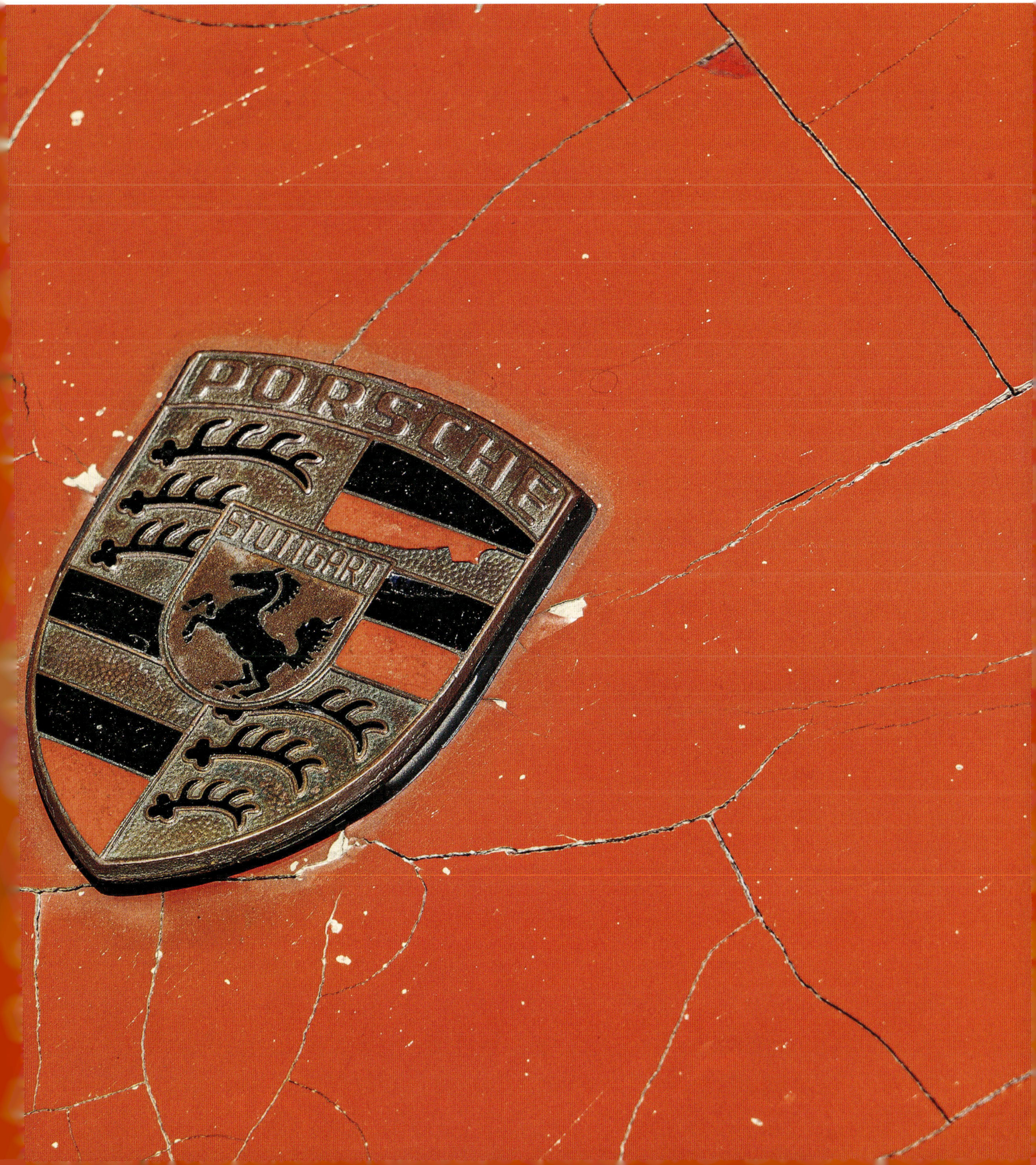
PORSCHE
STUTTGART

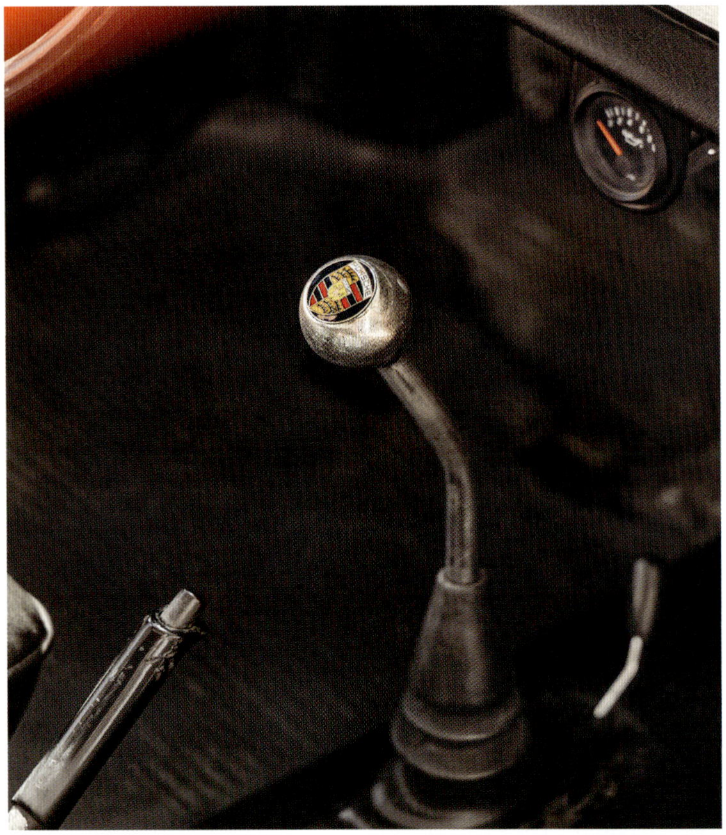

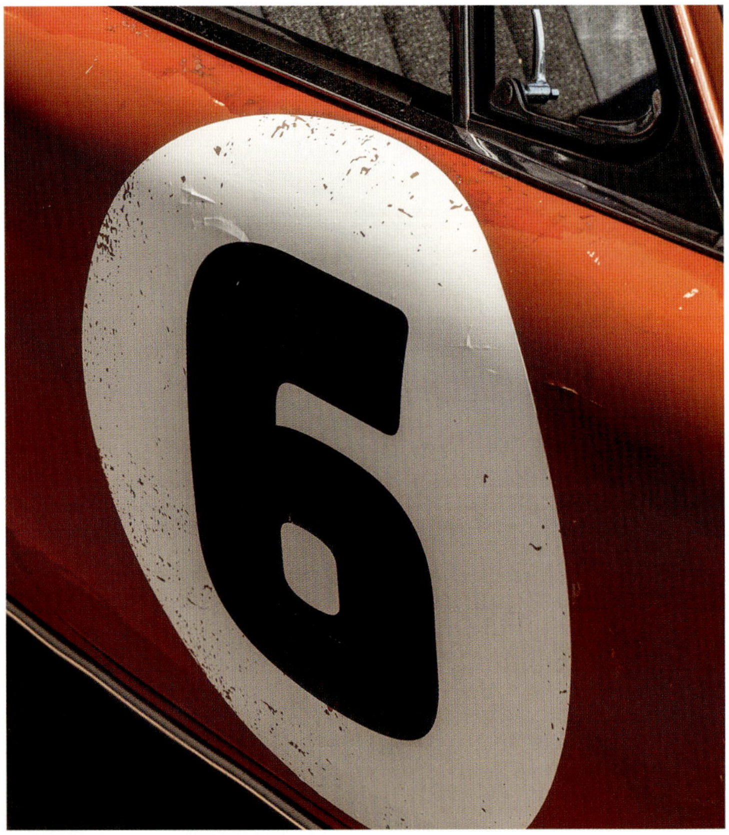

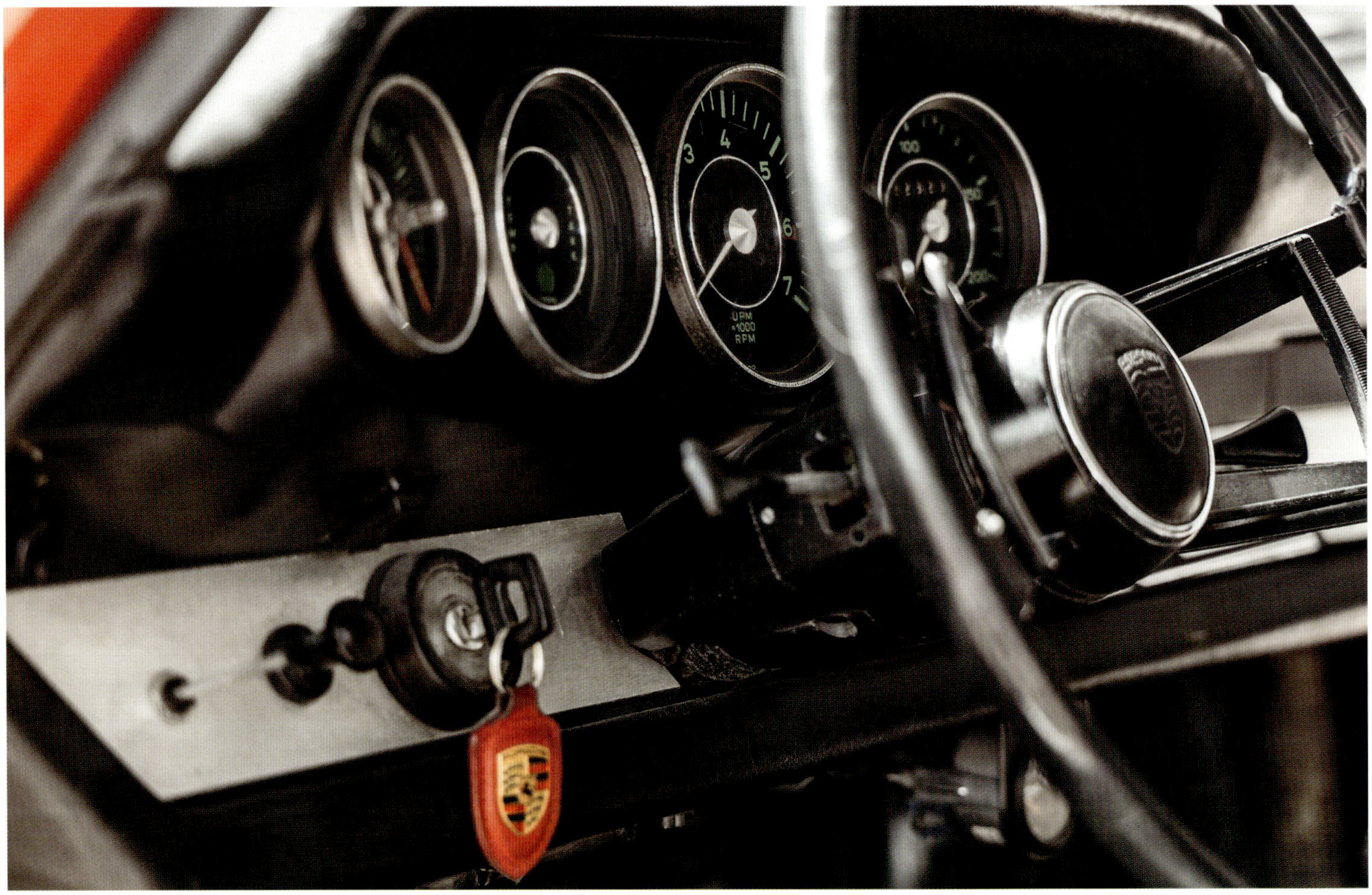

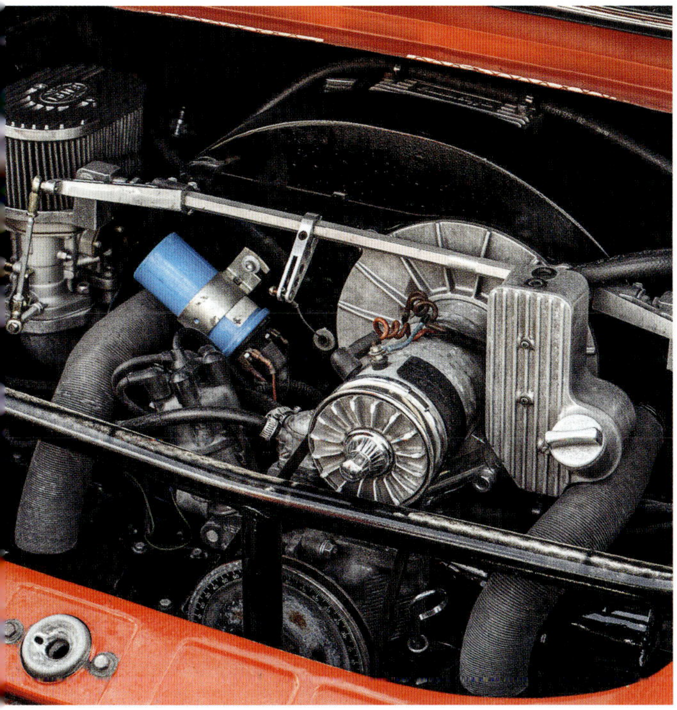

912 PATINA
BY THE NUMBERS

CREATION 1965

FLAT CYLINDERS 4

CC 1,835

HP 110

"It resurfaced in the 2000s, thanks to someone who was a Volkswagen fan, and who decided to fit a 356 engine in it. Another owner then took over. They rebuilt the sills but not the floor. I acquired this 912 in 2017, but I immediately broke the engine. Hence the high-performance engine that I rebuilt with a friend who's a specialist. It is really reliable, and I have driven the car to numerous rallies all around Europe."

Above all, this 912 has a unique feature: the patina! The bodywork is completely original, weathered by time and worn by the elements. It bears the scars of a life lived, and that's what gives it such special charm. It's like an old, battered armchair that has seen the children grow up but that cannot be replaced. "The number 6 on it is the number of the date of birth of my son, Abel. He was born on 6 January 2016. I had a Beetle before, this is my first Porsche. I completely rebuilt it at the end of 2023 to get rid of the rust, but I kept the original patina. The original paint was Polo Red – it was very popular at the time – and in the 1970s, it was given a light recoat. With sun and time, those two layers ended up developing into this really superb patina." Beyond its timeless beauty, what Samuel loves most is that his Porsche continues to live its life without him needing to worry about the path it takes: it's a real Outlaw because you can put the key in and set off on a tour of the whole country without worrying about where you might park up. You can use it however you like and never stress about it – the worn-in patina is exactly what makes it so carefree to enjoy. And you can't put a price on that. You're always stressed if you've got a spotless car. With this one you can park on a gravel lot, you can drift it, without worrying about the paint job.

"One last tale: when it came out of the repair shop, the front-left wheel came off while I was driving – fortunately not very fast. The wheel had bent up the wing, but I put it back, straightened the bodywork as much as I could and we were back on the road. It would have been a tragedy in a pristine Porsche. But not this one: it's got its patina, so there's nothing to worry about!"

1 2

3

1. Time's wear and tear mark every part of this weathered 912.

2. The number six represents the birthday of Sam's son, Abel.

3. Four VDO dials with green lettering evoke a past that's still present.

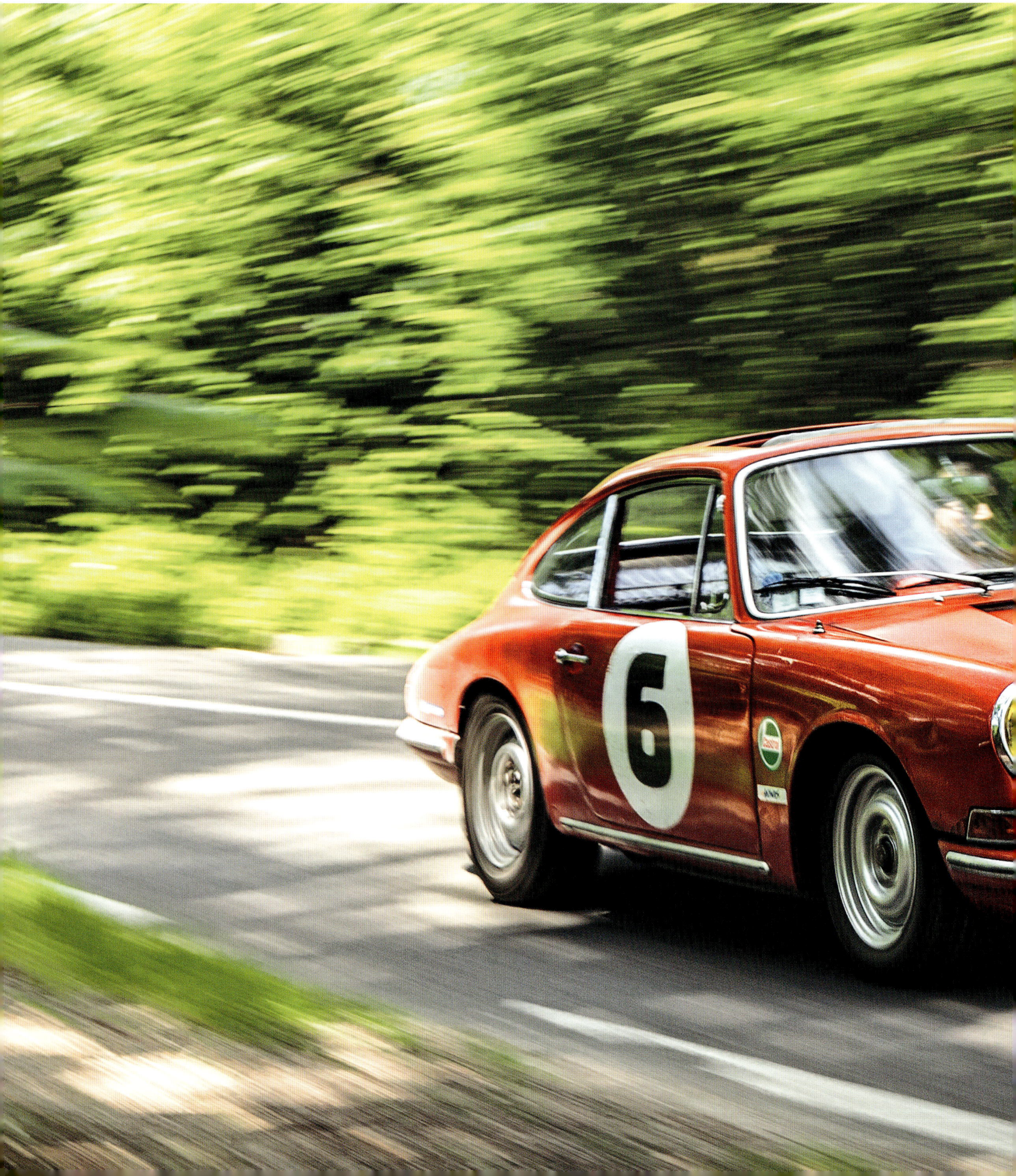

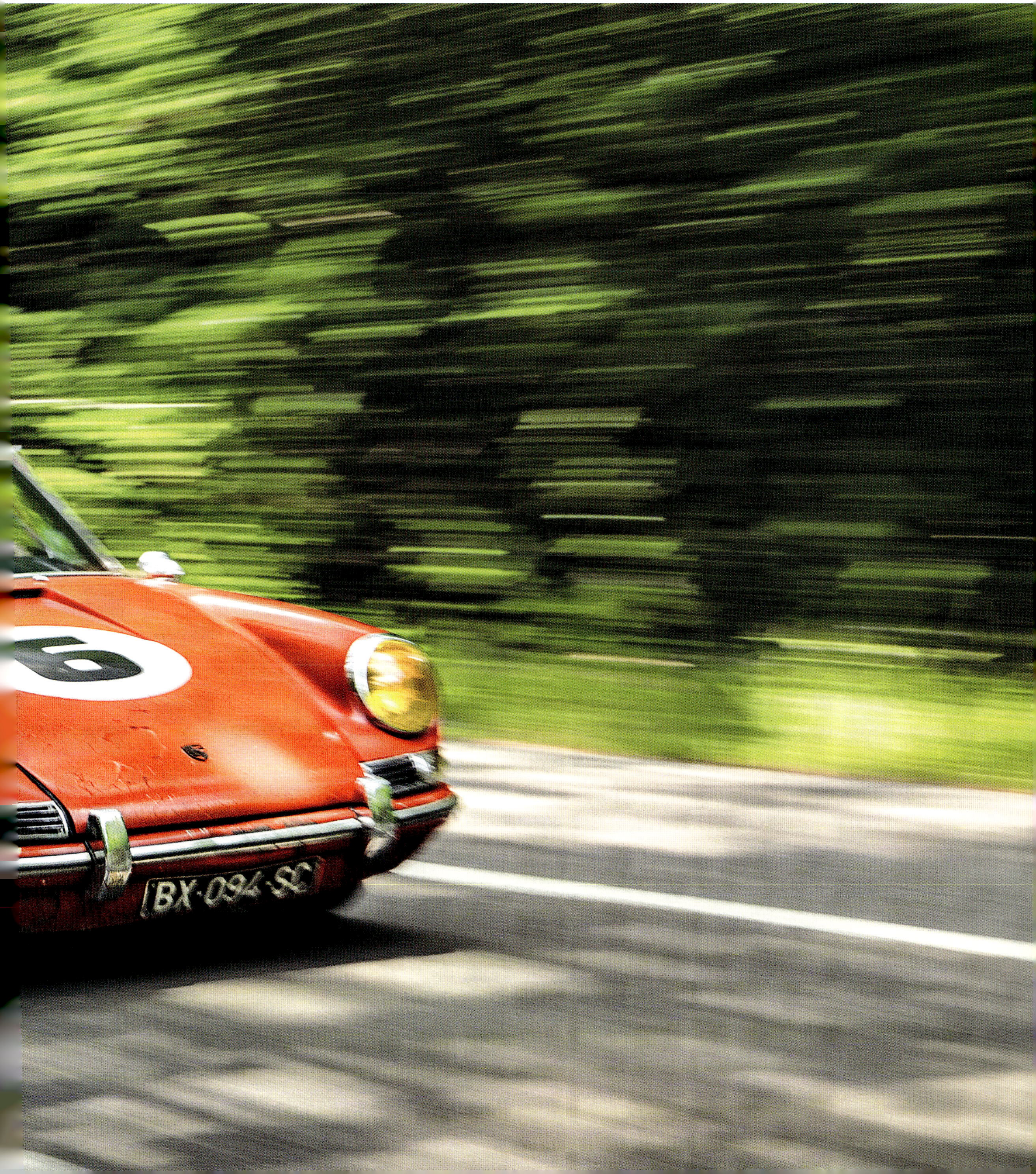
BX-094-SC

911 TARGA

DIVA REFINED

Combining the elegance of backdating with inspiration from a 1966 Porsche 911 Targa to transform this 964 into a restomod-style conversion, without betraying the pure style of a classic car of this calibre. That was the challenge faced by Diva – and it deserves a standing ovation! Turns out a 420 hp Outlaw can be refined …

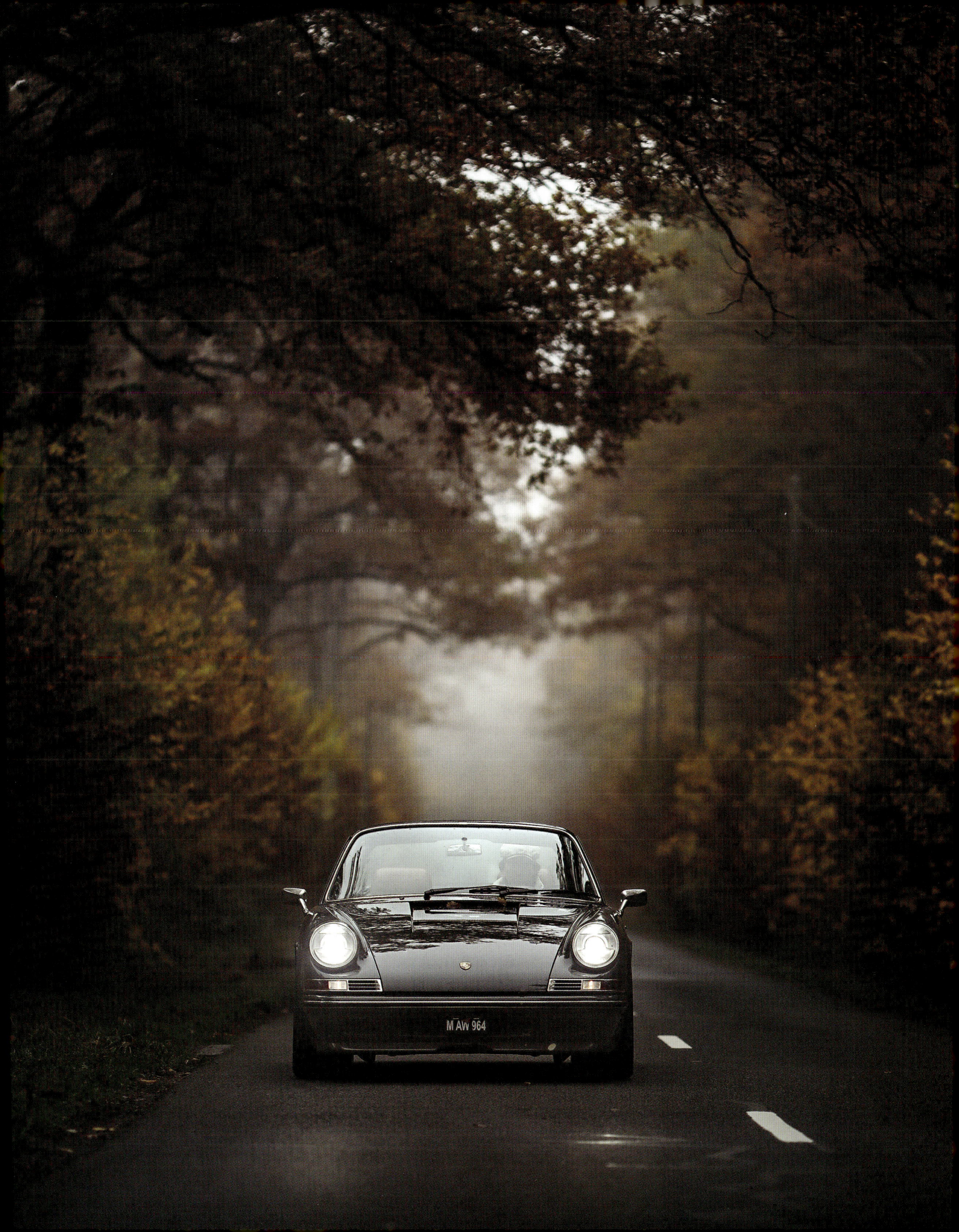
M AW 964

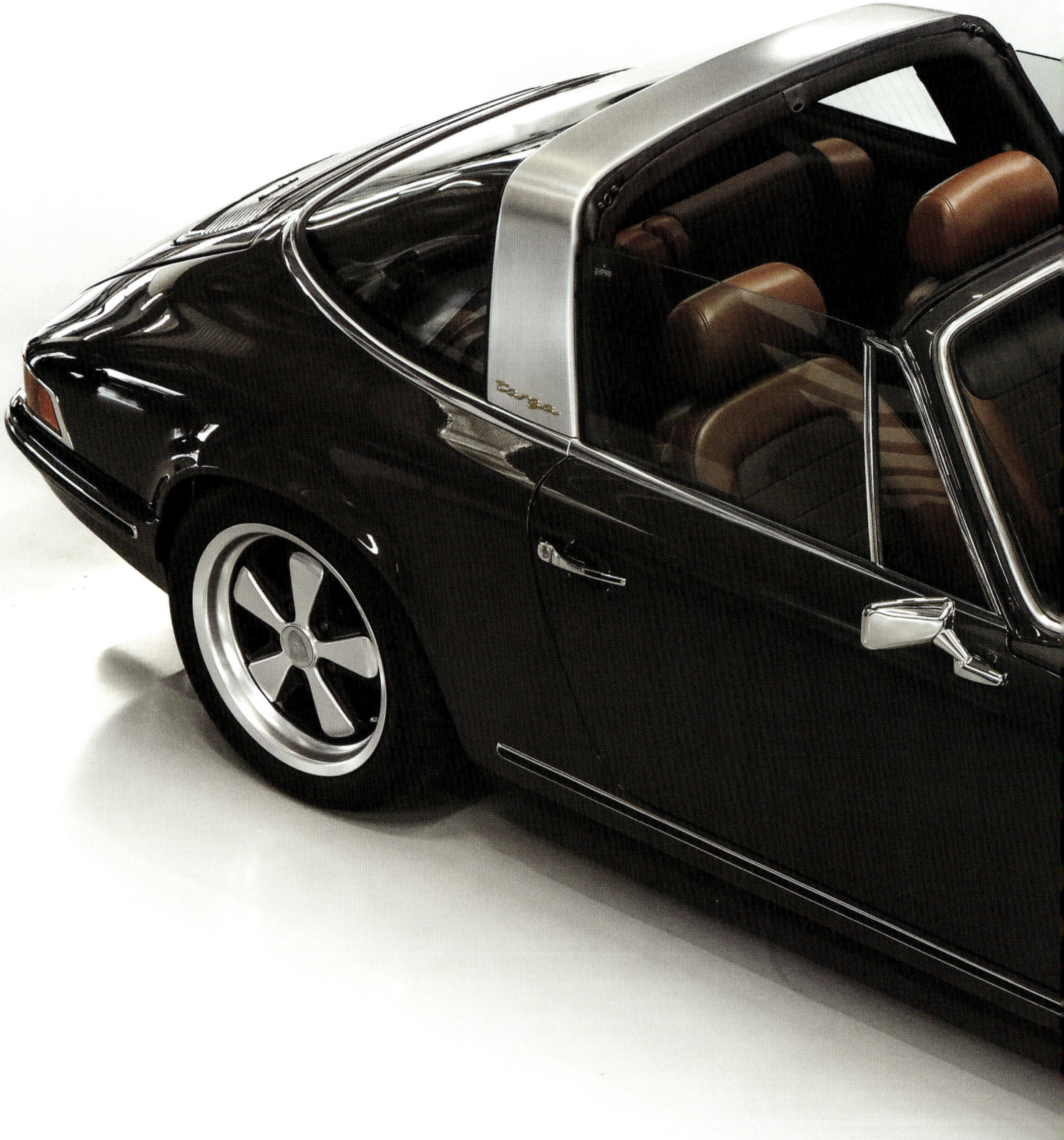
targa

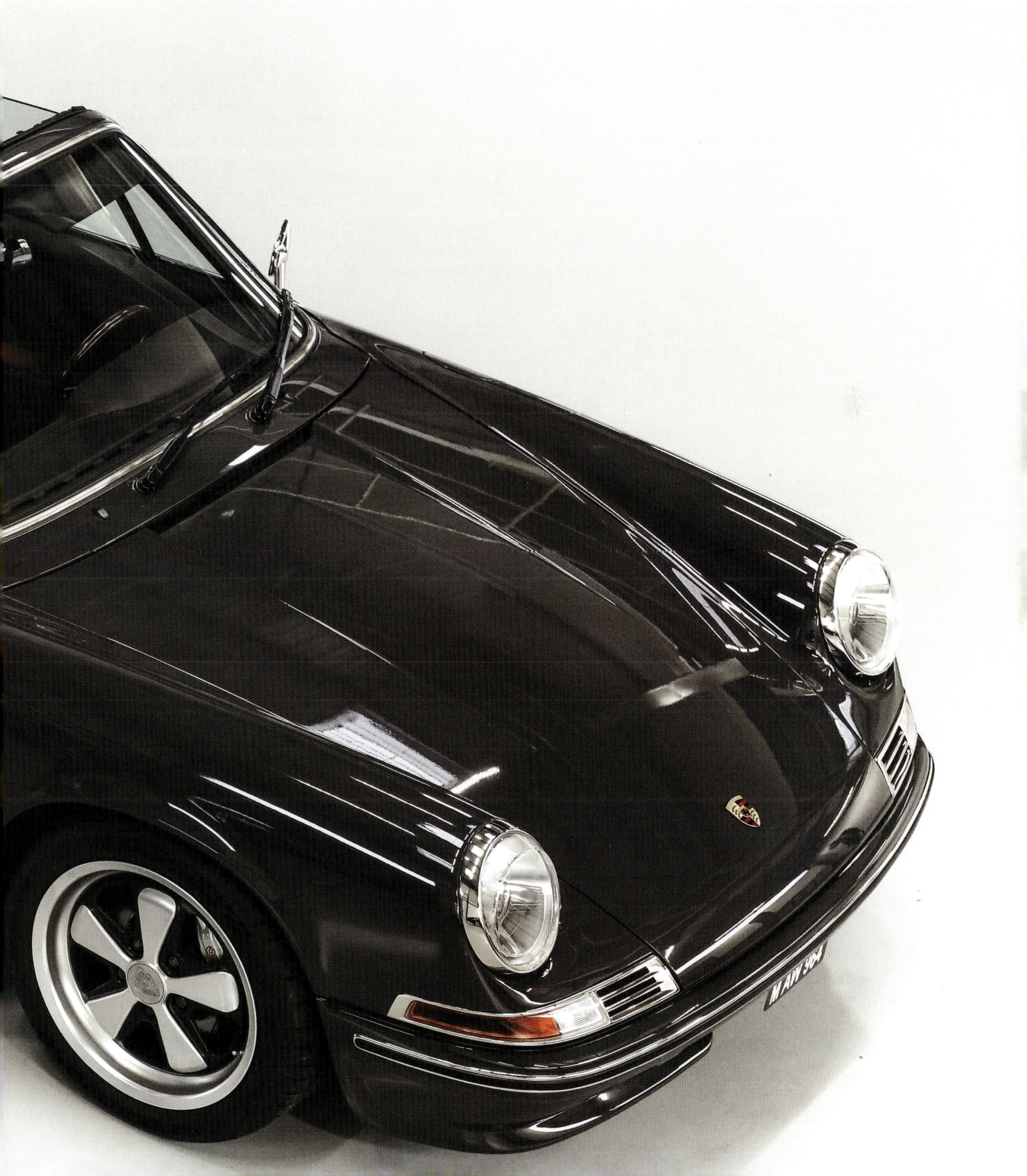

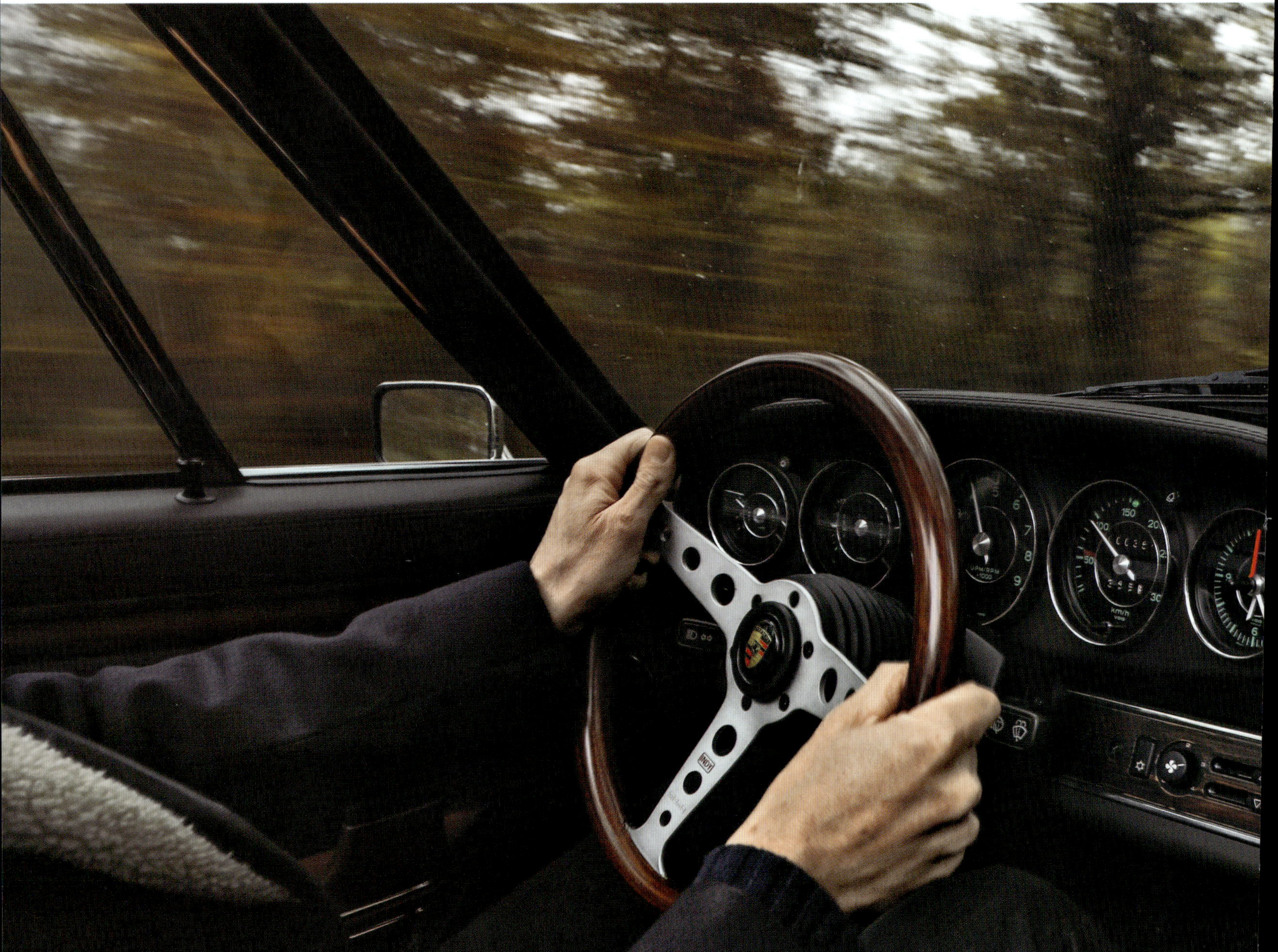

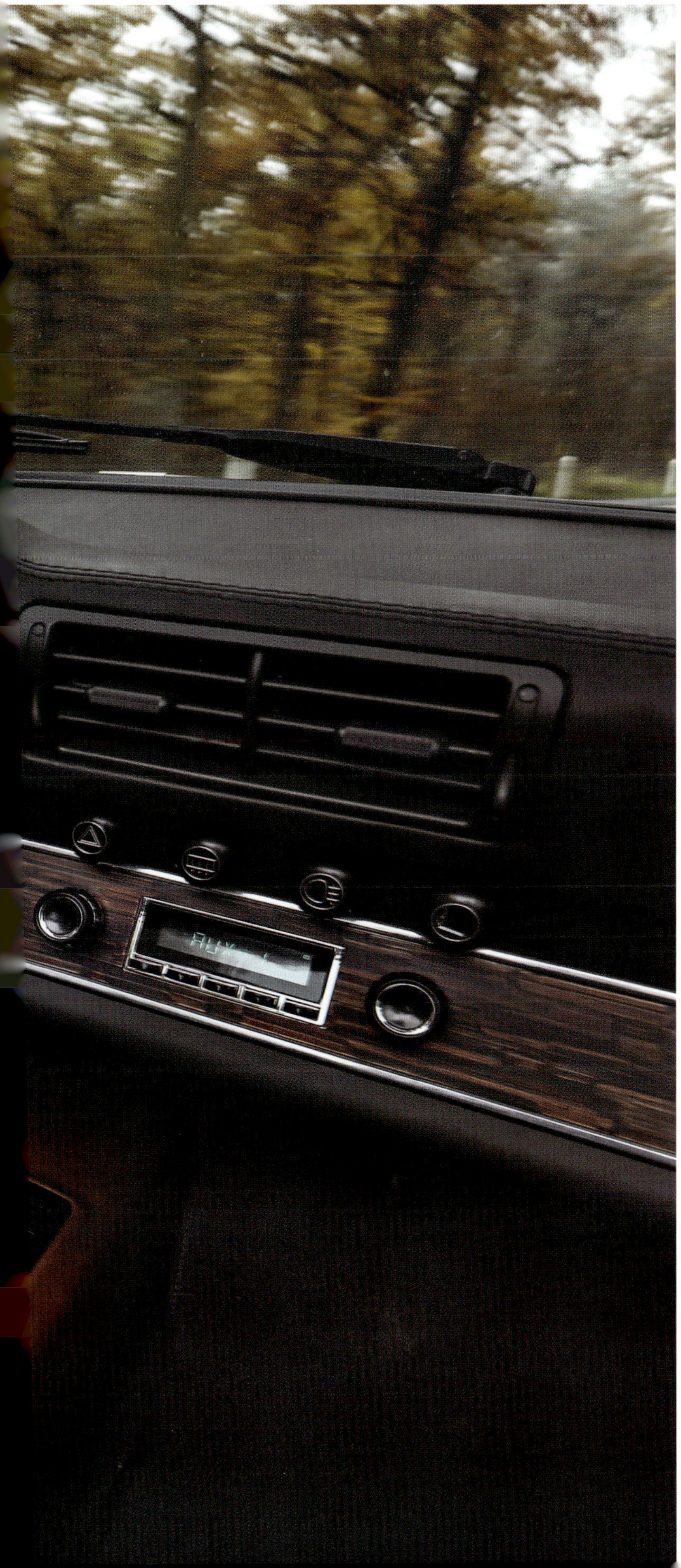

THIS TARGA REPRESENTS THE PINNACLE OF QUALITY, ENHANCED BY FRENCH ELEGANCE.

"I always wanted to design my own car," explains Sébastien Crubilé, the owner of this simply sublime Diva. "And it evolved through the experience I gained with the technological challenges I have faced and the races I took part in. It was always in the back of my mind, without me thinking too much about it. Then, one day, one of my clients, who owned a 2.8-litre Porsche 935, told me that what he wanted was a classic car that he could drive every day. During our discussion, he talked about his fondness for the lines of the 1966 Targa, but he said he found those cars to be outdated, technologically and dynamically. As he was explaining this to me, I got the idea in my head that I could build him an amazing car – beautifully finished and that runs like a dream!" Basically, a car that was like a backdated Porsche, but with modern, high-performance mechanics, like a restomod! "The idea is a bit like that of Rob

Dickinson – aka Singer – who rebuilds 911s like this in the United States. But he keeps the narrow wheel arches, which are so much more elegant than the Californian style of flared wheel arch Porsches. I wanted to keep the clean lines that run from the front headlights to the rear lights of the car." Something along the lines of a classy, elegant Outlaw, with the refinement of a beautiful jewel and mechanics with the precision of a Swiss watch. "I thought of a Porsche with two sides: gentle and elegant in appearance, but incredibly powerful and aggressive when pushed. Along the lines of Doctor Jekyll and Mr Hyde!"

The starting point had to be a Porsche 964 Targa, produced between 1989 and 1994. To maintain consistent proportions between the flat wheel arch design and the 17-inch wheels, the car was widened by 3 cm (1.1 ins) overall, which involved numerous complex modifications. The rims are authentic, contemporary Fuchs. They were repainted entirely, in order to subtly balance the colour distribution. The suspension is Bilstein and the brakes are custom-made by Brembo. With a diameter of 332 mm (13 ins), the discs are 10 mm (0.4 ins) larger than standard models – the maximum size possible with the 17-inch rims. On the mechanical side, the good old air-cooled flat-six with two valves per cylinder had a displacement increase from 3.6 litres to 4.2 litres.

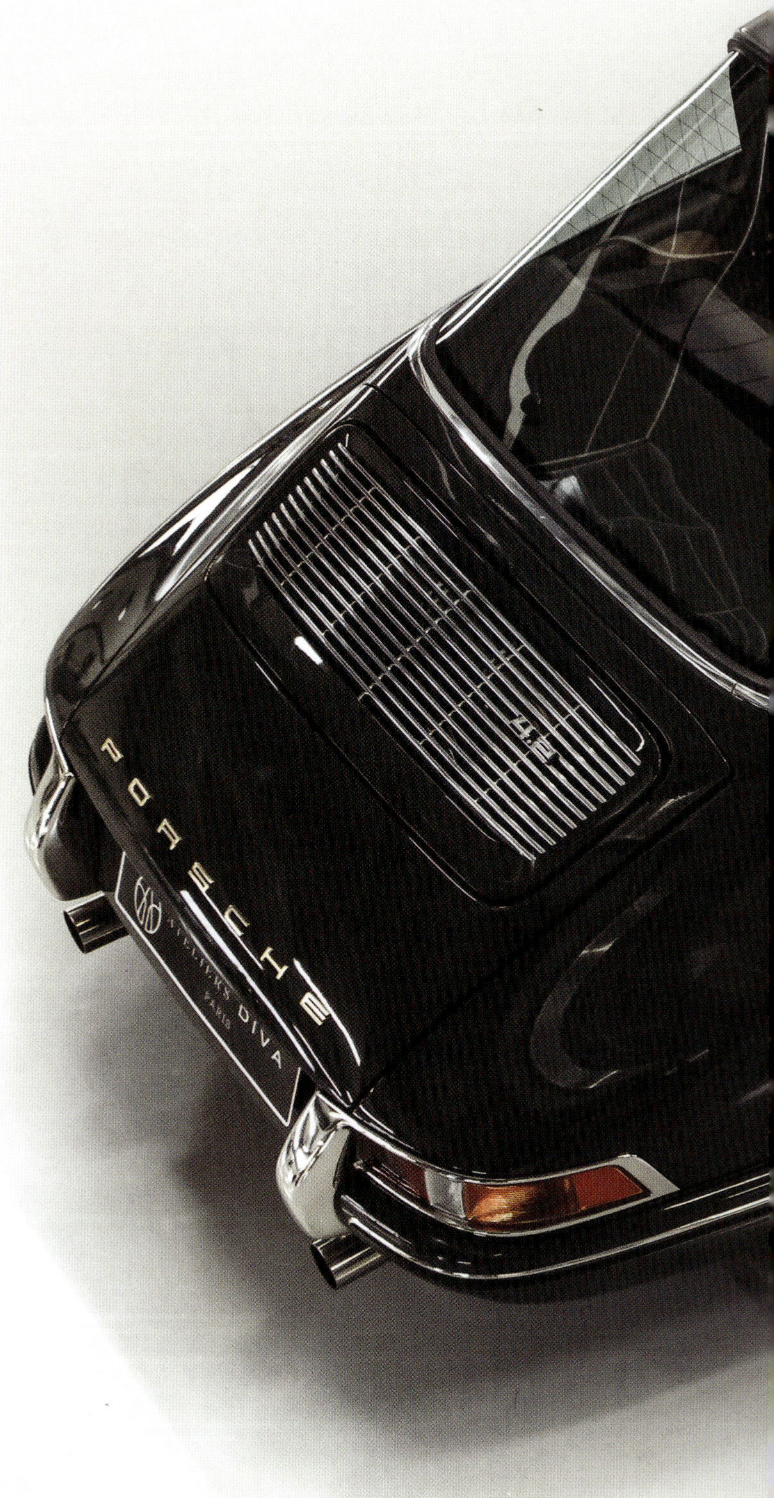

DR JEKYLL AND MR HYDE – IN A 911 TARGA.

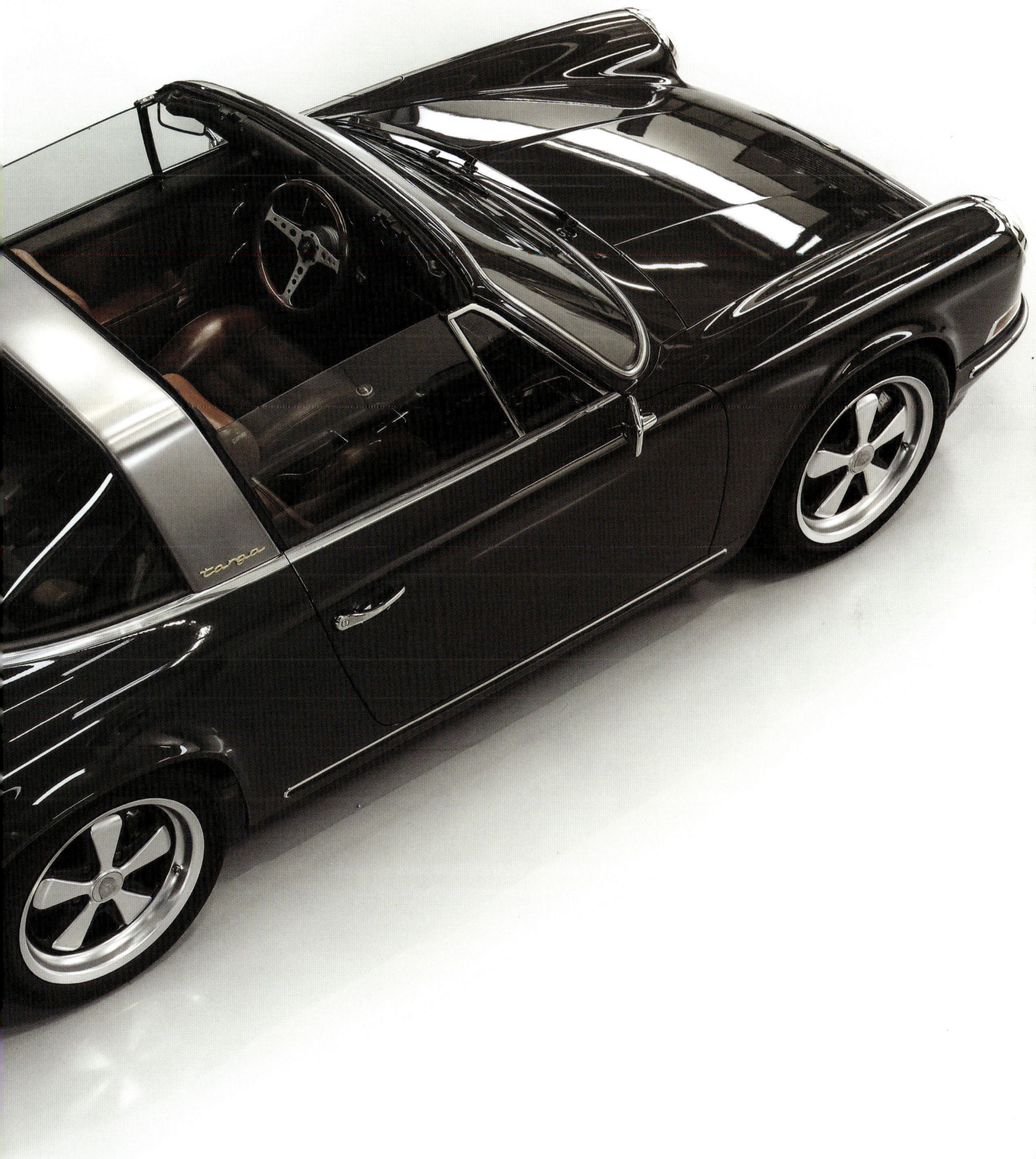
targa

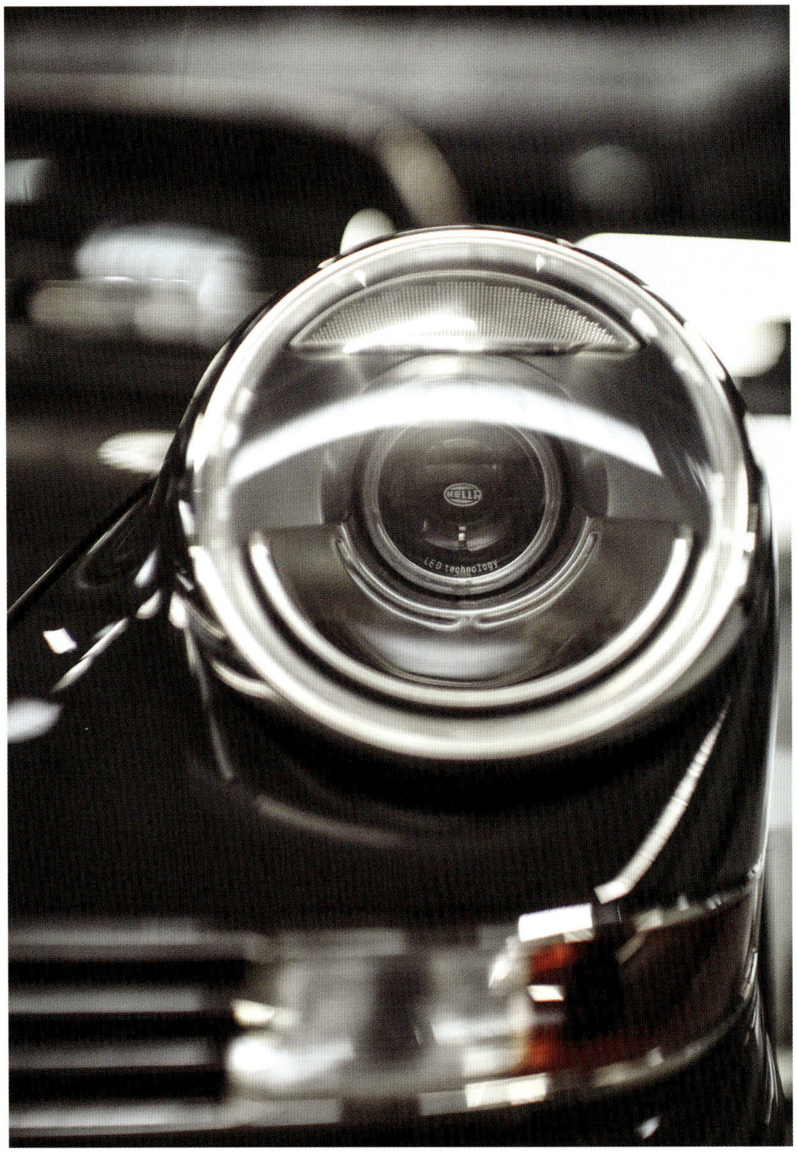

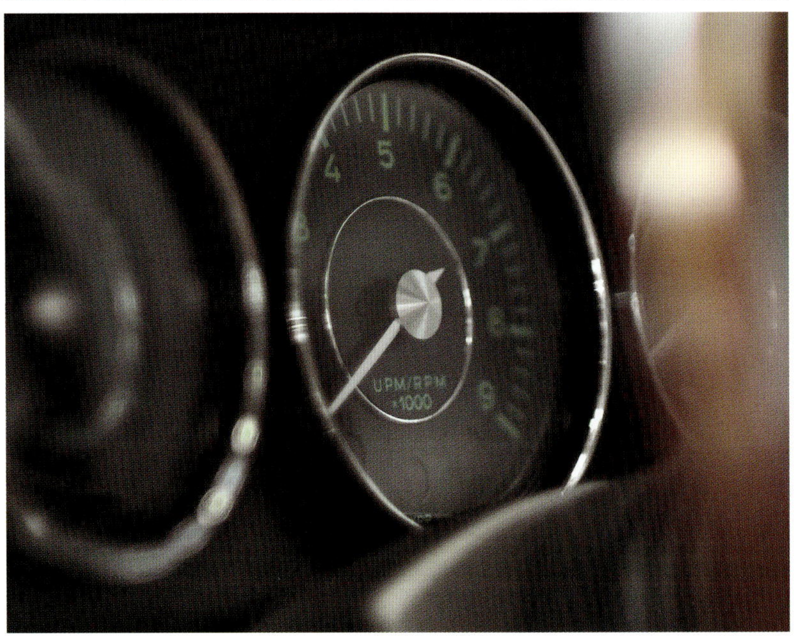

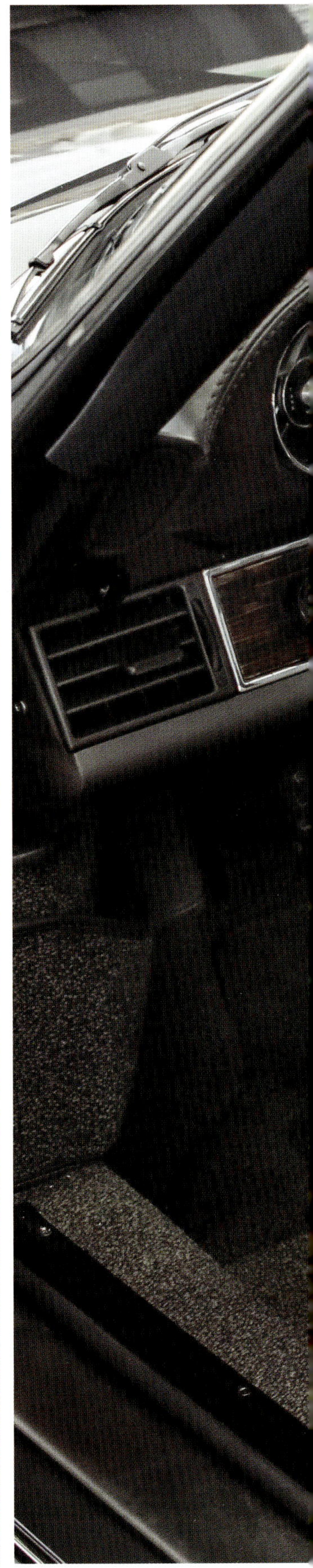

1. The headlights are an unmistakable signature feature of the 911.

2. The vintage VDO-style dials add an essential touch of refinement.

3. The atmosphere takes you to a comfortable sanctuary that's bursting with energy.

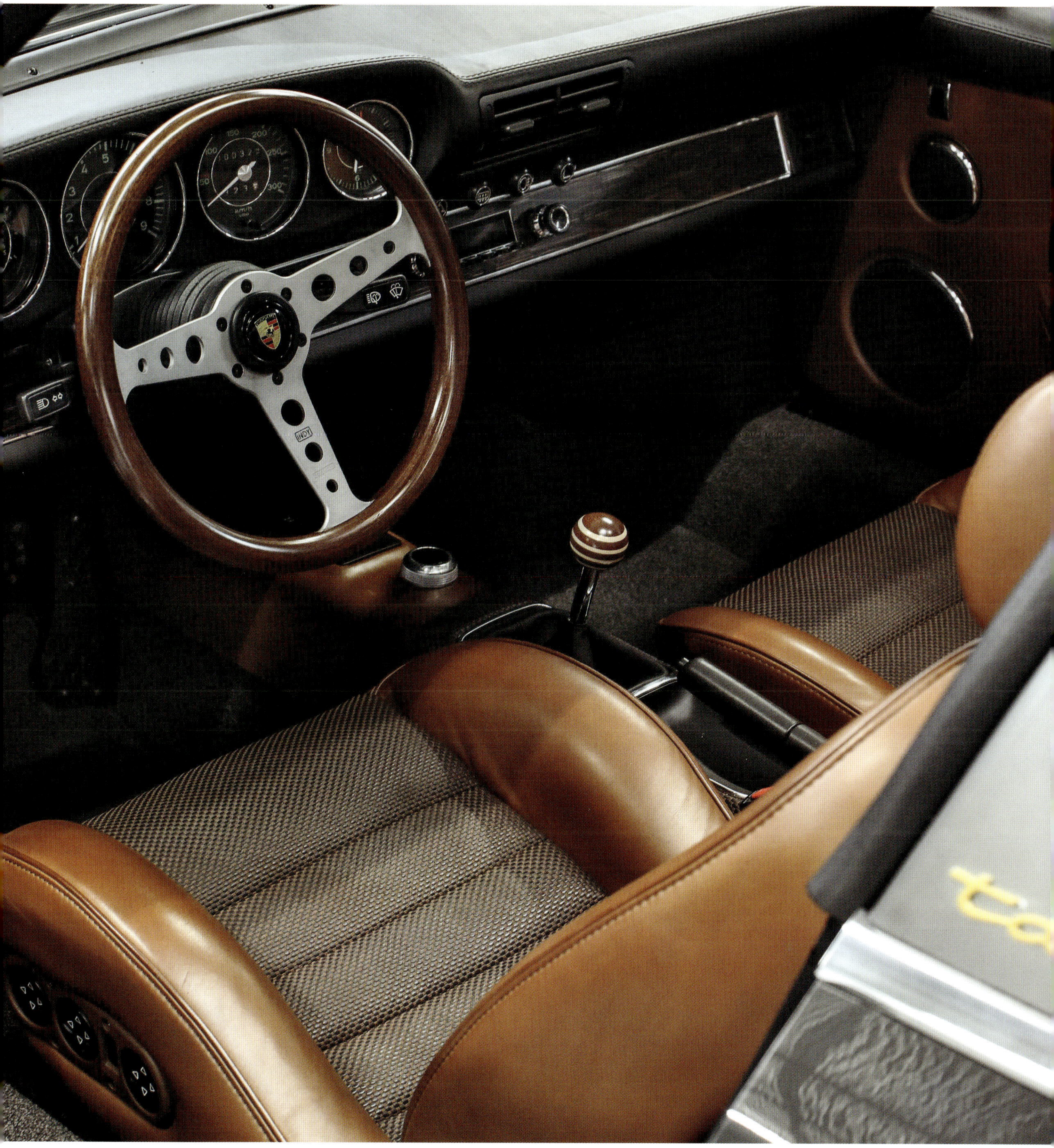

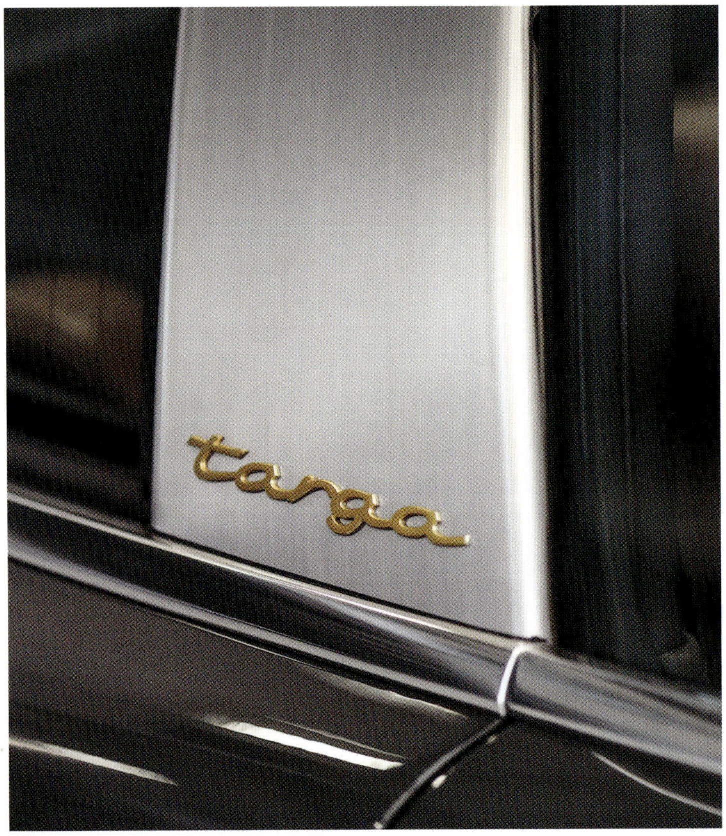
targa

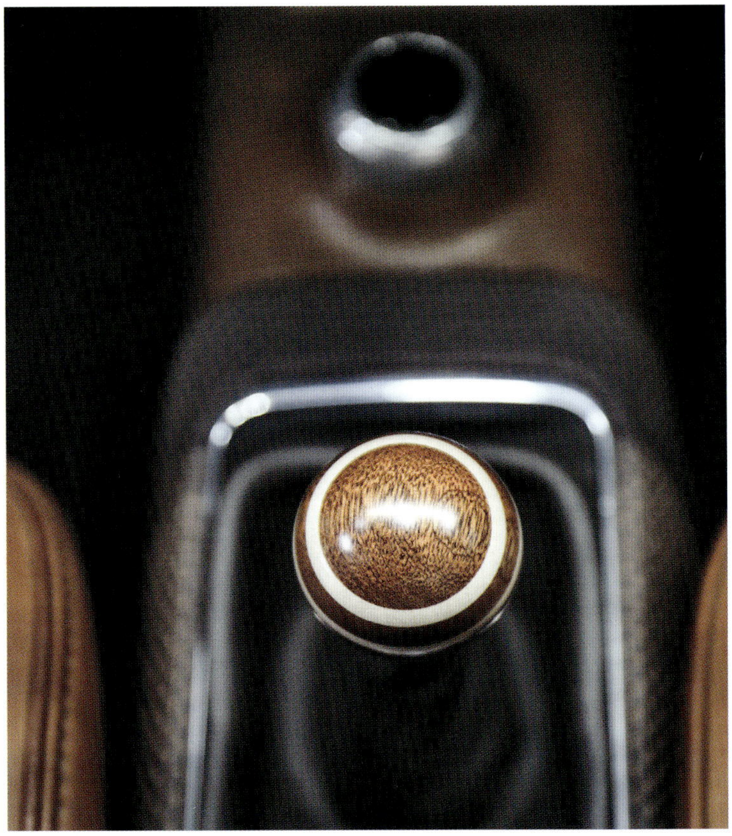

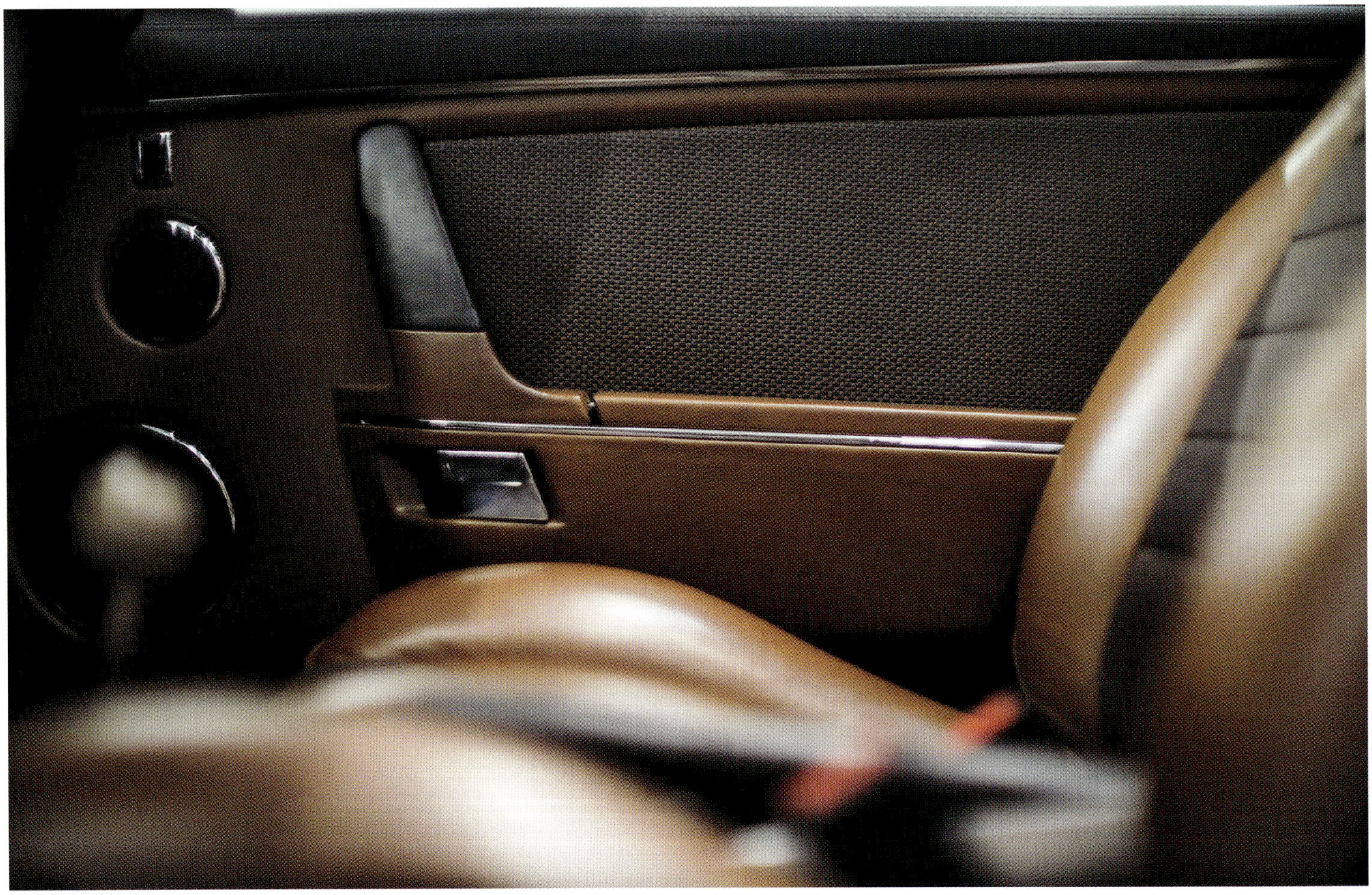

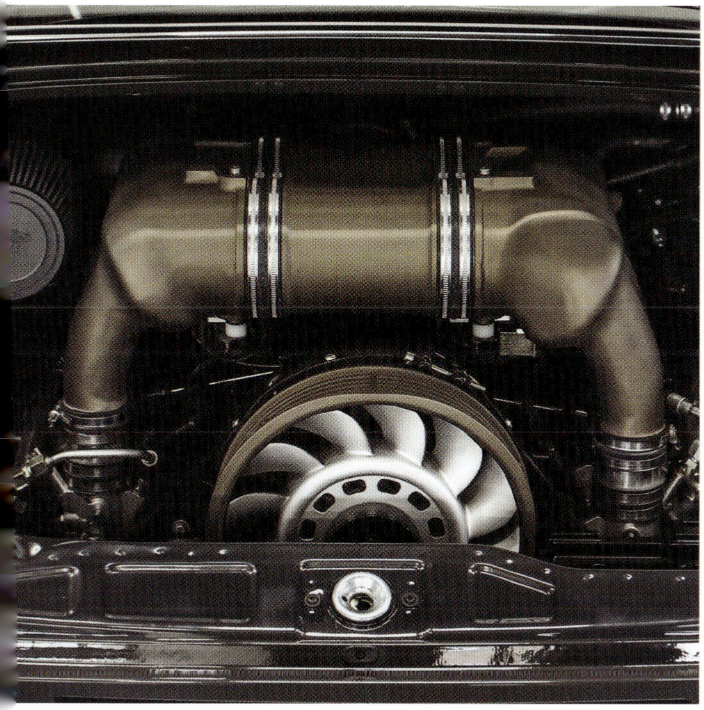

That's good for a power output of up to 420 hp! Did someone say maxi restomod? It also had a really robust ceramic treatment, which lets the metallic finish that Sébastien loves so much shine through, while also giving a rich, deep colour. "Up to 5,000 rpm, the Diva pulls harder than the 4.0-litre 997 GT3 RSR race cars I drove at Le Mans." Sébastien happily notes. The 4.2-litre, flat-six engine is fiendish, delivering power with a ferocity you would never expect from such an elegant car. To top it all, the Diva has a button – near the wooden gear lever – that lets the driver choose between four modes, ranging from discreet to the uncompromising racing mode. As for the interior, you can make the most of the Targa's removable roof to feel the air rushing by at full speed. There is leather everywhere, positively inviting you to sit comfortably in club chairs that look like something from a charming boudoir in a luxury hotel. But when the flat-six engine roars to life and this Porsche starts to cut through the air in front of it, the luxury makes it feel like you are on a Riva Aquarama speedboat. Its wooden steering wheel and gear lever are in keeping with the Targa's natural elegance. The green-numbered dials, as made by VDO at the time, were produced in Eastern France by a specialist who offers the perfect vintage touch. To further enhance the listening experience, Sébastien called on Focale, the French hi-fi experts, to provide the sound system for the Diva. Going truly above and beyond in the exceptional preparation of this 911, Sébastien fulfilled his dream by achieving, without compromise, the ultimate goal of a life devoted to the Porsche marque: his own 911 Targa with a 4.2-litre, flat-six engine! Who ever said that an Outlaw couldn't be refined?

911 DIVA
BY THE NUMBERS

CREATION 1991

FLAT CYLINDERS 6

CC 4,200

HP 420

1. Targa is a name that has evoked a certain elegance since 1966.

2. The gear knob offers a choice: settle back and soak in the ambiance, or drive like you're racing.

3. A high-end finish surrounds you.

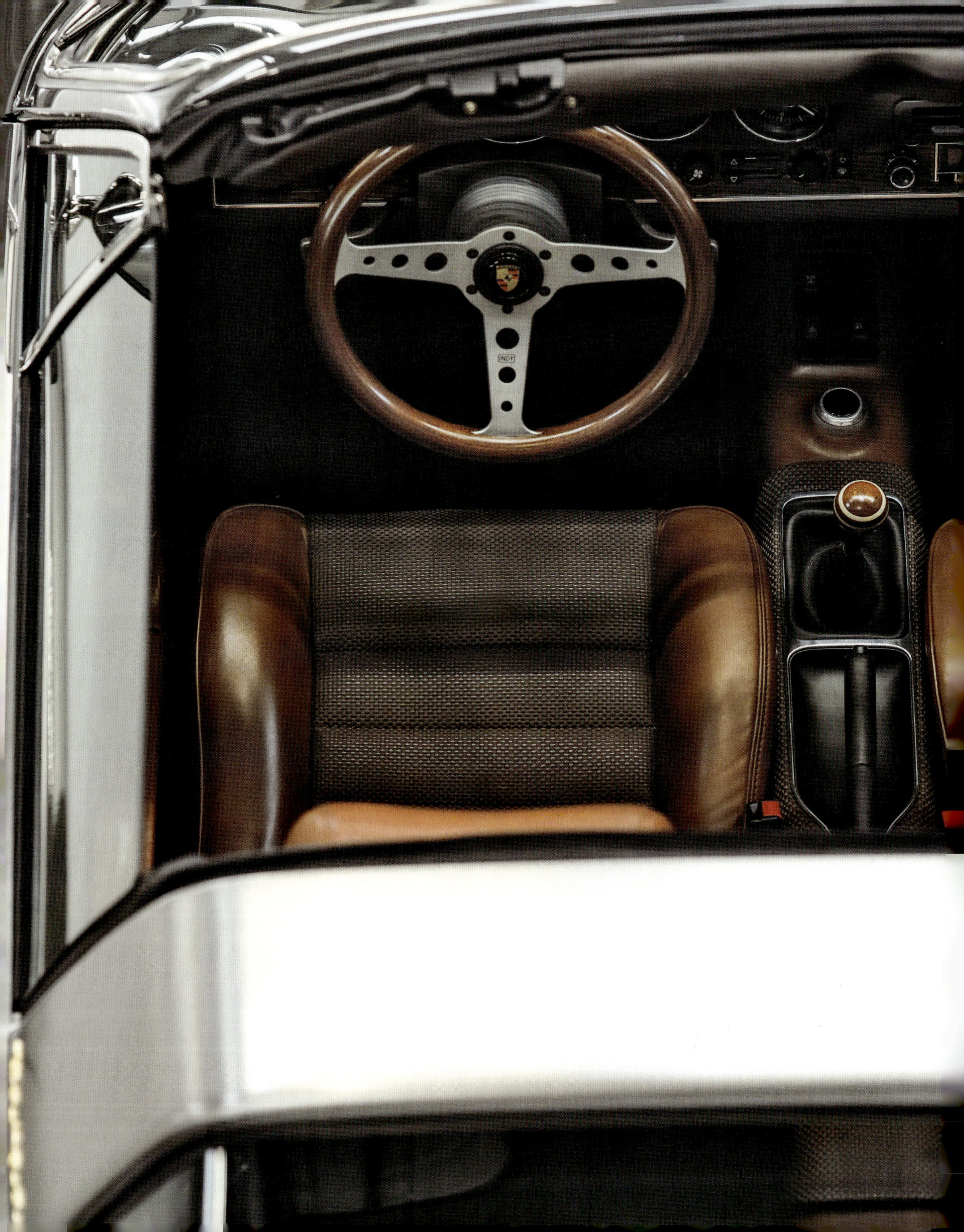

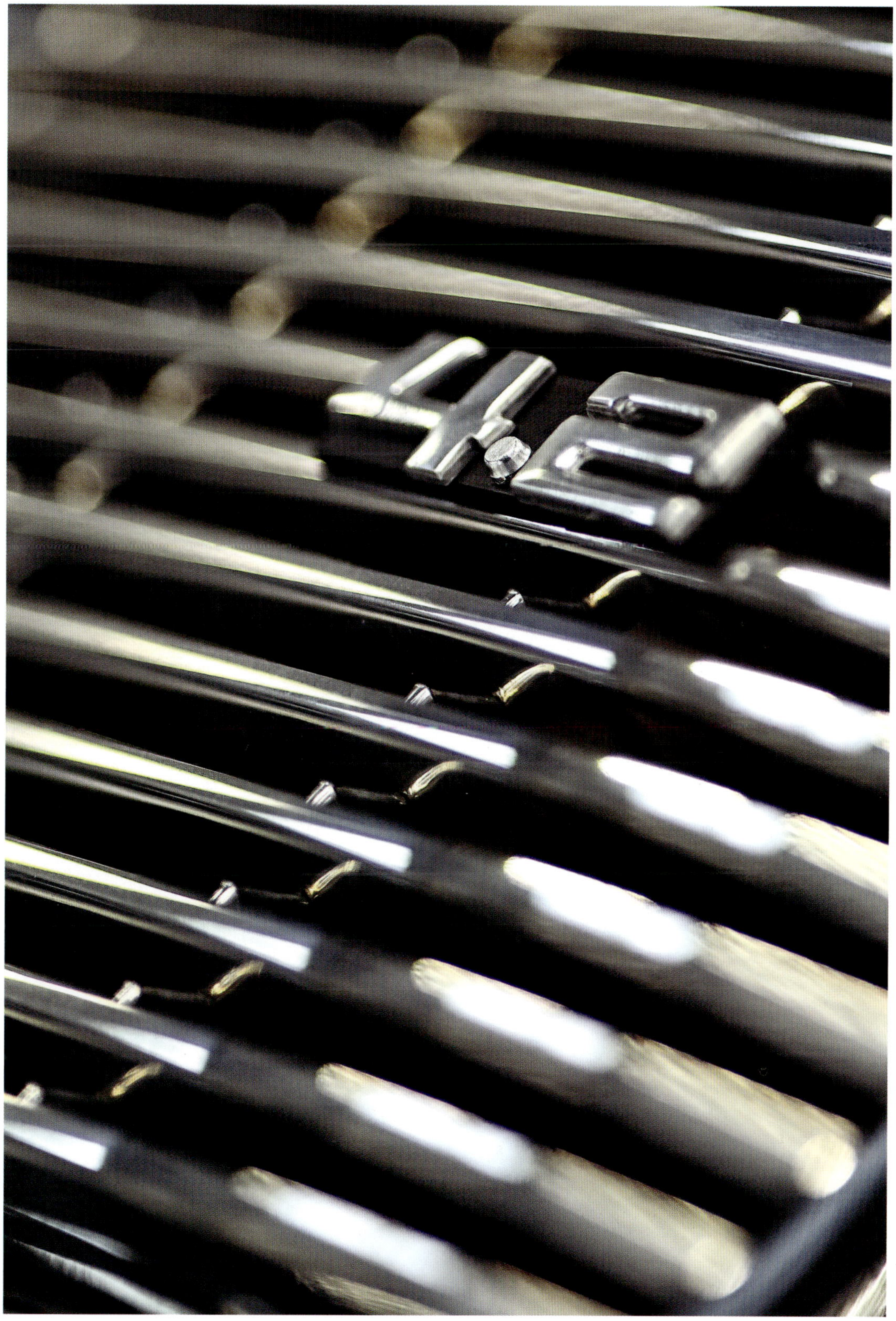

Above: 4.2 litres of displacement for a flat-six-cylinder engine that develops a whopping 420 hp!

Opposite: Bird's-eye view from the removable roof of this 911 Targa onto the fabulously neat, tasteful cockpit.

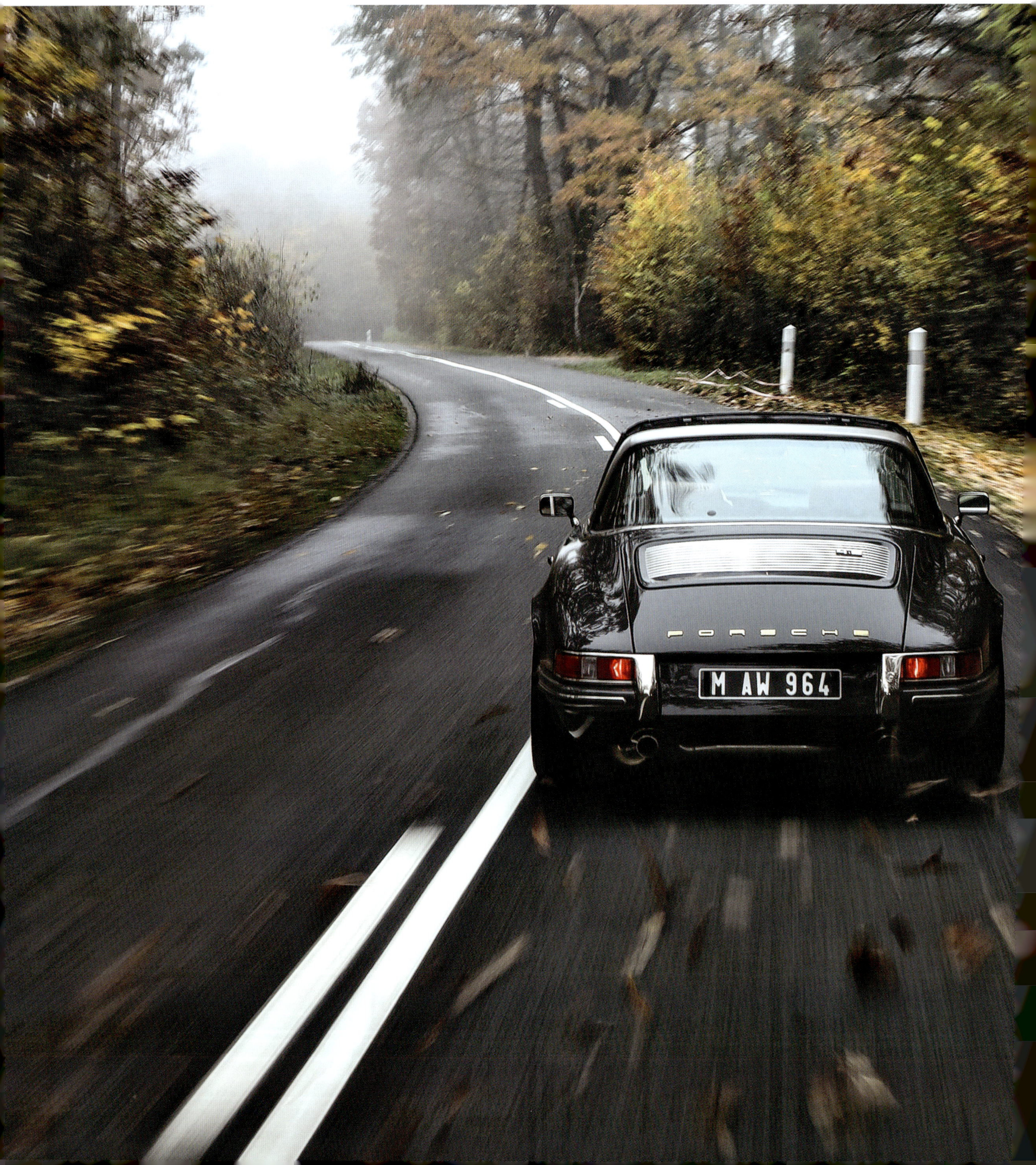
PORSCHE
M AW 964

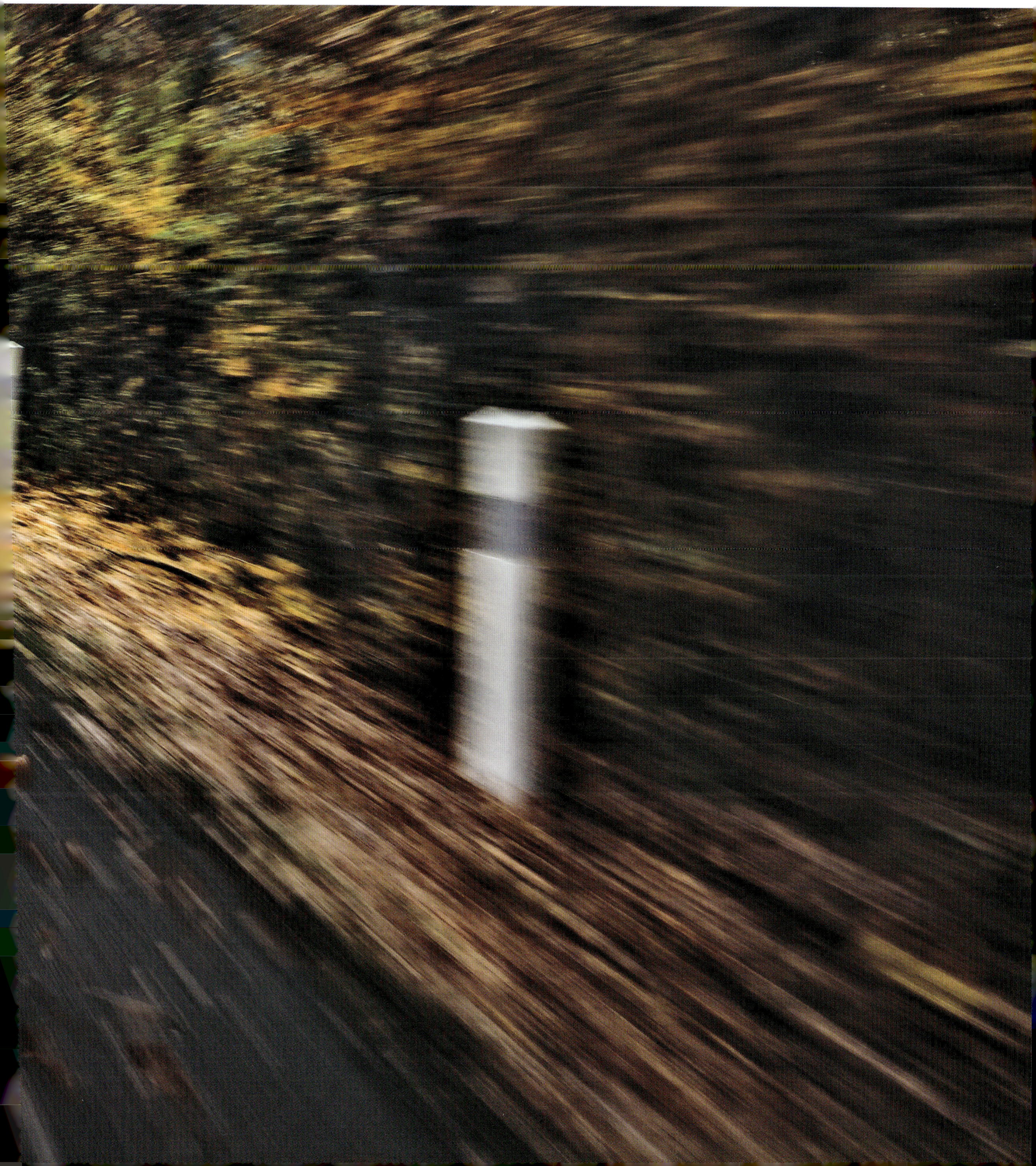

944 HOLLY SACRED FLAME

The story of this 994 is like a Phoenix reborn from the ashes. Designed for the track, it evolves with each new tattoo that Baptiste grafts onto it over the course of its wild life. And that's just for starters …

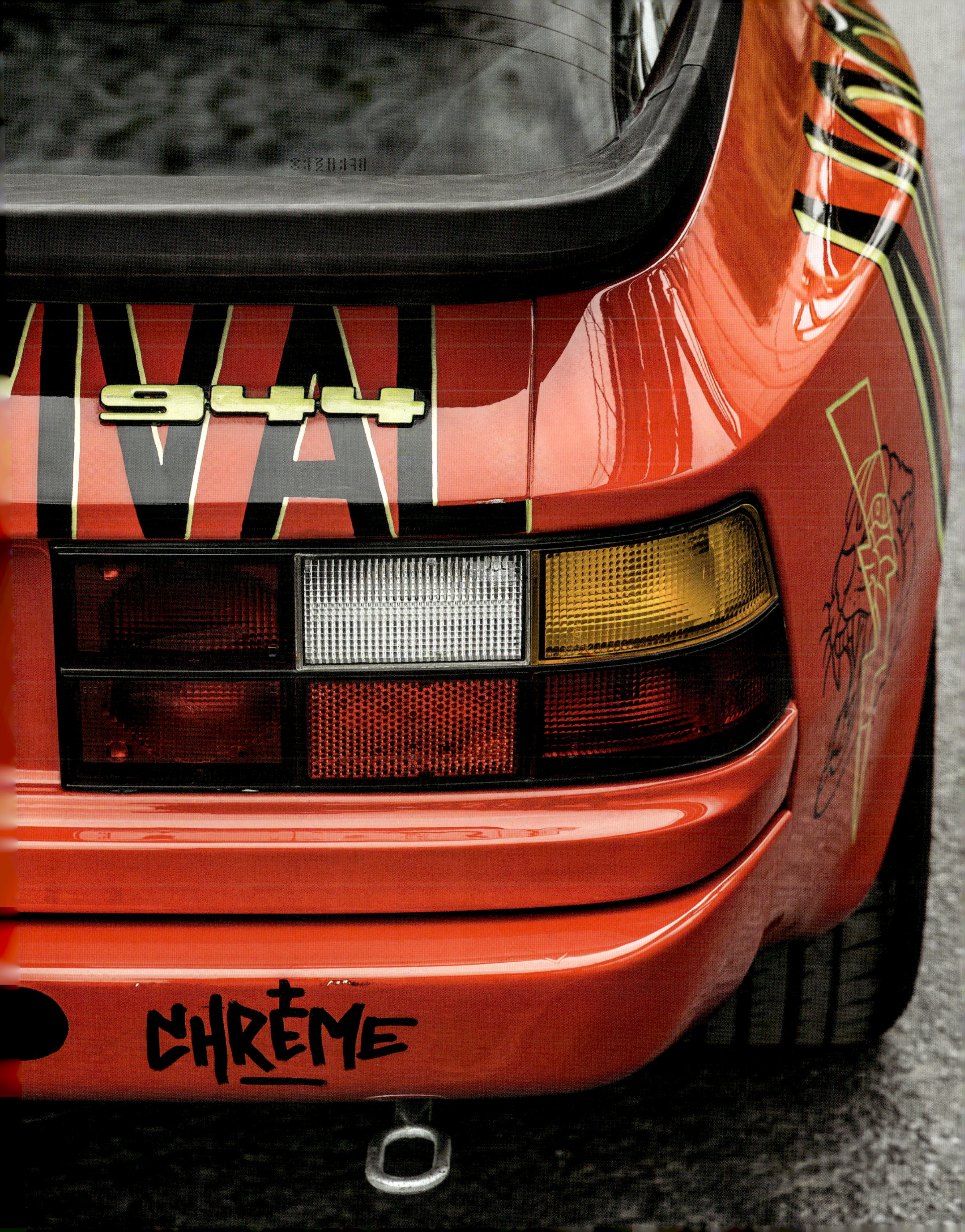
944
CHRÈME

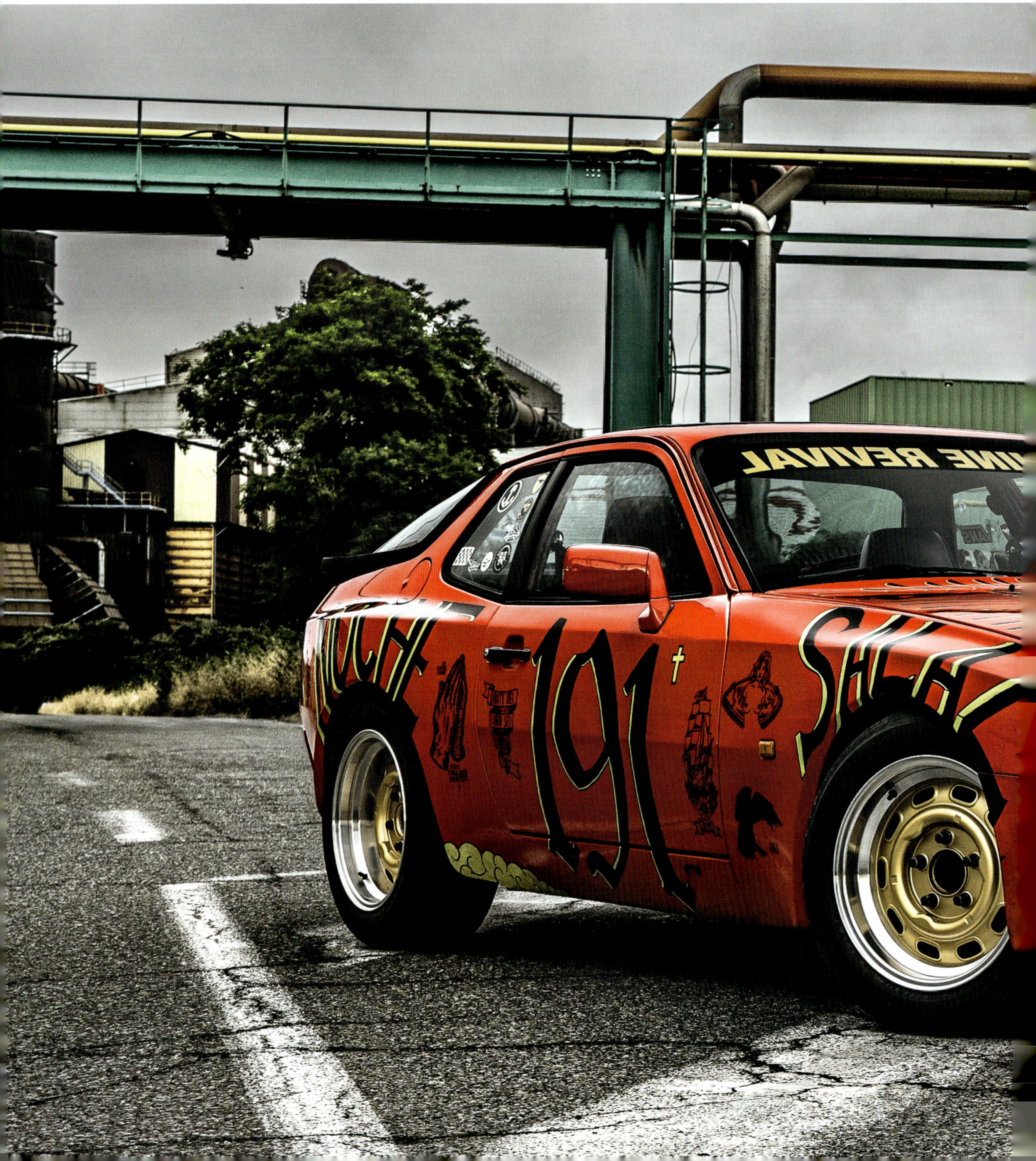
191

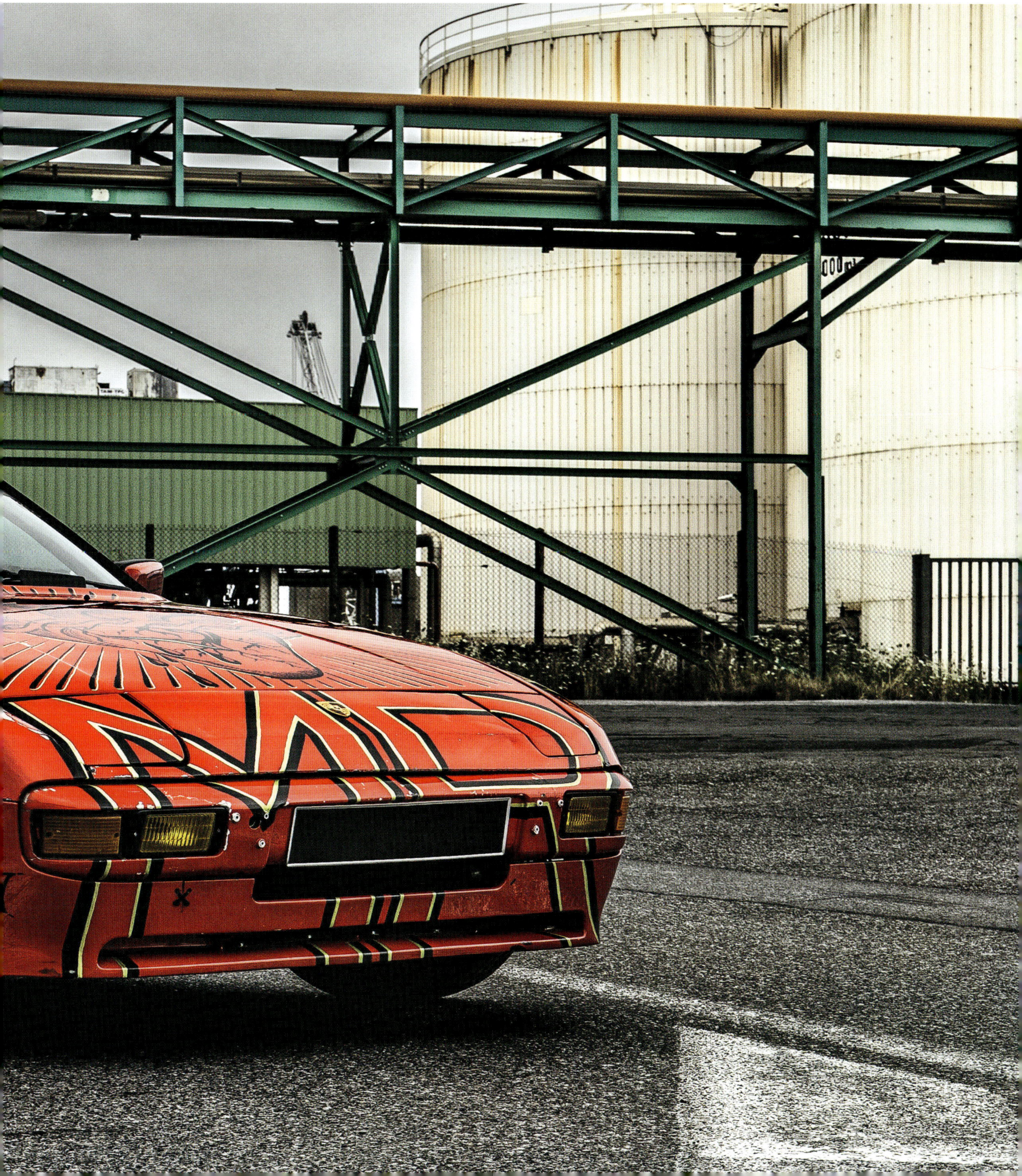

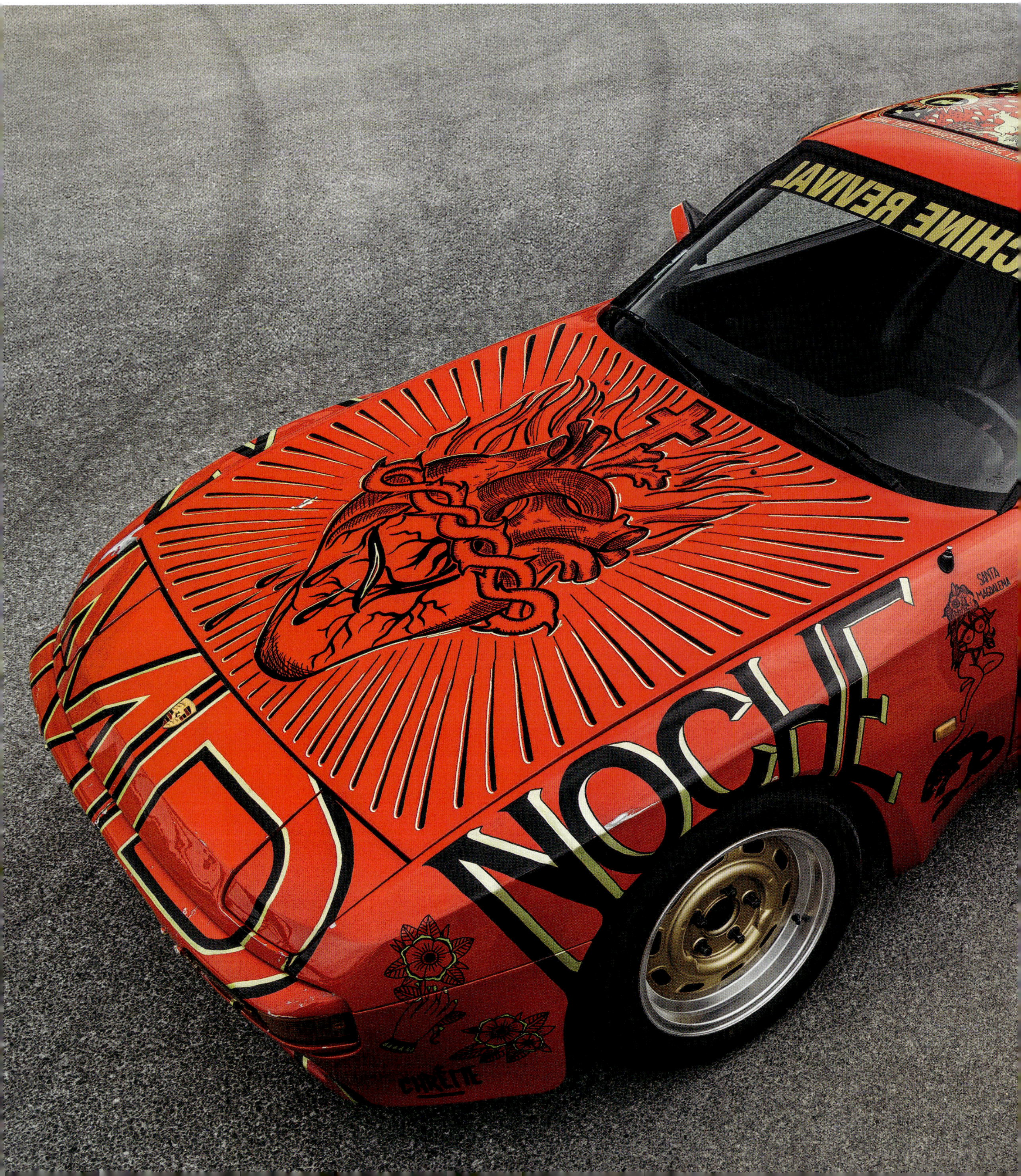
NOCHE

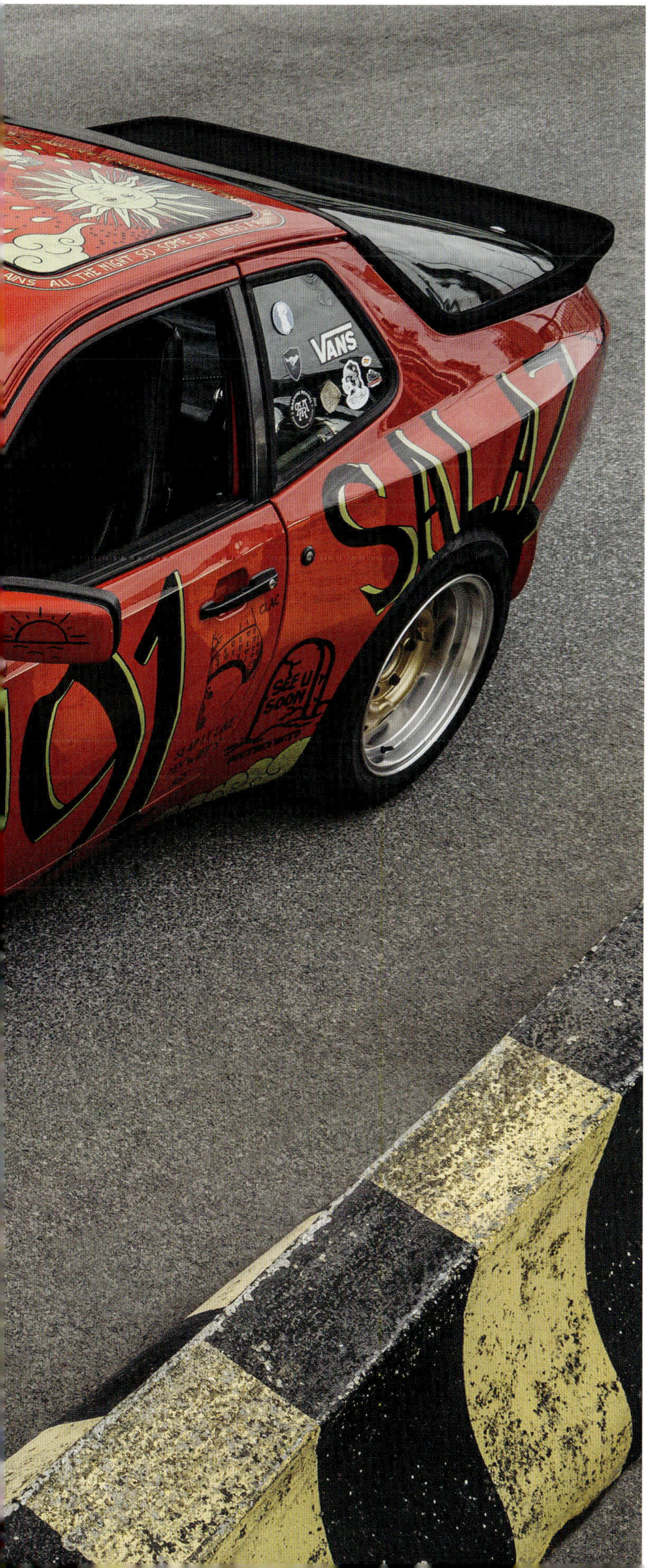

NOCHE SALAZ MEANS "WILD NIGHT" . . . QUITE A PROMISE!

A Porsche sits abandoned. Its engine no longer starts. The paintwork is damaged. It is a 944 that dates back to 1984. For purists, we are talking about a front-engined Porsche. They were first produced in 1982 to bridge the performance and price gap between the 924 (released in 1976), and the 928, which launched in 1978. The bodywork was based on the 924, but with more pronounced, aggressive lines. With nearly 160,000 units sold by 1991, when it was replaced by the 968, the model served its purpose well. But among flat-six enthusiasts it lives very much in the shadow of the iconic 911. However, in view of the cost of those 911s, the 944 is starting to garner a lot more interest, and not just among "youngtimers".

Baptiste was drawn to this unusual Porsche, which had been left standing for almost two years. At the age of 29, after a career in thermal engineering in a design office, he resumed his studies to transform his passion into his profession. He enrolled in the prestigious Sbarro school – named after its founder, automotive legend Franco Sbarro – and became the designer he always wanted to be. Today, he works reimagining Porsches, designing prototypes and special parts. The 944 intrigued him. It called to him. He wanted to do something about it – get it running, for starters. He swapped it for a motorbike – a Honda XR600R – with Thomas, its former owner, who had also wanted to make a project of the car. And just like that, Baptiste was the owner of this 944. His first mission was to get that engine roaring again. It was fitted with a 2.5-litre naturally aspirated inline four-cylinder engine that produced 163 hp. Baptiste sold his old Audi 80 – his everyday car – in order to get the money to repair his new treasure: "I was a pedestrian with a 944 that didn't even start," he says laughing. He then threw himself into working on the car and spent two weekends in a row working on it. "In fact, this 944 had been through many owners before it broke down nine years before Thomas bought it. The mechanics who had worked on it had reversed the relays. Looking at the wiring diagrams, I just put the relays back in the right place and it started up straight away!

"I CHEATED DEATH, IN THE MOONLIGHT . . ."

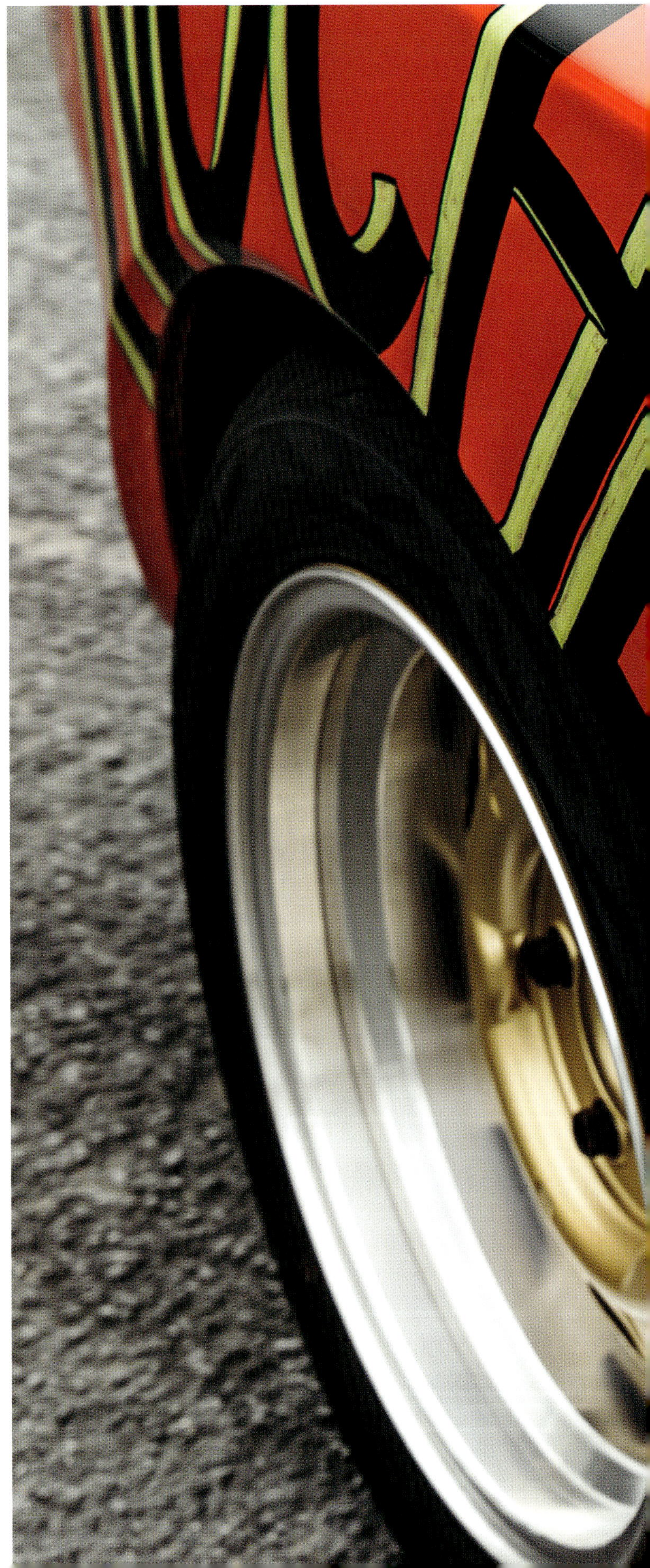

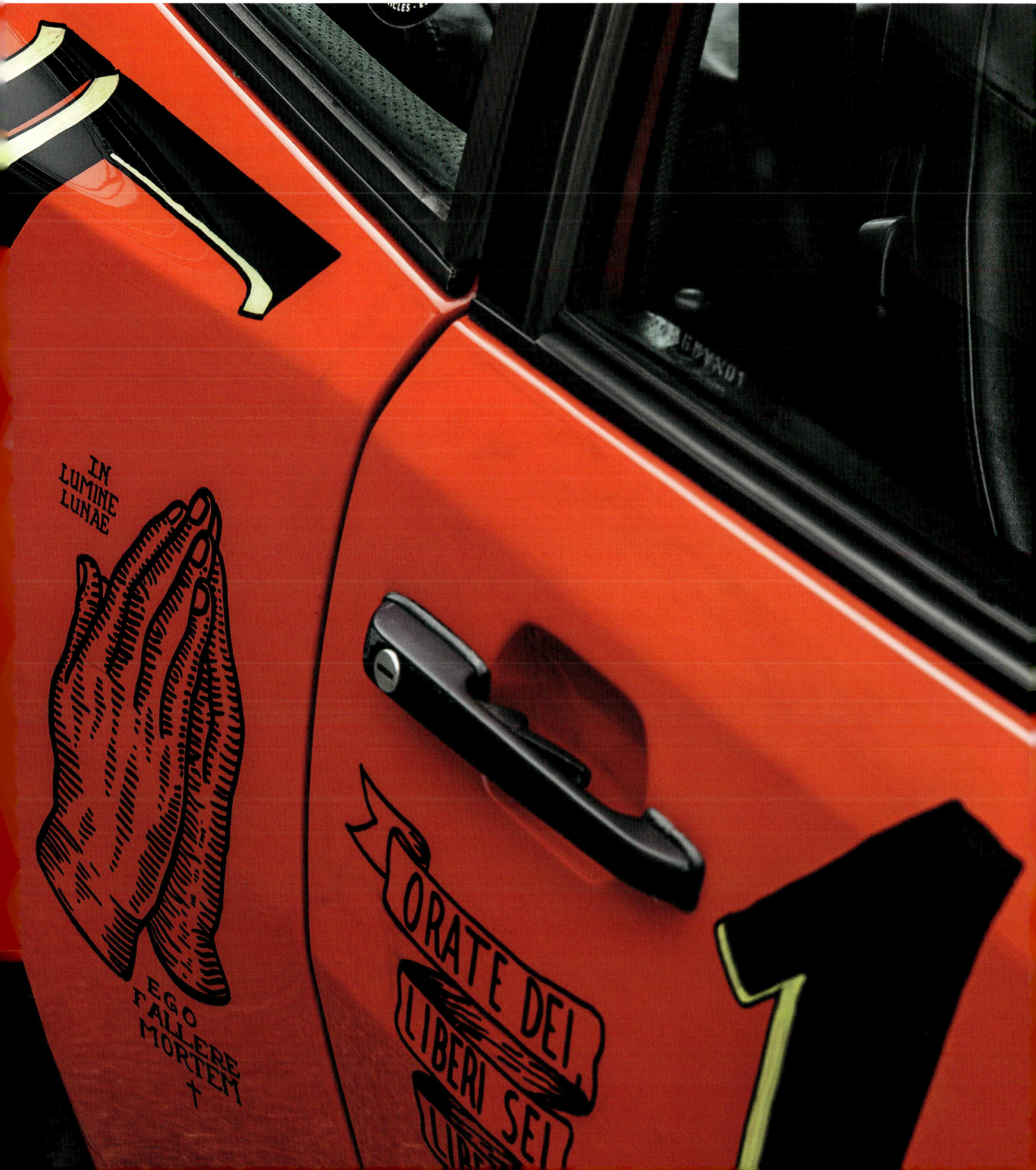
IN LUMINE LUNAE
EGO FALLERE MORTEM
ORATE DEI LIBERI SEI

"I then did a quick clean-up everywhere of everything that wasn't quite right. I went out the following weekend and I drove more than 600 miles, without any problems at all."

The verdict is in: "It's a real Porsche, for sure! One thing led to another, and this 944 ended up as my daily drive. It's a sports car, but it's a Porsche nonetheless, which means it's a car you can use every day without a thought, just like a 911. It is really a Swiss army knife of a car: you can take it to the track at the weekend, do your supermarket shop, put your surfboard in it – even sleep looking up at the stars." To begin customising the car, Baptiste removed the rear seats and door trim, along with all the insulation, and replaced them with door panels featuring just a leather strap. "I took out all the car's upholstery and covered it with perforated material, Alcantara style. The dashboard is still cracked. I wanted to keep it as understated as possible so that you wouldn't see it had been modified: everything was black, with no thick, coloured stitching. I didn't want it to be a stiff, formal ride; I wanted it to feel more like a real race car." That's why the text on the sun visor is written backwards – so that it can be clearly seen in the rear-view mirrors of the cars it is about to overtake.

BLOOD-RED PAINT PAIRS WITH THE DEEP-BLACK INTERIOR.

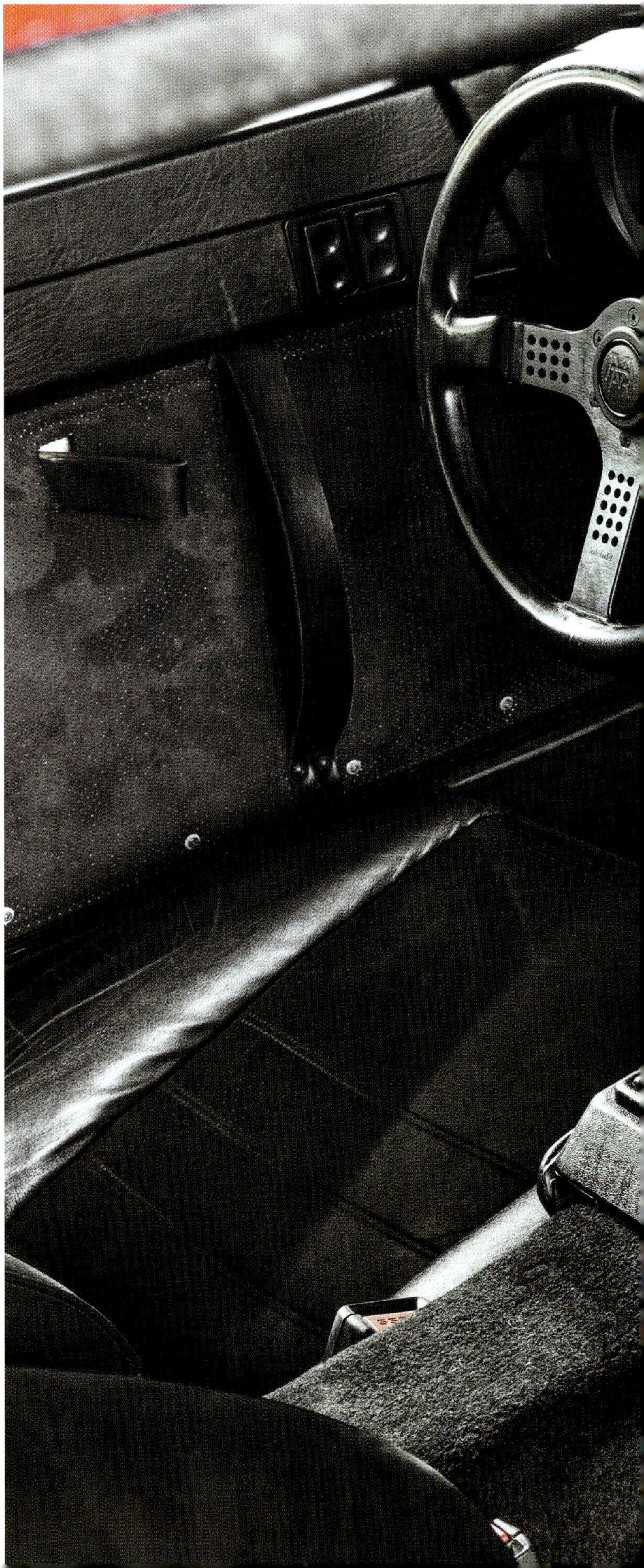

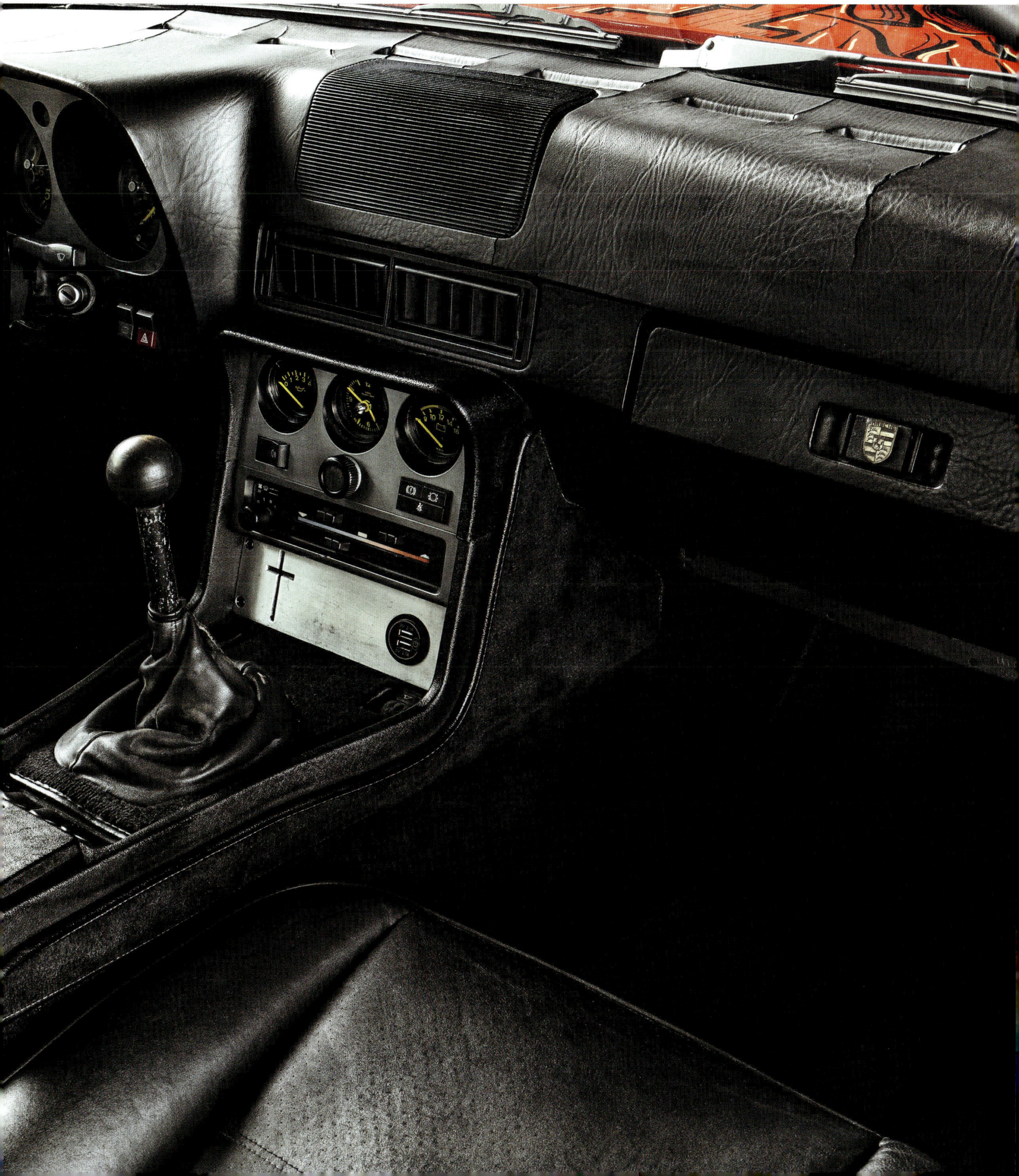

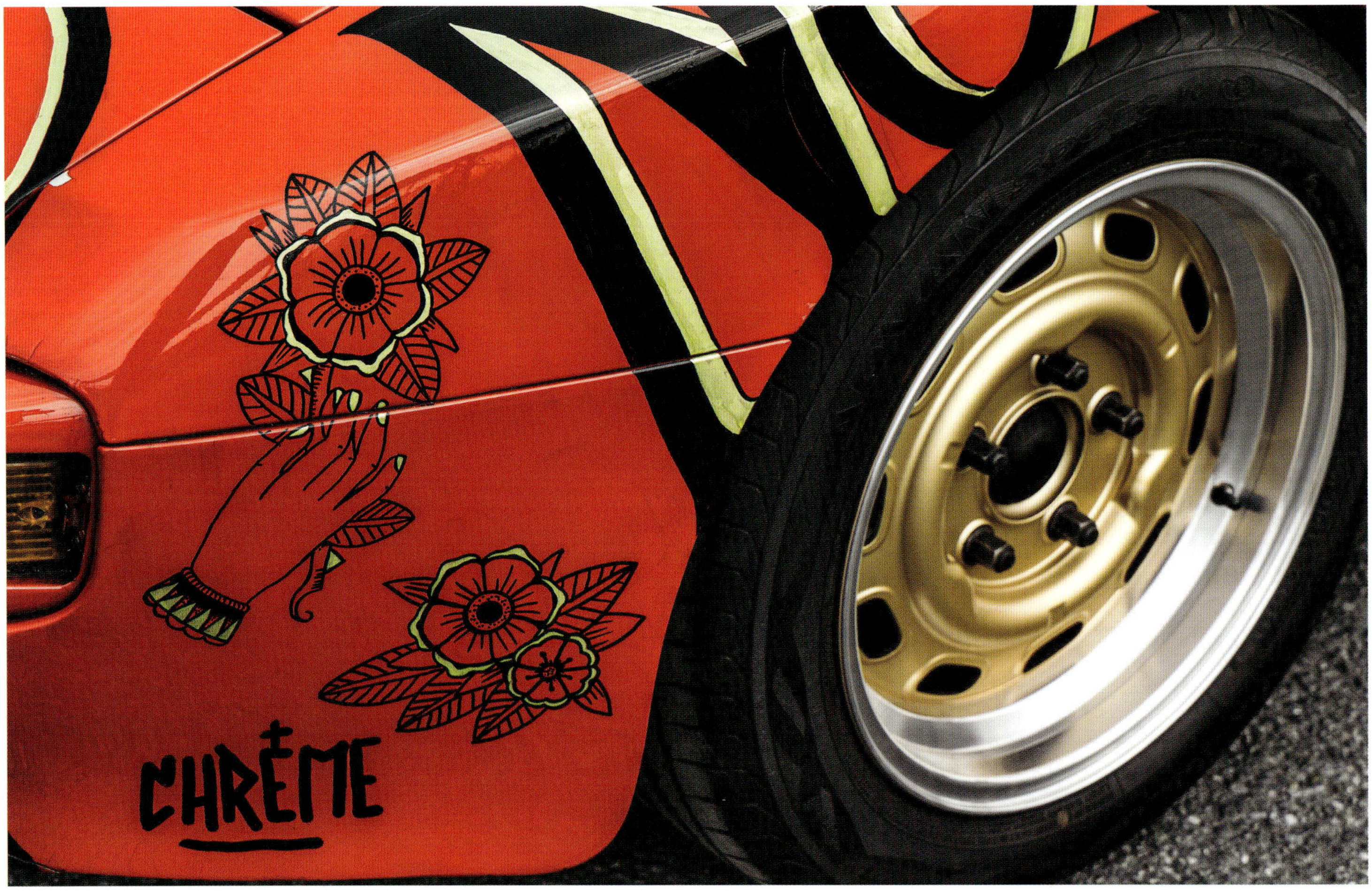
CHRÊME

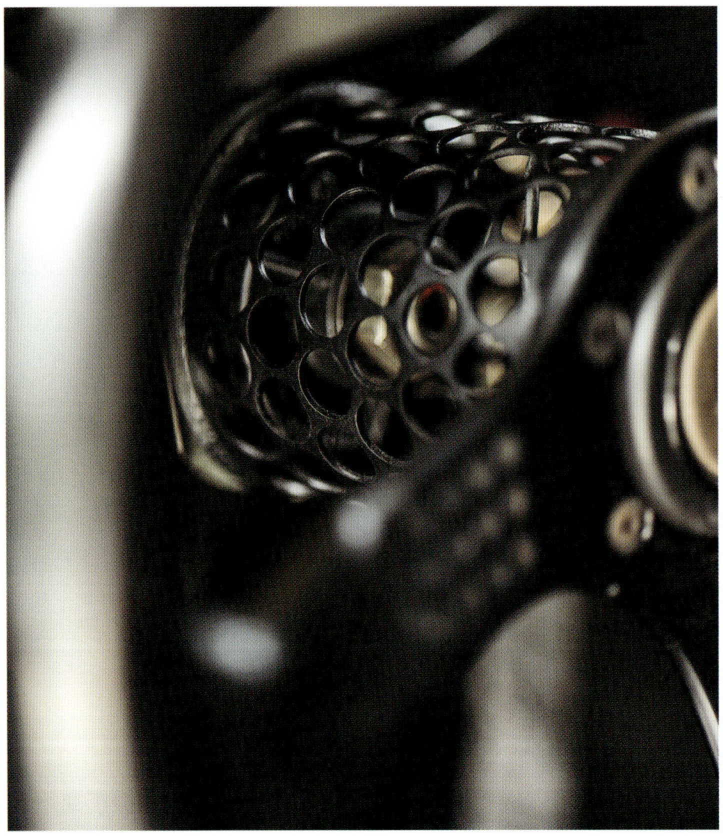

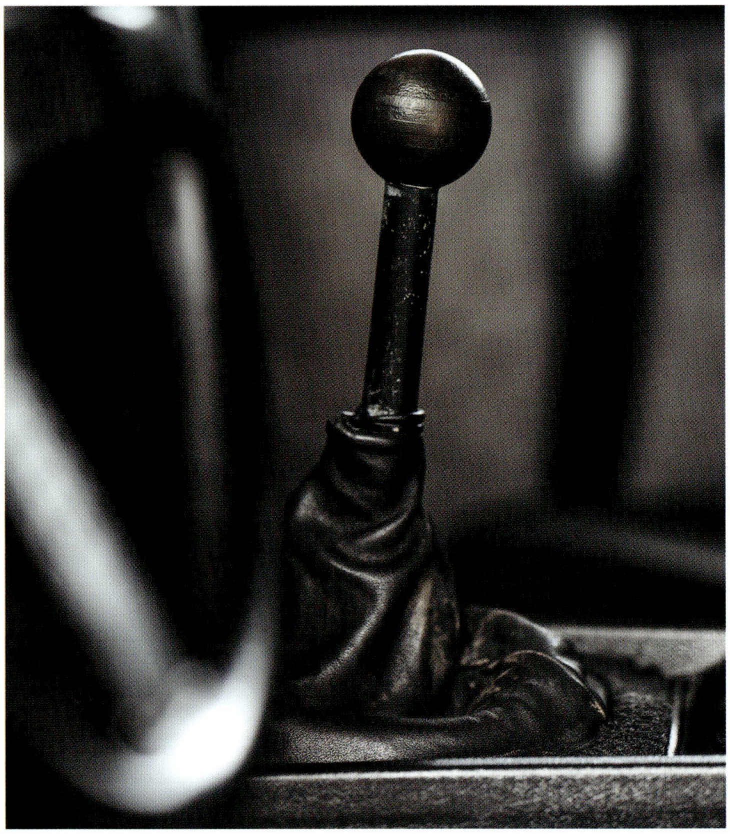

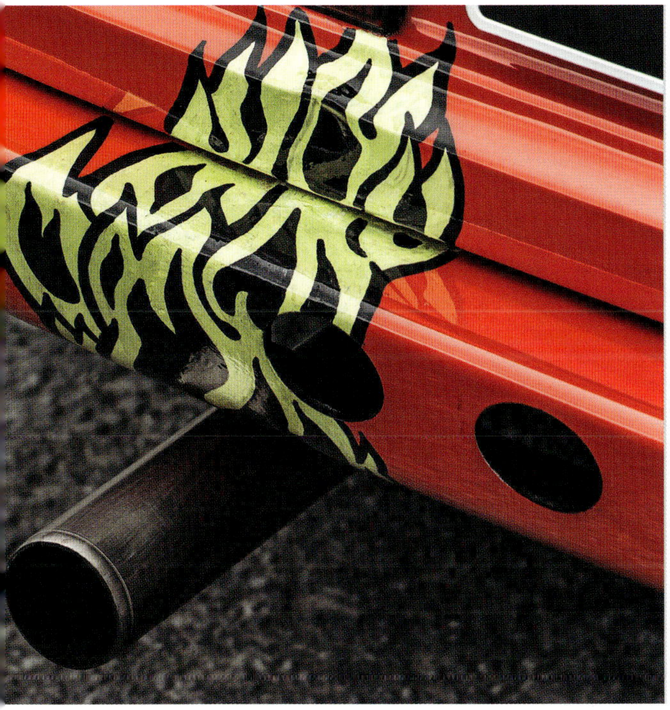

944 HOLLY
BY THE NUMBERS

CREATION 1984

IN-LINE CYLINDERS 4

CC 2,500

HP 163

"I installed a hand-made aluminium accelerator pedal and took the rubber off the other pedals, then put grip tape on them. The gear stick has been upgraded to a short-shifter for quicker changes, and it is topped with a black-and-red wooden knob." Finally, when it comes to the cockpit, the steering wheel was highly important: "I have no idea at all where it came from. I don't know what it was on before: it only had a horn on it, with the old logo with the Volkswagen castle. Maybe it came from a first generation Golf GTI? I think it's a MOMO ... I really liked it so I put it on, with just the Machine Revival logo in the middle."

Baptiste made a stainless steel exhaust system to give the car some voice, deep at low revs and high-pitched at high revs, lowered the ground clearance by 3.5 cm (1.3 ins), fitted two pairs of rims with a Porsche 906 and 908-style steel look – but made of solid aluminium – and that was that! The engine has – for now – remained stock: "It's crazy how well it runs. I haven't dyno-tested it, but it outpaces plenty of more powerful 944s. That is why I drew a heart on the front hood: that's the soul of the car, the light in the tabernacle;it has the sacred fire." Baptiste confesses his love for divine illustrations, in a religious style: "I'm not a believer, but I still think they are beautiful." As a true daily driver, Baptiste has lived a thousand lives in his car and experienced countless stories that aren't necessarily fit to tell ... "In the spirit of *The Hangover*, they are stories you wouldn't even want to share with your friends." Hence the words *Noche Salaz* in large letters across both sides; it means something like "wild night" in Spanish. The story is told through all the little tattoos on the car, which give this 944 its signature aesthetics. And the name? "Holly is for Hollydaily, referring to a porn actress..." A true Outlaw, whose life is only just beginning (again) ...

1. Chrême is Baptiste's artist name, and he signs all the illustrations on his 944 himself, as a testimonial ...

2. A dark mesh lurks behind the Volkswagen steering wheel.

3. The wooden knob on the gear stick is covered in black paint, looking like a lump of coal.

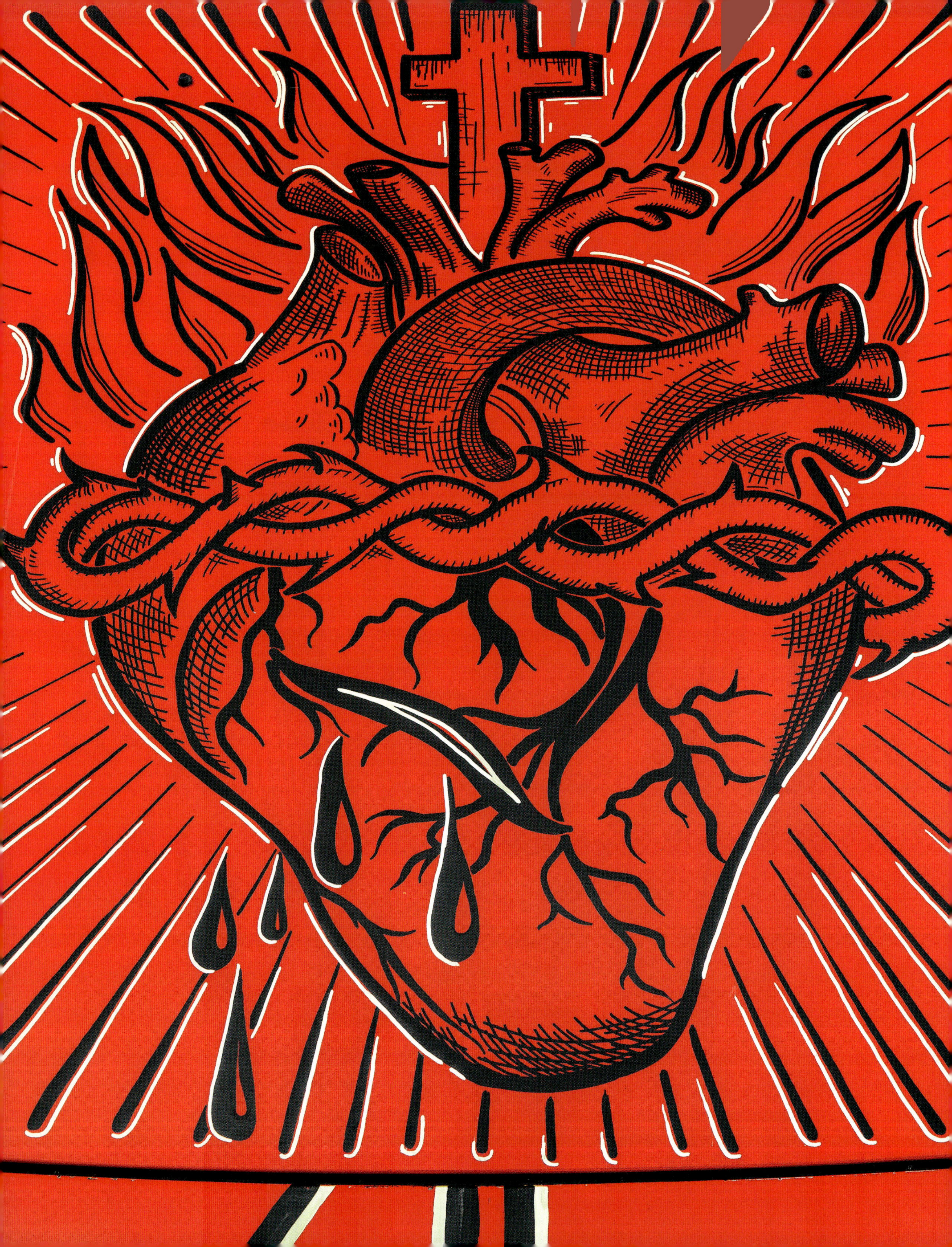

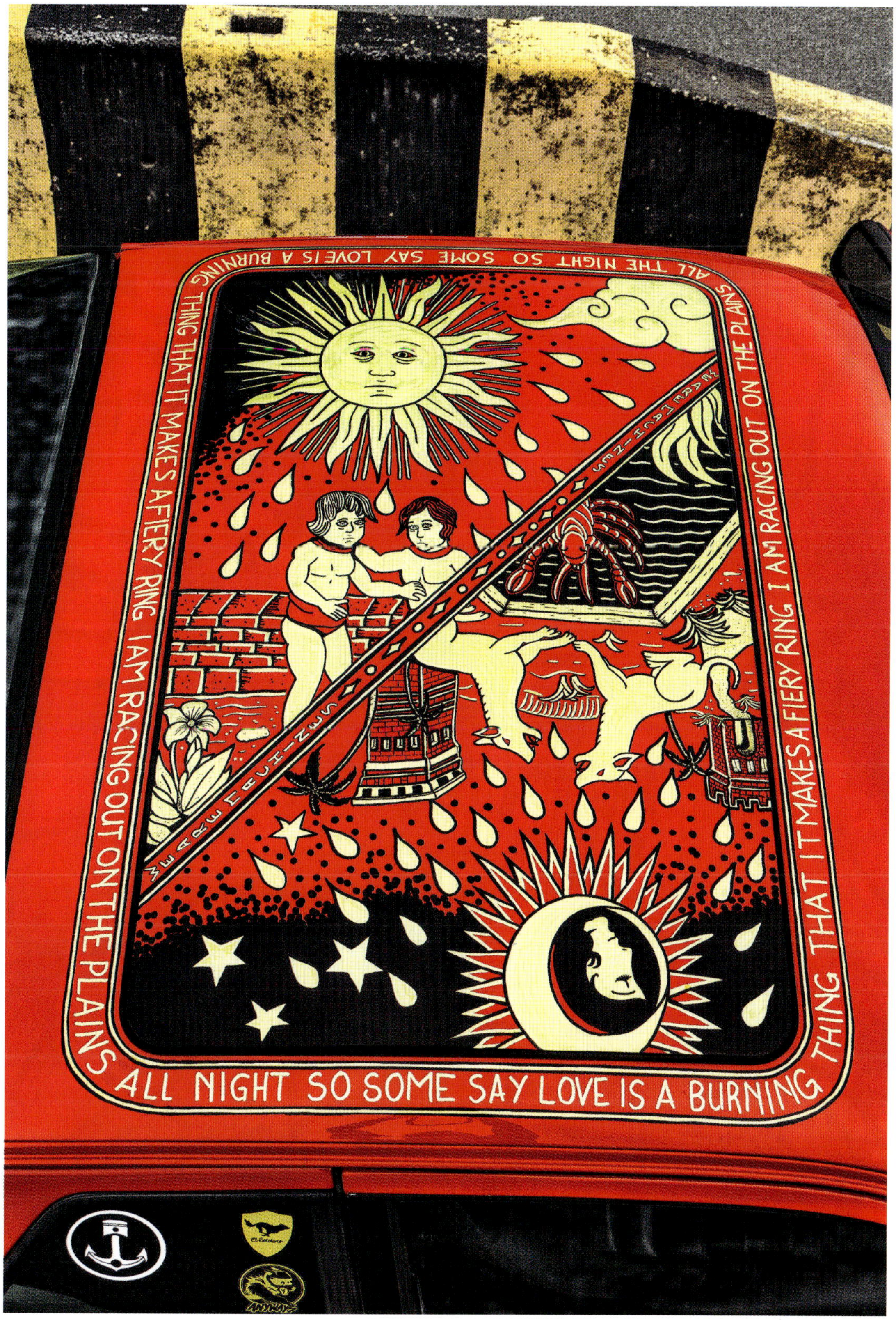

Above: A tarot card is painted on the roof of this Outlaw 944, featuring slightly modified lyrics from "Song for Zula" by Phosphorescent.

Opposite: The mechanical soul of this 944, the 2.5-litre, 163 hp, four-cylinder engine, hides beneath this Sacred Heart, as reinterpreted by Chrême.

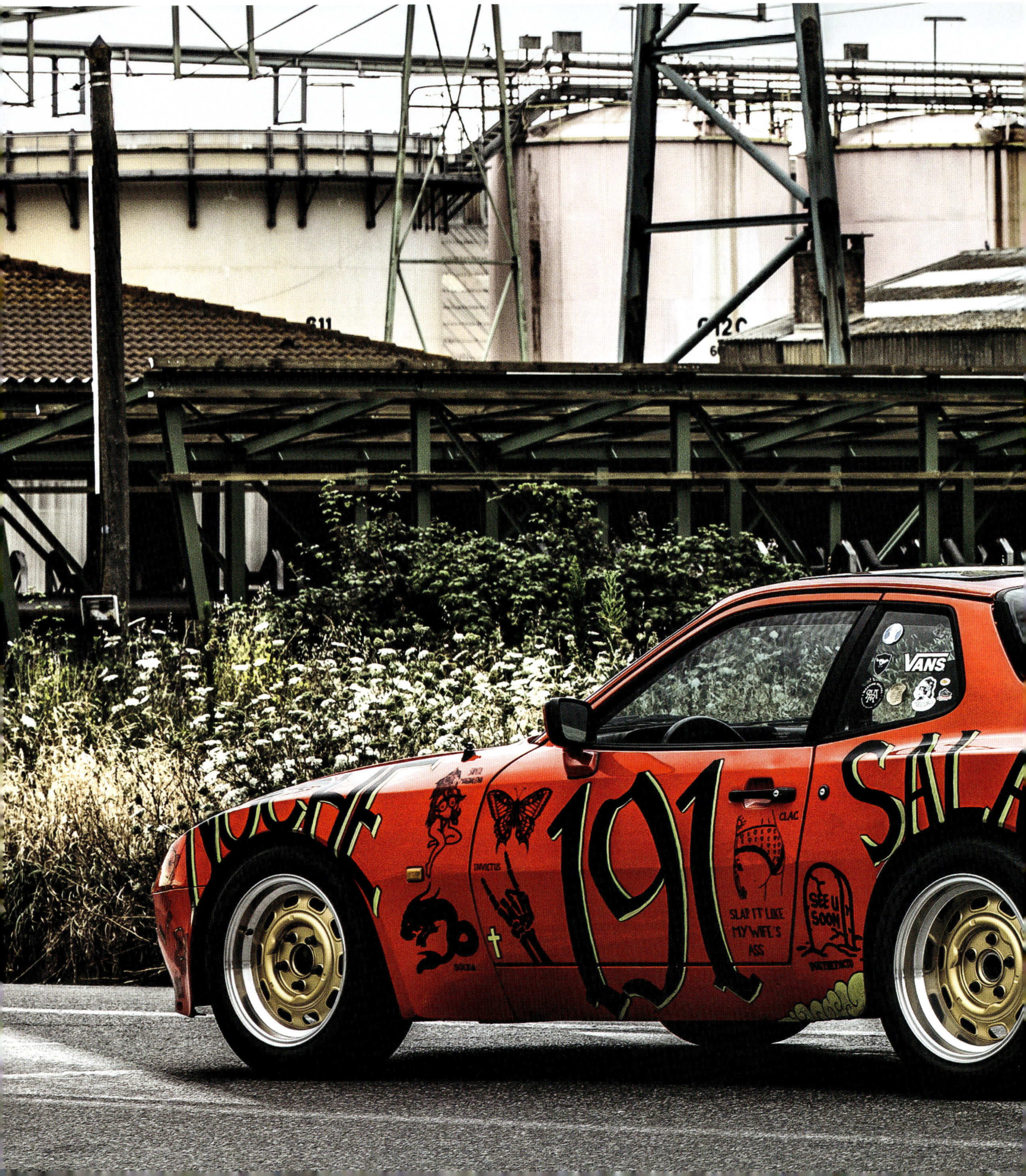
VANS
191
SLAP IT LIKE MY WIFE'S ASS
SEE U SOON

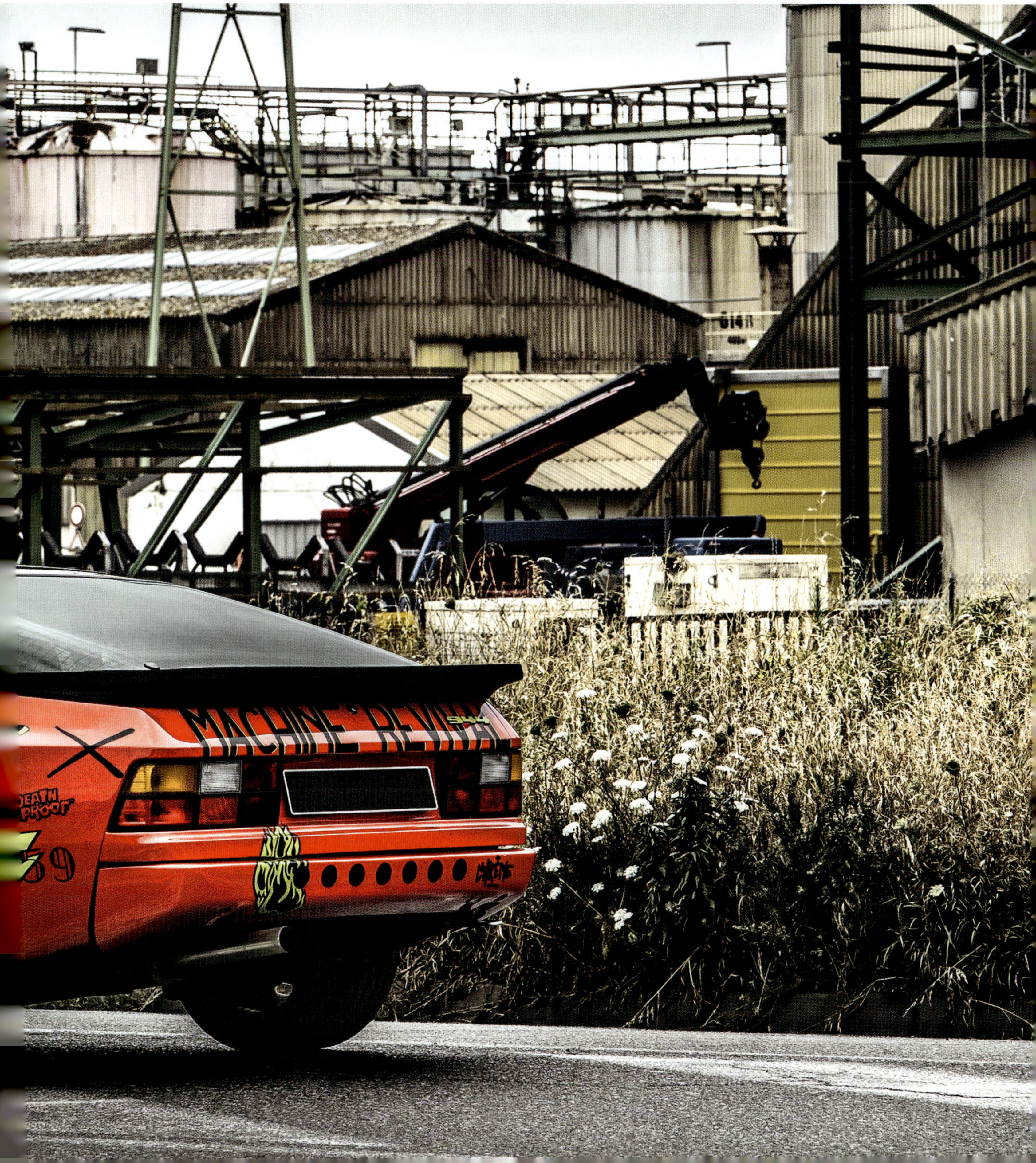
MACHINE

911
GISÈLE
THE *CHILL* OUTLAW

Who said an outlaw has to be fierce? Nicolas, who uses his 911 on a regular basis, chose to create a *chill* Outlaw, but still gave it a badass look with chic, elegant refinements.

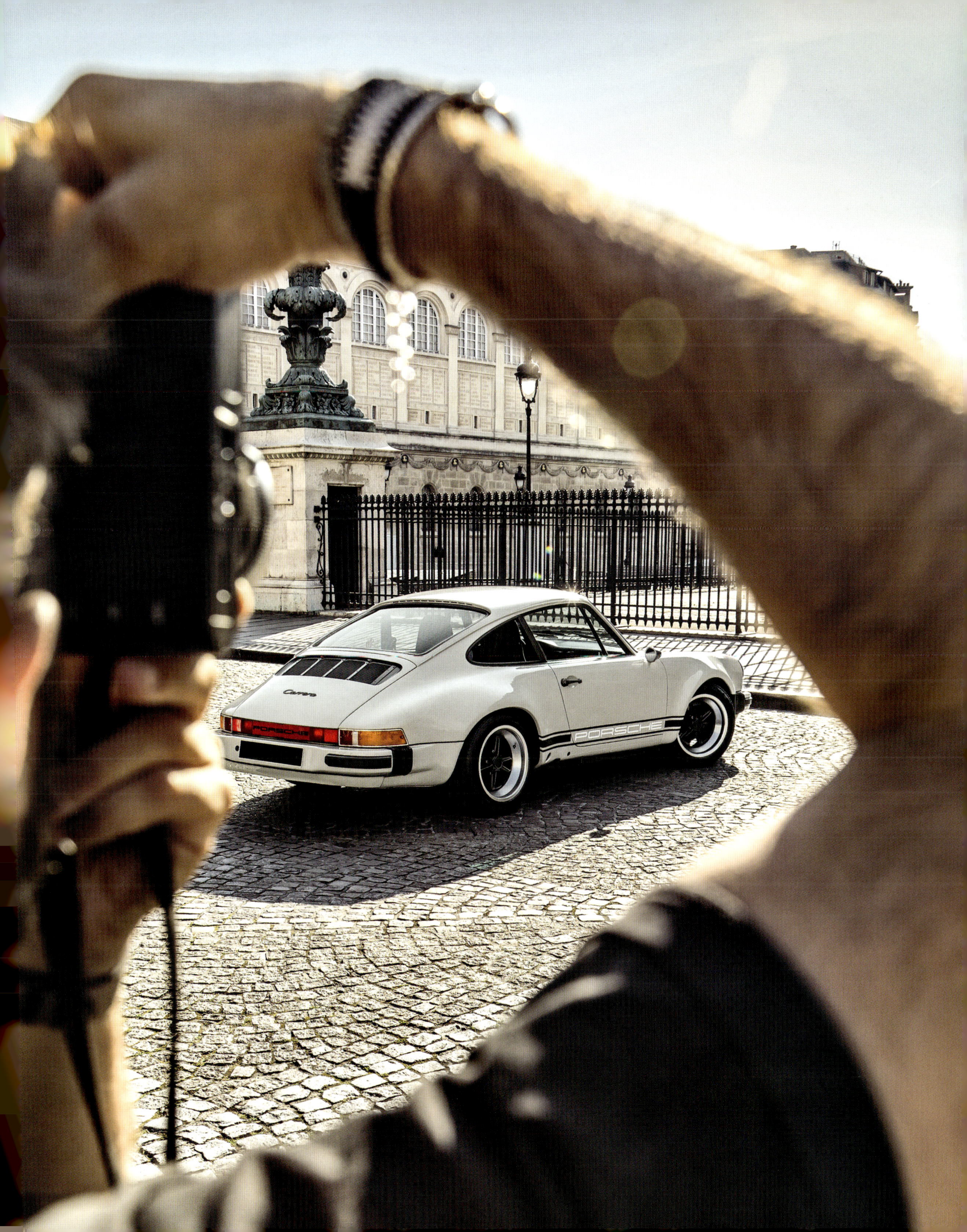
PORSCHE

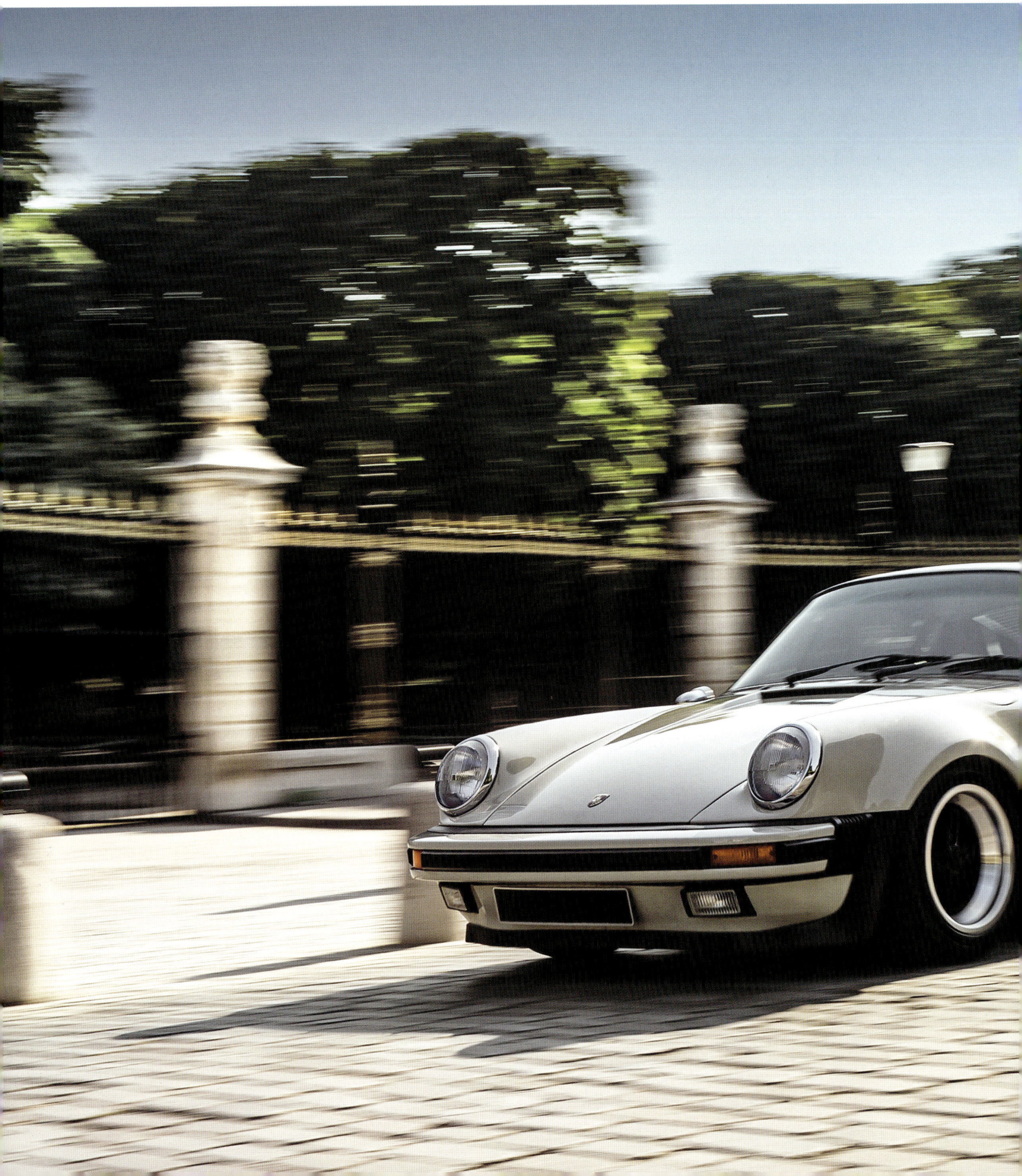

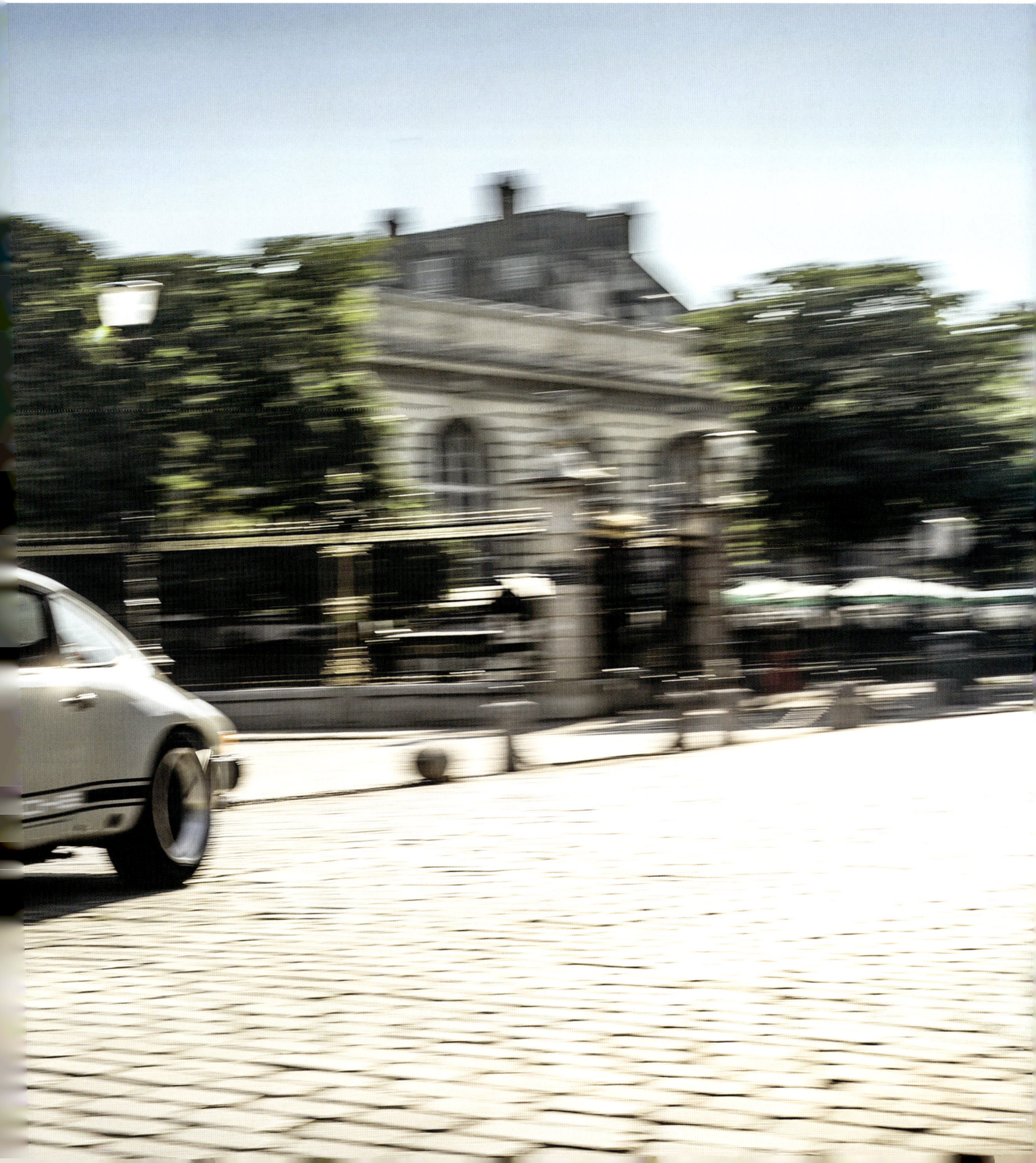

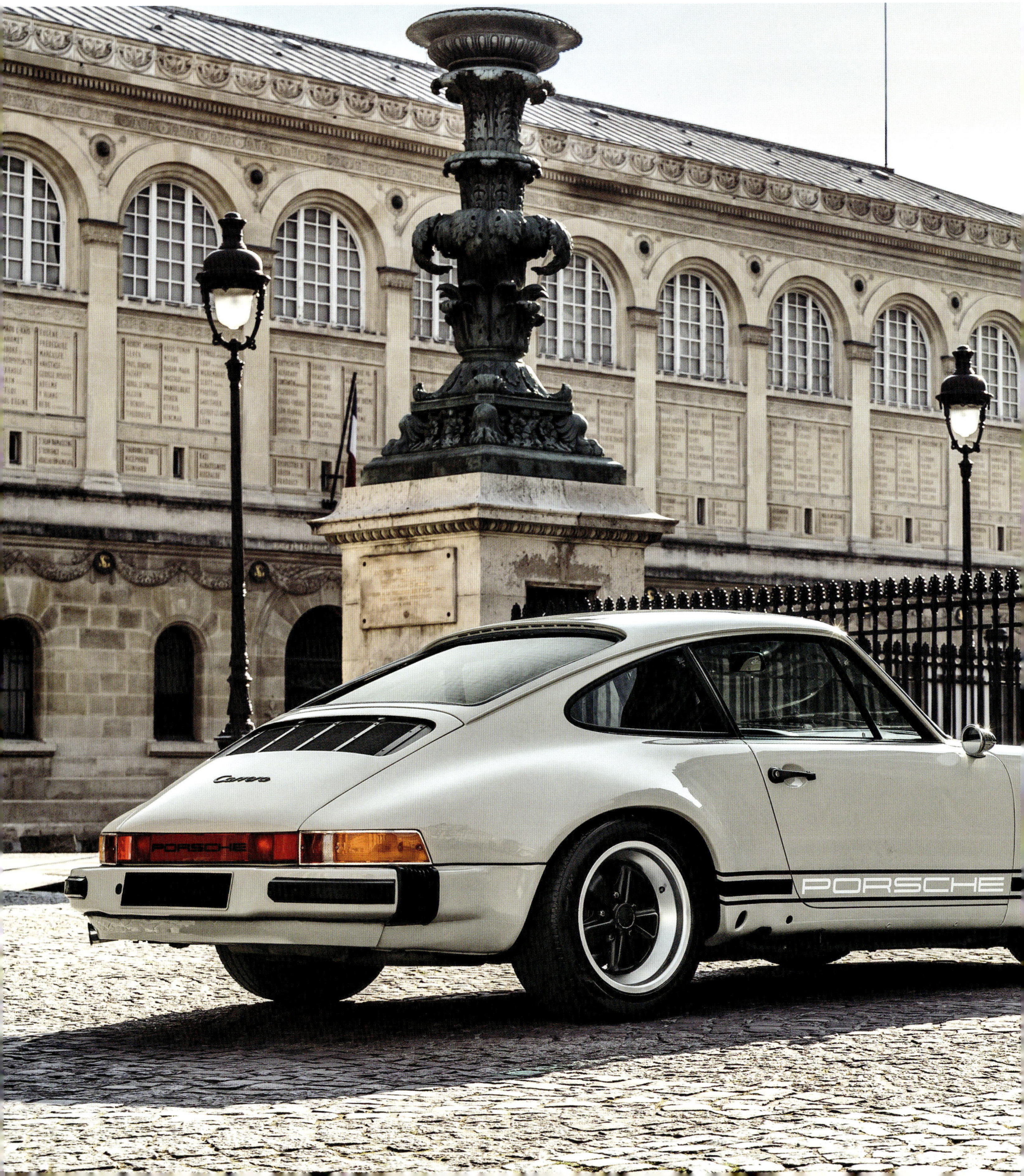
PORSCHE
PORSCHE

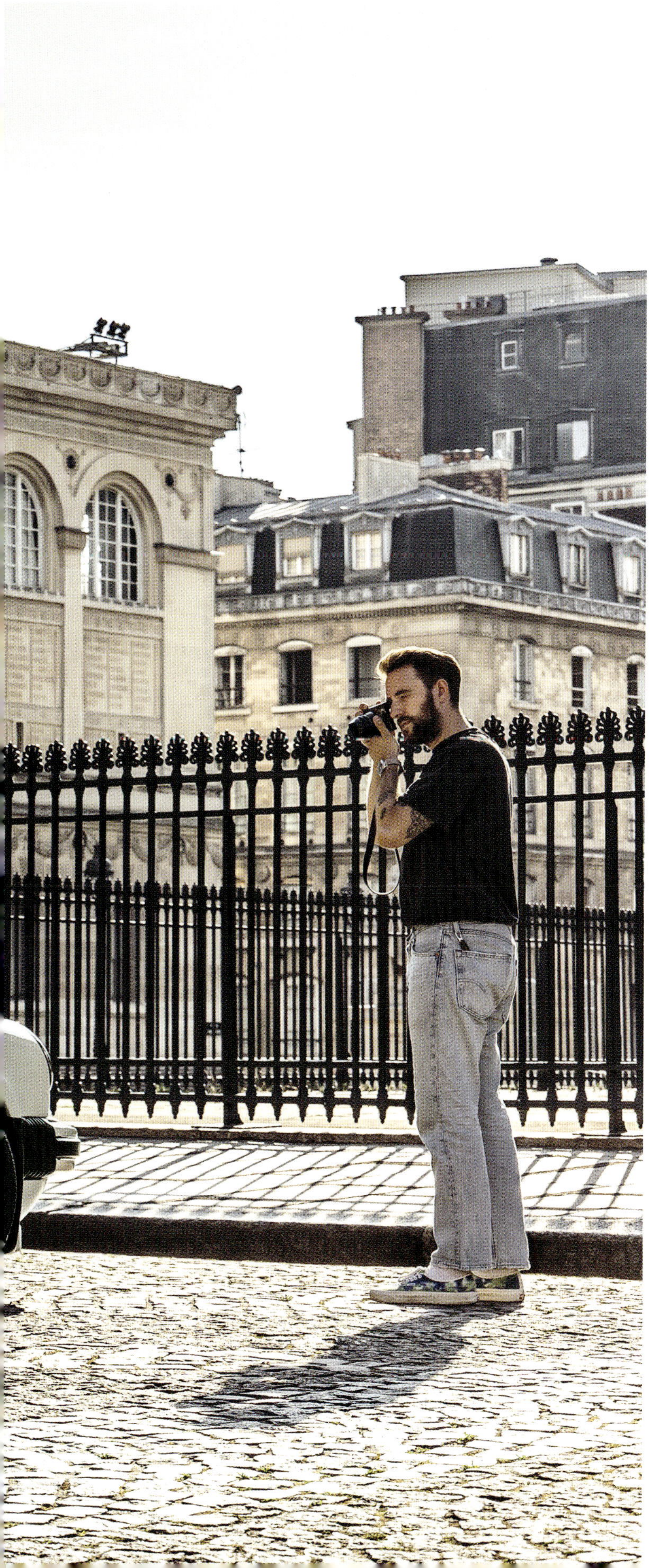

BREAKING FREE FROM THE RULES MEANS ADAPTING YOUR 911 OUTLAW TO YOUR OWN STATE OF MIND.

A chill outlaw, a quiet kind of outlaw. That's how Nicolas describes his car: "It has a sunroof, air conditioning, electric seats and windows," he says. "It has retained the comfort of the original car, which I drew upon when carrying out the restoration. I even fitted a Continental car radio with Bluetooth connection, but one with a vintage look so it doesn't stand out too much." Who said an Outlaw had to be a villain's car? This 1987 3.2-litre Porsche 911 Carrera SC with a G50 gearbox took a very different path for its concourse-level restoration. "It's an Outlaw because it's been widened, it's got much larger wheels, which makes it look like a 911 that's very low to the ground – significantly more than a classic 3.2-litre model. I took out all the rocker panels from under the doors to give it the cleanest, most streamlined look possible. The paint colour is not a Porsche reference, it's a shade of cream that took me more than two-

and-a-half hours to find on a paint shop's colour chart – from over 100 variations on that same colour theme. The Porsche stickers on the doors are white to be clearly different from other classic models that have monochrome Carrera or Porsche logos there. I fitted the small chrome bullet mirrors because they best suited the style of this 911. They are certainly not the best, particularly the one on the right – I can't see anything in it. Fortunately, the car is so open to the outside that I can simply look around to check for blind spots. I also fitted LED lights on the front, to see well at night. Because that's what makes this an Outlaw: I use it on a very regular basis." Living in Paris, Nicolas does not use this 911 as his everyday car, but he takes it out whenever he can, regardless of the type of roads he plans to drive on: "It's not my daily ride – it's too difficult to get around Paris by car – but last weekend I drove more than 300 km (186 miles) in it, getting back home after dark. I have no hesitation about driving it as often as I possibly can. I clock up a lot of miles, and not just on the motorway. Last year I went out to the Bardenas Desert in Spain. In fact, that was kind of my initial idea: to give it a badass look and a bit of a desert style, while still being able to have as much fun as I wanted behind the wheel."

CONTEMPORARY COMFORT FOR EVERYDAY USE.

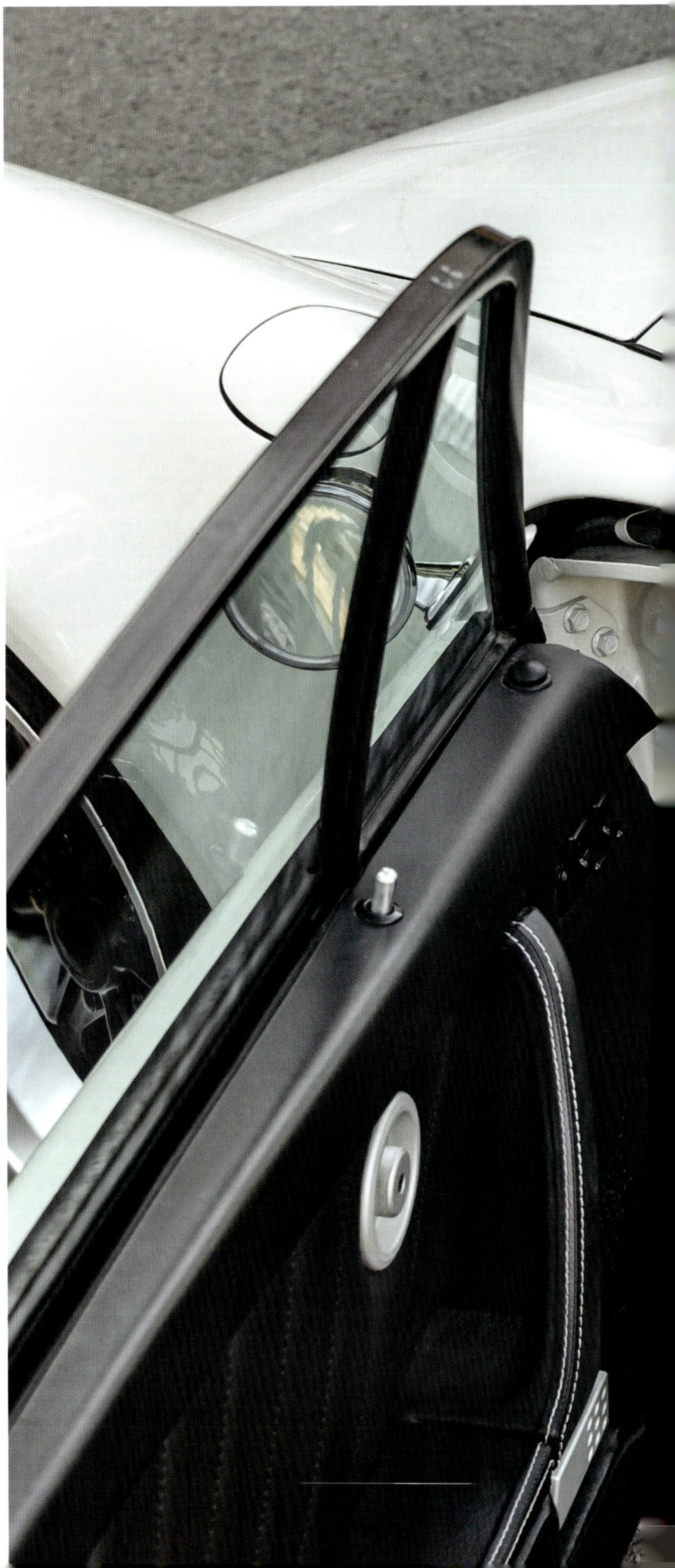

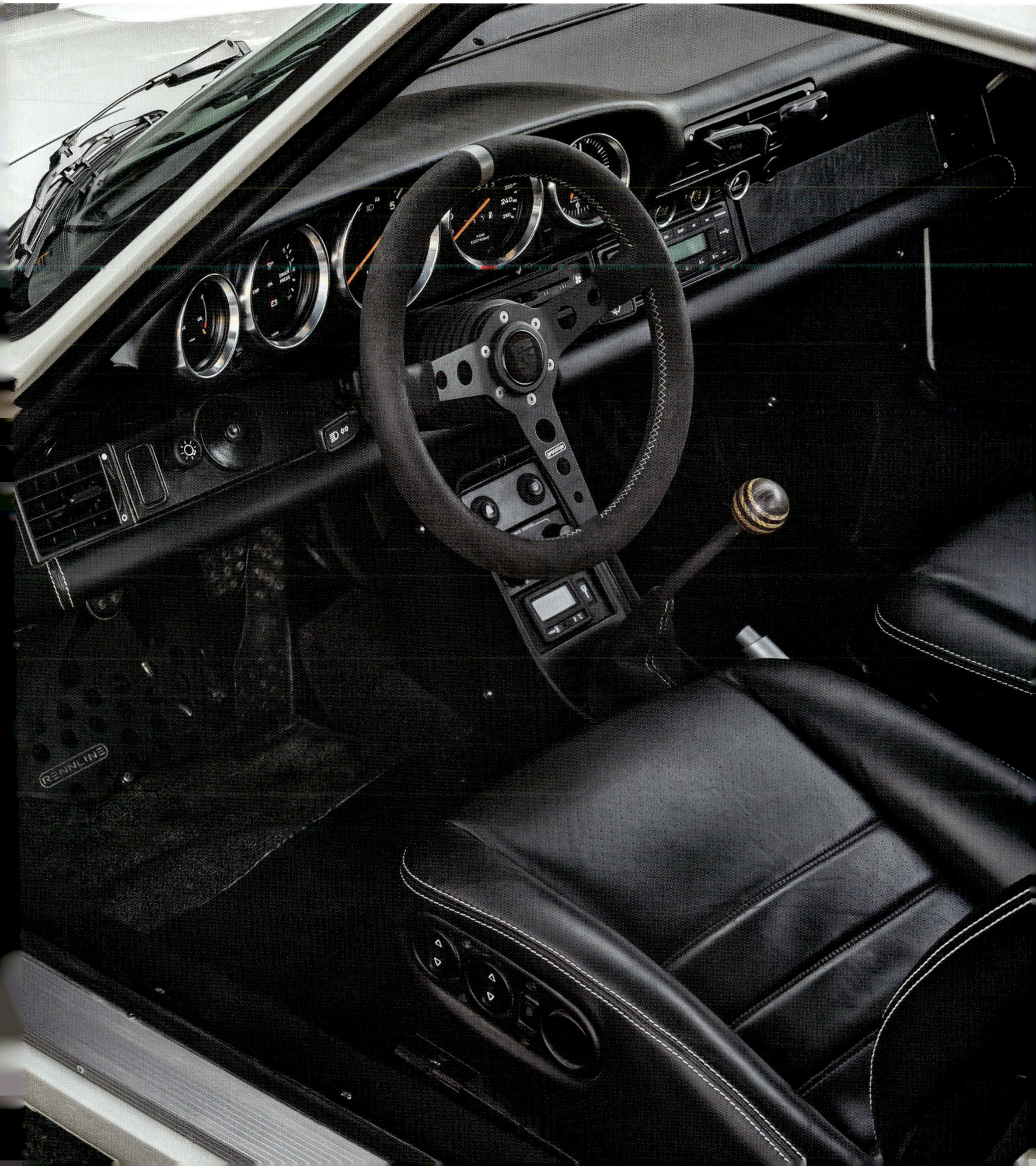

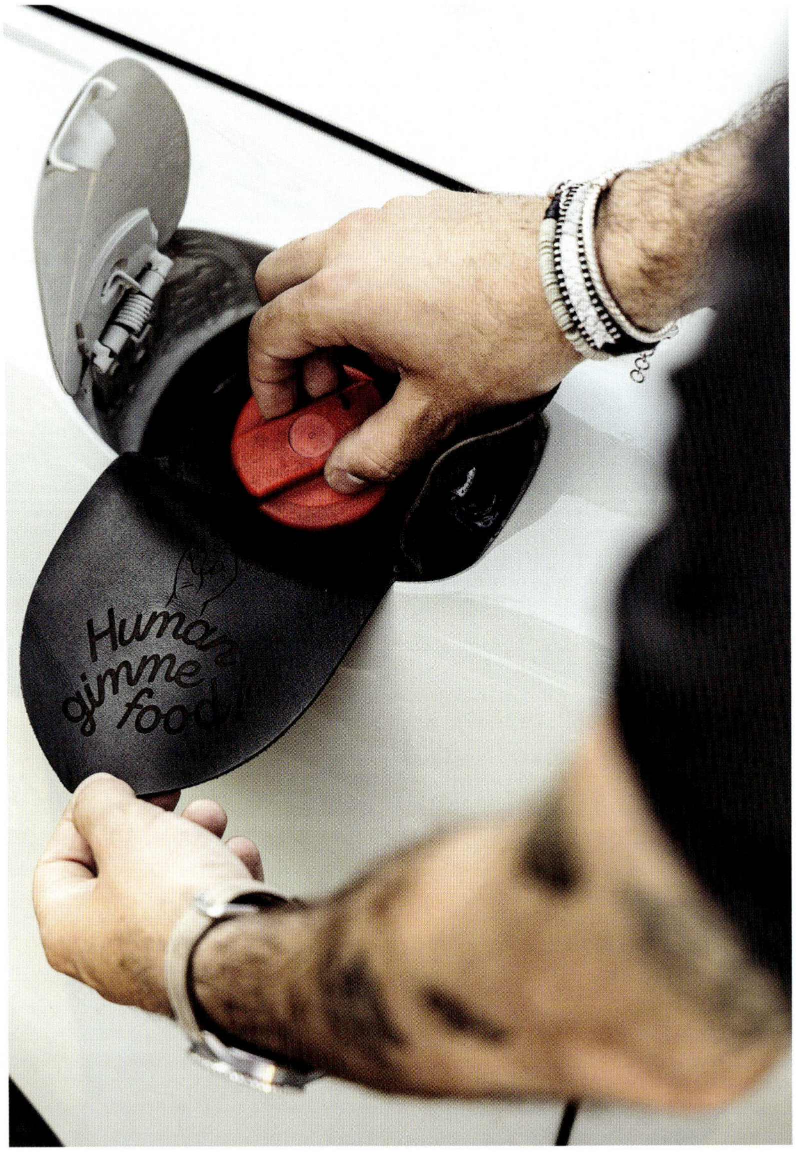

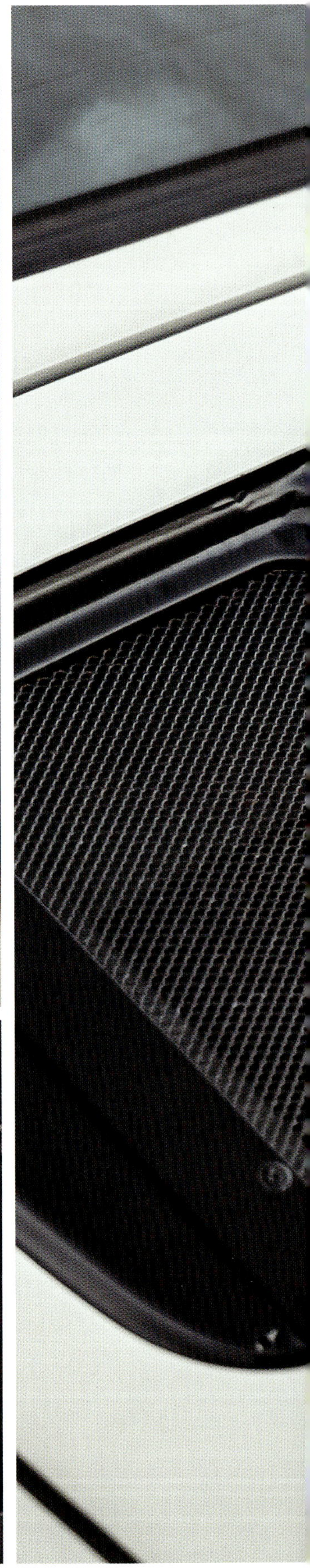

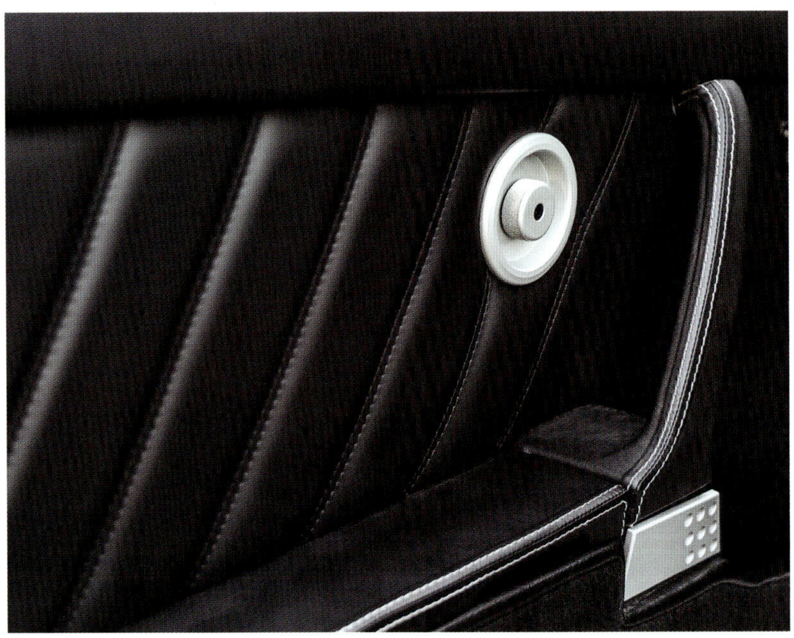

1. You have to keep this 3.2-litre Carrera SC 911 well fed.

2. The door locks blend in perfectly with the black leather.

3. Top tip: the grill is made of wire mesh and matching metal bars painted black for a rugged look!

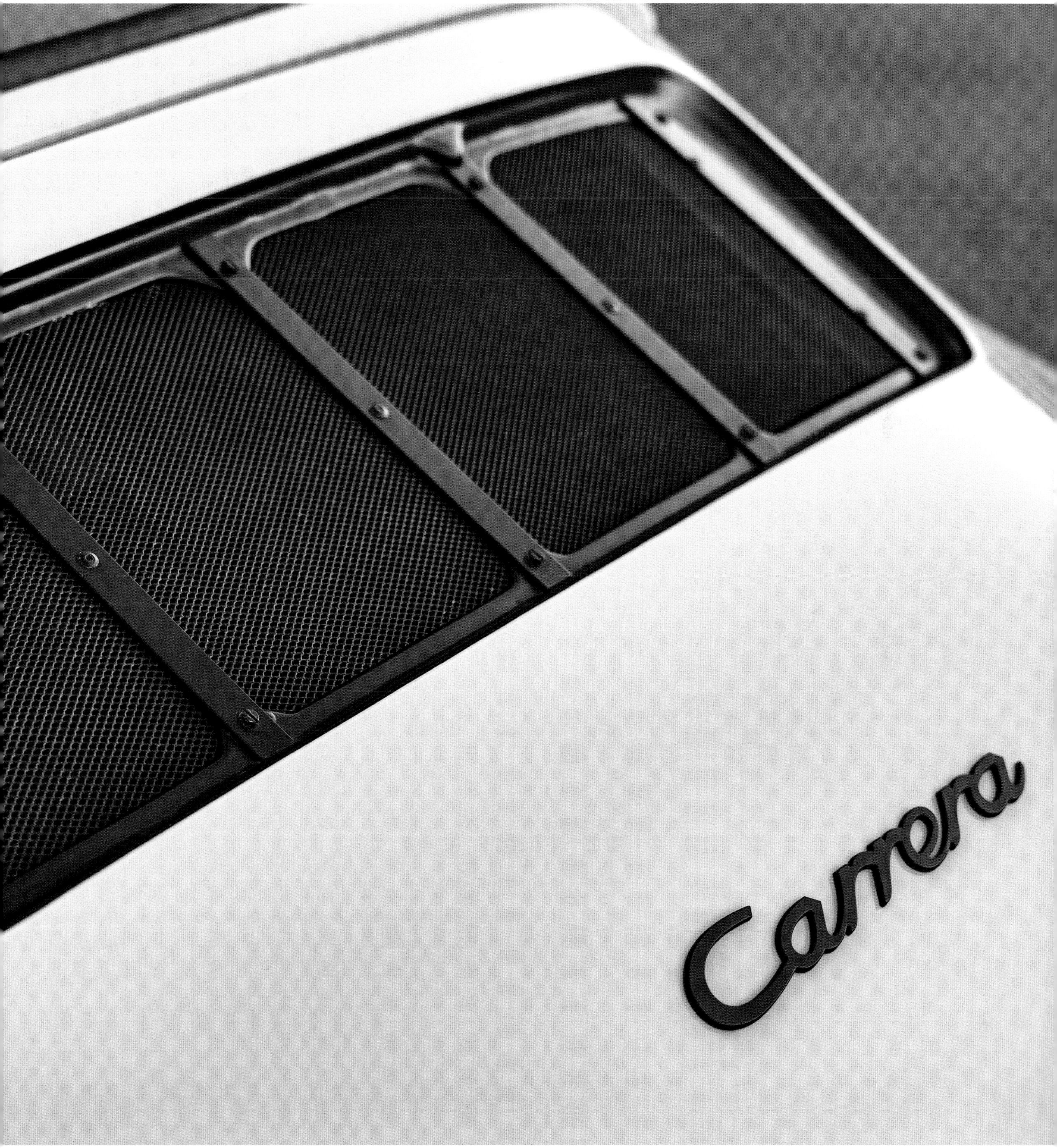
Carrera

Nicolas is a content creator. That's to say he's an influencer who makes his living by showcasing his life on social media. He began his career after following the advice of one of his teachers at the ISEG Digital/Marketing Communication School, which he attended in Bordeaux in 2010: "'Start your own blog, talk about things you like and maybe one day it will come in handy,'" Mr Chapelle told us. The next day, I started my blog, which I called *le petit Français* [the little Frenchman], because everyone was coming up with names in English. It enabled me to find internships at advertising agencies and to start my professional life working for various brands. But at one point, I had to choose between my life in advertising and my life as a content creator. I chose the latter a little over seven years ago and I'm still pursuing it on Instagram and TikTok." And so, his wish to rebuild a Porsche 911 to his liking turned into a collaborative endeavour. "COVID happened. It was time to realize my childhood dream. Philippe, a friend who now works at CarJager, suggested I look for a 3.0-litre or 3.2-litre Porsche from the 1980s to start the adventure, for reasons of reliability and maintenance. That's how I found this Porsche 911 with the 3.2-litre engine, the bottom end of which had been recently done up. It was clean, but the paintwork wasn't original and wasn't very well done. There were drips under the bonnet and the door seals, which gave me some scope for negotiation on the price.

EVERYTHING HAS BEEN CAREFULLY THOUGHT OUT, TO MAKE LIFE EASY ...

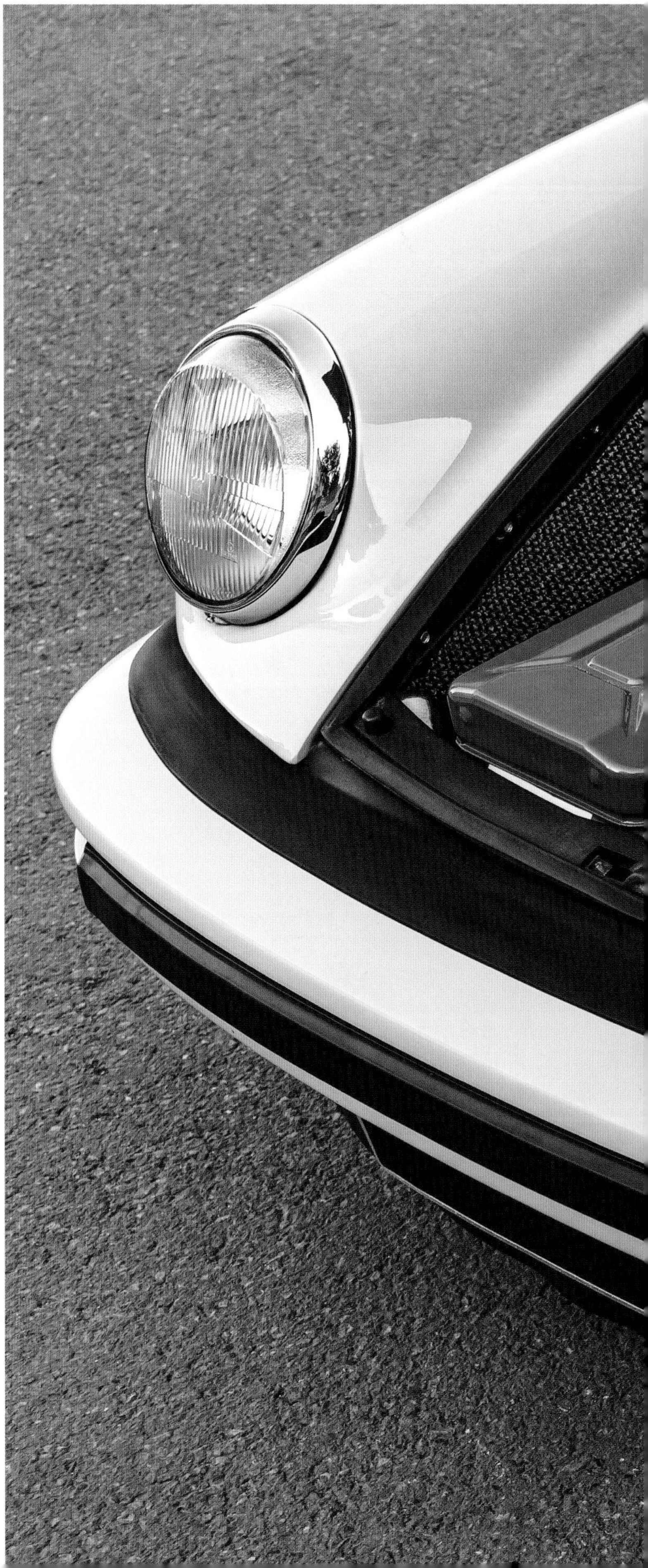

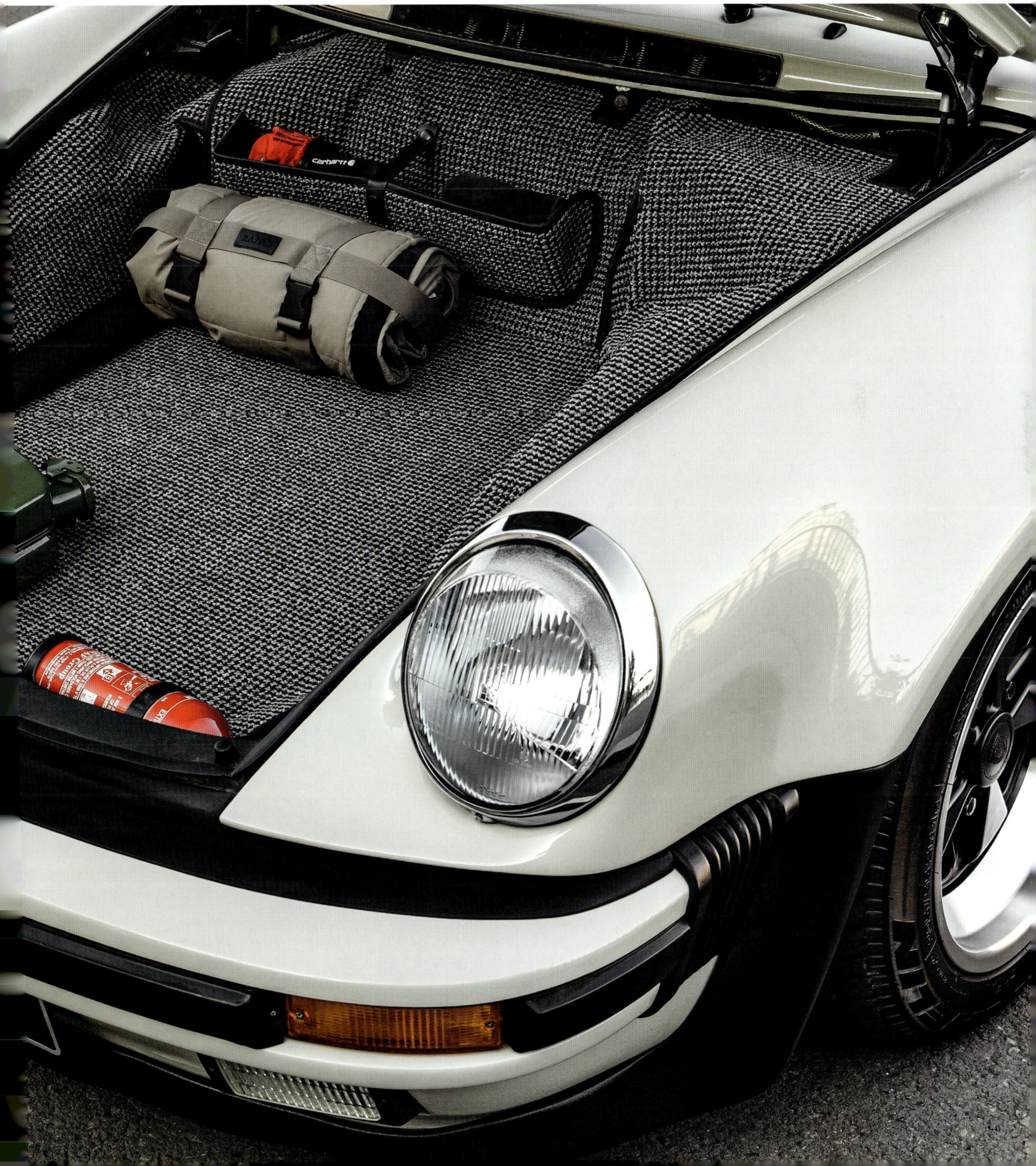

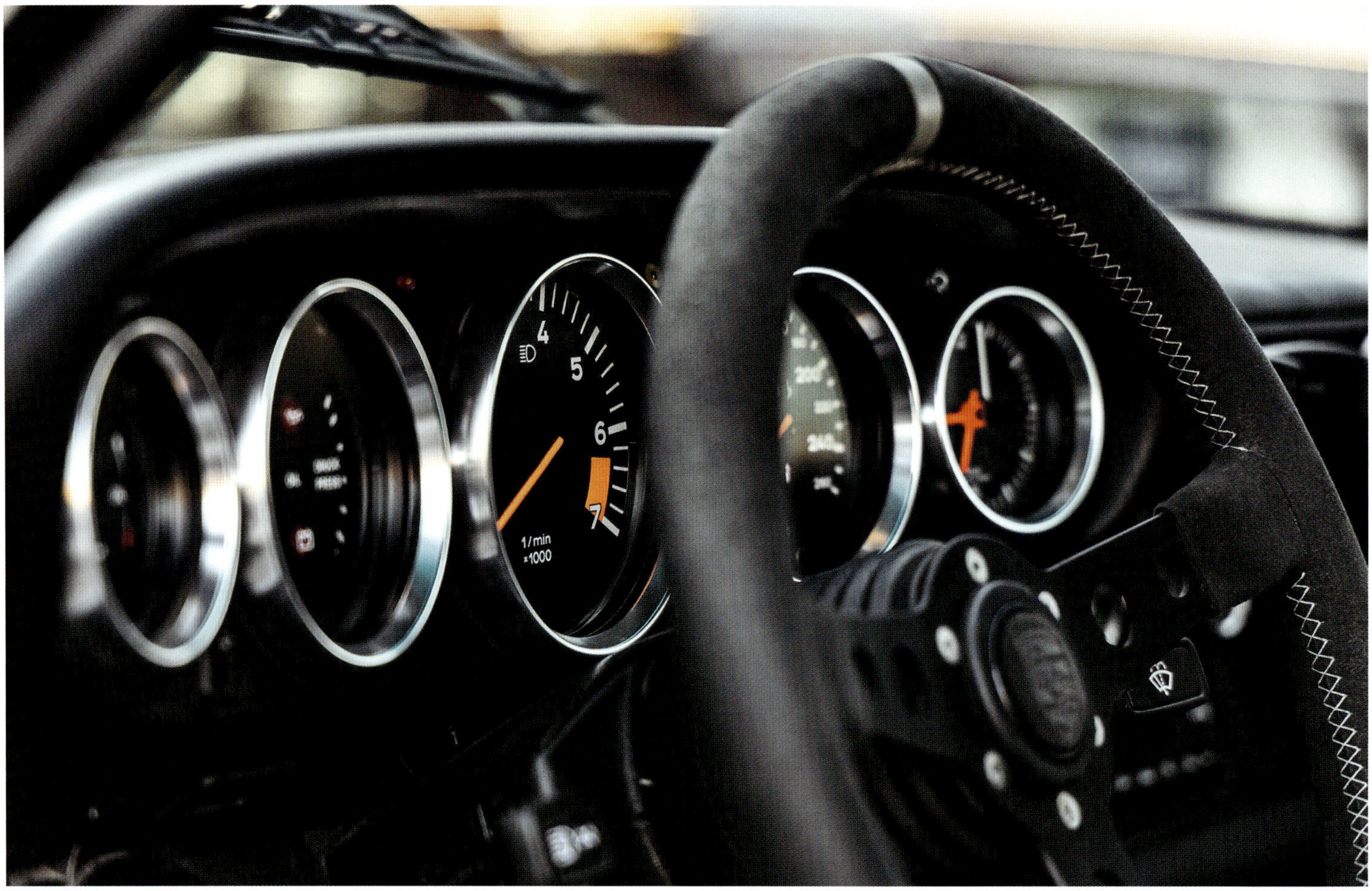

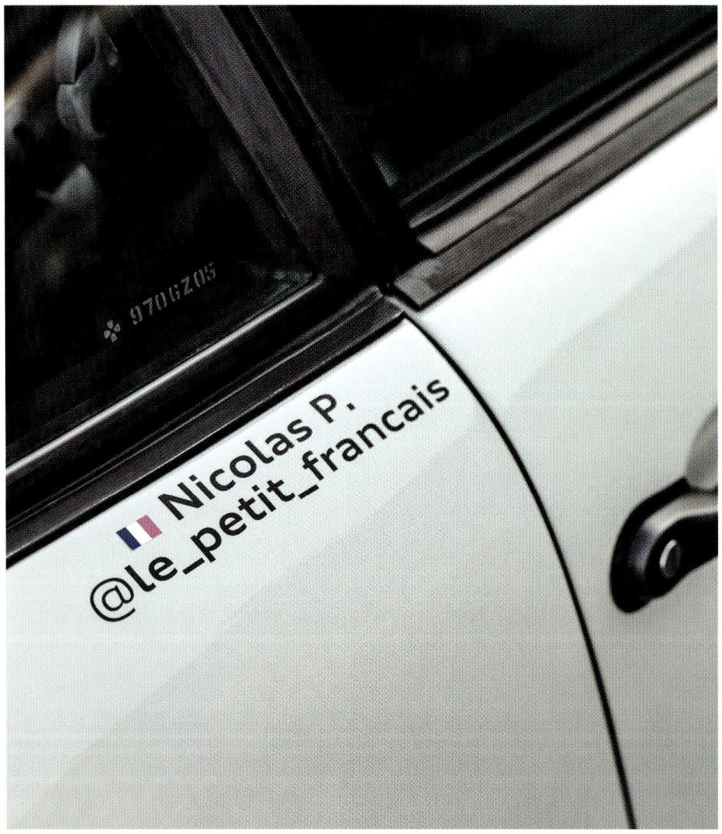
Nicolas P.
@le_petit_francais

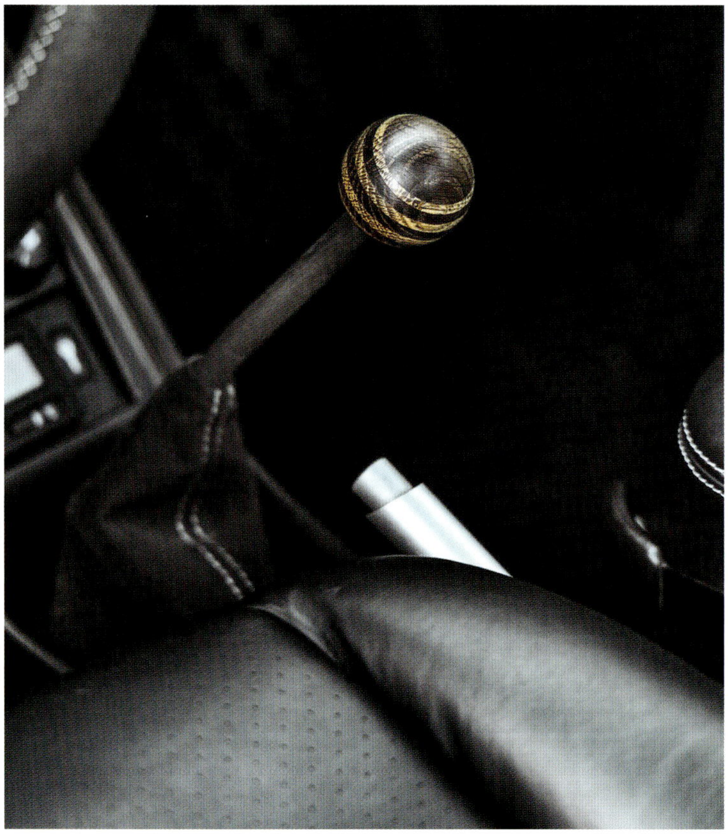

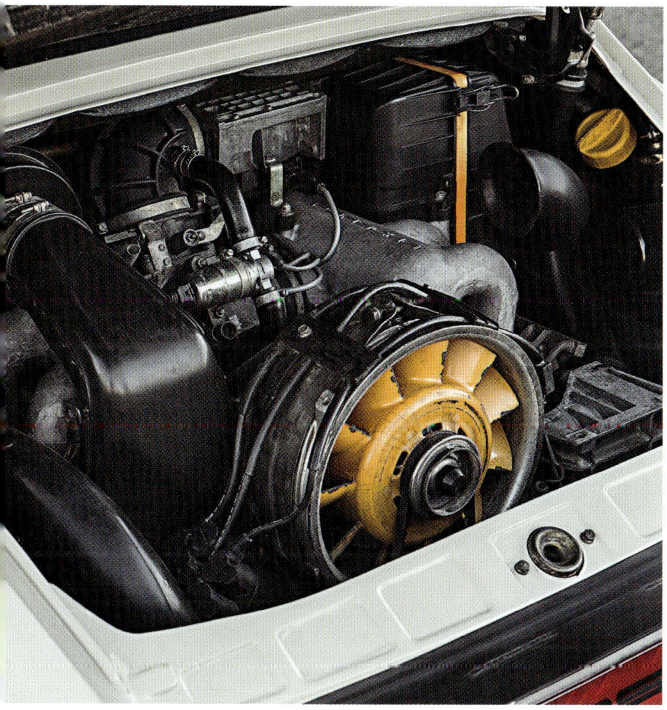

"And then it all came together. Not long after lockdown, I took it to my friends, Christophe and Loïc, at General Cars Vintage, near Tours. I then asked my buddies at GDB. tv, le Garage des blogs ("the garage of blogs") , if they would host videos of my Porsche restoration on their channel, in parallel with my own accounts. I told the whole story from start to finish, which took at least six months. That's pretty much all we did, or nearly – working on it non-stop. And so with my friends, we ended up deciding on the name Gisèle, because it sounded a bit German, like someone from the 1980s."

It has a very Outlaw look, with front wings from a 911 Turbo and rears from a 2.3-litre ST. They incorporate, respectively, 215 mm [8.4 ins] and 245 mm [9.6 ins] tyres on 16-inch rims. The interior was meticulously crafted, right down to the smallest detail, featuring Rennline footrests for driver and passenger as well as racing pedals. A custom-made MOMO Prototipo steering wheel was added, with grey stitching and a central stripe at 12 o'clock in the same colour scheme. It features brushed aluminium and a few shiny parts that complement the black upholstery, which has the Porsche logo on the headrest. There are a few other touches here and there, such as a rear hood grille in wire mesh. It is painted black with matching metal bars for a unique, bold look. Not to mention the little mat by the fuel tank hatch with the slogan "human gimme food" on it. To sum up, this 911 has a personality unique to its owner, whose name – just like a racing driver's – is proudly displayed near the rear quarter-panel, with a French flag: Nicolas P. @le_petit_francais.

911 GISÈLE
BY THE NUMBERS

CREATION 1987

FLAT CYLINDERS 6

CC 3,200

HP 231

1. The five dials are topped with aluminium rings to retain the sporty, elegant look of this 911.

2. The owner's name of this Chill Outlaw 911 is found near the rear quarter-panel.

3. The wooden gearknob is a must-have for the authentic touch.

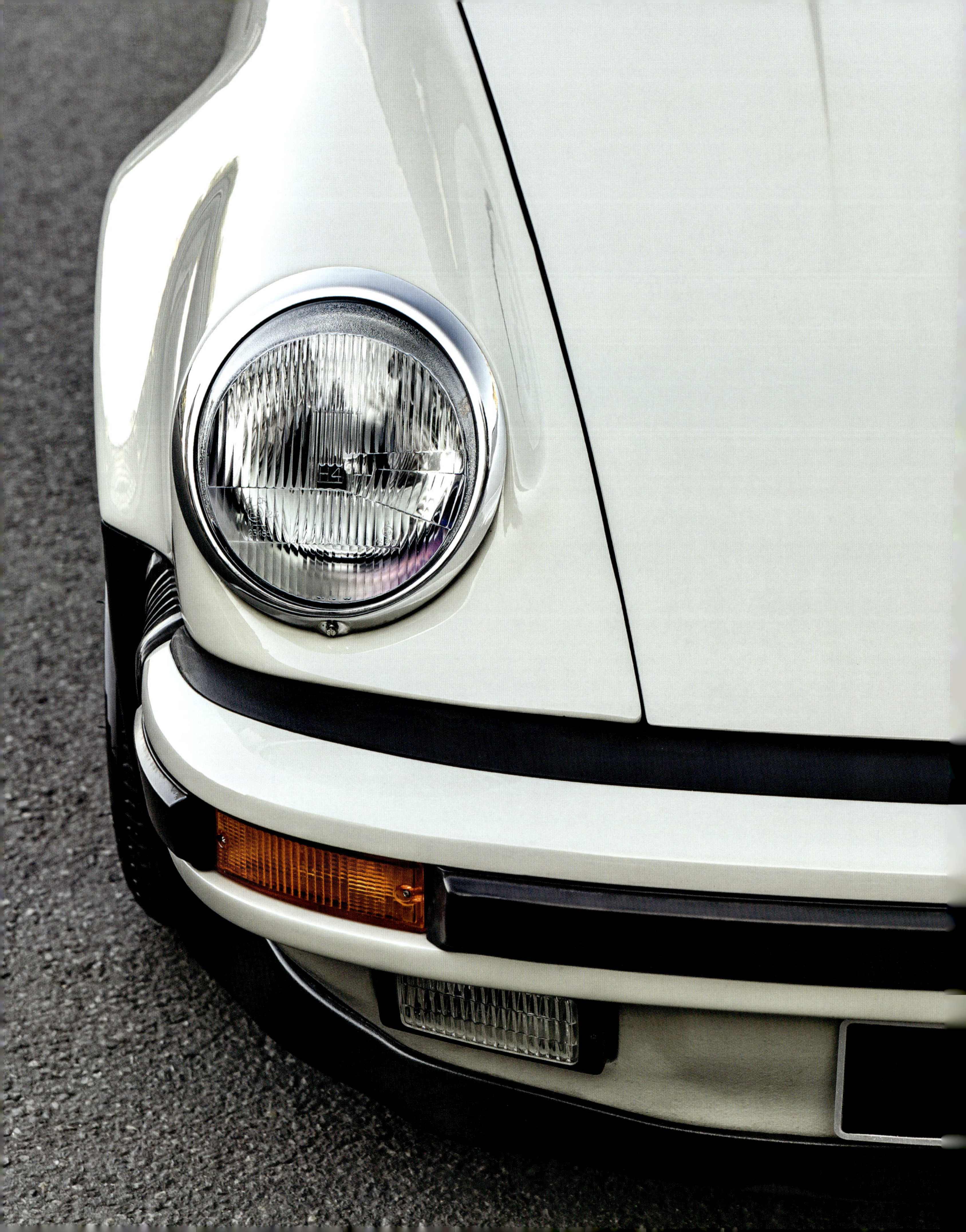

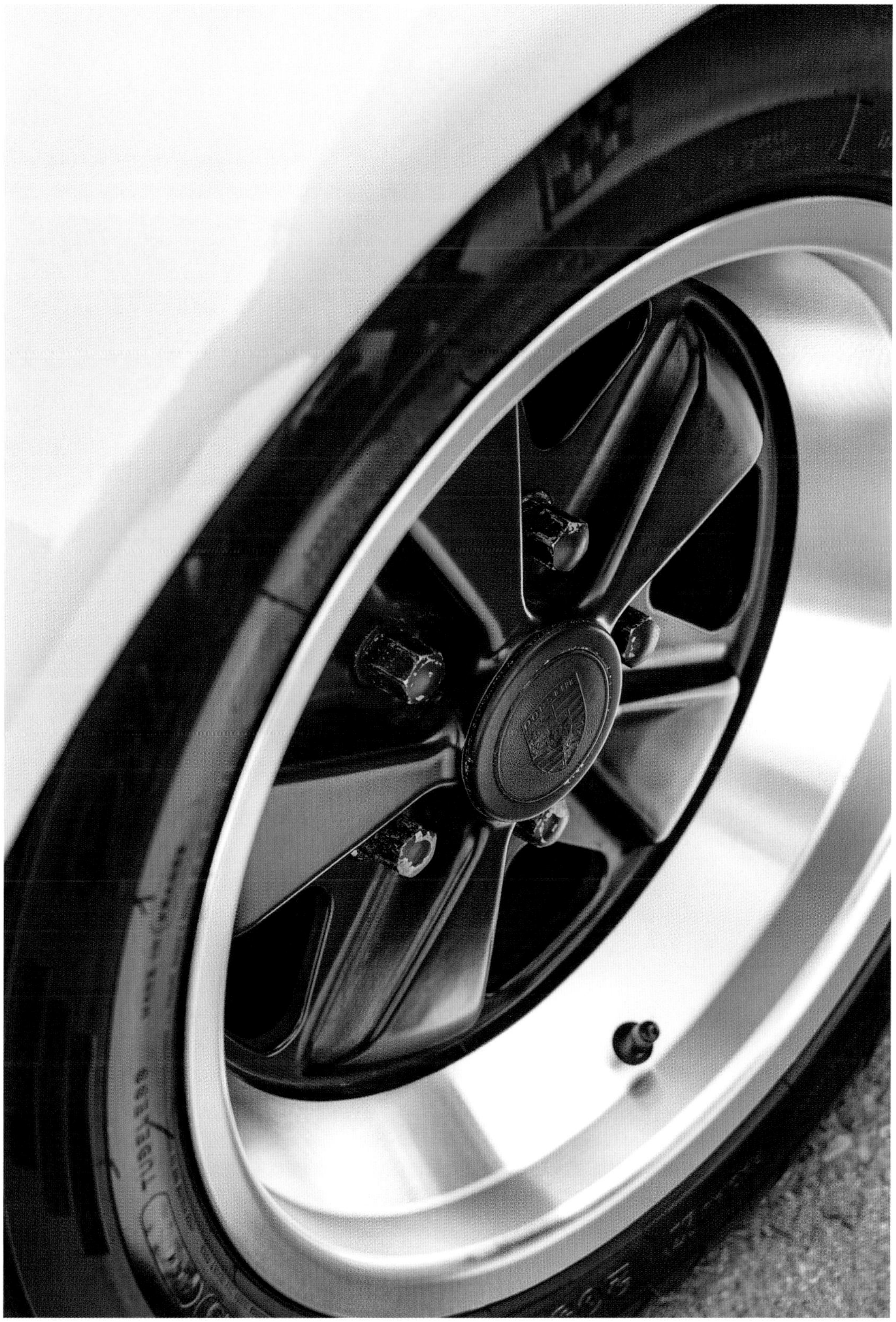

Above: 16-inch rims fit under the front wings of a 911 Turbo and the rear wings of a 911 2.3 ST.

Opposite: It's not a Porsche colour, but a cream shade applied in a direct gloss finish that gives a different look depending on the light.

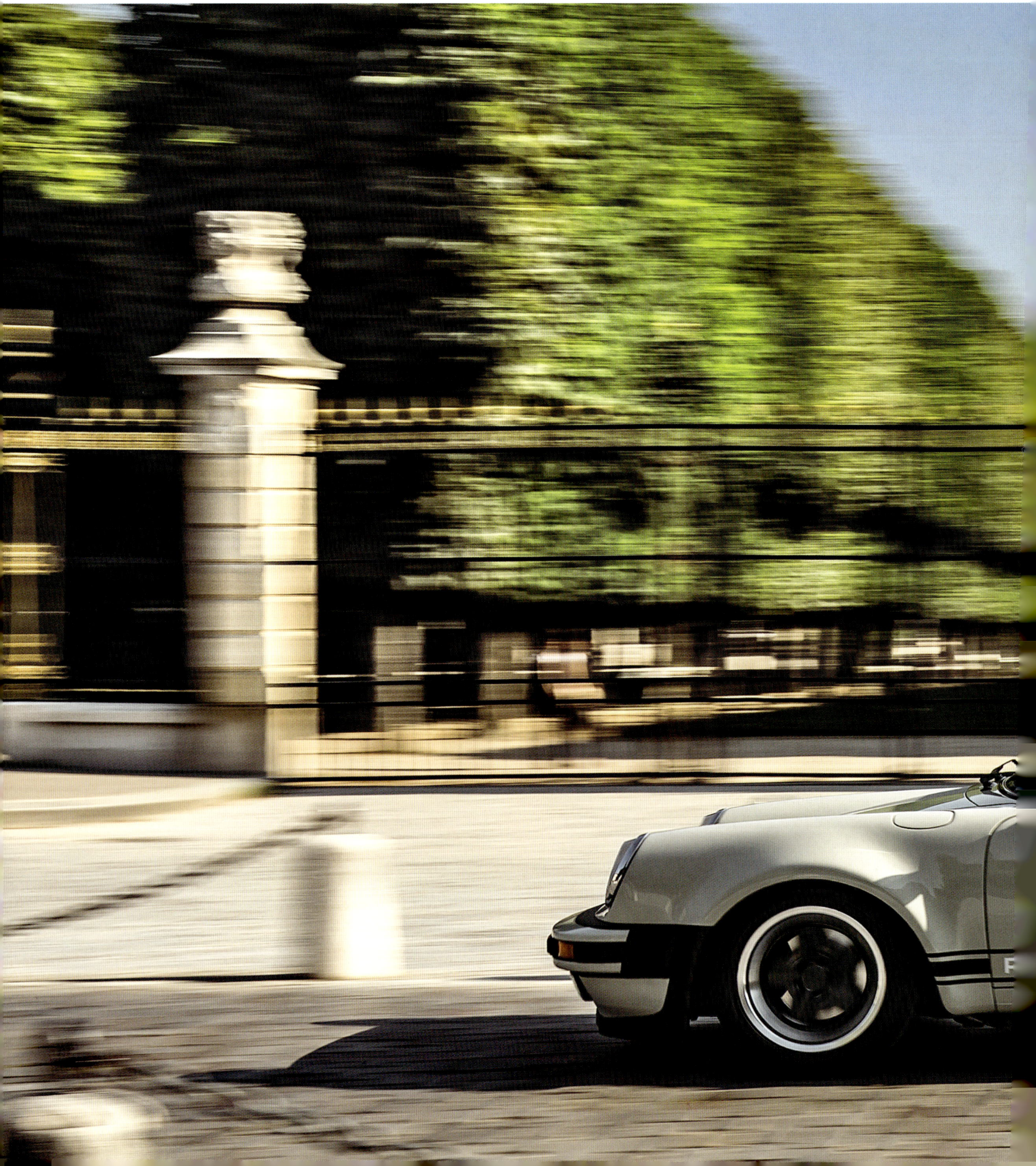

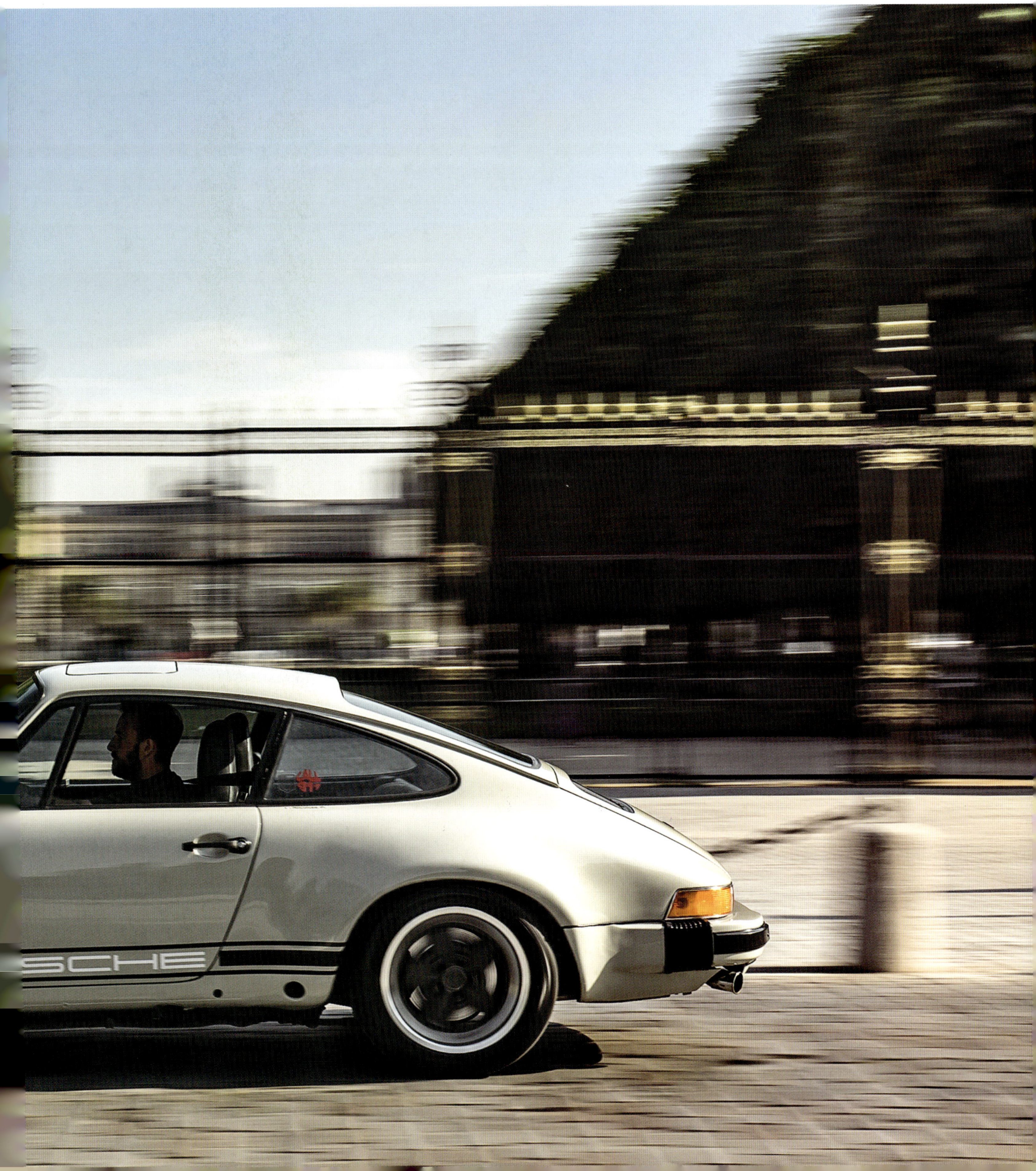
SCHE

928

NARDONE

A WAKING DREAM

In the spirit of Outlaws and their racing style, you can distinguish between backdating, which gives a modern Porsche a vintage appearance, and a restomod, which adds a high-tech edge to an older car. Nardone recreates the 928 as you might dream one up today.

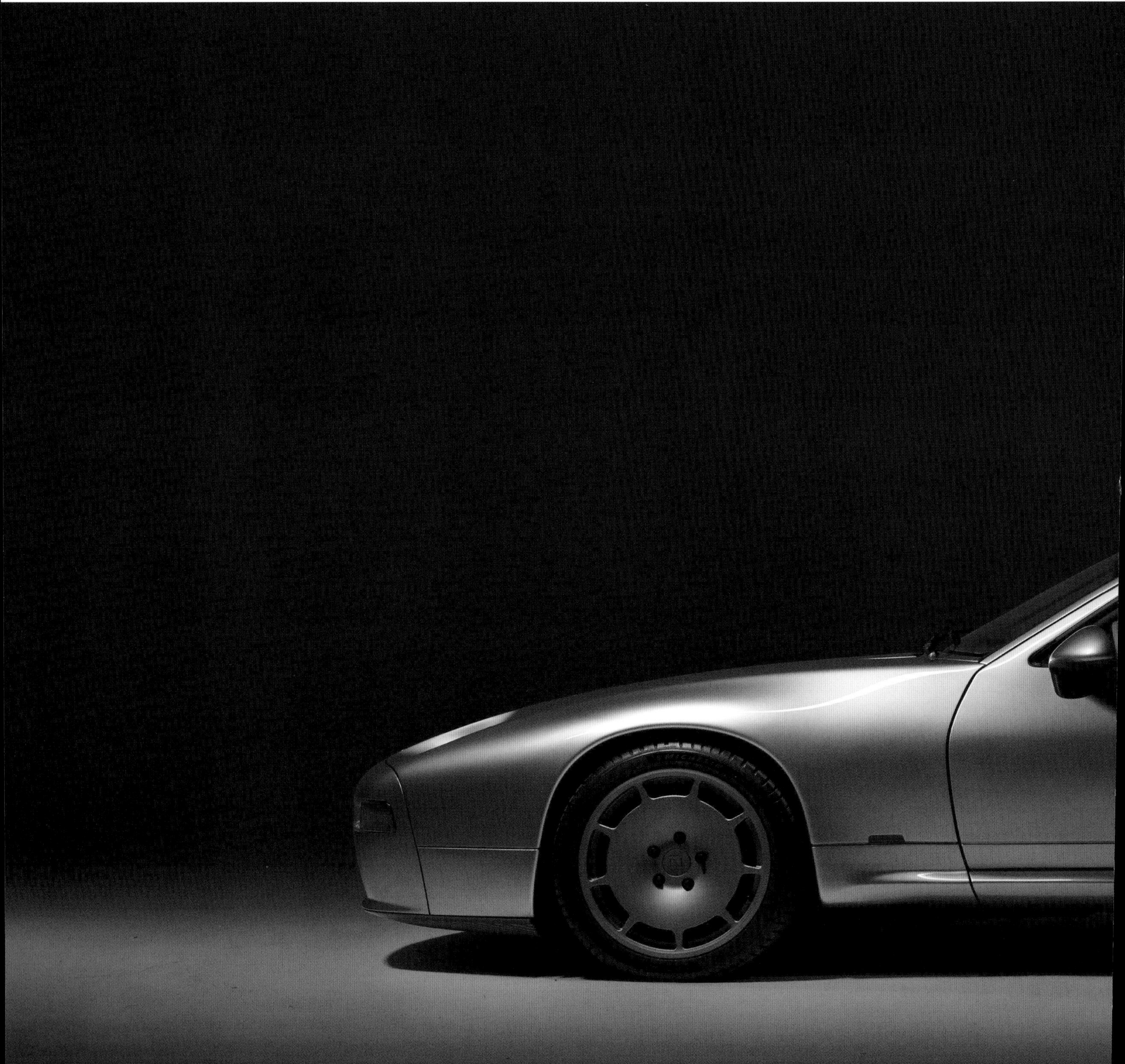

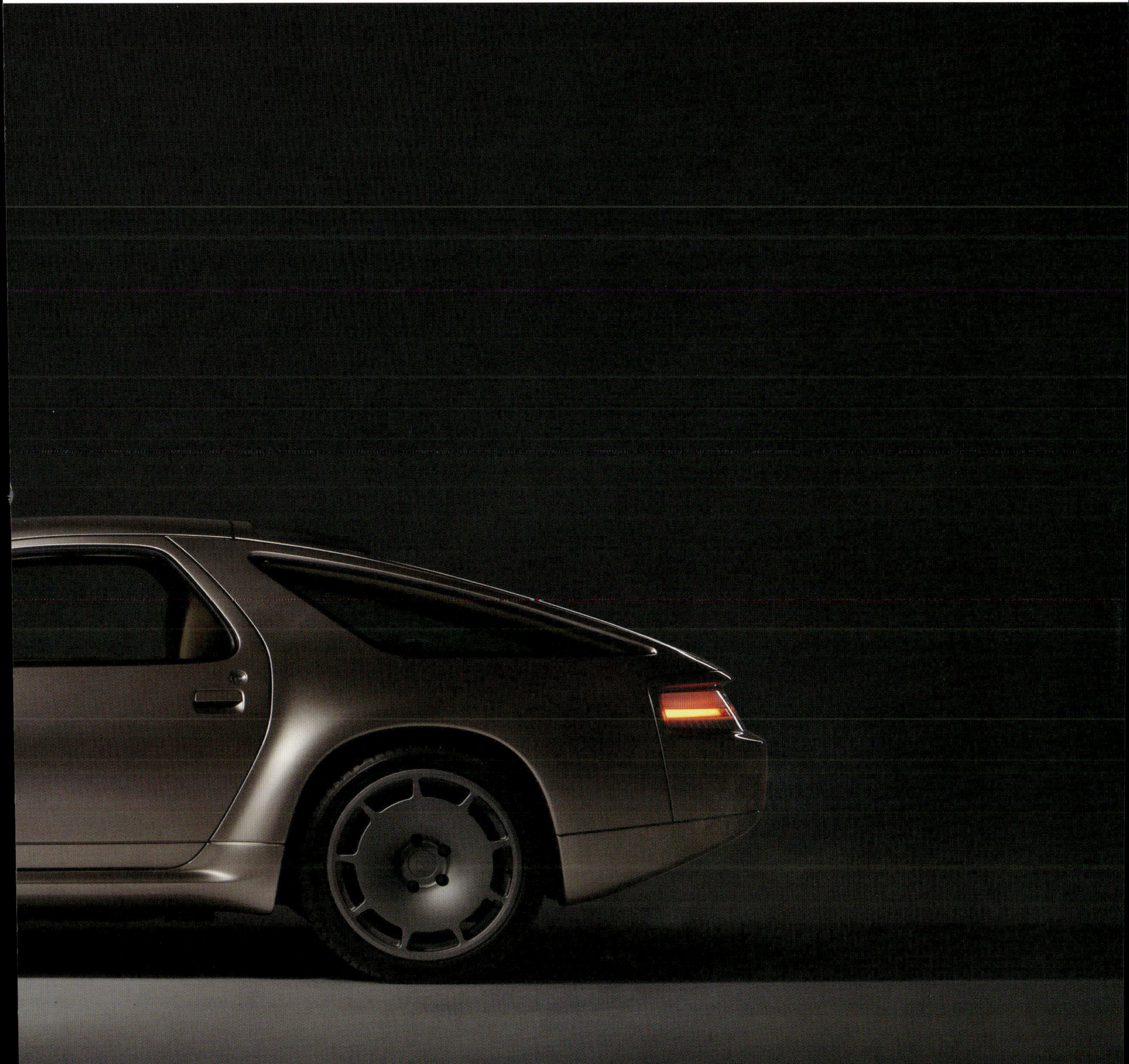

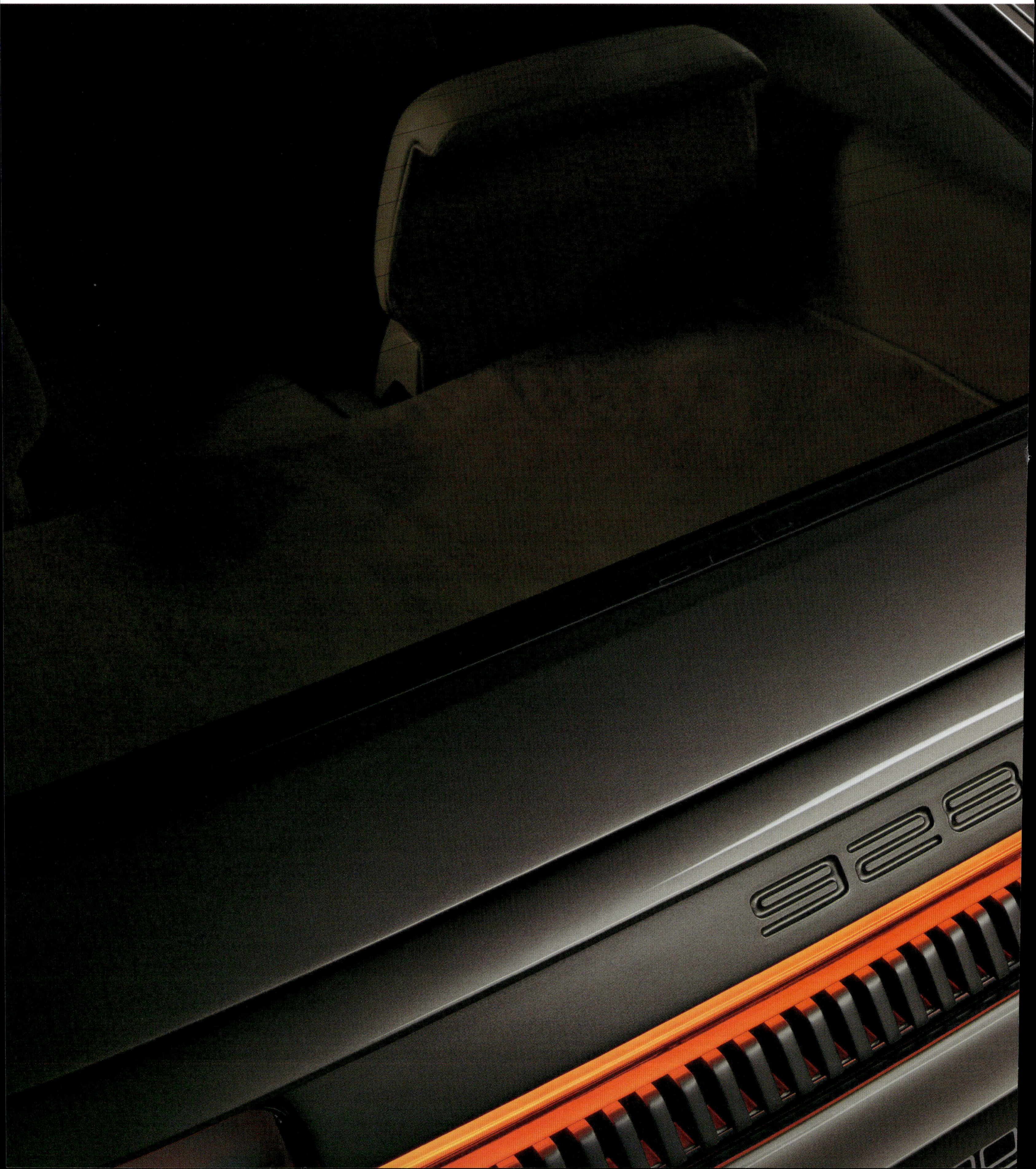

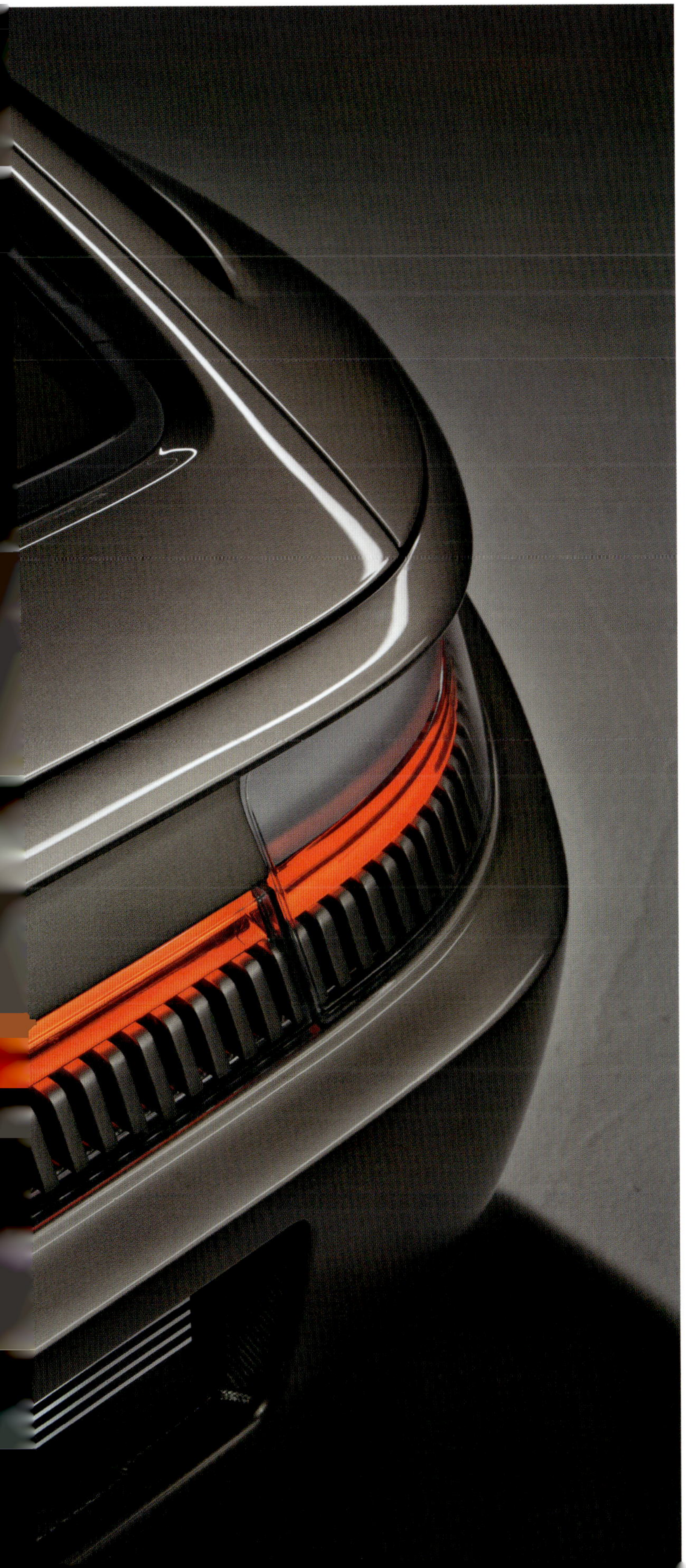

THE 928 WAS AN ORIGINAL OUTLAW THAT, IN ITS DAY, SHATTERED ESTABLISHED PORSCHE CONVENTIONS.

"When I was nine, I was on vacation, somewhere near Valencia, in Spain, when I saw an unusual car with all these big glass panels." The car, which left a long-lasting impression on Thierry, was a Porsche 928. Since it came out in 1978, this particular Porsche has always been a very unconventional vehicle. Named Car of the Year on its release, it made history in the Stuttgart factory. Its innovative and futuristic design for the time earned praise and recognition from the automotive world. But its front-mounted V8 engine meant it was a vehicle that was shunned by Porsche enthusiasts who exclusively worshipped the 911 and its rear-mounted flat-six. In spite of this, it became the spearhead of the front-engined Porsche era. Its road-handling qualities made it an excellent 2+2 coupé, and the GT provided comfortable travel for its passengers at a steady pace. It was manufactured until 1995, and roughly

60,000 units of the 928 were produced. But after that? Nothing. There was no follow-up – what happened to the modern 928, updated with all the latest technology? No matter: Thierry was working tirelessly on a new car that he had been envisioning for more than three years. This 928 is not just some stylish facelift of a classic car, however legendary it may be. It is a masterpiece that goes well beyond established conventions, and it features more than 3,000 completely new parts. "For me, this car is the Hermès of automobile restoration. It is a restomod which uses the best craftsmen, the best engineers and the best specialists in order to realize the dreams of a child who is all grown up!"

The basis for the car is a 928 S4. They were produced between 1984 and 1991 and were one of the last models to come out, just before the GT and GTS that continued the line until 1995. It has a 5.0-litre V8 engine that delivers 320 hp. "We limited our 928 to 450 hp, but 80 per cent of the 522 Nm torque is available from 2,000 rpm." Those are jaw-dropping numbers, but they come as no surprise given Thierry's desire to achieve perfection. "We rebuilt the entire engine from scratch, using over 300 new parts, but we kept the same displacement and the original casing. We replaced the pistons, fitted titanium

THIS RESTOMOD IMAGINES WHAT A MODERN 928 WOULD BE LIKE.

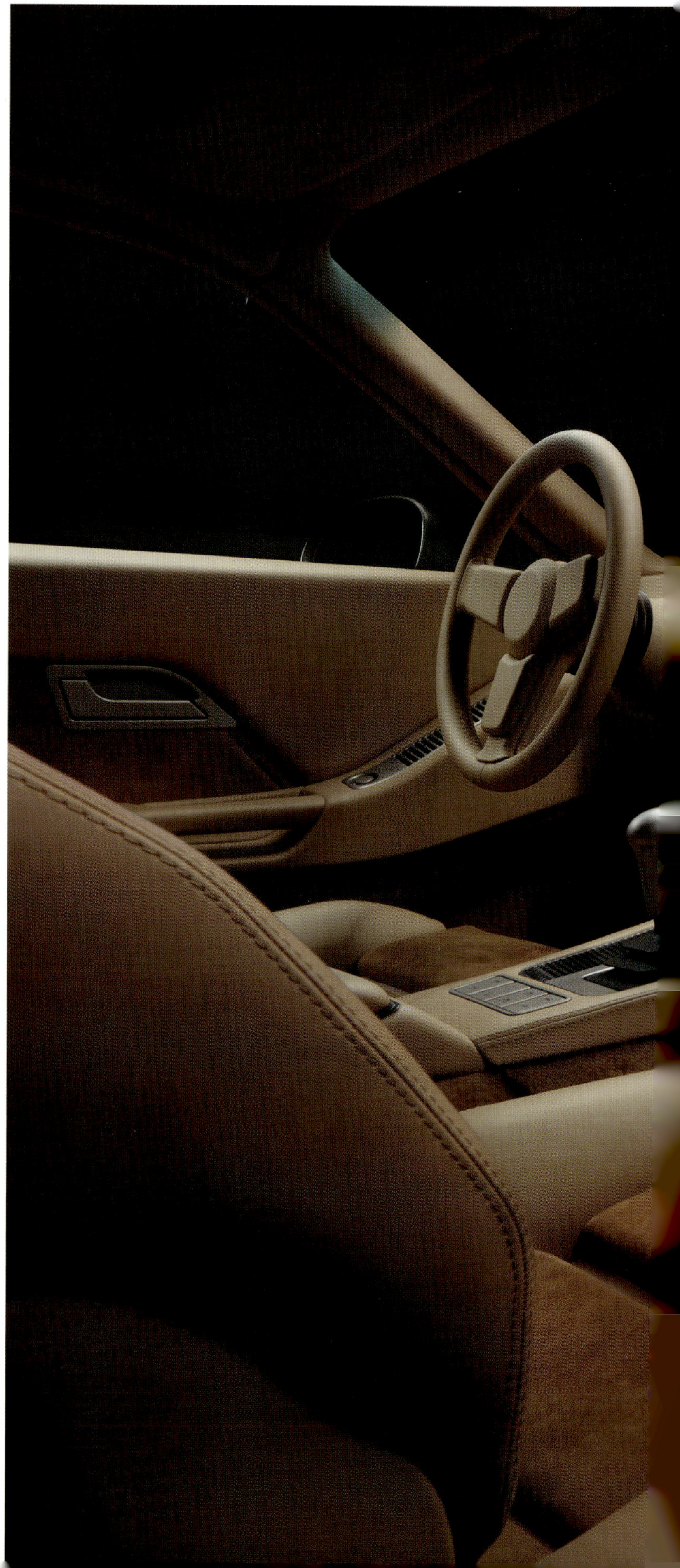

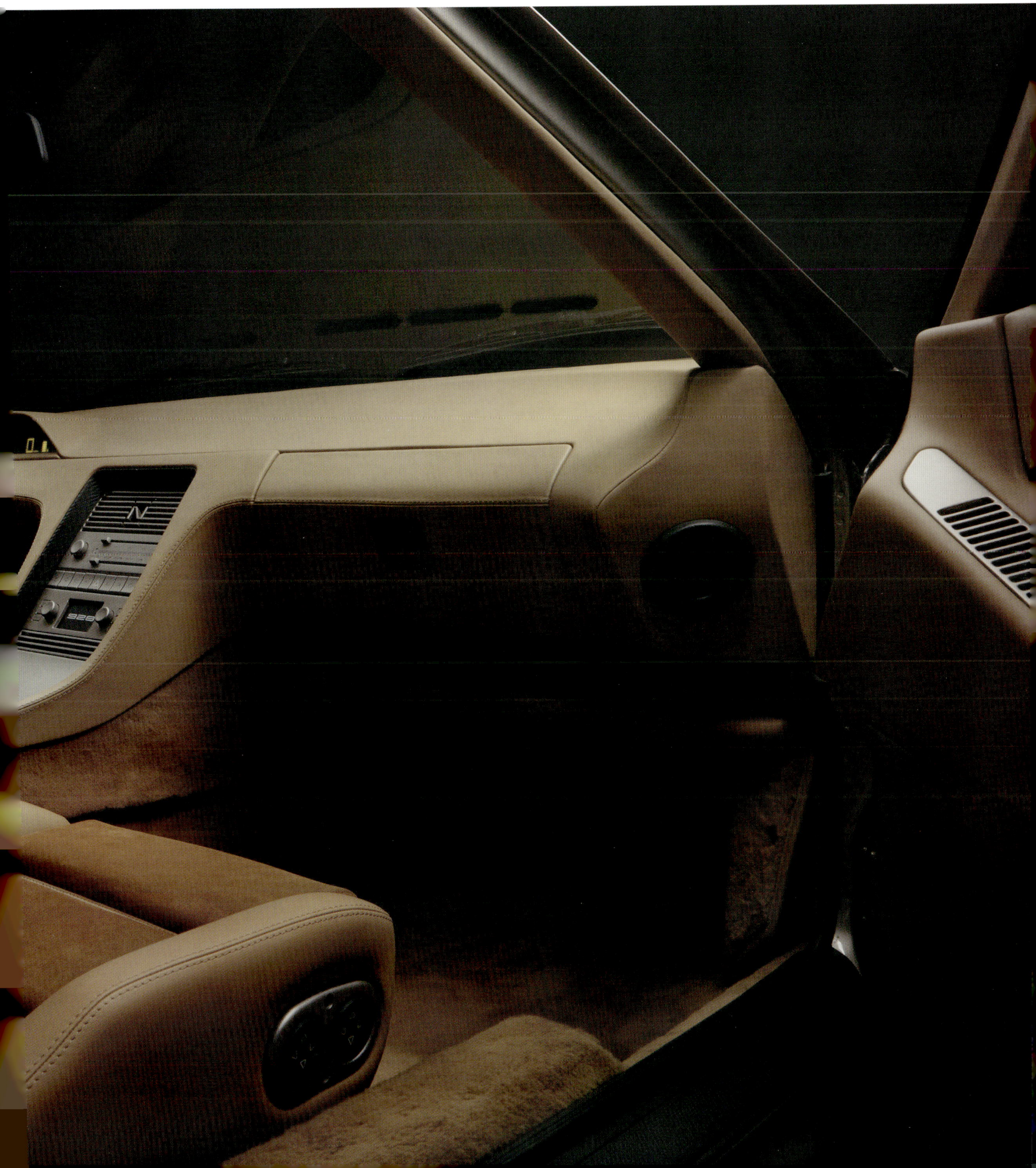

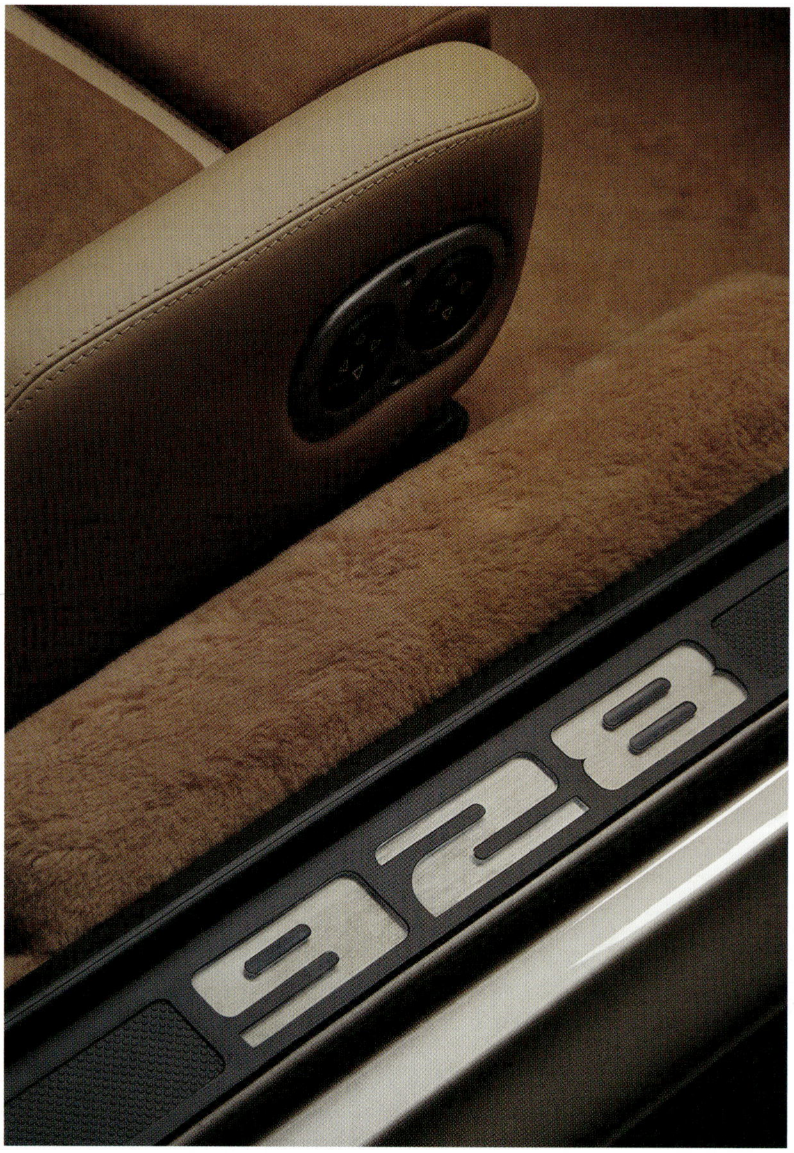

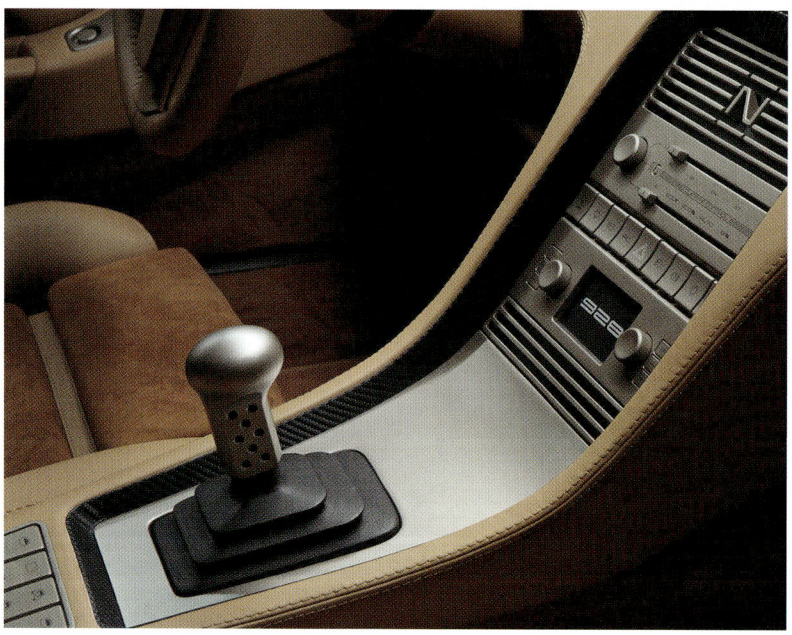

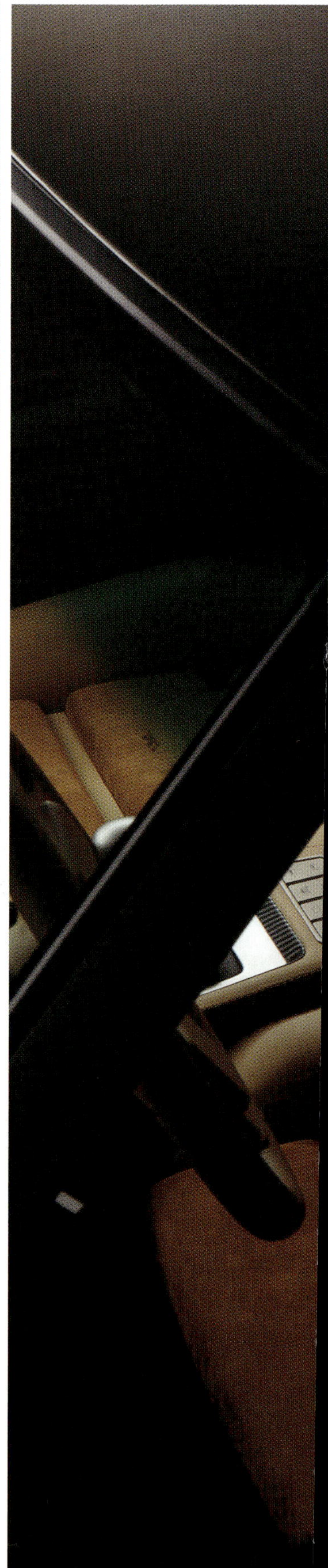

1. The name serves as a reminder that the front-mounted engine is a V8!

2. Below the gearstick is 450 hp to leap into action!

3. This 928 preserves the "youngtimer" feel of the 1970s with a modern, elegant interior.

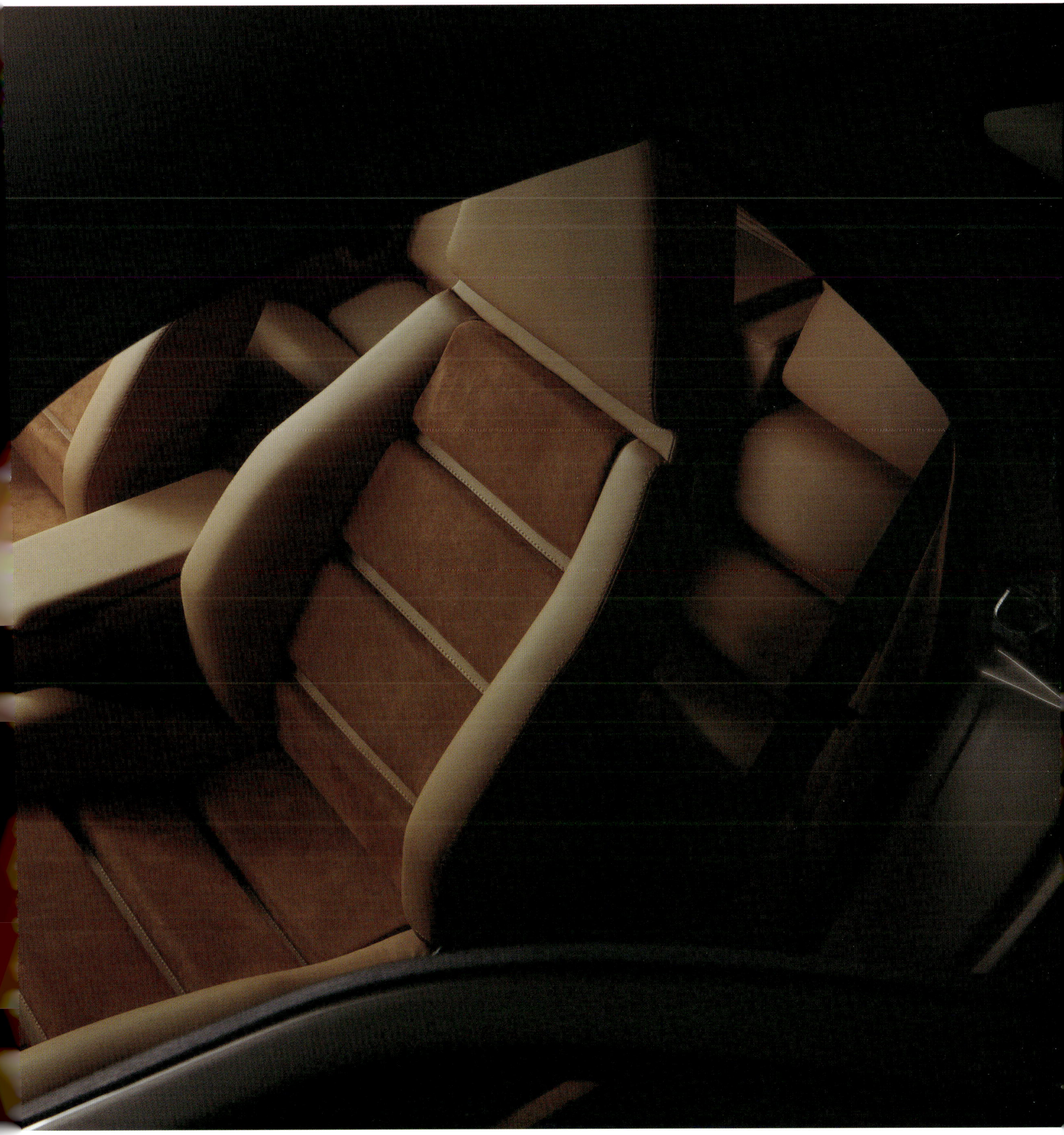

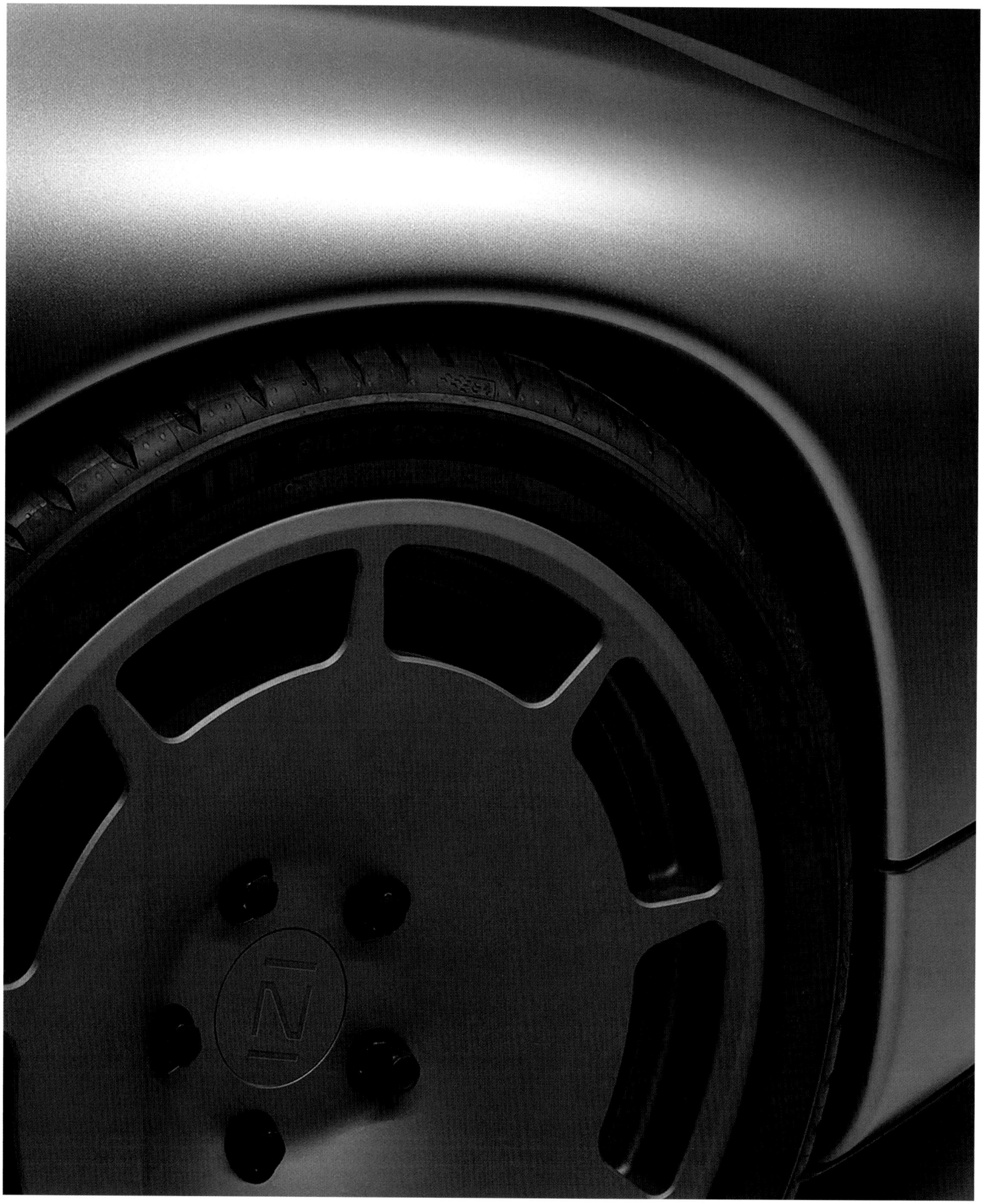

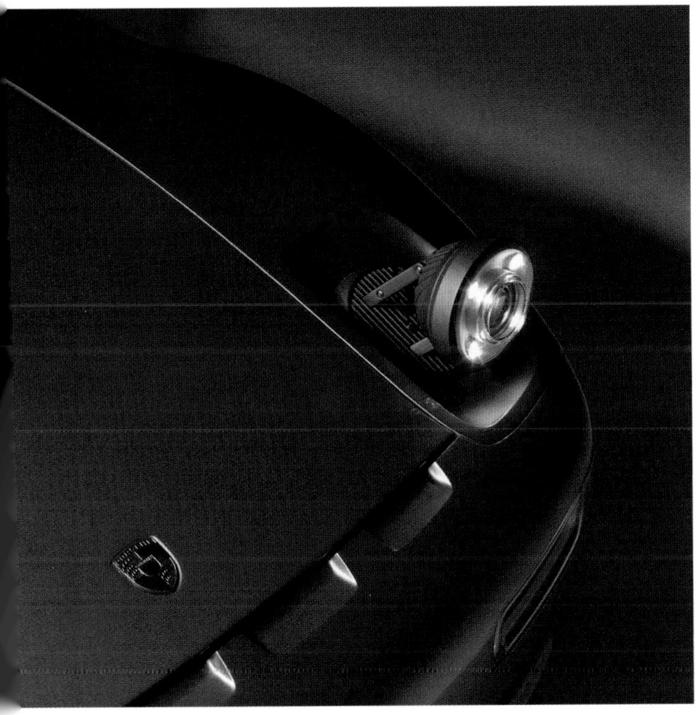

928 NARDONE
BY THE NUMBERS

CREATION 1987

V-SHAPE CYLINDERS 8

CC 5,000

HP 450

con rods and sodium-filled valves, modified the crankshaft, installed a modern fuel-injection system with one ignition coil per cylinder, high-tech engine management, custom camshafts – with mechanical rather than hydraulic supports – to handle the extra 1,500 rpm." To handle this surplus of power, the chassis was completely redesigned. "We widened the track widths in line with the new design by creating new hubs that were machined from solid blocks, as well as new axle stubs. We redesigned the original running gear with more modern specs to ease the load on the front end. We fitted 18-inch forged wheels, a reinterpretation of the 16-inch 'manhole' wheels that originally featured on the 928." Every single part was carefully considered, crafted, concealed, reimagined and tested before being installed: "We replaced the original steering rack, because its ratio was far too high – it was detrimental to the steering wheel feedback. We sent it to a specialist who works on this aspect for all WRC rally cars, and gave them our wants and needs. We wanted to achieve a feel similar to that of the 993. Those steering racks are known to be the best for air-cooled 911s." The chassis is a highlight of this super-high-end restomod: "We strengthened the chassis by adding a carbon shell, not to save weight – it weighs about 5 kg (11 lbs) – but to stiffen the structure, a bit like a roll cage."

Inside, the cabin is utterly luxurious, and the utmost care has been taken to make it as elegant as possible. "The central console and the instrument panel are completely new. The gearbox has six gears instead of five, which required a total of 198 parts. Only the housing is original." The beautiful sound has not been overlooked: inside, there is a system with 11 high-precision speakers and there's a custom exhaust that makes the V8 engine really sing. And so Thierry's sweet-dream restomod, lulled by the hum of its engine, became a reality.

Opposite: Breaking the rules to reinvent a 928 is a very Outlaw-style approach for a very neat restomod.

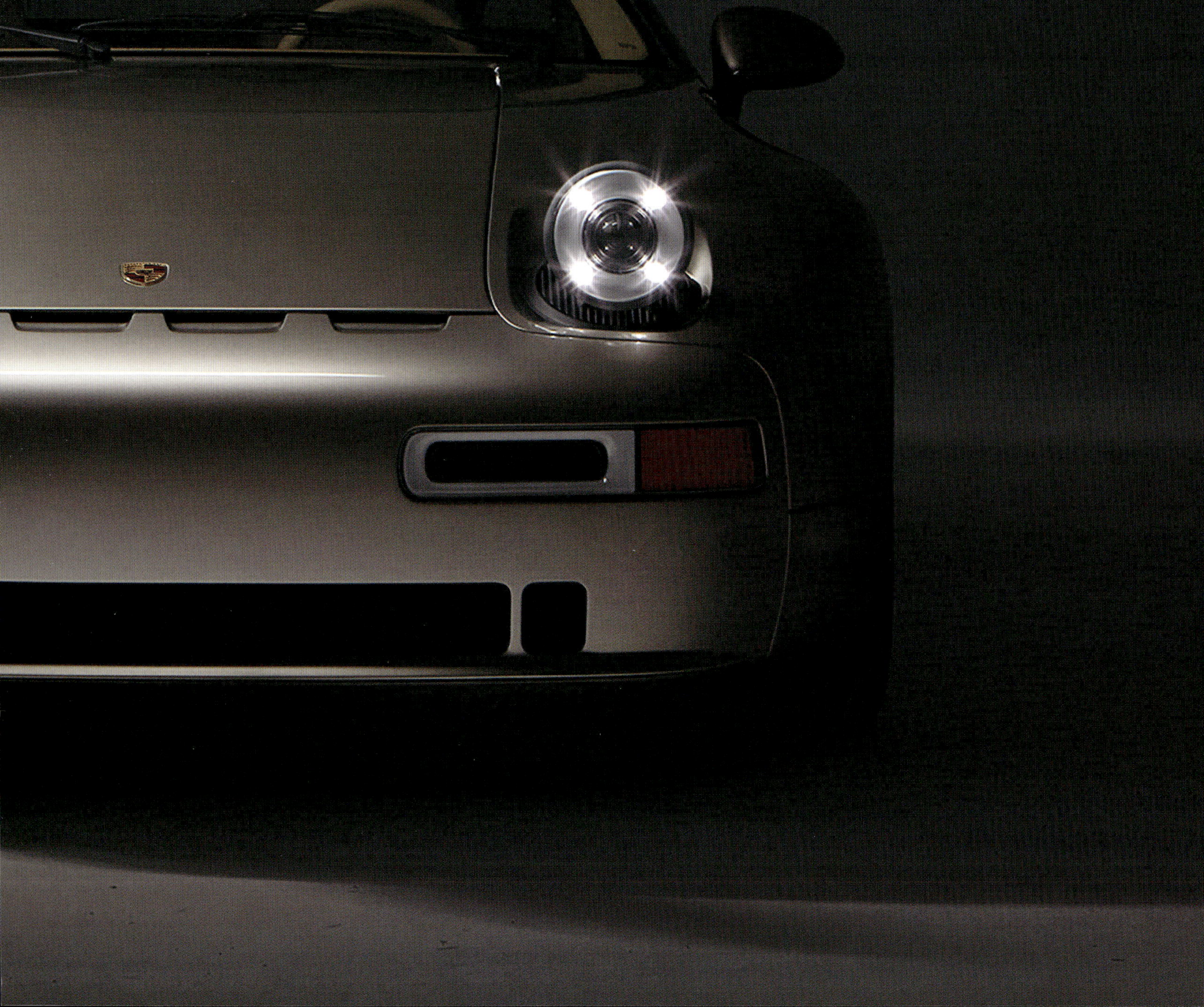

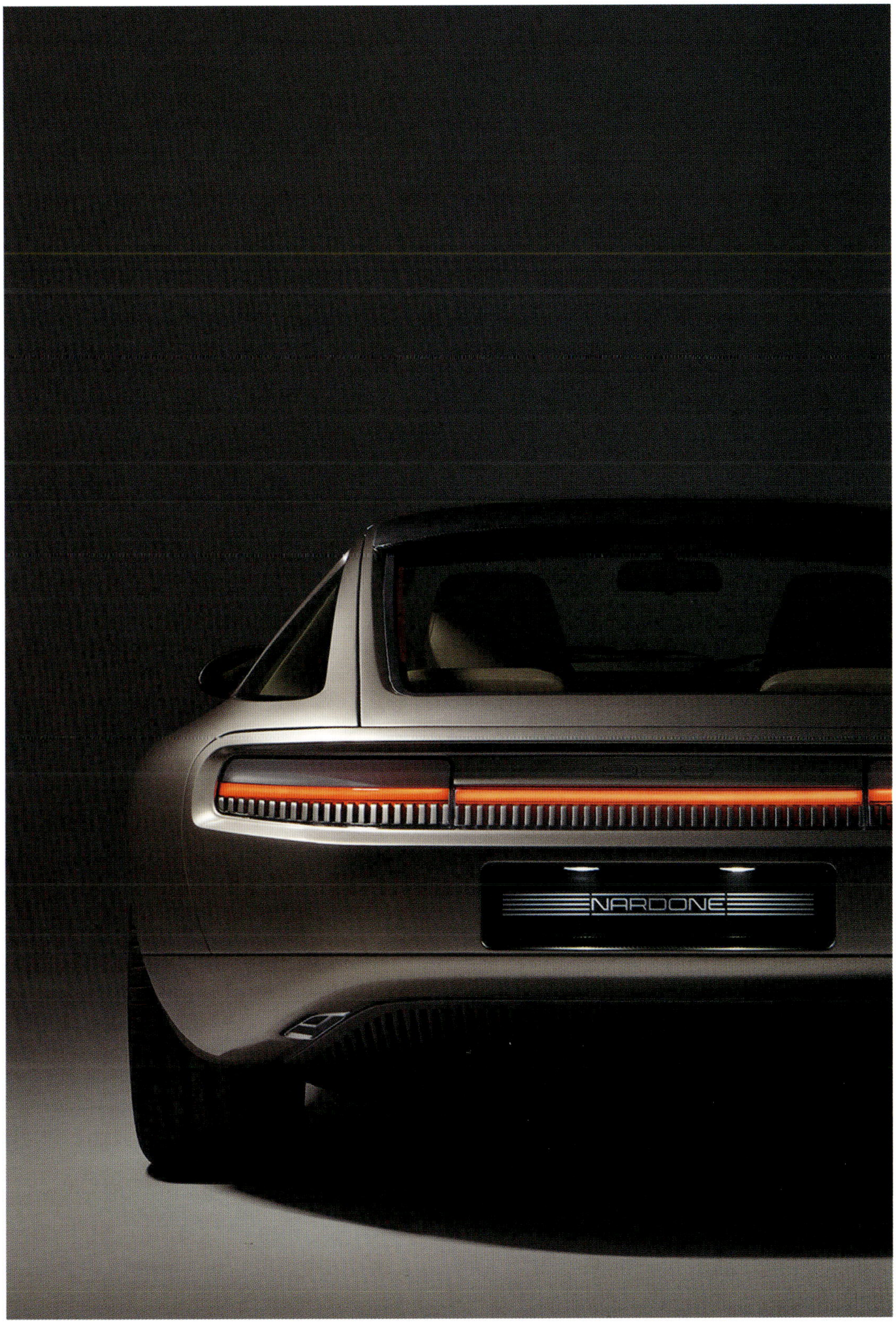

Above: A long, thin LED strip lights up the rear of the car, giving a futuristic look to this thoroughly reimagined 928.

Opposite: The iconic 928 headlights tilt forward, and have an ultra-modern design.

A WORD FROM THE AUTHOR AND PHOTOGRAPHER

The aim of this book is to share the passion for Outlaw Porsche modification, from backdating to restomod, with a racing spirit. The cars in this book represent a selection of Outlaw Porsches, based on our favourites.

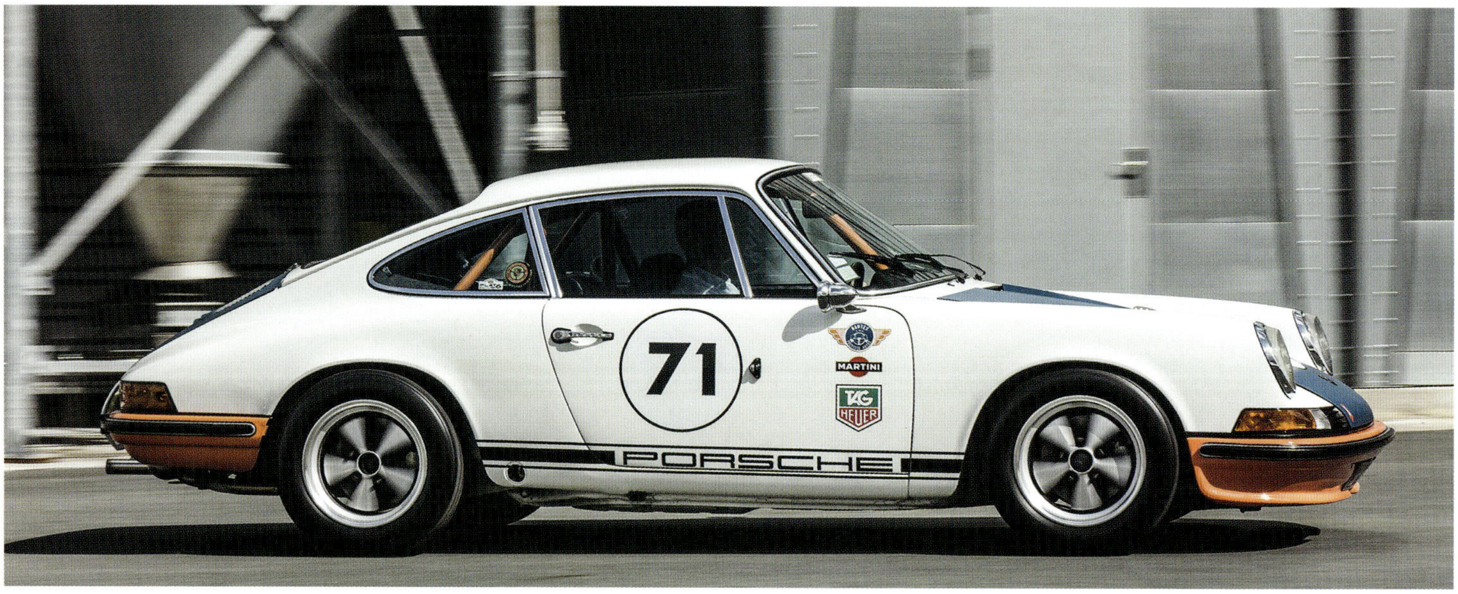

PHOTO CREDITS

All photographs by Thomas Cortesi, apart from the following:
Page 3: reprinted with the permission of Gerry Blyenberg
Page 14, #2: Ted Gushue / Petrolicius
Page 17, #2: Michaël Levivier
Page 25, #2: reprinted with the permisssion of Renaud Lechalier

---

This edition published by Welbeck Illustrated
An Imprint of HEADLINE PUBLISHING GROUP LIMITED

1

Cataloguing in Publication Data is available from the British Library

ISBN 9781035440917

Printed and bound in China

MIX
Paper | Supporting responsible forestry
FSC® C104723

Management: Ariane Lainé-Forrest
Editorial Manager: Camille Dejardin
Art direction: Clotilde Roussin
Graphic Design: Magali Levivier (ML&Co.)
Proofreading: Camille Salomon
Production: Lea Legnice
Repro: HYPHEN
Translation: Roland Hall

Headline's policy is to use papers that are natural, renewable and recyclable products and made from wood grown in well-managed forests and other controlled sources. The logging and manufacturing processes are expected to conform to the environmental regulations of the country of origin.

HEADLINE PUBLISHING GROUP LIMITED
An Hachette UK Company
Carmelite House
50 Victoria Embankment
London EC4Y 0DZ

The authorised representative in the EEA is Hachette Ireland,
8 Castlecourt Centre, Dublin 15, D15 XTP3, Ireland (email: info@hbgi.ie)

www.headline.co.uk
www.hachette.co.uk